STRATEGIC
OPERATIONS

STRATEGIC OPERATIONS

Competing Through Capabilities

Robert H. Hayes
Gary P. Pisano
David M. Upton

THE FREE PRESS

NEW YORK   LONDON   TORONTO   SYDNEY   TOKYO   SINGAPORE

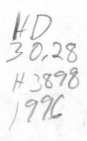

THE FREE PRESS
A Division of Simon & Schuster, Inc.
1230 Avenue of the Americas
New York, N.Y. 10020

Designed by Michael Mendelsohn of MM Design 2000, Inc.

Manufactured in the United States of America

printing number
10 9 8 7 6 5 4 3 2 1

Library of Congress Cataloging-in-Publication Data

Hayes, Robert H.
 Strategic operations: competing through capabilities / Robert H.
Hayes, Gary P. Pisano. David M. Upton.
  p. cm.
 Includes index.
 ISBN 0–684–82305–5 (hardcover)
 1. Strategic planning. 2. Industrial management. 3. Production
management. 4. Manufacturing resource planning. I. Pisano, Gary
P. II. Upton, David M., 1959– . III. Title.
HD30.28.H3898 1996
658.4'012—dc20   95–40209
                  CIP

ISBN 0-684-82305-5

CONTENTS

PART III. SELECTING, DEVELOPING, AND EXPLOITING OPERATING CAPABILITIES

SECTION A. SELECTING CAPABILITIES AND DRAWING ORGANIZATIONAL BOUNDARIES

SECTION B. DEVELOPING CAPABILITIES

SECTION C. EXPLOITING CAPABILITIES: STRATEGIC HINGES AND LONG-TERM FLEXIBILITY

Preface

A S WE WRITE THIS, the concept of Operations Strategy is still, in human terms, barely past adolescence. In years, it is younger than most of the MBAs who study it today. So it is not surprising that this young idea—like these young people—has been undergoing almost continual growth and elaboration throughout its short life, as it both tested itself against the real world and as that world evolved. Today operations strategy is facing perhaps the greatest challenge in its short history, as it finds itself in the crossfire of debate about the basic conceptualizations of its two core disciplines: operations management and strategic planning.

This debate has its roots in the dramatic changes in the world's competitive environment and in the nature of industrial competition that have occurred over the past decade. The swelling number of global competitors and new entrants has caused competition to become increasingly ferocious, and technological change is inundating even the most innovative companies. Sobered by the apparent ineffectiveness of traditional theories, practitioners and academics alike began to reexamine the bases upon which successful firms have been able to build and *sustain* their competitive advantage. Such advantage, they have discovered, rests less on a firm's ability to identify and defend an apparently attractive market position than on the cultivation of organizational capabilities that enable it to create and deliver a product or service that is regarded as exceptional—even unique—by its customers.

As a result, top managers who have tended to think of their strategic role primarily in terms of selecting which industries or markets to enter are now refocusing their attention inward—seeking to revitalize their internal operations and nurturing their ability to deliver outstanding products and services. Achieving this kind of revitalization is often excruciatingly difficult, they find, and requires a major overhaul in practices, mindsets, and people. This is because in many companies the operations function has traditionally been regarded as subsidiary to marketing, finance, or R&D, so it has become reactive and unimaginative. It is our belief (and a major reason for our writing this book) that operating capabilities provide such powerful sources of competitive advantage, in a wide range of manufacturing and service contexts, that organizations can no longer afford to confine operations to such a reactive role.

Our goal is not simply to convince the readers of this book that operating capabilities *can* be a competitive weapon. Many managers and academics already appreciate and understand this. Our primary objective is rather to provide students and executives with a body of analytical concepts, frameworks, and tools for making specific operating decisions in a way that develops, nurtures, and exploits their firm's strategic operating capabilities.

The Operations Strategy Course: Antecedents

This book has many antecedents. Professor John McLean developed a course called Advanced Production Problems at the Harvard Business School during the late 1940s. To explain why companies within the same industry are often observed to adopt very different approaches to manufacturing, McLean adopted what he called "the industry approach." By devoting a number of classes to a single industry, McLean was able to demonstrate to his students that companies within the same industry often choose very different competitive strategies and that these different strategies inevitably lead to different decisions and policies relating to such important manufacturing issues as the location of facilities, production control methods, vertical integration, and the administrative structure of plants. That course, and the basic notions conveyed in it, had a powerful impact on the students who took it—among them a young Wickham Skinner.

A dozen years later, Skinner found himself teaching the same course (which he soon renamed Manufacturing Policy). The U.S. manufacturing environment had changed dramatically since he was a student. Whereas U.S. industry dominated the world scene in the 1950s, when foreign managers came in droves to study the latest manufacturing equipment and methods, in the mid-1960s Skinner sensed that American companies were no longer managing their manufacturing resources as effectively as they once had. Rather than providing sources of competitive advantage, their manufacturing organizations were increasingly seen by senior executives as sources of problems and constraints—"millstones," to use Skinner's term, around the corporate neck.

Seeking to help his students and colleagues understand what had gone wrong, and in the process provide a clearer, more actionable conceptual framework to convey the philosophy of manufacturing competition embedded in McLean's course, Skinner combined the notion of "important [manufacturing] choices" with competitive strategy. The kernel of his argument was that: (a) different companies have different strengths and weaknesses and can choose to compete in different ways (and therefore adopt different "yardsticks of success"); (b) similarly, different production systems (the composite of decisions in a number of key decision areas) have different operating characteristics; (c) therefore, rather than adopting an industry-standard production system, the "task" for a company's manufacturing function is to construct a production system that, through a series of interrelated and internally consistent choices, reflects the priorities and tradeoffs implicit in its own specific competitive situation and strategy.

That basic conceptual framework—despite the passage of 25 years, the emergence of a totally different world order for industrial competition (including the emergence of the "service economy"), and a continual barrage of skepticism and questioning—has proven to be remarkably robust. Most of those who write on the subject of operations strategy have adopted it, implicitly if not explicitly. Yet, while this basic framework provided a vision of the potential contribution that a company's operations organization could make to its competitive success, it left vague a number of key issues. Testing the basic framework and answering these remaining questions gave rise to a growing body of research and case studies, carried out by both academics and practitioners. More recently, these issues have been complicated further by the emergence of a *new* paradigm for manufacturing—one based on the "lean manufacturing" approach adopted by a number of elite Japanese companies and exemplified by Toyota. And their resolution was further confused by another controversy that was beginning to arise about the basic concept and purpose of competitive strategy itself.

The modern paradigm for competitive strategy is based on the notion of *strategic fit*, and evolved out of a melding of the famous "corporate strengths & weaknesses, opportunities & threats" (SWOT) framework that had been advocated by Andrews [1971] and others with the tools and concepts of industrial organization economics. The goal of business strategy, seen through the prism of this framework, was to seek a sustainable competitive advantage by entering (or positioning oneself within) industries and businesses that were either structurally attractive or could be made so through deliberate management actions.

Using the SWOT framework, managers could derive an appropriate competitive strategy and establish competitive priorities. The Operations Strategy framework, as it existed in 1980, could then be used to translate those competitive priorities into a set of supportive manufacturing decisions and policies. On the other hand, the two frameworks appeared to become increasingly incompatible during the early 1980s. Not only were they separated by their problem focus (simplistically: *where* to compete versus *how* to compete there effectively), but also by their conceptual approaches. Whereas the roots of the competitive strategy framework were in industrial organization economics and were based on industry-level studies, the manufacturing strategy framework was based on the specific nature of manufacturing and technology at the firm level.

The clear separation between the two frameworks is apparent from a quick scan of the two most widely used books on their respective subjects: Porter[1] and Hayes and Wheelwright.[2] Both were written at roughly the same time and cover many of the same topics—but they employ entirely

---

[1]M. Porter, 1980. *Competitive Strategy* (New York: The Free Press).

[2]R. Hayes and S. Wheelwright. 1984. *Restoring Our Competitive Edge: Competing Through Manufacturing* (New York: John Wiley & Sons).

different sets of tools. This is in stark contrast to the days when John McLean first taught his Advanced Production Problems course, and troubled many of those who tried to operate at the natural interface of strategy and operations management.

Despite the considerable insight the competitive strategy framework provided for both scholars and practitioners, it was essentially static in nature. Just as the old notion of comparative advantage could not explain the rising power of Japanese industry in world competition, neither could this position-oriented definition of competitive advantage explain (except sometimes in retrospect) the success of individual Japanese companies. Their approach to competition not only changed, sometimes with bewildering speed, from low-cost to high-precision to flexibility to innovativeness, but through such changes they often were able to transform the nature of competition within a whole industry.

Clearly, any modern course about Operations Strategy has to cover a much broader agenda than that of similar courses offered a decade ago. Not only did we want to include much of what had been learned about the subject—as traditionally framed—over the years, but we also wanted to reconcile the issues raised in our students' minds by the apparently conflicting ideas they were being exposed to in discussions of "lean manufacturing," competitive strategy, and "core competencies." This is what we attempted to do in the course upon which this book is based.

The cases in this book are drawn from all over the world. We have been fortunate in having had the opportunity to develop material about important issues facing companies in Australia, Germany, Holland, Japan, Korea, Mexico, Puerto Rico, and the United Kingdom, as well as the United States. While the perspective of the book is global, it is useful to reflect on the experience of the United States during the 1980s since this illustrates many of the issues that face companies throughout the world. The United States was one of the earliest Western nations to recognize that it had fallen behind in manufacturing and begin to search for new approaches. Others soon followed, and now even Japan, under growing competitive pressure from its Asian neighbors (as well as "retooled" Western companies), has had to reexamine many of its traditional approaches to operations management.

The American Experience

During the late 1970s and early 1980s many American industries came under fierce attack from foreign competitors. First steel and consumer electronics, then automobiles (that largest of U.S. industries and the symbol of its collective industrial might), followed by machine tools, banking, computer peripherals, office machines, and—the pride of American technology—integrated circuits: all rapidly lost market share to foreign imports. By the mid-1980s the U.S. merchandise trade deficit had soared to over $150 billion a year, and within a few years America went from being the world's biggest creditor nation to its biggest debtor. And the reasons for this decline sounded a common refrain: imported products and services provided higher quality *in the eyes of American customers*, better reliability and lower lifetime costs, better value for the money, and greater responsiveness to customers' increasing demands for product variety. In short, the common weapon that foreign competitors were using to attack U.S. producers was simply their ability to design and deliver products and services faster, more efficiently, and more effectively.

It was quickly discovered that operations had become—slowly and almost unnoticed—the Achilles' heel of many American companies. During the 1960s and early 1970s American managers had turned their attention away from competition based on superior operations and toward a fascination with marketing gimmicks, financial wizardry, and the development of grandiose strategies. The best young managers gravitated to "where the action was," and directed their attention more to buying and selling other companies than to creating and delivering superior products and services. So when the attack came, many companies were woefully unprepared to confront it. Their factories and equipment were aging, their workers dispirited, and their senior managers were intellectually as well as culturally removed from the intricacies of operations. As a result, they had fallen behind their foreign competitors on practically every competitive dimension: their products cost more, had higher defect rates and looser tolerances, took longer to deliver, and were less innovative.

In such a situation the traditional concept of Operations Strategy—which emphasized trade-offs among competitive priorities and the need to focus operations on a narrow range of priorities—seemed irrelevant. After all, if your company is lagging behind its competitors in terms of cost, quality, innovativeness, and other competitive dimensions, you are in danger of losing out regardless of how carefully you choose your emphasis. As a result, during the 1980s some began to argue that manufacturing strategy had become passé. Engaged, as it were, in hand-to-hand combat, U.S. industry responded with a shotgun approach, embarking on a flurry of manufacturing improvement programs.

Every self-respecting company, it seemed, wanted to become "world class" by initiating "lean manufacturing/operations" practices such as Total Quality Management, Employee Involvement, Just-In-Time workflow control, and Quick Product Development. They began "benchmarking" the performance of their own manufacturing and business processes against those of other companies that were recognized as leaders in those processes, and sent study teams of managers off to Japan and Europe to investigate the best practices wherever they could be found. If attempts to continually improve existing processes were felt to be insufficient, some companies began experimenting with "reengineering"—the radical restructuring of their entire approach to business.

And over the next decade many of them apparently succeeded: their competitive situation began to improve—although sometimes not for the intended reasons. The defect level of U.S.-made products and services was reduced, in some cases to near-Japanese levels. Companies cut costs, largely by downsizing, slashing overhead, outsourcing, and rationalizing facilities. Inventory levels and delivery times decreased. Key suppliers were integrated more tightly into both production scheduling and product development. A combination of productivity improvement, relatively slow growth in wage rates, and a weakening U.S. dollar (the Japanese yen, for example, more than doubled in value against the dollar between 1985 and 1995) buttressed the cost competitiveness of U.S. goods. New products and services poured into the market at an increasing rate. As a result, U.S. manufacturers stemmed the onslaught of imports and even began regaining market share in such key industries as autos, machine tools, integrated circuits, and construction machinery. Clearly, many U.S. companies had relearned "the basics" to the point where they were back to at least competitive parity with foreign producers.

Yet, despite all these improvements, by 1992 America's negative merchandise trade balance had surpassed $100 billion again, even though the U.S. dollar had weakened to historically low levels against the German mark and Japanese yen. And the fact that some U.S. producers had been able to regain world leadership did not necessarily imply that they had become net *exporters*. Personal computers provide an interesting case in point. Even though the U.S. industry's percentage of world shipments of personal computer systems rose from under 60 percent to over 70 percent between 1985 and 1994, it still ran a trade *deficit* of over $15 billion in 1994—because these systems were composed largely of imported components and peripheral devices. Over time the U.S. companies evidently had reduced their role to design, assembly, and marketing. Just as disturbing, study after study indicated that only about one third of all the operations improvement programs that U.S. companies had undertaken were regarded—by their own managers—as successful.

Clearly, remastering "the basics" of cost, quality, flexibility, and responsiveness was not enough. Nor, even, was the achievement of "world class" status in operations. Something else was needed, both to provide the next boost to corporate competitiveness and to avoid the drain of resources into activities that produced little apparent value. It was time, once again, to think about the *strategic* mission of operations.

The most important role of a strategy, of course, is to provide direction to an organization and channel its resources in the most productive directions, the goal being to achieve a sustainable *advantage* over competitors. Although benchmarking, adopting the best practice, and becoming world class could all assist a company in achieving parity with its key competitors, none could assure it of any enduring advantage over them. Such an advantage would have to come from somewhere else. That something else, we propose, is the guidance provided by a coherent and energizing operations strategy. While our concept of operations strategy has its roots in the work of Skinner and others, it is also much more explicitly dynamic. For example, whereas the traditional framework of operations strategy emphasized static choices among competitive priorities (e.g., you can be either low cost or flexible), the framework presented in this book focuses on *choices among improvement paths* and the creation of operational capabilities that lead to more favorable trade-offs over time.

The Operations Strategy Course: Content and Organization

The course we developed at Harvard was essentially a third-generation Operations Strategy course. The first generation was Skinner's Manufacturing Policy course, which was organized around selected industries. In the mid-1980s, Professor David Garvin developed and taught a popular second-generation course called Operations Strategy. It was focused primarily around different modes of competition (e.g., low cost, high quality, etc.) and drew upon the Manufacturing Policy course as well as several others developed and taught by Professors Kim Clark, Robert Hayes, Earl Sasser, and Steven Wheelwright. We three took over that course in 1991 and have since, with the help of our students, developed new frameworks to illuminate its evolving themes and new cases that reflect the course's increasing emphasis on infrastructure decisions and the building of organizational capabilities. Most of the course that was taught in early 1994 comprises material written during the previous three years. Close to a thousand MBA students have tested most of these materials, and we feel it is time to make them available to a broader audience.

This book comprises four basic blocks of materials. The first, and shortest (although it is larger than it appears here, because a follow-on case is contained in the companion *Instructor's Manual* and can be incorporated into a course) provides students with a general overview of the issues to be covered in the book, and the basic framework to be used in analyzing those issues. The second module illustrates the impact of different facilities and process-technology decisions on a company's ability to compete in different ways—e.g., low cost, high quality, high flexibility, etc., while the third module focuses on the impact of *infrastructural* decisions on its operating performance.

The final module, which comprises about half of the course, addresses the role of an Operations Strategy in guiding the development of specific operating capabilities, and is composed of three submodules. The first of these deals with the problem of deciding *which* capabilities a company should invest in developing. The second focuses on how companies go about *cultivating* selected capabilities over time, and the third on ways some companies have been able to *exploit* such capabilities for competitive advantage—or, alternatively, allowed them to waste away.

While we have chosen a structure for this book that is somewhat different from its predecessors, the notes, articles, and cases in it can be organized in many ways. A number of themes recur throughout this material and its cases, drawn from real-world experience, seldom deal with just one kind of problem or decision. Thus, while we have attempted to arrange them in a coherent order, they often cut across the structure we have chosen and thus provide opportunities for a variety of learning experiences. For example, issues associated with developing organizational capabilities and managing flexibility draw from material presented throughout the course.

We want to express our appreciation to all the people—managers, academics, and students—who have contributed to our understanding of this subject, and especially to our colleagues at the Harvard Business School for their insights, criticisms, and intellectual support. We are particularly indebted to the School's Division of Research, which funded the research and course development that provided the foundation for both our course and this book. Any errors or omissions, of course, remain our responsibility—as does the potential embarrassment we may feel ten years from now as we look back on what we have written here and realize, from that enlightened perspective, how much we still have to learn about Operations Strategy.

THE CONCEPT OF
OPERATIONS STRATEGY

Overview

*I*N MOST ORGANIZATIONS—both private and public, whether engaged in making products or delivering services—the bulk of their human and financial resources are invested in their operations functions. Within "operations" we include all those activities required to create and deliver a product or service, from procurement through conversion to distribution. Most of the people employed by an organization (including most of those considered "managers") are engaged in the operations function, and most of its physical assets reside there. An Operations Strategy is a set of goals, instructions, and self-imposed restrictions that together describe how the organization proposes to develop and direct all the resources invested in operations so as to best fulfill—and possibly redefine—its mission.

In the case of a private company (our focus throughout this book), this mission is usually expressed in terms of survival, profitability, and growth and is pursued by trying to differentiate itself from its major competitors in some desirable way. A company's Operations Strategy, therefore, has to begin with a statement specifying how it proposes to create for itself that chosen form of competitive advantage. By helping weld together the massive but disparate resources invested in operations into a cohesive, purposeful whole, such a strategy can make it possible for the company to compete *through* operations—rather than around operations (or in spite of it), as do many companies. The problem most companies face when attempting to create such a strategy is not that the task is too complex or difficult. Paradoxically, they often appear to believe that it is too easy—that they can easily seek out and emulate the best practices of so-called world-class companies. The seductive appeal of *ideal* approaches can be a trap, however. The past decade or so has seen a fierce (and often highly emotional) debate about the relative merits of two philosophies of operations that are essentially polar opposites. Neither, it is now becoming apparent, is right for all companies in all circumstances.

The Elusive Search for the "One Best Way"

Until the early 1980s, most American managers thought about manufacturing (whether or not they were directly associated with it) in terms of a

3

paradigm whose roots went back well over a hundred years. The "American system of manufacturing," with its emphasis on mass markets, standard designs, and mass production using interchangeable parts, revolutionized manufacturing in the middle of the last century. Modified and elaborated by the principles of "scientific management," as promulgated by Frederick Taylor and his disciples, as well as by such great industrialists as Andrew Carnegie, Isaac Singer, and Henry Ford, this new paradigm was the foundation upon which the United States built itself into an industrial powerhouse by the 1920s.

The ideas that work was most efficiently done when divided up and assigned to specialists, that managers and staff experts should do the thinking for workers (so they could concentrate on "doing"), that every process was characterized by an innate amount of variation (and hence an irreducible rate of defects), and that communication within an organization should be tightly controlled, so as to avoid possible confusion, and should proceed through a hierarchical chain of command—were accepted as dogma. The "best" manufacturing process was assumed to be based on long runs; it utilized equipment that was specialized for each stage of the process and whose capacities were matched as closely as possible, and it used inventories to buffer different stages both from each other and from the erratic behavior of suppliers and customers. Work should be organized and conducted systematically, in a logical sequence, and under tight supervision. In the minds of most top managers of that era, such practices—which collectively comprised a cohesive operations strategy—defined the "one best way" (to borrow Taylor's phrase) to design *any* manufacturing or service delivery sytem; it was the ideal toward which all should strive.

Rebuilding from the shambles of World War II, however, Japanese companies began to create an entirely different approach to production. Short on capital and manufacturing expertise, blessed with few natural resources, and faced with small, fragmented markets, they were forced to design new practices that reflected both their lack of resources and the chaotic conditions of their economic environment. Over time, they developed an approach to manufacturing that was claimed by some to be uniformly superior to "the American system/Taylorism."

Their "lean production" system was characterized by an emphasis on speed and flexibility rather than volume and cost. People needed to be broadly trained, rather than specialized, and work in teams to identify and solve operating problems. Staff was "overhead" and overhead was bad. No amount of rejects was acceptable; the organization should work tirelessly to reduce rejects to zero. Communication should take place informally and horizontally, among line workers rather than via prescribed hierarchical paths through the organization. Equipment should be general purpose and organized in cells that produced a group of similar parts or products, rather than specialized by process stage. Production throughput time was more important than labor or equipment utilization. Inventory, like rejects, was considered "waste." Supplier relationships should be long-term and cooperative. Activities associated with product development should be done concurrently, not sequentially, and should be carried out by cross-functional teams.

Does this new philosophy of operations represent, at last, the holy grail—the true "one best way" to organize and manage operations? We argue that it is not, any more than was the apparently discredited "American system." The problem is not that this new approach is wrong. It has worked for many companies. But the competitive landscape is also littered with companies that have been bitterly disappointed by their experience with these same practices. And even if a company successfully implements one or more of them, this does not assure that it will be successful financially. For example, the winners of the national Baldrige Award, which recognizes U.S. companies that have been unusually successful in improving their quality, productivity, and customer satisfaction, have done well on average—however, some of them have experienced notable failures. One of the early winners, for example, entered Chapter 11 soon after receiving the Baldrige, and others (like General Motors, IBM, and Westinghouse) soon thereafter began experiencing highly visible problems.

Even more disturbing, a number of Japanese companies are beginning to question many of these same approaches, which have become virtually synonymous with "Japanese manufacturing." They have found not only that any one of these programs may not be equally effective in every situation, but also that widespread use of some of them can create problems for society as a whole. For example, the extensive conversion to JIT, which requires frequent shipments of small quantities between suppliers, producers, and customers, is saturating the road system in Japan. Toyota's newest factory in Japan utilizes neither the JIT system (which Toyota itself pioneered) nor mixed-model assembly—at least partly because they create stress for factory workers, who are increasingly difficult to recruit. Honda and Nissan, after having received worldwide recognition for their ability to compress their product development times, are now reported to be lengthening them again. And other Japanese companies are openly questioning the value of product proliferation.

The real problem is that adopting JIT, TQM, or some other three-letter acronym is *not* a strategy for manufacturing. Nor is aspiring to "lean production," "continuous improvement," or "being world class." And it certainly is not putting teams in charge of everything (as residents of Boston, we feel compelled to report that just having teams does not automatically mean that you will win a lot of critical games). All these approaches are essentially imitative in nature. The purpose of an Operations Strategy, however, is to specify the kind of *competitive advantage* that a company is seeking in its marketplace and to articulate how that advantage is to be achieved. How can a company achieve any sort of advantage if its only goal is to be "as good as" its toughest competitors?

Proactive Operations

Again and again in our conversations with the senior managers of companies that are experiencing competitive difficulties, we hear comments indicating that their operations function plays an essentially neutral or reactive role—always waiting for others to set the direction and take the lead or, worse, being expected somehow to make up the delays and deficiencies resulting from the incomplete or flawed activities of other functional groups. In such companies the role of operations is essentially restricted to that of an implementer and fixer.

In other cases, either because the company's operations organization refuses to accept such a subservient role or because it too often fails to deal effectively with the crises it is routinely handed, the situation sometimes deteriorates to the point where the operations organization begins to play an adversarial role within the company, forcing it to redirect time and energy away from external competitors to resolve a recurring series of internal conflicts. Usually such bickering is ascribed to "poor communications" or the "natural friction" between different personality types. (Salespeople, it is argued, tend to approach problems, and behave, differently from those who gravitate to being engineers or accountants.)

We argue that another—and possibly more important—reason is that the different functional groups are likely to be pursuing different goals and strategies and/or to perceive their roles differently. Another purpose of an Operations Strategy, therefore, is to help a company's operations organization define the common ground where it can play a proactive and collaborative role with other company functions.

In this, our initial exposition of the process by which a company might go about creating such an organization, we focus on four basic principles: *fit, focus, learning,* and *role.* We will devote most of this introductory section to the first two: fit and focus. In later sections we will shift our attention to the more dynamic aspects of Operations Strategy, emphasizing the notions of learning, which involves both the continual improvement of existing skills and the selection and development of new ones, and expanding the role that an operations organization can play in its company. We focus particular attention on its less visible role as the source of distinctive operating capabilities that are strategically valuable not only because they provide specific operating advantages, but because they are difficult for competitors to acquire or imitate.

Fit: Strategic Coherence and Internal Consistency

The notion of "fit" is based on three premises. (1) Different companies (or business units within a company) may choose to compete—that is, attempt to differentiate themselves from their major competitors—in different ways. (2) Different ways of configuring, equipping, and managing an operations function can make it easier or harder for a company to achieve a given form of differentiation. (3) Therefore the primary goal of an operations strategy is to seek congruence (fit) between the company's chosen approach to competition and the way its operations organization is designed, organized, and managed. Each of these premises will be explored and elaborated on in more detail in the paragraphs that follow.

Competitive Differentiation

With the myriad choices customers have today when making a purchase, how do they decide which product or service to select? Different customers are attracted by different attributes. In order to appeal to those who are interested primarily in the cost of the product/service, some companies attempt to achieve a competitive advantage by offering the *lowest price*. Others prefer to attract those customers who want *higher quality*—in terms of performance, features, or appearance—even though this might necessitate a higher price. Still others seek to differentiate themselves through superior *flexibility, dependability, speed* of response, or *innovativeness*. A given company may try to match (or stay within some specified range of) its competitors on several competitive dimensions, and thereby offer the "best value" or other form of compromise between competing attributes. But when it comes down to the final attempt at persuasion—the moment of decision at the grocery store shelf, say—it hopes the customer's choice will be swayed by its product's (or service's) specific form of superiority.

Therefore, an Operations Strategy must begin by stating, in terms that are easily understood throughout the company or business unit, how it wants to differentiate itself in its chosen marketplace. Such a statement is usually embedded in the unit's Competitive Strategy, where it is sometimes expressed in terms of the "sustainable competitive advantage" that is being pursued. A Competitive Strategy, however, also includes additional statements about "positioning" (that is, which industry—or segment of an industry—the company will compete in), the extent and form of diversification, and so on. Such issues are of little concern in the early stages of crafting an Operations Strategy, as the unit's position is regarded as given and the only question is how to compete most effectively in that position; we will return to this issue later in this book, when we discuss how the development of distinctive operating capabilities may affect a company's decisions regarding what kind of new businesses to enter. The fact that other business units belonging to the same company might choose to compete in different ways or in other industries is also of little relevance—unless the company makes the mistake of trying to have the same operations organization service the needs of two or more very dissimilar business units.

Once the form of competitive differentiation is specified, management must then ensure that the business unit's operations organization is configured and managed in such a way that it can provide that form of differentiation most effectively. There is no "one best way" for dealing with *any* business problem—whether the activity involved is making a product, selling it, designing a management control system, or raising capital. In each case one must make choices that reflect one's objectives, resources, capabilities, and context. An operations organization is no different. Like an engineered product, it cannot do everything well. Therefore, it must be designed in such a way that it does what it is supposed to do in a particularly appropriate and effective way, while placing less importance on other performance attributes.

For example, one does not tell an auto designer simply to "design a car." She will immediately want to know how the car is primarily going to be used: for high-speed, long-distance drives on superhighways, say, or for carrying large loads, or for traversing rough terrain, or for commuting in crowded urban areas, or for high speed and responsiveness on country roads. Different uses imply different designs: the classic "road cruiser," van, station wagon, pickup truck, subcompact, or sports car. An attempt to "cover all the bases" typically results in a mongrel design that doesn't do anything particularly well. So the trade-offs the designer is continually forced to make must be both internally coherent and consistent with the priorities given her.

Just as an engineered product reflects the combined influence of a variety of design parameters (whether they be expressed in terms of electronics, mechanics, chemistry, or biology), so an operations organization reflects the influence of its own sort of design parameters. Some of these are *structural*, in that they represent decisions regarding the organization's physical attributes, such as the amount of production (or service delivery) capacity that it is expected to provide. Others are termed *infrastructural*, in that they describe the policies and practices that determine how the physical aspects of the organization are to be managed. In that sense, they are analogous to the software that determines how a computer's hardware is used. Hardware and software decisions interact in a variety of sometimes quite subtle ways. As an obvious example, the amount of capacity that a given set of floor space and equipment can provide depends on whether it is operated one shift a day, five days a week, or around the clock (21 shifts a week)—an infrastructural decision. It also depends, of course, on the process yield/defect level, which is affected by the facility's equipment and sourcing policies (both structural decisions), as well as by its employee selection and training policies, its quality systems, workflow scheduling practices, and measurement/reward policies—all elements of its infrastructure.

Capacity and Facilities. Besides the amount of raw capacity that is to be provided, other types of structural decisions specify how that total operating capacity is to be broken up into individual facilities: how big they are and how many, where they are located (near major customers? raw materials? low cost labor? etc.), and how each is to be specialized (by product? by process stage? by technology? by geographic scope?). Some of these decisions are much less pertinent for service companies, which require a high degree of direct interaction with customers, since that kind of capacity cannot be stored or transported. For example, an unused airplane seat cannot be saved and used on the next flight, or used by a simultaneous flight to a different city. But even service companies usually have certain "backroom" functions that do not require direct customer interaction or can be performed remotely via telecommunications networks, and these functions require the same kind of facilities decisions as manufacturing companies.

Process Technology. Another major type of structural decision involves the process technology that is to be employed in each facility. At one level this requires a choice among different types of processing equipment (which, it should be remembered, usually has been designed by someone outside the company who has in mind a specific proposed use and desired operating characteristics). At another level, it should specify how this equipment is to be arranged in the work area, connected together, and coordinated. For example, the same set of equipment can be organized as independent workstations, permitting a variety of process flow paths that result in a wide range of products or services (a so-called "job shop"), or as one connected processing line down which all products flow continuously. Each choice, of course, implies a matching set of structural and infrastructural decisions.

Sourcing. A final aspect of an operations organization's structure involves its decisions about how much of the total work that is required to create and deliver the product/service will be done internally and how much of it will be purchased from outside organizations. Some companies choose to be highly vertically integrated—producing most of their own component parts and services. Others prefer to purchase most of their needs from the outside, thereby limiting the amount of internal processing required and the amount of capital invested. Tied in with this decision are a number of other, partly infrastructural decisions pertaining to the way the company's outside suppliers are to be selected and managed.

It should be emphasized that the choices made for each of these different decisions have varying effects on a company's operating costs, quality, flexibility, dependability, and new product capabilities. If it wants to be able to respond to small orders of customized products and rapid changes in customer requirements, for example, it probably should configure itself so that it has excess capacity, its facilities are tightly coordinated (or individual facilities are focused on supplying the needs of specific customers), it organizes its processing equipment and people more like those of a job shop than a continuous flow line, and it has suppliers who are able to react quickly to changing requirements. If, on the other hand, it wants to be able to offer low cost and the latest technology, it probably should concentrate the production of those items that require large amounts of capital investment and technological expertise into one or two facilities, possibly located near engineering universities or other technical centers, and seek out suppliers who are able to match its needs.

Infrastructure. A company's operations infrastructure is composed of its policies regarding workflow scheduling (and, when the product or service is storable, inventory management), quality assurance, human resource management (for both operators and managers), performance measurement, capital budgeting and equipment selection, new product development, and interfacility coordination. Each of these sorts of policies often has repercussions and implications for other infrastructural decisions (performance measurement systems, in particular, seem to affect everything else!), but, as we have seen, they also interact with structural decisions. Although many companies, like economists, tend to devote the bulk of their attention to the more quantifiable issues associated with structural decisions, a company's infrastructure is at least as critical to its success—and it is usually even more difficult, expensive, and time-consuming to change.

Just as the trade-offs made by the designer of an engineered product must be both interrelated and consistent with its intended use, so must a company's structural and infrastructural decisions mesh together and combine to reflect the way it has chosen to compete. This is the "fit" that an operations strategy must ensure. However, achieving such consistency in an operations organization is much more difficult and complex for a company than it is for a product. Whereas the decisions and trade-offs involved in designing a product are usually made over a relatively short period of time by a small group of people who work closely together and often are located near one another, the kind of structural and infrastructural decisions described above are usually made at different points in time by entirely separate groups of people, who often are physically distant from one another and may seldom interact in the normal course of business. Hence, the company's competitive priorities and operations strategy need to be clearly communicated to all these groups, and individual structural and infrastructural decisions need to be monitored for consistency by senior managers.

Strategy as an Art Form

Understanding the basic principle of the importance of fit does not by itself, of course, solve the specific problem faced by an individual management group, any more than an understanding of the basic laws of physics solves the problem of how to design an automobile. None of the structural and infrastructural choices described above—the design parameters for our engineered operations organization—is cleanly delineated in terms of its impact on different competitive dimensions. A given design choice may clearly favor certain competitive dimensions (cost and dependability, say) and hinder others (such as quality or customer responsiveness), but there usually are gradations in these effects and its impact on still others may be highly debatable. The rich array of trade-offs required can be made in a variety of imaginative ways, as we will see throughout this book.

Two different companies, although trying to implement a similar set of competitive priorities, may make very different design choices in the process of putting together two equally effective operations organizations. One, for example, may rely primarily on structural decisions (facilities and equipment choices, say) in its attempt to meet a given set of competitive priorities; another may rely primarily on infrastructural elements (a Just-In-Time production scheduling system coupled with a Total Quality Management program, say) in pursuit of the same set of priorities. In this sense, designing an effective operations organization is an art form—constrained here and there by technological and organizational possibilities and guided by informed guesses—just as is product design. Hopefully, some of this this ambiguity will be reflected in your classroom discussions just as it is in corporate conference rooms. But ambiguity does not mean confusion or "anything goes." Throughout this course we emphasize repeatedly the basic principles that underlie these kinds of decisions, and provide guidance as to the reasonable alternatives that managers should consider as they attempt to mold their organizations in creative ways.

Focus: "Fit" in the Small

The notion of "focus" follows naturally, almost inevitably, from the concept of "fit." The essential idea behind it is that "each [competitive] strategy creates a unique [operations] task," as Skinner phrased it in his classic article, "The focused factory" (Skinner, 1974). There he argued that a single factory, even if equipped with the most modern machinery and systems, will inevitably experience almost irreconcilable inconsistencies and conflicts, and a loss of overall effectiveness, if it attempts to serve multiple markets, each of which is being pursued using a different competitive strategy. Such a factory, he conjectured, could only be converted into a competitive asset by breaking it up into two or more focused facilities, for each of which the "entire apparatus is focused to accomplish the particular manufacturing task demanded by the [specific] strategy . . ." This concept, with its emphasis on simplicity, clarity, and reducing overhead, foreshadows today's ideal of "lean manufacturing."

If different situations call for different approaches to configuring and managing an operations organization, then it is unlikely that the same operations organization will be equally effective for making different products, or delivering different services, for businesses that compete in markedly different ways. Just as a company must choose, train, and manage a sales force differently if its primary task is to sell expensive pieces of capital equipment to experienced engineers, as opposed to (say) selling inexpensive consumer disposables to unsophisticated buyers, it needs different types of operations organizations for different missions. It is not that it is *impossible* for the same operations organization to produce and deliver two different kinds of products/services that are to be sold in two different ways; many companies (too many, we think) operate this way. However, one cannot expect that organization to perform both tasks *equally well*, or as well as could two different organizations that each focuses its attention on the needs of a specific type of product/service and competitive strategy.

At the most extreme level, this notion of focus may suggest breaking up a factory (or service delivery organization) that is producing a number of products for different markets using a variety of technologies into two or more separate factories, each devoted to a smaller number of relatively homogeneous products and/or technologies. Many managers, when confronted with such a proposal, object on the grounds that it will be prohibitively expensive. They argue that multiple facilities usually require duplicate floor space, equipment investment, and overhead structures. But many companies have found just the opposite to be true—that focusing their facilities often causes their operating and overhead costs to *decrease*. If, for example, one's original facility is situated in an expensive (in terms of land, labor, construction, or transportation costs) location, and a given product can be produced in a less expensive location, then setting up a new facility to produce that product or service may turn out to be cheaper in the long run than continually adding floor space to the original plant as more and more work is piled into it.

Similarly, equipment that is specialized to the needs of a specific kind of product or service is often less expensive (and/or easier to build internally) and easier to operate than multipurpose equipment that has a broader range of capabilities and frequently must be changed over from one product to another. Finally, placing dissimilar product groups in the same factory does not reduce overhead, it simply covers it up under a single roof. Increasing the complexity of a facility by continually adding new products and services to it creates the need for more and more overhead—to resolve conflicts, coordinate production schedules, break bottlenecks, and estimate product costs. Companies that break up a big, complex facility into separate, tightly focused smaller facilities usually find that their total overhead costs decrease.

But a substantial portion of these advantages can often be obtained through less drastic means. At a minimum, one may be able to achieve considerable simplification simply by dividing a given facility into separated work areas—sometimes called "plants within a plant." A "manufacturing cell," composed of a relatively small group of people who are devoted to the needs of a related group of products, is an extreme example of this approach. Each work area will have most, if not all, of its own equipment, its own workers, its own work-scheduling and performance-measurement systems, etc. The basic premise behind the current drive to "reengineer" organizations is that the key to efficiency is to tie together (and preferably colocate) all the individual groups and functions that are involved in performing a complete process—for example, the steps from materials procurement through production to delivery to customers.

As with the case of fit, however, the principle of focus is easier to explain than it is to implement. Even though a company may agree that it needs to become more focused, the question remains, "How?" It can focus either around product lines, for example, or around process stages/technologies, geographic areas, and markets or customer groups, but it cannot focus along several dimensions simultaneously; that is, choosing to focus along any one dimension (e.g., product lines) means giving up focus along another. Once this decision has been made, it must decide *how much* focus is desirable. At one extreme, each product, part, or component service could be assigned to a separate organization—usually an infeasible approach. At the other, all operations could be performed at the same location. Companies engaged in delivering services that require direct interaction with customers (and therefore cannot be stored or transported) are sometimes forced to this extreme, and then begin to experience problems as they expand their range of service offerings; we will see an example of this later in this book in the "McDonald's Corporation" case.

Once a desired form of focus has been achieved, the organization must guard against losing it. Business organizations are continually buffeted by new demands and opportunities. Under pressure to react quickly, and swayed more by the obvious short-term benefits of enlarging—and complicating—an existing operation than by the longer-term, less tangible benefits of keeping it simple and focused by creating a new organization, the natural tendency of managers is to pile more and more products, technologies, and competitive priorities onto the existing facility. In that sense, business organizations tend to become steadily more complicated over time, analogous to the way entropy (disorder) naturally increases in thermodynamic systems. To guard against this tendency, companies have employed a variety of techniques. Some, for example, have found it useful to set up specific "charters" for different facilities or divisions. These charters not only specify what the company wants its divisions to do, or become particularly proficient at (developing into so-called "Centers of Excellence"), but also alert them to the types of activities that they are *prohibited* from undertaking without express permission from a higher level in the organization.

Learning: "The Best" is the Enemy of "Ever Better"

Despite the care with which an Operations Strategy is crafted on the basis of such notions as "fit" and "focus," it may not be successful. How can one explain, for example, the fact that even though several airlines may adopt very similar competitive strategies, choose the same model of planes, use the same ground crews at each airport, and adopt very similar passenger reservation systems—some turn out to be far more successful than others? Or, to make the point even clearer by removing all the potentially confounding variables, consider the familiar sight of a group of sailboats that approach the starting line of a race together. All are the same make and model, each is similarly equipped and crewed, all follow the same course, driven by the same wind and currents, with the same objective in mind. All, in short, have the same competitive strategy and have matched it with the same operating system. Yet, at the end of the race some boats are in front while others are far behind. And usually, if one watches the same group of boats race again and again, the same ones end up in front a disproportionate number of times.

If "fit" and "focus" aren't enough, what other concept(s) must be added? A number of different writers have proposed additional considerations, such as "the ability to implement" and "organizational commitment," but we suggest most are subsumed in the notion of *organizational learning.* In the 1970s most discussions of learning were conducted within the somewhat narrow confines of the so-called "learning (or experience) curve." Predicting the nature of the cost reductions that could be expected to result from various competitive strategies, and the resulting impact on corporate growth and profitability, was the subject of a flood of articles during this period. One—Abernathy & Wayne (1974)—folded this kind of analysis into the Operations Strategy paradigm, using the example of Henry Ford's Model T to illustrate both the cost-reducing power of the learning curve and how Ford's total preoccupation with being the lowest-cost producer in the industry inevitably led to a loss of product flexibility. This opened a window of opportunity to Alfred Sloan at General Motors, reinforcing the notion that an operating system that is good at one thing is likely to be weak at something else.

But learning involves more than simply improving one's performance along specific competitive dimensions, such as cost, quality, and flexibility. It also incorporates the possibility of developing entirely new organizational capabilities. Such new capabilities may cause an organization to adjust its competitive strategy, and therefore to shift the relative emphases placed on these competitive dimensions. In short, organizational learning not only improves the effectiveness of an Operations Strategy, it may over time lead to profound changes in that strategy. In addition, companies usually find that they can proceed along different paths as they pursue the development of certain new capabilities, and each path may create additional capabilities—or impair existing ones. We return to such issues in a later section, where we develop the concept of "strategic hinges."

Role: Expanding Expectations and Initiatives

Individuals often switch among several roles in the course of a day: dutiful daughter or son, supportive spouse, strict parent, obedient subordinate, demanding boss, etc. How they behave—what options are available to them, how assertive they are, and how they interact with others—is fundamentally affected by the particular role they are playing at a given time. Similarly, two operations organizations are likely to behave very differently, even though they operate in the same industry and are equipped and staffed similarly, depending on how they perceive their roles and/or are perceived by other groups within the company. Therefore, a critical aspect of an Operations Strategy is changing the way the operations organization thinks about itself and is regarded by others. If it sees its role as being simply a "good corporate citizen" or "team player," and is therefore willing to wait for requests and directions from others, it will never become a proactive force within the company no matter how much this is desired. On the other hand, attempts by it to play a more forceful role when other groups expect it to be reactive (or even submissive) will lead to continual friction and infighting.

Skinner's original notion was that the proper role for an operations organization was essentially supportive in nature. He stated that "the purpose of manufacturing is to serve the company" by configuring itself so that "its entire apparatus is focused to accomplish the particular manufacturing task demanded by the company's strategy and marketing objective." As one examines the best companies in the world (the so-called "world class" companies), however, it becomes apparent that their operations functions play a somewhat different role. Rather than simply carrying out their assigned mission, they appeared to have the authority to redefine that mission. The best companies, that is, did not just ask operations to fill a predetermined role. They challenged (and supported) their operations organizations to become so good that they generated new opportunities for the other functional groups. In the process of identifying and exploiting such opportunities, these elite operations groups were able to participate in—even instigate—the reformulation of the company's competitive strategy and pressure other functions to react to its initiatives. We will discuss this larger role, and put it into the context of the other kinds of roles that manufacturing could be asked to play, later in this book.

An Overview of Part I

This first module, Part I, "The Concept of Operations Strategy," introduces most of the themes that are raised in this Overview, and are then expanded upon in later modules. It consists of four cases in addition to this reading. The first, "Chandler Home Products (B)" is part of a series that follows the evolving competitive environment and operations strategy of Chandler's European organization from 1962 to the present. The (B) case picks up the story in 1979 and looks at the decisions it faced then. A follow-on case is contained in the *Instructor's Manual* and can be used in later classes to carry the still-evolving Chandler saga five years further ahead.

The second and third cases describe the dilemmas faced by two service companies, each of which is trying to define the appropriate scope and focus of its operations. The first addresses the mounting problems being faced by the Engineering Inspection & Insurance Company, which has built its competitive strategy around offering more customized insurance for boilers and other machinery—and at the same time reducing the amount of risk it assumes—by inspecting all items before issuing policies on them. In an increasingly competitive environment, however, this practice is leading to higher costs and longer delays in issuing policies than is true for its major competitors. There is increasing tension between its marketing and inspection functions, as they debate whether the company's historical strategy should be changed, and the implications such changes would have on its operations.

The third case in the module looks at several issues facing the McDonald's Corporation. It has built its success around offering a limited set of menu items and creating operating systems that ensure a high degree of consistency in their preparation—both over time and across different restaurants. Now, faced with a declining growth rate and tougher competitors, some of which are carving out niches in its mass market and others that are offering a broader array of product offerings, McDonald's must decide what, if any, changes it should make in its strategy. This decision is complicated by an internal proposal to make various changes in its operations for environmental reasons.

The final case describes the dilemma faced by the American Connector Company. A recent attempt to benchmark a Japanese competitor (DJC) reveals that it had been able to reduce its manufacturing costs dramatically over the previous six years. Although DJC's total costs currently are still higher than ACC's, largely because of the higher cost of raw materials in Japan, the manufacturing costs of the U.S. factory that DJC is proposing to establish would be far below ACC's if it were able to duplicate the manufacturing strategy that has been so successful in Japan. This case vividly contrasts not only the different strategies adopted by the two companies, but the different roles of the manufacturing organizations in each, as well as the rates of learning that each has been able to achieve as a result. A follow-on case describing the changes that the manager of ACC's U.S. factory is proposing to make it its operation is provided in the *Instructor's Manual.*

References

Abernathy, W., and K. Wayne (1974). "The Limits of the Learning Curve." *Harvard Business Review* (September–October): 109–119.
Skinner, W. (1974). "The Focused Factory." *Harvard Business Review* (May–June): 113–121.

CHAPTER 1

Chandler
Home Products (B)

"A FEW MONTHS AGO the head of our European organization asked me to recommend whether we should expand my plant again or locate a new production facility somewhere else in Europe. I studied the situation and alternatives for a few weeks and then suggested that this recommendation be made by someone outside my organization. There were simply too many conflicting interests involved, and I think I would have been regarded as being too biased.

"I am very proud of my plant's performance over the past four years. We have been able to maintain our prices and delivery reliability in the face of inflation, exchange rate fluctuations, new products, and political uncertainty. The arguments that led to the construction of this plant over 15 years ago, and the concentration in it of the production for most of our sales in continental Europe, are equally valid today. The plant is not too large, either in comparison with other manufacturing plants in Holland or in comparison with our own U.S. plant in Peoria. We have room to expand, and I am convinced that the costs of expanding here will be less than anywhere else in Europe."

Roland van Zwieten, Manager of Chandler Home Products' Com-plant ("Common Market plant") in Nijmegen, Holland, raised his hands expressively and smiled. "You see, I am biased! So my boss agreed with me, and that's the reason a Booz, Allen[1] team is working here now."

Chandler Home Products

Chandler Home Products was a privately owned, family-controlled corporation headquartered in Peoria, Illinois. Chandler's lines of household care products were marketed worldwide. Though no company figures were

---

[1] Booz, Allen & Hamilton, a U.S.-based multinational management consulting firm.

This case was prepared as a basis for class discussion rather than to illustrate either effective or ineffective handling of an administrative situation.

published, industry observers estimated Chandler's 1978 sales at over $1 billion. Approximately 1,500 different products were sold in almost 50 countries. More than half of Chandler's sales were made outside the U.S.A. Of these a majority were recorded in Europe. Van Zwieten's Complant alone produced almost 150 different product formulations. Since most of these were sold in more than one size, the total number of SKUs (stock keeping units) was in excess of 650.

The bulk of the company's business was concentrated in four product areas: floor care products, furniture polish, air fresheners, and insecticides. Although the percentage varied by product line and by country, roughly 60% of Chandler's sales were in the form of aerosols (sold in pressurized cans), a quarter were in liquid form (sold in cans and bottles), and the remainder were solids. Chandler's strategy had been to seek a dominant market position for its products, while maintaining premium prices, through product innovation and the heavy use of advertising. High gross margins (these varied considerably from country to country, but 60% was not unusual) were needed to finance the costs of R&D, advertising and channel support while still providing adequate returns. The company tried to maintain a profit-to-sales ratio of 5% after taxes.

In recent years attempts had been made to diversify into the personal care field with deodorants and shaving gels. Household care products had also been extended into laundry aids and air fresheners. Introducing new lines of products was part of an overall effort to become less dependent upon Chandler's traditional household care products. The markets for these traditional products had matured in the developed countries and promised inadequate future growth. Moreover, the large market shares which Chandler commanded in its traditional product lines were likely to be the target of increasing competitive assault. Competing in new markets, however, frequently pitted Chandler against such international giants as Procter & Gamble, Unilever, and Gillette.

Despite the fact that the markets for many of its products were maturing, and the overall rate of economic growth in the developed countries of the world was predicted to be less than 3% over the foreseeable future, Chandler hoped that the introduction of new products and the growth of markets in developing countries would enable it to maintain a sales growth rate of 15% per year. It intended to finance most of this growth through internally generated funds, so as to maintain its debt/equity ratio at the current level. This would require careful control over costs and investments, since a 15% sales growth could not be maintained if there were any deterioration in either its profit/sales or its sales/assets ratios. As part of its overall program for maintaining, even improving, profitability, the company intended to gradually shift its resources from low-profit, low-growth products to those that promised higher profits and higher growth. Proposed capital investments were expected to promise a return on investment of at least 25% before tax.

Chandler Europe

The decade of the 1960s witnessed a significant expansion of Chandler's European operations. While some European subsidiaries predated World War II, none had represented a major source of revenues until this growth period. Thereafter, existing subsidiaries grew in size and new subsidiaries rapidly blossomed throughout Western Europe.

Although most of the products sold in Europe were based on products developed in Peoria, the mix of sales differed greatly from country to country. Even neighboring European subsidiaries often significantly differed both in size and in the relative popularity of Chandler products in the diverse product categories in which they competed. Products were adapted to local consumers by means of local brand names, and sometimes even their formulations were modified to meet local preferences. Thus, the distribution of the income levels in a country, together with national tastes in home furnishing, greatly influenced the product offerings of the local Chandler subsidiary. Some foreign subsidiaries even sold products which had been developed specifically for their own use and which were unavailable in the U.S.

Country managers had considerable autonomy in determining their individual product lines. They could add, drop, reposition, or emphasize products according to their perception of local market conditions. Major product or marketing decisions (e.g. dropping a product, an unusual pricing strategy, etc.), of course, had to be justified before Mr. Genet, Chandler's Executive Vice President for European Consumer Goods.

In 1978 roughly 85% of Chandler's European consumer goods sales took place on the continent, while the U.K. accounted for the remainder. About a third of the sales in continental Europe came from Chandler's French subsidiary. The next largest subsidiary was Italy, whose sales were about half of France's, followed by Spain and Germany. An organization chart for the activities under Mr. Genet's jurisdiction is contained in Exhibit 1.1.

The Decision to Build the Complant

Before 1962 each subsidiary had been responsible for its own production. Following a major study by Booz, Allen & Hamilton it was decided to consolidate European production into two plants. One would be the existing facility at Buxbridge, England (about 50 miles from London) which would be responsible for the production of all of Chandler's products for the U.K. The other would be a new facility, the Complant, located in Nijmegen. This plant would be responsible for the production of the aerosol and liquid products for all of Chandler's EEC subsidiaries (the U.K. was not then a member of the Common Market).

The study which resulted in the decision to build the Complant was

Exhibit 1.1 Chandler Home Products (B)
Organization for European Consumer Sales

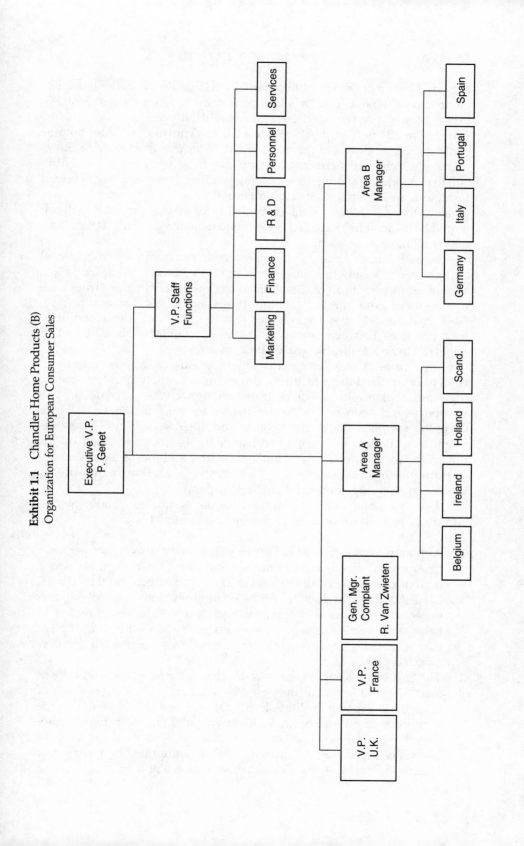

triggered by a recognition of two partially related trends in the European environment. First, Chandler's European sales were growing at a rate in excess of 40% per year and therefore would be expected to quadruple (from $6 to $24 million) by 1965 if not before. This forecast sales volume could not be produced in the existing Chandler manufacturing facilities, many of which were inefficient, already operating near capacity, and difficult to expand. Expanding these existing facilities, moreover, was expected to require an investment in additional plant and equipment which was greater than Chandler's total current European investment. Finally, it would be difficult to locate and train adequate managers and staff personnel for all these expansions.

Second, Europe appeared to be progressing smoothly towards its goal of free trade within the group of Common Market countries which accounted for almost all of Chandler's sales on the continent. Tariffs were to be reduced to 40% of their previous levels and quotas abolished by mid-1963. By the end of 1966 it was hoped that all tariffs and other discriminatory practices between member countries would be abolished. This appeared to be a realizable goal in 1962.

As a result, Chandler's management wondered whether the usual risks of centralized manufacturing (for example, supply problems resulting from a plant shutdown or transportation/customs restrictions) in Europe would soon be no greater than they were in the U.S., where Chandler supplied the entire country from a single facility. These risks might even be less in Europe because of the back-up provided by the Buxbridge plant, which was Chandler's largest and most modern manufacturing facility outside the U.S. Unlike most of its European facilities, moreover, Buxbridge had ample room to expand.

The consulting study confirmed Chandler's intuition, and provided additional reasons for moving to consolidated production.

1. Although overall growth in Europe would average over 40% per year, this growth varied widely among countries. Moreover, there was a high degree of uncertainty about the growth rate in several countries. Consolidating production for all countries into one plant was expected to help smooth the total load. It would be easier, that is, to balance production in a single, well-designed and well-managed plant than to balance production simultaneously in several small country-oriented plants.

2. The cost of building a centralized manufacturing plant would be at least $500,000 less than the cost of adding an equivalent amount of capacity to existing facilities. Partly this savings would be due to the economies of scale associated with buying eight modern, highly automated filling lines and auxiliary materials-handling equipment instead of expanding the capacity of older equipment or adding new lines at several locations. Construction costs at a new, carefully chosen

site would also be less than at the congested sites where most of Chandler's plants were located. These sites, however, could easily be converted into regional warehouses for Chandler's products.

3. A consolidated plant would be large enough to justify the construction of an on-site polymer plant and large-scale chemical processing and storage facilities. This would enable Chandler to reduce its reliance on outside suppliers and gain more control over its total costs.

4. The annual operating cost of the new plant would also be considerably less than the total cost of operating separate plants. The Booz, Allen study showed that such savings would amount to almost $1.8 million by 1965, or over 20% of total annual costs. A large part of this savings came from the same economies of scale mentioned previously (fewer production workers, a single production control department, etc.), but the major part was expected to come from centralized purchasing of raw materials and containers (the cost of the packaging materials in a typical product was about one-and-a-half times the cost of the chemical ingredients), and from being able to buy in bulk directly from manufacturers as a result of the proposed ability to process these materials in Chandler's own facilities.

5. A centralized plant using modern automated equipment, managed by experts, and utilizing modern testing equipment and a well-equipped laboratory would ensure high and, more important, standardized quality for Chandler's proliferating product line.

6. Finally, a centralized plant would simplify and speed up the development, debugging, and introduction of new products.

After an analysis of several countries the study team decided (somewhat to its surprise, since it had begun with the expectation that either France or Germany would be the most logical location) that Holland would be the best country in which to locate the new plant. Several possible locations in Holland were studied in detail, and Nijmegen was finally recommended for a variety of reasons, including access to raw materials, its proximity to markets via existing rail lines and highways (the distance from Nijmegen to Milan, Italy, for example, was about the same as from Peoria to Philadelphia), labor costs, tax rates, and political and social stability.

As a result the decision was made to buy 70 acres in a newly developed industrial park in Nijmegen, together with options on an adjoining 30 acres. The plant was built and in operation by mid-1964. Since it served the entire regional market, Complant was separated organizationally from the marketing activity in Holland. Its manager reported directly to the Executive V.P. for European Sales.

The transfer price was set equal to Complant's full manufacturing cost plus 10%. Each marketing subsidiary paid for the cost of transporting its goods from the Complant.

At the time of the Booz, Allen study Spain was not a member of the

Common Market, and there was no indication that it would become a member in the foreseeable future. Therefore the Complant did not attempt to service the Spanish market, which set up its own filling operations near Madrid. In 1979 this small plant, employing just over 80 production workers, was the only other Chandler production site on the continent. This plant had been modernized and expanded in 1978, a year which also saw Spain make considerable progress towards its goal of joining the EEC in the late 1980s.

History of the Complant since 1964

The performance of the Complant had fully met Chandler's expectations over the period of 1964–1978. As Chandler's European sales grew by a factor of 10, to over Dfl. 400 million, the Complant was expanded 5 times. It currently represented a total investment of Dfl. 90 million.[2] With each expansion the additional production space was integrated completely with the existing space, which usually required the shifting around of some equipment and departments to implement the new work flow. In early 1979 the plant was in the shape of a large square containing roughly 400,000 square feet of floor space. Storage tanks containing chemicals and propellants were on one side. These led directly to the chemical mixing and processing department, where the formulas for each product were prepared and stored. At the appropriate time these mixtures were piped to the adjoining area which contained the liquid filling and aerosol filling lines. Following the same flow pattern, filled bottles and cans then were transported to the storage area and then to packing and shipping. Finished products exited the plant on the opposite site from where raw materials entered. Complant's inventory turnover in 1978 was about 7 times for both raw materials and packaging materials. Finished goods turnover was even higher.

The heart of the plant was the 10 bottling lines and the 3 aerosol filling lines. These were operated two 8-hour shifts a day, five days a week. The periods between and after the two shifts were used for cleaning and equipment maintenance. Although it was difficult to put a precise figure on the "capacity" of the plant, since this depended greatly on the production mix (which included the product mix, the size mix, and the mix between aerosol and liquid products), Mr. van Zwieten estimated that under the current production mix the plant was operating at somewhat under 90% of capacity. "We are currently producing about 115 million units per year (where a unit is one can or one bottle of whatever size)," he stated, "and following our current operating procedures we probably could produce as many as 130 million units: 90 million aerosol and 40 million liquids. Beyond that point we would have to increase capacity in some manner." The breakeven point for the plant, he estimated, was about 90 million units.

[2]Dfl. 1.00 = $.50 in early 1979.

There was ample room to expand the plant, he stated, since the total working space required by current operations only utilized about 17 of the 70 acres that Chandler owned. Any plant expansion, however, could not be incorporated easily into the existing plant, but would probably have to be constructed as a separate adjoining work area. This would present no problems, in his view, because whether or not the expansion took place he was planning to move the chemical storage tanks from the side of the building where they currently were located (which was the side closest to a nearby village which had been gradually expanding towards Chandler's site) to the opposite side of the building for reasons of safety. He was planning to replace some of the storage tanks with bigger tanks during this move, and the production flow in the plant would also have to be redesigned.

The plant currently employed about 420 people (of which about 260 were permanent production personnel), which represented a small portion of the total work force in the area and was smaller than the work forces of several other companies in the region. Chandler's Buxbridge plant employed over 700 people (but only 315 in manufacturing), and its home plant in Peoria currently employed over 2,000 people, working three 8-hour shifts per day.

Complant had been able to build a considerable amount of flexibility into this work force because of van Zwieten's use of students from the nearby university as temporary workers. They usually represented somewhat less than 10% of the total work force (although this could rise to much higher levels). These students were delighted with the opportunity to make extra money and were willing to work on an "as available" basis. Hence they served to increase the job stability of the regular workers. The Buxbridge plant was able to make use of such workers to about the same degree as Complant. In Spain there was even more reliance on such workers. So far there had been no opposition from local authorities or unions to this practice, which allowed Chandler to respond to sales fluctuations by changing the production level and thereby maintain relatively low inventories of finished goods. This both reduced capital costs and avoided the need for sophisticated control systems.

No radical change in skills or operating procedures would be required by the addition of new filling lines. A manufacturing cost breakdown is provided in Exhibit 1.2.

There had as yet been no attempt at central coordination of Chandler's European plants. Nor was there any standardization of manufacturing cost systems, inventory control techniques, or quality control procedures. This was largely due to the fact that Spain's special status as a stand-alone plant outside the EEC had restricted the possibility for such coordination to Complant and Buxbridge. Individuals within these two plants had good personal relationships, and such informal contacts appeared to provide a satisfactory degree of communication and coordination.

Exhibit 1.2   Chandler Home Products (B)
Cost of Sales Breakdown by Category

	Percentage Base Budget 1978/79
– Materials	63.6
– Direct Labor	6.2
– 25% of direct Production Overheads	1.7
– 25% of Finished Goods Warehousing	0.4
– Freight Europlant to Marketing Companies	5.0
TOTAL: DIRECT DELIVERED COST	**76.9**
PLUS:	
– 75% of Direct Production Overheads	5.2
– 75% of Finished Goods Warehousing	1.1
– Environmental Control	0.4
– Production Planning	0.9
– Purchasing	0.8
– Engineering	0.8
– Quality Assurance	1.1
– Management Information Services	1.2
– Finance	1.0
– Administrative Management	0.8
– General Services	1.2
– Interest	0.9
– European Service Charges	0.9
– Profit Sharing	1.2
– European Mark-up	5.6
TOTAL COST OF SALES MARKETING	**100.0**

Evaluating Complant's Performance

During the period 1970–1977 the Complant had successfully weathered three, almost simultaneous, major crises: the explosion in petrochemical prices in 1974–1975 following the Arab oil boycott in late 1973, a similar explosion in the basic hourly wage in Holland that occurred soon thereafter and which raised the Dutch rate from one of the lowest in Europe to one of the highest, and the European recession of 1974–1975 which reduced Chandler's continental sales (in terms of number of units) by over 20%. Throughout this period the plant had never had a loss year.

Measures of the plant's performance in combatting these cost increases during a period of highly variable but generally rapidly rising sales is contained in Exhibit 1.3, which presents indices of various volume and cost categories for each year since 1970. Mr. van Zwieten particularly emphasized the fact that while the overall cost of living in Holland had

Exhibit 1.3 Chandler Home Products (B)
Summary of Complant Sales and Cost Performance Indices

	1971	1972	1973	1974	1975	1976	1977	1978
European Sales (Guilders)	100	125	148	190	195	238	227	226
Number Units Produced	100	117	127	155	123	157	160	160
Sales/Total Employees	100	124	150	161	169	188	186	190
Units/Production Worker	100	116	137	114	123	123	123	123
Labor Cost/Unit	100	89	85	113	126	137	152	160
Overhead Cost/Unit (Mfg. & Admin.)	100	83	110	113	172	156	176	180
Raw Materials Cost/Unit	100	99	99	132	151	150	147	150
Packaging Materials	100	107	112	123	136	139	130	130
Total Manufacturing Cost/Unit	100	102	106	123	145	145	144	148
Inter-Company Price Index	100	104	106	115	137	134	134	136
Cost of Living Index (Holland)	100	108	116	126	139	152	161	170

risen by 70% during the period 1971–1978, Complant's average price per unit had only increased 36%. Moreover, neither Complant's average cost per unit during this period nor the percentage breakdown of its cost were significantly different from that of Chandler's English plant, despite the considerably lower wage rate in the U.K. (see Exhibit 1.4).

Such comparisons between Chandler plants were somewhat suspect, however, because the products produced at each plant were usually quite different in terms of both formula and packaging. Different plants also used different standard costs (whose origins were sometimes hazy), and different methods for breaking down and allocating shared costs. Overhead costs were usually assigned on the basis of a standard percentage of direct manufacturing cost in each plant, but again these percentages varied from plant to plant.

At least part of Complant's ability to insulate itself against inflation was attributable to the fact that it sourced its materials from a number of different countries. Less than 35% of its purchases came from Holland, while the U.K., Belgium and Germany each accounted for about 15% of purchases, and slightly under 10% came from France. This diversity of sources contrasted with the sourcing policies of the English and Spanish plants, where almost all purchases were made within the host country.

Although over 50% of the purchases at Chandler's European plants were from vendors who also supplied at least one of the other plants, there was no formal coordination of purchasing among them (although there was some informal exchange of information). Partly this was due to the fact that a high percentage of purchases were from the large petrochemical

Exhibit 1.4   Chandler Home Products (B)

5 Year Comparison of Cost per 100 units in Guilders of Complant and U.K.

	1970/71		1971/72		1972/73		1973/74		1974/75	
	Cost of Production per 100 units	INDEX 70/71 = 100	Cost of Production per 100 units	Index 70/71 = 100	Cost of Production per 100 units	Index 70/71 = 100	Cost of Production per 100 units	Index 70/71 = 100	Cost of Production per 100 units	Index 70/71 = 100
I. U.K. cost in Sterling:										
Raw material cost	2.27	100	3.02	133	3.22	142	4.38	193	5.97	263
Component cost	4.21	100	5.41	128	5.94	141	6.95	165	7.62	181
Direct Labor & overhds.	2.20	100	2.76	126	2.53	115	3.41	155	4.16	189
Total cost of prod. £	8.68	100	11.19	129	11.69	135	14.74	169	17.75	203
II. U.K. cost in Guilders:										
Average exchange rate £	8.631	100	8.366	97	7.519	87	6.399	74	5.928	69
Raw material cost	19.59	100	25.27	129	24.29	124	28.01	143	35.46	181
Component cost	36.34	100	45.26	125	44.70	123	44.33	122	45.06	124
Direct labor & overhds.	18.99	100	23.09	122	18.99	100	21.84	115	24.69	130
Total cost of prod. DF1.	74.92	100	93.62	125	87.98	118	94.18	126	105.21	140
III. Complant cost in Guilders:										
Raw material cost	22.98	100	22.94	99	22.89	99	30.33	132	34.70	151
Component cost	37.40	100	40.10	107	41.89	112	46.00	123	50.86	136
Direct labor & overhds.	16.42	100	16.18	99	16.63	101	18.55	113	25.62	156
Total cost of Product.	76.80	100	79.22	103	81.41	106	94.88	124	111.18	145
IV. Comparison of Total Production Cost:										
U.K. DF1.	74.92	100	93.62	125	87.98	118	94.18	126	105.21	140
Complant DF1.	76.80	100	79.22	103	81.41	106	94.88	124	111.18	145

multinationals, whose organization and policies tended to preclude any integrated sourcing arrangements.

One of the keys to efficient manufacturing at any of Chandler's plants, according to Mr. van Zwieten, was the avoidance of short production runs. Short runs and frequent changeovers reduced throughput and, therefore, caused average costs to rise. Illustrating this concern, Complant had a policy of offering substantial discounts to its sales subsidiaries on some low-volume products in exchange for their accepting a year's expected sales volume in a single shipment. He also resisted as much as possible any increase in the number of products (and sizes) produced at his plant, because both indirect and direct manufacturing costs appeared to be more dependent on the number of product codes produced than on the total production volume.

The relationship between the Complant and the national marketing organizations had not been entirely without friction. In 1975, for example, the manager of the Italian marketing organization prepared a carefully reasoned argument that the exchange rate between the Dutch guilder and the Italian lira had deteriorated so badly that his product costs were much higher than those of his major Italian competitors. Moreover, his transportation costs were the highest of any Chandler subsidiary in Europe. Therefore, he argued that he no longer could price his products competitively in Italy.[3] The alternatives, he stated, were either to lose market share (in what was then Chandler's fastest-growing subsidiary), to utilize the services of local "contract fillers"—companies who owned liquid filling lines and would perform the filling function (using ingredients imported in bulk from Complant) for a negotiated price, such as was being done increasingly in England, or to negotiate a new pricing arrangement with Complant. One proposed modification would be to reduce Complant's 10% "profit margin" to 5%; another would be to equalize the unit transportation costs to all subsidiaries (which would have the effect of charging the Northern European subsidiaries more per unit and Italy less). He estimated his total intercompany transportation costs in 1976 at $800,000, or about 6% of his total costs. This was almost twice the percentage at any of Chandler's other subsidiaries.

These arguments had forced Chandler's top management to review carefully both the philosophy behind the Complant and how it was working in practice. After careful consideration, and the recognition that differing transportation costs and exchange rates did put certain subsidiaries at a disadvantage, it was decided to maintain the basic policy of centralized production although Italy was given more flexibility to use outside fillers under certain circumstances. Partly this decision was based on the fact that the Complant was then operating at less than 60% of capacity and, therefore, a major reduction in the demand from Italy would have an impact on product costs for all of Chandler's subsidiaries on the continent.

[3]See case "Chandler Home Products" (Harvard Business School case 9-377-232).

Although there was some concern that the use of contract fillers and multiple production points would lead to a loss of control over product quality, by early 1979 about 15% of Chandler's sales of products on the continent (primarily in Italy) was being handled by outside fillers.

The 1979 Capacity Expansion Decision

In mid-1978 Chandler European management developed sales projections for the 1980s reflecting its belief that unit sales would grow at an average rate of 6–7% per year during the decade. The annual growth rate was expected to be somewhat higher than this average during the first half of the decade, as several major new products were introduced, and then was expected to slow down. This forecast assumed no major crises in Europe's economic or socio-political environment. Although sales in different countries were expected to grow at somewhat different rates, no major changes were expected in their shares of total European sales by 1990—that is, the sales map of Chandler Europe was expected to look roughly the same in 1990 as it did in 1978, although it would be about twice as big.

Despite this apparent stability, there were expected to be important shifts in the product mix during this period. Liquids and solids were expected to grow somewhat faster than aerosols, which would drop to about half of total sales. New products (products introduced since 1975, that is) were expected to account for over 40% of total sales by 1990, but it was also expected that aerosols, solids and liquids would remain the basic packaging forms for Chandler's products (see Exhibit 1.5 for a summary of Chandler's European demand forecasts).

Total European manufacturing capacity in 1979 was about 200 million aerosol units, 80 million liquid units and 20 million solid units, assuming two-shift operations and 100% machine utilization. This represented "peak capacity," however. In order to maintain the flexibility to respond to short-term market shifts and production bottlenecks Chandler preferred to size its plants on the basis of an average capacity utilization of bout 85%. In mid-1979 both aerosol and liquid production were nearing 90% utilization at Complant (whereas the production of solids represented only about 50% of capacity). If its sales projections proved accurate, Chandler's manufacturing organization maintained the average output per filling line currently being achieved, and no increase in the reliance on outside fillers was allowed, it was estimated that at least two additional aerosol lines and four additional high-speed liquid filling lines would be required somewhere in Europe by 1990.

Buxbridge (which supplied a number of African and Middle Eastern export markets as well as the U.K. market) currently had annual capacity for 80 million aerosol units, 25 million liquid units and 8 million solid units. Although its sales to domestic markets were growing more slowly than Complant's, export sales were expected to rise rapidly. There was

Exhibit 1.5   Chandler Home Products (B)
European Sales Forecasts
(In Million Units)

	1980	1985	1990
Liquids			
• Contintental Europe			
– EEC	40	69	90
– Non-EEC	7	14	20
• UK	11	17	25
	58	100	135
Aerosols			
• Continental Europe			
– EEC	90	115	144
– Non-EEC	22	40	45
• UK	33	35	36
	145	190	225

some reluctance, however, given the historic instability of the regions to which it was exporting, for Chandler to justify increased production capacity solely to supply this projected growth in exports.

There was a strong reluctance to move to a three-shift work schedule at Complant, as was used in the Peoria plant, because it was felt that it would be difficult to attract sufficient people of the desired quality to work the third shift. Nor would university students be available for such work. Van Zwieten felt that such an arrangement would also increase the congestion and confusion in the plant to such an extent that efficiency and quality would both suffer. Chandler top management, he observed, had recently emphasized the importance it placed on the "high quality of the working life" in its plants. He pointed out that even though workers only worked 8 hours in a day, they were actually in the plant for 9 hours or more (because of breaks for lunch, coffee, cleaning up, etc.), and therefore three 8-hour shifts would complicate worker schedules and threaten the cooperative atmosphere he had tried to develop. Also, since equipment maintenance and the cleaning of the plant were being done during the off-shift hours when the plant was idle, removing this idle time would not cause total working hours to increase by the 50% that one might expect.

Since the manufacturing costs at Buxbridge and Complant were quite similar (see Exhibit 1.4), there appeared to be little advantage to transshipping products between them (the cost of transshipment averaged about 10% of Chandler's manufacturing cost). Similarly, the high Spanish import duties precluded shipment into Spain, at least until it achieved full EEC membership. Chandler's European management had also come to the tentative conclusion that the economies of scale involved in the production of aerosol products were such that Complant should continue to be the sole source for these products on the continent (outside of Spain). It was estimated, for example, that a modern aerosol filling line would cost about Dfl. 8 million, and would increase total aerosol capacity by about 40 million units per year. The question was whether additional liquid filling capacity should also be located at Complant. A modern high-speed liquid filling line would cost about Dfl. 3 million and would add about 20 million units per year to liquid capacity.

Some interest had been expressed by various members of Chandler's European organization in locating this new liquid filling capacity either in Italy or Southern France. Their argument was that, apart from avoiding the potential danger of "putting too many eggs in one (Complant) basket," a new plant in Southern Europe would tap a lower cost labor market, reduce transportation costs and offset the growing protectionist sentiment that was being expressed in several European countries—particularly France.

Van Zwieten, however, felt strongly that the most economical location for such an expansion was at Complant. He pointed out that this would minimize the investment required since no land would have to be purchased in Nijmegen, whereas about 10 acres (4 hectares) would be required for a minimum-sized stand-alone plant. The price of good commercial land (in industrial parks or a location similarly conducive to industrial operations) was at least Dfl. 1.5 million per hectare throughout Europe. On the other hand, even if Chandler did have to buy additional land in Nijmegen, under the terms of its option it could purchase an additional 12 hectares (30 acres) adjacent to its present site at a price of Dfl. 300,000 per hectare.

As regards equipment cost, van Zwieten stated that since almost all the equipment was imported from the U.S. or Common Market countries, the cost would be roughly the same no matter where it was located. As a result, he felt that the cost of a 20 million unit expansion in liquid filling capacity would cost at least Dfl. 12 million if a new plant were built, but only require an additional investment of Dfl. 6 million at Complant. An analysis of Complant showed that the synergistic effect of an additional aerosol line was at least 10 MM units higher than if such a line was put in isolation. Synergy of liquid filling was expected to be less severe. Furthermore, Complant now had sufficient liquid capacity to justify a blow-molding facility that would allow it to produce its own plastic bottles. This would give it a cost advantage compared with any other European plant.

Expansion at Complant would also limit the total number of overhead personnel required, for the reasons previously mentioned. Van Zwieten estimated that a minimum-sized new plant, with total annual capacity of at least 20 million units, would require from 50 to 100 total workers of which about 20% would be almost exclusively involved in plant administration. Such a plant would not be as automated as Complant, and would have a higher proportion of monotonous jobs. It was also unlikely, in his opinion, that the new plant would have access to university students who were willing to work on a temporary basis, as he did. Finally, a plant in southern Europe would not have the same access to petrochemicals and packaging materials that Complant had because of its proximity to several major ports and refineries.

As a result, despite the lower labor costs in both France and Italy (the labor cost in France, for example, came to just over half of the Dutch cost when fringes and direct supervision were included), the direct manufacturing cost at a French or Italian liquids plant was estimated to be slightly greater (0-2% for liquids, 6-10% for aerosols) than that at Complant. The cost of raw materials and components was generally higher in France and Italy than in Holland (except for plastic containers in Italy because of governmental aid on plastic raw materials). Over time, however, the gap between Italy and Complant was closing.[4]

Adding distribution costs tended to complicate the issue, of course: the delivered cost to French customers from a French plant, for example, would be slightly less than from Complant, while the delivered cost to German customers would be considerably more. These differences would be affected in the future both by changes in the relative wage rates in France and Holland and the exchange rate between the French franc and the Dutch guilder. There seemed to be no way of predicting whether the differences in total delivered cost would move enough in favor of a French (or an Italian) plant to justify the additional investment required.

Contract Filling

The only realistic alternative to increasing production capacity was to increase drastically Chandler's reliance on outside contract fillers. Currently about 15% of liquid sales on the continent were being filled by outside companies, although less than 1% of aerosol sales were filled outside. The U.K., on the other hand, utilized contract fillers for 30% of sales without apparent problems. There were some who argued, therefore, that at least part of Complant's apparent capacity squeeze could be alleviated by increasing its dependence on outside fillers. The cost of this service differed by country and by product type. In the case of liquid products, for example, contract fillers in France typically charged 5–10% less than the Complant price, while Italian fillers often charged 20–30% less.

There were two major arguments against such a move. First, there was concern that the perceived quality of Chandler's products and customer service (which was the cornerstone of its marketing strategy and the justification for its higher prices) might suffer. Second, the costs of

[4]

	Plastic material index	
	Nov. '78	June '79
Outside supplier	100	152
Complant supplier	119	156

inspecting and coordinating outside fillers increased rapidly as their number increased. Van Zwieten argued, in fact, that the cost of contract filling was considerably more than it appeared because of the increase in indirect costs that this caused at Complant. There was particular danger, he felt, in allowing contract fillers to take over 100% of the production of any product because the Complant's ability to solve production crises at a contract filler was heavily dependent on the body of expertise maintained within his plant.

The problem was complicated by the fact that a number of Chandler's products used proprietary formulations. Chandler management was very reluctant to risk the secrecy of these formulations by giving them to contract fillers. This reluctance was particularly strong in the case of Chandler's new "high-technology" products, and weaker in the case of older, low-technology products.

Restricting its attention only to those products which could be contracted out safely, Chandler decided that 14 million units of liquid products would be potential candidates for outside filling by 1980, 10 million of which would be in France and Italy. This number would increase to 42 million by 1990, of which 26 million would be in France and Italy. Although 25 million units of aerosol products were potential candidates for outside filling by 1990, there was less economic justification for doing so. Current quotes from most contract aerosol fillers, even in France and Italy, indicated higher delivered costs than Complant's.

The Booz, Allen & Hamilton Proposal

When the consulting firm of Booz, Allen & Hamilton was asked to make a recommendation where and how to expand the production of liquid products, it agreed to do so but only within the context of an overall evaluation of Chandler's manufacturing strategy for European production. It suggested an overall planning horizon of 1990, and promised to provide detailed proposals through 1983/84, including recommendations regarding organizational structure and staffing. These proposals would take into consideration a number of guidelines that represented different aspects of Chandler's overall strategy (see Exhibit 1.6).

Exhibit 1.6   Chandler Home Products (B)
Chandler Competitive Guidelines

---

1. Meeting well-defined customer needs in niches thropugh creative marketing is the over-ruling factor of success.

2. Incoming years, we must be able to develop and introduce large numbers of new products in a *timely manner*.

3. We must be able to respond *quickly* to changes in market needs and competitive actions.

(continued)

Exhibit 1.6 *(conyinued)*

4. Our product quality, wherever possible, should be clearly distinguishable as superior to the competition in terms of performance, packaging and design finish.

5. Customer service is a critical sucess factor in the market place. It must be competitive—or better. Exceptional customer service could be a major sucess factor, but generallyy the appropriate level of customer service should be dtermined by balancing marketing requirements with manufacturing/distribution/inventory costs.

6. We must develop/maintain expertise in process technology across an important share of our product line. We should maintain state-of-the-art capabilities in some manufacturing areas to insure a degree of technical pre-eminence in the organization.

7. We want both a very high degree of manufacturing flexibility to rspond to changing market conditions, and competitive landed costs with important local competitors.

CHAPTER 2

Engineering Inspection & Insurance Company

This company needs to make some major changes. But it's been successful doing things a certain way for so long, it's hard to get the top people to understand the necessity for change, or the nature of the changes that might be required.

—A recently appointed Branch Manager

HEADQUARTERED IN Spokane, Washington, the Engineering Inspection & Insurance Company (EIIC) inspected and insured a wide range of industrial equipment, ranging from small compressed air tanks and apartment building furnace boilers to 5,000 horsepower chemical plant compressors and large steam turbines. It was founded in 1952 by Warren Rodman, a former U.S. Navy engineer who had developed a thriving business providing inspection services for local businesses. In addition, if a property insurance company received a request to insure a non-standard piece of equipment, and did not have sufficient in-house inspection capacity or expertise in that region, it sometimes made use of experienced independents like Rodman. After several years, during which he built up a sizeable clientele and hired and trained a number of associates, Rodman came to the conclusion that he was making more money for other people than for himself. Because of his skills, the insurable losses incurred by the insurance companies that wrote policies based on his inspections were averaging substantially less than the insurance premiums paid to them. Securing the financial backing and expertise of a wealthy businessman who had extensive experience in the insurance industry, he began offering to insure the equipment belonging to some of his long time clients.

Professor Robert H. Hayes prepared this case as the basis for class discussion rather than to illustrate either effective or ineffective handling of an administrative situation. It is based on an earlier version prepared by Research Assistant Robert L. Banks, under the supervision of Professor W. Earl Sasser. Some numbers have been disguised; others have been estimated by the casewriter.

The company that resulted grew rapidly until by 1991 it operated through a network of 20 branches, located largely west of the Mississippi River and concentrated in the Pacific northwest. That year the total annual premiums written by the U.S. boiler and machinery insurance industry approached $1 billion, 80% of which was accounted for by the top five companies; the giant Hartford Steam Boiler company alone had a market share of over 35%. Against this formidable competition EIIC had been able to build its premium income to over $65 million a year. (See Exhibit 2.1 for a financial summary.)

During early 1991, EIIC CEO Ernest Cole and several other top-level officers had begun to wonder whether the quality of the service they were providing their customers was keeping pace with changing market requirements. One symptom of a possible problem was high employee turnover in several areas of the company; another was the length of time needed to prepare some policies. The time required to deliver a completed policy after an agreement to insure had been signed recently had been averaging between 40 and 50 days in some branches, and in a few instances delivery had taken as long as a year, half the duration of a typi-

Exhibit 2.1 Comparative Income Statement[a] (dollar amounts in millions)

	6 Months 1991[b]	1990	1989	1988
Underwriting Income				
Premiums written	$33.2	$62.4	$61.0	$55.8
Change in unearned premiums	(2.9)	(.3)	(2.7)	(1.3)
Premiums earned	$30.3	$62.1	$58.3	$54.5
Underwriting Expenses				
Losses and loss adjustment expense	12.2	21.5	18.1	13.7
Taxes (excluding federal income)	1.4	2.5	2.2	2.1
Commissions	5.0	10.1	9.5	8.9
Inspection	6.4	12.4	11.2	10.7
General	6.5	12.4	11.0	10.5
Total underwriting expense	$31.5	$58.9	$52.1	$45.9
Underwriting gain (loss)	(1.2)	3.2	6.2	8.6
Net investment income	3.0	5.2	4.7	4.4
Net income—Canadian subsidiary	(.2)	.5	.7	.6
Income before federal income taxes	$ 1.6	$ 9.0	$11.5	$13.6
Federal income taxes				
Current	(.6)	1.8	2.6	4.6
Deferred	.2	.1	.9	0.0
Total federal income taxes	$ (.4)	$ 1.9	$ 3.5	$ 4.6
Net Income	$ 2.0	$ 7.1	$ 8.0	$ 8.9

[a] Fiscal year ends December 31.
[b] Unaudited.

cal EIIC policy. During this time period, the customer was insured under a loosely structured agreement known as a "binder" rather than under a specific policy, and did not have to make any premium payment. Competitors that did not inspect, in contrast, could often deliver policies in less than one week.

As of mid-1991, EIIC insured more than one-half million separate objects in 50,000 different locations. The coverage normally provided by the company included provisions for actual dollar losses arising from acci-

Exhibit 2.2   Analysis of Premium System Policy Master File
Chart #1: Premium Size (by policy)

Premium Size ($000)	Number of Policies	Percent of Total Policies	Percent of Total Premium
0-.1	3,077	3.7%	0.3%
.1-.5	56,477	67.5	22.6
.5-1	11,953	14.3	12.2
1-2	6,504	7.8	13.3
2-3	2,204	2.6	7.8
3-5	1,753	2.1	9.4
5-10	1,113	1.3	9.6
10-25	489	0.6	8.2
25-50	85	0.1	3.1
50-100	25	0.0	1.8
Over 100	29	0.0	11.6
Totals	83,709	100.0%	99.0%

Chart #2: Number of Objects per Policy

Number of Objects Insured	Number of Policies	Percent of Policies
1	20,687	24.7%
2	17,404	20.8
3	11,344	13.6
4	7,206	8.6
5	4,637	5.5
6-9	9,426	11.3
10-24	7,445	8.9
25-49	3,683	4.4
50-99	1,327	1.6
100-499	513	0.6
500-999	10	0.0
999+	27	0.0
Total	83,709	100.0%

dental damage to or due to the equipment in question, various forms of liability coverage, and indemnification against the loss of profits due to machinery failure. The company's accounts varied in terms of size of premiums, the magnitude of the risk incurred by EIIC, the number and location of objects, and many other factors. A summary comparison of these characteristics is presented in Exhibit 2.2. As a result of its extensive and comprehensive inspection service, combined with its ability to tailor policies to the needs of individual clients, EIIC had been able to charge higher premiums (averaging about 10% for similar equipment) than most of its competitors. Moreover, in each of the last five years the company had experienced lower losses per premium dollar than all but one of the top five companies, and during most of that period it had grown at a faster rate than the industry average.

In order to make use of some of the underutilized capacity of its inpection engineers, EIIC began providing an independent "Professional Inspection Service" (PIS) in 1988 to supplement its regular activities. PIS was offered to manufacturing firms on a fee basis and involved an EIIC inspection of a boiler or pressure vessel as it was being constructed. This service was often performed at the request of either an equipment purchaser or a government agency to monitor a vendor. In addition, PIS was often consulted by manufacturers regarding the development or modification of construction codes. In 1991, the division was contributing about $5 million to annual revenues.

Industry Trends

There were several industry trends and characteristics that affected EIIC's operations. The property/casualty insurance industry, of which boiler and machinery insurance was a small segment, had generally approached selling insurance in two ways. One way was to deal directly with the insured customer through a salesman who was a full-time employee of the company; Allstate, State Farm, and others who used this method were called "direct writers."

The second way was to sell through independent agents. The agent was hired on a commission basis and the insurance companies using this method—called agency companies—employed few or no salesmen themselves. EIIC traditionally had been an agency company and still used agents for almost all of its transactions. There had been a long term trend for direct writing companies to use agents more frequently and, conversely, for agency companies to do more direct writing of policies. Yet, argued Mr. Woodrow Martin, vice president for Agency, "The agent will always be a part of our distribution channel, even though we are moving slowly towards more direct selling."

EIIC used both local and national agents, though it wrote much of its business with the larger insurance brokers such as Marsh & McLennan and Johnson & Higgins. There had been an increasing trend towards consolidation among agents, as well as more "packaging" of insurance policies—that is, combining a wide range of risks. "If we don't deliver a policy in a reasonable period of time," noted Denver branch manager Donald Hill, "then the agent can't wrap it up with his other coverages. So we're holding up his premium cash flow of, say, $100,000 even though we're taking only $5,000."

Additionally, there had been a trend towards self-insurance as insurance costs increased. "Sometimes, even in a big corporation, a guy will gasp at the idea of $500,000 for boiler insurance," explained Mr. Martin. "He will ask, 'what do we need that for?' Then the company might drop its insurance and effectively become self-insured."

Still, EIIC was not as worried as some companies in its industry. "No matter what," noted Mr. Martin, "we can always sell our loss prevention service. Consumerism and OSHA (the Occupational Safety and Health Act) both put pressure on corporate managers to manage their risks more effectively. Our service is not restricted to providing insurance policies."

Besides these trends, along with other insurance companies EIIC had to deal with their industry's historical cyclicality. After a few years of prosperity companies typically started underselling each other and drove industry profits down. "The last two years have been disastrous," noted Mr. Cole. "There has been a lot of price cutting , and we estimate the industry as a whole lost money on their insurance activities last year. Most companies did show some profit because of their income on investments, but they lost money on insurance."

Part of EIIC's competitive problem was that, whereas machinery insurance was but a tiny part of the business for most insurance companies, it was essentially EIIC's *only* business. "Some of our competitors go to a broker and look at our bid on a policy and simply undercut it by 5% or 6%," explained Mr. Roger Cutter, vice president for Engineering. "Now that's a hell of a competitive situation, even though they can get burned real bad. When their losses get to a point where everyone notices, they tell their salesmen to stop cutting prices so much."

Organization and Personnel

The EIIC organization consisted of five major functional areas reporting to President Cole: agency (sales, marketing and branch office operations); engineering (inspection); underwriting; finance and legal. The underwriting, finance and legal divisions operated from the home office, while the two other areas were primarily represented in branch offices. The company's 20 branch office managers, who were mainly responsible for sales and office administration, reported directly to Woodrow Martin. Branch managers did not directly supervise the inspection staffs in their branches; instead the chief inspectors reported directly to Roger Cutter, the Engineering Vice President, who also had profit and loss responsibility for the PIS division. Branch managers, through their office managers, supervised branch underwriting operations, generally a routine clerical function. The home office underwriting staff was headed by the vice president for Underwriting, Mr. Ronald Fox. It monitored the quality of underwriting operations at the branch offices and advised on significant or specialized risks. Despite these reporting relationships, the branch managers retained profit and loss responsibility for all the activities in their branches.

If conflicts arose at the branch level as to the advisability of taking on a specific risk, the problem normally was resolved at the branch office level. Unresolved disputes were sent to the home office for a decision; if the vice presidents could not agree, there was provision for the dispute to be placed before the Underwriting Committee, composed of five senior officers, for final resolution. This procedure was used only in isolated cases and for very large risks.

Inspection

EIIC's distinctive competence was embodied in its inspection service. "We offer an inspection service that is unmatched in the industry," commented President Cole. "There are only a handful of other companies with a great interest in loss *prevention*, as opposed to just loss *insurance*; that's also Hartford Steam Boiler's great strength, by the way. EIIC prided itself on its customer response time; it claimed that if an accident occurred, an EIIC inspector could be on the site in less than one hour, depending on location. "If somebody's boiler goes off," explained Cole, "they want us there in a hurry, and we are. This is one of the strengths of the branch office system. Our inspectors are in virtually every major community west of the Mississippi."

Each branch had one chief inspector who was in charge of the branch's inspection activities. Reporting to him were between one and three supervising inspectors and to them, approximately eight field inspectors per supervisor. The chief inspector was responsible for all inspection activities, accident investigations, and claim adjustments. Inspectors normally submitted all inspection reports to their supervising inspector for review. The engineering department felt that this added an extra measure of experience and expertise to each inspection.

The 350 inspectors deployed throughout the branch office system were almost entirely "practical" engineers—that is, trained to be able to diagnose and repair, rather than design, heavy machinery. In almost every state it was necessary to pass an exam to become a licensed boiler machinery inspector. Like the company's founder, inspectors were still largely recruited from Navy and Merchant Marine ranks; many had retired from the service while in their late thirties after 20 years of service. Often the inspectors had been engineering officers on vessels, and most tended to be "jacks-of-all-trades" rather than specialists. "Our inspectors, by the time they reach a certain level, are expected to be able to inspect anything that we insure," noted Roger Cutter, "from simple air tanks to complex four-color rotogravure presses." The company generally did not hire college graduate engineers as inspectors, because "graduate engineers don't like to get their hands dirty, and sometimes we do things that aren't very pleasant."

Inspectors' salaries began at approximately $27,000 per year. The company provided a car of the inspector's choice (within certain limits) and paid the vehicle's operating costs. EIIC estimated that these additions increased the "real" salary to over $31,000, plus all normal fringes. Training an inspector in EIIC's methods required approximately one year and cost over $20,000 in lost time and out-of-pocket expenses. Salary experts had assured the company that its salary scale was competitive within the insurance industry. Despite this, the company was experiencing a high turnover among its inspectors: about 17% in 1990. Mr. Cutter explained:

> We have a problem similar to that of IBM: it serves as a training ground. Our inspectors are in demand by other companies— construction, architectural and such—and many of them either work on a cost-plus basis or can simply afford to pay more for inspectors.

Moonlighting was an accepted fact of life for most inspectors. Various company employees estimated that between 50% and 75% of EIIC's inspectors held down some form of part-time job. Roger Cutter did not feel that this was detrimental to company operations.

> We have no objection to it as long as it does not interfere with normal activities and does not create a conflict of interest with the company. As long as an inspector is available for an emergency at 2 a.m., we don't care if he drives a taxi or raises chickens on the side.

Inspector Duties and Responsibilities

An inspector's four main duties were ranked according to priorities. The highest priority was responding to accidents. If a boiler went down, crippling an entire plant, it was crucial to both the insured and to EIIC that the plant become operational in the shortest period of time. The second priority was completing a First Inspection Order (FIO). This was the inspection required when a company was put on binder; it had to be completed prior to the issuance of a formal policy, so an inspector had to get into an insured's premises quickly and determine whether the risks were insurable ones. EIIC's inspectors spent somewhat over 50% of their time conducting FIOs. The third priority went to inspections required by law, and the fourth was routine inspections done as part of the loss prevention service. The frequency of inspection varied depending on the equipment involved. These priorities sometimes created conflicts. For example, when an accident occurred, an inspector had to cancel other appointments or find substitute inspectors in the branch to assist him or her.

If a branch was asked to inspect a piece of equipment with which it had little experience, the inspectors could contact the home office engineering staff for assistance. This staff of 30 engineers comprised a corps of specialists who assisted the branches with inspections, surveys, accident investigations and administrative functions.

Inspection territories varied according to geographical location. Inspectors in the San Francisco branch office, for instance, might each have a territory a few square miles in size while their counterparts in the Denver branch might each cover several hundred square miles. Travelling time ranged up to 30% of an inspector's total time, though a typical figure was 15%. In addition, Mr. Cutter estimated that inspectors spent 15% of their day writing reports. Each inspector was completely responsible for scheduling his or her workday, though they did have to provide certain inspections within a given time period. In most branches, inspectors rarely came into the office, conducting most company business by mail, fax, and telephone from their homes. Cutter felt that this freedom to plan one's own time was an attractive fringe benefit for inspectors.

The time required for inspections ranged from five minutes for standard risks, such as an air tank, to more than a week for a large complex turbine or compressor. A chief inspector familiar with the types and number of objects in his territory "works up what he feels is a proper workload for each of his inspectors," explained Mr. Cutter. "This is done by hand, but by people who know the territory and who know what has to be done." Typically, inspectors averaged between 35 and 50 inspections per week. Somewhat over 10% of EIIC's insured objects were considered "complex," and these were distributed relatively evenly throughout the branch system.

To minimize the cost of claims for damages resulting from business interruptions, the engineering department often could expedite repairs. "Our people know who's who in the many companies that supply heavy machinery and we can get those things moving in a hurry," explained Roger Cutter. "Once, when a 4,000 horsepower motor failed in a chemical plant, we knew where there was another one sitting idle and we shipped it in about four days. It would have taken eight months to get a new one."

While chief inspectors were portrayed as being slightly lower on the organization chart than branch managers, they maintained veto power over the risks to be insured. If a risk did not meet company standards, the chief inspector could prevent it from being insured, although in cases where the client was large and the reason for rejection small or correctable, the risk could be insured for "agency reasons" at the discretion of the home office. Not all employees felt that this veto power was an optimal situation. According to one: "The *de facto* social system is that the chief inspector runs the branch manager's life. That creates enormous problems. The engineers see themselves as the saviors of the company, the technicians who keep the lunatic salesmen and underwriters honest."

Underwriting

Underwriters at EIIC appraised objects to be insured and determined what premiums, deductibles and other financial conditions—if any—would make the object an acceptable risk. The home office staff included a vice president, Mr. Fox, an assistant vice president and three regional underwriters who had overall responsibility for the underwriting activities of between six and seven branches each. Additionally an underwriting services staff of seven performed research and rating services for the regional managers at the home office; they also collected and analyzed data on the performance of the branch underwriting departments. (See Exhibit 2.3.)

Each branch employed between 5 and 12 underwriters (an average branch had 8) who evaluated lower risk objects by performing the largely clerical function of "rating," that is, making underwriting decisions according to prescribed rules and procedures established by the home office. Larger risks were evaluated by the home office staff. The branch underwriters did not normally accompany the agents or the inspectors in the field to see standard items; they took the rates for such low risk items directly from a rate sheet or, increasingly, from personal computers.

Exhibit 2.3 Sales Commission, Inspection Costs, and Loss Ratio (grouped by size of annual earned premium per object)

	Annual Earned Premium per Object[a]					
	$75	**$150**	**$400**	**$1000**	**$5000**	**$20,000**
Sales commission	18%	16%	16%	13%	11%	7%
Inspection costs	30	22	19	16	10	4
Loss ratio	25	33	35	35	42	52
Contribution to profits	27	29	30	35	37	37
Total dollars (000,000 of annual earned premium (based on policies in force as of August 15, 1990).	$8.8	21.4	22.7	7.9	3.8	3.0

[a]The casewriter divided the half million objects insured into six categories by size of the annual earned premium for each object. The categories are identified by the estimated average earned premium per category. The simpler, more standard objects were, naturally, on the lower end of the scale; the more complex objects were on the higher end.

Administratively, branch office underwriters reported to the branch managers, although they received guidance from the home office underwriting department.

Underwriters faced five alternative choices with regard to a policy. He or she could: (1) take the risk in question; (2) reject it; (3) adjust the premium and/or deductible amounts to compensate for unusual risk exposure; (4) adjust the coverages applicable to certain objects to be covered; or (5) have the objects physically modified with the help of the engineering department to ensure conformity with regulations. This last option was exercised more frequently at EIIC than it was at most other insurance companies.

Premiums for larger risks usually were negotiated between EIIC and the insured party, and the home office underwriters usually went out into the field with an engineer to inspect the object personally. "You can gain a far better insight into just what it is you're insuring if you go out and see the damn thing instead of sitting here listening to someone else's description," explained Mr. Fox. He was concerned, however, about the motivation and morale of the branch underwriters and their high turnover rate (greater than 20% a year). Not only was their job frustrating because they lacked decision-making responsibility, but most believed there was no long term career path in underwriting.

Sales

The sales function was the branch manager's primary responsibility. Each branch employed sales personnel called "special agents," whose main task was to call on independent insurance agents and induce them to sell EIIC coverage rather than that of competitors. A typical branch employed seven or eight special agents, though the number varied depending on the number of accounts and the amount of premium revenue the branch generated.

The special agent had several responsibilities. One was to attract new accounts; a second was to ensure the renewal of the policies already in force. In addition, they served as conduits for any policy changes that customers might initiate. The special agents dealt with a wide range of risk and premium sizes, though the bulk of their business was in the smaller risk area. Various employees disagreed as to who EIIC's real customer was. According to one branch manager, the independent agent was the only true customer. "On small policies we rarely send special agents out to the insured party, so the independent agent is the only real customer. On larger accounts, boiler insurance may account for only be a small part of the total premium, so the insured isn't too concerned about who writes it. Either way, the independent agent controls the account." Mr. Martin, the Agency vice president, disagreed. "Some people say we have two customers, the independent agents and the ultimate purchaser of the policy," he explained. "I don't see it that way. Our customer is the insured. The independent agents are just our marketing arm. "

From Request to Delivery

When a request for insurance was presented by or solicited from an independent agent (producer), the special agent assigned to that account performed a cursory inspection (survey), the insured filled out an application for insurance and EIIC issued a binder covering the insured until the completed policy was delivered. When a binder was issued, the special agent requested the inspection department in his or her branch to do the inspection required prior to policy issue by submitting a First Inspection Order (FIO) to the supervising inspector. Only after the FIO was completed by the field inspector and approved by the supervising inspector, did the company proceed to write the policy. If irregularities were discovered during the course of inspection, the special agent was notified as to the nature of and possible remedy for the fault.

If the policy involved a fairly straightforward risk (which was true for about 90% of the cases), the information on the application form was transferred onto a computer connected by telephone line with the home office. Usually policy information was transmitted back to the branch and a completed policy assembled and sent out within 24 hours. Both the policy data and inspection information were then turned over to the records department where the required inspection slips were prepared. These slips were entered into the field inspectors' "slip books," which indicated when each object would require further inspection.

Inspection territories for field inspectors were assigned geographically, a situation which one office manager felt was less than optimal: "There is little flexibility, planning, or coordination in the engineering area. If 50 FIOs—high priority items—came in one day, they could all conceivably go to two inspectors. The other inspectors would continue to perform their routine work." Each inspector possessed a set of slip books that contained information about the objects insured in his or her territory, and relied on them as their primary source of data.

Branch managers generally felt they faced three related problems. One was that, while the home office had set a goal of 14 days for policy delivery, at many branches this goal was being met only on the simplest policies. The second was closely related: inspections were often completed later than originally scheduled. A medium-sized branch might average 26 days for a First Inspection Order to be completed, 10 days for the supervisory inspector to approve the completed FIO, 5 days to underwrite the risk after the supervisory inspector's approval, and 2 days for filing, recording data and other miscellaneous tasks. The third problem was that interpersonal conflicts often arose between branch managers and their chief inspectors. According to branch managers, if a chief inspector "went by the book" on all risks big or small, the likelihood of conflict was great.

Rethinking Organizational Structure and Strategy

In mid-1991 there was a growing sense of unease throughout the company. Although the slowdown in sales growth and decreasing profitability could be blamed to some extent on the difficult market environment that was also causing difficulties for their competitors, a number of EIIC managers sensed that the "old formula" wasn't working as well as it once had. After many years of growing faster and achieving higher profits than its competitors, the company's results were falling toward the industry average. Employee morale seemed to be low, turnover was rising, and disputes were becoming increasingly acrimonious.

One branch manager expressed an opinion shared by most of his colleagues:

> There was a time when we made most of our own decisions and we had a good record of producing policies. Today the home office tells us how to produce policies, what kind of systems to use, and so on. Yet my turnaround time is worse, and my chief inspector refuses to work with me in improving it. He ought to report formally to me. Otherwise, I have responsibility without authority."

Another argued, "Our tradition is to inspect everything, but most of the things we insure don't need to be inspected. We ought to have the authority to eliminate inspections in those cases.

Roger Cutter was vehement in his reaction.

> That would be like putting the fox in charge of the chicken coop. We are where we are today because of our inspection expertise. Inspection is our company's middle name. If we make inspection optional, and at the discretion of the branch manager, they will find all sorts of excuses for eliminating it. Inspection is how we differentiate ourselves in this business. And it's the reason our loss ratio is less than that of most of our competitors.

A young underwriter commented:

> The people in this company really know their business. But dissent is not popular and there are rigid party lines. Some tough old nuts are in charge here, and they picture themselves on the bridge of a battleship. Nobody 20 years their junior is going to tell them what to do.

CHAPTER 3

McDonald's Corporation 1992

Operations, Flexibility and the Environment

W HETHER IN Moscow or Massachusetts, the same experience would greet a customer in any of the 12,611 McDonald's quick-service restaurants worldwide. McDonald's had distinguished itself in the quick-service industry through its remarkable consistency across all units. To competitors and customers alike, the Golden Arches—the corporate emblem that adorned every restaurant—symbolized pleasant, quick service and tasty, inexpensive food.

In the United States alone, McDonald's served over 20 million customers every day.[1] Although such a number testified to the restaurant chain's success, it also suggested a troubling question for management. With McDonald's already serving so many customers, how could it possibly attract more business? External pressures reinforced the dilemma. Demographic trends were reshaping American eating habits while competitors were attacking the quick-service giant from all sides. From chains specializing in speed and service, to those offering wider variety and those that featured deeply discounted menus, McDonald's faced competitors poised to challenge the industry leader on all fronts. McDonald's had built its success on a legendary operating system that amazed competitors

---

[1] With 250 million people living in the United States, McDonald's was serving roughly 8% of the U.S. population daily.

This case was prepared by Professor David Upton and doctoral student Joshua Margolis as a basis for class discussion rather than an illustration of either effective or ineffective handling of an administrative situation. Data have been disguised.

The information presented in this case does not necessarily represent the opinion of McDonald's Corporation. Thanks are due to Terri Capatosto and Shelby Yastrow of McDonald's along with Jackie Prince and Fred Krupp of the EDF. The following provided background material for this case: John F. Lowe, *McDonald's: Behind the Arches* (New York: Bantam Books, 1986) and Lois Therrien, "McRisky," Business Week, October 21, 1991.

and the financial community by generating an average annual return on equity of 25.2% from 1965 through 1991, and an average annual earnings growth of 24.1%. However, sales per unit had slowed between 1990 and 1991, causing management to wonder whether the company's operating system, so vital in guaranteeing uniform quality and service at every McDonald's outlet, was suited to the new circumstances the company faced.

Consumers were changing: in addition to an increasing, yet variable, concern for "healthy" food, there was a growing concern for the environment among consumers. A study of Americans in the summer of 1989 had found that 53% of those questioned had declined to buy a product in the previous year because they were worried about the effects the product or its packaging might have on the environment.[2] Aware of the growing importance of environmental stewardship, McDonald's had recently undertaken a bold collaboration with the Environmental Defense Fund, which seemed to offer some concrete methods by which operations could adapt to the benefit of the environment.

Top managers considered three vexing challenges:

- To what extent should McDonald's change its operations strategy to accommodate the growing need for flexibility and variety in products. Was it merely tweaking—or a dramatic change—which would support the company's volume growth objectives?
- To what extent would environmental concerns compromise McDonald's traditional strengths and complicate an already challenging competitive situation?
- Finally, could the lessons learned in the recent collaboration with the EDF help McDonald's as it sought solutions to the continuing competitive challenge?

The Speedee Service System

Dick and Mac McDonald opened their first drive-in restaurant in 1941, relying on carhops—waiters who went from car to car—to take orders from patrons parked in the restaurant's large lot. In 1948, the brothers abandoned their popular format and introduced self-service windows, 15-cent hamburgers, french fries, and milk shakes. They standardized their preparation methods (in what they termed the "Speedee Service System,") with exact product specifications and customized equipment. Every hamburger, for example, was prepared with ketchup, mustard, onions, and two pickles; the ketchup was applied through a pump dispenser that required just one squirt for the required amount. Ray Kroc, who held the national marketing

[2]Frances Cairncross, "Costing the Earth," pp. 190–191. Harvard Business School Press, 1992.

Exhibit 3.1   McDonald's Original Menu

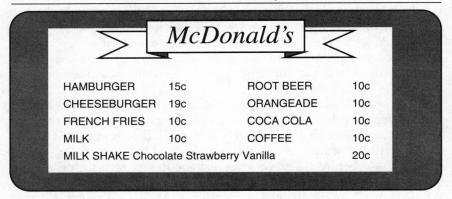

rights to the multimixers used in the restaurants to make milk shakes, met the McDonald brothers in 1954. He was so impressed by their restaurant and its potential that he became a national franchise agent for the brothers, and founded the McDonald's chain. Like the McDonald brothers' first restaurant in San Bernardino, California, the McDonald's chain featured a limited menu, low prices, and fast service. From the moment in 1955 when he opened his first McDonald's, in Des Plaines, Illinois, Kroc made the operating system his passion and his company's anchor. Whereas many competitors could prepare products that were similar to McDonald's, most focused on recruiting franchisees, whom they promptly ignored, and on identifying the lowest-cost suppliers. Kroc, on the other hand, sought (i) to make sure McDonald's products were of consistently high quality, (ii) to establish a unique operating system, and (iii) to build a special set of relationships between the McDonald's corporation, its suppliers, and its franchisees (see Exhibit 3.1).

Getting it Right—Again and Again

McDonald's designed its operating system to ensure consistency and uniformity across all outlets. Operating procedures guaranteed customers the same quality of food and service visit after visit, store after store. Every hamburger, for example, was dressed in exactly the same way: mustard first, then ketchup, onions, and two pickles. One competitor, who operated 250 Kentucky Fried Chicken restaurants, marvelled at McDonald's record of consistency:

> I've been to McDonald's in Tokyo, Vienna, and Australia, and I get a great sense of having the same product from each one of their locations. Most people haven't been able to bring the discipline needed in fast food to get that type of consistency.

McDonald's operating system concentrated on four areas: improving the product; developing outstanding supplier relationships; improving equipment; and training and monitoring franchisees. In its quest for improvement, McDonald's revolutionized the entire supply chain, introducing innovations in the way farmers grew potatoes and ranchers raised beef, altering processing methods for both potatoes and meat, and inventing efficient cooking equipment tailored to the restaurant's needs. Most revolutionary, perhaps, was McDonald's attention to detail. Never before had a restaurant cared about its suppliers' product beyond the price, let alone the suppliers' methods of operation.

McDonald's was able to spend as much time and effort as it did in perfecting its operating system because it restricted its menu to ten items. Most restaurants in the 1960s and 70s offered a variety of menu items, which made specialization and uniform standards rare and nearly impossible. Fred Turner, one of Kroc's original managers and later Senior Chairman of McDonald's, stressed the critical importance of menu size in attributing success of the company's operating system:

> It wasn't because we were smarter. The fact that we were selling just ten items, had a facility that was small, and used a limited number of suppliers created an ideal environment for really digging in on everything.

Turner developed the first operations manual in 1957, which, by 1991, reached 750 detailed pages. It described how operators should make milk shakes, grill hamburgers, and fry potatoes. It delineated exact cooking times, proper temperature settings, and precise portions for all food items—even prescribing the quarter ounce of onions to be placed on every hamburger and the 32 slices to be obtained from every pound of cheese. French fries were to be 9/32 of an inch, and to ensure quality and taste, no products should be held more than ten minutes in the transfer bin.

McDonald's patrolled suppliers and franchisees scrupulously. The meat in McDonald's hamburgers, for example, had particular specifications: 83% lean chuck (shoulder) from grass-fed cattle and 17% choice plates (lower rib cage) from grain-fed cattle. Fillers were unacceptable. Whereas other restaurants merely accepted what suppliers provided and complained only when meat was visually inferior, McDonald's routinely analyzed its meat in laboratories.

In 1991, McDonald's spent $26.9 million on its field service operation to evaluate and assist each of its restaurants. Each of the company's 332 field service consultants visited over 20 restaurants in the U.S. several times every year, reviewing the restaurants' performance on more than 500 items ranging from rest room cleanliness to food quality to customer service. Turner was the first corporate employee to visit and evaluate each restaurant, and, as early as 1957, he summarized his evaluations by assigning a letter grade to a restaurant's performance in three categories: quality, service, and cleanliness (QSC). For more than thirty years, therefore, McDonald's had prided itself on QSC and a fourth letter—V for value.[3]

McDonald's meticulous attention to detail and careful analysis of quality and procedures did not come from an unbending need for regimentation. Instead, McDonald's sought to study every component of its operation to learn what worked and what failed, to determine how best to offer consistently good service and food. Whereas other chains ignored both franchisees and suppliers, McDonald's sought to elicit commitment from them—commitment that required not only adherence but experimentation. Turner explained:

> We were continuously looking for a better way to do things, and then a revised better way to do things, and then a revised, revised better way.

Suppliers

A simple handshake secured every arrangement between McDonald's and a supplier, and symbolized the way McDonald's revolutionized the entire relationship. Jim Williams, head of Golden State Foods, which supplied McDonald's with meat, contrasted the traditional supplier-restaurant relationship with the changes McDonald's introduced:

> Deals and kickbacks were a way of life. How long you let a guy stretch out his payments was more the determining factor of whether you got the business than the quality of the product you were selling. Kroc brought a supplier loyalty that the restaurant business had never seen. If you adhered to McDonald's specifications, and were basically competitive on price, you could depend on their order.

When McDonald's first approached the established food processing giants, such as Kraft, Heinz, and Swift, the restaurant chain received a cold response. The established suppliers refused to accept McDonald's concepts and specifications and continued to concentrate solely on the retail market. Only small, fledgling suppliers were willing to gamble on McDonald's, and in turn, McDonald's created a whole new set of major institutional vendors. Each McDonald's restaurant ordered 1,800 pounds of hamburger meat per week and 3,000 pounds of potatoes. By meeting McDonald's strict standards and price requests, suppliers were guaranteed future volumes from a burgeoning restaurant chain. Kenneth

---

[3]Franchisees could not be graded on value because it violated antitrust regulations, which prohibited rigid pricing and required independent business owners be given the latitude to set prices on their own.

Smargon, whose Interstate Foods supplied McDonald's with shortening, described the novel relationship that developed:

> Other chains would walk away from you for half a cent. McDonald's was more concerned with getting quality. They didn't chisel on price and were always concerned with suppliers making a fair profit. A lot of people look on a supplier as someone to walk on. But McDonald's always treated me with respect even when they became much bigger and didn't have to. That's the big difference, because if McDonald's said "Jump," an awful lot of people would be asking "How far?"

Suppliers grew alongside McDonald's and were thus carefully attuned to the company's needs. As one supplier commented, "You've got to be deaf, dumb, and ignorant to lose McDonald's business once you have it."

Franchisees

McDonald's referred to its 3,500 U.S. franchisees as its partners for good reason. By 1992, McDonald's generated 39% of its revenues from franchise restaurants. When Ray Kroc first sold franchises, he made sure that his "partners" would make money before the company did, and he insisted that corporate revenue come not from initial franchise fees but from success of the restaurants themselves. That philosophy continued to be at the center of McDonald's franchise and operating practices.

Franchise owners did indeed see themselves as partners, developing such products as the Filet-O-Fish sandwich and the Egg McMuffin in the 1960s and the McDLT in the 1980s. Franchisees also formed powerful regional cooperatives for both advertising and purchasing. Their regional advertising budgets enabled them to "customize" local promotions while also supporting national programs, and the buying cooperatives gave franchisees a channel for challenging suppliers to be innovative, even when those suppliers were meeting corporate requirements.

Together with corporate management and suppliers, franchisees infused McDonald's with an entrepreneurial spirit. All three partners balanced one another, just as the entrepreneurial inventiveness within each balanced their collective emphasis on disciplined standards of quality.

Cooking Up Products

Nothing exemplified the success of McDonald's operating system like the development of its food. From french fries to Chicken McNuggets, McDonald's had distinguished its menu offerings by drawing both on the rigorous operating system, with its focus on uniformity, and on the orchestra formed by corporate management, suppliers, and franchisees.

In Pursuit of the Perfect Fries

When McDonald's first began operating, french fried potatoes accounted for approximately 5% of the entire U.S. potato crop. By 1985, french fries accounted for more than 25% of the U.S. market. McDonald's had made french fries standard fare for an American meal, but more important for McDonald's, french fries became the restaurant chain's most distinctive item. Ray Kroc was well aware of the importance of the chain's fries:

> A competitor could buy the same kind of hamburger we did, and we wouldn't have anything extra to show. But the french fries gave us an identity and exclusiveness because you couldn't buy french fries anywhere to compete with ours. You could tell the results of tender loving care.

McDonald's did indeed apply tender loving care in preparing its french fries. At first the company simply monitored the way french fries were cooked in its restaurants, trying to determine the exact temperature and settings that yielded the best french fries. They discovered, however, that temperature settings on the fryers had little connection to the temperature of the oil in the vat once cold potatoes were dropped in. By putting temperature sensors in the vat and on potato slices, McDonald's charted temperature readings during the cooking process. When a batch of cold, wet potatoes was thrown into a vat of melted shortening, the shortening's temperature dropped radically. Each batch of fries fell to a different temperature, but, McDonald's researchers discovered, the fries were always perfectly cooked when the oil temperature rose three degrees above the low temperature point. This discovery enabled the company to design a fryer that produced perfect french fried potatoes every order.

The initial research team eventually learned that potatoes also need to be cured for three weeks to produce perfect french fries: in that period of time the sugars within potatoes convert into starches. To prevent excessive browning and permit uniform crispness through the fry, McDonald's only accepted potatoes with a 21% starch content. Members of the company's field operations staff visited produce suppliers with hydrometers, a floating instrument that measured the starch content of potatoes when immersed in a bucket of water.

As the number of McDonald's outlets grew to over four hundred in the early 1960s, the company's potato consumption surpassed six million pounds a year. That gave McDonald's and its suppliers sufficient purchasing power to influence growers of Idaho Russet potatoes to adhere to planting practices that yielded potatoes with high starch content. McDonald's also began looking for potato processors willing to invest in storage facilities with sophisticated temperature controls.

In the early 1960s, Jack Simplot, a major potato grower who supplied

20% of McDonald's potatoes, approached McDonald's with an idea for improving the chain's french fries. He agreed to spend $400,000 to put Idaho Russets in cold storage during the summer, when they typically were not available. During the summer months, McDonald's relied on California white potatoes, less suited to production of crisp french fries. Although his gamble failed, and all of the stored potatoes rotted, Simplot returned with another, bolder suggestion in 1965. He recommended that McDonald's consider converting from fresh to frozen potatoes. Reluctant though the company was to tamper with its renowned french fries, Ray Kroc recognized the distribution problems involved in supplying fresh potatoes to his growing chain. Simplot pitched his idea to Kroc on the basis not of price but of quality, as he later explained:

> They were having a hell of a time maintaining potato quality in their stores. The sugar content of the potatoes was constantly going up and down, and they would get fries with every color of the rainbow. I told him that frozen fries would allow him to better control the quality and consistency of McDonald's potato supply.

McDonald's studied the freezing process carefully, learning that the traditional process robbed structure and flavor from french fries. Ice crystals would form in the potato during freezing, rupturing the starch granules. McDonald's developed a process to dry french fries with air, run them through a quick frying cycle, then freeze them. This reduced the moisture in the frozen fry while preserving its crispness. Simplot volunteered to build the initial production line that implemented this process, and by 1992, his company supplied McDonald's with 1.8 billion pounds of french fries—close to 50% of the chain's domestic potato business. Only a small, local supplier when he first approached McDonald's, Simplot's organization grew to a $650 million frozen-potato-processing giant.

McDonald's even improved the way restaurant crews filled orders for french fries. Operators had complained that employee productivity suffered because the metal tongs traditionally used to fill french-fry bags proved clumsy. In response, a McDonald's engineer, Ralph Weimer, designed a V-shaped aluminum scoop with a funnel at the end that enabled operators to fill a french-fry bag in one motion and, in addition, align the fries in the same vertical direction within the bag.

Fast Break from Competitors: Breakfast and the McMuffin

In June 1976, McDonald's franchisees introduced the chain's most significant new product: not just a new menu item but a new meal, breakfast. Most operators were sufficiently busy keeping their restaurants open between 11:00 A.M. and midnight, but a Pittsburgh franchisee looked at these hours as a limitation that offered an opportunity:

> We were paying rent, utilities, and insurance twenty-four hours a day, but we were only open for business for half that time. We had all those morning hours before 11:00 A.M. to do some business.

This franchisee began opening his restaurant at 7:00 A.M., serving coffee, doughnuts, sweet rolls, pancakes, and sausage. Without detracting from McDonald's existing menu, he generated entirely new business.

Other franchisees would agree to extend morning hours only if they happened upon a breakfast item that promised enormous sales growth. Herb Peterson, a franchise operator in Santa Barbara, California believed that to launch a new meal, McDonald's required a unique product that could be eaten like all other McDonald's foods—with the fingers. He turned to a classic egg dish—Eggs Benedict—for inspiration.

In 1971, he developed a sandwich and a special utensil that could, in classic McDonald's style, guarantee foolproof production of the sandwich. A cluster of six Teflon-coated rings could be used on a grill to give eggs the rounded shape of an English muffin while giving them the look and taste of poached eggs. When a slice of cheese and bacon were added, McDonald's had developed the cornerstone product of its breakfast menu: the Egg McMuffin.

McDonald's rolled out a complete breakfast menu in 1976, featuring the Egg McMuffin, hotcakes, scrambled eggs, sausage and Canadian style bacon. McDonald's had again distinguished itself from competitors, none of whom responded until the mid-1980s, by which time McDonald's held a virtual monopoly on breakfast, which accounted for 15% of average restaurant sales.

McDonald's once again turned to suppliers for support in developing the Egg McMuffin; some were responsive while others lost a revolutionary opportunity. Pork processors worked with McDonald's to build equipment that could cut round slices of bacon instead of strips.

Chicken Comes to the Golden Arches

In the late 1970s, McDonald's official chef, Rene Arend, tried to develop an onion product—deep-fried chunks of onion—but the variation in onion supplies made it difficult to control quality. Instead, CEO Fred Turner suggested that Arend substitute bite-sized chunks of deep-fried chicken.

McDonald's immediately turned to two suppliers to help develop the product in record time. Gorton, the original supplier of fish for McDonald's Filet-O-Fish sandwich, was selected to solve the breading and battering challenge as it had done previously with fish. McDonald's handed the most difficult challenge to Keystone, one of McDonald's meat suppliers: find an efficient way to cut chicken into bite-sized, boneless chunks. Arend, meanwhile, developed four sauces to accompany the nuggets. The collaborative effort between McDonald's and its suppliers produced breakthroughs that made the new product, Chicken McNuggets, not only possible but unique: a modified hamburger-patty machine that cut boneless chicken into nuggets, for example, and a special batter that gave the nuggets the taste and appearance of being freshly-battered.

By March 1980, just five months after beginning work on McNuggets, McDonald's was testing them in a Knoxville restaurant. Within three years of introducing Chicken McNuggets throughout its chain, McDonald's was deriving 7.5% of domestic sales from its newest product. The giant of the hamburger business had suddenly become the second-largest chicken retailer in the food-service industry, positioned behind Kentucky Fried Chicken. Keystone's efforts on behalf of McDonald's again provided proof of the success bred by loyalty: by 1992, Keystone had 65% of McDonald's chicken business, transforming the meat supplier into a major chicken producer as well.

Competitors and Growth

McDonald's had built the most successful quick-service franchise in the world, maintaining phenomenal growth for over 35 years. Distinguishing itself from other chains by adhering tenaciously to an operating system focused on uniformity, it worked with its franchisees and suppliers as partners to improve the operating system and introduce new products. But as management reviewed McDonald's performance in recent years, many wondered if the company's traditional strategy still suited the dramatic changes it now seemed to face.

McDonald's share of the U.S. quick-service market had dropped from 18.7% in 1985 to 16.6% in 1991, even though the company gained sales from a bigger quick-service "pie." Despite this, between 1988 and 1990, sales per U.S. outlet dropped an average of 3.7% in real dollars. After years of double-digit income growth, McDonald's 1991 net U.S. income grew just 7.2% to $860 million. It was estimated that by 1995, profit from overseas outlets would surpass profit from U.S. outlets. Overseas business, in fact, showed the greatest growth in recent years, with operating income rising from $290 million in 1987 to $678 million in 1991. Although international expansion clearly offered McDonald's its most fertile frontier, McDonald's had to concentrate on U.S. operations. There were 2,500 franchisees in the United States, over 8,814 restaurants (1,416 company-operated), and 25% of company revenues came from franchise fees based on a percentage of sales. U.S. business accounted for 60% of profits and it simply had to be bolstered.

Moreover, McDonald's had to consider demographic trends. Hamburger consumption had dropped from 19% of all restaurant orders in 1982 to 17% of all orders in 1990 (Hamburger consumption at McDonald's had nevertheless increased over the same time period.) Increasingly, though, consumers were becoming more conscious of nutrition and having dietary options without compromising taste. The change in dietary preference was, however, certainly not universal, and there was a strong constituency of customers who continued to enjoy McDonald's traditional fare.

The quick-service industry had grown at an average annual rate of 8.7% in the 1980s but was projected only to keep pace with inflation during the 1990s. Perhaps most confusing in its implications, the number of meals eaten off the premises of quick-service restaurants had increased from 23% in 1982 to 62% in 1990. McDonald's responded with double drive–thru windows to keep pace with changing consumer preference, as well as new venues for its restaurants, such as schools, sporting arenas, museums, airports and hospitals. It also developed new smaller restaurants, less expensive than its traditional designs, which could service customers profitably in "seam" areas between existing McDonald's restaurants.

New Competition

The once-simple quick-service market had been complicated by the entry of specialist competitors who had emulated McDonald's strategy to capture their own segment of the market. Michael Quinlan, Chairman of McDonald's, acknowledged just how fierce the competition had become. "Our competition is much tougher, no question about it. And not just in numbers but in quality." McDonald's most menacing competition no longer came from Burger King, Wendy's, or Kentucky Fried Chicken—the traditional rivals.

Chili's and Olive Garden catered to customers searching for full service and greater variety. Both were family-style restaurants where patrons sat down to be served. Menus offered a wide variety of foods, yet prices remained competitive with those at McDonald's. (See Exhibit 3.2 for McDonald's menu.) Casual dining restaurants were likely to grow in the 1990's as their most frequent patrons—people between the ages of 40 and 60—increased in number by about 20 million.

Two hamburger chains, Sonic and Rally's, offered drive–through service only and specialized in delivering burgers fast. For four years Sonic sales per restaurant grew an average of 11.3% per annum, and in 1991 alone, sales per unit increased 13%. There were 1,150 Sonic units and 327 Rally's.[4] Taco Bell featured Mexican food and a menu with 26 items under one dollar. Along with Kentucky Fried Chicken and Pizza Hut, Taco Bell was owned by PepsiCo and had seen the greatest increase in sales of

[4]Therrien, "The Upstarts Teaching McDonald's A Thing or Two," *Business Week*, October 21, 1991, p. 122.

Exhibit 3.2   McDonald's Menu: 1992

APPROVED NATIONAL MENU ITEMS - Listed on Menu Board
(Effective 6/1/92)

Regular Menu Items

1. Hamburger
2. Cheeseburger
3. Quarter Pounder with Cheese
4. Big Mac
5. McLean Deluxe (and cheese option) (8, 12, 16 oz.)
6. McChicken Sandwich
7. McNuggets - 6 Piece
8. McNuggets - 9 Piece
9. McNuggets - 20 Piece
10. Happy Meal - Hamburger
11. Happy Meal - Cheeseburger
12. Happy Meal - 4 pc. McNuggets
13. Filet
14. Chunky Chicken Salad
15. Chef Salad
16. Garden Salad
17. Side Salad
18. Small Fries
19. Medium Fries
20. Large Fries
21. Lowfat Milk Shakes
22. 1% Milk
23. Drink - Child Size (12 oz.)
24. Drink - Small (16 oz.)
25. Drink - Medium (21.9 oz.)
26. Drink - Large (32 oz.)
27. Orange Juice
28. Coffee (8, 12, 16 oz.)
29. Decaffeinated Coffee Fresh Brewed
30. Hot Tea
31. Iced Tea (12, 16, 21.9, 32 oz.)
32. Apple Pie
33. Chocolatey Chip Cookies
34. McDonaldland Cookies
35. Sundaes
36. Cones

Breakfast Menu Items

1. Egg McMuffin
2. Sausage McMuffin w/Egg
3. Big Breakfast
4. Hotcakes and Sausage
5. Sausage Biscuit
6. Sausage/Egg Biscuit
7. Bacon/Egg/Cheese Biscuit
8. Breakfast Burrito
9. Hash Browns
10. Apple Bran Muffin (fat free)
11. Cereal (Wheaties & Cheerios)

APPROVED NATIONAL "VALUE MENU COMBOS" Listed on Menu Board
(Effective 6/1/92)

Regular Menu Breakfast

1. Big Mac, Lg. Fry, Med. Drink
2. 2 Cheeseburgers, Lg. Fry, Med.
3. Quarter Pounder w/Cheese, Lg. Fry, Med. Drink
a4. McChicken, Lg. Fry, Medium Drink

1. Egg McMuffin, any size drink
2. Bacon, Egg & Cheese Biscuit, any size drink
3. Sausage McMuffin w/Egg, any size drink
a4. Sausage Biscuit w/Egg, any size

aThe #4 position can be used as a flexible option with provided options being McLean Deluxe, 2 Chicken Fajitas, Filet-O-Fish, or Hotcakes during Breakfast.

any quick-service chain in the late 1980s. By learning from McDonald's, Taco Bell shifted food preparation to outside suppliers, reduced kitchen space in its outlets, and used a cost-based strategy to compete—prices were always kept low. Between 1988 and 1991, Taco Bell served 60% more customers and sales rocketed 63%.

Early Responses from McDonald's
McDonald's drew on its traditional strengths to respond to competitors' challenges and customers' new habits. Careful product development, closely gauged to customer tastes, again formed the focus of attention as McDonald's turned to suppliers and franchisees for assistance. To address concerns about nutrition, McDonald's had introduced salads, chicken, and muffins. In conjunction with Keystone and Auburn University, it developed the first-ever 91% fat-free burger, McLean Deluxe. Keystone also convinced McDonald's to experiment with chicken fajitas, which proved an instant success in initial tests. The chicken arrived precooked and seasoned, so it only required heating and did not slow operations. The fajitas sold well in market tests and were soon scheduled for national introduction.

Just as McDonald's had spent five years perfecting its breakfast menu for national roll-out, the company spent seven years developing a pizza suitable for its restaurants. Meticulous product development included design of advanced technology, as it had when McDonald's engineers introduced a special french-fry scoop and a grill that prepared hamburgers in half the time by cooking them on both sides simultaneously. Now McDonald's engineers had invented a pizza oven that could cook McDonald's Pizza in under five minutes. In addition, McDonald's was developing new staging equipment—high-tech temperature and moisture controlled cabinets—that would allow parts of a product to be prepared ahead of time without detracting from food quality. Toasted buns, for example, could be stored in these containers without becoming dried out.

In early 1991, McDonald's returned to a value menu, cutting prices an average 20%. Cheeseburgers sold for only 69 cents and McDonald's Happy Meals™—complete children's meals (sandwich, fries, drink, and toy in a colorful box)—for just $1.99. As a result, sales of hamburgers increased by 30% and customer counts rose. Revenues and profits, however, increased less dramatically.

These initial moves suggested a fundamental tension between McDonald's expanded efforts to provide greater value, on the one hand, and enhanced variety, on the other. As Fred Turner noted, "We're a penny-profit business," and with a value menu, volume was critical. That made the chain's hallmark of speed more vital than ever, yet a wider variety of menu offerings posed the risk of slowing each unit's service. Variety and value had to be carefully balanced. Management's challenge was to sustain McDonald's painstaking attention to products and service in achieving that balance.

Flexibility and Growth

McDonald's had achieved success by focusing on a simple formula: limited menu, low prices, and fast service. The Golden Arches symbolized a uniform product—primarily burgers, fries, and shakes—delivered in a consistent manner. Whereas uniformity and consistency had formed McDonald's focal point for thirty-five years, the company's new advertising slogan seemed to suggest a subtle yet significant shift: "*What You Want Is What You Get at McDonald's Today.*" Catering to customers had always been the company's focal point, but to meet changing and divergent customer needs, McDonald's was exploring many different options, and management thought a basic question had to be answered. Would the chain's new concern with flexibility in meeting customers' changing needs require a fundamental change in McDonald's bedrock strategy? Or was this just a new, albeit incredibly complicated, situation once again adaptable to the company's traditional approach?

Early responses to new customer desires and intensifying competition represented just a piece of the company's maelstrom of creative activity. Further efforts were in progress as well. For example, McDonald's had developed a number of new building prototypes, from drive-through-only models to compete with Rally's and Sonic, to small cafes suitable for small towns. Menu diversification offered the greatest area of experimentation. A wide range of items were being tested, including lasagna, carrot sticks, corn on the cob, fruit cups, and oven-baked chicken. McDonald's was also looking for new ways to address nutritional concerns revolving around calcium deficiency and sodium and fat reduction.

McDonald's changes to date had not threatened its traditional operating system, but increased variation throughout the chain—whether in menu offerings, building plans, or eating experience—would pose formidable challenges to McDonald's in maintaining its remarkable quality control and speed of service. The operating system had been constructed to ensure uniformity, quality, and speed at all McDonald's restaurants. If the chain intended to offer a wider variety of foods, such as spaghetti and meatballs or baked chicken, it could disrupt an operating system built around a limited menu.

McDonald's traditional rival, Burger King, afforded an example of the dangers contained in variety. Burger King flame-broiled its hamburgers, which some perceived would be tastier than McDonald's grilled burgers—*if* the flame-broiled Burger King burgers were cooked correctly. But flame-broiled hamburgers were inconsistent in quality, however, and Burger King was not able to implement an operating system that could sustain consistency across all units.

Increasing variety posed another potential dilemma for McDonald's. As the chain responded to pricing challenges from competitors like Taco Bell, higher volume became imperative. To generate higher volume at each restaurant, speed became even more important, and speed could not be risked on a cornucopia of new products. Although the new menu items McDonald's had thus far tested, such as chicken fajitas, had not clogged operations and were well-received by franchisees, McDonald's had to guarantee similar smoothness with some of the more exotic products under consideration, whether chicken, spaghetti, or corn on the cob.

The sheer number of additional products could also detract from the speed of service. McDonald's perfected its operating procedures and equipment in part to accommodate its work-force, whose annual turnover rate was greater than 100% (this was, nevertheless, the lowest in the industry). While McDonald's commitment to training continued to set the industry standard, no McDonald's outlet could afford to engage in complicated preparation processes for new products that might work at cross-purposes with speed of service.

If those challenges did not prove sufficiently daunting to the quick-service giant, it also had to consider restaurant image if it hoped to expand its business through enhanced variety. McDonald's had built its image as the place for hamburgers and quick-service—not for other food and not for casual dining. If people sought Mexican food, they would go to Taco Bell. If people wanted pizza, they would go to Pizza Hut. If they wanted to sit down to a leisurely, reasonably priced meal, Olive Garden, Chili's, Perkin's, TGI Friday's, and Friendly all came to mind before McDonald's. Not only did McDonald's have to extend its own image, it also had to confront the established reputations of competitors.

These challenges appeared especially troubling because dinner presented perhaps the final frontier of potential growth. Only 20% of McDonald's sales came from dinner, and to entice customers to visit the Golden Arches for dinner required a new menu—as it had for breakfast—and even a different ambiance. To defend against competitors, McDonald's could not introduce dinner items one by one. Competitors could tout their specialties and thus respond easily. McDonald's, therefore, had to present an entire dinner menu at once, and the earliest possible date for such a roll-out appeared to be the spring of 1993.

Dinner differed in other ways too. Lunch and breakfast customers were most concerned with speed and convenience, but dinner was more of an event, and customers expected full meals and more complete service. Table cloths and table service, for example, did not seem out of the question. With 62% of 1990 quick-service sales coming from off-premises eating, compared to just 23% in 1982, the trends for lunch and breakfast seemed to be headed in the opposite direction.

While these competitive pressures mounted, a new challenge had been growing: protecting the environment. While many companies had seen the outbreak of environmentalism in the late 1980's as a threat—McDonald's saw an opportunity: the chance of knitting a responsible environmental policy into its evolving operations strategy.

Management considered all of these challenges and knew McDonald's would like to maintain the same core menu, operating systems, and decor. The chain would nonetheless have to allow greater latitude across units and provide a broader variety of products and experiences for the customer. But would there still be such a thing as a standard McDonald's?

Stepping into the Future: McDonald's and the Environment

"We're not wild-eyed zealots who are going to give away the store, but we'll always ask, 'Are we doing the right thing?' And remember, we live where we work, and we care about where we live."

—Keith Magnuson, Director of Operations Development

One recent development proved that there still could be a standard McDonald's, despite the most basic changes in operating procedures. On October 10, 1989, Ed Rensi, president of McDonald's U.S.A., met with Fred Krupp, the Environmental Defense Fund's executive director, at EDF's request. EDF recognized McDonald's substantial existing initiatives in recycling, and its critical role as an industry leader. McDonald's recognized EDF's expertise in solid waste management and the importance of seeking expert opinions.

When McDonald's accepted EDF's suggestion to help assess the company's solid waste stream and explore ways to reduce it, McDonald's was making a bold move. It was engaging a new partner to help address environmental concerns, one aspect of the increasingly complex situation in which the company now found itself. For a private corporation of McDonald's stature to collaborate with an environmental organization entailed significant risk and required a willingness, by both parties, to consider new ways of thinking about operating practices. The partnership, however, turned out to be a noteworthy success, generating advances in areas beyond waste reduction. "We went about finding environmental solutions," commented Bob Langert, "and we discovered efficiencies we never saw before."

The Newest Partner: Environmental Defense Fund

The Environmental Defense Fund (EDF) was founded in 1967 on Long Island, New York, to stop the spraying of DDT, a pesticide which threatened birds by causing their eggshells to thin. By 1990 EDF had become one of the nation's most respected and effective public-interest organizations working to protect the environment. It had over 200,000 members and recorded more than $18.5 million in 1991 revenues. Although most widely known initially for its legal work, especially its suits against private companies and the government, EDF now had twice as many economists and scientists as attorneys on staff. In the 1970s and 1980s EDF produced studies linking sulfur emissions to acid rain, lobbied successfully for legislation reducing the lead additives in gasoline, and designed several water conservation projects. EDF had helped fashion the Clean Air Act of 1990, taking a controversial stand by working with the government to create policy and by recommending market-based incentives to reduce pollution. The organization's sound economic and scientific studies and its practical approach garnered respect from all sides of environmental issues. However, actually collaborating with a private company—especially McDonald's, often referred to as the symbol of today's disposable society by many organizations in the environmental community—entailed tremendous risk and EDF, after all, would take no money from McDonald's. Jackie Prince of the EDF outlined EDF's views:

> Despite all the risks, we felt it was worth it—we *have* to explore a variety of different strategic alternatives and look for approaches which will find solutions and produce results for the environment.

Waste Reduction Task Force

In August 1990, four senior managers from McDonald's joined two staff scientists and an economist from the Environmental Defense Fund to form the Waste Reduction Task Force. In April 1991, the task force released its comprehensive report, which not only covered every aspect of McDonald's solid waste stream but also offered testimony to a successful relationship.

Bob Langert was one of the members of the task force and acknowledged the stereotypic suspicions both sides had at first. Quickly, however, McDonald's and EDF came together and began thoroughly examining solid waste at McDonald's. "We didn't decide to get married on first sight," recalled Langert. "At some point we came together. It was a mating game." To build rapport and gain a true understanding of McDonald's business, EDF participants were given access to all corporate information and even worked in a McDonald's for a day. For its part, McDonald's felt that a separate department dedicated to environmental issues would only belittle the company's efforts, so all environmental initiatives were to be directed through operations development.

The task force designed an action plan that met three criteria. First, the plan was comprehensive, covering all materials and all aspects of McDonald's operations. Second, it offered incremental solutions. "There is no single answer, no grand-slam home run," Langert mused. "While we were looking for this grand solution, though, we grasped the scope of the problem." The task force therefore identified an array of solutions, each complementing the other. Third, the plan made environmental action an ongoing activity at McDonald's: the report outlined areas where McDonald's developed new environmental criteria to be considered on a par with other business considerations. The joint task force delineated 42 distinct initiatives revolving around the environmental hierarchy of reduction first, reuse second, and recycling third. A set of management mechanisms accompanied each initiative to incorporate it into McDonald's standard operating procedures and ensure accountability.

The 42-step waste reduction plan included initiatives such as the introduction of reusable shipping containers and other materials, substantial packaging changes, use of unbleached paper products, new and expanded recycling efforts, composting trials, and employee retraining. Together, these initiatives would cut the waste stream at the chain's 8,500 U.S. restaurants by more than 80 percent.

Through careful study, the task force calculated that each McDonald's generated an average of 238 pounds of on-premise solid waste per day, or .12 pounds per customer. That did not even include the solid-waste generated by take-out customers, who represented 40% to 60% of store business. (See Exhibit 3.3 for characterization of McDonald's solid waste). Although McDonald's was perceived by some as an environmental demon because its products were all served in disposable containers, the task force determined that 80% of the chain's solid waste was in fact produced behind the counter. Its challenge, as a result, loomed even larger than expected: McDonald's could not simply tinker with the packaging of its products. Whatever course McDonald's pursued, its efforts to reduce solid waste could not disrupt any unit's service, had to involve numerous suppliers, and required sufficient flexibility to accommodate franchisees operating in different regions.

McDonald's sought to set ambitious goals for its franchisees while permitting sufficient latitude for each unit to achieve those goals. "We can allow for local autonomy," commented Langert, "as long as we're being as aggressive as possible." It would be left to each franchisee to determine the most viable means for achieving goals. In densely populated states, such as Massachusetts, California, and New York, franchisees might address solid waste issues by relying heavily on recycling. McDonald's units in Texas, on the other hand, might find lower landfill fees and less reason to explore recycling as vigorously, and instead focus primarily on composting.[5] Here too Langert offered a realistic outlook.

> Some percentage of the 42 initiatives will fail. We might not get it right the first time, but we'll test again. Composting may be difficult at first, so we'll learn to develop new packaging that can in fact be composted better.

[5]Composting is a natural biological process. In open-air piles or vessels, microbes break down organic materials into a soil or humus. Organic materials include items such as coffee grinds, egg-shells, food scraps, and soiled paper packing.

Exhibit 3.3 Summary of McDonald's On-Premise Waste Characterization Study[1]

OVER THE COUNTER (OTC)		BEHIND THE COUNTER (BTC)	
	% of Grand Total		% of Grand Total
Uncoated Paper	4%	Corrugated	34%
Coated Paper	7%	Putrescibles	34%
Polystyrene	4%	LDPE	2%
Non-McDonald's Waste	4%	HDPE	1%
Miscellaneous	2%	Liquids	2%
		Miscellaneous	6%
TOTALS	21%		79%

GRAND TOTAL
238 lbs./day/restaurant
0.12 lbs per customer served

DEFINITIONS AND EXAMPLES	
OVER THE COUNTER	Waste in the customer sit-down area and from outside waste receptacles
BEHIND THE COUNTER	Waste behind the register counter, including kitchen and storage rooms
POLYSTYRENE	Hot cups and lids, cutlery, salad containers
MISCELLANEOUS OTC	Condiment packaging
CORRUGATED	Shipping Boxes
PUTRESCIBLES	Food waste from customers, egg shells, coffee grounds, other food scraps
LDPE	Low-density polyethylene film wraps and plastic sleeves used as inner packaging in shipping containers
HDPE	High density polyethylene plastic mostly used for jugs, e.g. syrup jugs
LIQUIDS	Excess, non-absorbed liquids measured during waste audit
MISC. BTC.	Durables, equipment, office paper, secondary packaging other than corrugated boxes

[1]Based on a two-restaurant, one-week-long waste audit performed 11/12–11/18/90 in Denver, CO and Sycamore, IL. Figures have been adjusted to reflect conversion from sandwich foam to paper wraps. Adapted from Page 31 of the Task Force Report.

The task force evaluated possible actions according to their effect on four parties, each considered of equal importance: customers, suppliers, franchisees, and the environment. Shipping pallets provided an example of a transparent change McDonald's made (with minimal impact on operations) and was now encouraging suppliers to make. Standard pallets had been used an average of 1.8 times, creating an expense on two ends: constant replacement and landfill fees. McDonald's adopted a durable pallet that could be used between 30 and 40 times, reducing waste, decreasing costs, and having no effect on operations.

Although the task force sought foremost to reduce the materials McDonald's used and the solid waste it generated, it stressed the importance of examining the full lifecycle of all materials. The task force identified ways to reduce environmental impacts arising during initial stages—raw materials acquisition, manufacturing, and distribution—as well as during actual use and handling after use, whether discarded, reused, or recycled. To make sure that recommended actions had a net positive effect on the environment, the task force scrutinized each solid waste reduction option from the perspective of lifecycle assessment (see Exhibit 3.4).

Brown Bags. The changes inspired by environmental analysis came after deliberation over all the alternatives, deliberation that demanded more than scientific calculation. For example, one supplier presented McDonald's with a bag that was 17% lighter and thus used less material and generated less waste. Another supplier, however, offered a bag containing 65% recycled newsprint, which subsequently led to a bag constructed from 100% unbleached, recycled material—50% post–consumer waste and 50% post-industrial waste. After careful evaluation, the task force recommended the 100% recycled bag, which contained the least amount of virgin material. Because the new bags used

Exhibit 3.4 Scope of a Lifecycle Assessment

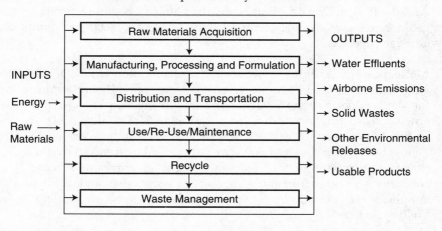

Each of the phases of the lifecycle are examined with respect to inputs and outputs, environmental impacts arising from them, and potential improvements that could reduce such impacts

Source: Society for Environmental Toxicology and Chemistry, "A Technical Framework for Lifecycle Assessment," Washington, D.C. January, 1991.

unbleached material, they were brown instead of white. Initial customer reaction was tepid, yet the task force discovered in restaurant testing that once consumers understood why the bag looked different, they felt good about it. McDonald's did in fact adopt the 100% recycled bag, suddenly recognizable in its advertising campaign and thoroughly explained in brochures available at each restaurant.[6]

Corrugated Boxes. Corrugated boxes made up one of the two largest components of McDonald's on-premise waste, accounting for 34% of solid waste by weight. Every McDonald's restaurant went through 300 to 400 corrugated boxes per week. As it had done so often in other areas of its operations, McDonald's again turned to suppliers. Boxes contained an average 21% recycled content, but McDonald's commissioned an outside consultant to survey the paperboard industry's capacity to increase that level. Suppliers worried that additional recycled content would weaken the boxes and make them more expensive and heavier. One small supplier, though, approached McDonald's with a new box containing 21% old newsprint. With the consultant's findings and a sample box in hand, McDonald's fixed an ambitious objective of 35% recycled content for its corrugated boxes. In September 1990, McDonald's mandated a 35% level for all suppliers and established a system to monitor and track adherence to this goal. Environmental criteria were now as important as all other criteria in McDonald's review of supplier performance.

By making such challenging demands, McDonald's did more than extend its dedication to quality into the environmental realm. McDonald's created a market for the recycled materials its stores would be generating. And the few McDonald's outlets that had already begun recycling corrugated boxes already realized reductions of $250 to $600 per month on garbage collection.

McRecycle U.S.A. Prior to McDonald's collaboration with EDF, McDonald's had announced its McRecycle U.S.A. program. This program called for McDonald's to spend $100 million annually on using recycled products when constructing, renovating, and equipping McDonald's outlets in the United States. Almost 350 new McDonald's were built every year in the United States, and close to 1,000 were remodelled. Just as McDonald's was doing in mandating 35% recycled content in corrugated boxes, the company was strengthening a market for recycled materials. Over 500 suppliers and manufacturers had already registered to participate in McRecycle U.S.A.

Sandwich Packaging. McDonald's generated tremendous controversy

---

[6]McDonald's Corporation/Environmental Defense Fund Waste Reduction Task Force, *Final Report*, April, 1991, p. 94.

when it decided to abandon the polystyrene clamshell it had been using to package its sandwiches since 1975. But the decision represented the most careful analysis the task force completed on any one issue and perhaps the most environmentally conscientious move McDonald's had ever made. By shifting to quilted wraps, McDonald's reduced the volume of waste from sandwich packaging by 90% and the volume of shipping packaging by over 80%.

McDonald's selected its packaging on the basis of three criteria: availability, functionality, and cost. To be suitably functional, sandwich packaging had to perform highly in four areas. First, it had to provide proper insulation to keep the food warm for a specified time in the holding bin. Second, the packaging had to keep the food tasty and moist without allowing it to become either soggy or dry. This was called "breathability." Third, food-packaging was evaluated for its handling ability. Did the packaging sustain product integrity—did it, for example, allow employees and customers to handle the sandwich in a sanitary manner? Fourth, packaging had to meet standards of appearance. It had to permit printing and graphics that would enable crews and customers to recognize the sandwiches quickly.

To evaluate the quality of sandwich packaging, McDonald's conducted a battery of tests. The company measured internal food temperatures as well as temperatures at different time intervals. The company used blind taste-tests and moisture analysis. McDonald's also judged grease resistance, product appearance, locking mechanisms, and folding characteristics. Every form of food packaging came with a set of procedures for wrapping the food and with training materials that connected preparation of the menu item with the appropriate method of packaging.

To these rigid standards the Waste Reduction Task Force added a new set of specifications. Every form of packaging would be evaluated according to the reduction it represented in materials and in production impacts (such as energy use and emissions). Packaging was also judged for its use of reusable material and recyclable material, as well as for its recycled content and use of materials that could be composted.

To improve performance of its packaging, McDonald's had, in 1975, switched from paperboard sandwich packages to polystyrene (foam) clamshells. Contrary to the confusion surrounding McDonald's switch from polystyrene packaging in November 1990, McDonald's did not return to paperboard packages. It introduced a thinner, paper-based wrap, once again making a switch based on performance criteria, which now included environmental standards.

The new sandwich packaging consisted of a three-layered wrap: an inside layer of tissue, a sheet of polyethylene in the middle, and an outer sheet of paper. Unlike paperboard containers, the layered wrap performed as well as the foam clamshells on the traditional packaging criteria and met higher environmental standards: it promised a large reduction in solid waste.

Just prior to the switch, McDonald's had announced an ambitious program to test plastic recycling in conjunction with plastic manufacturers. The switch from clamshells, therefore, elicited sharp reactions in the media. Immediate response accused McDonald's of pandering to public misconceptions about the environment. McDonald's was accused of exploiting the clamshell's notoriety as an icon of the throwaway society, eschewing the less popular and more difficult solution. "Had we only been out to score with the public," Langert retorted, "we would have returned to paperboard, which is actually worse for the environment but is perceived by the public as preferable to plastic." The analysis of alternative packaging did include an assessment of existing and potential recycling of foam clamshells. (See Exhibit 3.5 for comparison of sandwich packaging)

Nonetheless, McDonald's had serious qualms about the switch. Moving away from foam clamshells affected five suppliers, and two in particular felt a significant impact. The company hated to abandon a supplier and wondered how the move might affect its relationships with other suppliers. McDonald's considered those relationships sacrosanct, but relationships with suppliers all revolved around providing the best available product. In fact it was an existing supplier that approached McDonald's with the layered wrap in the spring of 1990 after two years of preliminary testing.

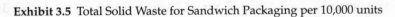

Exhibit 3.5 Total Solid Waste for Sandwich Packaging per 10,000 units

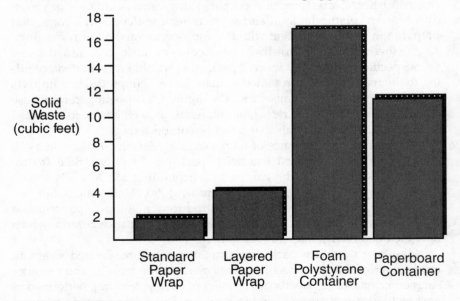

Adapted from "Resource and Environmental Analysis of Sandwich Wraps" by Franklin Associates, Ltd. for Perseco, 1991.

From the spring of 1990 until the wrap's introduction in November, both the supplier and McDonald's tested and developed the packaging further. When it met standards for heat retention, appearance, moisture control, and waste reduction, the wrap was tested in several McDonald's restaurants on the Quarter Pounder with Cheese.

Meanwhile, McDonald's asked EDF to compare the environmental merits of the new packaging to foam clamshells. The layered wrap promised three areas of reduced waste when contrasted with the clamshell. First, the volume of the boxes in which the layered wrap was shipped paled in comparison to clamshells. Second, production of the wrap entailed less industrial pollution than that associated with the manufacture and handling of polystyrene. Third, the layered wrap was itself of lower volume, so it promised to reduce the impact of waste disposal.

Plans to recycle polystyrene could hope to capture only the foam from products eaten on the premises of a McDonald's, so even if each restaurant could recover every clamshell used on site, that would constitute just a 40% to 50% reduction in disposed waste. In contrast, the layered wraps themselves represented a 90% reduction in volume over clamshells. When compared on energy use, air emissions, waterborne wastes, and solid waste generation, the layered sandwich wrap appeared far preferable to polystyrene foam: the wrap required 85% less energy, generated 40% less air emission, produced 80% less discharge into water, and 60% less solid waste (See Exhibit 3.6 for overall environmental comparison of packaging alternatives). Despite the clear choice implied by both performance tests and environmental studies, the task-force report carefully described McDonald's switch to layered wraps:

> It is critical to note that McDonald's decision to phase out polystyrene packaging and substitute paper-based wraps cannot be evaluated as a generic "paper vs. plastic" issue. . . . Not all plastics or paper materials are created equal. Therefore, the specific nature of the materials involved—their mode of production, their current rate of recycling, and so on—dramatically affects their relative environmental consequences and must be carefully taken into account in any comparison.

Planning for the Future

As McDonald's managers reviewed the work of the task force, they wondered what lessons they might draw from the experience with the task force. Had it all been worth it?—or was this just a distraction from the competitive pressures challenging McDonald's as it strived to maintain its growth targets? Was this just a transient issue, like the energy crisis of the seventies, or should it become a primary goal of McDonald's future oper-

Exhibit 3.6 Environmental Comparison of Packaging Alternatives

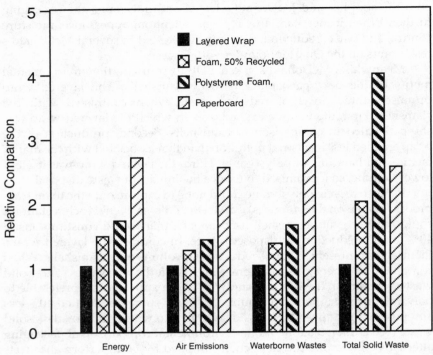

Note: The presentation of data in this chart for 50% recycling of polystyrene foam is hypothetical. Such a rate is far from being achieved anywhere in the US, and therefore represents a highly optimistic assumption—one that is far higher than even the goal of the polystyrene industry itself to be recycling 25% by 1995. For ease of presentation, impacts are shown relative to the layered wrap, which was assigned a value of 1.0.

Adapted from Waste Reduction Task Force, *Final Report*, page 41.

ations? Throughout the effort, one member of McDonald's top management recalled, McDonald's never forgot its business. "We're in the business of making hamburgers—of serving quality food at a low price. We're not in the packaging business." That business was growing more complex even without the environmental initiative. McDonald's was faced with unprecedented challenges for variety and flexibility in its service. The choices were clear. First, the company could rely on its traditional recipe based on consistency and quality through standardization, one which had made it the paragon of success in the quick-service business. Alternatively, McDonald's could make some changes in its basic strategy—by allowing even more franchisee autonomy and continuing to provide a growing variety of offerings and service in its restaurants. But how far was too far?

On October 1st, 1992, Burger King announced a dinner menu, and that it would begin table service between 5 p.m. and 8 p.m. in its company-owned restaurants.

CHAPTER 4

American Connector Company (A)

"*L*OOKS BLEAK." Those were the words Denise Larsen, the Vice President of Operations at American Connector Corporation, said calmly as she read the report on a competitor's plans to build a new electrical connector plant in the United States. The competitor, DJC Corporation of Japan, had become a dominant supplier of electrical connectors in its home market in recent years, after building what was rumored to be one of the most efficient connector plants in the world. However, despite its success in Japan, DJC was barely a contender in the U.S. market. The company had no plants in the U.S. and only a small sales force there. Larsen knew that this could all change quickly. As she explained to her assistant, Jack Mitchell, a recently graduated M.B.A.:

> There have been rumors the last few years that DJC would build a new plant here to launch an attack on the U.S. market. But with the market so crowded with competitors and burdened with excess capacity, no one took them seriously here. Either way, we figured that we still had a cost advantage. But if your report is right, and if DJC can operate a plant here like the one they have in Japan, I think DJC could quickly grab some market share here.

Larsen was worried because she felt American's position was particularly vulnerable at the moment. She was chiefly concerned with the company's connector plant in Sunnyvale, California since it had been struggling with a series of operating problems during the past year. Costs at Sunnyvale were increasing while quality seemed to be deteriorating. In the past month, she and Andrew Li, the new plant manager there, had discussed ways to improve the plant's performance. Now she wondered whether the DJC situation called for a completely new manufacturing strategy.

Professor Gary Pisano prepared this case with assistance from Research Associate Sharon Rossi. The case was prepared as the basis for class discussion rather than to illustrate either effective or ineffective handling of an administrative situation. Data have been disguised for purposes of confidentiality.

The Electrical Connector Industry in the Early 1990s

Electrical connectors were devices made to attach wires to other wires, attach wires to outlets, attach wires, components or chips to PC boards, or attach PC boards to other boards. A connector typically had two main body parts—a plastic housing and metal socket pins or terminals. The housing was usually made of a plastic resin such as a polyester, nylon, or polycarbonate. The metal pins could be made and plated with a number of

Exhibit 4.1   A Sample of Connector Products by Type

Figures 1-3: Component/Chip-to-Board Connectors

  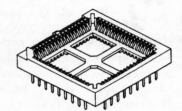

Figures 4-6: Board-to-Board Connectors

Figures 7-8: Wire-to-Board Connectors

Figure 9: Wire-to-Wire Connectors

different metals, ranging from tin to gold. Exhibit 4.1 illustrates several basic product designs.

The connectors were used in a variety of product applications, including military and aerospace electronics, industrial electronics, telecommunications equipment, computer and office equipment, automobiles, and consumer electronics and appliances. Each application—often each producer—called for different connector specifications. In 1990, there were over 700 standard connector product lines in North America alone. Standard designs were those which had been established by the International Institute of Connectors and Interconnect Technology (IICIT), the National Electronics Distributors Association (NEDA), or by end use industries. Other designs were custom-produced, usually on a one-year contract with a single connector company and were often accepted as industry standards after the contract expired. Since each type of connector had its own set of specifications, suppliers which produced many types of connectors (sometimes hundreds or thousands of models) for different industries were finding it difficult to meet the increasing number of specifications. In 1992, attempts were made to standardize product specifications among the many different industry associations.

Because connector types were made of different materials and varied from low- to high-technology, they varied dramatically in price, as well. For example, a simple connector such as a phone jack sold for only a few cents, whereas a custom designed connector such as one used in military electronics sold for several dollars. The cost of connectors used in any product typically counted for 2% or less of the cost of the end product.

In the 1970s, the U.S. connector industry[1] had experienced very rapid growth as firms built up capacity to meet the growing demand (particularly for computer applications). But when demand slowed in the mid to late '80s, there were too many suppliers and too much capacity. Price competition intensified as more offshore producers entered the U.S. market.

In the 1990s, the U.S. connector industry was characterized as a hostile environment. There were more than 900 suppliers and sales continued to slacken. In 1991, sales were down 3.9% from the previous year, while the ten industry leaders were on average down 7.9%. The abundance of suppliers gave customers leverage to demand reduced prices, improved quality, and faster delivery. At the same time, many customers were working to reduce the number of suppliers they did business with. OEMs that previously dealt with 10 or 12 connector vendors had reduced their suppliers to as few as four. Pressures spurred a trend of mergers and acquisitions in the industry and analysts predicted that the number of connector suppliers in the U.S. might drop to 400 or fewer by the end of the 1990s.

Electrical connectors were very engineering intensive products and

---

[1]The "connector industry" included three types of interconnect products: connectors, cable assemblies, and backpanels. While American Connector and DJC Corporation produced all types of interconnect products, the Sunnyvale and Kawasaki plants manufactured only connectors.

were critical to product performance. As electronic circuitry became more miniaturized and operated at higher speeds, new connectors had to meet more demanding requirements for space, weight, cost, quality, reliability and performance.

In 1991, worldwide sales of interconnect products totaled roughly $16 billion. The top ten worldwide leaders accounted for $6.67 billion, but the total industry (1,200 competitors) was very fragmented. The dominant company in the industry was AMP, Inc. It held 16% market share with sales of $2.6 billion in 1991. The second tier of companies consisted of six other companies, each of which had sales in the $500 million to $800 million range. DJC and American Connector were among the second tier companies worldwide. Companies in the third tier had sales in the $250 to $500 million range. In total, there were 28 firms with sales greater than $100 million.

Profile of DJC Corporation

The DJC Corporation produced a variety of electrical connectors used in computers, telecommunications, and consumer electronics. For these applications, DJC produced four basic types of connectors: wire-to-wire, wire-to-outlet, item-to-board, and board-to-board.

There were several aspects characterizing DJC's competitive strategy in most of its product lines. First, the company cultivated and maintained close links with the major computer, telecommunications, and electronics companies and distributors in Japan. These relationships represented an important entry barrier in the Japanese connector market. Secondly, the company's design strategy emphasized simplicity and manufacturability over innovation. Early DJC product designs were based on reverse engineering of other companies' designs, including those of American Connector. As one former manager of DJC explained:

> In 1965, we copied other companies' products. Americans made good products and the U.S. market was the most advanced in the world. Our R&D was geared entirely toward analyzing U.S.-made products, copying improvements as they were made. By 1975, our quality was as good as theirs. After that, the production process became the basis for competition.

However, DJC's design strategy went beyond simply copying U.S.-made connectors. The company paid very careful attention to customer and user needs in adapting American designs to the particulars of the Japanese market. For example, DJC connectors were designed for maximum compactness since this feature was very important to Japanese OEMs, particularly those producing consumer electronics. DJC also adapted the designs to economize on raw materials (which were nearly twice as expensive in Japan as they were in the United States) and to simplify manufacturing. Features which did not add perceived value to customers (such as color-coded housings) were eliminated.

Finally, and perhaps most importantly, DJC viewed highly efficient manufacturing as absolutely critical to its competitive strategy. The company historically relied upon manufacturing as the major means to achieve their overall profit goals. As one former Managing Director of DJC described it:

> In electrical products, high quality is a prerequisite for success. With large established competitors fighting for a maturing market, a low cost position becomes necessary for long term success. Manufacturing excellence is the source of both and has therefore been at the heart of DJC.

The importance of manufacturing to DJC was reflected in the organization of the company (see Exhibit 4.2). For example, Mr. Okada, the head of production, was responsible for the operations of four domestic factories and reported directly to the company president, Mr. Esaka. In addition, the balance of power between manufacturing and the sales/marketing division was clearly tipped in favor of manufacturing. For example, sales/marketing had little power to alter production schedules, product mix or lead times. As one former manager at DJC explained: "Sales sometimes needs an unscheduled delivery, but manufacturing just does not allow it. There isn't even any debate."

DJC's President, Mr. Esaka, was considered to be a dominant, hands-on leader. He was hand-picked by DJC's founder to become the company's president in 1971. Many within DJC viewed Esaka as *the* decision maker within the company. As one former executive put it: "Our strategy is pure and strict, driven by Esaka himself. People may bicker back and forth . . . but everyone knows they are personally responsible to achieve the goals set out by the president."

The Kawasaki Plant

During the early 1980s, the Japanese connector market experienced increased labor and raw material costs, a rising yen, and increased import penetration. Amidst these conditions, top executives at DJC were concerned that the company might not be able to maintain its historical 50% gross margins in the connector business. This concern led Mr. Esaka to formulate his vision of a plant which could achieve "the ultimate rationalization of mass production." His vision called for a highly automated, continuously operating plant which could meet the following three goals: First, the plant must achieve asset utilization of 100%. Secondly, yield on raw material must reach 99%. Finally, customer complaints could not

Exhibit 4.2 DJC Corporation: Organizational Chart (1991)

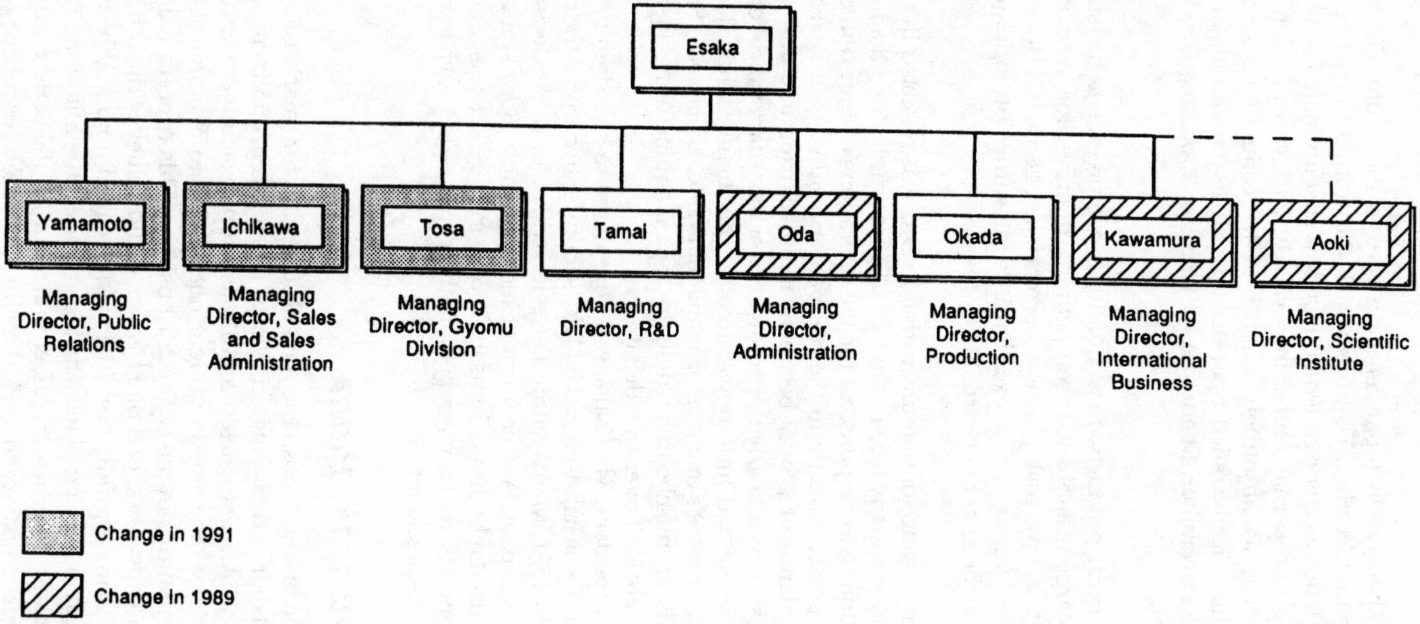

Esaka

| Yamamoto | Ichikawa | Tosa | Tamai | Oda | Okada | Kawamura | Aoki |

Managing Director, Public Relations

Managing Director, Sales and Sales Administration

Managing Director, Gyomu Division

Managing Director, R&D

Managing Director, Administration

Managing Director, Production

Managing Director, International Business

Managing Director, Scientific Institute

Change in 1991

Change in 1989

Source: Company Financial Reports

exceed 1 per million units of output. While cost was not stated as an explicit goal, everyone understood that if the above three goals were met, the plant would be one of the lowest cost producers in Japan.

DJC chose to build its "ultimate" new plant in Kawasaki, Japan; the plant was completed and began operating in 1986. Management chose the Kawasaki site for several reasons. From a logistical point of view, Kawasaki offered the advantage of being located close to the major Japanese electronics companies. In addition, perhaps more importantly, Kawasaki was near the major raw material suppliers. This was particularly important because it was anticipated that most raw materials would be delivered from vendors on a daily or weekly basis. The Kawasaki area also had an ample supply of relatively young, highly skilled workers.

The Kawasaki plant was designed to produce a maximum of 800 million connectors per year, assuming 100% utilization. Initially, the plant produced only 80% to 90% of this volume. About 75% of this output was sold in Japan and 25% was sold in developing Asian markets outside of Japan. The plant operated 24 hours a day, seven days per week, 330 days per year. The main advantage of running the plant on a nearly continuous basis was that it avoided start-up and shut-down costs.

To successfully operate the plant on a continuous basis, as well as meet Esaka's yield and quality goals, Kawasaki management carefully integrated decisions and policies related to the product and process technology, workforce, production control, quality, and organization.

Plant Layout. The Kawasaki plant was organized into four large cells, each of which was responsible for producing one of the four general types of connectors (wire-to-wire, wire-to-outlet, item-to-board, and board-to-board). With the exception of plating, all of the processes needed to manufacture a complete connector were located in each cell. Plating was organized separately in order to fully utilize the high fixed cost equipment and to protect the rest of the factory from exposure to corrosive chemicals and noxious fumes.

Each cell contained anywhere from two to six production lines, with each line consisting of terminal stamping, housing molding, assembly, and packaging. Each production line was responsible for producing a specific family of the cell's products. Successive processing stages in each line were located close to one another and in a straight line in order to minimize materials handling steps and to reduce as much as possible the distance work-in-process had to travel. For example, each plastic molding press in a cell was located only a few feet from the line's assembly operations. Operations were synchronized so that completed housing parts flowed almost continuously (via small bins) between each molding and assembly line. Because molding and terminal stamping equipment had shorter cycle times than assembly equipment, these processes were run below their top speeds in order to synchronize parts fabrication and final assembly.

Assembly operations were almost completely automated. After assembly, connectors were inspected and transported a few yards to the cell's packaging area. In packaging, connectors were sealed individually in plastic on strips containing 2,000 units.[2] Each strip or "tape" was loaded onto a large reel. The central shipping department was responsible for packing each customer's order for shipment. The Kawasaki plant delivered to many customers on a daily basis and some of the largest customers received shipments every few hours.

Product Technology. Product design reflected the goals of continuous and reliable operations and the need to economize on raw materials. Before commencing production at Kawasaki, product designs were thoroughly analyzed to determine ways in which the product might be made easier to manufacture and use less material. For example, product design of most connectors was standardized to reduce the number of product variations. In 1991, the plant produced only 640 different stock-keeping-units (SKU's), a relatively small number for a plant its size. The limited number of product variations, it was believed, reduced the costs and complexity associated with shorter production runs. To economize on the use of raw material, designers adapted some types of connectors to use pins plated with tin rather than gold. Though gold was the most reliable and durable material, tin was far cheaper and worked well in low power applications. To further simplify production and reduce costs, DJC packaged its connectors only on tape and reels. This packaging was particularly suited to customers with automated production environments, and it did not inconvenience customers with manual operations. DJC's engineers undertook extensive value-engineering to identify and implement cost saving design changes which did not compromise product quality or performance. These design changes are discussed in Exhibit 4.3.

Process Technology. Process design activities reflected several basic principles. First, while the plant was to be highly automated, significant resources were devoted to what DJC called "pre-automation." Pre-automation referred to the activities required to make the production process suitable for highly reliable automation. It reflected the philosophy that a production process could only be automated after it was completely understood, properly designed, and properly laid out. To automate before might mean automating a process which was inherently inefficient or unreliable. During pre-automation, process flows were carefully analyzed to determine ways in which the process could be streamlined and inventories eliminated. Worker movements and motions were also studied to identify ways in which the process could be made more efficient. Pre-

---

[2]Reels of 1,500 units were considered standard in the industry.

Exhibit 4.3 Analysis of Kawasaki's Material Cost Savings, Given American Connector's Design

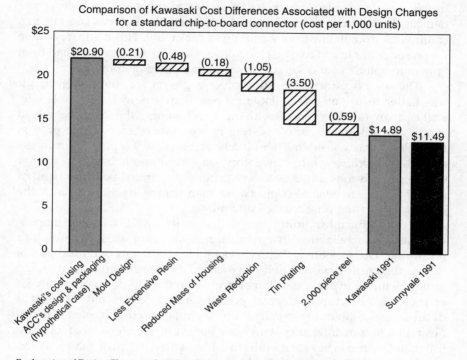

Comparison of Kawasaki Cost Differences Associated with Design Changes for a standard chip-to-board connector (cost per 1,000 units)

Explanation of Design Changes which Resulted in Material Cost Savings

• Mold Design: By using shorter and narrower "runners" (i.e. the channels which carried plastic resin into the mold chamber), DJC was able to reduce the consumption of raw material in molding.

• Less Expensive Resin: DJC's engineering department found that certain expensive resins used in plastic housings could be substituted with much lower cost materials, without any significant degradation in product performance, reliability, or durability.

• Reduced Mass of Housing: DJC altered connector designs (e.g., thinner walls) so that any unnecessary mass in the plastic housing could be eliminated.

• Waste Reduction: Includes material costs saved by reducing defects in both plastic housing molding and terminal stamping, as well as damage incurred during material handling.

• Tin Plating: Whenever possible and whenever it would not reduce product performance. DJC plated terminals with tin rather than with gold or other higher cost metals.

• 2,000 Piece Reel: DJC packed 2,000 pieces onto a packaging reel (instead of 1,500). This resulted in lower consumption of reels.

Note: Cost changes represent difference in material costs only, does not include manufacturing efficiencies.

Source: Company Documents

automation activities also included specifying raw material quality and process tolerance levels.

There were several examples of how pre-automation problem- solving affected the process. The warehouse was centrally located to simplify material flows and to economize on space. The amount of warehouse and floor space was intentionally limited so that there would be no room for excessive raw material or in-process inventories. To simplify material flows, each injection mold for plastic parts had a dedicated press and each press was dedicated to a single assembly line. Each assembly line was laid out in a continuous straight line from stamping to packaging. This made it possible for one operator to run two assembly lines. Only after the process had been "pre-automated" would steps be taken to implement automation.

The second principle guiding process design was the notion that it was better to use an old, reliable process than a new, less reliable one. Rather than taking chances with new technology, the plant relied on continuous improvement of existing proven processes. Reliable process technology was considered absolutely essential to keeping the process running smoothly, without inventory, on a continuous basis. To further ensure smooth runs, processes were generally operated below maximum speed.[3] Emphasis was also placed on maintaining equipment with the goal of eliminating unscheduled downtime.

A third principle guiding process design at Kawasaki was the emphasis on absolute reliability in upstream molding processes. According to one former DJC executive, "DJC views molding as the most critical part of the manufacturing process and has focused its efforts there." Its molding group included experts in polymer physics and many former employees of mold manufacturers. Several policies and decisions reflected DJC's desire to make molding virtually faultless. Molds were subjected to rigorous repair and maintenance schedules. For example, every mold received full maintenance every six months in addition to daily basic maintenance. Molds were also replaced relatively frequently to reduce the chance of failure and to allow mold technology to be upgraded. The average life of a mold at Kawasaki was three years. Taking into account purchase costs, maintenance costs, and costs of repair, Kawasaki's average annual cost per mold was $29,000.[4] The plant achieved mold yields in excess of 99.99%.

A fourth element of Kawasaki's approach to process technology was its reliance on in-house technology development. DJC's strong in-house process engineering competence was a result of both historical conditions and of strategic choice. One former employee described the historical conditions shaping the company's in-house process engineering expertise: "Because we were a small company and couldn't afford to buy equipment, we built a lot of it ourselves. There were extensive workshops in every factory."

During its early years, the company developed ideas about manufac-

[3]For example, an assembly line in the Kawasaki plant ran at 200 units/minute. By comparison, a similar line in American Connector's Sunnyvale facility ran at 500 units/minute.

[4]In comparison, American Connector's Sunnyvale plant spent approximately $40,000 per mold per year and molds averaged eight years of useful life.

turing by looking at the operations of emerging Japanese role models like Toyota. The decision to develop technology in-house was also strategically motivated. In Japan, contractual agreements with equipment vendors preventing resale to competitors were not common. Thus, DJC worried that its ability to achieve a competitive edge in process technology would be severely limited if it relied too much on equipment vendors. Indeed, part of this strategy was shaped by observing American Connector's experience with equipment vendors. As one DJC engineer recalled: "American Connector didn't develop their (connector) assembly machine themselves, they asked an equipment manufacturer to help them design the machine. That same equipment company then offered to sell us the identical machine." Thus, while the Kawasaki plant might buy standard equipment from vendors, it would make all proprietary design modifications in-house. In addition, Kawasaki designed all of its molds in-house and manufactured about half of them in-house as well (the most complex molds were all produced in-house). Kawasaki's goal was to eventually build 100% of its molds in-house.

A final element of Kawasaki's technology strategy was the inter-functional coordination of all its technology development activities. The plant's "Technology Development Division" was responsible for coordinating and managing the activities of the product planning section, the materials section, process engineering, and the molding technology group. Each section was assigned a specific set of goals. For example, it was the job of process engineering to design and modify new equipment and to identify opportunities for automation. However, it was the job of the Technology Development Division to ensure that all of these sections were working in concert to achieve a consistent set of explicit goals. These goals included: efficient resource utilization, design quality and manufacturability, smooth manufacturing introduction, shorter development cycle, and continuous process improvement.

One example of how this worked in practice was the development of a new resin to improve connector durability. The materials planning group solicited input from the product planning group on customer needs and requirements. Through this contact, the materials group learned that a more durable connector would help differentiate DJC's product in the customer's eyes. This led to a discussion with members of the R&D group about possible material breakthroughs which might create a more heat-tolerant and damage-resistant connector. At the same time, the materials group also held discussions with the process engineering group to learn about the potential new materials and the requirements of the manufacturing process. A new resin which improved connector durability emerged from this joint effort.

In the same way that the Technology Development Division coordinated various functions to improve product characteristics, it integrated the efforts of product planning, materials, process engineering and molding to reduce material costs and improve processes. It was estimated that if Kawasaki were to use American Connector's product design and packaging, material costs would total $20.90 per thousand units. However, because the Technology Development Division eliminated several design features of the product which used material but did not add value to the customer and implemented several waste reducing changes in the production process, the current Kawasaki material costs were only $14.89 per thousand units. This cost was still above American Connector Sunnyvale's $11.49 per thousand, but relevant raw materials were approximately twice as costly in Japan than in the United States. Exhibit 4.3 contains an analysis of these improvements.

Sourcing. Kawasaki maintained close relationships with a few suppliers of its key raw materials. These suppliers had to meet rigorous quality standards and were required to certify the quality of their products in every delivery. When Kawasaki received a shipment from a supplier, materials were used directly in production without further inspection. Suppliers were expected to further improve their quality over the long term. A manager of one of Kawasaki's Japanese suppliers commented: "Japanese customers will complain if the material causes problems in the manufacturing process and they meet with us frequently to discuss problems. DJC is our most demanding customer. . . . They complain constantly." Quality improvement was considered a joint effort between Kawasaki and its suppliers. Any supplier which was having difficulty meeting specific requirements received technical support from Kawasaki.

Kawasaki's sourcing policy also demanded frequent delivery. Most of the raw materials (including resins for the housing, metals for the pins, and packaging) were delivered on a daily basis. The rest were either delivered weekly or monthly. Frequent deliveries allowed Kawasaki to maintain raw material inventories that averaged only five days.[5] The low level of raw material inventory, in turn, allowed Kawasaki to have a relatively small warehouse and to reduce the amount of resources devoted to managing and controlling raw material stocks. While the procurement department relied on just-in-time deliveries, it used an M.R.P. program to plan longer term material requirements.

Quality Control. The Q.C. Division pursued five objectives: improving quality control standards, improving the process inspection system, improving the precision of molded components, improving the quality of product designs, and reducing the plant's waste. Most of its work, which included modifying equipment, was done in conjunction with the Technology Development Division.

---

[5]In comparison, raw material inventories at American Connector's Sunnyvale plant averaged 10.8 days.

Production and Inventory Control. To minimize yield and capacity losses associated with changeovers, production runs were scheduled to be as long as possible. On average, a production run of a particular model lasted one week, though some product lines were run on an almost continuous basis. Long runs were possible because of the limited number of SKU's produced at the plant. To further facilitate long runs, Kawasaki's plant had complete control over its schedule and mix and refused to make changes for unplanned orders.

As mentioned earlier, all aspects of the process and the plant layout were designed to achieve a smooth flow of materials and to minimize work-in-process inventory. With this design, management expected they would need to devote relatively few resources to inventory control. For the most part, this proved true: Kawasaki's processing lead times and work-in-process inventories each averaged two days.[6] However, Kawasaki maintained a relatively high finished-goods inventory of 56 days.

Workforce. One of the explicit goals of the Kawasaki plant was to gradually reduce the number of direct production workers as well as support and overhead staff. Management expected that as the plant became increasingly automated, fewer direct production workers would be needed. Similarly, the number of employees dedicated to controlling various activities in the plant were also expected to decline as processes became more reliable, as inventories decreased, and as the overall complexity of the plant environment declined.

The general approach to selecting workers was to hire new graduates from high schools (for lower level positions) and from universities (for higher level positions). All employees hired into the Technology Development Division had to have a university degree. Kawasaki offered wages which were somewhat above the average for recent graduates in Japan. The goal was to attract people with generally high skills and aptitudes ("raw talent") who could be developed on the job. New hires received extensive training both through formal programs and through a job-rotation system designed to broaden their skill base. The average worker in Kawasaki shifted positions once every three years. Production workers were directly responsible for *all* activities affecting conversion and material flows and were not specialized to particular processes or functions.

While Kawasaki's wages were above average for new graduates, they were below average for experienced workers. Thus, while the compensation system and the opportunities for training tended to attract relatively

---

[6]Processing lead time was the time it took for a batch of connectors to be completed (i.e., placed in finished goods inventory) once the first processing operations on the batch were commenced in either molding or terminal stamping. Processing lead time included waiting time between operations.

Exhibit 4.4 Organizational Chart of Kawasaki Plant

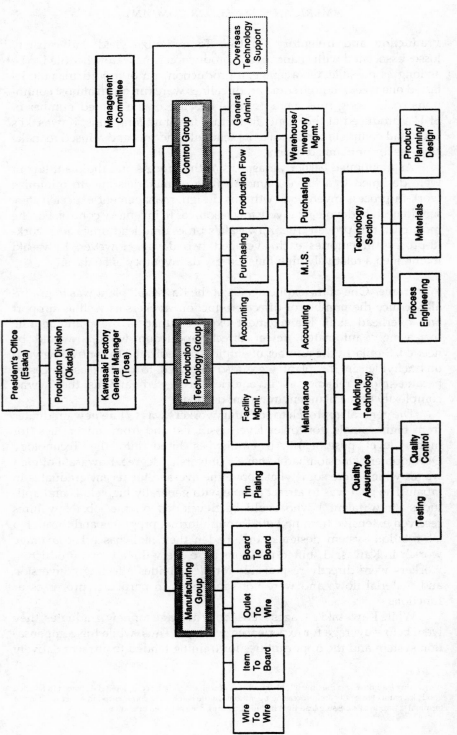

Source: Company documents.

qualified young workers, it tended to discourage workers from staying at Kawasaki for a long period of time. Many Kawasaki workers tended to leave the plant after the age of 35. The average employee stayed at Kawasaki for 9 years, while the average for large Japanese companies was 14.5 years.

Organization. While Esaka was the driving force behind the Kawasaki plant, the plant operated under a high level of autonomy from corporate. Esaka set the goals, but left the plant manager completely free to pursue those goals in any way he chose. Exhibit 4.4 provides an organizational chart of the Kawasaki plant.

The philosophy of pushing decision-making autonomy down in the organization followed at the plant as well. While the plant manager and his top staff were responsible for longer term planning issues facing Kawasaki, most tactical problems were solved by production employees. The number of employees dedicated to various control and support activities (such as accounting, production and inventory control, materials handling, etc.) was relatively low because all of the plant's technology and operating policies were designed to reduce the sources of problems that create a need for control staff. For example, a relatively continuous process flow eliminated much of the need for materials handling personnel. High process reliability made it unnecessary to employ mechanics for repair. Similarly, lack of work-in-process inventory greatly reduced the need for inventory control workers. Kawasaki's success in achieving this aim is reflected in data on the relative number of employees in various job functions (see Exhibit 4.5 for a comparison of Kawasaki and Sunnyvale). Only 32% of the employees at Kawasaki were in indirect labor positions. Of those in indirect labor positions, most were employed in Technology Development.

Exhibit 4.5   Comparison Of Labor Use (1991)

	Kawasaki 94 Employees	Sunnyvale 396 Employees
Indirect Labor		
Control	11.7%	16.7%
Technology Development	12.8%	6.8%
Materials Handling	3.2%	10.4%
Mechanics	4.3%	11.9%
Direct Labor (Production)	68.0%	54.0%
Total	100.0%	100.0%

Note: Kawasaki production estimated to be 700 million units.
Sunnyvale production estimated to be 420 million units.

Profile of American Connector Company

American Connector operated four plants in the U.S. and two in Europe. Each of these plants produced the four basic types of connectors and each serviced a particular customer segment. On the whole, the company's competitive strategy was characterized by its emphasis on both quality and customization. In the marketplace, the company had established a reputation as a high quality supplier; its products were recognized for superior design and performance, in particular. Customers' engineers often commented that American Connector (ACC) provided excellent technical solutions. Within the company itself, quality was a point of pride; management and workers alike believed that quality was American Connector's key to competitive success.

ACC considered its customization strategy to be an extension of its emphasis on quality. Beyond just meeting manufacturing specifications, quality at ACC meant conforming to the customers' needs. Custom orders made up 15% of the company's total production volume.[7] Employees worked closely with large customers to develop more unique solutions to specific connector problems. For example, engineers at ACC developed a socket for memory chips that made it much easier for end users to later upgrade to higher memory. For arrangements such as this, ACC's designers would collaborate with the customer's engineers early in the development cycle. Many of ACC's custom products had become industry standards.

Historically, ACC had been very profitable, sustaining margins as high as 52%, but management realized that they needed to put forth greater effort to compete globally, increase growth, and maintain profitability in the future. Between 1983 and 1988, the company invested several hundred million dollars worldwide in new plants and equipment to support the strategy. Unfortunately, increased competition in the industry, coupled with slacking demand for connectors made it difficult for the company to reach its growth and profit goals in 1991. While sales had grown from $252 million in 1984 to $800 million in 1991, gross margins had eroded from 52% to 43% during the same period.

The Sunnyvale Plant

American Connector opened the Sunnyvale plant in 1961 in order to serve the emerging electronics-based industries in and around Silicon Valley. Initially, the plant was housed in a small leased facility and had an annual capacity of only one million connectors per year. In 1963, as demand for connectors in the electronics industry began to accelerate, operations were moved to a newly built facility on the site of the present factory. Since that time, the plant was expanded several times in order to accommodate

---

[7]This figure did not include prototype production runs which accounted for less than 1% of production.

Exhibit 4.6 Productivity Comparisons (1991)

	Kawasaki 94 employees	Sunnyvale 396 employees
(a) Connector Output per Square Foot (in thousands of units) Per Square Foot of Map Space	15.1	10.9
(b) Connector Output per Employee (in millions of units)	7.45	1.06
(c) Fixed Asset Utilization (%)		
Plant Not Operating*	5.7%	28.6%
Non-scheduled	13.2%	23.5%
Process Failure	1.0%	8.9%
Preventive Maintenance	2.0%	2.4%
Process Changeover	2.0%	4.8%
Quality Losses	0.7%	1.6%
Effective Utilization	75.4%	30.2%

* Assumes maximum available time of 24 hours/day, 350 days/year (8,400 hours). Equal to (350 – days plant is operating)/350.
Source: Company documents.

rapidly growing demand. To maintain flexibility, the company tried to expand capacity at the Sunnyvale site ahead of expected growth in demand. Capacity was usually added when long term forecasts indicated that utilization would exceed 85% for sustained periods.[8]

The last major expansion occurred in 1986, bringing capacity up to 600 million units per year. At the time, it was thought that capacity would again have to be expanded in 1990 and tentative plans were laid for a completely new factory. However, 1986 proved to be a peak year in the connector market's long period of extraordinary growth. Beginning in 1987, slowed growth in demand resulted in excess capacity industry-wide, so plans for a new factory were immediately halted. Utilization at Sunnyvale plant sunk as low as 50% in 1988, but rebounded to 70% by 1991. Using current demand forecasts, the plant was expected to reach 85% utilization by 1996 (Exhibit 4.6).

Because of the depressed market conditions, the Sunnyvale plant had made no major investments in capacity or new technology since 1986. This was becoming a primary concern to the plant's production engineering staff. Bob Williams, the Director of Production Engineering explained:

> This plant has always been a technology leader. We've never hesi-
> tated to buy the latest production equipment if we thought it
> could help us improve quality or productivity. I know things have

[8]Sunnyvale calculated capacity utilization assuming a 3-shift per day, 5-day per week operation, for 50 weeks of the year. This was the normal operating schedule of the plant.

been tight the last few years, but I'm beginning to worry that some of our equipment is no longer leading edge stuff. In the past two years, some nifty new molding presses have hit the market, but our finance people won't let us buy them. Over the long term, we're really going to hurt ourselves if we don't get more aggressive in procuring new equipment.

The Sunnyvale plant produced the four major types of connectors used in computers, telecommunications equipment, and scientific instruments. Taking into account all of the combinations of housings (which varied by shape and color), the pin configurations, pin platings, and packaging formats, the plant produced about 4,500 different models.

The plant was divided into 5 production areas: terminal stamping and fabrication; terminal plating; plastic housing molding; assembly and testing; and packaging. The typical production flow went as follows. First, a batch of terminals was cut and stamped out of metal wire or strips in the terminal fabrication area. Terminals were then transported to a holding area, where they were kept until they were ready to be plated. Meanwhile, the molding department would fabricate a batch of plastic housings. Given the high rate at which they could be molded, a batch of housings was almost always ready for assembly before the terminal plating operations were completed. Thus, housings were sent to the work-in-process holding

Exhibit 4.7 Comparison of Manufacturing Costs (Kawasaki vs. Sunnyvale)

DJC vs. American Connector
Cost of Goods Sold
For a Standard Chip-to-Board Connector
(dollars per 1,000 units)

	DJC/Kawasaki 1986	ACC/Sunnyvale 1986	DJC/Kawasaki 1991	ACC/Sunnyvale 1991
Raw Material, Product	14.32	10.40	12.13	9.39
Raw Material, Packaging	3.27	2.25	2.76	2.10
Labor, Direct	7.63	...	3.02	...
Labor, Indirect	2.30	...	.75	...
Total Labor	...	8.53	...	10.30
Electricity	2.47	1.80	1.40	.80
Depreciation	7.63	5.52	1.80	5.10
Other	4.12	4.41	4.24	6.10
TOTAL	41.74	32.91	26.10	33.79

Note: ¥135 = $1, 1989 exchange rate used to convert from yen to dollars.

Exhibit 4.8 Cost Indices, United States/Japan (1991)

Expense Item	Index
Raw Material, Product	.60
Raw Material, Packaging	.60
Labor, Direct	1.10
Labor, Indirect	1.10
Electricity	.80
Depreciation	1.00
Other	1.00

Source: Company documents.

area until plated terminals were completed. When terminal plating was completed, the batches of plated terminals and housings were sent to the assembly area where housings and terminals were mated. For most products, Sunnyvale used an automated assembly process. However, for very low volume products (about 10% of Sunnyvale's total volume) manual assembly was required. A completed batch of connectors was then tested and sent to packaging. Sunnyvale offered a very wide range of packaging formats, ranging from a 10-piece plastic bag to 1,500 piece loaded reel. The processing lead time for a batch of connectors was typically 10 days for standard items and two to three weeks for special order items. Some runs ran as long as one week, but most product lines were run for 1.5 to 2 days. Sunnyvale maintained a finished goods inventory of 38 days.

Each area had its own production supervisor who reported to the plant's Director of Manufacturing. The key responsibility of area supervisors was to ensure that their respective areas met the production schedule. The Production Control Department (PCD) was responsible for scheduling the plant's aggregate production and for coordinating production across the five production areas. Using marketing forecasts and data from the finance department, the PCD set an annual production schedule which specified monthly production targets. The total level of production and the mix of products for any given month was updated three months in advance and each production area was advised. The production schedule for any given day was supposed to be "frozen" thirty days in advance. Thus, for example, on October 15 each area would receive its exact production schedule for November 15. In reality, however, the schedule was routinely changed to accommodate rush orders and requests from important customers. It was not unusual for some schedule changes to occur on a weekly and even daily basis. While such changes in the schedule could be disruptive, most of the supervisors in the plant understood the importance of maintaining flexibility. Brad Wornham, Director of Production Control, noted:

We've always prided ourself on being responsive to customers' needs and sometimes that means changing your production schedule at the last minute. You have to understand that many of our orders are for connectors which our engineering group designed specifically for a customer's new model. It's almost impossible for our customers to predict demand for their products with any degree of certainty. If they wind up with a real winner, we've got to be able to supply it or they can take the design to someone else. When that happens, our engineering people and our marketing people go crazy.

Sure, I wish we could get better information from our big customers. But, realistically, we can't demand it. If you want to compete in this business, particularly in today's market, you've got to be able to meet customers' delivery requirements. The guy who had this job before me believed that the schedule was sacred and should never be changed. He was always butting heads with marketing and engineering. In the end, marketing and engineering won and he has, as they say, moved on to other opportunities.

In recent years, Production Control had come under increasing pressure to schedule production runs in a way that would reduce work-in-progress (WIP) inventory. In the past, high WIP was not viewed as a problem because any extra inventory carrying costs were easily covered by growing sales. In the current climate, however, excessive WIP was considered a burden that the plant could ill afford to carry. Brad Wornham explained:

We've always kept a good amount of WIP in this factory. The set-up times in molding and plating operations don't make it economical to produce every one of our products in the exact quantity required every month. Instead, molded housings and terminals for every one of our products is produced in some minimum efficient batch size. Whatever parts are not needed in assembly that month stay in the WIP stockroom until they are needed.

I know finance is getting worried about the costs of all this WIP, but it buys us some flexibility. We don't like to keep finished goods inventory because of obsolescence. But if we keep housings and terminals in WIP, we can respond quickly to unexpected orders without keeping a lot of finished goods. Finance has suggested we try shorter production runs, but they don't like what that does to our utilization figures. Our average run in molding is already down to 1.5 days. If we go any shorter, it's really going to affect costs.

In recent years, production scheduling had become an increasingly stressful task as the number of individual products manufactured at

Sunnyvale expanded. In 1984, the plant produced about 3,000 different connectors; this figure had risen to 3,500 in 1986 and to 4,500 in 1991. To keep on top of the increasingly complex production schedule, the Production Control staff had expanded steadily over the past 6 years from 42 to 65. Some of the pressure on the staff was also relieved in 1988 when the plant invested $500,000 in a new computer system and software for production scheduling.

Quality had been identified as an area offering major opportunities for improvement. As a company, American Connector had an outstanding reputation for quality. As Bob Williams put it: "Our customers' engineers love us because of our superior design and their production people love us because we deliver nearly perfect connectors and never miss a scheduled delivery." However, some within ACC were becoming concerned about the way Sunnyvale was pursuing quality. Within the plant, defect rates were relatively high (about 26,000 per million units of production in 1990) and final inspection was responsible for making sure these didn't reach the customer. As one test technician described: "When it comes to quality, we do it the old fashioned way—we inspect it." In recent years, the new manager of the Quality Control department had made some attempts to implement Statistical Process Control and other more defect preventive measures, but these efforts had made only minimal progress. Some of the production supervisors felt that many of the defects were a result of new product designs which used increasingly complex pin configurations and required extremely high tolerances for molding. Yields on newly designed products entering production for the first time were sometimes as low as 55%. However, yields typically improved to about 98% once a product was in production for at least one year.

The Options

As she reviewed the data, Denise Larsen contemplated different scenarios and responses. She asked both Jack Mitchell and Andrew Li for their opinions. Jack Mitchell commented:

> From what I can see, DJC will kill us if they can operate a plant like Kawasaki in the U.S. We need to completely change our approach to manufacturing if we intend to stay competitive. We can't afford to wait and see if DJC will build a plant here or how it will work— we need to strike first and model our own operation into one like Kawasaki. There is no reason we can't do it here before they do.

Andrew Li looked skeptical. He responded:

> I don't see any need to panic. It's not going to be easy for DJC to implement their operating strategy in the U.S. I'm willing to bet

that their new plant here will be completely different from the Kawasaki plant. In any case, we already have a team working on a plan to cut costs. They will have a formal proposal ready in a few days. Before we do anything radical, let's look at the proposal and consider whether it will work.

PART II

DESIGNING AN OPERATIONS STRATEGY

Facilities and Process Technology Strategies

D ecisions to open or expand plants, install new equipment, or adopt advanced process technologies represent some of the most expensive and risky investment companies make. The figures can be staggering. A typical new drug now costs approximately $300 million to bring to market and may require the same amount of investment again in a new plant and equipment over the drug's commercial life. New semiconductor production facilities can cost over $1 billion and have a useful economic life of just a few years. In the automobile industry, investments in tooling for new models now routinely run into the multibillion dollar range. Often these investments have to be made long before a company knows whether a product will be a success in the marketplace. And, once made, such investments are difficult to undo. Yet, while investments in plants, equipment, and technologies can be enormously expensive and risky undertakings, companies simply cannot avoid them. In today's increasingly competitive global markets, a firm cannot survive for long if it is shackled with inadequate capacity, run-down and poorly located facilities, and outdated and uncompetitive process technologies.

In this module, Part II, we examine how effective facilities and process technology strategies can help build a competitive advantage. Earlier, we referred to these decisions as "structural elements" of an operations strategy. A third structural element, vertical integration and sourcing, is examined in a later section of this volume that focuses on selecting capabilities.

The materials contained in this Part II reflect the complexity managers have to deal with in making facilities and process-technology decisions. This involves more than simply spending money on new facilities, advanced equipment, or the latest process technologies. It also goes well beyond plant rationalization programs, the closing of inefficient plants, or moving production off shore. To have a lasting impact on a company's competitiveness, facilities and process-technology investments and decisions must provide the foundation upon which the company will build the specific operating capabilities that are critical to its success. Creating such capabilities requires managers to think of an investment in a new plant, or a decision to change a process technology, not as "once-and-for-all" solutions to fixed problems, but as part of a sequence of actions along a conscious *path* of operating improvements.

Facilities Strategies

A facilities strategy involves decisions about the configuration of a company's plant or service-unit network. It encompasses such issues as the number, size, and location of individual plants or operating units, the roles of each unit (in terms of products or services produced, processes utilized, or markets served), and the flow of materials and information across units. There are immeasurable ways a company can configure such a network. Some companies use a single, large plant to produce its entire range of products or to serve its entire global market; others have multiple plants, with each plant serving a different purpose (e.g., serving a specific geographic region, producing a particular range of products, or utilizing a given process technology). The "Chandler" case in Part I, the introductory module, provided a flavor for these types of decisions. As indicated in that module, no form of plant network works best for all companies under all circumstances. Different strategic goals and competitive circumstances require different configurations.

Almost every company makes *decisions* about facilities, but whether they have facilities *strategies* is a different matter. Too often, companies' decisions to open or close plants in particular locations are driven by short-term pressures to add capacity, cut costs, reduce labor costs, or gain a tax concession. Uncertainty about technology, markets, or competitors' actions also can lead firms to take a highly reactive posture toward expensive capital investments in facilities. When companies do not have a facilities strategy, each individual plant decision may make sense on its own merits, but over time such an approach can create an unwieldy and scattered collection of plants that do not collectively contribute to the company's competitive capabilities.

We see examples of this approach in two cases in Part II. A series of capacity-driven expansions over the years has led Applichem, a chemical manufacturer, to open various plants around the world. It is unclear at the time of the case what strategic role each of the plants plays individually. Moreover, since the plants are operationally isolated from one another, there have been few opportunities for them to share information and collectively create common capabilities. ITT-Automotive followed a similar approach as it expanded production from Europe to the United States to serve the rapidly growing market for antilock brake systems. According to one protagonist in the case, during this period of rapid market growth the primary goal was installing enough capacity to beat its largest competitor (Bosch); this took precedence over optimizing process technologies or finding ways to share best practices across plants in the network. In both the Applichem and ITT cases, a changing competitive

environment is forcing both companies to shift their thinking from providing *capacity* to creating *capabilities*. These issues reappear in the Medical
Products Company case in a later module.

Process Technology Strategies

A facilities strategy provides the logic for creating the physical architecture
of the company's operations. Developing the right physical architecture is
a critical first step in allowing operations to serve the strategic mission of a
business. A manufacturer of diesel engines, which are too heavy to be
economically transported by air, cannot compete on its ability to provide
just-in-time delivery if its plants are located thousands of miles from its
customers, regardless of how it operates individual plants. Likewise, a
company in the very-low-margin commodity chemical business cannot
hope to survive if its plant network is burdened with permanent excess
capacity. However, regardless of how well its plant network is designed, a
company will not be successful if the process technologies used within its
plants do not provide the technical capabilities to execute its strategy. A
company wanting to compete on the basis of quick response might do well
to locate its plants close to its customers (a facilities decision); but it will
not be able to execute this strategy if it uses production technology that is
costly and time-consuming to change over from one product to the next.
Because decisions about facilities and decisions about process technologies are highly interdependent components of a company's operations
strategy, the cases in this module deal with them together rather than as
separate issues. In most of these cases, process-technology decisions have
implications for facilities, and vice versa.

As in the case of facilities, there is a big difference between making
process technology decisions and having a process-technology *strategy*.
Investments in process technologies often follow a similar pattern as that
described above for facilities. Specific decisions, such as buying a new
piece of equipment or investing in process R&D for a new product, often
get made on a case-by-case basis. Process engineers or other technical
specialists are made responsible for selecting equipment, improving
processes, or developing new ones. To ensure that their engineers do not
become enamored with commercially unsound (even though technically
elegant) projects, financial analysts evaluate the required investment
against corporate return-on-investment and risk criteria.

The problem with this approach is that by making technology choices
the domain of technical and financial specialists, process technology issues
are not integrated into operations' broader strategic mission. Thus,
although each individual investment decision looks sound from both a
technical and a financial perspective, the sequence of choices may not
create a set of technical capabilities that are a good fit with other aspects of
the company's operating strategy (such as the skill level of the workforce

or the location of plants). The individual accomplishments do not cumulatively form a sound basis for pursuing the company's chosen competitive strategy.

At a very basic level, a company's process technology should provide it with the capabilities to produce products or services that have some desired mix of superior characteristics (e.g., lowest cost, most innovative or highest performing, quickest response, lowest rate of defects). There is no best approach to making process technology decisions any more than there is a best approach to facilities or any other aspect of a company's operations. Since different competitive priorities require different operating capabilities, different approaches to process technology will be taken by companies that choose to compete in different ways. An explicit process-technology strategy can provide a framework that guides individual process-technology decisions and ensures that these decisions cumulatively contribute to a set of desired competitive capabilities. The cases in this module provide examples of five types of decisions that comprise a company's process technology strategy. These are discussed briefly below.

1. Level and Allocation of Process R&D Investment. Even within the same industry, companies differ in their mix of product and process R&D. Partly, this is because companies with different strategies have different opportunities for investing their scarce capital. For example, in the pharmaceutical industry, companies that focus on inventing and developing novel therapeutic compounds ("patented drugs") tend to focus a greater share of their R&D resources on product discovery and development than on process development. In contrast, pharmaceutical companies that specialize in producing existing drugs that have come off patent ("generics") tend to allocate more of their resources to process development, since their ability to produce these products at low cost is the chief basis of their competitive advantage.

Even when companies compete in a similar fashion, they may choose different levels of process R&D investment because they differ in their assessment of the potential competitive contribution of process capabilities. For example, among pharmaceutical companies that compete primarily on introducing novel drugs, some companies choose to invest more aggressively in process R&D in order to create future entry barriers and build capabilities that enable the development of complex new compounds. Process R&D investments can be essential even for companies that compete on bases other than that of low cost. Even in industries like pharmaceuticals, luxury automobiles, and electronics, where cost is seldom the primary basis of competition, investments in process technology can have an important influence on competitive outcomes. The "Eli Lilly: Manufacturing Process Technology Strategy" case provides an introduction to the issue of how much to spend on process R&D and how to allocate it. The case also raises issues relating to the potential strategic role of process-technology competence and appropriate ways of evaluating process R&D investments.

For most companies, choosing the appropriate level of process R&D investment has constituted almost the sole focus of their process-technology strategies (just as their facilities strategies have focused only on establishing the amount of production capacity). However, it is possible for two companies to choose the same levels of process R&D investment, and yet be developing and utilizing their process capabilities very differently. Other types of choices that companies must make in shaping process capabilities are discussed below.

2. Timing of Process R&D Investment. Another choice that companies make is how they will time the spending of their process R&D investments relative to their product life cycle. Some companies might choose to focus their process R&D efforts on products that are still in development in an attempt to perfect the process before the product hits the market. Other companies prefer to minimize their investments in process R&D until there are some signs that a product will be commercially successful. Such companies tend to subscribe to the philosophy that it is impossible to design an optimal process until the company has accumulated a sufficient amount of actual commercial production experience with the product. Finally, some companies choose to hold off most process R&D until a product has reached its "mature" phase, where differentiation tends to revolve around cost, conformance quality, service, rapid delivery, or some other dimension of manufacturing performance.

One framework that is helpful in thinking about investments in process technology is the product-process life-cycle model (Abernathy and Utterback 1978). This model posits that the rate of product innovation and process innovation varies in a predictable way over the life of an industry. The rate of product innovation tends to be highest during the early part of an industry's life cycle. However, once a dominant design emerges, opportunities for radical innovation recede and the terms of competition shift toward costs. It is during this cost-competitive phase that companies shift their attention to process innovation. Although academic studies of this have focused primarily on documenting this relationship, the model clearly has normative implications. (Abernathy and Utterback 1978, Utterback 1994).

While the product-process life cycle model can be a powerful lens through which to view the interplay between technical change and competition, it prescribes a relatively narrow role for process technology. Process innovation is viewed as being largely concerned with *cost reduction*. Yet new process technologies can offer a wide range of benefits, including improved quality, an ability to produce a wider range of products, and faster responsiveness to customer demands, as well as lower cost. Thus, process innovation can be important throughout a product's life cycle, but its nature and focus may change as competition evolves.

The product-process life-cycle model may also be more applicable for assembled products (such as automobiles) than for process-intensive products such as chemical, plastics, or advanced materials. In these contexts, the nature of the product is strongly intertwined with the process technology, and product innovation is usually simultaneous with process innovation. The biotechnology and semiconductor industries provide excellent examples of situations where process innovation and product innovation proceed simultaneously.

Several of the cases in this module deal with the strategic role of process technologies in competitive environments where product innovation is critical. In "BMW," "ITT-Automotive," and both "Eli Lilly" cases, we see companies that have traditionally competed on the basis of product innovation, but that are facing increasing pressure along such dimensions as cost, quality, and responsiveness to customers. New approaches to process technology are contemplated in light of these new demands, but must be evaluated against the companies' continued desire to maintain their advantages in product innovation.

3. Choice of Production Technologies. The first two dimensions of process-technology strategy discussed above can be thought of as answering two questions: *how much* to spend (level) and *when* to spend it (timing). A third element of a process technology strategy is *which* production technologies to invest in. Choices about detailed aspects of process technologies occur on an almost daily basis (e.g., should a particular part be fabricated through injection molding or thermo molding?), but large, difficult-to-reverse commitments to broad process architectures occur less frequently. When such choices are made, they can represent a watershed in a company's competitive position or even in the history of an industry. Ford's decision in 1914 to adopt the moving assembly line as a process for producing automobiles represented such a watershed. It not only dramatically changed the cost structure for the automobile industry, but committed Ford to a trajectory of lower-cost, high-volume production of increasingly standardized models. This strategy worked very effectively until General Motors began to attract customers by offering product variety and differentiation. Ford's process architecture was so inflexible to product variation that it was forced to shut down all production in 1926 just to change over to the production of a new model. Another example would be the introduction of Pilkington's float glass process in the 1950s, an innovation that fundamentally altered the competitive structure of the glass industry.

This module explores choices concerning two types of process architectural decisions that have confronted a wide range of companies in the past several years. One is the choice regarding the appropriate level and nature of *automation,* an issue examined in "ITT-Automotive." The other issue, arising in "Eli Lilly: Flexible Facilities 1993," is the degree to which companies should design their facilities to be flexible enough to produce a wide range of new products versus designing for the production of a specific product (i.e., a product-focused factory). Advances in software, electronics, and programmable machine tools have created a variety of opportunities for companies to pursue automation and to achieve higher degrees of flexibility. In the 1980s, many U.S. companies turned to such advanced systems in hopes of protecting themselves against foreign competition. However, it has become clear that investing heavily in advanced production technologies does not necessarily guarantee competitiveness. General Motors, for example, invested massively in factory automation during the 1980s, yet could not stop the erosion of its domestic market share. GM's experience was not unique.

In a study of the drivers of productivity in nine factories, Hayes and Clark (1985) found that investments in new capital equipment could be twice as costly as expected and often led to surprisingly long-term *decreases* in total factor productivity. Yet there were significant differences across the plants in their sample. Factories that were able to achieve long-term improvements utilized new equipment and new process technologies in concert with changes in their operating *infrastructure,* including material flows, inventory policies, scheduling, and quality procedures. They also found that these infrastructural elements had a significant impact on the overall productivity of the plant. Rationalizing plant networks, one of the most widely used structural approaches during the 1980s, also turned out to be no panacea. Part of the problem appears to be the loss of focus that occurs when remaining plants in a network are forced to take on the products and processes from the plants that were closed. In other cases, companies found (after it was too late) that they had closed plants that had cultivated essential operating capabilities.[1]

Investment in FMS is another example. During the 1980s, companies spent billions of dollars on these sophisticated systems in hopes of becoming better able to compete on the basis of flexibility, and thus to gain some advantage over foreign competition. These high expectations were often followed by frustration and ultimately by disappointment. In some cases, disappointment resulted from the issue discussed above: an FMS could not make a company's operations more effective unless the operational infrastructure also changed to facilitate flexibility (Jaikumar 1985). However, many companies also discovered that certain new production technologies did not always provide the specific operating capabilities required to pursue their chosen competitive strategy. Many found that they had bought the wrong capability. For instance, while early FMS's could quickly changeover from one existing part to another, they could be very inflexible when it came to producing entirely new component designs, a serious impediment to companies that based their competitive

---

[1] See, for example, "Michigan Manufacturing Corp.: The Pontiac Plant (1988)," HBS case #9-694-051.

edge on product innovation. These experiences reflect another theme running throughout the volume, namely, the need to match operating capabilities with broader strategic goals.

4. Locus of Organizational Learning. Building and implementing new process capabilities is ultimately an exercise in learning. There are numerous studies documenting the tendency for cost or some other metric of manufacturing performance to improve with cumulative production experience (see, e.g., Wright, 1936; Hirsch, 1952; Rapping, 1965; Alchian, 1959; Lieberman, 1984). This "learning curve" has had a powerful impact on the formation of competitive strategies and operating strategies. It has also provided managers with a framework for thinking about manufacturing improvement (a subject covered in more detail in a later module). Experience influences performance through many routes. In labor-intensive contexts, workers may become more familiar with and adept at performing certain operations. In more capital-intensive environments, process engineers many be able to use data accumulated from production experience to optimize equipment designs or process parameters. Altering product designs to improve manufacturability is another way in which learning is manifested through experience. Investments in process R&D during the product-development phase can help an organization move down the learning curve even before commercial production commences (as in Eli Lilly, ITT, and BMW).

Opportunities to improve processes not only arise in different forms, but also occur in different venues within an organization. For example, when an organization focuses its efforts on developing processes before the launch of a product, most of the learning is done by process developers in the R&D laboratories. In an organization that does little formal process R&D before launching a product, but instead emphasizes "learning-by-doing" through actual production experience, most learning takes place on the shop floor.

Where should an organization do its learning? An obvious answer is: everywhere. After all, isn't learning good, and thus more is better? Unfortunately, as we explore in this module, some approaches to learning may be incompatible with others, and thus hard choices must be made. In "BMW," a new approach to prototyping that is designed to better simulate the production process during product development is likely to have the effect of shifting learning from the plants to the prototype and pilot-assembly operations. An important issue in that case is whether a focus on such process issues will interfere with the company's pursuit of product innovation. In "ITT-Automotive," on the other hand, a strategy of requiring that a new product be produced using the same highly automated production technology throughout the world necessarily limits the ability of individual plants to make changes in the process technology. This strategy essentially has the effect of shifting the locus of organizational learning from the shop floors of foreign plants to the central engineering center in Germany.

5. Process Development Roles of Plants in Multiplant Networks. Increasingly, companies operate a network of manufacturing or service facilities located around the world. Since these plants are, in effect, the customers of the process technology, process-technology strategies must deal with basic questions concerning plant roles and relationships. To what extent should process-technology choices and decisions be delegated to individual plants, centrally coordinated, or even centrally dictated? In this module, "Applichem," "ITT-Automotive," and "Cummins" all deal with managing process technology and learning within the context of global multiplant networks.

References

Abernathy, William J. (1978). *The Productivity Dilemma*. Baltimore: The Johns Hopkins University Press.

Abernathy, W. J., and J. M. Utterback (1978). "Patterns of Industrial Innovation." *Technology Review*, Vol. 80, No. 7 (January–July): 40–47.

Alchian, A. (1959). "Costs and Output," *The Allocation of Economic Resources: Essays in Honor of B. F. Haley*, M. Abramowitz (ed.). Stanford, CA: Stanford University Press: 23–40.

Hayes, R. H., and Clark, K. B. (1986). "Exploring the Sources of Productivity Differences at the Factory Level," in K. B. Clark, R. H. Hayes, and C. Lorenz, (eds.), *The Uneasy Alliance: Managing the Productivity-Technology Dilemma*. Boston: Harvard Business School Press.

Hirsch, W. (1952). "Manufacturing Progress Function." *Review of Economics and Statistics*, Vol. 34 (May): 143–155.

Jaikumar, R. (1986). "Post Industrial Manufacturing," *Harvard Business Review* (November–December): 69–76, Reprint No. 86606.

Lieberman, M. (1984). "The Learning Curve and Pricing in the Chemical Processing Industries." *Rand Journal of Economics*, Vol. 15, No. 2 (Summer): 213–228.

Rapping, L. (1965). "Learning and the World War II Production Functions." *Review of Economics and Statistics*, Vol. 48 (February): 98–112.

Utterback, James M. (1994). *Mastering the Dynamics of Innovations*. Boston: Harvard Business School Press.

Wright, T. P. (1936). "Factors Affecting the Cost of Airplanes." *Journal of Aeronautical Science*, 3 (February): 122–128.

CHAPTER 5

Applichem (A) (Abridged)

The Gary [Indiana] plant had had obvious problems for years. It was an ineffective operation. It had a fiefdom type of management. The people had grown complacent and inefficient. They had lost their technical curiosity. And the state-of-the-art technology was in Frankfurt. In the late '70s, when I was business manager, I tried to get them to invite Ari (the Frankfurt manufacturing and technology expert) to Gary. After months of talking, they finally invited him to get me off their backs.

In the fall of 1981, we [top management] had a meeting reviewing our 10 year plan. I said that I was going to shift production of Release-ease and another product from Gary to Frankfurt as fast as possible. I almost got punched in the mouth for that. We had been working on the Gary plant for years. But we hadn't accomplished anything!

J. S. (JOE) SPADARO, Vice President and Director of the Plastics Business, was discussing the conditions in Release-ease manufacturing that had led him to request a study of comparing productivity at Applichem's four Release-ease plants. He had requested the study in June 1982, and it had been finished in September 1982.

Spadaro had joined Applichem in 1956 when he was 27. His bachelor's degree was in mechanical engineering, and he had held several jobs prior to joining Applichem, including managing a machine shop, but not

This case was abridged by Professors Jan Hammond and Gary Pisano from the Applichem (A) case, written by Professor Marie-Therese Flaherty. This case was written as the basis for class discussion rather than to illustrate either effective or ineffective handling of an administrative situation.

including anything related to the chemical industry. His first assignment had been in Italy where he spent 10 years; then he had spent 5 years in the U.K. before returning to work at corporate headquarters in Chicago.

Company Background

Applichem was a manufacturer of specialty chemicals founded in Chicago just before World War II. Most of its products were devised by Applichem's applications engineers as solutions to specific customer problems. Applichem's Research Department subsequently refined the product and process— in successful cases—to arrive at a product with broader application.

Applichem had a strong functional orientation, even though some matrixing had been introduced to the organization during the mid-1970s. There is evidence of matrixing in the June 1982 organization chart presented in *Exhibit 5.1*. Business Managers for two businesses reported to a Group Vice President and four Area Vice Presidents reported to the Chief Operating Officer. Each Business Manager led four business teams, one for each of the four Areas. Each Area business team was headed by one full-time manager. On each team were a financial manager, a marketing manager, an R&D manager (who usually focused on new product introductions) and an operations manager. The functional managers also held line jobs in their respective Area organizations. The operations and marketing managers, like employees in the manufacturing plants and sales and marketing organizations, reported up through the Area organizations. Finance and R&D reported up through the functional organizations. For example, John Benfield, Operations Manager for the Plastics North America Business Team in 1982, reported through two boxes on the organization chart in *Exhibit 5.1:* directly to Joe Spadaro and through several people to the Vice President of the North American area.

Business Background

Release-ease was a specialty chemical that Applichem had developed in 1952 in response to a customer's request. The customer had asked Applichem to formulate a plastic molding compound that would release easily from metal molds after compression molding. Release-ease was sold as a dry powder.

Making molded plastic parts is much like making molded jello. Both jello and the plastic molding compound are hot liquids when poured into the mold; both harden as they cool. Both tend to leave residue on the mold after they are unmolded. However, washing a jello mold is easy, and the mold is rarely needed again immediately. But molds for plastic parts are

Exhibit 5.1 Organization Chart, June 1982

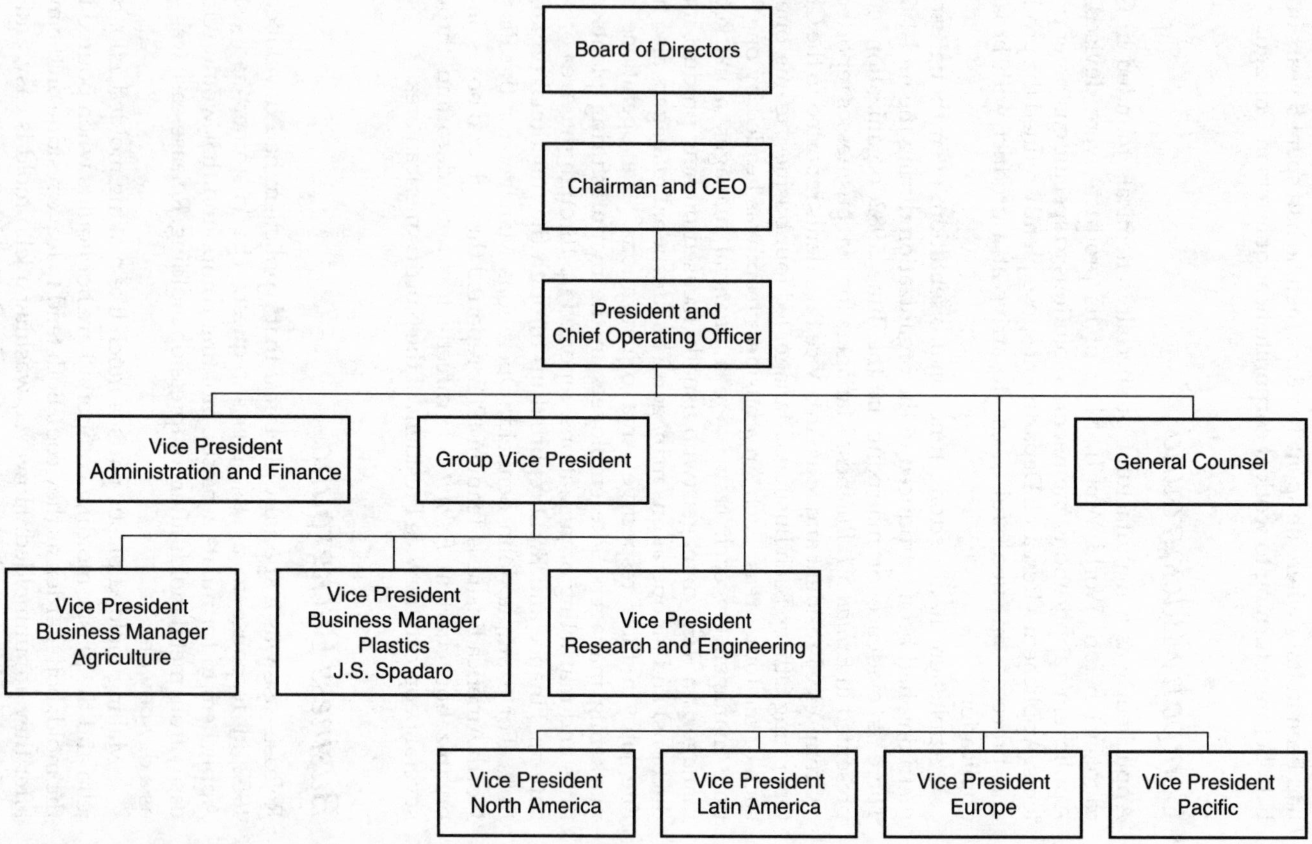

- Board of Directors
- Chairman and CEO
- President and Chief Operating Officer
  - General Counsel
  - Vice President Administration and Finance
  - Group Vice President
    - Vice President Business Manager Agriculture
    - Vice President Business Manager Plastics J.S. Spadaro
  - Vice President Research and Engineering
    - Vice President North America
    - Vice President Latin America
    - Vice President Europe
    - Vice President Pacific

precision stainless steel; they can be difficult to clean; and they are used repeatedly, with unmolding and cleaning often the bottleneck in the molding process.

When a customer requested help in cleaning molds quickly, Applichem applications engineers came up with "Release-ease." It was a chemical to be added in low concentration to the plastic molding compound during its manufacture so that the molded parts would be easier to separate from the mold and would leave the mold cleaner. Release-ease was widely used in molding plastic parts.

Applichem had held the patent for Release-ease, and the product family had been a steady sales and profit generator for the company through 1982. Applichem had done little focused research on the Release-ease product or process after about 1953. What product and process changes had been made were instigated and implemented by manufacturing people in the plants. And most of those changes had been made by Aristotle (Ari) Pappas, Manager of Release-ease manufacturing at the Frankfurt plant.

The specifications of Release-ease varied slightly among regions. Over the years, as customers encountered problems in their molding processes, Applichem's applications engineers had worked with them to identify changes to Release-ease or to the customer's manufacturing process that could relieve the symptoms. The process was one of trial-and-error. Customers were also continually finding ways to reduce the concentration of Release-ease while achieving the same results. In 1982 Applichem's market research group expected little increase in worldwide demand for Release-ease during the next five years.

Market requirements for Release-ease varied by region. In Europe suspendability of the particles in liquid came to be an important property, and most promotional literature stressed this property. Competition was more fierce in Europe than in the U.S., and quality and product specifications were more closely monitored there. Several managers were convinced that Release-ease made in the Frankfurt plant met specifications better than that made in other plants. There were two other important differences in customer use in Europe and the rest of the world. First, European customers made sure to consume Release-ease within one year of purchase, whereas some final customers in the U.S. would use it as long as three years after manufacture; customer use in other regions varied between the two extremes. Second, European customers purchased Release-ease in 50-kilo bags, but customers in the U.S. and Japan used packages in many sizes from 1/2-kilo on up.

Release-ease sold at an average price of $1.01 a pound. Applichem's Release-ease sales by region, production by each of the four plants, as well as exports and imports by region (all in millions of pounds) were as follows:

	Sales	Plants	Actual 1982 Production	Exports by Region	Imports by Region
North America	29	Gary	14.0	0	15.0
Western Europe (incl. Middle East and Africa)	20	Frankfurt	38.0	18.0	0
Latin America	12.3	Mexico	17.2	4.9	0
Pacific and Rest of World	11.9	Sunchem	4.0	0	7.9
Total	73.2		73.2	22.9	22.9

Applichem's strongest competitor was a large U.S.-based chemical company whose only plant for making a close substitute for Release-ease was located in Luxembourg. Its sales in Europe were strong and it made some export sales to the U.S. and Latin America. But Applichem had by far the largest market share and the mystique associated with having patented the earliest available form of the product. A third U.S.-based company provided some competition in the U.S. but J. (John) Benfield, Operations Manager for Applichem's Plastic North American Business Team, said that he thought that the latter company was not seriously committed to the business for the long run. He noted that the company had a plant with some excess capacity that it was using in 1982 to produce its version of Release-ease.

In Japan Applichem was the only company whose product had been approved by the Japanese regulators. Joe Spadaro expected that eventually there would be some other products sold in Japan, even if only exports from Europe.

Technology

Release-ease was manufactured using a 4-step process: reaction (particle formation), cleaning, drying, and packaging. In the reaction step the raw materials (several of which were hazardous, flammable, and therefore not transportable internationally) were combined in a precise sequence under pressure and heat to form the Release-ease. The Release-ease was then precipitated out to form a slurry. The timing of introducing materials into the pressurized vessel ("kettle")—as well as the temperature and pressure which prevailed, the feedrates, heat removal, and agitation—affected the size and composition of the forming Release-ease particles. The quality of the Release-ease, the amount of raw materials, and the characteristics of the process were unaffected by the source of energy used in the plant. So steam, natural gas, oil and electricity were combined differently at different plants to minimize local energy costs.

The second step was to clean and isolate the Release-ease particles from the slurry. This was done by moving the slurry on a conveyor belt made of mesh so that the liquid fell through the belt to the trough below, leaving wet Release-ease particles on the belt. In the third step, Release-ease particles were dried; in the fourth step the Release-ease powder was packaged in bags on an automated filling and packaging line.

Laboratory samples were taken for analysis at the end of each of the reaction, cleaning and drying steps. It usually took four hours for operators to get laboratory results. Since waiting between the cleaning and drying steps impaired product properties, Release-ease particles moved continuously between cleaning and drying. The laboratory test information was used to classify the material after it was processed. Material that was off-spec was reworked in some plants; in other plants some of it was reclassified as QC-3 (QC-1 was the category used for product which conformed to specs) and sold at a lower price.

Throughout the process there were possibilities for yield loss. For example, in the reaction step some raw materials were added in powder form; these could be lost as dust on the floor and in the air. In the cleaning step, particles might be filtered out with the liquid and impurities. Recapturing waste materials was an important source of yield increases; the manufacturing people typically improved recapture gradually over years of work. Waste levels could also be an important health and safety measure.

The average yield of Release-ease from raw material A was a key indicator of the overall performance of the Release-ease manufacturing processes at different plants. The yield was defined by dividing the actual number of pounds of active ingredient in the final product by the number of pounds of active ingredient which would be in the Release-ease if all the key raw material A were converted to active ingredient. Yields were usually expressed in percentages. Benfield explained,

> Plants designed for larger volumes of output generally have higher yields. Raw material A might not wind up in the final product for one or both of two reasons: (1) There might be physical losses (waste) during the process. For example, the percentage of residual raw material A per pound of Release-ease produced in a drum container (used in low volume processes) would be greater than that left in a railroad tank car (used in high volume processes). (2) The available raw material A might not be converted during the process. Larger scale processes have less waste than smaller scale processes. But the proportion of available raw material A converted to Release-ease is determined by how well the process is run, regardless of scale. A well-run, low-volume (around 5 million pounds a year) process would have an average yield on A of 91 or 92 percent; a well-run, medium

volume plant would have an average yield on A of 94 to 95 percent; a well-run, high volume plant would have an average yield on A of 98 to 99 percent.

Usually, the manufacturing process was run 24 hours a day, 7 days a week, because shutting down the process required expensive cleaning of the reaction kettles and the dryers where Release-ease particles stuck. Similarly, changing the size of bag in the packaging line could require as long as a day.

One of the main quality measures for the final product performance was the percent of active ingredient in the powder, since high active ingredient correlated well with good application properties, especially for U.S. markets.

The Plastics North America Business Team estimated that in 1982 it would cost about $20-$25 million to build another plant like that in Gary, Indiana. And they expected that such a plant would have a useful technical life of about 20 years if properly maintained.

The Manufacturing Plants

The *Gary* plant was managed by the North American Area. The plant was located in Gary, Indiana, (just outside Chicago) in a neighborhood where immigrants from Eastern Europe had settled during the early twentieth century. The plant was founded in 1905 and purchased in 1951 by Applichem as the company's first large manufacturing facility. Many people who worked in the Gary plant in 1982 had followed 6 to 10 other members of their families who had worked there over the generations. They were loyal to the plant and to the plant manager, who had grown up in the neighborhood and called himself the "Gary kid."

Release-ease was the first product Applichem manufactured in Gary, and the process had changed incrementally as the market for Release-ease had changed. Most equipment for the process used in 1982 had been installed between 1959 and 1964. It was designed to run a wide range of product formulation and package types. In 1982 Gary ran 8 formulations of Release-ease and about 80 package sizes, whereas the Frankfurt plant, for example, ran only 2 formulations of Release-ease and one 50-kilo package.

The Gary plant manufactured 19 product families in addition to Release-ease. It had a total of 1,000 non-union employees, down from about 2,000 during the mid-1960s. It had a Release-ease design capacity of 26 million pounds a year, and around 60 people manufactured 14 million pounds of Release-ease in 1982.

The *Frankfurt* plant was managed by German nationals who reported through the European Area, and supplied customers located in Europe, the Middle East, and Africa as well as other Applichem plants. It made 12 product families in addition to Release-ease. The plant had 600 employees in 1982, and it made about 38 million pounds of Release-ease a year. Its design capacity was 47 million pounds a year. It had two processes for manufacturing Release-ease: one installed between 1971 and 1974 and one installed in about 1961, with later major modifications to increase capacity. The processes featured computer control of the first process step and extensive solids recovery and waste treatment. Frankfurt bulk-shipped Release-ease to other company plants which then packaged it and shipped it to customers.

Release-ease manufacturing in Frankfurt was managed by Ari Pappas. He was a Greek national who had headed Release-ease manufacturing at Frankfurt since the mid-1960s. He knew Joe Spadaro and several other members of Applichem's top management team from the 1960s, when they had worked in Europe. Pappas had a technical bent; and he had worked with customers, the Applichem Technical Center in Europe, and his own employees to improve the yields and reliability of the Release-ease he made.

The *Mexican* plant was part of a wholly owned subsidiary of Applichem. It was managed by Mexican nationals, who reported to the vice president of the Latin American Area. It supplied the Mexican market and in the early 1980s began to supply some markets in the Far East. The plant processed about 17.2 million pounds of Release-ease during 1982, and had a design capacity of 27 million pounds a year. All its Release-ease was packaged in 50-kilo bags. The process had been installed in 1968 with extra drying capacity introduced in 1978. It was similar in design to the Gary plant, and manufactured 6 product families in addition to Release-ease.

Although educational levels of the Mexican operators were generally lower than those of operators in the other plants, John Benfield explained that the Mexican operators had some technical depth and were able to maintain process improvements suggested by Ari.

Sunchem was Applichem's 50% Japanese joint venture which owned and operated a manufacturing plant in Japan for Release-ease and one other product for the plastics industry. It was managed by Japanese nationals and reported to Applichem's Pacific Area. It was founded in 1957 and had supplied the Release-ease requirements of Japanese customers after that. Its manufacturing process had been redesigned in 1969, when some automation and waste recovery systems had been introduced. Its volume was constrained by its dryer capacity in 1982. The Japanese plant processed many 1/2-kilo and 1-kilo packages. The plant had a rated capacity of 5 million pounds a year, and it produced 4 million pounds in 1982. Within Applichem the Japanese plant was generally thought to be technically excellent. Employees there did more development work than in other plants: they had a product test laboratory, a plastics engineering lab and a workers' dormitory for single men. Japanese managers said that they required more environmental protection measures than the other plants. Their plant was, for example, the only Applichem plant with scrubbers for processing gaseous wastes.

There was no union at this plant although there generally were industry—as opposed to company—unions in the Japanese chemical industry. In 1979 the plant manager had written to U.S. management to explain why an unusually large number of employees was needed in Japan relative to similar Applichem plants elsewhere. He wrote:

> Work rules and regulations seem to be more severe than those in other countries. For example, the Japanese Fire Prevention Law prescribes that all work requiring the handling of flammable raw materials be performed by those having a license for doing such work. There are a wide variety of operations requiring similar licenses, including those in which we handle high pressure gas as in refrigerators, toxic substances, and organic solvents, as well as drying operations being performed where oxygen is not sufficient. A number of plant operators will have to attend training courses to acquire such licenses.
>
> Also, we know that one operator has been taking care of running several kettles at the Gary plant. One operator would not be enough to handle all kettles here because our workers do more work with the kettles.
>
> Finally, in accordance with a strong recommendation by the Shift Work Committee of the Japan Industrial Hygiene Institute, manufacturers are required to allow a temporary sleeping time of two hours a day to all who are engaged in midnight work.

The Cross-Plant Productivity Study

John Benfield had managed the study comparing productivity at the different plants. He reflected on the study:

> The report got things on an even keel. It set the agenda. Until then our managers at one plant rarely encountered managers from sister plants. And they never gave much attention to improving their process on the basis of what other plants had done.
>
> Although the standard costs and volumes of Release-ease were easily available for each plant, the technical information needed for the study was not available. Allocating indirect labor over products was a major problem. The Japanese and Gary employees, for example, complained throughout that they simply had low volumes which caused their overhead allocations to be too high. Yield information was available, but only the technical people in the plants had it. The study was able to identify precise

labor productivity differences among plants and to set an agenda for improvement.

It was important to have financial and technical people in all the plants work together developing the numbers. We argued back and forth during the process, trying to ensure that everyone in the plants agreed with the numbers. For example, to satisfy some concerns at Gary, where a lot of time is spent packaging Release-ease in small packages, packaging was studied separately for all plants. And the Japanese over-estimated their material usage in their standards because they did not want to be caught short. So we took their usage numbers from their actual experience year-to-date.

Over the four months that we worked on the report before it was published in September 1982, a lot of time went into it. The individual plants are not interested in repeating the comparison project. In fact, some said that they hoped it was never done again. It was a pain.

Exhibit 5.2 presents the breakdown and comparison of manufacturing costs for Release-ease at Applichem's four plants in 1982 as it appeared in the study. Exhibits 5.3 through 5.5 present some of the data that Benfield's group used in defining and computing the cost figures presented in Exhibit 5.2. The costs in Exhibit 5.2 are manufacturing, as opposed to delivered, costs. Annual volume of Release-ease was a plant's forecasted volume of Release-ease for 1982. Indirect costs were allocated over all the products in each plant; the standard cost of Release-ease included the allocated indirect costs. The operating costs were derived by dividing a plant's annual budget for the corresponding element of expense for all Release-ease production by the annual volume. Raw material prices and exchange rates were those used in the plants' 1982 business plans. Benfield said,

Although exchange rate changes have a significant impact on comparative raw materials costs stated in dollars, the impact is lessened due to the fact that more than half of the raw materials are available in competitive international markets. We estimate that over the long haul only 30 to 40 per cent of the raw material cost is directly influenced by exchange rate changes. A variety of energy sources are used by the plants depending on local price and availability. The high local electricity costs at Sunchem reflect Japan's generally high energy costs.

Two employees from the Gary plant commented on the study. T. E. (Tom) Schultz was a project manager in development engineering at the Gary plant when John Benfield was assembling the productivity study. He had joined Applichem in 1978 just after completing his Bachelor's degree

Exhibit 5.2   Comparison of Worldwide Release-ease Manufacturing Cost
(U.S. dollars per hundred pounds of Release-ease)

	Plants			
Expense	**Mexico**	**Frankfurt**	**Gary**	**Sunchem**
Raw Materials				
A	27.00	24.02	27.96	29.62
B	14.57	11.69	13.52	20.41
C	16.39	9.03	6.92	24.68
D	5.89	3.75	6.48	5.50
Other	11.20	4.51	5.95	11.65
SUBTOTAL	75.05	53.00	60.83	91.86
Raw Material Overhead	—	—	2.65	—
Operating Costs				
Direct Labor, Salary & Fringes	2.38	5.78	8.46	12.82
Depreciation	.95	1.05	1.60	3.23
Utilities	1.20	1.11	1.94	3.67
Maintenance	1.60	1.34	3.71	3.77
Quality Control	.64	.57	1.54	2.77
Waste Treatment	1.37	.64	1.02	10.61
Plant Administration	1.11	2.91	1.22	4.07
Development	—	.38	.97	2.48
Supplies	2.25	—	.77	.56
Building Expense	—	1.12	.64	.36
Other	2.20	1.01	.29	6.22
SUBTOTAL	13.70	15.91	22.16	50.56
SUBTOTAL: COST BEFORE PACKAGING	88.75	68.91	85.64	142.42
PACKAGE, LOAD, & SHIP	2.38	3.35	13.78	4.56
TOTAL COST	91.13	72.26	99.42	146.98

Notes:
1. Operating costs include indirect labor and associated material costs other than raw materials.
2. Raw material overhead in the Gary plant includes incoming inspection, handling, and inventory carrying costs related to raw materials. For other plants those costs were included in Operating Costs.

in Chemical Engineering. In the period before Applichem's U.S. Controller took over, Schultz and Gary's Production Manager for Release-ease began work to improve productivity in the Release-ease area. By the time John Benfield requested information for the Productivity Study, they had it nearly ready. The entire process of getting the data ready for the study took about two person-years. But Schultz had been enthusiastic about the study because he had believed that corporate managers were seeking to identify the best process ideas from all the plants and to implement them wherever they were relevant throughout the Applichem manufacturing network. Tom Schultz said:

There were several difficulties in comparing cost, usage, and yield statistics across plants—even data assembled as carefully as Benfield did. For example, the Gary plant was designed to manufacture prototype samples for customers; most products in the Release-ease family had first been manufactured in Gary. Also, being an old product, Release-ease has folklore in Gary. There was also a body of opinion to the effect that older product [greater than two years] suffered some degradation in applications performance. As it was not unusual for product in the U.S. to be in the distribution channel for two years, Gary placed great emphasis on achieving a high level of active ingredient in the product at time of

Exhibit 5.3   Selected Productivity Comparisons for Release-ease Production

	Plants			
	Mexico	**Frankfurt**	**Gary**	**Sunchem**
Labor (Number of People)				
Direct	20	46	24	14
Indirect	25	40	34	17
Utility Usage (per million pounds product)				
Steam (metric ton)	2.09	3.18	2.74	NA
Natural Gas (cubic meter)	—	—	78.40	—
Oil (liter)	98.00	74.20	—	214.20
Electricity (kilowatt hours)	298.20	245.00	344.40	463.40
Utility Costs, ($ per unit purchased)				
Steam (metric ton)	$25.00	$20.56	$23.43	NA
Natural Gas (cubic meter)	—	—	$0.18	—
Oil (liter)	$0.32	$0.35	—	$0.31
Electricity (1000 kilowatt hours)	$40.00	$45.00	$56.00	$79.00
TOTAL UTILITY COSTS ($ PER MILLION POUNDS)	$12,012	$11,116	$19,365	$36,675
Raw Materials				
Pounds of Raw Material per hundred lbs of product produced				
A	20.4	18.9	20.75	19.14
B	51.21	47.82	53.8	48.23
C	55.97	50.28	53.6	49.49
D	26.40	24.21	28.77	25.07
%Active Ingredient in product	85.6%	84.4%	84.6%	85.4%
Average Yield on Raw Material A	94.7%	98.9%	90.4%	98.8%
Volume (million lbs)				
1982 Production Volume	17.2	38.0	14.0	4.0
Annual Design Capacity	27	47.0	26	5.0

manufacture. We were also very leery about implementing some of the changes that the Frankfurt plant had made because we were afraid that our product shelf life might be adversely affected. As Frankfurt's product stayed in the distribution channel for at most one year, its emphasis on producing a high active ingredient product was less than ours and it was more adventuresome in adopting process changes.

You know, when I joined the Gary plant it seemed that we had the lowest costs of any plant. But then the exchange rates changed a lot. And the productivity study came along just when we looked bad . . . I wonder when the exchange rates will swing back and make Gary look good again.

W. C. (Wanda) Tannenbaum was a financial analyst at the Gary plant during the productivity study. She had joined Applichem in 1981, after completing an undergraduate degree in Business from the University of Illinois. She noted that the study was very technically oriented, that she was involved only to "look it over." She explained:

At Applichem we use fully allocated standard costs for operations management. For sourcing we used out-of-pocket costs. The data needed for the study were available, but not in accessible form. For example, we had many monthly reports, but no data was

Exhibit 5.4   Average Transportation Costs from Plants (¢/pound) to Regional Markets

| Plants | Regional Markets | | | |
	North America	Western Europe	Latin America	Pacific & Rest of World
Mexico	11.0	11.1	7.5	14.1
Frankfurt	10.5	2.0	12.9	13.3
Gary	5.0	10.1	11.5	12.6
Sunchem	14.0	14.3	13.3	2.0

Notes:

1. On average, it cost 12.9¢ to transport a pound of Release-ease from Frankfurt to Latin America and 11.1¢ to transport a pound of Release-ease from Mexico to Europe. The price of transport depended on distance, type of transport, and the volume transported. Where there were differences in transport costs between two locations, they were due to differences in the volumes Applichem had historically shipped in each direction between the locations and differences in import duties.

2. These costs include duty into various countries. In 1982 the duty into each country was the following percent of the value of Release-ease imported for the following sample countries:

Mexico	Canada	Venezuela	Germany	U.S.	Japan
60%	0%	50%	9.5%	4.5%	6%

Exhibit 5.5 History of Exchange, Inflation, and Wage Rates

	Mexico	Germany	U.S.	Japan
Average Annual Exchange Rates: (currency/$1US)	(Pesos)	(Deutsche Mark)	(Dollar)	(Yen)
1982	96.5	2.38	1.0	235.0
1981	26.2	2.25	1.0	219.9
1980	23.2	1.96	1.0	203.0
1979	22.8	1.73	1.0	239.7
1978	22.7	1.83	1.0	194.6
1977	22.7	2.10	1.0	240.0
Average Annual Price Indices (1980 = 100)[a]				
1982	194.2[c]	114.1[d]	113.7[d]	103.2[c]
1981	124.4	107.8	110.6	101.4
1980	100.0	100.0	100.0	100.0
1979	80.3	93.0	86.1	84.9
1978	67.9	88.7	76.3	79.1
1977	58.6	87.7	71.0	81.2
Average Gross Money Wages (Before Income Taxes, Social Security Contributions, and Benefits) (local currency per hour)[b]				
1982	99.42	14.64	8.50	1424.86
1981	63.46	13.92	7.99	1372.77
1980	48.11	13.18	7.27	1292.66
1979	39.91	12.36	6.69	1203.80
1978	34.17	11.73	6.17	1134.00
1977	29.70	11.14	5.68	1061.00

[a] *Source: International Financial Statistics*, International Monetary Fund.
[b] *Source:* Business International Corporation, *Worldwide Economic Indicators*, One Dag Hammarskjold Plaza, New York, NY.
[c] Wholesale prices
[d] Industrial prices

cumulative. And standard costs were redefined only once or twice a year, so it was just about impossible to get actual costs for Release-ease by month.

The allocation of indirect costs was a big problem for the study—especially for a plant like Gary. It was not designed to be a real streamlined operation. It was designed to be a batch operation for research and specialty products. Its equipment is unique, and Release-ease manufacturing is spread out all over the place. You just can't compare it with plants that make commodities.

CHAPTER 6

The Cummins Engine Company

Starting Up "B" Crankshaft Manufacturing at the San Luis Potosi Plant

Introduction

*I*n mid-1992, after several months of rather routine activities and decisions, Joe Panella's job suddenly started getting more difficult. He and his "B-crankshaft Start-Up Team" were responsible for coordinating the installation of a manufacturing line to make crankshafts for Cummins Engine Company's "B-series" engines at its facility in San Luis Potosi, Mexico. In addition to designing the new crankshaft machining line, procuring and installing the appropriate equipment, recruiting and training workers and engineers, and designing new logistics flows and procedures, the team found itself increasingly caught in the crossfire of competing interests and priorities within the far-flung and complex Cummins organization. Mused Panella,

> The thing that makes the kind of issues we're encountering now so difficult is that they don't involve determining who's (or what's) right and who's wrong. Both sides have valid points, and are probably each "right" in their terms. But the different "right" answers lead us in different directions. So we have to choose among different degrees of rightness, and balance the needs of different parties—all of whom are good, experienced, and well-meaning people—against the needs of the company as a whole. But since our team is drawn from a number of different organiza-

Professor Robert H. Hayes prepared this case as the basis for class discussion rather than to illustrate either effective or ineffective handling of an administrative situation.

tional units within Cummins, we often find ourselves disagreeing about what those needs are and which are the most important.

Right now, for example, we're trying to mediate the issue of machine capabilities, which has led to a conflict between the original budget developed by the manufacturing engineers at our U.S. crankshaft manufacturing plant and the stringent performance standards that the San Luis plant has embraced. The company as a whole has been losing money for the past several years, and is therefore taking a very cautious approach to investments in new equipment. On the other hand, not only has the Mexican plant been very profitable, but by enthusiastically adopting and implementing our new Cummins Production System (CPS), which incorporates many of the latest manufacturing philosophies and approaches, it has achieved one of the best productivity and quality records within the company. But some of the used equipment that we are being asked to adapt to B crankshaft machining isn't capable of achieving the precision demanded by the CPS.

There's also the issue of which measurement gauges to use in inspecting crankshaft dimensions, which have to be extremely precise. The obvious approach would be to use the same air-gauging system that is used at our Fostoria plant, where the crankshaft is currently being produced. Doing that would permit similar procedures and facilitate comparisons when we start producing the crankshafts here. On the other hand, that system is quite sophisticated, and requires both a high degree of skill and very tight control over environmental factors. Moreover, the supplier of that equipment doesn't have an office in Mexico. The alternative is to use a contact-gauging system, but some people are concerned that its use might compromise the quality of the crankshaft. What are you supposed to do when the "experts" disagree?

The San Luis Potosi Plant

Mexico had long been Cummins' largest market outside the United States. About a third of the automotive diesel engines operating in the country bore its nameplate, and Cummins' share of the market for electrical generators was about 60%. In 1980 the company entered into a joint venture with Diesel Nacional (DINA), Mexico's state-owned producer of trucks, buses, and diesel engines, to build a new diesel engine assembly and components machining plant. DINA owned 60% of the joint venture and took an active role in its management.

The new plant was built in San Luis Potosi (often referred to within the company by its initials: S.L.P.), a 400-year-old but fast-growing colonial city of about one million people located on the high plain (elevation 6000 feet) roughly halfway between Mexico City, 250 miles to the south, and Monterrey. S.L.P. had the advantage of being on the main north-south road (along the route of the old Pan-Am highway) connecting Mexico City with the United States at Laredo, Texas. The plant began operations in 1984, initially assembling engines at a rate of two per day.

In the protected Mexican market of the mid-1980s, the joint venture had only one domestic competitor and supplied virtually 100% of the engines installed by Mexican assemblers of heavy duty trucks. Although the company made a profit each year—largely because of aggressive pricing—the plant was plagued with quality and other operating problems. Morale was low, turnover was high, and a status quo mentality prevailed; people were afraid to try anything new. Moreover, the plant was regarded as a poor supplier by other Cummins entities.

By late 1986, the administration of President de la Madrid had signalled its interest in selling off government-owned enterprises, and Cummins had decided that achieving its quality and performance standards was unlikely to happen within the joint venture arrangement. Therefore, Cummins began negotiating the purchase of DINA's share, reaching its objective in September 1987. The new wholly owned subsidiary was renamed Cummins, S.A. de C.V. (CUMMSA).

Freed of the severe budget limitations and bureaucratic requirements of the former government joint venture, and now able to pay salaries competitive with other private sector companies, CUMMSA's top management immediately began to implement new approaches for dealing with its quality, productivity, and delivery problems. Many of the activities performed at CUMMSA's headquarters in Mexico City, including engineering, purchasing, supplier development, human resources, and finance were moved to the plant to improve cross-functional communication and put these people close to where the products were made. Working conditions at the plant were improved, salaries were increased, teamwork was encouraged, hierarchical barriers were knocked down, and attempts were made to increase union involvement and cooperation in the new focus on quality and delivery.

Improvements were quickly obtained; within two years, for example, the rejection rate for cylinder heads shipped to the Cummins plants in Indiana dropped from 40% to less than 1%. But the rate of improvement increased markedly after 1990 when, under the leadership of Plant Manager Norman Brown, the plant began implementing the new Cummins Production System, which emphasized cleanliness and orderliness, involvement of people, functional excellence, synchronized production flows, shortened leadtimes, and visual controls. "The three core concepts behind CPS," commented Brown, "are teamwork, setting high standards for quality and customer service and not compromising them under pressure, and pushing for continuous improvement in all activities."

Material flows were reorganized to reduce distance travelled and time required, a Just-In-Time "pull" production control system was implemented, and employee teams were organized to identify and propose solutions to problems. Internal education programs were also expanded; in 1989 CUMMSA's top managment set a goal of 12 training days per employee per year—about five times more than had been carried out in 1987. This target was achieved in 1991.

The plant's steady improvement led Cummins to decide to manufacture additional parts at S.L.P.; for example, in 1989 the production of cylinder heads for the K series engines was moved from Komatsu in Japan without problems or disruption in shipping schedules. As a result, CUMMSA's annual sales had more than tripled between 1987 and 1991, to over $180 million, as heavy duty engine sales grew to nearly 10,000 units a year and exports of engine parts also increased. In 1991, CUMMSA produced and sold 44% more engines than in the previous year, while adding only three people to its payroll (to a total of 604). Its profit after tax was more than 11 times higher than in 1987, even though engine prices (in U.S. dollars) had been reduced an average of 20%. The "teardown quality" index for the engines assembled at the plant rose from under 92% in 1987 to 99.8%, production throughput time was cut in half, to just over three days, and on-time delivery rose from 51.4% in 1989 to almost 93%. Moreover, compressing material flows and reducing inventories (for example, the assembly area for the big NT engine was reduced by almost 50%) freed up several thousand square meters of floor space that were available for the production of additional products.

In mid-1992 the spotless plant employed 363 shop floor workers and 99 engineers, technicians, and administrative people. Most of the workers had at least a high school education or had graduated from a government-sponsored training program for mechanics. In addition to assembling NT and C series engines for domestic consumption (none of these engines were exported), the plant machined and assembled water pumps, machined cylinder heads for the NT and K engines, and manufactured vibration dampers. The plant was surrounded by attractive landscaping, which included a grassy soccer field. In addition to paying the highest wages in the area (equivalent to about $1.50 per hour in 1992), the plant offered a number of fringe benefits whose cost was equivalent to about 70% of the average wage. In addition to the usual retirement and health benefits, for example, most of the workers commuted to work on company buses and paid only 25% of the cost of the 500 hot meals served each day in the plant's modern cafeteria. The normal workweek was 45 hours (five nine-hour days).

Each quarter the plant management shared with its employees the sales, production, and financial information that had just been sent to Cummins headquarters. Employee turnover was about 1.2% per year, and the plant had never had a layoff. Relations with the union (the Confederation of Mexican Workers, or CTM in Spanish) were excellent.

The union was primarily interested in insuring job stability and growth—although it pushed hard in wage negotiations to keep CUMMSA's wages among the very highest in the S.L.P. area. The union seldom initiated disputes about work issues, nor did its leadership show concern about jurisdictional matters or about people being moved from job to job. In fact, it supported activities that increased the skills and responsibilities of its members. Contracts were negotiated every other year, and a wage adjustment was agreed to in the off year.

CUMMSA's financial success had resulted in its San Luis Potosi employees being among the highest compensated factory workers in Mexico during 1992. Under Mexican law, each legal entity had to distribute 10% of its profits before tax among all its employees in proportion to their wages and hours worked. In 1992 this distribution, based on the company's 1991 results, amounted to over twice the annual salary of the average factory worker.

Rakesh Sachdev, CUMMSA's chief financial officer, was optimistic about both the Mexican economy and the future of his own organization.

Mexico's industrial expansion is bound to continue, due more to the fundamental changes that have been made in its manufacturing sector than to its current low labor and engineering costs. The Mexican workforce is steadily becoming more productive. Quality is increasingly being emphasized in the workplace, and workers are being trained to master highly complex engineering and manufacturing tasks. One of the most significant factors that impact us is the cost of purchasing raw and semi-finished materials—which, in our case, are primarily imported from the U.S. While material costs in Mexico historically have been high, they are coming down as more production moves here.

Depending on the part to be manufactured and the volumes involved, Mexico may or may not be the low-cost source today. Mexico will probably continue to be dependent on the United States and other countries for many components, such as steel forgings and castings, for the foreseeable future. This interdependence will create opportunities for both Mexico and the United States. As far as capital costs are concerned, they're high within Mexico, but a company like Cummins is able to source capital from anywhere in the world.

To promote exports, the Mexican government permits companies to import materials and equipment without paying import duties (normally 22%), provided those materials and equipment are used to produce exported products. This is accomplished through the PITEX (Program permitting Temporary Importation for Export) system. The customs officials carefully record each imported item and check it off when it is exported, and you have to specify in advance roughly when this will occur. All this requires meticulous records and lots of paperwork, and errors (even corrections to the original) are not permitted. Training people in the United States to understand why this is so important has taken more time than we expected.

One of the ironies associated with this system is that it can penalize suppliers that have distribution centers in Mexico. You won't be eligible for the PITEX savings, for example, unless you arrange to purchase the parts from a point across the border!

Another benefit that is available to a company like Cummins is the ability to sell Export Credits, called "DIVISAS." Car companies in Mexico have to maintain a certain ratio of exports to imports, roughly 1.7 to 1. If they can't meet that requirement they can buy export credits from other companies—like Cummins—that are not required to meet the same export-to-import ratio as they do. This has resulted in an active market in DIVISAS, which has made it possible for us to reduce our cost of purchased material for exported products by up to 4%. The benefits from the sale of DIVISAS and programs such as PITEX are constantly changing, however, so it is probably not advisable for a company to count on them when making business decisions regarding Mexico.

As far as the future is concerned, we still have some unoccupied space in the plant and our rate of productivity improvement continues to free up workers. So we've entered into discussions with Cummins headquarters to move a rebuild operation for B and C series engines here from the States. That's a highly labor intensive job, where used engines are completely disassembled, each part is thoroughly checked out and remachined or replaced if necessary, and then the engine is reassembled and tested. As it reaches mature volume levels in about five years, this operation would require more than 300 workers. And we've also had some very tentative discussion with a couple of the automobile assembly plants here in Mexico about supplying them with machined parts that they're currently importing from the United States.

Problems threatened on the horizon, however. The opening of the Mexican market had encouraged imports from Caterpillar, Navistar, and the recently-reinvigorated Detroit Diesel. As a result, Cummins engines faced stiff competition in Mexico. The signing of the NAFTA (North American Free Trade Agreement) was expected to lead to additional reductions in tariffs and encourage these and other competitors to both increase their exports to Mexico and consider establishing manufacturing operations there.

Company Background

Cummins Engine, with annual sales of about $3.5 billion, was one of the premier producers of heavy duty diesel engines in the world (see Exhibit 6.1 for financial background). Its engines were offered as either standard or optional equipment by every major North American truck manufacturer, as well as by the major producers of construction, mining, and farming equipment.

Together with other diesel engine producers, Cummins had experienced turbulent times since the late 1970s growing out of two shifts in the competitive environment. First, the growth of the total market for diesel engines had slowed and emphasis had shifted away from Cummins' most popular engines to smaller, lighter weight, and more fuel efficient designs. Second, competition intensified as both existing and new (largely Asian) competitors fought for a share of this market. Cummins reacted with a series of manufacturing improvement efforts, new product development programs, and financial restructurings.

In the early 1980s, for example, it instituted programs to improve delivery times and achieve world quality standards while cutting manufacturing costs by 30% through a combination of plant rationalizations, outsourcing of components, and personnel and floorspace reductions. In 1984, as this program was still being implemented, Japanese producers attempted to increase their share of the U.S. market for medium-sized truck engines by quoting prices 40% below Cummins'. Refusing to allow itself to be undersold, the company dropped its own prices to competitive levels while maintaining heavy investments in R&D; at the same time it redoubled its efforts to improve its manufacturing competitiveness and introduce lower cost, more fuel efficient models. During the battle for share—and survival—that ensued, Cummins (like most of its competitors) experienced a series of operating losses. In 1992 it hoped to show a profit for the first time in five years.

By then the company was able to boast that its product line, consisting of both redesigned models and three new engine families, offered the most advanced diesel engine technology in the world. As a result of their superior operating performance (as measured by reliability, durability, and fuel economy), they not only held share in Cummins' traditional markets but gained share in those where the company had not had a significant presence in the past.

Each mountain climbed, however, revealed new mountains ahead. The toughened emissions requirements that went into effect in 1991 had been met, but the more stringent ones that would be required in 1994 were widely regarded to be "10 times more difficult" to achieve. The company gritted its teeth and committed itself to continuing heavy expenditures on R&D and efforts to improve manufacturing efficiency and quality. Both Cummins' top management and capital market observers were concerned

Exhibit 6.1 Summary of Consolidated Financial Information for 10 Years ($ millions, except per share amounts)

	1991	1990	1989
Results of operations:			
Net sales	$3,405.5	$3,461.8	$3,519.5
Cost of goods sold	2,776.7	2,857.1	2,856.9
Gross profit	628.8	604.7	662.6
Selling, administrative, research and engineering expenses	619.3	631.7	607.4
Interest expense	42.5	43.9	51.8
Other expense (income), net	12.7	8.4	(17.2)
Unusual charges			
Earnings (loss) before income taxes	(45.7)	(142.2)	20.6
Provision (credit) for income taxes	16.9	25.0	22.2
Minority interest	3.0	(2.1)	4.5
Earnings (loss) before extraordinary credit and cumulative effect of accounting changes	(65.6)	(165.1)	(6.1)
Extraordinary credit	—	27.4	—
Cumulative effect of accounting changes	51.5	—	—
Net earnings (loss)	(14.1)	(137.7)	(6.1)
Preferred and preference stock dividends	8.0	13.7	
Earnings (loss) available for common shares	$ (22.1)	$ (151.4)	$ (15.9)
Per common share:			
Earnings (loss) before extraordinary credit and cumulative effect of accounting changes:			
Primary	$ (4.96)	$ (14.47)	$ (1.52)
Fully diluted	(4.96)	(14.47)	(1.52)
Net earnings (loss):			
Primary	(1.49)	(12.25)	(1.52)
Fully diluted	(1.49)	(12.25)	(1.52)
Cash dividends	.70	2.20	2.20
Common shareholders' investment	34.29	37.37	39.77
Average number of common shares (millions):			
Primary	14.8	12.4	10.5
Fully diluted	14.8	12.4	10.5
Operating percentages:			
Gross profit	1.85%	17.5%	18.8%
Return on net sales	(.4)	(4.0)	(.2)
Financial data:			
Working capital	$ 219.2	$ 263.4	$ 224.2
Property, plant and equipment, net	953.0	921.2	890.1
Total assets	2,041.2	2,086.3	2,030.8
Long-term debt and redeemable preferred stock	443.2	411.4	473.7
Shareholders' investment	623.8	669.3	559.2
Supplemental data:			
Property, plant and equipment expenditures	$ 123.9	$ 147.0	$ 137.9
Depreciation and amortization	127.2	143.4	135.0
Number of common shareholders of record	5,900	5,900	5,700
Number of employees	22,900	24,900	25,100

Effective January 1, 1991, the company changed its accounting to include in inventory certain production-related costs previously charged directly to expense. The company also changed its method of depreciation for substantially all engine production equipment to a modified units-of-production depreciation method.

In 1990, the company purchased a portion of its outstanding zero coupon notes resulting in an extraordinary credit of $27.4 million.

Source: 1991 Annual Report

about the impact such expenditures were likely to have on the company's ability to meet its financial goals.

Manufacturing Organization

Cummins assembled diesel engines at six major facilities (one of them a joint venture with another company) in North America. Each facility produced a limited range of engines and was supplied through a central purchasing office at its Columbus, Indiana headquarters. A major in-house producer of mechanical components for these plants was its Atlas subsidiary, which had two plants in the United States and one in Brazil. More and more components were being outsourced from a global network of suppliers. Supplying each assembly plant with all the components and materials it required, therefore, necessitated complex administrative and logistics processes.

Until recently, for example, Atlas had produced the bulk of the crankshafts used in Cummins engines. During the 1980s, however, it had turned to external suppliers from as far away as India. Outsourcing decisions required a careful balance of competing concerns. On the one hand, the main Atlas factory in Fostoria, Ohio, was regarded as having higher costs than other Cummins facilities. On the other, past experience had taught Cummins that unless it established strong partnerships with single source suppliers, it risked being exploited by price increases.

The B Crankshaft Decision

In 1991 Cummins forecast that worldwide demand for its six cylinder B (5.9 liter) and C (8.3 liter) engines would almost double over the following five years. Most of this increased demand would take place in the United States, as both Ford and Chrysler had decided to switch to Cummins engines from their current source. The crankshafts for these engines were produced primarily at Atlas's Fostoria plant. Smaller amounts were purchased, at delivered prices that were generally about the same as Fostoria's, from two other external suppliers—one in Brazil and the other in the United Kingdom. The capacity of all these facilities, however, was not expected to keep pace with the increasing demand.

In particular, the crankshafts for its B engines represented a potential bottleneck. The capacity of all current suppliers was estimated to be only 400 to 460 per day—not much more than current requirements and far less than the 800 crankshafts per day (200,000 per year) that were expected to be needed by 1995. Moreover, it was unclear whether Cummins' external suppliers would be willing to commit the funds required to expand capacity. Three alternatives for breaking this bottleneck were considered: 1) expand capacity at the existing Fostoria plant; 2) build a new facility near the CDC engine manufacturing plant, Cummins' joint venture with J.I.

Case in North Carolina; or 3) begin production at a new Atlas-CUMMSA joint venture to be housed in the area freed up when the S.L.P. plant's NT engine assembly line had been compressed.

Adding capacity at the Fostoria plant would not provide the required return on investment, while the investment required to build a new crankshaft production facility near CDC in North Carolina was considered prohibitive. The last alternative promised the lowest investment and operating costs (see Exhibit 6.2). In addition, it would offer Cummins the potential opportunity to displace local crankshaft manufacturers who were selling crankshafts to Mexico's fast growing vehicle manufacturing sector. Potential customers included Chrysler, Ford, G.M., Nissan, and Volkswagen.

But the Mexican alternative also would take the longest time to implement because of the problems associated with equipping a production line from scratch and training workers to produce a component that was much more complex and precise than any they had ever made before. It was anticipated that the earliest date production could begin there would be the first quarter of 1993, and that it would take at least another year to ramp up to 250 per day. Therefore, in order to make up the production shortfall that would be experienced during the transition, an investment of almost $1.0 million would be required at the Fostoria plant in order to increase its capacity temporarily from 275 to 325 per day.

After considering many factors, Cummins decided to add a new crankshaft production line in Mexico that would be able to produce 375 B crankshafts per day by 1995. It would be located in a 40,000 square foot area of the S.L.P. plant and, at capacity, would employ about 110 factory workers on three shifts, supported by 31 salaried workers in Mexico. An additional five people would be required in the United States to coordinate the materials flows required. Setting up the facility would require the installation of 45 pieces of equipment, of which two would be transferred

Exhibit 6.2   Crankshaft Manufacturing Cost Comparisons

| | Manufacturing Cost per Unit at: | | |
	S.L.P.		Fostoria
	@ 150/da	@ 300/da	
Materials	$141.2	$141.2	$139.3
Direct Labor	9.9	8.8	102.8
Overhead	39.9	22.3	38.9
Freight	22.5	22.5	0
Depreciation	19.9	15.1	5.5
Total	**$233.4**	**$209.9**	**$286.5**

Source: Company records (disguised).

from Fostoria to S.L.P. and the remainder would be a mix of purchased new and used machines. Fourteen million dollars were budgeted for these purchases, and another $2.5 million was provided for the costs associated with coordinating the installation and managing the start-up. The manufacturing cost of a crankshaft produced at S.L.P. depended somewhat on the rate of production, but was anticipated to be about $210 when the line was at full capacity—almost $80 less than Fostoria's manufacturing cost.

In addition to these cost savings, adding the B Crankshaft line produced tax savings, according to Rakesh Sachdev.

> The line's investment and start-up costs, which are substantial during the first two years of the start-up, will be offset somewhat by lowering our Mexican income tax and profit sharing obligations—totalling 45% of the start-up expenses. If we'd made the same investment in the United States, on the other hand, we would not have benefitted from that tax shield because Cummins' U.S. operations have not been in a tax-paying situation for the past several years.

Crankshaft Manufacturing

The crankshaft (see Exhibit 6.3 for a schematic) of a modern diesel truck engine was one of its most intricately shaped and technically demanding components, requiring both careful handling and extremely high precision throughout a series of tightly specified and linked steps. Constant monitoring of dimensions was required during all these steps. A deviation anywhere along the line could have repercussions that reverberated throughout the remainder of the process.

The process began with a forged steel blank costing about $100, which was imported from a U.S. supplier (the same company that currently supplied the Fostoria plant). Although Mexican suppliers existed for the cast steel blanks that were used as the basis for manufacturing automobile engine crankshafts, there was no domestic source for forged blanks (castings did not have the strength or durability needed for long-running and heavily loaded truck engines). After cleaning, the crankshaft's main bearings (the load-bearing round surfaces that rotated around its central axis) and pins (the surfaces that transferred the reciprocating power of the pistons to the rotating crankshaft) were rough machined, first on a center drive lathe and then a rough milling machine to +/-10 thousandths of an inch. Then they were individually hardened using electrical induction heating. The heat and stresses created during this operation were then relieved through heat treating, in which the whole crankshaft passed through a furnace.

These induction hardening and heat-treating processes served to

Exhibit 6.3 Atlas 6B Crankshaft Project

ATLAS 6B CRANKSHAFT PROJECT
CLASSIFICATION OF CHARACTERISTICS
CUMMSA ENGINEERING

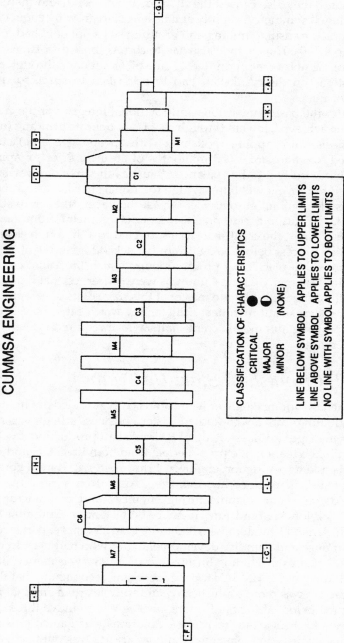

CLASSIFICATION OF CHARACTERISTICS
CRITICAL ● APPLIES TO UPPER LIMITS
MAJOR ◐ APPLIES TO LOWER LIMITS
MINOR (NONE)

LINE BELOW SYMBOL APPLIES TO UPPER LIMITS
LINE ABOVE SYMBOL APPLIES TO LOWER LIMITS
NO LINE WITH SYMBOL APPLIES TO BOTH LIMITS

DWD A. CONTRERAS   ISSUED & REV. M.A. MEJIA   APPD J. JESUS GALLAGA   03 REVISION (26/OCT/92) toughen the crankshaft's surface and relieve its internal stresses; on the other hand, they also caused the shaft to "bow" (bend, and therefore lose its rotational symmetry) slightly and its length to grow by about 0.06 inch. Therefore, the ensuing milling and grinding steps not only had to achieve tolerances of 0.001 inch, they also had to correct those distortions. In addition, precise holes that permitted engine oil to circulate through a variety of locations on the crankshaft had to be drilled to specified depths at complex angles.

After the basic dimensions and rotational integrity of the crankshaft had been achieved, it went through a series of delicate grinding (on grinding wheels) and lapping (polishing with an abrasive tape) steps that achieved tolerances of +/- 3 millionths of an inch. Prior to lapping, the crankshaft also had to be "balanced," just as the tires of a car had to be balanced to prevent wobbling at high rotational speeds. Instead of adding weights, as on an automobile wheel, however, the crankshaft was balanced by drilling out precise amounts of metal from non-critical surfaces. Finally, the crankshaft was subjected to a thorough cleaning and inspection process before being carefully packed for shipment.

The whole machining process required such precision, control, and discipline that many within Cummins were concerned that it might be too difficult for the S.L.P. plant to master at this stage of its development. Only one other crankshaft manufacturing facility was located in Mexico, but it was producing automobile crankshafts, which required far less demanding tolerances.

The B Crankshaft Start-Up Team

Joe Panella, a young engineer who had recently rounded out his education by graduating from a well-known Eastern business school, was made the project manager for the start-up of B Crankshaft production. In early 1991 he acquired a team made up of people from both the S.L.P. and the Atlas Fostoria plants. A senior engineer from Fostoria, Karen Forster, was appointed U.S. engineering manager. Also from Fostoria came Ken Reynolds, as senior manufacturing engineer, and manufacturing engineers Dick Johnson and Jim Heyman. Bert Hand, a Cummins engineer from the United Kingdom who had more than 25 years experience in quality assurance and supplier development, and who had been in charge of the S.L.P. plant's machining businesses since 1984, was named the on-site project director. CUMMSA's top management, recognizing that the crankshaft project was more sophisticated and complex than any that had been attempted before at the S.L.P. plant, also agreed to move three of its best engineers to the start-up team. Jose Contraras was named on-site manufacturing engineering manager; Manuel Zacarias was put in charge of on-site quality management; and Juan Jose Hernandes was made head of maintenance. Representatives of the corporate purchasing department and the Cummins plants that would become the customers of the new crankshaft line were also associated with the team.

Looking back on their early experience with the transfer, various team members commented:

Karen Forster:

The main problems we've encountered here are the obvious ones: the different language and culture. Even though we all speak and understand a little Spanish now, and many of our Mexican colleagues speak some English, we're never really sure if we and they understand each other—even when we phrase things very simply. We think something has been decided, or somebody is going to do something, and later we find it has fallen through the cracks. Then, the next time, in order to make sure that they understand what we are trying to communicate, we tend to ask lots of questions. But sometimes this leads to a different kind of misunderstanding, because it appears that we don't trust them.

Also, we tend to be rather direct, and like to get right to the point when dealing with some issue. But Mexicans tend to approach issues in a more roundabout way and feel more comfortable about talking business with someone once they've established a personal relationship with that person. It's important not only that you know the person you're dealing with well, but you also should know about their family and the various other activities they're involved in.

But in many respects they are more flexible than our Atlas-Fostoria workforce. It is generally much more difficult, for example, to persuade workers in the States to give management the flexibility to change work assignments and adjust jobs that we have in Mexico. And in Mexico the use of videotaping people at work for training purposes is common practice, while in the States it is not easily done.

Basically, we can get product to or from Fostoria in from five to 10 days: two days from S.L.P. to the U.S. border, two days from the border to Fostoria, and one to five days getting across the border, depending on whether the paperwork is right and the customs gods are smiling. Our regular weekly shipments tend to go through pretty quickly; it's the irregular shipments that experience delays. In general, Mexican customs officials assume you're doing something illegal and it's up to you to prove you're not. You have to be extremely precise, and sometimes the language difference trips you up (all documents have to be in Spanish). For example, one time we imported a bunch of highly polished carbide inserts; the customs officials insisted they were mirrors!

Ken Reynolds:

The skill level and work ethic of our Mexican employees are excellent. They are also a very proud people. You can be very demanding, and can count on them to respond with enthusiasm, as long as you enlist their involvement in getting the job done. They also like to celebrate accomplishments—more so than in the States—with parties. Taking the time to show appreciation, even for little things, really pays off.

On the other hand, their cultural heritage is one in which hierarchical position is quite important; bosses are typically treated with great deference and their orders are seldom questioned. As a result, it was sometimes hard at first to get them to participate in solving a problem or making a decision. And, whereas in the U. S. we tend to choose group leaders who are decisive, "take charge" kind of people, here we have to be careful that they not become too autocratic.

The Center Drive Lathe

According to Joe Panella: "One of the main problems we've encountered so far with transferring this technology to Mexico was created during the formulation of the Project Authorization Document (PAD). Essentially, the manufacturing engineers who prepared the PAD kept cutting and cutting until the investment required was reduced to a level that could be approved in the context of the company's financial situation. To get the investment down they assumed we could make use of—or rehabilitate—a lot of used equipment from existing plants. But much of this equipment was simply too old to provide the precision required by the B crankshaft.

For example, the center drive turning equipment that had been identified for us was over 30 years old. It can't hold the in-process tolerances required. The Atlas-Fostoria people say, "So what. This is the rough machining stage, so you don't need close tolerances. You can machine the parts to the correct tolerances in later stages.

On the other hand, under the CPS system that the S.L.P. plant has adopted, every machine in the place is supposed to be "Cpk capable." The Cp refers to the ratio of the tolerance range required by a part to the range of the precision that the machine is capable of. That ratio reflects the machine's "capability," and naturally we want it to be as large as possible. The k refers to the percentage of the product's tolerance range that the process mean is off center. You would like that always to be zero, of course, but machines do wander off center. Cpk, then, is a combined measure that indicates roughly how far the process can wander off center without causing an unacceptable level of rejects; the higher the Cpk, the better (see Exhibit 6.4). The goal of our CPS is to have all machines operating at a capability level of 1.33 Cpk or better. That means that if the process is carefully monitored there's almost no chance that we will generate a part that doesn't fall within the required tolerances. Every piece of equipment in the plant has a color-coded sticker on it that specifies its Cpk, so it's pretty obvious if a machine doesn't meet the required level of capability.

Of course you can sometimes compensate for an error early in a process by exercising extra care later on, but this adds complexity and possible sources of errors. Insisting that each machine be Cpk capable is therefore a form of discipline—like insisting on

Exhibit 6.4

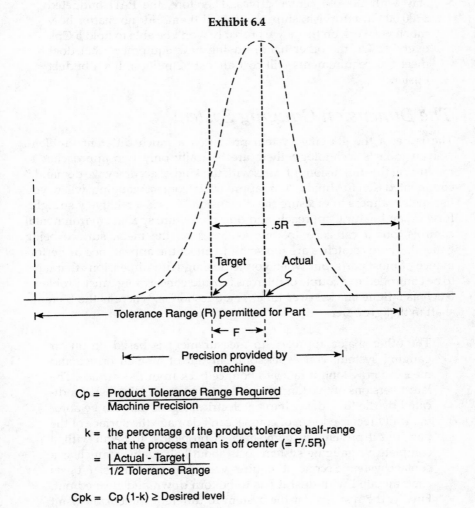

$$Cp = \frac{\text{Product Tolerance Range Required}}{\text{Machine Precision}}$$

k = the percentage of the product tolerance half-range that the process mean is off center (= F/.5R)

$$= \frac{|\text{Actual - Target}|}{1/2 \text{ Tolerance Range}}$$

Cpk = Cp (1-k) ≥ Desired level

zero defects. If you allow deviations, you get caught up in endless negotiations. S.L.P. has trained their workers that this is bad. Now, because of budget constraints, we're asking them to compromise their values.

Fostoria had used old center drive equipment for many years, and their highly trained workforce had learned how to produce acceptable parts by "tweaking" the equipment, so it was felt that using far more sophisticated and expensive equipment could be avoided. It was estimated that the scrap caused by the old center drives would be higher in S.L.P. than in Fostoria because S.L.P.'s operators were less experienced. But since the cost of this additional scrap could not be substantiated, the decision was made to stay with the old center drives. Therefore, the PAD budgeted $300,000 to refurbish, ship, and install them. But no matter how much we work on them, we probably won't be able to hold a Cpk over 1.0. On the other hand, buying new equipment that does meet our requirements will cost almost $2 million. It's a budget buster.

The Dimension Gauging System

The issue of the gauging system presented a much different problem. "Given today's technology, there are basically only two approaches to measuring the dimensions of parts with the kind of accuracy we demand," commented Ken Reynolds. "One approach is 'contact' gauging, where you use metal calipers to measure the dimension. This is a relatively straightforward and natural approach, and doesn't require special environmental controls, but it can lead to tiny scratches on the metal surface being gauged. These scratches are too small to affect the appearance or performance of most parts, but when you're dealing with dimensions that have to be controlled to a couple of microns it could conceivably cause problems (such as fatigue cracks) over time. The question is, where is the B crankshaft in that grey area?

The other major approach to measurement is based on an air gauging system: you expel some air out of a small orifice and measure how long it takes to bounce back from the surface. The latest versions of this kind of system translate the dimension indicated by the time delay into an electrical signal that can be automatically recorded. Air, of course, can't damage the surface of the part, but it presents its own series of problems. To begin with, a complete air-gauging system costs about half again as much as a contact system. Second, it requires very clean conditions; if it gets contaminated with dust it has to be torn down and cleaned out. Finally, the response of the system to different dimensions isn't exactly linear, so it is only accurate within a rather narrow range and has to be calibrated very carefully. Partly as a result of this, you will get slightly different readings from an air-gauging system than you will from a contact system. If we went to air gauging, therefore, we would need a workforce and support staff that were very well trained and experienced in this particular process.

At our Fostoria plant they use an air-gauging system, which they got from the Dearborn Gauge Company (which makes by far the best system) and with which they've been very satisfied. In fact, our Jamestown plant is now in the process of switching over from contact to air gauging. The problem is, not only is there concern that an air-gauging system may be too difficult for our S.L.P. organization to maintain—at least, at this early stage of its experience with crankshaft manufacturing, but Dearborn Gauge doesn't have a facility in Mexico. If we start having problems, it may take some time to get their service people down here, and when they come they probably won't be able to speak Spanish.

The alternative is to use a $70,000 contact gauging system from Marposs, a company that Cummins has lots of experience with and that does have a plant in Mexico City. But this will lead to somewhat different measurements being generated by our new B crankshaft line, and will complicate the transfer process. We'll continually have to determine whether the differences we see between the dimensions Fostoria obtains and those we get here are due to process differences or measurement differences.

CHAPTER 7

Building Competitive Advantage through a Global Network of Capabilities

Andrew Bartmess

Keith Cerny

*T*HE TRANSITION TO GLOBAL COMPETITION in many U.S. manufacturing industries has added significant complexity to facility location decisions. Unfortunately, few companies have responded well to this challenge. Many plant location decisions made during the past decade could be characterized as tactical, stop-gap actions which resulted in short-lived benefits and in company facility networks that are unbalanced, inefficient, or ineffective. The financial performance of the resulting plants has frequently been disappointing. Typical management comments include:

> Our savings were significant initially, but wage rates at our overseas plants have risen consistently, and at the current exchange rates our savings are almost insignificant.

> We save a lot on labor over there, but we have also added a lot of new people here to support the foreign plants and additional finished goods to support our customers.

> The process of communicating with our (South American country) plant is incredibly burdensome. They are almost never in synch on engineering changes and timely new product releases are next to impossible.

The authors would like to thank Professor Steven Wheelwright of the Harvard Business School for his patient guidance and assistance during the development of this article. The research work for the article was completed while both the authors were students at the Harvard Business School.

There have, however, been some exceptions to this pattern. A few companies have made location decisions that have fostered the development of critical capabilities and created lasting competitive advantage. The resulting plants fit into well-conceived facility networks which solidly support the companies' businesses. It is not surprising that the decision processes utilized by these firms are quite different from those of most others. By understanding the nature of the processes used by these companies, and the key differences from more typical processes, managers can:

- implement better plant location decisions for the company as a whole by recognizing the importance of this decision to the overall firm;
- improve decision making regarding which products, processes, or organizations to relocate overseas, and thereby better grasp the implications of such a move;
- facilitate the interactions between internal functions (e.g., Design, Manufacturing, and Marketing) and with external suppliers and markets; and
- support critical capabilities in the company that are an ongoing source of competitive advantage.

The Beginnings of a Traditional Approach

In 1990, Kodak's Business Imaging Systems Division (BIS) found itself facing increasing pressure from foreign competition. Japanese competitors were experiencing growing success with small-sized, low-priced microfilm capture and retrieval equipment. To engineers and managers at Kodak, the design of these machines seemed "cheap." The frames of the competitive products were of lower gauge metal than Kodak's and flexed noticeably when lifted. In addition, power supplies and other components were smaller, and functionality was much more limited. But despite these apparent shortcomings, foreign customers and price sensitive domestic customers were beginning to switch to these competing brands, thereby eroding BIS's market share. Marketing management responded to this trend by putting pressure on Manufacturing personnel whom they felt were responsible for producing products which were "not competitive." This pressure quickly grew as the Division General Manager also became concerned with Manufacturing's cost position.

In responding to this concern, Manufacturing management determined that changes to production methods and sourcing, the traditional sources of manufacturing cost reduction, could not yield the savings required to be competitive with the Japanese products. It happened, however, that the Manufacturing Director had recent experience starting up a plant in Taiwan to produce optical components for another Kodak division. Others in the BIS manufacturing management team had similar experience. As a result, they were aware of the large difference in production worker wage rates between their current U.S. plant and the overseas facilities (approximately $12 versus $3). They were also aware that in some locations materials costs could be reduced by 10% or more. In addition, the Kodak optics facility in Taiwan had excess space available. Manufacturing some products overseas seemed to have the potential for creating short-term savings of the magnitude that BIS required.

Due to the pressure from upper management and from Marketing, Manufacturing management felt an urgent need to take action, and a high-level manufacturing manager was asked to assess the impact of moving some operations overseas. He began by looking for a plant location selection framework and by examining methodologies that had been used to make past plant location decisions. These consisted primarily of models which applied subjective weights to a long list of factors characterizing each location (e.g., political risk, labor availability, union activity, and infrastructure). The locations with the highest scores were then considered most seriously.

BIS's early response to its competitive situation displays many of the key characteristics of a "traditional" approach to the manufacturing facility location decision.

- *Static "Snap-Shot" Analysis*—The analyses which accompany typical plant location decisions tend to be focused on *current* wage rates and *current* material costs. The analysis makes a good attempt at understanding the costs and benefits of a location at a given point in time but ignores how these may change in the future.[1] There is also typically no ongoing process to examine the viability of the company's facility network; the individual location analyses performed are unrelated reactions to independent internal or external stimuli.
- *Stop-Gap Response*—Plant location decisions, particularly those to locate overseas, are often made as a short-term response to a competitive threat. Overseas wage rates can seem miraculously low ($1–2 in some countries vs. $10–15 in the U.S.) and can appear very tempting to a manager facing foreign cost competition. A new plant located in a low factor-cost country can seem like an attractive way to level the playing field, at least in the short term.
- *Single Functional Focus*—The plant location decision is addressed almost solely by the company's manufacturing organization, usually with only minor outside functional input to address pricing and tax issues. This high degree of autonomy leads to three main weaknesses in the decision making process:
  - *Overemphasis on Direct Labor Costs:* The common obsession of the manufacturing function with direct labor costs, largely due to traditional cost accounting systems, has been well documented.[2]

The result has been numerous plant location decisions based primarily on direct labor costs.

- *Focus on Options Implementable by Manufacturing Alone:* Rather than looking for reductions in cost across the entire business system (e.g., design changes or overhead reductions), the manufacturing function tends to focus on significant changes that it can implement directly. Once again, a plant relocation will appear to offer the potential for a "quantum leap" reduction in manufacturing costs.

- *Neglect of Impact on Other Functions:* Since the plant location decision is made by individuals most familiar with manufacturing issues, they often underestimate the impact that a plant location decision may have on the company as a whole.

- ***Focus on External Environment and Resources***—Traditional decision analyses focus almost exclusively on the characteristics of the locations being considered. Extensive and detailed evaluations of wage rates, material costs, utility costs, transportation costs, infrastructure, and taxes are fairly common. Analyses which address the impact of the facility location on the internal workings and "capabilities" of the company are not.

The Capability Focused Approach

At any given point in time, the products and competitive position of a firm are important. In the dynamic competitive environment facing most manufacturers today, however, products are quickly obsolete and static competitive positions are rapidly overtaken. In such an environment, the only real source of competitive advantage is the ability to respond consistently to changing markets with new products and ever-improving competitiveness. A firm can achieve this ongoing renewal by identifying, developing, and maintaining its critical "capabilities."[3]

Capabilities are a company's proficiency in the business processes which allow it to constantly distinguish itself along the dimensions that are important to its customers. For example, in a high-tech industry, the ability to quickly develop new state-of-the-art products with features and performance that deliver value to customers creates an enduring advantage. In a commodity industry, by contrast, it may be the ability to constantly reduce costs that creates the lasting competitive edge. Capabilities like these are resident in the company's people and are supported by its procedures, culture, and infrastructure. Firms seeking sustainable success in today's competitive environment must focus on building and nurturing these capabilities. Exhibit 7.1 presents examples of successful companies and the capabilities which support their success.

Clearly, a capability creates no competitive advantage if it is easily

Exhibit 7.1 Example Capabilities for Selected Companies

Company—Industry	Nature of Competition in Industry	Example Capabilities
Applied Materials—Semiconductor Equipment	Technology driven with high requirement for customization and service	• Rapid, high-technology product development and rollout • Rapid production/delivery of highly customized product
Cooper Tire—Replacement Auto and Truck Tires	Near commodity market. Difficult for buyer to discern differences in products. Buying decision based on price and dealer recommendation	• Low cost product design and manufacturing/continual cost control and reduction • Constantly improving customer service
Analog Devices—Analog and Digital Semiconductors	Analog circuits bought on technical performance. Talented analog designers create most of the customer value and are a scarce resource	• Attracting, developing and retaining talented employees
Sun Microsystems—Workstations	Easily copied products. Competition based on latest available technology	• Rapid, high-technology product development and rollout • Operational flexibility
Motorola—Semiconductors and Electrical Equipment	Technology, cost and quality	• Continuous quality improvement • Rapid, high-technology product development and rollout • Operational flexibility
Tandy/Radio Shack—Electronic Equipment/Toys Manufacturing and Retailing	Price and availability of latest "fad" products	• Market trend identification capability to quickly and consistently spot market trends • Operational flexibility

achieved by competitors. Thus, the *critical* capabilities are those that are difficult to develop. This difficulty is created by three common characteristics:

• *Complexity*—Critical capabilities tend to be developed in business processes that are highly complex. Developing them involves patient "organizational learning" over a long period of time. Thus, a company with a head start in this learning process is difficult to overtake.

- *Organizational Diffuseness*—Critical capabilities involve processes which nearly always cut horizontally across the functional groups in the company, and frequently involve external groups (see Exhibit 7.2).[4] As a consequence, they cannot be developed by hiring away a few key individuals.
- *Well-Developed Interfaces*—Critical capabilities depend as much on the way that individuals/organizations have learned to work with each other as they do on the particular expertise of the individuals/organizations themselves. As a result, a competitor could staff each of the functions involved in a critical process with the most talented individuals available and still not develop a capability.

Developing and maintaining critical capabilities demands relationships between all groups involved in critical processes that are dynamic and responsive. In particular, rich, constant, and frequently informal communication must replace the arm's-length, periodic, and contractually oriented mode that often characterizes the relationship between these groups. This type of association can be extremely difficult to conduct at a distance.[5] As a result, the configuration of a firm's facility network, which determines the geographical proximity of each of these groups to the others, can support or undermine its critical capabilities. If facility location decisions are to result in benefits that are sustainable, it is essential that this need for co-location be recognized and addressed.

Like the traditional approach to facility location, a capability-focused approach works to exploit the costs and benefits of external conditions and factors, but, unlike the traditional approach, it also attempts to foster both the internal and external relationships that sustain critical business processes. While the traditional approach takes a static view of conditions and benefits, the capability-focused approach attempts to capture benefits that are dynamic and self-renewing. The traditional approach tends to view the plant location decision from the lone perspective of the manufacturing function, while the capability-focused approach takes the cross-functional business process view. Finally, the objective of the traditional approach is often tactical competitive improvement, whereas the capability-focused approach targets long-term strategic advantage.

Traditional location analyses often include complex mathematical models that determine the location which minimizes a firm's total cost by balancing such elements as factor costs, transportation costs, and taxes.[6] It is exactly this same kind of balancing/optimization algorithm that is required by the capability-focused approach, although different terms are included. Certain benefits are derived by locating each of a company's functions near external entities like customers, suppliers, competitors, and governments. Certain benefits are also derived from locating each of a company's individual functions near one another. The magnitude of each of these benefits differs by industry and by company. The timing of bene-

Exhibit 7.2 Common Capabilities and Supporting Interfunctional and Interorganizational Links

Capability	Supporting Links
Rapid, high-technology product development and rollout	• Manufacturing and Design • Design and Leading Edge Customers • Design and Suppliers of High Technology Purchased Parts
Rapid Production/Delivery of highly customized product	• Manufacturing and Design • Sales and Design • Customers and Sales • Sales and Manufacturing
Low cost product design and manufacturing/continual cost control and reduction	• Manufacturing and Design • Marketing and Design • Customers and Marketing • Accounting and Manufacturing • Production workers and Management
Continual Quality improvement	• Manufacturing and Design • Demanding customers and Manufacturing • Demanding customers and Design • Production workers and Management
Attracting, Developing and Retaining Talented Employees	• Human Resources and All Other Functions • Management and Employees • Management and Human Resources
Constantly improving customer service	• All functions and Demanding customer groups • Sales and Design • Sales and Manufacturing • Service and Design • Service and Manufacturing • Distribution and Manufacturing
Operational Flexibility	• Manufacturing and Design • Manufacturing and Customer • Manufacturing and Sales/ Distribution • Information Systems and Manufacturing

fits is also an important element in determining the overall return. Achieving capability-driven financial returns may require several years, but once achieved they will endure. The financial benefits from relocating to a low factor cost country are nearly immediate, but they are transient. The objective of the plant location analysis should be to identify the network that combines these benefits in such a way that the net present value of future cash flows to the company is maximized.

Other authors have proposed approaches to the plant location decision which evaluate elements beyond the external conditions considered in the traditional approach. Markides and Berg criticize the traditional approach to site selection and particularly the decision to manufacture overseas for domestic markets.[7] They outline the hidden costs in such an approach including the impact on domestic product development skills. Kogut considers the requirement for operational flexibility in global competitiveness in his approach.[8] Neither of these, however, proposes an approach to manufacturing site selection based on the development of critical competitive capabilities. Porter comes closest to a capability-focused approach by considering the role that "strong domestic rivals, aggressive home-based suppliers and demanding local customers" play in spurring continual innovation.[9] He does not, however, address the role that the relative location of a company's internal functional groups plays in supporting its competitiveness. Nor does he address the internal mechanism through which a company converts the influence of a challenging external environment into useful internal abilities.

Two Contrasting Approaches to the Plant Location Decision

The cases of two high-tech companies during the past decade provide a good illustration of the traditional and capability centered approaches to the plant location decision.

Seagate Technology Inc. Seagate Technology is recognized as the firm which made hard-disks affordable for personal computers by bringing volume production and in-house component manufacturing capabilities to the industry. During the early 1980s, it leveraged this capability into a dominant position in the market. By the summer of 1984, however, Seagate faced a severe crisis. Falling personal computer sales had forced its customers to cut orders back sharply. Seagate's largest customer, IBM, was insisting on a price cut, and had begun to manufacture some of its own disk drives. The price of Seagate's principal product fell by 45%. President David Mitchell responded to this situation with a series of actions which many, at the time, felt saved the company. Moving disk drive assembly offshore to Singapore was the most significant of these changes. The result was an almost immediate 30% cost reduction. In fiscal 1985, even though Seagate's sales dropped to $215 million from $344 million the prior year, the company was still able to show a small profit.

Exhibit 7.3 displays Seagate's profitability prior to and since the time of this decision. Although the company did very well in the two years following the overseas move, performance since that time has been disappointing. The headline of an April 1991 Wall Street Journal article covering the earnings of Seagate and a major competitor proclaimed: "Conner Peripherals Says Profit Doubled: Seagate Earnings Fall."[10] During the summer of 1991, Seagate dismissed 1650, more than 20% of its non-manufacturing work force, in an effort to cut costs in response to further price competition. In September of 1991, David Mitchell abruptly resigned as President and Chief Operating Officer, apparently as the result of pressure from the board of directors.

Many of the forces which resulted in the sharp change of fortunes for Mitchell and Seagate from the mid-1980s to the early 1990s are more easily understood by examining Seagate's approach to the decision to move manufacturing overseas.

Exhibit 7.3   Seagate Technology Inc.,
Return on Sales

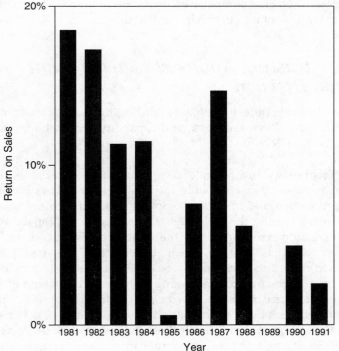

Static "Snap-Shot" Analysis. The primary driver for Seagate's move overseas was the competitive cost advantage which could be achieved with the significantly lower wage rates available there at the time. Unfortunately, other disk drive manufacturers soon followed Seagate to Singapore, reducing Seagate's advantage. In addition, the ensuing competition for production workers resulted in double-digit annual wage rate increases and the necessity to offer benefits like child care reimbursement and free medical care.[11] In 1987, Seagate built a new disk drive assembly facility in Thailand where wage rates were again much lower (starting wages were approximately $0.50 per hour). This facility was assembling a majority of the company's drives by mid-year 1988, but the pattern of increasing wages immediately commenced at this location as well.

This pattern of a company relocating to a low labor cost location, only to be forced to move again as costs in that country rose, has been a common one in industries as diverse as Winchester disk drives, toys, textiles, and ball bearings.[12] Many companies in these industries have made a series of plant location decisions, each seeking out the location that minimized their products' manufactured cost at the time of the decision. When these conditions changed the advantage vanished.

As these companies have discovered, where one company can relocate for a wage advantage, others can follow, and the result is a self-perpetuating cycle. Maquiladoras in Mexico, for example, have seen wage rates rise as companies compete for local skilled labor. Currencies in Taiwan, Singapore, and Korea have all showed sustained appreciation in the second half of the 1980s (between + 25% and + 50% over this period), and this appreciation has increased local costs in these countries when they are converted to U.S. dollars.[13] These changes have been, in part, the natural result of the economic success brought by foreign investment and increased national income. By building plants in developing, low factor cost countries, U.S. companies alter the very conditions that attracted most of them initially, as they contribute to the development of these countries' economies.

Stop-Gap Response. In moving manufacturing overseas to Singapore, Seagate responded to pressing immediate competitive threats. It was rewarded with a quick cost reduction. At the same time, however, it was significantly altering its ability to compete long term. It was particularly affecting the ability of the company to develop and introduce innovative new products in a timely manner. A quote from a March 1987 Business Week article is revealing:

> There were risks. Mitchell knew that transportation costs would soar, communication between U.S. engineering and foreign plants would be hard, and controlling quality would be harder. The solution, he decided, was to bring 50 to 100 foreign workers to

Seagate's Scotts Valley (Calif.) headquarters and teach them how
to assemble the new drives before production began.[14]

The solution described clearly does little to respond to anything other than
the immediate start-up concerns of the new facilities.

Single Functional Focus. Seagate's decision to move was based almost
exclusively on manufacturing concerns and issues. The decision was
driven by David Mitchell, who had experience prior to Seagate managing
the Asian plants of Fairchild Camera & Instruments Corp, and who was
described in a 1987 Fortune article as "a manufacturing man."[15] As
discussed earlier, he apparently gave little consideration to the impact of
the move on the other functions important to the company's long-term
success.

The difficulties inherent in viewing the plant location decision as exclusively a manufacturing issue are significant. Manufacturing is not a separa-
ble set of activities, distinct from all other functions; the interaction between
manufacturing and product development is particularly important. In the
automotive industry, for example, Clark and Fujimoto found that success in
manufacturing and success in design are correlated, and that a product's
design plays a role that is at least as important as manufacturing in determining its cost and quality level.[16] The ability to influence these factors is far
greater when a product is being designed than after it has been released to
manufacturing. A plant location decision that fails to consider development
issues can easily harm the company's ability to produce cost-competitive,
quality products in the long run.

A manufacturing-focused decision can also be particularly detrimental to a company's ability to develop products with leading-edge technology. In industries like disk drives, product and process technologies are
tightly linked. The challenge of making increasingly smaller disk drives is
as much a manufacturing problem as it is a technological one. As a result,
the communication link between manufacturing and development is critical to the timely development of new products in this environment. When
development is located far away from the associated manufacturing facilities, the day-to-day communication between these two functions can be
impaired.[17]

Focus on External Environment and Resources. For Seagate, the benefits
of moving manufacturing to Singapore were based entirely on the economic conditions and resource costs in that country. Little consideration
was given to the impact of the move on the company's internal capabilities. The move did not enhance Seagate's capability in low-cost manufacturing, but rather only gave it access to lower labor costs (which were also
instantly available to any other company who moved overseas). As
discussed earlier, there is a great deal of evidence to suggest that the move

weakened, or at least sustained an existing weakness in, Seagate's capability to maintain the pace of technological development required for success in this industry. Throughout the late 1980s and early 1990s, Seagate has consistently been months, and in some cases over a year, later to market than competitors with significant new technologies. This problem is the primary cause of Seagate's poor financial performance in recent years, and remedying it is the focus of the company's current improvement efforts.

Applied Materials Inc.: An Alternative Approach

In the late 1970s, James Morgan, the CEO of Applied Materials—a U.S. producer of semiconductor manufacturing equipment—became dissatisfied with his company's progress in the Japanese market.[18] At the time, his company was using the Japanese trading company Kanematsu Electric to sell in Japan, with unimpressive results. As he analyzed the situation, he came to the conclusion that succeeding in Japan would be critical to his company's long-term success worldwide. In the process of learning to be successful in the demanding Japanese market, Morgan felt that his company would develop capabilities which would benefit it in its global operations.

Semiconductor manufacturing equipment is very complex and involves state-of-the-art technology. The equipment is also highly customized based on customer requirements. These requirements must be quickly and thoroughly understood and then satisfied using the latest available technology. As a result, success in Japan was based on two factors, technology and relationship, and Applied's limited success in Japan at the time was based purely on technology. With the trading company arrangement, Applied would never be able to develop the critical customer relationships required for success in the market. A long-term commitment to the Japanese market through local direct operations was required in order to build lasting relationships with Japanese customers.

On the basis of these concerns, Morgan established Applied Materials Japan (AMJ) in late 1979. Initially, he established only a Sales operation staffed with local nationals, but the benefits were significant. In its first year, AMJ increased sales by 100% over the level achieved the year before by the trading company. By 1983, AMJ provided one third of Applied's total sales and Morgan was ready to take the next step. That year, Applied began construction on the Narita Technology Center in order to bring both R&D and Manufacturing operations to Japan. This step allowed Applied to improve the level and responsiveness of its support to Japanese customers by using customer-focused design teams and developing in-depth customer knowledge. It also allowed the company as a whole to benefit technically from direct exposure to the world's most demanding customers and the industry's latest breakthroughs.

By 1990, a time when most U.S. competitors (who were still utilizing

Japanese partners to sell in Japan) were having very little success in the growing Japanese market. Applied Materials was the Japanese market leader in a majority of its technologies. It was also the only company in the top 5 worldwide semiconductor equipment suppliers that was not Japanese (all 5 were U.S. companies in 1980). A quote from Applied's 1990 annual report sums up this story well:

> This global strategy . . . has also exposed our products and organizations to the toughest customers and competitors the world has to offer. This experience has tested us in ways not yet understood by most organizations.

This approach to the facility decision is altogether different from the conventional approach pursued by Seagate. The decision for Applied Materials was based on its view of the strategic market direction, not on current competitive issues and resource prices. The decision was made in response to a projection of future conditions, not a snapshot of the current situation. The decision was made by the CEO, based on marketing, product, and operational issues, not by a manufacturing executive based on direct labor rates. Finally, the decision for Applied Materials was based on the capabilities that conditions in the new location could help the company to build, not on the conditions themselves.

The goal of this strange approach to the facility location decision is to build a network of capabilities, rather than just a network of facilities. This network is specifically designed to support the company's business and market strategies on an ongoing basis. It is structured as much for what it can "teach" the firm, as it is to take advantage of external location resources. It is dynamic, and is maintained as an ongoing element in a company's strategic plan.

Key Steps Towards Building a Network of Capabilities

Exhibit 7.4 outlines an approach for identifying a company's critical capability set, and then for developing a facility network that will support these capabilities. The approach starts in Step 1 by examining the company's distinctive competitiveness and the nature of the markets in which it competes. The objective is to identify the value (e.g., low cost, leading-edge technology, extensive customer service) that the company intends to deliver to its customers. Once this value is identified, the objective in Step 2 is then to identify the business processes in the company that can give it an advantage over its competition in delivering this value. These are the critical processes in which capabilities can exist. Step 3 examines these processes and identifies where they cross the boundaries

Exhibit 7.4 Building a Network of Capabilities

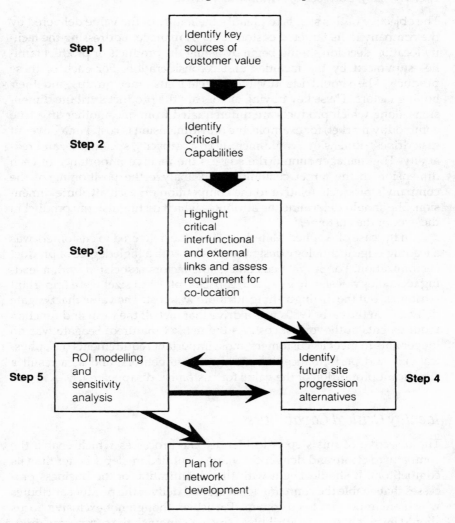

Step 1 — Identify key sources of customer value

Step 2 — Identify Critical Capabilities

Step 3 — Highlight critical interfunctional and external links and assess requirement for co-location

Step 5 — ROI modelling and sensitivity analysis

Step 4 — Identify future site progression alternatives

Plan for network development

between internal functions or with external groups. The relationships that exist at each of these boundaries are then scrutinized to determine: Is the relationship critical to the process? and if critical, does the relationship require geographic proximity for success? In Step 4, alternative plant locations, and sequences of plant locations, are developed with the objective of best balancing the requirement for proximity of each of the critical relationships. Finally, in Step 5, a return on investment model is utilized to assess the financial implications of each alternative. A detailed discussion of each of these steps follows.

Identify Key Sources of Customer Value

The objective of this step is to identify the nature of the value delivered by the company to its targeted customer set. A manager addressing the facility location decision should begin by listing the products or product families supported by the facilities under consideration. For each of these products, she should identify the targeted customer groups and their buying factors. These key buying factors are the product attribute dimensions along which products are differentiated from one another. In a true commodity market, for example, the only dimension is cost. For a buyer of disk drives, dimensions could include cost, capacity, speed, size, and reliability. The manager should then assess the relative importance of each dimension to the target customers and analyze the positioning of the company's products relative to the competition on each attribute dimension. She should determine the attributes which distinguish the product in the eyes of the customer.

In the case of Applied Materials, the value delivered to customers was a leading-edge technology design combined with a high degree of product customization. For Seagate customers, the factors associated with a leading technology design (e.g., speed, capacity, physical size) were important attributes, but the distinguishing attribute was cost. The value that Seagate delivered in the early 1980s was a drive that met all the form and function requirements at the lowest cost. As the market matured, Seagate was no longer able to meet its customers' most important requirements (i.e., physical size and performance) as quickly as competitors, and as a result a significant proportion of the value for customers disappeared.

Identify Critical Capabilities

The objective of this step is to identify the processes which enable the company to create and deliver the value identified in Step 1 better than its competitors. It should begin with the identification of the business processes that enable the company to create and deliver the product attributes which are important to customers. Particular, though not exclusive, focus should be given to those attributes which distinguish the company's products from the competition and influence customers to select it.

It is important to focus on the processes that create the attributes that customers value on an ongoing basis; these may not necessarily be the processes which are creating the product today. For example, if customers buy a particular product because it is the least expensive, one might conclude that the efficient, automated process which manufactured the product is the source of the value for the customer. However, when this product is obsolete, or when the competition imitates the manufacturing line, this efficient automated process, though still intact, will no longer be a source of value. On the other hand, a design process for low-cost products, or a capability in developing automated manufacturing processes, or even organizational processes which drive continual cost reduction, can deliver products with a competitive cost advantage on an enduring basis.

Once the processes which create value have been identified, the "critical" processes should be isolated. "Critical" processes are those that cannot be easily duplicated by the competition. Competitors should not be able to match the process by hiring away key individuals or through heavy investment. As noted earlier, the typical barriers to imitation include the complexity of the process involved and the fact that the expertise in the process tends to be organizationally diffuse.

In businesses like software design, the work of a few talented individuals may create nearly all of the value that the customer perceives in the product. In cases such as this, the *critical* capabilities that the company possesses may be the processes and systems which create the working environment and rewards that keep these individuals motivated and content. This capability provides an enduring competitive advantage for the company over competitors who could not retain these essential employees. These processes are very complex and involve individuals throughout the organization. As a result, they are not easily imitated.

For Applied Materials, the process which delivered value to customers was the product development capability, including the process of working with customers to understand their requirements thoroughly before pushing the envelope of technology to provide a state-of-the-art solution.

Highlight Key Interfunctional and External Links

Having identified the critical processes around which capabilities exist, the manager can identify the key interfunctional and external links required to support them. To begin the step, the manager should construct a simple flow chart that depicts at a high level the major steps in the process, including the physical and informational flows between these steps. After developing the process flow, the manager should identify the locations where the process crosses either functional boundaries or the boundaries between the company and outside groups.

Particular attention should be given to interfaces with demanding outside groups which can give the company insight into the future competitive requirements in the industry. These can be leading-edge customers who will have requirements that may portend the future needs of most other companies in their industry (e.g., Japanese semiconductor manufacturers for Applied Materials). It may also be with a government agency in a regulated environment or with key technology suppliers in a fast moving high-tech industry (e.g., Intel for early Sun Microsystems products).

The manager must then assess the criticality of each of these interfunctional and interorganizational links. These can be evaluated by identifying the major failure modes for the link (e.g., lack of communication, communication delay, introduction of errors, loss of information) and the probability of failure under normal circumstances. The impact of each failure on the value delivered to the customer by the process must then be assessed. If a significant impact is at all likely, the link must be considered critical.

Common critical links include the link between development and manufacturing for high-tech product and the link between marketing and development for a consumer product. Companies in different industries have different critical external and internal links. In the toy or shoe industries, the ongoing day-to-day interaction required between manufacturing and other functions such as marketing or development is less crucial than in a high-tech area (such as disk drives or semiconductor manufacturing equipment). For Applied Materials, the link between R&D and the demanding Japanese customer base was essential for its global success. Similar critical links can exist with key suppliers, government agencies, and financial institutions.

The need for geographic proximity in each of these critical relationships should then be evaluated. Several factors influence the degree to which proximity is required to support inter-group communications and relationships.

- *Complexity of Information:* The more complex the information that must be regularly communicated between groups, the greater the need for proximity. By its nature, complex information is difficult to communicate. It may require multiple communication cycles, several different communication media, or even for the parties involved to look each other in the eye to ensure that the message has been understood. In addition, complex information is more easily communicated incrementally through time than it is in large batch "transmittals." Each of these requirements is facilitated by proximity.
- *Required Level of Interaction:* Communication which requires significant interaction drives a greater requirement for proximity than communication that does not. Several factors can affect the need for interaction including the predictability of the communications content (i.e., relationships in which similar information can be communicated in a similar format month after month as opposed to more variability) and the requirement for one-way vs. two-way information flow.
- *Similarity of Background and Expertise:* It is much easier for individuals with similar backgrounds and experience, who "speak the same language" (either figuratively or literally), to conduct a relationship at a distance. In instances where differences exist, it is frequently difficult for each individual to know what information is important to the other individual and what is not. When these individuals are distant

from one another, they are forced to filter the information communicated to fit into the available communication opportunities. They may unknowingly filter out important information.

- *Requirement for Trust-Based Relationship:* In many cases, particularly those involving external parties, effective communication requires the individuals to trust one another. In these instances, there is typically no obligation on the part of one individual to communicate to the other, and there may even be disincentives for communicating. This type of relationship is nearly impossible to develop and maintain at a distance.
- *Concreteness of Information:* In some cases, information is difficult to verbalize. Customer feelings and emotions and the subtleties of a foreign culture are good examples. In cases like these, there really is no substitute for being there.

Here it is very tempting to think that technology provides an alternate approach. In reality, electronic mail, facsimile, and telephone communication work well only after initial relationships have been established. Even then they cannot support the rich, constant nature of the communication required in the relationships which support capabilities.

For Applied Materials, the complex nature of the required interaction between several internal functions (Sales, Design, Manufacturing) and its most demanding customer set required geographic proximity to be effective.

Identify Future Progression Alternatives

The manager should plot each of the major "links" between important internal and external groups on a two-dimensional map (see Exhibit 7.5). They should be plotted across the dimensions of current level of proximity (continuous scale from local to long distance) and the need for proximity (identified in the previous step). It can be easily seen that the ideal area is the upper right hand one, and the worst area is the lower right.

The ideal progression of moves can now be identified (Exhibit 7.6). There will probably be a large gap between the current network and the ideal network which co-locates all links with a high need for proximity. Some groups cannot be moved easily, either because they are external to the company or would be very expensive to relocate. These should be highlighted, since it is unlikely that they can be moved. We refer to these groups as anchor points since they are the fixed points around which the network must be built.

At this stage, the manager should identify high leverage moves around anchor points that create maximum strategic value and move toward the ideal network. These moves should be considered as an evolution over time. A large toy manufacturer in Indonesia, for example, might

Exhibit 7.5   Example: Applied Materials in Late 1970s

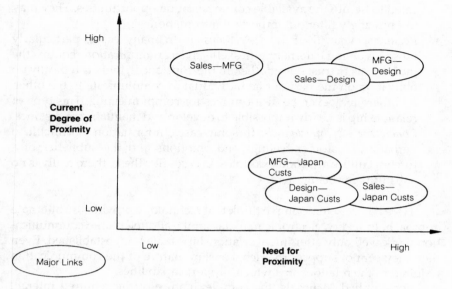

map out a long-term sequence of country moves that responds to projected increasing labor costs. In the case of Applied Materials, James Morgan elected initially to move Sales to Japan. This initiated the development of direct relationships with the Japanese customer base, and sales in the market grew dramatically as a result. The links between development/manufacturing and the Japanese market were also critical, but the market was too small initially to support their presence. After the market growth driven by the move of Sales to Japan, however, this was no longer a problem. The move of Development and Manufacturing to Japan soon followed.

It is important that the analysis here extend beyond the next move to include potential sequences of moves that could take place over the next several years. In many cases, the move after next (or even the move after that) may influence what the best next move should be. For example, if a company had a long-term objective of entering a previously untapped market with sales and manufacturing operations, it might make sense to locate a small design team there in advance of the other groups to develop a customized product set. This "next move" makes sense when considered as a step in a sequence, but it would not make sense in isolation. Tax laws, political considerations, changing economic conditions and learning requirements can each create situations where optimizing a sequence of moves will drive superior results than considering each move only after the optimal prior move has been selected.

Exhibit 7.6 Example: Applied Materials Move Sequence

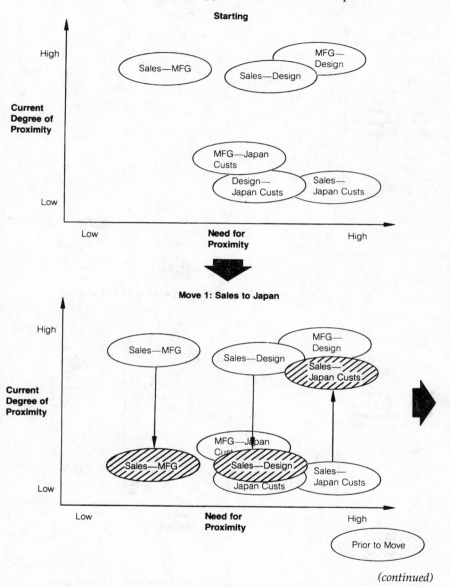

(continued)

Return on Investment Modeling and Sensitivity Analysis

A return on investment (ROI) analysis should be used to quantify the financial implications of alternative facility networks, and it should incorporate as accurately as possible the costs and benefits associated with these networks. Distant location of functions or groups requiring a high

Exhibit 7.6   Example: Applied Materials Move Sequence *(cont.)*

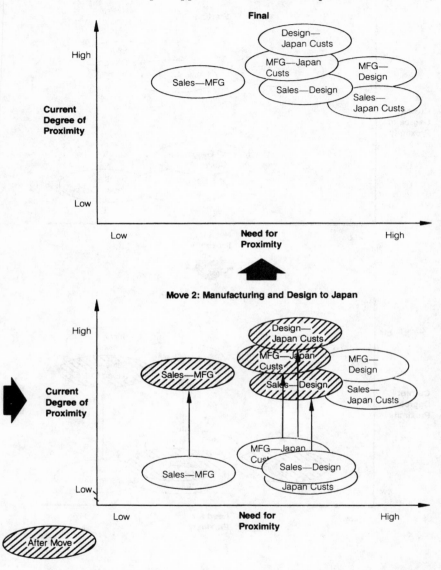

degree of interaction will lead to inefficient communication and higher costs. For example, Markides and Berg quote a survey commissioned by the National Tooling and Machinery Association that suggests offshore manufacturing can add 3% to product cost for additional paperwork, and up to 35% for unanticipated design changes.[19] Conversely, strengthening the network of capabilities may lead to increased margins or sales, and these financial impacts may be modeled as well.

While these figures can be explicitly included in the ROI calculation, a careful qualitative analysis should also be used to "reality check" the results. To be accurate, this ROI analysis must meet several requirements.

- *The ROI model must take a cross-functional perspective, including costs and savings to the company as a whole.* For instance, an overseas plant will generally cause costs for the distribution function to rise, as a company with predominantly U.S. customers must pay for additional duties, and longer shipping distances, and must fund a larger inventory pipeline. The company must also consider the substantial additional costs that will be incurred by almost all functions due to added complexity. These costs include currency management, adherence to local regulations, and expatriate support. They also include all other costs created by the introduction of distance, including differences in time zone, language, and culture in both communications and logistics channels.

- *The model must also account for changes in local economic conditions.* The manager must forecast future exchange rates by using a simple model based upon purchasing power parity, interest rate parity, or return to real exchange rate equilibriums. This information must be used to assess both the company's and competitors' situations over time. As Lessard and Lightstone have noted, even domestic producers have exchange rate exposure since their overseas competitors' cost structures will be affected by exchange rate shifts.[20]

  Political risk assessment must also be incorporated into the analysis. Desta has summarized the most common approaches and has proposed a framework that precisely defines the notion of political risk and explicitly incorporates the developmental aspirations of the country being invested in.[21] Levi has suggested an interesting quantitative approach for countries facing potential confiscation of overseas investment.[22] His derivation concludes that the impact of potential confiscation can be computed by multiplying cash flows by the probability that the firm will survive each year (i.e., 1-probability of confiscation), divided by the sum of the discount rate and the probability of confiscation), divided by the sum of the discount rate and the probability of confiscation. The analysis assumes that the probability of confiscation does not vary from year to year.

- *Wage rates, taxes and transfer pricing, and overhead savings must be handled correctly.* These aspects of the analysis present three particular complexities. The first is the choice of wage rate to use in the model. Raw local labor costs are deceptive, since they do not account for the lower productivity of low factor cost country workers relative to the United States. An accurate approach requires the adjustment of labor costs for the relative productivity within the appropriate economic sector of the country being considered. Changes in local wage rates over time should also be estimated, since these have risen sharply in many developing countries in response to foreign investment.

The second area of complexity is the choice of effective tax rate and transfer price; these areas are important to the final result, and a successful manager will need to involve his or her tax staff early to understand and fully exploit all opportunities. Finally, in evaluating overhead savings, only those savings that are relevant for the company as a whole should be included. Fixed costs such as buildings and systems do not disappear directly when a plant moves overseas, although the company's cost accounting system may at first suggest that this is the case.

One end result of this analysis should be an understanding of the external condition scenarios under which each alternative network makes sense and under which it does not. Another result should be to identify the level of benefits (e.g., improved future sales or margins) which must be derived from improved internal capabilities to justify the costs of the location alternatives. Management can then make a judgment on each alternative's likelihood of success and level of risk. It can also then make an informed decision on the network configuration for the company in the short term and the planned development of this network in the future. If the results are not satisfactory, management can cycle back to the previous step to search for a network that improves the level of high-leverage co-location and produces good returns on investment.

A Change of Approach for BIS

The manager charged with the BIS plant decision completed his review of past site selection methodologies and judged them inadequate. To him, the past approaches seemed excessively subjective, since they did not identify the real impacts of various site alternatives on BIS's business, and they ignored the effect of potential sites on key business processes. He then set about finding an approach which would address the real impacts of potential plant locations to BIS and to Kodak as a whole.

He decided to undertake an ROI analysis of the proposed foreign plant locations to understand the full economic picture. What he discovered surprised him: the products produced by this division did not have the scale or direct labor content required to make a move to a low factor cost country pay off. Three primary factors accounted for the result.

- *Labor Rates:* Although the raw labor rates were low, productivity was as low as 20% of U.S. levels. Thus, for example, although the basic wage rates in Singapore in 1988 were US$3.09 per hour, the productivity-adjusted wage rates were US$6.40 per hour.[23]
- *Overhead Structure:* Only about 35% of the total allocated overhead

dollars were due to hourly direct labor; the rest were either fixed costs (such as tooling and information systems, which were not affected by an overseas move) or salaried manufacturing support (typically experienced engineers). Overseas wage differentials were much smaller for engineers than they were for assembly workers. In Malaysia today, for example, experienced engineers earn about M$4000 (US$1600) per month and typically also receive use of a car and housing subsidies. Hourly employees often earn as little as M$400-800 (US$160-320) per month. As a consequence, the savings on overhead costs driven by engineering wage rates were much smaller than those driven by the wage rates of hourly assembly workers.

- *Cost Increases Over Time:* In many of the proposed sites, projected currency appreciation over time resulted in increases in labor and material costs. Even in countries with no such appreciation, the results were affected by what Ken Ohmae refers to as the "expense of cheap labor."[24] As he notes, "the chip-makers have learned first-hand what CTV and textile industries discovered earlier: inexperienced labor must be trained, and, once trained and experienced, labor does not stay cheap very long."

The BIS approach then began to evolve from a fairly traditional one to one which was more capability-centered. As the team charged with the decision began to delve into the details of what a Taiwanese plant would really mean to their business they found:

- The designs of their low-end products had excessive functionality and ruggedness, both of which drove excess cost. The products were also too large to be a good match for global customer requirements. In addition, a large segment of domestic customers were also changing from a high-feature orientation to a high-value orientation.
- Successful competitors' products for the U.S. market were not manufactured in low factor cost countries.
- The core capability set implied by the Division's competitive strategy required that Manufacturing and Engineering be co-located, and a transplant Division Engineering outpost in the country to support the foreign plant did not seem economically feasible.
- Cost advantages which were at least equal in magnitude to the benefit of low foreign wages (and more durable) were available, without moving, through improving the manufacturability of product designs.[25]

On the basis of these findings, the Kodak facility location team grew to include multiple functions including representatives with responsibility for engineering and marketing. The team decided that although a low factor cost manufacturing site for current products made little sense, an Asian presence was important to improve the company's understanding of the requirements of this important, high-growth market. It was also felt that the competitive Asian environment and skilled engineering workforce could help Kodak to develop improved internal low-cost manufacturing capabilities.

BIS eventually elected to move a few engineers to Taiwan to coordinate the development of a low-end product for the local market. The development effort was staffed with local engineers. This design effort is currently in progress and proceeding on-schedule. A small scale manufacturing operation, for this product only, will be initiated progressively as it is required to support the engineering effort and eventual production volumes. In parallel with this effort, BIS is working to improve the design of its current, U.S.-manufactured product line to improve its cost competitiveness and to match it more carefully to global customer requirements.

Conclusion

A capability-focused approach to the facility location decision can be used to create a network of capabilities that includes plants as an integral part. The resulting networks will support the company's competitive advantage on an enduring basis. Ironically, broadening the analysis to include non-manufacturing issues will help to enlist the manufacturing organization as a true contributor to the company's strategic capabilities. This capability-focused approach is far more difficult to implement than the traditional one, and the financial improvements may not appear as quickly. The end results, however, are lasting and cumulative. They can transform a company's operational stance from reactive and defensive to being a key element in a premeditated strategic plan.

Notes

1. For a good approach to assessing the competitive impact of changes in cost structure over time, see Arthur A. Thompson, Jr., "Strategies for Staying Cost Competitive," *Harvard Business Review* (January/February 1984).
2. See, for example, Robert S. Kaplan, "Yesterday's Accounting Undermines Production," *Harvard Business Review* (July/August 1984). See also Robin Cooper and Robert S. Kaplan, "Measure Costs Right: Make the Right Decisions," *Harvard Business Review* (September/October 1988) and Michael J. Fradette et al., "Cost Accounting Overhaul: Making Your Financial Reports the Linchpin of Strategic Decisions," *Corporate Controller* (November/December 1988) for a brief discussion of traditional systems and a good overview of activity-based costing.
3. See George Stalk, Philip Evans, and Lawrence E. Shulman, "Competing on Capabilities: The New Rules of Corporate Strategy," *Harvard Business Review* (March/April 1992) for an excellent description of capabilities.
4. The definition used here for capabilities contains some elements in common with the notion of core competencies as advanced by C. K. Prahalad and Gary Hamel, "The Core Competence of the Corporation," *Harvard Business Review*

(May/June 1990). As the authors note on page 82, "Core competence is communication, involvement, and a deep commitment to working across organizational boundaries. It involves many levels of people and all functions."

5. A similar point is made in a study by Craig S. Galbraith documented in "Transferring Core Manufacturing Technologies in High-Tech Firms," *California Management Review*, 32/4 (Summer 1990), which found that when core technologies were transferred between facilities, a correlation existed between the distance separating the facilities and the time required for the receiving plant to match the productivity level of the originating plant.

6. Morris A. Cohen and Hau L. Lee's "Resource Deployment Analysis of Global Manufacturing and Distribution Networks," *Journal of Manufacturing and Operations Management*, 2 (1989) represents an excellent example of this type of model.

7. Constantinos C. Markides and Norman Berg, "Manufacturing Offshore is Bad Business," *Harvard Business Review* (September/October 1988).

8. Bruce Kogut, "Designing Global Strategies: Profiting from Operational Flexibility," *Sloan Management Review* (Fall 1985).

9. Michael Porter, "The Competitive Advantage of Nations," *Harvard Business Review* (March/April 1990).

10. Jim Carlton, "Conner Peripherals Says Profit Doubled; Seagate Earnings Fall," *Wall Street Journal*, April 18, 1991, p. B8.

11. Evelyn Richards, "Looking for the Asian Edge: Low-Cost Foreign Labor Helps a U.S. Disk-Drive Maker Lead Its Industry," *The Washington Post*, June 17, 1990, p. H1.

12. "The Non-Conformist," *The Economist*, August 22, 1992.

13. Between 1987 and 1988 alone, average hourly labor rates expressed in U.S. dollars increased 24% in Taiwan, 16% in Singapore, and 37% in Korea. U.S. rates, by contrast, increased by just over 3%. Sonia Nazario, "Boom and Despair," *Wall Street Journal*, September 22, 1989, p. R26.

14. Richard Brandt, "Seagate Goes East—And Comes Back A Winner," *Business Week*, March 16, 1987.

15. Lynn Fleary, *Fortune*, March 30, 1987, pp. 91–96.

16. See Kim B. Clark and Takahiro Fujimoto, *Product Development Performance: Strategy, Organization, and Management in the World Auto Industry* (Boston, MA: Harvard Business School Press, 1991).

17. See, for example, Kenichi Ohmae, *Triad Power: The Coming Shape of Global Competition* (New York, NY: Free Press, 1985), pp. 5–6.

18. This section draws upon the book by James C. Morgan and J. Jeffrey Morgan, *Cracking the Japanese Market: Strategies for Success in the New Global Economy* (New York, NY: The Free Press, 1991).

19. Markides and Berg, op. cit.

20. Donald R. Lessard and John B. Lightstone, "Volatile Exchange Rates Can Put Operations at Risk," *Harvard Business Review* (July/August 1986).

21. Asayehgn Desta, "Assessing Political Risk in Less Developed Countries," *The Journal of Business Strategy*, 5/4 (1985): 40–53. The article also presents a good overview of the strengths and weaknesses of traditional approaches to political risk analysis.

22. Maurice D. Levi, *International Finance* (New York, NY: McGraw Hill, 1990), pp. 389–390.

23. Matt Moffett highlights a similar finding for plant locations in Mexico in "Culture Shock," *Wall Street Journal*, Global Business, September 24, 1992, p. R13.

24. Kenichi Ohmae, op. cit., pp. 5–6.
25. This notion is not new, but as Dixon and Duffey point out, "while *recognition* of design's importance in keeping U.S. industries competitive in global markets has begun to increase, the actual *response* continues to be almost entirely in manufacturing: automation of existing processes, material and labor cost reductions, quality control, and so on." John R. Dixon and Michael R. Duffey, "The Neglect of Engineering Design," *California Management Review,* 32/2 (Winter 1990): 19.

CHAPTER 8

Eli Lilly and Company

Manufacturing Process Technology Strategy (1991)

*I*N OCTOBER 1991, Joe Cook, vice president of Production Operations and Engineering at Eli Lilly and Company, leaned back in his chair to collect his thoughts before the upcoming Manufacturing Strategy Committee meeting. Cook believed that manufacturing could play a greater role in reinforcing Lilly's competitive position in the pharmaceutical industry. To accomplish this, Cook was considering several appealing opportunities. Among the possibilities, he was most drawn to a program aimed at upgrading Lilly's manufacturing process technology.

The environment for making such a proposal at Lilly was encouraging: for three decades Lilly's revenue had consistently expanded, but 1990 had broken old records. Pharmaceutical sales jumped 26%, the highest rate in 34 years. Net income had climbed 20% and earnings per share were up 22%. To support this growth, capital expenditure, mostly for manufacturing, had been boosted by 82%, following a 49% increase in 1989.

Nevertheless, the committee could choose among many potentially lucrative investments, including more product R&D. Along with marketing, R&D was regarded as the linchpin of corporate strategy in most pharmaceutical companies; generally, senior management had either science or marketing backgrounds. In 1990, Lilly increased R&D expenditures by 16%, to 13.5% of sales, following an 18% increase in 1989. Manufacturing's traditional focus had been on providing sufficient capacity and developing better sourcing strategies. Cook's proposal regarding process technology, therefore, would have to be backed by persuasive evidence to win support over competing opportunities.

Doctoral student Jonathan West wrote this case as the basis for class discussion rather than to illustrate either effective or ineffective handling of an administrative situation. Selected data have been disguised to protect the proprietary interests of Eli Lilly and Company.

Background

Colonel Eli Lilly founded Eli Lilly and Company in 1876 with total capital of $1,400 and four employees, including his 14-year-old son, Josiah. Defying then-standard practice, Colonel Lilly sought to make medicine according to recognized scientific criteria: precise formulation, accurate compounding, standardization by assay, full disclosure of ingredients on the label, and honest claims.

The formula was successful. The company rapidly became a leader in the pharmaceutical industry, and 115 years later was the second-largest pharmaceutical concern in the United States and the eighth-largest world-wide. Its prosperity had long been based on a combination of strong research and careful management. A scientific division was formed in 1886, and a department of experimental medicine in 1912. In 1991, Lilly, with headquarters in Indianapolis, Indiana, sold a broad line of human health care and agricultural products. It was committed to all essential aspects of the industry: discovery, development, manufacture, and marketing. Over one-third of its 1990 sales came from outside the United States: the company manufactured and distributed its products in 25 other countries and sold them in more than 110 countries. Pharmaceuticals accounted for 71% of total sales in 1990, while medical devices and diagnostics (19%) and animal products contributed the rest. Exhibits 8.1A and 8.1B outline recent financial results.

Ten Lilly pharmaceuticals sold more than $100 million each in 1990. Lilly's Ceclor,™ the world's number-one selling antibiotic, saw a sales increase in 1990 alone of $100 million. Prozac,™ the world's top-selling antidepressant, was introduced in 1988 and rapidly became one of the company's top-selling drugs. In its first year on the market, Prozac's sales topped $100 million, faster growth than any other product in Lilly's history. Humulin,™ human insulin (and the world's first marketed human-health-care product based on recombinant DNA technology), was the company's third-largest seller.

The pharmaceutical industry was the most profitable sector of the U.S. economy. Returns on equity had long been 50% higher than the median for the *Fortune* 500 and in the 1980s the gap had widened. Profits for most major drug companies surged in that decade, as world markets expanded and prices rose. In 1990, world pharmaceutical sales totaled $174 billion (U.S. sales were more than $50 billion), an increase of 14% over 1989, continuing a compound annual growth rate of more than 10% throughout the 1980s. Pharmaceutical sales in Europe had grown by 28% in 1990 alone. Between them, North America and Europe accounted for 61% of the total; Japan made up a further 25%.

Market expansion was expected to continue at 7.9% per year, adjusted for inflation, through the mid-1990s. People around the world were living longer and desired more and better health care. In 1990, 13% of the U.S.

Exhibit 8.1A   Balance Sheet, year ending December 31 ($ in millions)

Assets	1990	1989
Current Assets		
Cash and equivalents	$350.2	$323.0
Short-term investments	$400.6	$329.0
Accounts Receivable	$770.7	$732.1
Other receivables	$108.0	$113.7
Inventories	$673.0	$599.5
Prepaid expenses	$198.8	$177.1
Total current assets	$2,501.3	$2,274.4
Other Assets		
Investments	$480.7	$530.8
Goodwill & intangibles	$469.1	$453.6
Sundry	$755.0	$474.6
Property & Equipment (net of depreciation)	$2,936.7	$2,114.6
Total	$7,142.8	$5,848.0
Liabilities and Equity		
Current Liabilities		
Short-term borrowings[1]	$1,239.5	$134.0
Accounts payable	$259.9	$196.2
Employee compensation	$367.7	$290.9
Dividends payable	$143.8	$115.5
Other liabilities	$406.7	$323.1
Income taxes payable	$400.0	$269.1
Total current liabilities	$2,817.6	$1,328.8
Long-term debt	$277.0	$269.5
Deferred income taxes	$351.2	$300.4
Other liabilities	$229.5	$192.2
Shareholders' Equity		
Common stock	$177.6	$176.8
Retained earnings	$4,548.7	$4,065.4
Loan to ESOP	($109.9)	($122.9)
Currency adjustments	$28.6	($53.9)
Less common shares in treasury	($1,177.5)	($308.3)
Total	$7,142.8	$5,848.0

Source: Eli Lilly and Company, 1990 Annual Report

[1] The 1990 increase in short term borrowing was directly related to a special $1 billion share-and-warrant repurchase program announced and completed in 1990 as part of the terms associated with Lilly's earlier acquisition of Hybritech.

population was 65 or older, up by more than 10 million people since 1950, and other developed countries showed similar trends. Typically, people over 65 required three or four times more medical support than younger people. In addition, developments in medical technology, including

Exhibit 8.1B   Income Statement and Selected Ratios, year ending December 31
               ($ in millions)

Income Statement

	1990	1989	1988
Net Sales	$5,191.6	$4,175.6	$3,607.4
Cost of Sales	$1,523.3	$1,255.8	$1,125.3
Research and development	$702.7	$605.4	$511.6
Marketing and administrative	$1,426.2	$1,149.6	$1,019.5
	$3,652.2	$3,010.8	$2,656.4
Operating income	$1,539.4	$1,164.8	$951.0
Other income (net)	$59.6	$165.1	$129.7
Income before taxes	$1,599.0	$1,329.9	$1,080.7
Income taxes	$471.7	$390.4	$319.7
Net Income	$1,127.3	$939.5	$761.0

Selected Financial Ratios and Other Data

	1990	1989	1988
Net income (% of sales)	21.7	22.5	21.1
R&D (% of sales)	13.5	14.5	14.2
Return on shareholders equity (%)	31.2	26.9	24.3
Return on assets (%)	17.5	17.0	14.8
Long-term debt (% of equity)	8.0	7.2	12.0
Number of employees	29,900	28,200	26,700
Net sales per employee (thousands)	$173.6	$148.1	$135.1
Net income per employee (thousands)	$37.7	$33.3	$28.5
Capital Expenditures	$1,007.3	$554.5	$372.1
Earnings per share	$3.90	$3.20	$2.67

Source: Eli Lilly and Company, 1990 Annual Report

recombinant DNA and monoclonal antibodies, were yielding entirely new
approaches to diagnosis and treatment and were expected to produce a
mounting flow of new products.

Lilly's major competitors in North America included Merck, Bristol
Myers-Squibb, American Home Products, Johnson and Johnson, and
Pfizer. Worldwide, the largest non-American firms were European, includ-
ing Ciba-Geigy, Hoechst, Glaxo, Bayer, and SmithKline-Beecham. Most of
these had enjoyed growth rates comparable to or better than Lilly's.
United States-based firms accounted for 42% of world sales in 1990.

Companies in the pharmaceutical industry vied to be first to market,
especially when another firm was working on a similar product.
Competitors had a minimum two years' notice of imminent new drugs,

because New Drug Applications (NDAs) filed with the Food and Drug Authority took at least that long to gain an approval status. In addition, the first years of a drug's life often determined its long-term success. If a company could establish its product firmly in the minds of doctors before another hits the market, the follow-on products would have a more difficult product launch. Moreover, maintaining a reputation as industry leader was vital to attracting people, as well as to winning the confidence of doctors and establishing credibility in academia and in government circles. The key was to be seen as consistently producing quality products and undertaking leading-edge research.

Companies also competed vigorously with sales calls to doctors. In the 1980s, the number of pharmaceutical sales representatives employed by U.S. companies increased by 50%. Some companies maintained three or four sales teams in each region, so that each product could be fully represented to physicians. Pharmaceutical sales representatives often were highly trained; many were licensed pharmacists. Drug companies, however, rarely competed on price, except occasionally when confronted with generic substitutes.

Firms specialized in different kinds of drugs, or in different therapeutic classes, which allowed for some segmentation of the industry and reduced the threat of price competition. Lilly, for example, concentrated on insulin and antibiotics. This enabled it to develop strong links with particular universities and other centers of research. Specialization also improved the chance that new drugs in that therapeutic group would be widely accepted.

Industry Trends in the 1980s

Along with higher sales and profits, the 1980s brought important changes in the competitive environment facing Lilly and other pharmaceutical companies. Many at Lilly felt that the company's response to these shifts could determine its fate in coming years.

Globalization

Increasingly affluent—and aging—populations in the developed countries meant new customers for health care providers. National differences in health care markets were disappearing as most major medical problems were found worldwide. In addition, government regulators were beginning to communicate and coordinate their evaluation procedures. The European Community, for example, was developing an application procedure that would accelerate approval in European national markets. While this trend could expand the number of buyers, falling trade barriers could reduce prices to the lowest levels in Europe.

Rising development costs also spurred many pharmaceutical companies to seek larger markets. Complicated government approval and testing procedures drove up the cost of drug development. At the end of the 1980s, companies needed 8 to 12 years between discovery of a compound and the launch date of a commercial product. The number of patient trials required prior to FDA release for a typical drug had risen from 1,500 in 1980 to 10,000 in 1990. Average development costs per product had risen to an estimated $250 million, which included the considerable research and overhead outlays for the thousands of compounds that did **not** make it to the market.

Slower Rates of Innovation

By the mid-1980s, only one-third as many new products were introduced each year as had been during the 1950s. Although stricter regulatory requirements were partly responsible, some people argued that the pace of innovation had slowed as researchers found it increasingly difficult to identify promising new drugs. Industry experts estimated that only one of every 5,000 to 10,000 new chemical compounds discovered by researchers ever became a commercial product.

Government Involvement

In the 1990s, two forces seemed likely to push prices and profits lower. First, governments were becoming more interventionist. By 1991, the United States was one of only a few developed countries that did not significantly intervene in the free market system. Escalating medical costs in many countries sparked new calls for cost containment. Price controls, restrictive reimbursement schemes, managed health care programs, and greater government involvement in medical and pharmaceutical reimbursement, especially for the elderly, poor, and uninsured, threatened to squeeze margins. In 1991, half of U.S. prescription users had part of their costs paid by a third party, up from only 25% five years earlier.

At the same time, the public in many countries was demanding higher standards of environmental and product safety. Governments insisted on ever-tighter systems to prevent environmental contamination and reduce the risk of dangerous or contaminated drugs reaching consumers. In the United States, Food and Drug Administration (FDA) officials had to approve any change to the manufacturing process that might affect the product. In order to meet increasingly stringent regulatory requirements, drug companies were investing heavily on new capital equipment. In 1990, for example, Eli Lilly spent slightly over $1 billion on capital expenditures, an amount that exceeded that year's spending on R&D.

Meeting these new standards often required major investments. In August 1989, the FDA inspected one of Lilly's tablet and capsule manufacturing facilities at Indianapolis and mandated a substantial overhaul of operating procedures and documentation systems. Lilly estimated that several hundred new employees and over $70 million of capital expenditures had been needed to ensure that the new requirements were met throughout the company.

Shorter Product Lifecycle

The second force threatening to hold down prices was intensifying competition from generic drugs introduced after patents expired. In 1984, the U.S. Congress passed the Drug Price Competition and Patent Restoration Act, which enabled generic manufacturers to gain accelerated approval for their products; generic copies of many drugs could now be made available almost literally on the day the patent expired, depending upon how long the approval process for particular drugs had taken. In 1990, patents expired on drugs with annual worldwide sales of about $363 million. In 1991, $541 million worth of sales would go off patent, and in 1992 and 1993, the figures were expected to rise to $1.9 billion and $2.6 billion, respectively. Major generic competitors included Abbott Laboratories, Warner-Lambert, and American Cyanamid, as well as numerous smaller firms.

Patents ran from the date of issue, which preceded much of the approval process, and came some years before market launch. Therefore, the profit secured from new drugs was, even more than in the past, a function of how long firms could fully harvest their patents. Speed to market and manufacturing ramp-up could be critical to extending that period. Moreover, most companies could charge higher prices during the initial years of their patents, when they often faced little real competition.

These trends, coupled with more sophisticated and complex manufacturing processes, had increased the minimum-efficient scale of a new bulk active ingredient plant (the initial bulk material production step in most pharmaceutical products). Company officials estimated that the average capital commitment needed for a new bulk chemical site had increased from $200 million to $400 million during the 1980s. Moreover, the time line for building such a plant was lengthened by two years. It was estimated that these trends would continue to escalate in the 1990s and beyond.

Creating Pharmaceutical Products and Processes

The development of a new drug generally began with the discovery of a chemical compound in the company's medicinal chemistry laboratories (See Exhibit 8.2 for a typical schedule of development tasks). If scientists had sufficient experimental data to suggest the compound might be both safe and effective against a particular disease, the company would launch a full scale development effort. Initially, this involved experimental tests conducted only on animals. If animal derived data was promising, the drug would then undergo three phases of clinical trials in humans. Phase

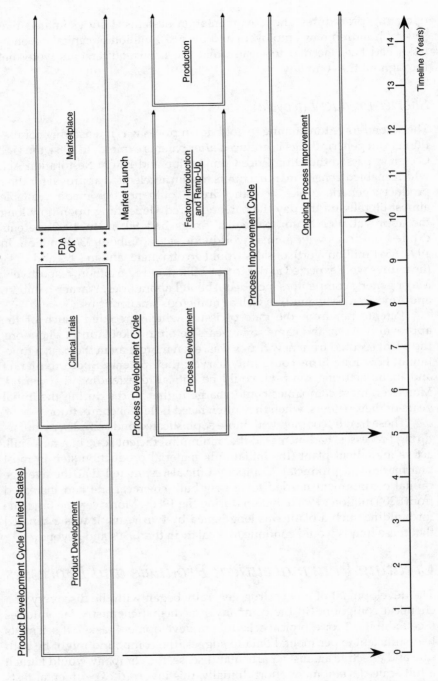

Exhibit 8.2 New Product and Process Development

I trials tested whether the drug was safe for humans at recommended dosages levels. Phase II attempted to demonstrate whether the drug actually worked for the application claimed for it. Phase III, typically the longest and most expensive set of clinical trials, simultaneously tested safety and efficacy of the drug, more thoroughly and in larger patient populations than the first two phases. At the end of Phase III, the company would file a New Drug Application (NDA) with the United States Food and Drug Administration (FDA).[1] The NDA was a voluminous document containing extensive data on the drug's safety and efficacy, as well as a thorough description and analysis of the manufacturing processes which would be used to produce both the drug substance (the chemical active ingredient) and the final dosage form of the product (e.g. tablet, capsule, liquid, etc.). The company could begin marketing the drug in the United States only after NDA received approval from the FDA.

Developing a Production Process for the Active Ingredient

An integral part of bringing a new drug to market was developing a production process to manufacture the active ingredient contained in the drug. The first step in developing the process was to figure out the sequence of chemical reactions required to synthesize the particular compound from a set of starting materials. There were normally many different possible routes for making a given compound and it was the job of the company's scientists in the Process Research group located in Indianapolis to identify the alternatives and to determine which ones might be viable for production. Process researchers generally started by deriving (through theory) a large set of alternative synthetic routes. The routes which looked most promising on paper were then selected for further testing, first in small scale laboratory equipment and later in the unit's pilot plant.[2] The Process Research unit was also responsible for supplying initial supplies of product for clinical trials. At the very beginning, small quantities were produced in the laboratories, but as clinical trials progressed and the requisite quantities increased, production would switch to its pilot plant.

At some stage of the project, when the quantities required to supply clinical trials would exceed the capacity of the pilot plant at Indianapolis, the process would be transferred to the Process Development group in Tippecanoe (about two hours from Indianapolis). Although the Process Research group would have designed the basic process and had shown it to be technically feasible by the time of this hand-over, the process was

---

[1] If the company wanted to market a drug outside the United States, it had to file a similar application with a similar regulatory agency in each country.

[2] The Chemical Research group's pilot plant contained vessels that were approximately 1/10 the size of commercial scale equipment.

normally a long way from being commercially viable. It was Tippecanoe's job to further refine the process, improve the yields, and adapt it to the requirements of the large scale commercial manufacturing environment. This involved such activities as optimizing reaction conditions, combining chemical steps, selecting reagents and solvents, designing new equipment (if necessary), and designing a process for handling waste by-products from the process. Process Development at Tippecanoe was also responsible for scaling-up the process to demonstrate that it would operate in a predictable and economic manner once transferred into commercial manufacturing. Scaling-up a chemical process was not always straightforward. For example, a process which worked perfectly well at small scale might not work at all when run in large scale vessels. It was the job of Process Development to identify and solve the underlying causes of scale-up problems. In most instances, scale-up problems could be overcome through small changes in the process. Occasionally, however, an entirely new process design would be required. On these occasions, chemists from Process Research group would become involved once again in the project and work jointly with colleagues in Tippecanoe to find an alternative approach to synthesizing the molecule. Since the NDA could not be filed without a well-defined process, scale-up problems arising late in the development cycle could potentially delay an NDA filing and the ultimate launch date of the new drug.

Once large scale manufacturability was demonstrated, the process would be transferred to one of the company's bulk chemical manufacturing sites. Lilly manufacturing facilities were located around the world (Exhibit 8.3 shows the location of Lilly's bulk chemical plants as well as the main fill and finish operations). Location decisions were heavily influenced by availability of technical staff, infrastructure (e.g. electricity, water, and other utilities), and tax incentives. To facilitate technology transfer, new products were normally manufactured at the company's bulk chemical plant in Tippecanoe, Indiana. Plants usually maintained their own technical services groups that were responsible for routine trouble-shooting and for making incremental improvements in yield. The Process Development group from Tippecanoe would also get involved in these efforts.

Although developing and scaling-up processes for new products was considered by many to be the most exciting work, improving existing manufacturing processes was equally important. In fact, most of Lilly's investments in process development were aimed at improving existing processes rather than developing processes for new products. Typical manufacturing improvements achieved after a process was operating in the plant included combining steps in the production sequence ("telescoping"), changing catalysts and solvents, developing additional process controls and control points, and refining parameter settings and operating procedures. Although such changes almost always required FDA approval, they could improve yields, reduce throughput times, eliminate

Exhibit 8.3 Manufacturing Plant Locations*

*Bulk chemical manufacturing facilities underlined. All others are fill and finish operations only.

costly inputs and solvent recycling requirements, and achieve significantly higher output, thereby reducing or eliminating the need for additional capital intensive production capacity.

Manufacturing at Lilly

During the 1980s, manufacturing priorities at Lilly had evolved through three phases. In the early and mid-1980s, the cost of an idle plant was a continuing topic of senior management discussion and steps were taken to balance capacity. In the second half of the 1980s, however, rising sales for several products (Humulin, Prozac, Ceclor, and others) shifted the focus to growth. Capital expenditures were boosted sharply to cope with burgeoning demand for the company's products. While much of this capacity was added at existing plant sites, the new capacity usually involved different processes or more advanced equipment and thus required major new investment and substantial conversion of older equipment and facilities.

In the late 1980s, management realized it had given manufacturing's contribution a relatively lower weight in corporate strategy. To remedy that deficiency, management looked at where and how capital investments had been made in the past and concluded that key manufacturing decisions had mostly been reactive; immediate needs had predominated over long-term coordinated planning. One result was that critical manufacturing technologies were spread across numerous smaller-scale plants, rather than concentrated at key world-scale plants. Another was that manufacturing had not been able to coordinate fully its activities with other functions. This was thought to have resulted in significant lost opportunities—both in developing manufacturing processes for new drugs and improving existing processes.

In late 1988, Lilly formed a Manufacturing Strategy Committee to help establish global manufacturing policies. The committee included top executives from manufacturing, engineering, R&D (development), marketing, finance, personnel, and international. The committee was to consider all aspects of manufacturing planning and their implications for the corporation as a whole, including human resource planning, process development, technology deployment, sourcing, capital investment, and vertical integration. (See Exhibit 8.4.)

By mid-1991, most committee members were confident that improvements in manufacturing could add substantially to the company's competitive position. To determine the best strategy, members agreed that they needed to sort out which options for improvement offered the greatest promise, long term as well as short term. It was decided that picking a

---

Exhibit 8.4   Manufacturing Strategy Committee (1988)

Manufacturing Vision

The Lilly manufacturing organization will provide a market advantage for the company by satisfying customers' requirements through recognized leadership and innovation in the worldwide development, production, and distribution of the highest quality products and services.

Manufacturing Strategy Committee Charter

- Serves as a focal point for all strategic manufacturing activities
- Coordinates, reviews, approves, and implements multi-year business planning
- Provides global direction for:

    —Capital investments
    —Human resources
    —Sourcing
    —Vertical integration
    —Technology management

Membership—All Senior Executives

Manufacturing
Engineering
R&D (Development)
Marketing
Finance
Personnel
International

---

central theme might provide the focus and leverage needed to energize Lilly's manufacturing strategy for at least the next five years.

Lilly's senior manufacturing managers were attracted to process development and improvement as a focal point for several reasons. *First,* if greater improvements in existing processes could be made, then the economic benefits of lower costs could be used to fund more new products and/or to maintain a strong market (and profit) position on mature products even after patent expiration.

Second, substantial process improvements achieved in the early years of a strong, new product would lead to two types of payoffs. One would be higher margins as a result of lower costs. The other would be lower capital investment requirements. Better technology might allow more flexibility, reduced cycle time, and/or improved yields, with important implications for the amount of capacity needed. Cook's staff had estimated that even a fraction of a percent increase in the overall yield of final bulk product in a typical manufacturing process could save $5 million of capital cost.

Even more important was the impact that process improvement could have on the total capital invested in a major new drug at its peak demand. Because market adoption for a new drug took time, even a very successful new product didn't reach its peak volume until five or six years following introduction. Anything that could be done in those initial years to develop a less capital intensive process technology or to increase the effective output of the existing process technology (by improving yields or cycle times, for example) could significantly reduce the peak year's investment in capacity.

In the bulk chemical processing stage of most drug products, the basic unit of capacity planning was the standard chemical "rig"—or tankage that could produce 2000 gallon batches. Although the cost of a new site varied widely, depending on the number of rigs to be included in that plant location, the type and complexity of the process technology to be employed, and so forth, Lilly estimated that an "average" new rig of capacity cost about $40 million, or $4 million per year if depreciated over 10 years. In recent years, some of Lilly's very successful drugs had required 4 to 6 rigs in their peak year. Thus, improvements that reduced the peak requirement by 20% to 30%—something that Cook's staff considered quite possible—would have a big payoff.

Third, if Lilly's process development group could increase its ability to fully participate in the early stages of product development, there could be substantial payoff. Not only could product development be steered toward more effective and efficient process technologies, but the product required for clinical tests could be produced more quickly. Since production would be done with a process closer to that to be used for volume manufacturing, the entire FDA approval process might be shortened and the new product approved for introduction sooner.

As the FDA began to act on its promise of shortening review times, there would be greater pressure on process development to complete its efforts sooner in order to be ready for product launch. In the pharmaceutical industry, getting a product onto the market even a few months sooner could be worth tens of millions of dollars in pretax profit.

Developing a Strategy for Process Technology

Traditionally, Lilly focused most of its process development resources on improving processes for products which were already on the market. For new products under development, process development investments were relatively modest and were generally concentrated during the later stages of Phase III clinical trials when it was much more certain the compound would eventually be marketed. The rationale for not investing more resources earlier in the development cycle was that 80% of the new compounds which entered Phase I clinical trials never made it to market. However, by Phase III trials the fall-out rate of product candidates generally fell to approximately 20%. Thus, it was believed that waiting until Phase III trials to invest significant amounts in process development offered the best economic pay-off.

While the payoff from developing and improving process technology was significant, the benefits would be neither easy to obtain nor cheap. Senior management would not be likely to commit substantial corporate resources to manufacturing process technology unless it could be convinced that the returns gained would be greater than those promised by other kinds of investment.

In order to provide the Manufacturing Strategy Committee with solid data and analyses, Cook decided to put together specific illustrations of each of the three types of process improvement efforts that had been identified. In addition, while he hoped that all three might eventually become central elements in Lilly's manufacturing strategy, he knew that senior management would probably initially agree to only one of them. By working through an illustration of each type, he thought the committee would be helped in deciding which to recommend.

As a starting point, he outlined what he considered the essence of each option:

Plan 1. *Increase the investment to improve the manufacturing processes for successful products that are already on the market.* These could be products facing price pressure from generics because of anticipated patent expiration, or products for which lower prices could win greater market share. A typical product which might benefit from this option would be a drug already on the market, with four years remaining before patent expiration.

Plan 2. *Commit to process improvement for a product (or products) that is not yet on the market, but which appears overwhelmingly likely to succeed.* This could be a product in Phase III clinicals which, based on Phases I and II clinicals, was estimated to have an 80% chance of being approved and commercially marketed. Such a product might have two more years of testing and approval before market introduction and then nine more years of patent protection after introduction.

Plan 3. *Commit substantial resources to a selected basket of products, very early in their development lifecycles.* This would entail investment in process development even before Phase I clinicals. It would be essential to invest in several products under this option, because only 20% of the product development projects put into Phase I ever got introduced to the market.

Because Lilly had never aggressively pursued these options, there was no historical data with which to evaluate and compare them directly. Recently, the company had retained an outside consulting firm to take a major Lilly product and estimate what the impact would have been if an aggressive process improvement effort had begun five years before market introduction. The results of this study enabled a systematic quantitative comparison of the three options.

The consultants started by gathering the actual data on a major successful new product introduced to the market in 1984 (see Exhibit 8.5). Lilly had patented the drug in 1974 and had started some process improvement efforts on that drug in 1979; for the next 12 years they committed approximately 5 full-time equivalents (FTEs) of process engineers per year to the endeavor. The consultants gathered data on the production volumes, cost of the process improvement effort, and unit costs for the product for each of those years. These data are illustrated in Exhibit 8.6 (shown as "current costs").

Next, the consultants conducted in-depth interviews and estimated the impact on costs of doubling that investment in process development during the first five years (1979–1984); in essence, they attempted to model Plan 2. The estimated cost of this effort and resulting unit cost improvements are shown in Exhibit 8.5 and included on the graph in Exhibit 8.6.

Cook also had asked his staff to work with the consultants in estimating the impact of increased, front-loaded process investment (Plan 2) on the total capital investment in capacity required to manufacture the same major product from 1979 out to the year 2000. The approach taken had been to estimate the productivity of a single rig assuming traditional process improvement levels, and then assuming more substantial, front-loaded process improvement efforts. Estimates for volume and process yields ("current" versus "Plan 2") are shown in Exhibit 8.7A.

To show the impact that front-loaded process improvement might have eventually on all of Lilly, the estimates for the drug were applied to

Exhibit 8.5 Process Development and Manufacturing Costs for a Major Drug (Market Launch 1984)

Current Costs vs. Estimates of Plans 1, 2, and 3

		Current Costs		**Plan 1**		**Plan 2**		**Plan 3**	
Year	Annual Volume (kg)*	Unit Cost ($/kg)**	Annual Process Dev. Expenses (1990 $m)	Unit Cost ($/kg)**	Annual Process Dev. Expenses (1990 $m)	Unit Cost ($/kg)**	Annual Process Dev. Expenses (1990 $m)	Unit Cost ($/kg)**	Annual Process Dev. Expenses (1990 $m)
1977	0		0.00		0.00		0.00		1.60
1978	0		0.00		0.00		0.00		1.60
1979	5,000	15,000	0.58	15,000	0.58	12,000	1.16	7,800	1.16
1980	1,000	14,000	0.58	14,000	0.58	10,320	1.16	7,150	1.16
1981	1,000	13,000	0.58	13,000	0.58	8,731	1.16	6,500	1.16
1982	1,000	12,000	0.58	12,000	0.58	7,334	1.16	5,850	1.16
1983	1,000	11,000	0.58	11,000	0.58	6,014	1.16	4,550	1.16
launch-1984	10,000	9,000	0.58	9,000	0.58	4,691	1.16	3,250	1.16
1985	10,000	7,000	0.58	6,790	1.16	3,283	0.58	2,600	0.58
1986	10,000	6,000	0.58	5,820	1.16	2,725	0.58	1,950	0.58
1987	10,000	5,000	0.58	4,850	1.16	2,180	0.58	1,300	0.58
1988	10,000	4,000	0.58	3,880	1.16	1,635	0.58	650	0.58
1989	25,000	3,000	0.58	2,910	1.16	1,096	0.58	520	0.58
1990	25,000	2,000	0.58	1,940	1.16	548	0.58	390	0.58

* *Includes pre-launch clinical supplies*
** *Unit costs exclude depreciation expense*

Exhibit 8.6 Pharmaceutical Unit Costs (based on Exhibit 5)

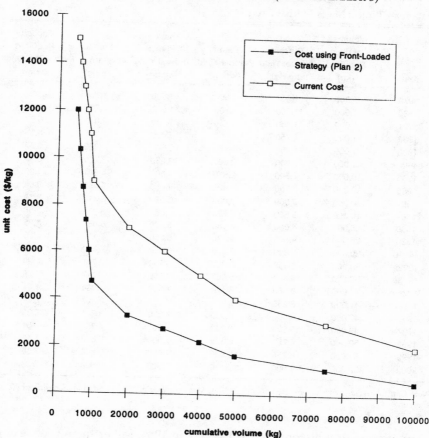

Lilly's total requirements for bulk chemicals from 1979 through 2000 for all products introduced in 1990 or before. These results are shown in Exhibit 8.7B.

Finally, Cook's staff brainstormed about what impact two other patterns of process improvement investment—those corresponding to Plans 1 and 3—might have. For Plan 1, which entailed increased investment in process development after market introduction, they concluded that adding five more process engineering FTEs in years one through five following market introduction (for the drug in Exhibit 8.5, this would be 1985–1989) would increase development costs by approximately $580,000 per year and reduce the production costs by 3% more as compared with the actual costs. For example, the unit cost per kilogram would be $6,790 in 1985, instead of $7,000. In addition, the anticipated yield improvement would increase the capacity of each rig by an additional 2% annually. Rig

Exhibit 8.7A   Capacity Planning and Investment in Bulk Chemical Facilities
Data for a Typical Major Market Drug

Year	Volumes of Drug Required (kg)	Current Annual Yield (kg/rig)	Plan 1 Annual Yield (kg/rig)	Plan 2 Annual Yield (kg/rig)	Plan 3 Annual Yield (kg/rig)	Capacity Required Current Yield (# rigs)
1979	5,000	1,500	1,500	1,500	1,725	3.33
1980	1,000	1,500	1,500	1,500	1,725	0.67
1981	1,000	1,750	1,750	1,750	2,013	0.57
1982	1,000	1,750	1,750	2,000	2,295	0.57
1983	1,000	1,750	1,750	2,500	2,869	0.57
1984—launch	1,000	2,000	2,000	3,250	3,730	0.50
1985	10,000	2,500	2,550	4,000	4,591	4.00
1986	10,000	2,750	2,805	4,750	5,452	3.64
1987	10,000	3,000	3,060	5,500	6,312	3.33
1988	10,000	3,500	3,570	6,000	6,886	2.86
1989	25,000	4,000	4,080	6,000	6,886	6.25
1990	25,000	4,500	4,590	6,250	7,173	5.56
1991e	30,000	5,000	5,100	6,500	7,460	6.00
1992e	33,000	5,250	5,355	6,750	7,747	6.29
1993e	36,000	5,750	5,865	6,750	7,747	6.26
1994e	40,000	6,000	6,120	7,000	8,034	6.67
1995e	44,000	6,250	6,375	7,250	8,321	7.04
1996e	47,000	6,500	6,630	7,250	8,321	7.23
1997e	49,000	6,500	6,630	7,250	8,321	7.54
1998e	50,000	6,750	6,885	7,500	8,608	7.41
1999e	51,000	6,750	6,885	7,500	8,608	7.56
2000e	52,000	7,000	7,140	7,500	8,608	7.43

Note: Capital investment for a new rig was $40 million. Assume capacity can be added in increments of less than one.

capacity would therefore be 2,550 kg/rig in 1985, rather than 2,500. Data on volumes and yields are shown in Exhibit 8.7A.

For Plan 3, their estimate assumed that, for the drug shown in Exhibit 8.5, process improvement would be staffed with 10 FTEs, at a cost of $1.6 million per year in 1977 and 1978. The pattern of increased, front-loaded investment would then be followed from 1979 onwards, assuming work on that drug was not terminated. This effort was estimated to lead to a 35% improvement in cost/kg in 1979 (as compared with the estimated costs achieved that year through the "front-loaded process investment" described in Plan 2) and 15% more output from each rig compared with the current output. For example, in 1979 yield per rig would increase to 1,725 kilograms and cost per rig would drop to $7,800. These cost and yield improvements would result from a better "start point" for that process (by the percentages estimated), and then the cost and yield curves would simply follow those estimated for the front-loaded (Plan 2) path shown in Exhibits 8.5, 8.6, and 8.7. If the drug was never launched, there would be

Exhibit 8.7B   Capacity Planning and Investment in Bulk Chemical Facilities
Data for All Lilly Pharmaceutical Manufacturing

Year	"Current" Yield (kgs)	Plan 2 Yield (kgs)	New Tank Volume Required (000s kg)	Projected Capacity Req'd "Current Yield" (# rigs)	Projected Capacity Req'd Plan 2 Yield (# rigs)
1979	1,500	1,500			
1980	1,500	1,500			
1981	1,750	1,750	50,000	29	29
1982	1,750	2,000	70,000	40	35
1983	1,750	2,500	80,000	46	32
1984	2,000	3,250	100,000	50	31
1985	2,500	4,000	130,000	52	33
1986	2,750	4,750	170,000	62	36
1987	3,000	5,500	210,000	70	38
1988	3,500	6,000	240,000	69	40
1989	4,000	6,000	270,000	68	45
1990	4,500	6,250	300,000	67	48
1991e	5,000	6,500	310,000	62	48
1992e	5,250	6,750	290,000	55	43
1993e	5,750	6,750	250,000	43	37
1994e	6,000	7,000	240,000	40	34
1995e	6,250	7,250	220,000	35	30
1996e	6,500	7,250	200,000	31	28
1997e	6,500	7,250	180,000	28	25
1998e	6,750	7,500	150,000	22	20
1999e	6,750	7,500	110,000	16	15
2000e	7,000	7,500	90,000	13	12

Note: Capital investment required for a new rig was $40 million.

no significant benefit—other than the experience gained—from having made that early process improvement investment.

With this information, the manufacturing management team was ready to evaluate each of the three illustrative options. The committee would then decide which one (or more) of these options should be incorporated into Cook's recommendations for Lilly's manufacturing strategy.

CHAPTER 9

Eli Lilly and Company

The Flexible Facility Decision (1993)

*I*N NOVEMBER 1993, Steve Mueller, manager of strategic facilities planning at Eli Lilly and Company, mulled over a difficult situation. Mueller had to make a recommendation to the company's Manufacturing Strategy Committee about the type of manufacturing facilities to construct for three new pharmaceutical products that the company expected to launch in 1996. The question about what *kind* of capacity to add for these three products had touched off a broad debate within the company about manufacturing strategy at Lilly.

In the past, Lilly had built a variety of types of facilities for new products. Some of these were dedicated to a single product, while others were designed to produce a specific set of products. Plants were considered "specialized" because they could only manufacture products for which they were specifically designed. Construction would begin as soon as the company was reasonably certain that the product would be commercialized, usually two to three years before product launch. The strategy had worked well in the past, but in the increasingly competitive marketplace of the 1990s, some believed that the company needed to revise its approach. Lilly's top management had set stringent goals to increase new product speed to market and to reduce the cost of manufacturing. The facilities strategy would have to be aligned with these goals.

One alternative to the current strategy was to build flexible manufacturing facilities which could accommodate virtually any of Lilly's new products. A facility of this type could suit all three of Lilly's new products and could serve as a "launch plant" for future new products. The concept was attractive for a number of reasons. In the past, there were cases in which the time required to design and build a specialized plant had delayed the launch of new products. Late changes in the process technol-

Professor Gary Pisano and Research Associate Sharon Rossi wrote this case as the basis for class discussion rather than to illustrate either effective or ineffective handling of an administrative situation. Some data have been disguised.

ogy for a particular product were also difficult to accommodate after specialized equipment was already installed. In addition, specialized plants entailed risk. Because plant construction had to begin well before the end of clinical testing, there was always the risk that the plant would be idle if there was a delay in the regulatory approval. Even worse, if a drug never made it to market, the plant would have to be retrofitted for another product. Nevertheless, the flexible plant strategy was not without its drawbacks. For example, flexible plants were much more costly to build and operate than specialized plants. While Mueller was attracted to the flexible plant concept, a number of questions raced through his mind. Could the higher capital costs of the flexible plant be justified on financial grounds in the increasingly competitive environment Lilly faced in the 1990s? How did it fit with new corporate goals of faster time to market and manufacturing cost reduction? Were there alternatives no one had yet identified? Steve Mueller wanted to have these questions answered in his own mind before making a recommendation to the Manufacturing Strategy Committee.

The Pharmaceutical Industry in 1993

In 1993, sales of ethical pharmaceuticals (prescription drugs) totaled $191 billion worldwide. While there were hundreds of companies in the industry, the top 15 competitors accounted for more than one-third of industry sales worldwide. In the United States, the world's single largest market, the four largest companies, Merck, Bristol-Myers Squibb, SmithKline Beecham, and Eli Lilly, accounted for 25% of the $50 billion in drug sales. Outside the United States, major markets included Japan (with an estimated 13% market share), Germany (6%), France (5%), Italy (5%), and the United Kingdom (3%).

One of the most critical activities for pharmaceutical companies was the discovery and development of novel therapeutic compounds. Companies' research laboratories typically screened thousands of chemical compounds in search of ones that had potential for treating or curing disease. Once a compound was shown to have therapeutic potential, it typically took a company eight to twelve years to develop it into a marketable product. This long process included first testing the product for biological activity and toxicity in the laboratory, testing for safety and efficacy in three phases of human clinical trials,[1] developing a process for commercially manufacturing the product, designing an appropriate dosage strength and formulation (i.e. tablet, capsule, liquid, etc.), and submitting the product for approval by federal regulatory agencies. In the United States, New Drug

---

[1]Phase I clinical trials determined the safety and pharmacological properties of a compound, by conducting tests on 20 or more healthy volunteers. Phase II clinical trials evaluated the effectiveness of a drug and isolated side effects. Phase II tests were typically conducted on several hundred (volunteer) patients. Phase III clinical trials measured the drug's effect on a large sample of patients (typically thousands of patients) over several years. Phase III trials determined the long-term side effects and provided information on the effectiveness of a range of doses administered to a mix of patients.

Applications (NDAs) were submitted to the Food and Drug Administration (FDA) for review. The fall-out rate of new drugs in development was extremely high. According to one study, of every 10,000 chemical compounds synthesized in the laboratory, only 10 could be expected to enter human clinical trials, and of these, only 1 would make it to market.[2]

In addition to the uncertainty about whether a product would be approved, there was uncertainty about the amount of a new drug that would be required for the market. Volume depended on a drug's potency and side-effect profile (which were determined during clinical studies) and market demand (which could only be estimated prior to launch). For a typical product, production volumes started relatively low in launch year, increased over time, and peaked at about the fifth year of commercial sales. A drug's 17 year patent usually ran out after the tenth year, so that sales tapered off as lower-priced generic substitutes became available.

Once on the market, pharmaceutical products were sold to hospitals, health maintenance organizations (HMOs), retail pharmacies, and physicians, each of which prescribed the drugs to patients. In hospital sales, the hospital pharmacy and therapeutics committee decided what products the hospital would stock. At HMOs, the buying decisions were similar, but these organizations were usually more cost-conscious. Three-fourths of the sales volume of ethical pharmaceuticals were sold to wholesale distributors. One-fourth of the volume was sold directly to hospitals, HMOs, retail pharmacies, and physicians.

Changes in the Industry Environment: "A New Marketplace"

The U.S. pharmaceutical industry had historically been one of the most profitable and fastest growing sectors in the U.S. economy. The average annual growth rate was 18% during the period 1982 through 1992, but was expected to slip to the 8% to 12% range in 1993 and beyond. Throughout the 1970s and 1980s, pharmaceutical company earnings and return-on-equity grew at a double-digit pace, fueled by many new product developments, strong patent protection, and pricing flexibility in the United States. Although sales volume declined by 15% since 1987, many companies were able to maintain revenue and earnings growth by raising prices.[3] Traditionally, average gross margins on products ranged from 70% to 85% in the U.S. and 60% to 70% in Europe.

[2]Sheck, L. (1984) "Success Rates in the U.S. Drug Development System," *Clinical Pharmacology and Therapeutics*, vol 36, no. 5: 573–583.

[3]Manufacturers of ethical pharmaceuticals received a 132% increase in prices (as measured by the Producer Price Index) during the 1980s, compared with the overall inflation rate of 22% for all finished consumer goods. (*Medical and Healthcare Marketplace Guide*, 1993 (9th edition), MLR Biomedical Information Services, p. 36)

Beginning in 1991, the pharmaceutical industry environment began to change. A set of new factors were at work that put pressure on drug margins from multiple directions: pricing flexibility was diminishing, the rate of innovation was slowing, competition within drug classes and from generic substitutes was growing. Investors acknowledged the negative impact of these changes, as pharmaceutical stock prices declined by 35% between 1991 and mid-1993.

Beginning in the late 1980s, the rate of new drug innovation began to slow throughout the industry. Even though most companies had dramatically increased the amount invested in R&D, development pipelines at companies were no longer deep with promising new compounds. Industry-wide, pharmaceutical companies were investing more in R&D— total R&D expenditures grew from $1.1 billion in 1975 to an estimated $12.6 billion in 1992—but the number of novel drug compounds launched during this period had risen only slightly.[4] Due to increasing regulatory requirements and the complexity of new compounds, the cost of developing drugs was also increasing. According to one study, the cost to develop a new drug was estimated to be $359 million in 1992 (taking into account the cost of the many compounds that never made it to market), up from $120 million 5 years earlier.[5]

The cost of manufacturing pharmaceuticals was also increasing. In the 1990s, manufacturing costs represented about 20% of sales, up from 10% in the early 1980s.[6] According to one forecast, the average cost of goods as a percentage of sales in the industry was expected to increase to 60% by the year 2000. There were several reasons for the escalating costs of manufacturing. In the United States, more stringent FDA regulations concerning product quality[7] required drug companies to invest in more sophisticated production equipment while Environmental Protection Agency (EPA) regulations were forcing them to invest in costly pollution control equipment and waste treatment facilities. Many new drugs were based on highly potent compounds and production of these required investment in costly containment facilities. In addition, as drug discovery and design technology advanced, drug researchers were able to synthesize more complex molecules in the laboratory; these complex molecules typically required more advanced production technology for large scale manufacturing. Finally, the increased cost of manufacturing was also attributed to under-utilization of facilities throughout the industry. These

---

[4]The number of new molecular entities (compounds with chemical structures different from those already on the market) approved by the FDA increased from 22 in 1984 to 26 in 1992, with a median of 23 compounds per year. (Standard & Poor's Industry Surveys, 9/9/93, p. H25.)

[5]*Pharmaceutical R&D: Costs, Risks, and Rewards*, U.S. Office of Technology Assessment, February 1993.

[6]"A Modern Smokestack Industry," *The Economist*, November 1992.

[7]Although regulations about quality were becoming more explicit, product quality was a "given" in this industry. All pharmaceutical companies' products were at least 99.8% pure.

increases were forcing companies to focus for the first time on the cost of manufacturing and the cost of manufacturing capacity.

Several other factors were at work that limited pharmaceutical companies' ability to recoup these escalating R&D and manufacturing costs through higher prices. One of these was government intervention. In 1993, the Clinton administration, in an attempt to curb the upwardly spiraling cost of health care, was proposing caps on price increases and caps on reimbursement for Medicare and Medicaid, measures which many people believed translated into federal price controls. It was uncertain how severely the federal policy would impact the drug industry, but it was clear that pricing flexibility would be diminished. By mid-1993, 17 of the leading U.S. pharmaceutical companies had voluntarily agreed to hold price increases on products to the Consumer Price Index.[8]

Potential government regulation was not the only force limiting pricing flexibility. Rapid growth of managed care providers was also having an impact. HMOs and other types of managed care networks represented an increasing share of health care providers, accounting for 64% of pharmaceutical purchases in 1992. This figure was expected to grow to 75% by 1995.[9] These and other large, centrally-administered customers were buying in bulk and often relied on formulary lists that limited purchases to only one or two drugs for a given condition; they were able to demand price discounts of as much as 60% from pharmaceutical companies. Third-party payers (including Medicare, Medicaid, and private insurers) were also gaining leverage on drug companies, as more and more included coverage of prescription drugs in their benefit plans. In 1991, 45% of prescription drug expenditures were funded by third-party payers, up from only 4% in 1960.[10]

Another factor pressuring drug margins was increased competition from the pharmaceutical companies themselves. More firms were working on developing similar compounds, making some therapeutic classes more crowded with potential substitutes. Mark Foglesong, executive director of manufacturing and facilities at Eli Lilly, described it this way: "Nowadays, everybody's playing in the same sandbox." The first drug of its kind to win approval set the market price and usually enjoyed a period of exclusivity before competing products were launched, but the period of exclusivity was shrinking. Foglesong added, "If you developed a blockbuster drug in the past, few firms were following on. Now, blockbusters have rapid followers." According to Peter Johnson, director of manufacturing planning at Eli Lilly,

> In the late '70s and early '80s, you could expect about five to six
> years of exclusivity before competitors launched a product with

---

[8]Outside the United States, drug prices were generally regulated by government. However, the evidence was mixed whether such regulation actually led to lower drug prices.

[9]*Medical and Healthcare Marketplace Guide* (MLR Biomedical Information Services) (9th edition) 1993, p. 34.

[10]Ibid.

similar therapeutic effects. That window has been cut in half. For example, with *Prozac* [an anti-depressant], we only had the market to ourselves for a little more than two years.

This shorter period of market exclusivity meant not only lower sales, but allowed less time for a company to recoup its R&D investment. Second entrants in the market for a particular indication, although branded and patented, had to discount their prices (34% on average) to attract market share. These "me-too" drugs had the effect of reducing prices across all products within the therapeutic class.

Additional pricing pressure was coming from the growing availability and use of generic drugs. Generic products were essentially copies of branded and patented products whose patents had expired. In the 1990s, more generic drugs were becoming available, eroding sales of branded and patented products. In 1993, roughly half of all prescriptions in the United States were filled generically, as compared with about 2% in 1980.[11] They were typically priced 30% to 60% lower than brand-name products. These lower prices could be charged because generic companies did not have to recoup R&D costs or sales and marketing expenses. In some cases, generics compelled pharmaceutical companies to drop their prices. Even when a company's own drug remained under patent protection, it could face price competition if a competitor's drug within the same therapeutic class came off patent and a generic version was introduced. It only took one generic entrant to subject the entire class of products to generic pricing pressure. Between 1993 and 1999, patents would expire on branded products with annual sales of $20 billion, and generic substitutes were expected to capture a significant share of these sales. There were few therapeutic areas free from generic competition. Analysts estimated that, by the year 2000, generic sales would triple to more than $12 billion, up from $4 billion in 1992.

As the period of market exclusivity decreased and price flexibility was reduced, companies began to understand the value of getting a new compound to market as quickly as possible, preferably before competitors. The value of getting a new drug to market one year sooner or one year later was equal to one year's net sales gained or lost. For a large market drug, one year's net sales could be as high as $175 million. To shrink time to market, companies were working on designing shorter clinical trials, the traditional "bottleneck" in the drug development process.

Eli Lilly and Company
Company Overview

Eli Lilly and Company, headquartered in Indianapolis, Indiana, developed, manufactured, and marketed pharmaceuticals, medical devices,

---

[11]Standard and Poor's Industry Surveys, 12/16/93, p. H4.

diagnostic products, and animal health products. Total company sales were $6.2 billion in 1992. Sales of ethical pharmaceuticals were $4.5 billion that year, ranking Lilly ninth in the world among drug companies, with a 2.5% market share. In the United States, Lilly ranked among the top six pharmaceutical companies. Two products, *Ceclor*, an antibiotic, and *Prozac*, an antidepressant, accounted for a large part of Lilly's pharmaceutical sales: *Ceclor* sold $950 million and *Prozac* sold $1.1 billion in 1992. Both were among the 15 biggest-selling drugs in the world. (See company financials in Exhibits 9.1A and 9.1B.)

In the 1990s, Eli Lilly was faced with competing in "a new marketplace." *Prozac* was the world's number-one selling anti-depressant in 1993. Although sales were growing steadily, recently introduced competing products, including Pfizer's *Zoloft* and SmithKline Beecham's *Paxil*, were beginning to capture an increasing share of the anti-depressant market. Lilly's *Ceclor* went off patent in 1992 and was surpassed in the same year by SmithKline Beecham's *Augmentin* as the world's leading anti-infective. All of the company's existing products had therapeutic substitutes on the market, and no "blockbuster" products were far along in the development pipeline. In 1993, Lilly's profit margins were 22%, but were expected to fall to 15% by 1996.[12]

Facing these fierce market conditions, management at Lilly believed that the company needed to better focus on serving the needs of customers and bringing new products to market faster, at lower cost. A set of company-wide goals were established concerning time to market and manufacturing costs. It typically took Lilly between 8 and 12 years to develop and launch a new drug. Several initiatives were underway to reduce development leadtime by as much as 50%. Another goal was to reduce manufacturing costs by 25%.

Some people within Lilly believed that the company would have to make major changes in how it developed and manufactured products in order to meet these targets. For example, to meet a product launch target in 50% less time, the company would have to get manufacturing facilities ready for production much earlier than it had in the past. Bill Smith, executive director of engineering, explained,

> To meet this new launch goal, we'll need to have our facilities ready much earlier. The reality of getting facilities ready fast means you almost have to start designing your production facility while the product is still very early in development. You also have to know what the manufacturing process is at this early stage.

[12]Nancy Hass, "Serious Medicine," *Financial World*, 11/9/93, p. 32.

Exhibit 9.1A Income Statement and Selected Ratios, year ending December 31 ($ in millions)

Income Statement

	1992	1991	1990	1989	1988
Net sales	6,167	5,726	5,192	4,176	3,607
Cost of goods sold	1,897	1,654	1,523	1,256	1,125
Research and development	925	767	703	605	512
Marketing and administrative	1,624	1,536	1,426	1,150	1,020
Restructuring/special charges	566	0	0	0	0
	5,012	3,957	3,652	3,011	2,656
Operating Income	1,156	1,768	1,539	1,165	951
Other income (net)	27	111	60	165	130
Income before tax	1,182	1,879	1,599	1,330	1,081
Income tax	355	565	472	390	320
Cumulative effect of acct'g changes	-119	0	0	0	0
Net income	709	1,315	1,127	940	761

Selected Financial Ratios and Other Data

	1992	1991	1990	1989	1988
Net income as % of sales	11.50%	23.00%	21.70%	22.50%	21.10%
R&D as % of sales	15.00%	13.40%	13.50%	14.50%	14.20%
Return on shareholders equity	14.40%	31.20%	31.20%	26.90%	24.30%
Return on assets	8.30%	17.20%	17.50%	17.00%	14.80%
Long-term debt as a % of equity	11.90%	8.00%	8.00%	7.20%	12.00%
Number of employees	32,200	30,800	29,500	27,800	26,300
Net sales per employee (000's)	$192	$186	$176	$150	$137
Net income per employee (000's)	$22	$43	$38	$34	$29
Capital expenditures	$913	$1,142	$1,007	$555	$372
Earnings per share	$2.41	$4.50	$3.90	$3.20	$2.67

Source: Eli Lilly and Company, 1992 Annual Report.

Mark Kamer, department head of process research and development, foresaw the need to change the way production processes were developed:

Under the new approach, we'll have to do a lot of development very early. We will also have to finalize the manufacturing process much earlier even if this means we wind up with less than optimal yields.

Meeting the 25% cost reduction goal also posed a challenge. Ed Smithwick, vice president of biochemical manufacturing, noted,

Exhibit 9.1B   Balance Sheet, year ending December 31 ($ in millions)

	1992	1991
Assets		
Current Assets		
Cash and short term equivalents	432.40	479.20
Short-term investments	295.90	303.20
Accounts receivable	898.60	834.70
Other receivables	152.50	291.30
Inventories	938.40	796.90
Prepaid expenses	288.20	234.00
Total current assets	3006.00	2939.30
Other Assets		
Investments (at cost)	242.50	276.20
Goodwill and intangibles	460.10	425.90
Sundry	892.10	874.70
Property and equipment (net)	4072.10	3782.50
Total Assets	8672.80	8298.60
Liabilities and Equity		
Current Liabilities		
Short term borrowings	591.20	690.20
Accounts payable	323.60	276.30
Employee compensation	272.80	295.10
Dividends payable	175.90	161.00
Other liabilities	575.30	410.30
Income taxes payable	459.80	439.10
Total current liabilities	2,398.60	2,272.00
Long-term debt	582.30	395.50
Deferred income taxes	169.70	415.60
Other liabilities	630.10	249.40
Shareholders' Equity		
Common stock	183.00	183.00
Additional paid-in capital	307.90	340.10
Retained earnings	4,743.10	4,693.00
Loan to ESOP	(263.90)	(286.20)
Currency adjustments	(70.20)	50.70
Less common shares in treasury	(7.80)	(14.50)
Total	8,672.80	8,298.60

Source: Eli Lilly and Company, 1992 Annual Report.

Twenty-five percent is a very big number considering that most of our costs of production are fixed. The only way to do it is to increase the volumetric efficiency of our existing plants so we can increase volumes without investing in more capacity.

Greg Davis, manager of finance, added:

We can nickel-and-dime for a 5% cost reduction. To make a 25% reduction, you really need a big jump in utilization. You either need to figure out how to make manufacturing capacity more productive or you need to reduce your asset base. Traditionally, this has not been a high priority for the company.

Lilly's Existing Operations Strategy
Facilities and Capacity

Eli Lilly operated 23 plants worldwide, including four plants in Indiana. Plants in the network were of two types: 1) bulk drug manufacturing facilities and 2) formulation, filling, and finishing. Bulk chemical manufacturing produced the active chemical and biochemical ingredients for a drug while filling and finishing operations formulated the active ingredients into a pill, capsule, liquid, or other form. Of the 23 plants in Lilly's network, eight plants were for bulk chemical manufacturing and fifteen plants were for filling and finishing operations. Fill and finish operations were geographically dispersed around the world. Operations were located this way in order to achieve local market presence and because filling and finishing specifications for a product varied by market.[13] In many countries, trade barriers made it more attractive to fill and finish domestically. In contrast, production of a particular active ingredient ("bulk drug") was usually concentrated into one or two plants, both to achieve economies of scale in large volume and because the active ingredients in a product did not vary by market. In bulk drug manufacturing, each plant contained several different production suites or facilities, each of which produced a specific product. Approximately 60% of Lilly's manufacturing assets were tied up in bulk facilities.

The process for making bulk drugs usually involved several different chemical steps, each of which took place in a different tank (sometimes called vessels or reactors). Ingredients were combined based on the chemical "recipe" in one tank, heated, mixed, or otherwise modified in the tank, then piped to another tank for another processing step, etc.[14] Tanks came in different sizes (typically 500 gallons to 4,000 gallons), with different controls, different temperature ranges, and different piping configurations.

In bulk drug production at Lilly, the standard unit of capacity was known as a "rig." A rig was the set of tanks and equipment required to process from start to finish 2,000 gallon batches. One of the challenges of capacity planning was that the output (in kilograms) of a rig varied by both the product and the particulars of the process technology. For example, for a very complex product, the amount of bulk drug produced from one rig might be only a few hundred kilograms. In contrast, another, much simpler product, might require only one rig to produce several thousand kilograms

[13]For example, a product might be formulated as a liquid in some markets and a topical cream in others.

[14]Production was not always continuous. In-process product was often stored in large drums between steps.

of bulk drug. Thus, in forecasting future capacity needs (in rigs), Facilities Planning had to take into account *both* the expected demand for a product (in kilograms) and the expected volumetric efficiency of the process (in kilograms per rig). In 1993, Lilly's products occupied about 12 rigs of capacity; by 2004, total capacity requirements were forecast to reach 46 rigs, assuming no changes in production technology and no process improvements. The smallest increment of capacity that could be built or added to an existing facility was one-quarter of a rig (or 500 gallon batches).

Bulk Drug Facilities Strategy

Historically, Lilly built a specialized facility or converted an existing one for each new product. In some cases, the company built multi-product facilities which were specialized for a specific set of products. All facilities, including single-product and multi-product plants, were for dedicated use, meaning they produced only those products for which they were designed. The type of equipment and size (capacity) of the facility were customized to the particular specifications of the product or set of products. For example, a single-product facility had specialized tanks, equipment, piping, and process controls that were configured to run the particular production process for a specific product. Because of the time and disruption to existing operations involved in adding physical capacity, new facilities were built to accommodate estimated peak demand for the product or set of products, which typically occurred five years after market launch. As a result, new facilities were typically underutilized for the first several years as product demand approached its peak. (See Exhibit 9.2.) In a multi-product plant, capacity could not be "swapped" among products; excess capacity for any one product could not be used to produce any other product.

A product stayed in its facility throughout its commercial life, which was usually about 15 years. In the past, demand for most products generally tapered off in about the twelfth year as both generic substitutes and newer, patented substitutes became available. As demand declined, the plant would again have excess capacity. At the end of the product's life, when Lilly would no longer manufacture the drug, the facility could be converted to produce another product. This changeover, referred to as a "retrofit," involved replacing tanks, equipment, piping, etc. and took about one year. During the changeover, the plant could not be used. The cost to retrofit was roughly equal to the cost to build a new facility.

In 1993, all of Eli Lilly's bulk drug commercial manufacturing plants were specialized. However, attempts had been made in the past to pursue a more flexible approach. Lilly had constructed some "generic" facilities that were not specialized for a product or set of products. Over time, though, these plants did not make production more flexible. According to Bill Smith,

Exhibit 9.2   Production Curve for a Specialized Manufacturing Facility

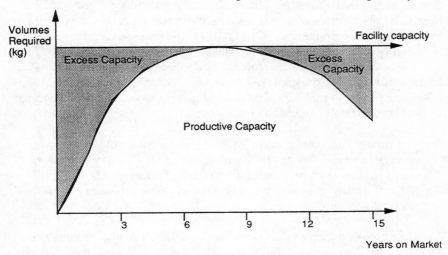

The flexible plant concept is really not new. In the past, we used to build plants that were capable of making a variety of products. But once a product was in, and volume began to increase, we would start to modify the equipment to improve yields, cycle times, and throughputs. What would start out as a flexible plant would gradually evolve into a specialized plant.

One of the chief concerns about the specialized facilities strategy was the time involved for design and construction. Because facilities were designed around specific products and processes, facilities engineering typically could not begin its work until process development activities were almost complete and the process technology was finalized. In addition, because a specialized facility could only manufacture one product, the company preferred not to start construction until there was a reasonably high probability that the product would make it to market. Unfortunately, this created severe time pressures in trying to launch new products. Art Morstadt, director of facilities delivery engineering, commented, "With the specialized plant, we're always under time pressure. There's always a crunch and facilities wind up on the critical path."

Bulk Drug Process Development

An integral part of bringing a new drug to market was developing a production process to manufacture the active ingredient. The challenges of process development had increased in recent years as molecules became more complex (and thus required more sophisticated process technology) and as the company sought to achieve large reductions in overall product development lead times. As Eldon Shuey, an executive director of Lilly Research Laboratories who was responsible for bulk process development in Indianapolis, commented: "Our goal is to get process development and availability of product for clinical trials off the critical path."

Lilly divided process development into three phases. (See Exhibit 9.5) In the earliest phase, the goal was to develop a crude process as quickly as possible in order to make the first several kilograms of bulk drug required to start clinical trials. As Eldon Shuey noted:

> The project can't move into Phase I clinical trials until we prepare enough material. We're rate limiting here. Our primary objective is to make enough material to get clinical trials started. Manufacturing cost and manufacturability are secondary issues we deal with later.

As a project progressed through clinical trials, it would become necessary to start developing a more manufacturable process. In the second phase of process development, chemists began to determine the sequence of chemical reactions which would be used in the manufacturing process. At the end of this second phase, the basic chemistry of the process would be "locked-down" (finalized) and process development activities would transfer from the Chemical Process Research group in Indianapolis to the Chemical Development group at Tippecanoe (located about two hours from Indianapolis). It was the job of the development group at Tippecanoe to undertake the final phase of development and refinement needed to make the process efficient and commercially viable at large scale. While Tippecanoe was a commercial manufacturing site, it also housed Lilly's larger scale pilot production facilities. This final stage of process development typically began during Phase III clinical trials and ended with the transfer of the process to the commercial manufacturing site.

Striving to reduce time-to-market, Lilly planned to significantly shorten the clinical timeline and would need to finalize the manufacturing process much earlier than it had in the past. In order to allow time for facilities to be designed and constructed, management expected that the final stage of process development would have to begin in Phase II clinical trials, instead of Phase III.

Sourcing

At Lilly, bulk chemicals requirements were met both through in-house production and through outsourcing. For a typical bulk drug, the company might outsource some of the steps of the chemical process, mostly those which were relatively simple and non-proprietary. Steps which were complex and proprietary (usually the final steps of the chemical process) were performed in-house.

Lilly considered its manufacturing capabilities to be an important competitive strength. The company believed that manufacturing in-house was critical for maximizing speed to market, assuring product quality, and guarding proprietary technology. It was also critical in impeding competitors. For example, *Ceclor,* one of Lilly's biggest-selling products, had to be produced in large volumes and required a very complex manufacturing process. The product went off-patent in 1992, but the company's expertise in manufacturing it gave Lilly an extra year of market exclusivity, since no generic manufacturer was capable of making it at a competitive price. With increasing excess chemical capacity in both the fine chemical industry and the pharmaceutical industry, Lilly was considering whether to outsource more of the process steps for older products.

Production Planning

In 1993, Lilly manufactured 13 different active ingredients in its bulk chemical and biochemical manufacturing facilities.[15] The scheduling of production took into account product demand, inventory levels, and production start-up and shut-down costs. The object of production scheduling was to optimize these three factors. For the most part, production runs were scheduled to maximize utilization. This meant long production runs, with interruptions only for scheduled maintenance. When a product was in the early or late years of its life, when sales volume was well below capacity, production runs might only be carried out during part of the year.

Because of the high gross margins of most products, however, it was absolutely critical that sufficient inventory be available. As one production scheduler described: "Although production scheduling seems quite complicated, it's really come down to a pretty simple dictum: Never stock out!" For this reason, the company carried a large inventory of finished bulk active ingredients.

Production scheduling was expected to get more challenging in the future for several reasons. In line with its new strategy, Lilly was hoping to dramatically increase the number of new products launched during the next decade. By the year 2004, the company could be producing as many as 37 active chemical ingredients. However, the nature of these products would be very different than those Lilly currently produced. Following a broad trend in the pharmaceutical industry, Lilly's new products were likely to be based on much more potent molecules. Because high potency molecules were used in much smaller dosage strengths, their production volumes were relatively low compared to Lilly's current products. At the same time, they actually consumed more manufacturing capacity per unit of output because they were typically more difficult to manufacture than

---

[15]Since each active ingredient could be formulated in a wide variety of ways (e.g. tablet, liquid, capsule, cream, ointment, etc.) and in a wide range of dosage strengths (e.g. 25 mg, 50 mg, 100 mg, etc.), the actual number of *final products* stocked by the company ran into the thousands.

older products. Because they were high value-added products, the high potency products of the future would be much more costly to keep in finished goods inventory.

The Manufacturing Facilities Decision

Alfatine, Betazine, and *Clorazine* were three products in development at Eli Lilly in 1993. Although there was still some uncertainty about whether they would receive FDA approval, the company anticipated launching the three new products in 1996. In 1990, Lilly's facilities planning group submitted a proposal to Steve Mueller describing the new facility for *Alfatine.* Mueller recalled:

> *Alfatine* was in Phase I clinical trials and the engineering group began to design a specialized plant for it. At this stage, the process development people began to warn us that the manufacturing process might change. Because of the *Loracarbef* project, they really hadn't had much time for *Alfatine.* As a result, the process was still very immature. We realized we needed to keep some flexibility in the design of the new facility. The need for manufacturing process flexibility for *Alfatine* led to broader discussion about whether we should be using flexible facilities for all our new products.

By the end of 1993, a final decision needed to be made regarding what *kind* of capacity to add for the three new products and beyond: *Should Lilly follow its current strategy of building specialized facilities or should flexible facilities be constructed?* To make this decision, Steve Mueller analyzed the input he had gotten from people in operations, finance, marketing, and facilities planning (shown in Exhibit 9.3), keeping in mind the importance of meeting the goals for a 50% shorter development cycle and a 25% reduction in costs. Mueller laid out two options and considered the costs and implications of each.

Option 1: Build One Specialized Facility Following the current strategy, Lilly would design and build one specialized facility for the three new products. In this plant, *Alfatine,* the largest-volume product, would have one full rig of capacity. *Betazine* and *Clorazine* would each have one-fourth rig of capacity, the minimum feasible scale for a facility.[16] All three products would remain in the facility throughout their 15 year lives. The total cost of building this three-product facility was estimated to be $37.5 million (Lilly depreciated manufacturing facilities over a 15 year period).

---

[16]Lilly also considered putting the new products into 3 single-product facilities, but because Betazine and Clorazine were small volume products, a single three-product was more economical. Three single-product facilities would have significantly higher operating costs than one multi-product family.

Exhibit 9.3 Manufacturing Facility Alternatives

OPTION 1: Specialized Facility

	Capacity in Rigs	Maximum Output in kilograms*	Construction Costs (millions)	Annual Operating Costs (millions)
Alfatine Capacity	1	16,000		
Betazine Capacity	0.25	4,000		
Clorazine Capacity	0.25	4,000		
Specialized Facility	1.5	24,000	$37.50	$6.80

OPTION 2: Flexible Facility

	Capacity in Rigs	Maximum Output in kilograms*	Construction Costs ($ millions)	Annual Operating Costs ($ millions)
Flexible Facility	3	14,625	$150.00	$9.48

*assuming average utilization (80% for specialized, 65% for flexible).

Operating costs for the facility were expected to be $6.8 million per year. See Exhibit 9.3 for a break-down of the capital and operating costs.

In the specialized facility, productivity per unit of capacity would be relatively high, averaging 16,000 kilograms of output per rig at 80% utilization. High productivity would occur because the plant was specifically designed and optimized for the set of products, resulting in better yields. Operators would become experienced in running the processes, resulting in fewer problems or batch failures. With dedicated equipment and operators, more learning would take place, so the plant would have a steeper experience curve. The absence of product changeovers would result in a smoother operation of processes overall. See Exhibit 9.4 for a schedule of demand and capacity.

However, building this type of facility would entail some risks. If any one of the products did not make it to market, part of the facility might have to be retrofitted to produce another product. If a manufacturing process was dramatically changed after construction had begun, a part of the facility might need to be redesigned or re-equipped to suit the new process. Since establishing the goal of 50% reduction in time-to-market, this risk was especially high. In order to meet the launch target, the facilities concept and design phase would have to begin about three months before final manufacturing processes were designed. (See Exhibit 9.5.) Construction would have to begin about 100 days before final product decisions were made. If the facility was not completed on schedule, a product launch could be delayed by weeks or months, costing millions of dollars in lost sales.

Exhibit 9.4 Ten-Year Projection for Demand and Manufacturing Capacity

Volumes Required Annually (bulk drug in kilograms)

	Year 1 1996	Year 2 1997	Year 3 1998	Year 4 1999	Year 5 2000	Year 6 2001	Year 7 2002	Year 8 2003	Year 9 2004	Year 10 2005
Alfatine	7,000	8,000	9,000	10,000	16,000	16,000	16,000	16,000	16,000	16,000
Betazine	2,500	2,700	3,000	3,100	4,000	4,000	4,000	4,000	4,000	4,000
Clorazine	500	500	750	750	1,000	1,000	1,000	1,000	1,000	1,000
Total	10,000	11,200	12,750	13,850	21,000	21,000	21,000	21,000	21,000	21,000

Capacity Under Option 1 versus Option 2 (in kilograms)*

	Year 1 1996	Year 2 1997	Year 3 1998	Year 4 1999	Year 5 2000	Year 6 2001	Year 7 2002	Year 8 2003	Year 9 2004	Year 10 2005
Option 1: Specialized	24,000	24,000	24,000	24,000	24,000	24,000	24,000	24,000	24,000	24,000
Option 2: Flexible**	14,625	14,625	14,625	14,625	14,625	14,625	14,625	14,625	14,625	14,625

Excess Capacity Under Option 1 versus Option 2 (in kilograms)

	Year 1 1996	Year 2 1997	Year 3 1998	Year 4 1999	Year 5 2000	Year 6 2001	Year 7 2002	Year 8 2003	Year 9 2004	Year 10 2005
Option 1: Specialized	14,000	12,800	11,250	10,150	3,000	3,000	3,000	3,000	3,000	3,000
Option 2: Flexible***	0	0	0	0	0	0	0	0	0	0

* Assumes average utilization (80% for specialized, 65% for flexible).
** Demand expected to exceed capacity in the flexible plant beginning in year 5, assuming no process yield improvements.
*** Flexible facility never has excess capacity since other products can be produced in it.

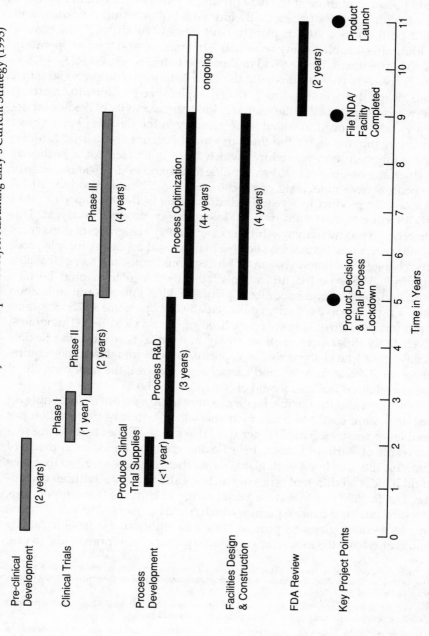

Exhibit 9.5 Sample Timeline for an 11-year Development Project Assuming Lilly's Current Strategy (1993)

202   STRATEGIC OPERATIONS

Option 2: Build One Flexible Facility Under this option, Lilly would build one flexible facility. Like the specialized plant, the flexible facility could produce all three of the new products. However, it would also have the capability to produce virtually any new bulk chemical product, and could be used as a launch plant for future new products.[17] The cost of building this flexible facility would be $150 million and annual operating costs were estimated to be $9.48 million. See Exhibits 9.3 and 9.4.

There were two reasons why the flexible facility would cost so much more (nearly three times as much) than the specialized facilities to construct. One reason was related to the relatively lower productivity of flexible capacity and thus the need to install more capacity in the flexible plant to meet volume requirements for the three products. Because specialized facilities used equipment and procedures which were optimized for a particular product, and because operators were able to develop in-depth knowledge of the process over time, a rig of specialized capacity could produce 20,000 kilograms of product in a year. In contrast, a rig of flexible capacity could only produce a maximum of 7,500 kilograms of product in a year. This difference in productivity was further exaggerated by significant differences in utilization rates. Because the flexible plant would produce multiple products, change-over time between products would consume some available capacity.[18] The expected utilization of the flexible plant would be 65% compared to 80% for a specialized plant.[19] Taking into account utilization rates, a rig of flexible capacity could actually only produce 4,875 kilograms of product per year, whereas a specialized rig would yield 16,000 kilograms. Given these differences in productivity and utilization rates, the flexible facility would need three rigs of capacity to meet initial volume requirements for *Alfatine*, *Betazine*, and *Clorazine*. In contrast, the total capacity of three specialized facilities would only require 1.5 rigs.

Not only did the flexible facility require more rigs, but each flexible rig was also more costly to build than specialized capacity ($50 million per flexible rig versus $25 million per specialized rig). Higher cost per rig was the result of various factors. In a flexible factory, tanks were made of complex alloys or lined with glass (rather than stainless steel) so that they could handle all different types of reactions and materials without corroding. The facility would have a wider range of controls (for temperature, pressure, etc.) and flexible piping, which could be changed to suit different process technologies and process flows. In addition, the flexible facility would also have to stock relatively exotic pieces of equipment, just in case

---

[17]A "market entry plant" or "launch plant" manufactured new products temporarily, typically for two to three years after launch. After this period of time, products were moved into their own dedicated manufacturing facilities.

[18]An average of four product campaigns would be run each year (each 11 weeks long), with 2 weeks of down time between each campaign for cleaning, repairs, and maintenance.

[19]However, the flexible plant's utilization rate would not vary with product life cycles as was the case for specialized plants. Once the flexible plant was operating, there was expected to be enough volume to keep it at 65% utilization.

they were needed for a particular process. Finally, the plant had to be designed with empty floor space so that equipment could be changed around or new pieces of equipment could be added without disrupting existing operations.

The flexible facility could produce *Betazine* and *Clorazine* for their entire product lives. *Alfatine* would be launched in the flexible plant, but demand for this product was expected to exceed the capacity of the flexible plant by 2001. Based on current demand and yield projections, *Alfatine* would require its own specialized one-rig plant in 2001. A decision could be made later whether to build a new plant, retrofit an old one, or keep the product in the flexible facility, based on actual demand and process yield improvements. If *Alfatine* did move to a specialized plant, other new products could be produced in the flexible facility. Subsequent products would be produced for two to three years in the flexible facility, then moved to specialized facilities as demand increased.[20] Forecasts indicated that there would be more than enough demand to fully utilize (up to 65%) the flexible facility.[21] In fact, if Lilly were to go with the flexible launch plant strategy, it would likely need to build several more flexible plants over the next 10 years to accommodate demand for new products. (See Exhibit 9.6.)

In spite of having lower yields and utilization, the flexible facility offered some significant advantages. Since a flexible facility was more adaptable, processes for making new products did not have to be finalized early in the concept and design phase of construction, as they did for a specialized plant. Mark Kamer commented, "The great thing about the flexible plant is that since design and construction of the facility are no longer issues, we can work on the process longer, without worrying about delaying the product launch."

Another advantage of the flexible plant was reduced lead-time for manufacturing new products. "The flexible plant takes facilities construction off the critical path," explained Art Morstadt, director of engineering facilities delivery. Although it would take 36 months to design and construct (the same as for a specialized plant), once the flexible plant was built, it could accommodate almost any new product without delay (other than the 2 week changeover/setup time). *Alfatine, Betazine,* and *Clorazine* would not get to market any sooner with the flexible plant, but subsequent new products could get to market one year earlier.

The flexible plant also offered the advantage of lower risk. If any of the three products failed in development, the plant decision was not jeopardized. The unutilized capacity could be allocated to any other new Lilly

[20]For each product that was transferred out of the flexible plant to a specialized facility, Lilly would incur costs of about $1 million for start-up, process validation, and source change registration with the FDA. Registration could take up to one year, so the specialized plant had to be ready in advance of starting commercial production. Process rework was not required for the transfer and process experience would not be lost.

[21]Even in the short-term, while volume for *Alfatine, Betazinel,* and *Clorazine* were increasing, the flexible plant's excess capacity could be absorbed by making some materials for Phase III clinical trials.

product, since it was flexible enough to accommodate almost all other processes.

Because the flexible plant offered benefits of lower risk, more time and freedom for process development and construction, and an extra year of sales on subsequent products, some people within Lilly believed that flexible plants were the ideal manufacturing strategy for the long term. "In the future, all of our plants should be more flexible," noted Morstadt.

Conclusion

Since the strategy of designing and building specialized plants had worked well in the past, Lilly had never before raised the question about what *kind* of capacity to add. Faced with a competitive new marketplace and stringent corporate goals for faster development and lower costs, many within Lilly thought that the current strategy had to change.

Steve Mueller thought over the situation. He knew many people within Lilly were attracted to the concept of flexibility, and he himself thought it offered a number of advantages. However, it was a complex decision, and one that would have implications for future product launches. "This decision is bigger than just these three products. It's not a one-shot deal. We're going to have many new product launches in the future and we need to decide if flexibility is the right strategy for all of these." Since product launches were deemed critical to Eli Lilly's future, Mueller wanted to think the issue over carefully.

CHAPTER 10

BMW: The 7-Series Project (A)

*A*s he accelerated past the security gates of BMW's Research and Engineering Center, Carl-Peter Forster, director of Prototype and Pilot Manufacturing, thought about the 7-series project meeting. It was June 12, 1991, exactly two years, eight months, and five days until the scheduled start of production of the completely redesigned 7-series luxury sedan. The project, code-named E-99, was reaching a critical milestone. Over the next several months, engineering prototypes[1] had to be designed, built and tested so that one last round of design revisions could be made in time for launch. Traditionally, BMW hand-built and assembled its prototype cars in its in-house prototype shop. The parts were carefully fabricated by highly skilled craftsmen in the company's model shops and by specialized outside vendors. Meticulous attention to detail resulted in prototype vehicles which very closely reflected the form and function that product designers had laid out in their drawings.

At today's meeting, however, Forster and the cockpit design team, headed by Dr. Hans Rathgeber, would decide whether to try a new process for building the cockpits[2] of the 7-series prototype vehicles (Exhibit 10.1). Under the new approach, prototype cockpit components would be fabricated by outside suppliers using more automated methods, more specialized tooling, and less skilled workers. A single supplier would then construct major subassemblies of the cockpit and ship these to BMW where they would be assembled into prototype vehicles on a pilot assembly line. Under existing practice, all assembly of prototype vehicles was done in the prototype shop.

Professor Gary Pisano prepared this case as the basis for class discussion rather than to illustrate either effective or ineffective handling of an administrative situation. Some data have been altered for purposes of confidentiality.

[1]A prototype was a full-scale, working model of the final product created during the development process.

[2]The cockpit of an automobile consisted of the dashboard, instrument panel, glove compartment, shift console between the driver and front passenger seat, trim components (such as the air conditioning grills), numerous ducts for the heating and air conditioning systems, conduits for wiring, and a supporting structure.

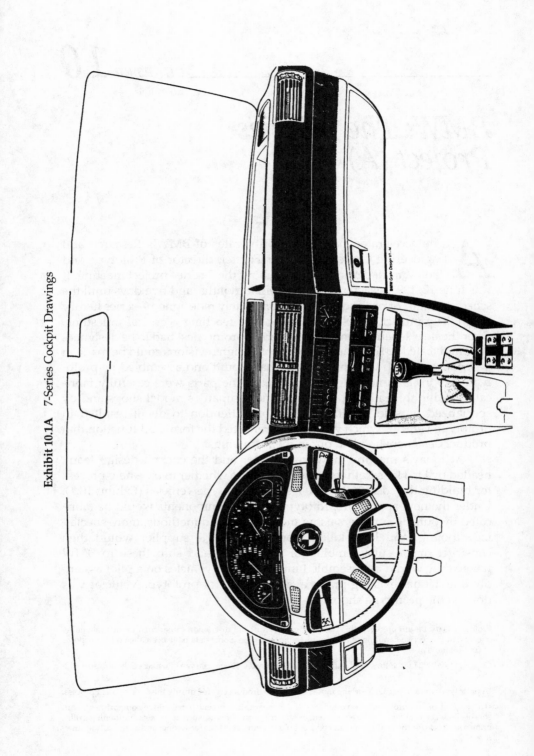

Exhibit 10.1A   7-Series Cockpit Drawings

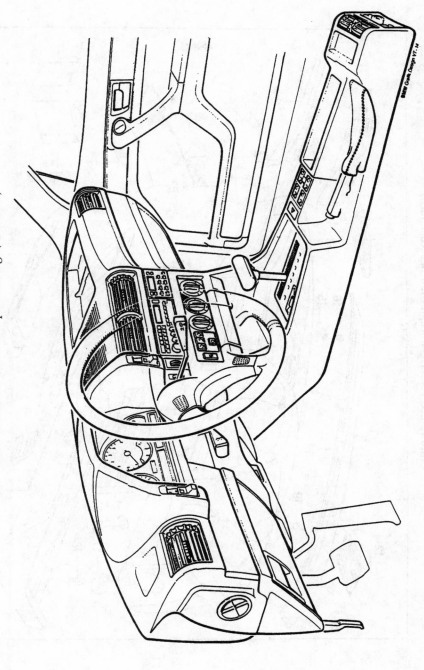

Exhibit 10.1B 7-Series Cockpit Drawings (continued)

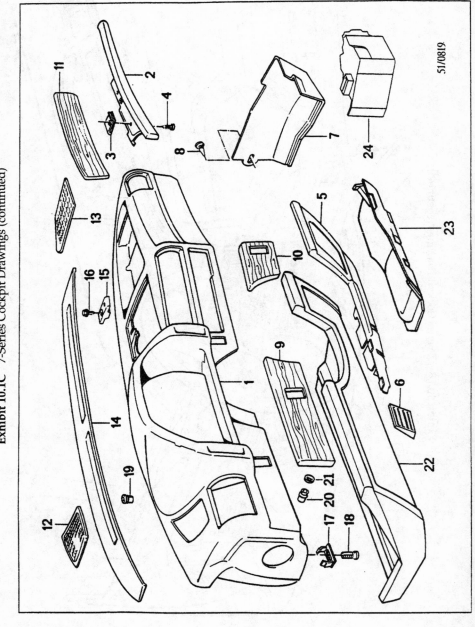

Exhibit 10.1C 7-Series Cockpit Drawings (continued)

51/0819.

Forster, Rathgeber, and others involved in the interior design of the 7-series believed that the new approach, despite its higher tooling costs and longer lead times, could drastically reduce the problems associated with bringing a new model into production and have a dramatic impact on product quality at launch. Yet, they knew there were risks. The redesigned 7-series would be a particularly visible new product for BMW. To be launched for the 1994 model year, the new 7-series was a "flagship" product and its success or failure would have enormous impact on BMW's image and standing in the increasingly competitive luxury car market.

Background

Bayerische Motoren Werke (BMW), founded in 1916 by Gustav Otto, the son of a pioneer of the internal combustion engine, began as a producer of aircraft engines.[3] In 1917, BMW registered its trademark blue and white rotating propeller still used today. In the late 1920s, BMW began producing cars. Sport racing competition enabled BMW's engineers to experiment with aerodynamic body styling, new suspension systems, high-performance engines, and numerous other automotive innovations. Through success on the race track and the introduction of several trend setting sporty roadsters from the 1930s to the 1950s, BMW built a reputation for high-performance engineering.

Despite these successes, BMW remained a relatively small specialist, more admired for its engineering and technical prowess than its commercial success. In 1959, BMW was so weak financially that it was nearly bought out by its much larger rival, Daimler-Benz. Instead, BMW was rescued by a $1 million investment from the Quandt family, who since that time was the majority shareholder. In 1966, with its larger, more sophisticated 02 series, BMW created a new automobile market segment that combined the high-performance engineering of sporty roadsters with the size, styling, and comfort of the European luxury sedan. This combination set BMW apart from its competitors and was largely responsible for the company's move into the world league of car companies in the 1970s.

From 1970 to 1990, sales volume (in DM) grew by a factor of 15, car production increased from 160,000 units per year to slightly over 500,000 units/year, and the work force trebled. Since 1959, BMW earned a profit every year; between 1980 and 1990, return on shareholders equity annually averaged 21%, and 1990 profits were expected to reach a record DM 700 million (Exhibit 10.2).

During this period the company also broke with its traditional strategy of following Mercedes' lead in pricing and styling. According to Claus Luthe, BMW's former chief stylist, "We had to get away from the boxy

---

[3]The company was originally founded under the name Bavarian Aircraft Works. The name was changed to Bavarian Motor Works in 1917 after Bavarian Aircraft Works merger with Rapp Motor Works.

Exhibit 10.2   BMW Selected Financial And Operating Data

BMW Group	1989	1990 (est.)
Production (units)		
Automobiles	511,476	519,660
Motorcycles	25,761	31,589
Automobile Sales (units)		
Domestic	190,363	200,418
Foreign	332,658	325,448
Automobile Sales (DM thousand)	20,855,144	20,885,802
Automobile Sales (units, by model line)		
3-series	270,500	265,400
5-series	202,300	211,600
7-series	50,200	48,900
Income Statement (DM, thousand)		
Net Sales	**26,515,351**	**27,177,615**
Increase in Inventories	124,257	462,167
Total Value of Production	**26,639,608**	**27,639,782**
Other Operating Income	775,420	986,124
Income from Investments in Subsidiaries	7,192	3,920
Interest Income	146,116	319,079
Total Revenues	**27,568,336**	**28,948,905**
Expenditures on Materials	15,280,148	15,749,312
Expenditures on Personnel	4,700,120	5,313,123
Depreciation	1,548,800	1,777,981
Other Operating Expenditures	4,346,140	4,261,297
Interest Expenditure	131,938	183,664
Net Income Before Taxes	**1,561,190**	**1,663,528**
Taxes	1,003,128	967,665
Net Income	**558,062**	**695,863**

look of our cars and create a model that people would want to look at and caress."[4]

In addition to styling, heavy investments in R&D put the company at the leading edge of technology in such critical areas as engines, pollution control, safety, chassis design, suspension systems, automotive electronics,

[4]*Forbes,* "The Company Behind the Image," November 27, 1989, p. 92.

and transmissions. Few other car companies in the world could match BMW in performance, handling, and safety; automotive critics regularly voted BMW's models the best cars in the world in their respective class. Juxtaposed to this background of advanced technology was a culture that prized the craft traditions of Europe. Skilled workers and technicians were still required to go through a rigorous three-year apprenticeship. BMW's chairman, Eberhard von Kuenheim, was proud of the apprenticeship program and the people it produced: "They think in hundredths of milli-meters. That's the foundation of our quality."[5]

Germany, the most important geographical market for BMW, accounting for over one-third of the company's total sales, was also where BMW competed head-to-head with the much larger Daimler-Benz in what many observers consider the most demanding and sophisticated luxury car market in the world. In Germany, BMW held a 7% share of the total market, and ranked fifth behind Mercedes, Volkswagen-Audi, Ford, and Opel. Over 70% of BMW's sales came from Europe, with the remaining 30% coming largely from the United States and Japan (where BMW was the leading automobile import).

BMW's three main assembly plants were in Germany in Munich, Dingolfing, and in Regensburg, its newest and most advanced plant. The main components plant was located in the German town of Landshut. Over 70% of BMW's suppliers were also in Germany. The company's engine plant was located in Steyr, Austria. All functions required to bring a car from concept to pilot production were housed in BMW's brand-new Research and Engineering Center in Munich. Completed early in 1990, it replaced 40 previous facilities scattered around that city.

Luxury Car Market

While BMW was only the world's 16th largest car maker, and held only a 1.5% share of the world market (Exhibit 10.3), it was a leading player in the luxury car segment,[6] where approximately one out of every 10 of the five million cars sold annually was a BMW. Companies in this market competed on tangible product characteristics like acceleration, handling, and comfort, and intangible ones like perceived quality and image. With some cars at the highest end of the luxury market retailing for prices in excess of $100,000, cost was clearly a less important factor in this market. In the United States, the fastest growing segment of the luxury car market was the $20,000 to $40,000 range. Between 1990 and 1995, this U.S. segment was expected to double in size to more than 400,000 sales per year. Exhibit 10.4 lists BMW's main model lines with corresponding competitive models.

[5]*Business Week* (Special Issue on Quality, January 1991) "Grill-to-Grill with Japan," p. 39.

[6]Generally the luxury segment was defined as the market for automobiles retailing above $20,000.

Exhibit 10.3 The World's Ten Largest Passenger Vehicle
Manufacturers in 1989

Rank	Company	Passenger Vehicle Production (units)[a]
1	General Motors	3,213,752
2	Toyota	3,055,101
3	Ford	1,677,081
4	Nissan	1,972,508
5	Peugeot	1,962,348
6	Fiat	1,958,953
7	Volkswagen	1,691,843
8	Renault	1,446,669
9	Honda	1,155,683
10	Chrysler	915,899

Source: *1990 Birds-Eye View of the Automobile Industry.* Toyota Motor Company.
[a]Figures for Peugeot, Volkswagen, and Fiat include total group production of
vehicles. The others include only production taking place in home country.

By the late 1980s, new competitors had begun to challenge the
European high-end producers. In 1986, Honda introduced its luxury car
brand, the Acura, followed in 1989 by Toyota (Lexus) and Nissan (Infiniti).
While their entry into this market seemed a natural progression, many
industry experts, including people within the European auto industry,
were skeptical: few believed that marques like Honda and Toyota, while
highly respected in the high-volume car segment, could compete with
Mercedes, BMW, or Jaguar in prestige. In fact, the image of Japanese cars
as highly reliable but not sophisticated was viewed as one of the biggest
barriers to entry. In 1989, BMW's von Kuenheim commented: "Building
luxury cars and a luxury image requires more than scissors and glue. Just
because Toyota and Nissan are introducing cars that *look* like BMW and
Mercedes doesn't mean they will succeed as we have."[7]

By spring 1990, however, clear signs indicated that the Japanese
would be serious contenders. Honda's Acura and Toyota's Lexus were
consistently topping the J.D. Power Surveys on Customer Satisfaction and
Initial Quality (Exhibit 10.5). Moreover the Japanese producers had
rapidly closed the performance gap with leading European makers.
Automobile critics were hailing the overall smoothness and comfort of
Lexus' ride as equal to and in some cases better than European models. At
the same time, Japanese luxury cars were being priced substantially below
competitive European models.

Even more disturbing to the European producers were Japanese
inroads into the increasingly competitive U.S. luxury market: between
1986 and 1989, their share jumped from 1.9% to 11.8%, while European

[7]*Forbes*, "The Company Behind the Image," November 27, 1989, p. 89.

Exhibit 10.4   BMW's Model Lines and Selected Competitors

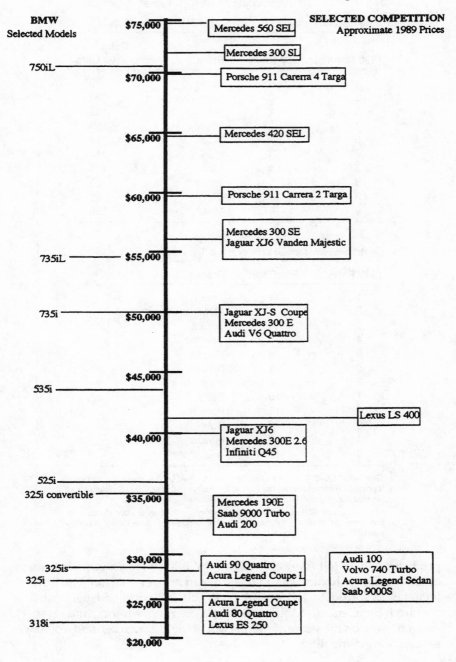

BMW
Selected Models

SELECTED COMPETITION
Approximate 1989 Prices

$75,000 — Mercedes 560 SEL

Mercedes 300 SL

750iL

$70,000 — Porsche 911 Carerra 4 Targa

$65,000 — Mercedes 420 SEL

$60,000 — Porsche 911 Carrera 2 Targa

Mercedes 300 SE
Jaguar XJ6 Vanden Majestic

735iL — $55,000

735i — $50,000   Jaguar XJ-S Coupe
Mercedes 300 E
Audi V6 Quattro

$45,000

535i

Lexus LS 400

$40,000   Jaguar XJ6
Mercedes 300E 2.6
Infiniti Q45

525i
325i convertible — $35,000

Mercedes 190E
Saab 9000 Turbo
Audi 200

$30,000

325is   Audi 90 Quattro
325i   Acura Legend Coupe L

Audi 100
Volvo 740 Turbo
Acura Legend Sedan
Saab 9000S

$25,000   Acura Legend Coupe
Audi 80 Quattro
318i   Lexus ES 250

$20,000

Exhibit 10.5   Selected Data from the J.D. Power and
Associates Quality Surveys

Initial Quality Surveys of New Cars,[a] Top Ten Car Brands

1990 Rank	1989 Rank	Brand	Defects per 100 Cars
1	N/A	Lexus	82
2	2	Mercedes-Benz	84
3	1	Toyota	89
4	N/A	Infiniti	99
5	7	Buick	113
6	5	Honda	114
7	4	Nissan	123
8	6	Acura	129
9	19	BMW	139
9	8	Mazda	139

Customer Satisfaction Survey,[b] Top Ten Car Brands

1989 Rank	1988 Rank	Brand
1	1	Acura
2	2	Mercedes-Benz
3	4	Toyota
4	5	Cadillac
5	3	Honda
6	6	Nissan
7	7	Subaru
7	10	Buick
9	15	Porsche
10	8	BMW
10	8	Mazda
10	12	Audi

[a]The Initial Quality Survey rates car brands based on the average number of reported problems during the first 60 to 90 days of ownership. Problem areas include steering and handling, engine performance and brakes.

[b]The Customer Satisfaction Survey polls owners one year after purchasing their new car. It covers mechanical problems and satisfaction with dealership service.

producers' share fell from 29% to 22%.[8] While BMW's share held steady, other European luxury car makers began to feel the impact. Britain's Jaguar was forced to sell out to Ford and 50% of Sweden's Saab was acquired by General Motors, Britain's Sterling Motors and France's Peugeot were on the verge of pulling out of the U.S. market, and Volvo was experiencing difficulties.

[8]*Fortune*, "Here Come the Hot New Luxury Cars," July 2, 1990, p. 60.

Strategic Issues

Seeing an increasingly competitive luxury car market in the 1990s, BMW's top management believed that three major strategic objectives had to be pursued: 1) increased product variety, 2) more frequent product introductions, and 3) improved quality of newly launched models.

Increased Product Variety

BMW management believed that customers should be offered a huge "a la carte" menu of options, colors, engines, and configurations. As Von Kuenheim explained, "Each customer can have a unique car."[9] The 3-series, for example, came in four different models (a two- and four-door sedan, a station wagon, and a convertible); each was available in 40 different body and style choices, customized with options for up to 14 different countries. By 1990 in Europe, BMW was making most of its cars to order. At the heart of this strategy was its new Regensburg plant. Commencing production in 1986, the plant was designed and automated to permit maximum flexibility: each of several hundred possible versions of 3-series models could be produced in an efficient lot size of one. The Regensburg plant produced 420 cars/day, but made the same car type only once every month.

More Frequent Product Introductions

On average, BMW introduced a completely new model line (or a new "series") every eight years, with development lead time (from concept to market) averaging six years. Existing model lines (such as the 3-series, 5-series and 7-series) were totally redesigned every four years, which generally involved substantial changes to the car's interior and exterior styling, and significant engineering changes in the engine, suspension, and other critical subsystems. Lead times for major redesign programs were also about six years. In contrast, Japanese competitors launched new and redesigned products in rapid succession, with lead times of approximately four years. For example, Lexus and Infiniti were expected to introduce a combined total of five new models over the following two years. Design strategy played a role here: Japanese automobile companies' philosophy was to introduce new models frequently, incorporating incremental changes in styling and technology. In contrast, BMW introduced major new models relatively infrequently but tended to make bold changes when it did. BMW, however, had recently altered its design strategy to emphasize accelerated product development. The new goal was to introduce a new engine, a new series, or a redesigned series every year.

---

[9]*Business Week* (Special Issue on Quality, January 1991), "Grill-to-Grill with Japan," p. 39.

Improved Quality of Newly Launched Models

In the past, BMW's launch quality had always been on par with or better than that of its major competitors, but the entry of Japanese competitors into the luxury segment was changing the standard for what was considered acceptable quality at launch. Forster explained:

> Five to 10 years ago, in the luxury segment, 10–15 customer complaints per car at model launch would have been considered acceptable. By the first year or year and a half after launch, you would have needed to get it down to 3–5 complaints per car. At BMW, we always met or exceeded these standards. Now, however, Lexus seems to be launching models with an average of 3–5 complaints/car. After about one year, they are down to 1.5 complaints/car. Customers have come to expect a much higher standard of conformance.

The Launch of a Redesigned Model

The development and launch of a completely new or redesigned model line was a complex, time-consuming, and expensive undertaking (Exhibit 10.6). Six years before the scheduled introduction, stylists in BMW's design studios began exploring various alternatives for the car's exterior appearance. BMW typically spent about two years in styling, longer than most other automobile companies, and far longer than the six months typically spent by the Japanese luxury car makers. Dr. Rathgeber, who had experience in this phase of development, commented:

> We spend more time and effort styling than almost any other car company. We're not only trying to get all the technical elements like aerodynamics, ergonomics, and safety just right, but we're also trying to create an aesthetically excellent and durable design, one that will still look fresh and be sellable in 12 years. It's a creative process and it simply can't be rushed. There are so many subtle details you have to consider. We look at everything and that's why it takes us so long.

After evaluating numerous drawings, and clay models, BMW's management would give final approval to the overall style and product concept. Product engineers then translated the product concept and style into a vehicle with the specified functional and aesthetic characteristics. This required designing and specifying the shape, dimensions, and materials of thousands of individual components, and the details of the production process, such as the type of tools that would be used to shape various

Exhibit 10.6   Product Development Cycle at BMW—An Overview

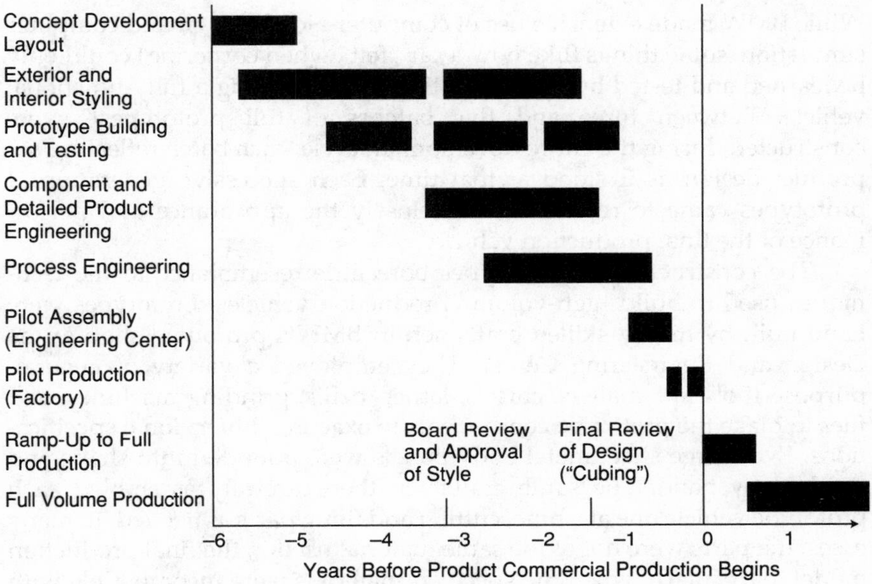

Concept Development Layout
Exterior and Interior Styling
Prototype Building and Testing
Component and Detailed Product Engineering
Process Engineering
Pilot Assembly (Engineering Center)
Pilot Production (Factory)
Ramp-Up to Full Production
Full Volume Production

Board Review and Approval of Style

Final Review of Design ("Cubing")

−6   −5   −4   −3   −2   −1   0   1

Years Before Product Commercial Production Begins

parts. Dieter Pfadenhauer, responsible for the engineering work on the interior trim of the 7-series, explained: "The detailed engineering is the really hard part. Anyone can design a concept. The question is, can you engineer the parts so that they will fit and they will work the way you want them to? Just to make a rear view mirror quiet is a world in itself!"

A vehicle under development was divided into 30 major subsystems or modules, such as the cockpit, interior trim, trunk, side doors, rear suspension system, and braking system. An interfunctional team of people from design, product engineering, production engineering, prototyping, vehicle testing, procurement, manufacturing, and other functions was responsible for each module of the car from start to launch. BMW had adopted this approach because it recognized that a well-engineered car required more than outstanding engineering; it also required strong interfunctional coordination. Because the product engineering phase was so complex, it proceeded through a series of cycles, each of which involved design, the building of prototype cars capturing the design, and the testing and evaluation of prototypes. Prototypes were tested and evaluated for such characteristics as performance, handling, safety, interior comfort and appearance, ride comfort, aerodynamics, exterior appearance and other aesthetic factors. What was learned in prototype testing was then incorporated into the next design cycle. At BMW, new products typically passed through three to five design cycles.

Prototyping at BMW

While BMW made extensive use of computer-aided design and computer simulation, some things (like how a car "felt" when cornering) could only be learned and tested by actually sitting in and driving a fully functional vehicle. Between three and five batches of full prototypes[10] were constructed during the entire development cycle, each batch reflecting the product design as it stood at that time. Each successive generation of prototypes came to resemble more closely the appearance and perfor-mance of the final production vehicle.

The construction of prototypes bore little resemblance to the tech-niques used to build high-volume production vehicles. Prototypes were hand-built by highly skilled craftsmen in BMW's prototype shop at the Design and Engineering Center. They employed a variety of general-purpose tools like mallets, chisels, lathes, drills, grinding machines, and files to make the prototype components to exacting dimensional specifica-tions. Even large sheet metal body panels were pounded into shape and finished by hand. The same craftsmen then carefully assembled each prototype vehicle one at a time, cutting and filing parts as needed. In many cases, the parts were not of the same material used in the final production model, particularly when the specified materials were incompatible with the production methods and capabilities of the prototype shop. For exam-ple, the prototype shop used fiberglass rather than sheet metal for the underlying support structure of the dashboard, as fiberglass could be quickly and easily molded without expensive tooling. Likewise, the outer layer "skin" of the prototype dashboard was made from an easily applied sheet of plastic rather than polyvinyl chloride (PVC), the material specified for the production vehicle, which required very complex tooling that was both expensive and time-consuming to procure. Later generations of prototypes contained some parts that were not manually shaped but were formed with "flexible" or "pre-production" tools. Although similar to production tools, these were less durable and could only be used at rela-tively low production speeds. Generally, the large body panels and other parts where the design had stabilized would be made from flexible tools. The vast majority of parts, however, including the cockpit and all the inte-rior trim, were still made by hand. Rarely were any prototype parts made from actual production grade tools, which could cost from five to 10 times more than "pre-production" grade tools.

Overall, BMW's highly skilled prototype builders were generally able to hand-make parts that reflected very closely the intentions of product designers. The process was not cheap, however; each complete prototype vehicle cost about DM 1.5 million.

BMW's approach provided maximum flexibility within the design cycle. Because specialized tooling was almost never needed, design

---

[10]Prototypes were typically built in batches of between 10 and 25 vehicles.

changes could be made relatively quickly and at low cost. For example, the prototype shop was often able to make new parts within one week after being notified of a design change. In contrast, if a prototype part were formed from "pre-production grade" tools, design changes would be both costly and time consuming. A complete set of pre-production tools would cost DM 7 million for just the cockpit parts and about DM 50 million for the entire car.[11] If design changes were great enough, these tools would have to be scrapped and new ones procured. The lead time to design and procure new tools could take six months.

The ability to make changes in the design relatively late in the design cycle was very important at BMW. Design changes were made relatively late in the cycle if top management believed those changes were desirable. Carl-Peter Forster explained:

> Our strategy is to be the leader when it comes to technical and styling innovation. If a late breakthrough is made in some area, like suspension, we want to be able to put it into the production model if at all possible. When we first introduced the 7-series in the mid-1980s, we decided to widen the entire car by 40 millimeters only 20 months prior to launch. This required us to re-design over one-third of the parts in the car. It was costly. But without this change, almost everyone agrees the car would have been totally wrong. It would have been too cramped and would never have succeeded in the market like it has.
>
> Some companies refuse to make such changes so late. Even if they later discover that it's not quite right, they go ahead with it anyway. We just won't do that. We won't compromise. The design must be exactly what we want.

The final design was typically frozen 16–18 months before the scheduled market introduction of the product. (The final design approval process at BMW was called "cubing.") At this stage, a large chunk of the production tools would be ordered and outside suppliers, who were usually selected a few months before, would begin to receive final engineering drawings. Then, final volume and pricing agreements with suppliers would be struck.[12]

Pilot Production and Manufacturing Start-up

During development, production engineers specified literally thousands of new fabrication and assembly processes, and designed hundreds of

---

[11]To put this figure in context, the total budget on the 7-series project for the production and procurement of prototype parts was DM 80 million.

[12]BMW's traditional procurement policy was to use multiple vendors for each part and to provide each vendor with a one-year contract.

millions of dollars worth of complex production tools. Implementing these in a high volume production environment represented a major challenge of product launch. BMW carefully managed the transition from final prototype to high volume production through three discrete phases: 1) pilot production in the Engineering Center's pilot plant, 2) pilot runs in the factory, and 3) gradual ramp-up to full-scale manufacture.

Pilot Production in the Pilot Plant

Nine months prior to launch, pilot assembly began in the Research and Engineering Center's small pilot production facility, under the supervision of Jurgen Hohbein, a former supervisor at the company's Munich plant. Although it was designed to simulate an actual production line, the pilot facility was much smaller, much quieter, and much more serene than a commercial facility. Here, 20 full-time relatively highly skilled workers, joined by visiting production workers from a high volume plant, turned out about one car per day. Only about three-quarters of the high-volume "production tools" were normally ready when pilot production began because of the relatively long lead times for procuring them. The other tools were "pre-production" grade.

During the six months of pilot production, workers learned about the assembly process and uncovered problems with tooling, parts, and assembly procedures. Pilot production vehicles, which were never sold to the public, were carefully inspected to reveal any problems. For example, certain assembly sequences might not be repeatable, or certain parts might not be joined with consistently high quality. Suppliers sometimes also had trouble making parts. Literally thousands of minor problems would be uncovered and investigated. In response, procedures, tooling, and even part designs had to be modified. Dr. Gunther Link, a production engineer responsible for procurement on the 7-series cockpit team, provided an example:

> When we first put the latest 3-series into pilot production, we discovered that the grills for the heating and air conditioning ducts fit too tightly. As a result, it took too much force to change the direction of the airflow. We didn't have this problem in the prototypes—it was only after we started producing them in any volume that we discovered that the specifications were off.

Most changes were relatively minor, but occasionally a major problem was uncovered. Carl-Peter Forster, who had previously been the program manager on the 5-series station wagon, recalled:

> On the 5-series wagon, to maximize the opening of the rear tailgate, we designed a very complicated hinge to be made out of

stamped sheet metal. In pilot production, we learned that under higher volume production the sheet metal could not be stamped in a way that made it strong enough to support the door. We had to change the design to one made of forged steel. Unfortunately, this delayed the introduction of the car by three months.

Factory Pilot Production Run

Once the process was debugged, pilot production was transferred to the factory where the new model would be produced. This was generally scheduled to occur three months prior to the start of commercial production. The team of temporary and full-time pilot workers moved to the plant to smooth the transition.

The line used for pilot runs in the plant would cease to produce commercial vehicles once factory pilot production began. This was done to avoid the confusion which might result if regular and pilot production were intermingled on the same production line. An initial run of 25 cars was made, followed by a final pilot run of 60 cars, and none of these were sold. The pilot runs in the factory were considered "dress rehearsals" for commercial production. It was supposed to be the last opportunity to fine tune the process, change tooling, and trouble-shoot. As Jurgen Hohbein explained, "Once you start commercial production, your goal is to ramp-up to full volume. You don't want to be shutting down the line to troubleshoot or to change tooling. It's very costly."

Full Production Ramp-Up

If no major problems were uncovered in the final pilot runs, commercial production would be authorized. Generally, BMW, like most other car makers, tried to start commercial production slightly ahead of market introduction in order to fill the distribution channels. Commercial production began slowly with output of the new model at only four cars per day. In the past, BMW had rapidly phased out production of the old model, but given the relatively low initial productivity for new models, this resulted in a temporary, but significant, drop in total output. To better utilize the high fixed costs of the plant (capital equipment and labor[13]), BMW decided, for some models, to maintain production of the old model until production of the new model could be brought up to full-volume. During this six-month transition, new models would be interspersed with old models along the assembly line. For example, initially one new model would come down the assembly line in-between 10 of the old models. Over time, the ratio between new and old would shrink, until

---

[13]German law made it very costly to lay off workers. As a result, when volume dipped from the introduction of a new model, the plant had to bear significant unabsorbed overhead.

the old models were phased out. Exhibit 10.7 illustrates the two ramp-up approaches.

While the "mixed-model" ramp-up permitted better utilization of fixed assets, it caused greater confusion and made logistics more complex. Further complicating ramp-up was the fact that not all potential production problems were discovered or solved during pilot production. Carl-Peter Forster explained:

> All our time in pilot production is spent identifying and solving the big problems. Do the parts fit? If not, we redesign the parts and

Exhibit 10.7   Comparison of Ramp-Up Strategies

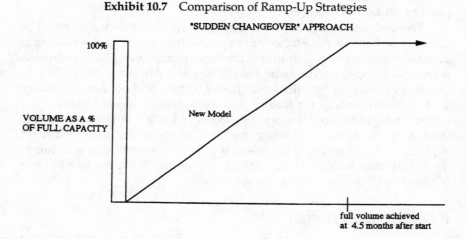

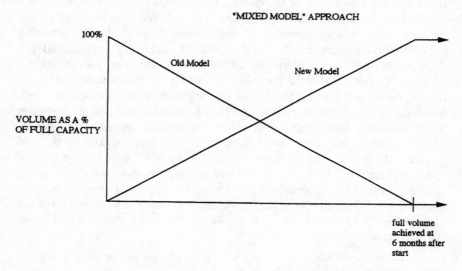

the tooling. Then, in theory, we are supposed to move on to the fine tuning: How does the surface look? Are the edges of the parts perfectly aligned? Unfortunately, by the time we solve all the big problems, we don't have much time left for fine tuning and a lot of minor problems have to be dealt with in production.

The minor problems only added to the confusion workers experienced, as Jurgen Hohbein noted: "When production on a new model starts, all the workers are very excited and want it to be perfect. When parts are not right or when paint is clogging the body holes, they get really frustrated because smooth assembly is hindered."

BMW's response was to assign additional engineers to help fine-tune the process and, if necessary, redesign parts. Additional engineers were also sent out to supplier plants to help solve problems arising in the production of parts. To lower the risks of imperfect cars reaching customers, plants were also provided extra resources during launch for quality assurance, inspection, and rework. As Hartmut Schulze, the member of the cockpit team representing production, commented: "We always produce high quality cars from the customer's viewpoint, but it comes at a great cost."

However, this approach was costly in other respects as well. Currently, it took BMW an average of six months to achieve full production volume. Some within the manufacturing organization felt that this time could be cut in half if more of the many minor production and quality problems were solved earlier. Dr. Rathgeber, who once worked in production, commented: "The speed of ramp-up is determined by how good your development process is." Parts that did not consistently fit or frequent changes in the production process tended to add confusion and made it more difficult for production workers to settle into a routine. Some within BMW were particularly worried that the current start-up process was incompatible with BMW's future manufacturing strategy, which included more automated, flexible, and sophisticated plants like Regensburg. Finally, and perhaps most disturbing to BMW management was that, despite intensive inspection and rework, the incidence of customer complaints about new models was higher than what was becoming the norm in the market, although greater quality problems with new models seemed to affect almost all automobile companies to varying degrees.

The 7-Series Cockpit Decision

Against this backdrop in early 1991, the cockpit module team began to think about ways to improve the quality of the cockpit for the new 7-series. From a design point of view, the cockpit, which contained over 97 parts, was both critical and complicated. Being the driver's interface with the car, the cockpit had an enormous impact on perceptions of the entire car. Seemingly minor design glitches, whether ergonomic (e.g., a hard-to-reach climate control switch), aesthetic (e.g. a knob appearing too big), or functional (a too-small air conditioning duct), could become serious liabilities in the marketplace. Functional aspects also presented an engineering challenge. Underneath the dashboard, heating and air conditioning ducts had be carefully laid out to minimize the consumption of interior space.

The cockpit was also a challenge for manufacturing. Because it was such a visible part of the car's interior, cockpit quality had to be excellent. To ensure nearly perfect fit and finish, extremely high precision processes were used to fabricate parts. A particularly difficult part to make was the dashboard, which consisted of three layers. The bottom was a sheet metal support structure, above which was a layer of foam; the top layer, the "skin," was molded polyvinyl chloride. Each required a different production process and its own tools and molds. The fit had to be virtually perfect, but as Rathgeber noted:

Getting the fit between the layers right takes a lot of trial-and-error. It's difficult to predict precisely how foam and plastic will actually behave when being molded. For example, little bubbles may form in a corner of the part and then you have to redesign the mold.

Rathgeber was convinced that good launch quality started in the development process. While there were many aspects of the development which could affect quality, he and his team began to focus on the prototyping process. Over the next several months, the team met with Carl-Peter Forster to discuss possible changes in cockpit prototyping.

A New Approach to Prototyping

Rathgeber and the cockpit team believed that the current process for making prototypes masked many design and manufacturing problems which only surfaced during pilot production and ramp-up. They thought that it was critical for prototypes to be built with technology, equipment, and workers that were more like those found in a factory environment. Dr. Link, who had previously worked as a manufacturing supervisor, stated: "You never know what a part is really going to look like or how it will fit until you make it with production tools. At least if we use pre-production tools in early prototyping, we can learn something about the part much earlier." Rathgeber added: "And if there's a problem with the tool design, the part, or the process, we still have time to correct it *before* actual production starts."

Link was also concerned that prototype parts were rarely procured from the vendors who supplied commercial production. The rationale behind this split sourcing was specialization. Prototype production was a low volume, quick turnaround business. Cost was not important, quality was defined by how well the part met dimensional specifications, and the appearance of prototype parts was not important. In contrast, suppliers for commercial production had to produce in high volumes and meet regular delivery schedules. Cost was a very important criteria for choosing a commercial supplier, who, in addition, had to produce parts that consistently met *all* design specifications.

Link felt there would be benefits of involving suppliers in both design and prototyping:

> Our suppliers can foresee problems in the production process and with parts which we miss. We should tap their expertise earlier. We should also have them make prototype parts so that they can learn about the part before they have to make it in volume.

Between January and June of 1991, the 7-series cockpit module team formulated a proposal to alter the process for prototyping the next and final batch of 7-series prototypes. This final batch, which would be assembled in six months, was to consist of 25 prototype vehicles.

Under the proposed approach, all cockpit components would be fabricated with pre-production grade tools. Thus, after each part was designed, a production engineer would design the tool or set of tools needed to make it. The tools would then be made to exact specifications. For the more complex parts, this cycle would take up to six months to complete. The total investment to design and make all the pre-production grade tools for the cockpit would be DM 7 million, with another DM 1.5 million for materials, labor, overhead, and outside services. In contrast, under the existing approach, a prototype part was made directly from the part designer's drawings and clay models. Specialized tooling costs were essentially zero, but the cost of material, labor, and overhead of producing 25 prototype cockpits came to DM 1.8 million.

The cockpit module team also proposed contracting with a single outside vendor to supply fully assembled cockpits for prototype, pilot, and commercial production runs. The vendor under consideration, a long-time supplier of cockpit parts, would still make some parts but it would also procure the remaining ones from subcontractors it or BMW chose. The supplier would also be in charge, for the first time, of some engineering design work, with the hope that over time it could take on more.

Finally, rather than having the prototype shop assemble the cockpits into the prototype vehicles, the team proposed having this done on the assembly line of the Engineering Center's pilot plant. The pilot assembly plant's workers, not the prototype specialists, would perform the requisite assembly operations.

Some within the design group worried that any attempts to use more sophisticated tooling and production processes to make prototype parts would severely constrain their flexibility and creativity. Because of the lead time for designing and purchasing a set of tools, concrete commitments to designs would have to be made about one year prior to each prototyping cycle (up to six months to design the tools and six months to procure them). Thus, if a batch of prototypes was scheduled to be produced 20 months prior to product launch, design commitments had to be made thirty-two months prior to launch. Currently, designers made their final commitments about one month prior to each prototype build cycle. They viewed a more sophisticated prototyping process as an unnecessary constraint. As one designer put it:

> It's true that the current prototypes are mainly crafted by hand, but they serve their purpose. They look, feel, and work just the way they are designed to. And the parts fit extremely well. Considering that they are just prototypes, they are really of quite high quality.

Carl-Peter Forster had been involved in the discussions about this proposal and was in general quite enthusiastic. He had long believed that prototyping could play a more proactive role in the development process. Nevertheless, he knew the issue was complex and a number of questions had to be answered. One concern was that the current design of the 7-series cockpit was far from frozen. A passenger's side air-bag might be added and the material for the dashboard's surface skin changed. Either one of these changes would require a whole new set of tools. Most of the DM 7 million investment might have to be written off and, with a six month lead time for pre-production tools, final generation prototype cockpits would end up having to be made by hand.

Forster also had to make some decisions about prototyping strategy for future projects. How far back in the development cycle should pre-production tools be used? He knew that some Japanese companies used pre-production tools for some parts of their very first prototypes. He also had to decide how broadly the concept of early tooling should be applied. If early tooling worked for the cockpit, should it done for other parts of the car as well? If so, which ones? Already the interior trim module team was considering investing DM 10 million in pre-production tools for the interior trim parts of the final generation 7-series prototypes. If the logic of early tooling was applied to all parts of the prototype, an investment of DM 50 million would be required. While this represented a significant investment, an internal study suggested that if the prototyping process being considered for the cockpit were adopted for all other applicable parts of the car, and if other preventive quality measures were taken, BMW would save at least DM 100 million per product launch.[14]

As these issues raced through his mind, Carl-Peter Forster entered the conference room. It was 7:59 AM. The meeting was about to begin.

[14]The DM 100 million in savings would come from reductions in excess direct and indirect labor, reductions in tool replacement costs, and lower warranty expenses.

CHAPTER 11

ITT Automotive

Global Manufacturing Strategy (1994)

D R. JUERGEN GEISSINGER, director of central industrial engineering at ITT Automotive Europe, prepared to make a difficult decision. Since joining ITT in December 1992, one of his primary responsibilities had been to oversee the development of the company's newest automotive anti-lock brake system, the MK20, at the company's headquarters in Frankfurt, Germany.[1] The MK20, to be launched in 1995, was predicted to be enormously popular, since it would be the lightest, lowest-cost, and most sophisticated automotive anti-lock brake system available in the world.

Now, in May 1994, ITT Automotive was preparing to begin commercial production of the MK20. Mass production would begin at the Frankfurt plant in October 1994. Highly automated equipment had already been purchased and installed there; test production was currently underway. Demand for the product was expected to grow rapidly and, by Summer 1995, the company planned to expand production to additional sites in the United States and Europe. Under the current plan, the manufacturing at all these sites worldwide would be highly automated, with processes identical to those used in Frankfurt.

Given the high volumes and intense cost pressures in anti-lock brakes, management had agreed on a basic imperative that the company would use highly optimized manufacturing processes for the MK20. However, there was some disagreement about the means to this objective; the extent of worldwide standardization and the appropriate level of automation for production were currently under discussion. Managers at the U.S. plants had some concerns about the plan and were urging top management to consider alternatives better suited to their own situations.

[1]MK20 is pronounced "Mark 20."

Professor Gary Pisano and Research Associate Sharon Rossi wrote this case as the basis for class discussion rather than to illustrate either effective or ineffective handling of an administrative situation.

As anti-lock brake systems rapidly became less expensive and more sophisticated each year, ITT Automotive was headed into a new era of higher-volume, lower cost manufacturing. The decision about the MK20 was seen as a watershed that would determine the company's global manufacturing strategy for the longer term. Characterizing the two sides of the debate, Dr. Geissinger said, "It's a conflict between whether to standardize or have a Plant Olympics."

ITT Automotive

ITT Automotive, part of the $23 billion U.S. conglomerate ITT Corporation, was a $3.5 billion global company headquartered in Auburn Hills, Michigan.[2] ITT Automotive was organized into eight different automotive product groups: 1) brake systems; 2) wiper systems; 3) fluid handling systems; 4) precision die castings; 5) structural components; 6) switches and lamps; 7) electric motors; and 8) aftermarket products (shock absorbers, brake components). See Exhibits 11.1A, 11.1B, and 11.1C for financial data and Exhibit 11.2 for an organizational chart.

ITT Automotive was further divided into ITT Automotive North America, based in Auburn Hills, Michigan and ITT Automotive Europe GmbH, based in Frankfurt, Germany. Within ITT Automotive Europe, ITT-

Exhibit 11.1A ITT Corporation Income Statement

In $ millions	1993	1992	1991
Sales and Revenues			
Products and Services	10,791	11,098	10,268
Insurance	10,338	9,862	9,242
Finance	1,633	2,017	2,026
	22,762	22,977	21,536
Costs and Expenses			
Products and Services	10,240	10,908	9,882
Insurance	9,619	10,375	8,726
Finance	1,371	2,798	1,932
Other	211	165	135
	21,441	24,246	20,675
	1,321	(1,269)	861
Interest expense	(147)	(169)	(177)
Other income (expense)	(261)	553	65
Net income (loss)	913	(885)	749

[2]ITT Corporation's seven other businesses included insurance ($10b), finance ($2b), defense, communication and information services, fluid technology, components, forest products, and hotels (each roughly $1b).

Exhibit 11.1B ITT Corporation, Income by Business Segment

In $ millions	1993	1992	1991
Sales and Revenues			
Insurance	10,338	9,862	9,242
Finance	1,440	1,414	1,321
Communication & Information Services	800	817	684
Automotive	3,580	3,498	2,933
Defense & Electronics	1,671	1,927	1,985
Fluid Technology	1,030	1,070	1,064
Hotels	3,184	3,109	2,826
Ongoing Segments	22,043	21,697	20,055
Dispositions & Other	719	1,280	1,481
Total Segments	22,762	22,977	21,536
Income (Loss)			
Insurance	719	(513)	500
Finance	271	175	343
Communication & Information Services	162	170	149
Automotive	164	118	71
Defense & Electronics	51	(82)	83
Fluid Technology	95	67	83
Hotels	78	(28)	33
Ongoing Segments	1,540	(93)	1,262
Dispositions & Other	105	(906)	(38)
Total Segments	1,645	(999)	1,224

Exhibit 11.1C ITT Corporation Balance Sheet

In $ millions	1993	1992
Assets		
Cash	1,136	882
Receivables	12,719	14,683
Inventories	963	1,108
Insurance investments	30,582	27,866
Finance investments	3,097	2,989
Reinsurance recoverables	11,577	11,322
Plant, property, & equipment, net	3,416	3,306
Other assets	7,070	6,407
	70,560	68,563
Liabilities and Stockholders' Equity		
Liabilities		
Policy liabilities and accruals	40,884	37,705
Debt	13,940	15,933
Accounts payable & accrued liabilities	4,293	3,957
Other liabilities	3,793	3,721
	62,910	61,316
Stockholders' Equity	7,650	7,247
	70,560	68,563

Exhibit 11.2 ITT Automotive Organizational Structure

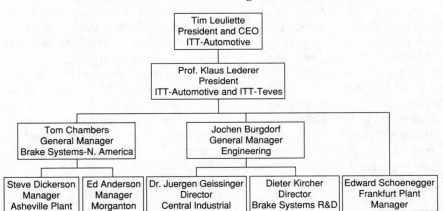

Teves (Teves)[3], also in Frankfurt, was the center for design and engineering of new brake and traction control systems for ITT worldwide. ITT-Teves produced anti-lock brakes, traction control systems, and total brake systems. A separate group in Auburn Hills, Michigan was responsible for application engineering for these products for the North American market.

Beginning September 1992, ITT Automotive embarked on a restructuring program aimed at strengthening ITT's bargaining power with vehicle makers and increase negotiating power with suppliers.[4] All of ITT's businesses involved in brakes and electrical systems were merged together and focused around the operations of ITT-Teves. Professor Klaus Lederer, former president of Alfred Teves, became the president of ITT Automotive Europe and assumed responsibility for the brake systems group (ITT-Teves).

In 1993, ITT-Teves was the world's leading supplier of four-wheel passenger car anti-lock brake systems (ABS) and traction-control systems (TCS). That year the company shipped 2.9 million four-wheel ABS and TCS, with combined sales of these products reaching $1.1 billion. ITT-Teves was the only automotive parts supplier ever to exceed sales of $1 billion.

ABS Technology: A Basic Description

Anti-lock braking systems (ABS) were computer-controlled brakes designed to improve a vehicle's stopping capability in emergencies by preventing wheel lock. When a driver brakes heavily (typically in an emer-

---

[3]Prior to 1988, ITT-Teves had been a separate company known as Alfred Teves GmbH, a pioneer in anti-lock brake systems. In 1988, Alfred Teves was acquired by ITT and became part of the Brake Systems group within ITT Automotive.

[4]Christopher Parkes, "Survey of World Automotive Suppliers," *Financial Times*, 6/28/93.

gency situation), conventional brakes "lock," often losing grip with the pavement. This causes the vehicle to slide or skid and prohibits the driver from steering in control. With an ABS-equipped vehicle, a driver can brake heavily but stop safely; the car (or truck) stops in a straight line, without skidding or sliding, and allows the driver to steer in control.

An ABS system typically contained these basic components: an electric motor, a hydraulic fluid pump, a valve block, a microprocessor controller, a wire harness, and wheel sensor assemblies. The motor, pump, and valve block (also known together as the master cylinder/booster), along with the electronic controller, were mounted on the inside of the firewall of the vehicle (in the engine compartment). The sensor assemblies were mounted on each wheel. See ABS diagram in Exhibit 11.3.

A vehicle's ABS is activated as soon as the ignition is turned on. As the

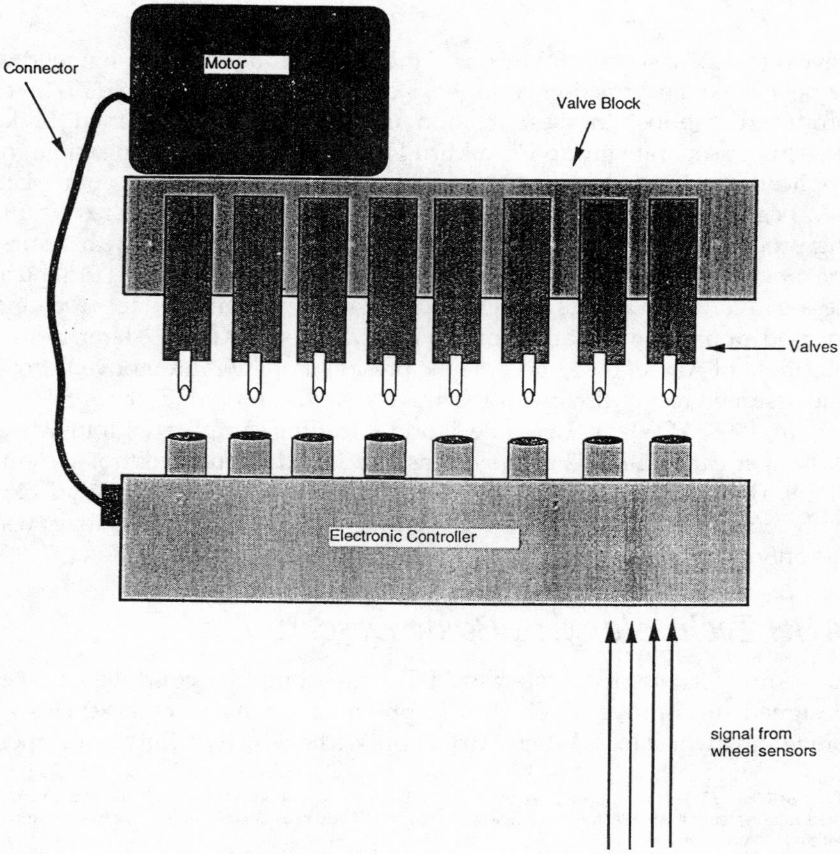

Exhibit 11.3   Basic Design of the ITT MK20 Anti-lock Brake System

car moves, sensors on each wheel continually measure wheel speeds. Under normal operation, the driver will not know that the ABS is there. However, if the driver brakes heavily and any one wheel or driveshaft begins to slow more than others, ABS takes action. The sensors detect the slow wheel (before it begins to lock) and transmit this data to the electronic microprocessor. The microprocessor then signals the solenoids to modulate pressure to the disc brake pistons and/or drum wheel cylinders. The solenoids open and close rapidly (about 15 times per second), thus preventing the wheel from "locking up." Modulated braking pressure allows optimal braking and allows the driver to remain in control of the vehicle.

Origin and Evolution of ABS

ABS technology was originally designed and patented in the 1940s. The first applications of ABS were developed for aircraft and for heavy trucks by 1950. In the 1960s, efforts were made to develop and commercialize ABS for automobiles, but these systems met with little success because of very high costs and low performance. With the development of inexpensive microprocessors in the 1980s, ABS for automobiles became feasible, pioneered by Robert Bosch GmbH and Alfred Teves GmbH. Bosch introduced the first automobile ABS system in 1984; Alfred Teves GmbH followed later that year with the MK2. Because of their high cost, these early systems were only installed on luxury automobiles such as the Ford Lincoln Continental (in the U.S.) or the Ford Scorpio (in Europe). Worldwide, less than 1% of cars produced in 1984 were equipped with ABS.

Six years later, in 1990, ITT-Teves introduced its second generation ABS, the MK4. This system operated with a standard vacuum booster (rather than a hydraulic booster, such as that used on the MK2), and could be adapted to add a traction control feature. The MK4 sold for nearly half the price of the MK2. Three years later, in 1993, ITT introduced the MK4-G, a lighter-weight system which had hydraulics designed in a closed circuit that were less sensitive to brake failure. The MK4-G sold to OEMs for the same price as the MK4. One year later, the company introduced the MK4-Gi. This system integrated the electronic controller and the hydraulics, and thus it was much smaller and lighter weight than the previous version. It was the world's first integrated ABS system. This system also had a smaller wire harness and much higher reliability. The MK4-Gi sold to OEMs for the same price as the MK4-G. See Exhibit 11.4 for illustrations of these brake systems. By April 1994, ITT-Teves had sold 10 million ABS units.

In the 1990s, demand for ABS was growing rapidly and costs were dropping as a result of two simultaneous trends: First, experience with the technology helped to lower costs. Second, consumers were increasingly concerned with vehicle safety and were willing to pay for features that

Exhibit 11.4   ITT Automotive's 3 Generations of ABS

MK2 (1984)

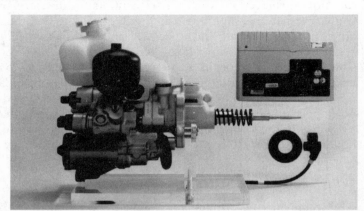

MK4 (1990)

MK20 (1995)

reduced hazards of automobile travel, therefore costs and prices dropped with increased economies of scale. (Exhibit 11.5 shows ABS price and volume trends.) With costs dropping and demand for safety features rising, ABS was no longer viewed as a luxury car feature. Automobile manufacturers called for systems to fit a wider variety of vehicles, including compact and subcompact cars. New ABS designs had to be smaller and lighter since smaller cars had less space available in the engine compartment. These systems had to be dramatically lower in price, as well. Thus, there was great demand for a lighter, more compact, low cost ABS system.

As demand for ABS grew, so did production volumes and market penetration. For example, 32% of all cars and 8% of all light trucks built in North America in 1992 were equipped with ABS, compared with 14% for cars and 2.3% for trucks one year earlier. ITT responded to this trend by opening up plants in Asheville, North Carolina (1989) and Morganton, North Carolina (1993). In some instances, however, demand was growing

Exhibit 11.5   ITT Automotive's ABS Production Volumes (1984–1995) and Price Trends

Production Volumes

	1984	1985	1986	1987	1988	1989	1990	1991	1992	1993	1994	1995
MK2	150	150	200	280	430	659	470	330	270	100	25	10
MK4, MK4G, MK4Gi							310	1000	1900	2800	3600	3500
MK20												700
Total ABS Units	150	150	200	280	430	659	780	1330	2170	2900	3625	4210

Price Trends (Indexed - MK2 introduction price equals 100)

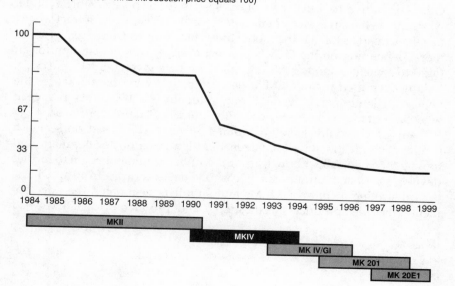

so quickly that orders outstripped capacity. In early 1993, for example, ITT had difficulty supplying sufficient units to Chrysler for its new LH vehicles. The Morganton plant was scheduled to supply the units, but had opened only recently and had not yet ramped up to full volume. Early order rates exceeded 80% of capacity (more than the plant could then produce) and the plant temporarily fell short of its orders. To supply Chrysler, ITT had to ship ABS from Europe until U.S. production ramped up further.[5]

While demand forced rapid ramp up of production volumes, technology advancements were forcing rapid obsolescence of ABS systems. As a result, product lives were shortening. For example, the MK2 (the company's oldest ABS) was on the market for roughly 6 years, whereas the MK4-G (a more recent system) was expected to remain on the market for less than 4 years.

Competition in the ABS Market

In 1984, when ABS for cars and light trucks were first introduced, Bosch and Teves were the only suppliers of ABS. Total sales of ABS that year were DM 300 million worldwide. Ten years later, in 1994, ABS sales had grown to DM 6.9 billion and the marketplace now included a number of competitors. Worldwide, major market shares were divided among ITT-Teves (27% share), Bosch (22%), Delco[6] (17%), Kelsey-Hayes (14%), Bendix (7%), and others (13%).[7]

Market shares for ABS suppliers were slow to change, as they were based on long-term contracts with OEMs (vehicle producers). Typically, an OEM committed to purchase a brake system for a specific vehicle model while that vehicle was early in its development phase. The contract would usually extend as long as the model life, which ranged from 4 to 7 years or more, depending on the OEM's product cycle. It was uncommon for an OEM to switch to another ABS supplier during a given model's life cycle. Volumes required by an OEM varied dramatically by the market for the vehicle: a large-market vehicle might require 400,000 units per year, whereas a small-market vehicle might require 50,000 units or fewer.

An OEM would usually commit to a new ABS based on seeing a prototype from the supplier. Given the high costs of development and tooling for a new ABS product, an ABS supplier would not begin to further develop the system until it had at least one major contract from an OEM.

In striking a contract, OEMs and suppliers negotiated the development schedule, product specifications, and product price. OEMs had

---

[5]Ward's Auto World, March 1993.

[6]Delco was owned by General Motors and supplied ABS for all GM vehicles.

[7]ITT estimates.

gained leverage in the early 1990s by reducing the number of suppliers they worked with.

Throughout the automotive industry, components manufacturers were feeling squeezed; margins eroded as OEMs gained leverage. For example, between 1985 and 1992, German vehicle prices rose 26%, while parts prices rose only 11% during the same period. Average return on sales among components manufacturers slipped from 5% in 1987 to 1.5% in 1991.[8] Average margins on ABS systems, which had been between 10% and 15% in the 1990s,[9] were also declining. Margins on conventional brake systems were about 6%.

To the OEM, the terms of competition in the ABS business were product performance,[10] product price, size and weight of the ABS, and degree to which the ABS could be adapted to different size vehicles. Most OEMs preferred to work with suppliers who were willing to adapt the ABS product specifications to meet the customer's needs. Other OEMs were more involved with the manufacturing process. In many cases, OEMs wished to view and approve a supplier's production facility and its process for a new brake system. Some even requested that the ABS supplier run dedicated production lines for their particular product.

International Differences

In 1994, ITT was a supplier for 30 automotive companies worldwide, and produced ABS for 60 to 75 different vehicles models. The products were supplied to automobile producers throughout the world, including customers in North and South America, Europe, and the Pacific Rim.

As a global supplier (and the only ABS producer in the world to have a presence on three continents), ITT encountered challenges in understanding and serving customers worldwide. Mark Sowka, manager of international projects, observed:

> In Europe, suppliers have close working relationships with the customer. You get a commitment from the customer early on. If you have a problem, you go talk to the customer and work something out. Volume requirements are between 2,000 and 400,000 units per year.
>
> In the U.S., there are the big three auto producers. The volume requirements for these customers are somewhere in the range of 50,000 to 400,000 units. They are sharp-penciled business people:

[8]Christopher Parkes, "Survey of World Automotive Suppliers," *Financial Times*, 6/28/93.

[9]Based on Varity Corporation's ABS margins (estimated by Sanford C. Bernstein & Co).

[10]There were actually only slight performance differences among ABS. These differences could rarely be detected by the driver.

they are fair, but very formal about things. If you have a problem, they go and check the contract.

In Japan, the customer will never give you a formal long term commitment, but they do everything in good faith. When you work with a Japanese customer, you are partners for life.

The MK20 Project

The MK20 Concept

Amidst this environment of rising customer demands and shrinking margins, in June 1992, ITT-Teves began to design a new generation of ABS. The goal of this design would be to meet market demands for a system that was low cost, lightweight, and compact. As Norbert Ocvirk, the MK20 project leader explained, "The concept for the MK20 was to keep the functionality that we had with the MK4-Gi, but make it smaller, lighter, and cheaper than we ever had before." Of these objectives, cost was the most critical. Max Seiermann, manager of technical services and coordination made this clear: "Ninety percent of this project was about getting costs down."

Once the initial design was prepared, ITT-Teves approached potential customers with a prototype of the MK20 in an attempt to attract a buyer. In late 1992, the company received a commitment from a major European automobile company to install the MK20 on its 1995 vehicles. This commitment gave ITT-Teves the go-ahead for developing the MK20.

Having committed to purchasing the MK20, the European customer set strict targets for the MK20. One target was to develop a product that it could buy for half the price of the previous generation, MK4-Gi. At the same time, the customer forced ITT to follow an equally rigorous development timeline: the first MK20 systems had to be shipped by January 1995. This timeline allowed 2 years for development (from concept to market), a significantly shorter amount of time than had been allowed for any previous generation. (In comparison, the company had taken 8.5 years to develop the MK2 and 3.5 years to develop the MK4.) To meet the product cost and launch targets, ITT knew it needed a new approach.

Dr. Geissinger recollected:

> Historically, product and process R&D were separate within the company. One group worked on the product design and the other group would just produce it. Over the past ten years, there has been such rapid growth in ABS that all we did was worry about volumes and about passing Bosch. While we succeeded with this strategy, the price for this was that there was not enough time to optimize all manufacturing equipment in advance of installation in the plant.

But change was underway with the MK20. Geissinger continued: "Looking to the targets now, it is necessary to optimize everything simultaneously—product, manufacturing, and quality."

Simultaneous Engineering

One of the new approaches that was introduced with the MK20 was the concept of simultaneous engineering. Because of the tight project schedule, this effort—concurrent product design and product engineering—was seen as critical in saving development time. Helmut Weis, project manager for manufacturing, said, "With only 2 years, we couldn't do the design and then figure out how to manufacture it. We had to have parallel efforts."

To start it off, Jochen Burgdorf, chief engineer and general manager of engineering, brought together teams of people representing Design, Engineering, Manufacturing, and Quality. Throughout the project, these teams met every one to two weeks to discuss the progress, solve problems, and negotiate timelines when necessary. Every six to eight weeks, the groups met with senior management, including Prof. Lederer, to give an update on the project progress.

Because the MK20 had an integrated design for the valves, hydraulics, and controller, the project required a new level of integration among engineers and designers.[11] Separate groups designed each component, but the simultaneous engineering effort brought these teams together in a way that had never happened before. Dr. Geissinger explained, "The architecture of the MK20 was quite different from earlier models. This required a new interaction between groups and it forced them to integrate their efforts."

Weis agreed: "Over the years at Teves, personal connections have developed between people that allows them to work together and attack certain problems. On the MK20, simultaneous engineering seemed to formalize these connections and made us more efficient." He explained that this effort required a new level of openness.

> Ten years ago, the company was divided between R&D and manufacturing. If an R&D guy had an idea, he would put it on paper and not share it with anyone outside R&D. There was always a fear that manufacturing might ruin things. Breaking down these barriers took time. With this project, people realized very quickly that if you talk to each other early, then there are no surprises.

Aside from improving communication among groups and allowing them to work in parallel, simultaneous engineering forced the teams to

[11]The valves, hydraulics, and controller all had to be completely redeveloped for the MK20 because of its radically different architecture.

eliminate some activities, thus speeding development even further. Karlheinz Haupt, manager of the development of ABS hydraulics and sensors, gave one example:

> In the past, we would make complete drawings before we built or tested any new parts. With the MK20, we could not wait for complete drawings. We made sketches and then worked in cooperation with people from manufacturing. Drawings were passed back and forth rapidly between our groups. We finished the design while they built the parts and tested them.

Although this cooperative effort was seen as a success, people at ITT believed there was still room for improvement. For example, Dr. Geissinger hoped that on future projects people from the manufacturing plants would become more involved. He explained: "In January 1993, I brought together the manufacturing engineering team, led by Helmut Weis. People from manufacturing, materials, and quality at each of the plants were invited to join. Unfortunately, not all the members took the opportunity to participate."

Design for Manufacturability

Because of strict product cost targets for the MK20, design for manufacturability (DFM) was integral to product design. ITT had used DFM concepts—in essence, designing for lowest cost manufacturing—on its other ABS designs, but the MK20 project (with its half-price target) required a bigger stretch than ever before.

One result of the DFM effort was fewer parts: the MK20 design had 130 parts, 50 fewer than the MK4.[12] Designers achieved fewer parts on the MK20 largely by integrating the pump and the valves into a single block, and by integrating the electronics with the hydraulic controls. They also introduced a "self-clinching" design for connecting components to the aluminum valve block. Rather than attaching them with screws or seals, components were punched directly into orifices in the valve block, clinched in place by the surrounding metal. The use of screws or seals was eliminated, reducing the number of parts and simplifying assembly.

It was impossible for DFM to eliminate all problems because, in solving some problems, others were created. For example, the integrated pump and valve block, including the new "self-clinching" components, were machined from one solid block of aluminum. The machining process was similar to that performed for ITT's other ABS products, but the operation was much more complex for the MK20. Because the valve block now

---

[12]In contrast, the company's first ABS, the MK2 system, had 400 parts.

contained the valves *and* the pump (as opposed to just the valves), the block had more orifices and more connector attachments. The increased complexity of the design made the valve block more susceptible to problems. For example, self-clinching required a perfect fit between the component and the orifice.

Some believed the design still had room for improvement in terms of DFM. Dr. Geissinger said, "For example, the valve block still needs to be assembled on five sides and connectors attached to all these sides. In theory, all the machining and connections should be made on one side of the block." He added, "We've had a lot of success on this project, looking at the short time for development of a new product, but to meet future challenges more improvements are necessary."

Modular Design

The MK20 was designed so that it could be constructed out of independent, interchangeable components, a concept known as modularity.[13] The primary benefit of modularity was to fulfill more customer requirements using the same components, but at lower cost.

The MK20 began with a basic, standardized platform. To produce an MK20 for any customer, there was one type of pump, two valve-block sizes, and three possible motors which could be specified. Within these standard platforms, all the valves and placement of orifices and connections were exactly the same. Using these 3 modules or components, ITT could easily produce 6 different basic types of MK20 systems. In comparison, the company produced 25 different basic versions of the MK4, a design that was also modular, but with many more modules.

With modularity, the goals of product compactness and lightness were also achieved. By integrating the electronic and hydraulic controls into a single unit and fitting them to the valve block, the product's dimensions shrunk to $16 \times 10 \times 10$ cm and weighed 40% less than the previous system, the MK4-Gi.

The modular design allowed the MK20 to accommodate other brake system enhancements, depending on customer requirements. The MK20 could easily be integrated with traction-control and electronic brake-force distribution (EBD) technology.[14] Another up and coming feature, stability control (FSR), would also be integratable with the MK20 platform.[15]

Designers expected that the MK20 was also prepared to accommodate

[13]Karl Ulrich and Karen Tung, "Fundamentals of Product Modularity," MIT Sloan School of Management, (1991).

[14]EBD is ITT Automotive's proprietary technology. The feature allows maximum deceleration under normal circumstances, below the "locking" threshold where ABS starts to work.

[15]FSR is also proprietary technology. This feature would prevent a car from rolling too far when the driver swerves too fast (such as in an emergency situation) or during a tire blow-out.

future changes and enhancements. They planned to continue using the same standardized platform, and expected that the next generation of ABS would hopefully not be dramatically different from the MK20. Any changes could be made by redesigning a specific component or components, rather than the entire product. By sticking with same basic design from generation to generation, the company hoped to be able to reuse about 50% of the MK20 production equipment on the next generation ABS. Reusing more of the equipment, rather than scrapping it, would provide a significant source of savings on tooling and capital equipment.[16]

Even though modularity and standardization made a great deal of sense for manufacturability and low cost, it was clear that following these principles required tradeoffs in reduced product variety and customization. For example, customers could no longer specify a unique valve size for their vehicle's ABS, since ITT had adopted a family of standard sizes for all systems. Mark Sowka, manager of international projects for brake systems engineering, gave this example:

> There have been some strong discussions with customers. We had one customer who specified a different orifice size for the valve. ITT's new standardized size wouldn't be compatible with that specification. One of our industrial engineers fought with the customer. He insisted that another size would be too complicated and insisted on sticking to one size. We try to accommodate specific requests as much as possible, but sometimes we have to say, 'I'm sorry, this is the family of sizes we make.'

There were also some elements that could not be standardized. For example, although most connectors were standardized throughout the industry, some customers still requested a unique connector type. For elements such as this, ITT was not in a position to push standardization. Sowka commented: "Standardization is our philosophy, but we sometimes have to deviate from it. We make the decision on a case-by-case basis. So far, we've been very clever in standardizing along meaningful dimensions."

Looking forward, ITT management was uncertain about how far to take the concept of standardized product design. Dr. Geissinger said, "The whole world is talking about standardization, but *whose* standard do we choose? Every car is different and every car manufacturer has unique requirements for its system."

As of January 1994, the company had MK20 contracts from a number of automotive companies, including BMW, Chrysler, Ferrari, Ford of North America and Europe, Honda, Jaguar, KIA, Mercedes-Benz, Mitsubishi, Peugeot, Renault, Saab, Volkswagen, and Volvo.

---

[16]Between the MK4 and the MK4-G, about 20% of the equipment had been reused; 80% had been scrapped.

Manufacturing Strategy for the MK20

Following the company restructuring in 1992, ITT Automotive in Europe began stepping up efforts to cut labor costs in response to customer demands for lower cost products. A key part of this plan, headed by Prof. Lederer, involved transferring manufacturing of highly labor intensive or relatively unsophisticated products (such as brake sensors) outside Germany. In mid-1993, the company announced plans to begin manufacturing in Portugal, Hungary, and China.[17]

Because the MK20 was viewed as a highly sophisticated product, requiring a high degree of operator skill, management decided final assembly could not be performed in a low-wage country. (For subassemblies, however, this was possible.)

Facilities and Capacity

With the growing popularity of ABS, ITT expected that demand for the MK20 would be significantly higher than any of its other brake systems, even with a life cycle of only 5–6 years. Management estimated that the company could expect to sell 25 million MK20 units worldwide over the product's life, more than eight times the volume of the MK2.

ITT planned to produce the MK20 in all four of its existing ABS plants: Frankfurt, Germany; Mechelen, Belgium; Morganton, North Carolina; and Asheville, North Carolina. As of June 1994, all four of these plants were up and running other ITT ABS products. Asheville was running at full volume to produce the MK4. Morganton produced both the MK4 and MK4-G; these products would be phased out of this plant over the 1990s, as volumes of the MK20 ramped up.

Following the pattern used for other new ABS products, production of the MK20 would begin first in Frankfurt. Initial test production runs would begin in October 1994 and the first shipments would be made to customers in January 1995. The three-month lag (October to January) would allow time for the company to ramp-up and solve any unexpected problems. This plant would focus on supplying customers in Europe.

The Morganton plant would be the second plant to begin production of the MK20, starting in June 1995. The Morganton plant would primarily supply customers in North America. In January 1996, the Asheville plant would begin production. Like Morganton, the Asheville plant would primarily supply customers in North America.

MK20 assembly equipment would be purchased and installed in modules (sets of equipment); one module was capable of producing one million ABS units. (See Exhibit 11.6 for timing and placement of capacity.)

---

[17]The choice of these production sites was also due in part to the location of customer plants. ITT's Chinese plant, for example, was being built in a joint venture arrangement to supply a nearby Volkswagen assembly plant.

Exhibit 11.6   Timing and Placement of MK20 Production Capacity

	Europe		North America	
	site	installation	site	installation
Module 1	Frankfurt	Q4 '94	Morganton	Q1 '95
Module 2	Frankfurt	Q3 '95	Asheville	Q1 '96
Module 3	Mechelen	Q2 '96	Asheville	Q1 '97
Module 4			Asheville	Q4 '97

Standardized Process Technology

A critical aspect of the manufacturing strategy was to use the same assembly process in all the plants. Using one process in all the plants would allow the company to source globally. The MK20 could be produced in any of its plants for any customer, depending on where capacity was available. This would allow the company to use capacity more efficiently on a worldwide basis. Capacity could also be shifted over time by moving equipment from one plant to another.

Using one process also had the advantage that plants could benefit from each other's learning. Dr. Geissinger explained, "Using one process allows the machines to become process capable much more quickly. You don't have to worry about having different problems at each site."

Global sourcing could also allow ITT to run preproduction series for customers long before commercial production actually began, and thus, ITT did not have to invest in production capacity in advance. For example, when one of the plants received a contract to supply a customer with a certain ABS model, the customer would normally wish to view and approve the manufacturing process at that plant one year before receiving the first shipments. With the MK20, ITT would use the same manufacturing process throughout the world, so customers could view and approve the plant in Frankfurt before production actually began at other plants. Geissinger explained: "With common technology across plants, we can supply customers with pilot production from one plant."

Automated Process Technology

A second critical aspect of the manufacturing strategy for the MK20 was to use a highly automated process for assembly operations. Depending on which version of the MK20 was being produced, assembly would require approximately 100 individual operations, including in-line tests.[18] While

---

[18]In contrast, the assembly of the MK4G required over 200 assembly operations.

previous product generations had used a mixture of automated and manual assembly,[19] the MK20 process was designed to be almost completely automated. At each workstation, robots would pick the necessary components, assemble them onto the workpiece, and then place the workpiece back on the conveyor belt so that it could be transported to the next workstation. Two people staffed each production line in order to perform the few assembly operations that could not be automated and to monitor the system. Designing the system for some level of human intervention also provided extra flexibility. If a workstation failed, these operators could step in and perform the necessary assembly operations until it was restored.

Since the MK20 would be produced in different variants for different customers, robots at each station had to be capable of performing a given assembly operation with a high degree of flexibility. Dr. Geissinger explained, "We're trying to use the most flexible robots we can. We want to bring customer-specific tooling to a minimum." Additionally, some versions of the product required distinct, supplementary operations. Thus, not all versions of the product went through the same sequence, or even the same number, of assembly operations. Some work stations would be bypassed by some or most of the work-in-progress.

To accommodate these variations in assembly operations, the conveyor system was designed to automatically route each workpiece to the right set of workstations. In addition, this system (called a "flexible path") was also designed so that if a workpiece arrived at a workstation which was currently busy, the piece would be re-routed to a free station or put back in the central work-in-process queue. The flexible routing system was considered the most novel, and perhaps most complex, aspect of the MK20 production process.

While the company had had experience with automation before, the MK20 clearly created some significant engineering challenges. For example, in writing the computer software that would manage the entire process, it was necessary to anticipate all of the possible modes of failure and variation in the process. The system was also designed for a high degree of reliability; if any one of the processes failed, all other operations would continue working. Operating this sophisticated system would require a higher level of skill than previous systems. Engineers and highly skilled technicians would be responsible for all system programming and maintenance.

Because of the complexity and novelty of the new process, the Frankfurt plant management planned to implement the process in phases. Bernd Rossbach, who would be responsible for supervising all eight MK20 lines in the Frankfurt plant, explained:

---

[19]For example, the process for assembly of the MK4-Gi had approximately 75% of the operations automated. The MK4, a much older product, used a much more labor intensive process with only about 40% of the steps being automated.

We are ramping up in three phases. In the first phase, which started in April of this year, we did all the assembly by hand. There was no automation. In phase two, which will run from June to August, we will automate some of the more simple assembly operations, such as robots that pick and place parts. Full automation will not start to be implemented until October of this year. That will give us three months to get ready for commercial production which must start on January 1, 1995.

The decision to use a highly automated process had been made in March 1993 when the product was first being designed. Automation was seen as critical to the manufacturing strategy for the MK20. It was viewed as the solution for achieving lower costs, producing higher volumes, and maintaining high quality. Karl Haupt said: "Automation was absolutely necessary for us to compete in Western Europe. It was our only chance to stay competitive." The MK20 assembly process would require 50% fewer operators than the more labor-intensive process used for MK4-G. (See Exhibit 11.7 for ABS cost structures.)

The quality assurance (QA) group strongly supported the use of a high level of automation in producing the MK20. Mark Reece of QA said, "The quality group loves automation. With automated processes like this, our processes are very much in control. We don't even need to use SPC anymore. We're way beyond it." From a quality perspective, automated processes were easier to check and monitor. This simplified QA activities and QA documentation requirements.

With automation, product quality would be improved. Mark Reece estimated that with automation first-time yields of 98% (pass inspection without rework) could be expected. Second time yield (pass inspection with rework) was expected to reach 99.7% to 99.8%. In contrast, ITT's older plants that used a full manual process had first time yields of 87% to 88%.

Exhibit 11.7   Cost Structure of the MK20 versus MK4-G Brake Systems

	MK20 Proposed Automated Process	MK20 Mixed Manual/Automated Process	MK4G Current Process
Total Manufacturing Cost Index	77	81	100
Costs as a % of total cost:			
Materials	70%	70%	
Direct Labor	10%	15%	
Overhead (incl. indir. labor)	13%	10%	
Depreciation	7%	5%	

Notes: Estimates based on costs in Germany.

The mixed manual/automated process assumes the same level of automation as the process currently used to produce the MK4-G.

Manual process plants which had been updated with better, more modern equipment had first-time yields approaching 96% to 97%.

Automation was also expected to reduce product costs as a result of better product quality. Less equipment would be required. Dr. Geissinger estimated that 25% percent of the capital equipment costs for the MK IV were related to quality assurance. Much of this expense, he believed, would be unnecessary with an automated process: "With automation, you get product quality built in."

Some flexibility would be lost with automated processes, but this was seen as a rational tradeoff: "It's true that manual processes are the most flexible. But, because of the short development cycle, we need to start up production in Germany. In Germany, it is too costly to use manual processes." Management believed that automation offered the best solution. Dr. Geissinger explained,

> It's not an option to go to a low-wage country because the product technology requires a high degree of skill. So, we prefer to stay in a country where workers are skilled. These countries are higher wage, but we will use automation to lower costs. Besides the skill issue, there is the issue that people need to be trained, technology has to be transferred, and you have to worry about quality.

Although start up of MK20 production was expected to be a challenge, the challenges were not increased because of the higher level of automation. Weis explained that, because the MK20 was such a drastically different design than previous ABS, starting up with automated processes would not be any more complex than starting up with more manual processes. He said, "With manual processes, ramp up would still be difficult because people would need entirely new skills. We want operators to have product-independent skills."

The Morganton Plant

Opened in January 1993, the plant in Morganton, North Carolina was ITT Automotive's newest plant. It was scheduled to begin producing the MK20 in June 1995. The production equipment for the MK20 had been ordered by the central engineering group in Frankfurt (as was standard procedure within the company) and was scheduled to arrive in the fourth quarter of 1994.

As of June 1994, the Morganton plant produced two of ITT Automotive's other ABS, the MK4-G and MK4-Gi. The process for the MK4-Gi employed a relatively high level of automation, almost as much as was planned for the MK20. The level of automation planned for the MK20 would go one step further, by introducing fully automated materials handling.

The Morganton workforce was generally comfortable with a high level of automation. However, management had concerns about the process proposed for the MK20. Ed Anderson, manager of the Morganton plant who had been with ITT Automotive for 17 years, expressed mixed feelings. On the issue of globally standardized processes, Anderson believed that the MK20 plan made sense, but went too far. "We need to standardize to some degree, but not to the point that manufacturing engineering is pushing for now," he said. Geff Hoots, senior manufacturing engineer, further explained:

> Certain customer-specific requirements can be different in the U.S. than in Europe. In many cases, meeting those requirements calls for using different manufacturing processes. For example, in the U.S., customers really prefer to have their own dedicated manufacturing lines, whereas in Europe, this is not the case.

Different supplier conditions between the United States and Europe challenged the rationale for standardized processes. According to Mike Vann, senior manufacturing engineer, there was much more variability in the quality of materials received from U.S. suppliers, compared with materials received from companies supplying ITT in Europe. For example, parts purchased from U.S. suppliers had a defect rate of 50,000 defects per million, whereas Frankfurt's defects per million from its suppliers averaged 5,000 per million. This difference meant that the process used in the Frankfurt plant could accept much tighter specifications or require fewer quality checks than that used in U.S. plants. Vann commented: "The U.S. supplier base is not ready for automation."

Anderson, Vann, and Hoots all agreed that automation for the MK20 was unnecessarily complex. For example, they believed that the new flexible path would require an enormous amount of control to keep track of all the pallets on the conveyor (containing ABS in-process). Further, they believed that the flexible path system, with its circling conveyor, would make it difficult to identify the source of quality problems and would create a hidden inventory buffer.

The high level of complexity created other concerns about skills required of the workforce. Anderson was concerned that new equipment would require a higher level of technical knowledge than the plant currently had. Hoots predicted, "The technical support we'll need will increase greatly, by 50% or more." For example, the plant currently employed technicians for maintenance, but the proposed MK20 process would require engineers to maintain it.

Anderson did not expect quality to improve with more automation, nor did he foresee the cost of inspection decreasing. "Now we have a manual process, followed by 100% checking. We will still need to have quality checks for the MK20. Because of the precision of the product, there are a lot of things that can only be detected with the human eye. We will always need some human intervention." Furthermore, he added, "whenever an automated process isn't working, you have to have a person there to back it up."

Anderson was also concerned that the MK20 equipment was not sufficiently flexible to change for future generations of ABS. "History tells us that the product will change every four years," he said. He foresaw that equipment would also have to change with each successive generation of ABS. Fully automated equipment for the MK20, including material handling conveyors, would not be a reusable investment. Vann agreed. "We've been through four 'worldwide' equipment design standards in this company in the last five years. A standard doesn't have much value for us if it changes every year."

Since opening in 1993, the Morganton plant had had a successful startup. With its non-union workforce of 438 people, the plant had achieved 95% uptime by June 1994. Anderson questioned whether further automation could significantly increase productivity: "If I'm operating here with a total downtime of 5%, what more can this buy me?"

Some of Morganton's success was attributed to the implementation of Kaizen, a continuous improvement program, in 1994. Anderson was concerned that a high level of automation and standardization for the MK20 could possibly reduce or eliminate further process improvements, hindering the Kaizen efforts. Because of the high degree of integration in the system, operators would no longer be permitted to rearrange equipment, alter material handling, or optimize processes as they saw fit, as had been done under the company's current Kaizen program. Limiting change, he believed, would eliminate the prospect of future improvements. One manager in the plant summed it up, "If you automate, you stagnate."

The Asheville Plant

Opened in 1989, ITT's Asheville, North Carolina plant was scheduled to begin producing the MK20 in mid-1997. The equipment for the MK20 production had been specified, but had not yet been ordered from suppliers.

As of June 1994, the Asheville plant produced the MK4. The manufacturing process for this product was semi-automated. About 60% of the 200 assembly operations were performed by people, the other 40% of the process was automated. Much of the materials handling was also manual, including picking of parts and moving of in-process parts between subassemblies.

The Asheville plant would start production of the MK4-G later in the year, as this product was being transferred from the Morganton plant to make room for the MK20 there.

The Asheville plant manager was Steve Dickerson, a Harvard MBA

('78) with 20 years experience at General Motors. He had joined ITT as the manager of the Asheville plant in May 1993.

The struggle, according to Dickerson, was that the design and engineering of the MK20 needed to be adapted to U.S. requirements. As he explained, design and engineering were in Frankfurt (including the design of equipment); application engineering was performed in Auburn Hills, Michigan; and the largest manufacturing site would eventually be his plant in Asheville, North Carolina. Dickerson said:

> Frankfurt's view is the Frankfurt plant. There, they have expensive labor in the range of $30 to $35 per hour, a union environment, and employees that are multicultural and multilingual which makes it difficult for managers. They have a tremendous incentive to design labor out of the process. From where I sit in Asheville, I see a non-union environment, labor costs of $20 per hour, and a single culture, single language workforce that is much easier to manage.

Dickerson was concerned also that automation would require him to significantly reduce the workforce at his plant. He commented, "If it all works, I have an employment problem. What do I do with all of the extra people?" He explained further, "The last thing we want to do here is have a layoff. The short mission statement we follow at Asheville is first, satisfy your customer, and second, love your people. My mission in life is to keep people employed."

Since he foresaw that automation would require fewer people than he currently employed, Dickerson had instituted a hiring freeze when he started in May 1993. "I'm working with my workforce to help them see what's coming. I told them that five years down the road we'll need fewer operators and more skilled maintenance people to program PLCs (programmable logic controllers). I told them to go out and get those skills." Many employees had responded to the offer; in 1994, the Asheville plant was spending $10,000 per month on employee tuition reimbursement.

Dennis White, manager of manufacturing engineering, had other concerns about the impact of automation. He said, "By introducing Kaizen we made big improvements in the plant as well as a culture change." The culture change he was referring to was the arrival of Dickerson as plant manager and the introduction of Kaizen. With these changes, the plant had undergone a dramatic transformation in the past year.

Dickerson had managed the Asheville plant out of crisis by introducing Kaizen philosophy. This philosophy included first establishing an environment of trust and openness, then working with people to "to make what we have the best it can be." By implementing Kaizen philosophy and using Kaizen teams, the Asheville plant had made dramatic improvements in operating performance. In addition to improving productivity by

Exhibit 11.8   Asheville Plant Performance Data

Productivity
ITT Asheville

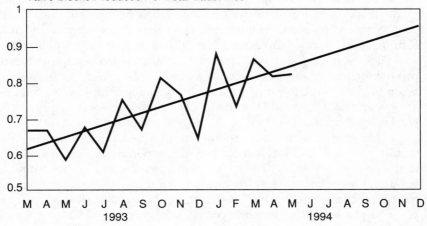

Valve Blocks Produced Per Total Labor Hour

Line NOK & Reject Rates
ITT Asheville

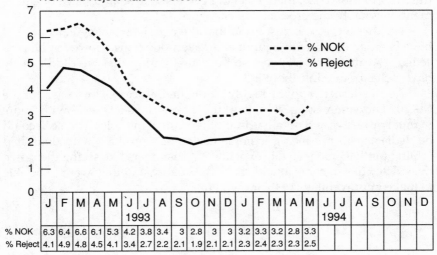

NOK and Reject Rate in Percent

	J	F	M	A	M	J	J	A	S	O	N	D	J	F	M	A	M	J	J	A	S	O	N	D
% NOK	6.3	6.4	6.6	6.1	5.3	4.2	3.8	3.4	3	2.8	3	3	3.2	3.3	3.2	2.8	3.3							
% Reject	4.1	4.9	4.8	4.5	4.1	3.4	2.7	2.2	2.1	1.9	2.1	2.1	2.3	2.4	2.3	2.3	2.5							

STRETCH GOAL = 50% ANNUAL REDUCTION IN REJECT RATES

Note: "Line NOK" (not okay) are parts rejected in-process. "Rejects" are finished parts or products that are rejected. Rejected parts and products are either scrapped or re-worked.

30%, the plant had increased days ahead of the customer measure from 0.2 days to 2 days and dramatically reduced the occurrence of defects. (See Exhibit 11.8 for plant performance data.)

Dickerson attributed most of this improvement to the effort and dedication of his workforce. He did not believe that more automated equipment would enhance plant performance much further. He said, "In the past year, we have made tremendous gains in productivity by doing Kaizen. I want to have equipment that utilizes the skills of my workforce."

Dickerson also did not believe that automated equipment could produce better quality products. "Quality is not a big factor, really. In assembly, there are cases where a machine does something better, but these are few and far between." He added, "Ultimately, quality depends on your workforce. People in Asheville care a lot about quality."

With more automation, Dickerson was concerned that the plant would give up flexibility across product generations and flexibility in terms of product mix. "There are high set up costs with automation because it takes time to clear the line and changeover." Flexibility was also critical for changes to product specifications. He explained, "Last year, this plant handled 3,000 engineering change orders on the MK4. This was a 4 year old product! Most are just engineering tweaks, but some are major changes. This puts a premium on flexibility with respect to the product. I need a process which can adapt."

Like Anderson in Morganton, Dickerson questioned whether the equipment could actually be reused for future generations of ABS: "From the MK4 to the MK20, there has not been a single shared piece of equipment. Inevitably, the product will change again."

He also expressed frustration that the people at Asheville could not have been involved with equipment design decisions. However, he conceded, "At that time we were so busy firefighting that we didn't really have a chance to think about it."

As an alternative to the highly automated processes proposed for the MK20, Dickerson suggested that the plants instead stick with more manual processes and organize into cells or small modules. Each cell could be dedicated to producing a single customer's product, with dedicated tooling for that customer. He explained, "Customers like seeing their own lines. They like to come in and check the quality, and they want to be able to make improvements to their own lines."

Systems and Organizational Processes

*A*s with the structural elements of an Operating Strategy, the various infrastructural elements (such as human resource policies, production planning and control systems, quality systems, and the way operating units are organized and measured) also must be molded to fit the firm's competitive strategy. Because the myriad decisions that combine, over time, to shape its infrastructure tend to be made at relatively low levels in the organization, involve little capital expenditure, and occur on a daily basis, many managers and academics tend to dismiss such decisions as merely "tactical" rather than strategic in nature. They regard such apparently ephemeral policies and systems as simply being supportive of, or ancillary to, the structural decisions, which command more top-management attention because they often require sizable investments and are physically impressive (and are counted as "assets" in the firm's balance sheet).

For most firms, this is a profound mistake. Their almost invisible infrastructure is just as important as—and often more important strategically than—their physical structure, just as a computer's software often has more impact on its overall effectiveness than its hardware. And infrastructural choices contribute just as directly to a firm's performance along certain competitive dimensions. As an obvious example, a performance measurement system that is focused primarily on cost variances and labor/equipment utilization rates will undermine any attempt to compete on the basis of superior quality or responsiveness to customer requests. Similarly, workforce policies that seek out low-cost labor, wherever it can be found, can easily hamstring attempts to use advanced technology or to compete on the basis of fast delivery. Policies that restrict movement among different jobs and/or provide little training or incentives to broaden operator skills will thwart "pull-type" workflow scheduling systems and quality improvement efforts.

A coherent infrastructure takes time to build, can be very difficult to change once in place, and in many cases provides the company's primary source of advantage over competitors that have adopted similar structures. Therefore, infrastructural issues *are* strategic in nature, even though they receive far less attention from strategists and planners. As we will see in the cases in this section, the cumulative effect of these decisions and policies determines the degree to which the potential embedded within a firm's structural hardware is exploited for competitive advantage. Over the past several years, we have seen a dramatic shift in the relative importance of structural and infrastructural elements. Companies that competed largely on the basis of cost have historically focused their attention primarily on structural issues, such as locating factories in low-cost regions and choosing processing equipment and sourcing arrangements that permitted economies of scale. However, as competition has shifted progressively to emphasize quality, flexibility, and speed, firms have come to concentrate more and more on infrastructural issues. Such competitive characteristics, they have found, cannot be assured simply by having advanced technology, and certainly not by sourcing products from remote overseas locations.

This has meant a dramatic shift in the skills demanded of operations strategists and managers. In the past, many operations managers were expected simply to be custodians of the assets entrusted to them, responsible primarily for "keeping the equipment running." Managers increasingly now confront a much broader challenge. More and more of the capabilities needed to provide sustainable competitiveness are grounded primarily in sound infrastructural policies and decisions. But there is much more to building an effective infrastructure than becoming "world class" or following the latest management fad. More important is building the right *kind* of infrastructure—one whose elements fit together well, one which works in harmony with the structural elements, and one which contributes to and reinforces the principal strategic objectives of the firm. In the cases that follow, we explore the way a few key elements of an operation's infrastructure—*human resources, quality, workflow planning and control,* and organization and measurement—can be forged together with structural elements to support difficult-to-imitate forms of competitive advantage.

Human resource policies determine such factors as the skill level of people in the operation, the nature and extent of their training, how and why they are committed to their work, how much (and how) they are paid, and how secure they are in their jobs.

Quality policies capture those features that determine how defective products and poor service are prevented, and how quality is monitored, measured, and improved over time.

Workflow planning and control systems determine the way work is planned, scheduled and controlled. They include not only the policies concerning what work is some at what time, but also the information and human processes that coordinate the work flow.

Organization and Measurement characterizes how the operation is organized: for example, whether control is distributed or centralized; the degree of autonomy of the various operational units and levels; how incentive systems are structured; and how integration across functions is assured.

How Does Infrastructure Differ from Structure?

As we described earlier in the book, the infrastructural elements of an operations strategy are characterized by a number of features and distinguish them from the structural elements. First, while both structure and infrastructure take time to develop, infrastructural elements demand a very different kind of effort. Rather than putting effort into planning, proposals, and grand designs, infrastructural capabilities are built through persistent day-to-day effort, often in the lowest parts of the organization.

Second, an operations infrastructure tends to be characterized by less tangible features than its structure; for example, an atmosphere of trust or particular customs and practices in the operation. By their vary nature, such characteristics take perseverance and dogged effort to change and cultivate. It is, rather frustratingly, much easier to buy a new plant than it is to walk into a plant and change its measurement system or to declare, "Top management has decided that, due to a change in our competitive strategy, there will now be a new attitude to quality in this plant" with any hope of success!

Third, the values that underpin an infrastructure are easily undermined: a few bad decisions can unravel many years of patient work. One peremptory decision to discipline an operator or override a production-control system can set precedents that fundamentally change the effectiveness of the organization. Shared understanding and trust take a long time to build, but only a moment to destroy.

The Interaction of Structure and Infrastructure

Even if a company's operations structure is well thought out, its effectiveness is strongly dependent on a consistent and coherent infrastructure. For example, the actual (as opposed to the rated) capacity of a plant depends not only on how many hours per year it is operated, but how effectively work is scheduled through it and how well its equipment is maintained. Similarly, the competitive advantage that a company can generate from a piece of standard technology is greatly enhanced if the people operating it work in an environment that encourages them to continually improve the equipment and how it is used. Even a Stradivarius violin will make an awful noise if played badly!

Achieving a competitive advantage from operations, however, requires more than having both a structural and an infrastructural strategy. It also requires that these strategies be *integrated*. Different structural approaches require different infrastructural policies. For example, consider a company competing on the basis of cost. One structural strategy would be to invest heavily in the appropriate type of automation; but this will only led to low cost if production is also scheduled around long run lengths (to minimize set-up costs) and a workforce is recruited that is sufficiently skilled (and well paid) to operate the equipment. An alternative approach that may be just as effective in creating a cost advantage would be to locate a labor-intensive process off shore (a structural decisions) in order to be able to access a lower-wage (and lower-skilled) workforce. In this example, whether a company is able to achieve low-costs depends on how well it integrates its structural and infrastructural strategies, rather than on its decisions within each category.

Infrastructure and the Role of Operations

Because the capabilities that a firm nurtures in its infrastructure are so often embedded deep in the organization, it is critical that a firm communicate clearly how its operations organization is expected to contribute to the firm's competitive strategy. A company that views its operations function primarily as a servant of other functions may, in spite of having a good operations structure, foster infrastructures that are incomplete, stunted, or rigid. In the absence of an expanded view of the role operations can play in the firm's competitive success, its systems, policies and procedures tend to become haphazard—the agglomeration of a series of uncoordinated decisions—or regress to "the way we've always done it." People who view their role simply as caretakers of expensive equipment, or who see their job as simply "keeping utilization high" will not be motivated to build systems and procedures that help the operation deliver superior performance on the principal competitive dimensions it seeks. When the importance of operations is widely understood and reinforced, throughout the workforce, it is much easier to build an atmosphere that encourages the development of quality procedures, work-planning methods and organizational structures that support the strategic goals of the business.

Throughout this module, there is a strong theme of *improvement and learning* to which we return later in the book. In each case, however, the primary question is one of *fit*—how the infrastructure each firm is trying to shape and cultivate supports the competitive mission of the operation.

The Cases and Readings

John Crane (UK) Ltd. is facing a slow, but consistent change in the way it competes, and, over a ten-year period, we see how its infrastructures has been molded to adapt from a cost/product technology-based competitive environment to one that values customization and quick response. This has meant visceral change for Crane. While some process technology changes have taken place, the infrastructural changes have been much more profound. The operators, steeped in the old methods, have been challenged to learn new skills, to work in manufacturing cells, and to understand the importance of keeping inventory low for responsiveness rather than just keeping their machines running. The case also allows us to see how production control systems must adapt to new competitive roles. Crane's old system was designed to maximize utilization (consistent with competing on cost), whereas it has now been shaped, slowly but surely, to support responsiveness and flexibility.

Crane's quality systems and organization also have been adapted to fit the new way of competing, and the firm seems to be on an ever-improving path to achieve its changing goal (albeit after a slow start!). Crane's improvement path is threatened, however, as its policy of elevating the operators' role comes into conflict with a new technology that threatens to de-skill them again. Management has to decide how to proceed at this juncture—by making a decision that is apparently tactical but has important strategic consequences. This case also shows how the *role* of operations can change over time: from an embarrassing, grudgingly-tolerated cost center, to the powerhouse of its competitive success.

Advanced manufacturing technology often demands the kind of deep-rooted organizational change that we see in the Crane case. In their article, "Manufacturing's Crisis: New Technologies, Obsolete Organizations," Hayes and Jaikumar explore the various kinds of infrastructural changes that companies may need to make in order to take advantage of the full potential of new manufacturing technologies.

AT&T Universal Card Services. This case describes the way UCS has developed its quality systems to deliver outstanding customer service—and hence meet its goal of "delighting" customers and differentiating itself from its fierce competitors. Not only does the "UCS" case provide an excellent example of the strategic deployment of quality systems, it also shows the meticulous attention to detail that strategic infrastructural development demands. Some decisions about compensation and measurement have come precipitously close to unraveling the gains made in service performance, as UCS attempted to "raise the bar" and improve quality even further. The case gives us an opportunity to explore the strategic importance of the way in which people are organized and measured, as well as the feasibility of sustaining improvement by continuously readjusting their compensation system.

Philips Taiwan. This thriving firm has grown from a Philips manufacturing satellite, originally located in Taiwan for low-cost production, to an innovative outpost at the center of the Asian computer industry. It has become clear that Philips Taiwan has developed new capabilities in product development and, in order to tailor its innovations more closely to the market, is deciding the extent to which it will use a powerful but cumbersome quality technique—Quality Function Deployment (QFD)—to deliver the right kind of quality to its customers. Philips Taiwan is also proposing organizational changes to speed up its new product development, given the progressive shift of the computer industry to Asia. This case asks the question: Should Philips retain control over Taiwan's innovation process at its corporate headquarters in Holland, and ensure a coherent product line around the world, or has the environment changed sufficiently to give its Taiwanese subsidiary much more autonomy in the innovation process?

Throughout the course, but particularly in this module on infrastructure, we have used the word *flexibility* to cover a broad range of capabilities and to denote a source of competitive advantage. But like quality, flexibility has many dimensions and it is important to be clear about the type of flexibility a firm needs to develop. There is little point in producing a broad product range (one way of competing through flexibility), when what the customer wants more is quick response. Different infrastructures are needed to support each capability. In "John Crane," for example, the infrastructure had to support an ability to be a responsive *customizer* while "McDonald's the firm had to decide to what extent its operations strategy could support an increasingly *broad product range*.

In his article, "The Management of Manufacturing Flexibility," Upton suggests a way of defining flexibility that allows one to be more precise when the word is used in an operations context—the first step in determining what structural and infrastructural changes need to be made. This framework will help us analyze situations where flexibility is an important issue throughout the rest of the course. Indeed, we have the opportunity to apply that framework immediately in the "Stermon Mills" case. Here we see a company that can no longer compete on the basis of cost and must therefore develop a new infrastructure and improvement path to compete on the basis of flexibility. But first it needs to decide what kind of flexibility it should offer, and how it should adapt its infrastructure to deliver the type of flexibility it selects.

In the increasingly volatile Japanese cosmetics market, the firm described in the "Kanebo" case also needs to improve its flexibility to provide quick response to its volatile and faddish market demand. To do this, it proposes combining an innovative new point-of-sale information system and a flexible manufacturing system. While these are largely structural decisions on the surface, the case makes it explores the kind of infrastructure that is required to complement these technologies when market information, and the ability to respond to it, are critical abilities.

The final case in this module, "Daweoo Shipbuilding and Heavy Machinery," describes a firm that is betting it competitive future on its infrastructure while its competitors are expanding by making huge structural investments in plant and equipment. Daewoo must decide if continued infrastructural improvement alone will be sufficient to maintain and build its market share. This case also shows us the strong interaction between structural and infrastructural elements of the strategy; as one

Daewoo manager puts it, "Productivity improvement *is* capacity expansion." Rescued from the brink of disaster in 1987, Daewoo is a shining example of a firm that has learned to build new capabilities through an indefatigable and determined focus on its workforce, its quality systems, its work-flow control systems and its organization. Indeed, we will return to this critical issue in the latter part of the book, when we explore the general subject of building and exploiting capabilities

CHAPTER 12

John Crane UK Limited

The CAD-CAM Link

*I*T WAS A CRISP July morning in 1990. As usual at this time of day, the M25 London Orbital Motorway was a parking lot. Bob Gibbon, Operations Director for John Crane UK Limited sat in his car, and thought about the previous day's meeting with John Carr, Engineering Systems Manager, and Alex Luboff, Engineering Systems Engineer. The CAD-CAM issue was getting to be a problem at John Crane's Slough[1] plant. Carr's team had demonstrated the feasibility of generating programs for computer-controlled production machines directly from the company's design database. At the same time, Crane's shop-floor operators had made astounding progress in learning to program the machines themselves from engineering drawings. They had become progressively more skilled over the past few years, chiefly as a result of their involvement in the manufacturing cells project, one of a handful of projects which had brought Crane manufacturing from mediocrity to world-class excellence. The operators were keen to continue to use their newly-acquired expertise.

Carr had put it plainly the day before: "We need to think about who should be writing these programs, now that we have a choice: should they be written automatically in Production Engineering, or should the shop-floor operators be writing them?"

The Crane Story

On March 9th, 1917, Crane Packing Company was founded in Chicago, Illinois by Frank Payne. The company's first product was invented by John

---

[1]Pronounced like *plough*.

Crane. He devised a system for sealing rotating shafts by packing material tightly around the shaft thus preventing the fluid surrounding the shaft from leaking out. Payne set up a British subsidiary of Crane in Slough in 1923. By 1989, John Crane UK Limited was the main European arm of John Crane International (JCI), whose 1989 profit before interest was £32m on turnover of £239m (£1.00 = $1.85 at the time of the case). JCI was owned by the TI Group, a British company with diversified engineering interests, and had defined its corporate strategy to be congruent with that of the TI Group as a whole:

> TI's basic strategic thrust is to be an international engineering group, concentrating on specialised engineering businesses, oper- ating in selected niches on a global basis, and commanding sustainable technological and market share leadership.
> —Christopher Lewinton, Chairman and Chief Executive, TI Group, 1989

John Crane UK Limited managed the EMA (Europe, Middle East and Africa) region of John Crane International. This region generated 30% of JCI's revenues. John Crane EMA had subsidiaries in Austria, France, Belgium, Germany, Holland, Italy, Sweden, Spain, Switzerland and a joint venture in China. It had numerous agencies in other countries as sales and distribution points for its products and services. In 1989, over 70% of its business came from outside the UK.

The Product: Mechanical Seals

Mechanical seals had become complex engineering products with a wide variety of applications. For example, they were used around the propeller shafts of submarines to prevent sea-water from leaking past the shaft and filling the vessel; they were used on the shaft of chemical pumps to contain the fluids being pumped. The most common use was in the water-pump of an automobile, to contain the coolant around the pump drive shaft. Despite the variety of applications, all seals performed a similar function. They provided a barrier between two regions through which a common shaft rotated (see Exhibit 12.1). Exhibit 12.2 shows some examples from Crane's product range. Crane supplied seals for most applications. Customers came with a particular sealing problem, and Crane provided a solution in the form of either a standard or custom seal, along with a hous- ing design if necessary. Sixty percent of seal sales were replacements for seals which had reached the end of their useful life. John Crane UK manu- factured 64% of the EMA region's seals by sales volume. The principal seal families are shown in Figure 12.1.

While there were many standard products, others were very special- ized and complex, requiring superlative engineering design. For example,

Figure 12.1 Product Families

Product	Application	1990 UK Production	
		Sales (%)	Typical Price (£)
automotive and appliance	e.g. automotive coolant pump	7	1
standard rubber bellows	water-based industries	21	15
standard wedge ring	petrochemical industries	31	30
special seals	various specialist applications	41	80

While there were many standard products, others were very specialized and complex, requiring superlative engineering design. For example, gas seals were special seals in a high-growth product category, on the "leading edge" of seal technology. These highly complex seals could cost tens of thousands of pounds, and demanded a high degree of production expertise.

gas seals were special seals in a high-growth product category, on the "leading edge" of seal technology. These highly complex seals could cost tens of thousands of pounds, and demanded a high degree of production expertise.

Exhibit 12.1 Mechanical Sealing

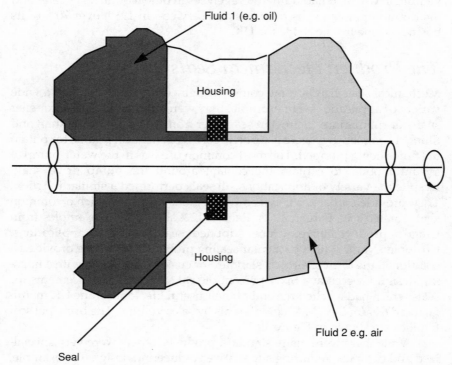

Exhibit 12.2   Examples of Products

The Market

Revenues from sales of seals manufactured in the UK in 1989 were £46m. Customers for mechanical seals generally belonged to one of the following three categories:

i. Projects

Project sales came from customers who were involved in building a large scale plant, such as an oil rig or chemical plant. Competition for these orders was intense since projects tended to be large and relatively few in number. Success in this market resulted in future sales of spare parts for the whole plant since the life of the pump being sealed was often five times longer than the life of the seal. Each seal would probably be replaced four or five times during the life of the pump.

ii. Original Equipment Manufacturers (OEMs)

OEMs (for example, pump manufacturers) bought seals to install in their equipment before they sold to their customers. Their products were manufactured to a firm schedule which meant that reliable delivery by Crane was essential. Again, competition was fierce, as the volumes tended to be larger and more stable, often forcing higher levels of price discounting. OEMs and Project sales shared similar levels of replacement business.

iii. End user

The majority of sales of seals and replacement parts were made to end users. Two extremes of this market were large multi-national companies which specified Crane seals in all their plants worldwide and owners of swimming pools which required seals for their filtration pumps. Larger users required reliable, though not always immediate, delivery. Small users required reliable seals with prompt replacement service.

In general, the market was conservative, and not eager to try out new products. This meant that there were some very long product life cycles: the 1A seal, one of the best selling seals, had been in the market for 40 years. At the same time, customers continued to push for improved responsiveness for applications design.

Competitors fell into four categories. First, and most important, were those similar to John Crane who offered a wide range of sealing solutions. Second were low variety, high volume producers. They concentrated on a very small range of seals, and often lost customers as soon as they had requirements out of the range of their expertise. Third, competitors in local markets often emerged from companies expanding from seal servicing. Finally, and increasingly more worrisome, were "pirate" competitors who put Crane's name on a substandard seal and passed it off as genuine. Crane held approximately 30% of the European market across the range of segments it currently served, and was widely considered to be the leader in seal technology.

Crane's market had evolved markedly over the previous ten years. There had been a steady shift away from standardized products to specially designed products which had grown from 7% of revenues in 1981 to 41% of revenues in 1989.

Manufacturing at John Crane UK

Most UK employees were based in the towns of Slough and Reading[2] (20 miles apart) in the southeast of England. There were 170 production employees in Slough and 70 in Reading. The main steps in manufacturing a mechanical seal were component production and assembly. Metal-machining was the dominant method by which Crane produced seal components, although it produced some by machining PTFE[3] (10% of value) and by pressing sheet steel (20% of value).

The two main processes for machining metal components were turning and milling. In a turning process, the component was rotated and cut by a stationary tool, while in milling, the component was held still and was cut by a rotating tool. Turning resulted in round, rotationally symmetrical features, while milled features were generally asymmetrical or prismatic. Because seal features were usually round (to fit around shafts), most of the productive effort was spent turning components on lathes or turning centers (which were sophisticated lathes). All machined components were turned as part of the production process, while only some components had milled features. A typical process for a metal-machined component was:

1. Make blanks from metal stock;
2. Perform first set of primary turning operations on turning center (called Op. 1);
3. Turn component around in the work holder, and perform the second set of primary turning operations (Op. 2);
4. Mill and drill features which cannot be turned;
5. Finish turn components to final tolerance; and
6. Store for later assembly (see Exhibit 12.3)

Component machining work was split into two categories: Make to Order (MTO) and Make for Stock (MFS). MTO comprised 35% of machined component production value and was produced in the Slough factory. MFS made up the remaining 65% and was produced in Reading. MTO was further split into "specials" (32% of MTO unit volume), which were components specially designed for a particular order and "standard" which had already been engineered (68% of MTO unit volume). In 1989, the Slough factory machined 34,000 components while Reading produced 400,000.

Assembly was relatively straightforward and in general Crane assembled to order. A mechanical seal comprised about 8 components assembled

---

[2]Pronounced like *heading*.

[3]PTFE (polytetrafluorethylene) was a low-friction polymer. PTFE machining was carried out in a separate facility as was sheet steel work. Automotive seals were also produced in a separate local facility in Slough.

Exhibit 12.3   Manufacturing Process for Metal Machined Components

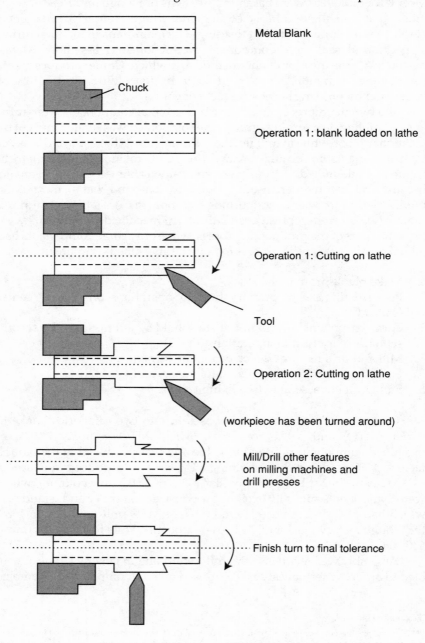

Metal Blank

Chuck

Operation 1: blank loaded on lathe

Operation 1: Cutting on lathe

Tool

Operation 2: Cutting on lathe

(workpiece has been turned around)

Mill/Drill other features
on milling machines and
drill presses

Finish turn to final tolerance

into a finished unit. There were nearly 100,000 finished assembly types even though there were only 6,000 standard components. While complex metal components were usually machined in-house, many components were produced by vendors (bought-outs). Bought-outs were often non-metallic and relatively simple: carbon faces or grub-screws for example. Though Crane manufactured a large variety of seals, only a few products were made in large volumes. This meant that much of Crane's manufacturing task was that of a job-shop: making a large variety of components effectively. Sixty-five percent of Crane's components had an annual demand of less than 10 per annum. This included all MTO components and half of MFS.

> When we talk about economies, they are economies of variety, not scale. We are not trying to increase production to spread our costs over any particular product. We are trying to minimise the impact which product variety has on us. If we can aggregate our products cleverly, we gain a great advantage.

The Reading Factory: 1981–1983

In 1980, most of the machines (in both Reading and Slough) were 20 to 30 years old. Capital investment had slowed to a trickle of about £50,000 per annum over the previous five years. There were many different machines to cope with the enormous variety of material sizes, batch quantities, and types of product. Machines in both Reading and Slough were arranged functionally: all the lathes were together in one area, all milling machines in another and so on (Exhibit 12.4 shows such a functional layout). Having machines of the same type grouped together in departments meant that components had to visit multiple departments, making the flow of components through the shop very complicated. Work would slowly wend its way through the shop spending most of the time sitting and waiting on the floor. A component could travel literally miles between the time the raw material went onto the floor and the time the component went into finished components stores. There was very little grouping of components in manufacturing. If anything, it was based on the volume of parts produced. Small volume components tended to be produced in Slough, and higher demand components in Reading, but there were many exceptions. A third factory in Havant handled medium volume components. Production costs were divided roughly evenly between these three factories.

In all factories, the objective was to keep machines busy. Shop loading was aimed at maintaining machine utilization. Unfortunately, the large number of components in process meant that there were very long lead times. Gibbon commented on the Reading factory.

> In Reading, we could have 8, 10 or 12 weeks worth of work sitting at a given machine. We often had to interrupt a batch to put on a

Exhibit 12.4 Old Shop Layout in Slough

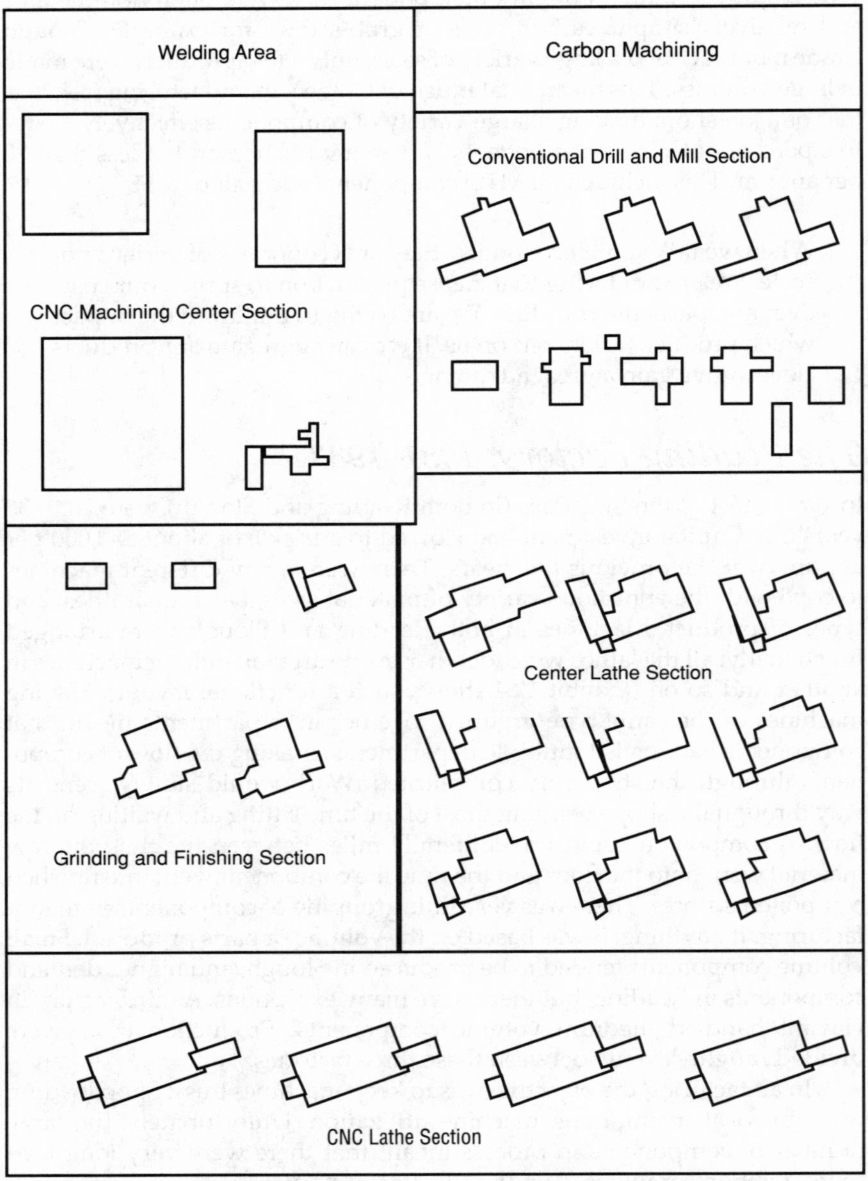

rush job, and the work-in-process reflected our lead times of about 3 months in make-to-stock (90% of value) and 6 months in make-to-order (10% of value). The mix gave rise to a complex logistical problem.

The Reading factory ran two shifts, five days a week, and made about 300,000 components a year. Components were being produced in a very wide variety of batch sizes; some of the larger batches were 2000–3000 components. Occasionally these long jobs were punctuated with rush orders, which usually meant re-setting some machines and losing considerable productive time.

In the middle of 1982, the Havant factory was burnt down by an arsonist. While this was a short-term disaster, it gave Crane a golden opportunity to resite and reorganize production. Havant production was brought to Reading. Gibbon, in his mid-twenties at the time, was made Production Superintendent and put in charge of the move. Reading was divided into a stock shop (for make-for-stock components) and a non-stock shop (for make-to-order components), to increase the visibility of make-to-order work by manufacturing it separately. This was the first attempt at grouping components within a factory. (The non-stock shop was moved to Slough in 1984). This separation greatly improved the visibility of non-stock work in the shop, and reduced the lead time for non-stock components from 26 weeks to 12 weeks. Within each of these shops, a number of changes were made:

> We wanted to use the opportunity to make production more flexible. We tried to make machines more similar to each other and we trained people to operate a number of machines.

The replacement labour was new. In the old factory, people on the shop-floor were either setters (who performed machine set-ups) or operators. The change in labour force meant that this tradition could be changed, and workers were employed as setter-operators rather than one or the other. While this was a small step, it meant a great increase in flexibility in the shop. Improvements were limited, since the machines were fire-damaged and the labour was new. Even with this hindrance, make-for-stock lead times were reduced to 6 weeks. Despite weathering the fire, and making improvements along the way, the way the Reading factory was being run was still a headache.

> As things were, we threw work at the shop because that's what the order point system demanded. In 1981, I had made a computer model of the factory using CAN-Q[4] [see Exhibit 12.5], so that we

---

[4]CAN-Q was a computer program which used queueing theory to mathematically model the flow of work around a factory. It gave information such as expected queue lengths and throughput times.

could understand our plant better and demonstrate the advantages of any changes in the system. We validated the model and found it accurate to within 2 or 3%. We explored the relationship between the amount of work-in-process on the shop floor and the output we got from the plant [see Exhibit 12.6]. This made it even clearer to me that the way we were loading work onto the shop was a big problem. I just couldn't win on this point!—people genuinely believed it was the production's fault that lead times were so long, rather than the policies we were using. Countering the traditional beliefs about shop loading was very difficult.

Gibbon was convinced that the policy of keeping the shops loaded down with work was hurting effectiveness and was causing long lead times. The results he had gleaned from the computer model further steeled his conviction that changes were needed. Frustratingly, he was unable to convince people that there could be a better way of doing things.

CNC and Cells in Reading, 1984–1986

Having had such difficulties changing shop-loading practices within the status quo, Gibbon changed tack and turned to new production technology and the problem of flow. The age of the machines in the Reading shop often made it difficult to hold tolerances and efficiently produce a high-quality product. Gibbon and his team set about justifying an investment of £350,000 in new, Computer Numerically Controlled (CNC) machine tools. As the name implies, a CNC machine has a dedicated computer controller which tells the machine all it needs to know to make a part, such as the spindle-speed, the position of the tools, the tooling to be used and so on. On traditional machines, the operators performed these functions using levers and dials. Computer-control was much faster and more reliable. The controller had a computer program (a *part-program*) for each part which the machine would make. This could be read into the controller's memory from punched tape, magnetic media, or another computer by a communications link.

Some non-CNC machines did a similar job using mechanical automation, but the set-up time for each batch was long, so these machines were relatively inflexible. CNC machines required only a change of program and the appropriate tooling to switch jobs. The new machines would thus be more flexible since the penalty of changing from one job to the next would be reduced. The machines also tended to be more versatile because they could make many more types of components than the old machines. This was a large investment for Crane and came at a time when capital was short. To be sure that the project was accepted, the justification carried out was unusually rigorous, thorough, and extensive.

The proposed investment in the new machines gave Crane the chance

Exhibit 12.5   A Glossary of Terms

2D-Drafting	The use of design systems which rely on two-dimensional representations of three-dimensional objects.
CAD	Computer Aided Design
CADAM™	IBM proprietary CAD system.
CAM	Computer Aided Manufacture.
CANQ	Computer Analysis of Networks of Queues: A simple, generalized mathematical model of a manufacturing system developed by James Solberg at Purdue University.
CAPP	Computer Aided Process Planning: The use of computers to generate methods for producing a product, either through interaction with the user (interactive) or automatically (generative).
CIM	Computer Integrated Manufacturing: The philosophy or tools associated with ensuring use of common computer information in products, processes and business systems.
CNC	Computer Numerical Control: A system for operating the axes and motors of machine tools using computers and electro-mechanical drives, rather than human motion. Sequences of motions are stored in a part-program and run on a CNC machine controller.
Discrete Event Simulation	The modelling of a system, usually on a computer, by describing the changes that occur to it at discrete points in time. Examples of computer software packages to do this are XCELL and SLAM™
Machine tool	A device for shaping or cutting a product which incorporates driven spindles, along with two or more axes of motion for either the tool, the workpiece, or both. Examples of machine tools are lathes, milling machines, and grinding machines.
Offline programming	The production of part programs without stopping the machine on which they are to run.
NC	Numerical Control: The precursor to CNC, which used paper tapes and electromechanical systems rather than computers.
Part program	The computer program which a CNC machine tool uses to direct its motors and axes, containing detailed instructions on how to produce a component.
Post processor	A computer program which adapts a generalized computer-based process plan to produce a part program for a particular machine tool.
Turning	A method of machining which involves rotating the workpiece and cutting it with a stationary tool. This is carried out on a lathe or a turning center.
Turning Center	A sophisticated lathe, which provides additional machine capabilities, such as driven tools.

Exhibit 12.6   CAN-Q Results

CAN-Q Results - Reading Shop - 1981		
Mean WIP (components)	Mean Lead Time (working days)	Mean Output Rate (components/day)
4970	15.1	329
7456	16.1	464
9941	17.1	581
12426	18.2	683
14912	19.3	771
17397	20.5	847
19882	21.8	912
22368	23.1	967
24853	24.5	1014
27338	25.9	1054
29824	27.4	1086
32309	29.0	1113
34794	30.7	1134
37280	32.4	1151
39765	34.2	1163
42250	36.0	1173
44736	37.9	1179
47221	39.9	1182

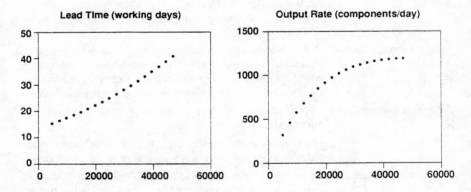

to look very carefully at the way it ran its production operation, and issues such as material flow were closely examined. During the project, in 1983, Crane looked at the prospect of a Flexible Manufacturing System (FMS): a complex system with an automated materials-handling system connecting unattended machines together, the whole shop being scheduled by a central computer. The team decided that the technology was too new, and too inflexible to adapt to Crane's needs. However, the process of carrying out the analysis for the FMS crystallized Crane's production-system needs.

A great deal of use was made of discrete-event simulation,[5] which now became an important instrument of persuasion. After considering all the alternatives, Crane decided to rely on the following to improve their manufacturing system:

- Manufacturing cells
- Advanced production technology (in the form of CNC machines)
- Better-trained people

Manufacturing cells were formed on the principle that machines in a shop should be located based on the parts they were producing rather than the type of machine they were. In effect, mini-factories were created within an existing plant. Gibbon set up 3 different types of cells in Reading, as shown in Exhibit 12.7. Components were grouped to be produced by particular cells. In Reading the groupings were made by distinguishing between those components which required only turning (turned rings) and those which required turning and subsequent milling (drilled rings). Rather than making a long, weary journey from department to department, batches of components passed quickly around a close-knit U-shaped "cell" of machines, visiting 2 or 3 of them. Each cell contained all the machines necessary to complete its type of job along with a small group of operators who ran the cell.

Union rules in the shop had always been that one machine should be tended by one person. However, the change in machine technology made this policy clearly unreasonable. Operators could often tend multiple machines if computers tended low-level operations. Operators assigned to work on the cells were thoroughly trained in the new technology. When the new machines were commissioned, performance targets based on learning curves were set for the operators, many of whom took these targets as a personal challenge. They became very committed to the project as they learned more about the technology and the new production system. The move towards cells meant a very different style of work for them. Instead of having the next operation for a batch on the other side of the shop and possibly several weeks away, the subsequent operation was performed a few metres away and possibly only minutes after the original operation. This link fostered cooperation between people on the shop-floor. Rather than sitting in isolation, plodding through an endless pile of work waiting for the same operation, people became aware of the total production process. Gerry Cusack, a Production Engineer at the time, pointed out:

> A big part of the success of this project came from the bottom. A lot of work was put in by everyone, but the people on the machines could have made it work or killed it off. They made it work.

[5]See Exhibit 12.5.

Exhibit 12.7   New Shop Layout in Slough

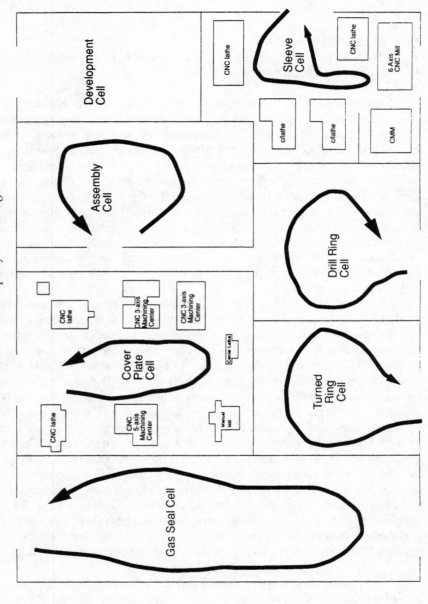

By mid-1986, the project was clearly a success:

> To be fair, it would have been difficult to fail using such new equipment. Even so, output per operator increased by 13%, and lead times fell by 65%. Both of these are key measures for Crane. People liked the project and the technology gained acceptability. We were on a roll!

The experiment had paid off. Not only had the introduction of cells and CNC improved performance, but it had, at last, clearly demonstrated the advantages of not overloading the shop with work. During 1986, batch quantities were reduced dramatically as manufacturing and stock management became more aware of these advantages. This new way of working was not without its problems, however:

> Operators were used to having a mountain of work in front of them: there was always something to do. Now, they had to get used to the idea that they only got work when it was needed. This was uncomfortable for some people.

To limit work in the shop, Crane painted 1.5 metre squares on the floor for finished work. That square also held the input buffer for the next operation. Operators were given a "make list" each week, but were also told that they could only put their finished work in the square while there was room: if it got full, they were to stop and find out why it wasn't being emptied. Four years later, the painted squares were long worn away, but the work-in-process continued to be as low as when they were fresh on the floor. The control system in Reading started to shift from a re-order point system (fixed quantity, variable time) to a time-phased system (fixed time, variable quantity). This meant that similar components could be grouped together more easily. These changes in production control decreased lead times by a further 50%.

Not everyone was happy with the new methods. About 5% of the operators just didn't like it: they preferred the old way of working. In general, however, the project resulted in an enormous improvement in morale. Operators helped to make video recordings of each other setting up machines so that they could improve their work-methods. They wrote, produced and edited a video tape of the cells, demonstrating how much better the manufacturing system was, now that the cells were in place. The title music they chose was Bachman Turner Overdrive: "You Ain't Seen Nothin' Yet".

Cells in Slough

In 1988, the lease ran out on Crane's London Road plant in Slough. Rather than renew the lease, the whole factory was moved to a new building in

Figure 12.2   Performance Improvement, 1981 to 1990

	1981	1990	Change
Turnover (£m)	28	70	+150%
Inventory/Sales			− 45%
Return on Assets			+120%
Sales/Employee (£000)			+130%
Lead time (days):			
MTO	180	7	− 96%
MFS	90	9	− 90%
Components produced (Reading)	300,000	400,000	+33%
Components produced (Slough)	10,000	34,000	+340%

Slough in October 1988. The experience of installing cells in Reading and the factory move meant that the time was ripe for moving to the cell system in Slough for production of non-stock components. The Slough operation demanded much more flexibility of its manufacturing system because of the sheer variety and novelty of components that were produced. Along with the move, several new CNC machines were bought, primarily turning centers. By July 1990, six cells were working in Slough on two shifts. These are shown in Exhibit 12.7. As in Reading, these cells produced components according to their geometry, although the gas ring and assembly cells were separate. The move to cells was a similar success in Slough. Operators were paid 25p per hour more for each new skill learned. Thus, a turner who could also mill could make £2.00 per day more by learning the skill. Mark Glennerster, Production Controller at Slough, commented:

> In the old plant, it was easy for work to be obscured by the general mess. With the cells though, everyone can see the work sitting in a particular cell waiting to be worked on—problems can't be hidden. It really is management by sight.

In the old plant, WIP could be dismissed as being on its way from one machining area to another. With the cell system, it is was obvious that WIP was the responsibility of the people in that cell which made the whole manufacturing system much easier to keep under control for both managers and operators.

Since 1981, Crane's continual manufacturing development had helped to greatly improve the EMA region's operating performance, as evidenced in Figure 12.2.

CIM at Crane

While the cells were being developed on the shop floor, changes were made in manufacturing philosophy at the top of the organization. By 1985, Computer Integrated Manufacturing (CIM) became an important issue.

By 1985, FMS was dead. Everyone read "The Goal." OPT and JIT were the fashionable things. The emphasis moved very much to the "Whole Business" issue and Computer Integrated Manufacturing was a natural progression.

Technologies such as Computer Aided Design (CAD) and Computer Aided Manufacturing (CAM) had been developed at Crane but management knew that such technology could also be bought by competitors. In its simplest terms, computer integration meant ensuring that computer information generated by one part of the company could be used directly in all others. For example, subsidiary companies needed to be able to access data from the central design database and the ordering system needed to be integrated with production planning. CIM was both a set of technologies and a philosophy. In 1985, it was common for people to carry boxes of computer-printout from one part of the Slough headquarters to another. This was the antithesis of the CIM philosophy. Management at Crane were convinced that instilling CIM "thinking" in the firm was the key. Gibbon pointed out:

> CIM meant the integration of the whole manufacturing business. We had simplified a lot of our processes, and automated them: the key was integration. CIM, for us, was CIM. Because it involved so many departments and personal interests, it really needed commitment and perseverance right at the top of the organization to carry it through. It's good to have as much technical understanding as you can at the top level—even when there is a lot of trust—top people need to know the technology so they can play devil's advocate. They also need enough technical knowledge to deal with all of the changes which take place, and not be overwhelmed by technology.

The push towards CIM was intense. A team with representatives from Finance, Engineering Design, Logistics, Production Engineering and Data Processing was assembled to look at business integration.

> Although the brief was business integration, CIM was our fashionable flag. We went away for a week to discuss it, and slowly we developed a CIM strategy. We assessed what we thought were the current and future needs of the business in terms of financial performance and satisfying customer demands. To improve, we used information and product flows along with lead times and development times and how we might reduce them. We then asked the Board to commit to a feasibility study.

The team recognized that a CIM "philosophy" was something too intangible to impart to the organization. It needed to be made clear by projects which would be pilots for the company's direction, and which would use CIM technology to achieve their ends. This process generated eight CIM foundation projects, as shown in Exhibit 12.8.

> CIM gave us a shared vision. The technology forced people to talk to one another, and made information transfer come naturally. The process of developing the projects was probably as important as the projects themselves. It gave people a more holistic view of the business.

One CIM project was the development of an expert system: The process of providing a customer with a seal suited to the particular application demanded considerable judgement and expertise on the part of the sales engineer. The knowledge required for seal-selection had become progressively more expansive and complex. Experienced sales engineers were not easy to find and there was considerable disparity amongst them. In general, older salespeople recommended standard "conservative" solutions, while younger, newer employees tended to suggest novel solutions using the latest seal technology. Sales engineers often disagreed about the best solution for an application. To resolve some of these problems, Crane developed an *expert system* for seal selection. This was a program which could run on a laptop computer, and could ultimately be carried by sales engineers to their customers. The program used Artificial Intelligence (AI) techniques to embody the expertise of the sales engineers as a whole, as well as the engineering department, and asked the user a response-dependent sequence of questions. After gathering the responses, the program would provide a seal suitable for the application, according to a standardized selection procedure. This and the seven other foundation projects steered Crane firmly on a course towards computer integration.

CIM became the central theme in the development of manufacturing at Crane. The link between CAD and CAM was one of the prominent motifs.

Computer Aided Design

In the late 1970s, Crane had a very traditional design office in which people sat at boards with pencils and erasers and produced the engineering drawings which conveyed their designs. By the early 1980s, it was clear that things had to change. The tremendous expertise which had been built up over the years needed to be used more effectively: customers required more responsiveness from Crane and their competition, and the time it took designers to produce drawings caused a bottleneck. CADAM™[6], a 2-dimensional drafting package which ran on a mainframe,

---

[6]CADAM is a trademark of IBM Corporation.

Exhibit 12.8   CIM Report

Computer Integrated Manufacturing, (CIM), is a never-ending road to continual business improvement. It requires us to be constantly aware of present and future developments in technology and to plan the future with these advances in mind.

However, to ensure that we make best use of these developments as they arise. It is very important that we get and keep our company in the right shape. To achieve this we have established 8 major projects which will form the foundation of our CIM strategy.

Because any company, including our competitors, can buy computers, CNC, CAD, etc., we must ensure that the benefit John Crane gains from such investments is greater than that achieved by our competitors.

The key to this success is YOU.

The adaptability, flexibility and ingenuity of every employee to make best use of these technologies and systems is the key to us maintaining our number 1 position in the world.

To date, the building blocks of CIM already in use (CAD,CNC, JIT, Mainframe, mini and microcomputer systems, etc.) and the subsequent corporate focus since we first committed ourselves to CIM in 1985 have made significant contributions to our corporate objectives.

Continuing to stay on top had to be our aim so the 8 CIM foundation projects are practical actions for further improvements to Crane's competitiveness now, and in the future.

We have set ambitious, but realistic targets and John Crane's board and senior management are committed to achieving them.

To realise these ambitions everybody has to play their part.

KEY CIM PROJECTS AND TARGETS

Projects	TARGETS (DECEMBER 1988)
1. CAD Development	Install CADAM in major subsidiaries
2. Expert Systems	Install Seal Selection System to Subsidiaries/Sales Offices
3. Made-in Non-Stocks	Lead time reduction - Sales order to supply order - 2 weeks - Standards - 2 weeks - Specials - 4 weeks
4. Made-in Stocks	Service Level - 95% Lead time reduction - 1 week
5. Order Processing System	Update
6. Just-in-time (JIT) Purchasing	Lead time reduction - Stock items - 2 weeks - Non stocks - 4 weeks
7. JIT Purchasing (by John Crane)	Lead time reduction - Stock items - weeks - Non stock items - 4 weeks
8. New Factory	Improved Communication Reduced Indirect Costs

was introduced in 1983. To produce a drawing using CADAM™, a designer sat at a workstation with a light pen and a button box, and produced the engineering drawing which expressed the details of the seal design. Many short-cut features in the software meant that designers no longer had to worry about time-consuming geometric constructions. The computer did these for them and freed them to concentrate on the design process itself. Much more importantly, CADAM™ allowed the designers to edit existing designs to produce a new one. For John Crane's business, this was a great boon. Very few of the "specials" were truly completely new designs; they were almost always adaptations of an existing design using perhaps a different material or a different dimension here and there.

By early 1985, the average time to produce an engineering design had been halved to one week, and by 1989, The CADAM™ mainframe system operating within the UK was used to generate all special and standard drawings for manufacture and assembly. The system soon allowed subsidiaries to access the design and gave them much faster and more accurate interaction with the design office.

Computer Aided Manufacturing

Traditionally, skilled operators had been able to make items directly from an engineering drawing (see Exhibit 12.9A and Exhibit 12.10) on manually-controlled machines. However, when the first CNC machines were bought and installed, programs were written by the Production Engineering Department. Production Engineers worked from computer-generated paper drawings and devised the tool paths required to produce the geometry in metal (see Exhibit 12.9B). Stand-alone microcomputers translated that plan and tailored it for a particular machine. Punched tapes were then produced and taken to the machine tool. Each manufacturer's machine tools required that slightly different dialects be produced to allow for particular physical designs and controllers. Programs which translated the code into the right dialect were called *post-processors*. Fortunately, Crane was using CNC machine tools from only a handful of manufacturers at the time, and post-processor software was available for all these machines.

Production Engineers became the link between the CAD system and the computer-controlled machine tools on the floor. The operators' jobs were made much more straightforward because they became responsible simply for running and tending the machines. Even so, they frequently re-checked the Production Engineers' work after the tape was read into the machine.

Despite the advantages of this manufacturing method, a number of Production Engineers were still dissatisfied with it. Alex Luboff commented:

It was ludicrous. We were drawing a component on CAD, print-ing this off onto paper and typing the dimensions back into

Exhibit 12.9   Stages of Design-Manufacturing links at John Crane UK Limited

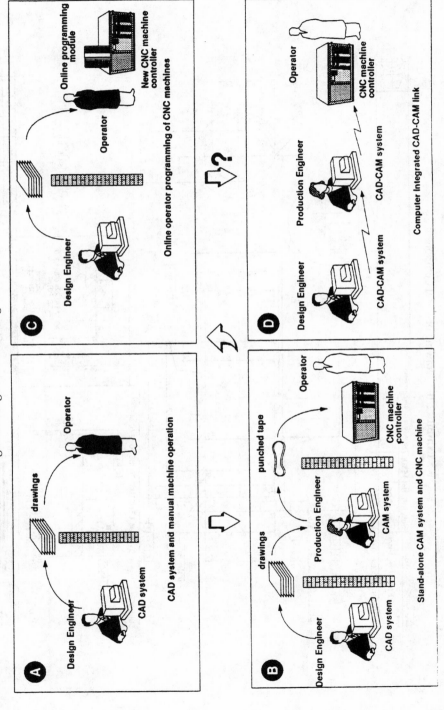

Exhibit 12.10 Drawing of a Seal Component

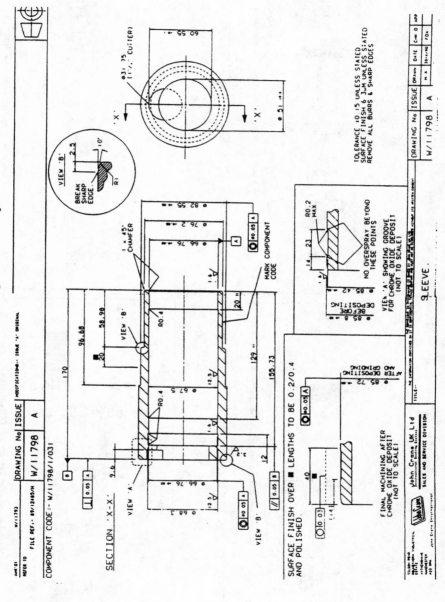

another computer to produce a part-program. It was time to buy a system that could automatically combine CAD and CAM. The CAD system did have the ability to allow machine-tool programmers to interact with the system and produce process plans and part-programs automatically, but at the beginning of 1987, CADAM™'s CNC software was very basic, and was seen by the Production Engineers as worthless for Crane's purposes—it just didn't produce usable programs. By the middle of the year IBM's CADAM™ group had announced vast improvements to their software and we agreed that this was the way to go. In 1988, a new mainframe computer was installed in Slough together with 16 workstations and the CADAM™ upgrade (including a package from IBM from which it was possible to create a post processor for any machine tool simply by filling in a questionnaire). We set ourselves a target of one year to set up the CAD-CAM system for all the machine tools in Slough. At the same time, six new turning centers were purchased, all with advanced on-machine programming facilities.

The new machine tools understood a different dialect of programming language and there was no software available to post-process the Production Engineers' plans on the stand-alone microcomputers. Fortunately, the machine tools could be programmed interactively at the machine console using a friendly, graphical language. Their controllers dealt with the post-processing internally. As there was no other way to produce programs for the machines, the operators were trained in this "online" programming (see Exhibit 12.9C). Meanwhile, engineers eagerly awaited the new CADAM™ CNC package. Disappointingly, it was much inferior to expectations. The engineering team was frustrated: many years of discussion with the supplier still had not produced a usable system. There were numerous software errors, and the engineers complained of "tediously slow" processing. It was also very difficult to create post-processors for the system, and engineers found that it lacked many features necessary for the type of work Crane did. Gerry Cusack pointed out that the process plans it produced were also a problem:

Take a sleeve for example—CADAM™ made cuts of equal depth when boring out a sleeve. A skilled operator makes very fine cuts towards the end of the job because a sleeve is a long, vibrating thin object. There's still some art in programming a CNC machine, and a computer can't capture it that easily.

The Engineering Systems group spent the rest of the year trying to trick and cajole CADAM™ into producing usable programs for the new machines. At the end of the year, they still faced the problem that they couldn't get "into" the software to alter it. It just could not produce programs as good as those the operators were producing.

By mid-1989, the project was put on hold in anticipation of an early 1990 re-release of CADAM™. The new version promised to provide licensees direct access to CAD data so they could write their own software, and offered an ideal chance for Crane to build its own CAD-CAM software to exact specifications. Bob Gibbon and the Engineering Systems team carried out a feasibility study of the new "Crane written" system when the new CADAM™ release arrived. By the beginning of February 1990, the development of the Crane CAM software was well underway and trials were resoundingly successful; by July, the software was nearing completion of the initial stage (turning for one type of CNC turning center). (See Exhibit 12.9D.)

Tests of the new software produced impressive results—at last, a Production Engineer could sit at a terminal in the drawing office, pull up a component's CAD drawing, generate a part-program and post-process it without errors. The engineers were elated: the CAD-CAM link had been forged.

The Situation in July 1990

Online Programming

The purchase of six new turning centers combined with the inadequacies of the CAD-CAM system had made further operator training a necessity. Operators became highly skilled in producing part-programs on the machines from paper drawings produced by the CAD system. The fact that only one department was involved in producing a part-program meant that lead time was much shorter. Programming and proving times improved because operators were familiar with both the part-program they had written and the machine it was being written for. Many of the operators pointed out that they found their jobs more satisfying when they were able to do the programming themselves. The new turning centers were distributed amongst the cells, and performed both Operations 1 and 2 on each job they produced. Operators estimated their programming time to be 30 minutes for Operation 1 and 15 minutes for Operation 2. Operator time was not a significant constraint, since CNC machines ran without interaction once the component was loaded.

The problem with online programming was that machines were not productive while the operator was programming on them. The combination of machine and operator cost approximately £100 per hour. While it was technically possible to program on the machines while they were cutting another job, the fact that jobs could be produced in very short runs made this impractical and difficult. A sample of operator time sheets showed an average of 1.96 jobs (batches) for each of the six turning centers per shift. Although a job may have been done before (in exactly the same way in some cases), operators often "re-programmed" the machine. This could be solved by storing and pooling tapes, but would operators trust each others' part programs as much as their own?

Machine controllers were idiosyncratic. When all the CNC part-programs were being written by Production Engineering, the operators only had to know how to run a machine. If they had to program machines as well, their flexibility in moving from machine to machine in the cell was reduced. While they were, in general, enthusiastic, a handful of operators disliked programming, and some were much better at it than others. Online part-programming also meant that design-for-manufacture problems often were not spotted until they held up an operator on the floor.

Offline Programming

The advantage of programming machines offline was that the machine could be running while the part-program was being prepared. Programming was carried out on a separate computer, allowing the machine tool's control computer to be used exclusively for production.

The stand-alone microcomputer-based offline programming was still used by Production Engineers for the older CNC machines. The new in-house software would enable them to produce offline programs for the new machines using data direct from the CAD system. The cost of employing a Production Engineer as a part-programmer was around £16,000 per annum. If the offline programming could be done from CADAM™ using the new software, then there would be no manual translation of dimensions from the drawing. This would improve quality by eliminating transcription errors, and the time it took the engineer to produce a part program would be halved in comparison to operators using the online method. It would also allow a more straightforward path for future computer integration: the component design, part-program and measurement program would all be derived from the same data file, integrating both the design and measuring processes with fabrication. Eventually, the costing system (for example) could be integrated using this link. The annualized cost of a CADAM™ workstation was estimated at £3000.

The CIM Cell Dilemma

Should part-programming be carried out offline, by Production Engineering on CADAM™ workstations in the Production Engineering office or by the operators using the machine's local control computers on the shop-floor? Paul Sefton was an engineer on the CIM team:

> Computer Integration is a sound philosophy for manufacturing, but to integrate, you have to do some standardization. Take the

expert system project for example—we can't get people to agree on a standard seal-selection procedure despite the fact that we need one badly[7]. Look at CAD-CAM: the operators have really put their weight behind improving things on the shop-floor, but they all do programming differently and its getting to be very inefficient. Perhaps they'll just have to stand aside now and let the Production Engineers write standard programs again. CIM will give Crane advantages that it just cannot let slip away.

Crane's CIM project was the cornerstone of its manufacturing strategy. Eventually Crane would be able to integrate all its manufacturing departments, allowing them to achieve "sustainable technological leadership" in manufacturing. The push towards CIM from the top of the company was clear and strong.

At the same time, the cells had been built by helping operators to become autonomous and responsible. Crane saw their commitment and energy as the central element of its improved manufacturing performance. In the main, they had taken to the task of programming their machines with great enthusiasm and were doing an excellent job of transferring the skills they had developed from years of manual work to computer-based machine tools. Now, there was an alternative to the online programming skills which the operators had learned: true integration with the CAD system.

Gibbon sat back amidst the juggernauts on the motorway and considered the dilemma.

[7] By 1990, the seal-selection expert system was still having difficulty gaining acceptance in the UK. Whereas sales engineers sometimes provided different solutions to each other, they could usually be relied upon to disagree with the expert system.

CHAPTER 13

Manufacturing's Crisis

New Technologies, Obsolete Organizations

Robert H. Hayes

Ramchandran Jaikumar

OREIGN-BASED COMPETITORS CONTINUE their assault on U.S. markets, exploiting their low wages or superior technological sophistication or both. Consumers are requiring ever-higher levels of quality and diversity, which has forced manufacturers to upgrade tolerances and designs, eliminate defects, and accelerate the rate of new product introduction. Meanwhile, just-in-time production systems are putting pressure on OEM suppliers to surpass their old standards of delivery and service. The challenges facing U.S. manufacturing companies are staggering.

Fortunately, manufacturing managers have new resources with which to respond to these challenges—a set of technologies that are collectively referred to as programmable automation. These include computer-aided design (CAD), computer-aided manufacturing (CAM), computer-aided engineering (CAE), flexible manufacturing systems (FMS), robotics, and computer-integrated manufacturing (CIM).

These advances promise to improve everything: cost, quality, flexibility, delivery, speed, design—everything. A recent study of FMS systems in 20 U.S. companies showed that they had reduced by more than 50% the amount of labor required to perform the same work, and reduced total product costs by as much as 75%. FMS installations have achieved significant reductions in the number of indirect workers and staff, in reject rates, and in time required to introduce products.

Robert H. Hayes is the William Barclay Harding Professor of Management of Technology at the Harvard Business School and chairman of the production and operations management teaching area. His latest book (with Steven C. Wheelwright and Kim B. Clark) is *Dynamic Manufacturing,* recently published by The Free Press. In his research and teaching, Ramchandran Jaikumar, an associate professor at the Harvard Business School, focuses on the management of advanced manufacturing technologies. His previous contribution to HBR, "Post-industrial Manufacturing" (November–December 1986), won the Frederick Winslow Taylor medal of the American Society of Mechanical Engineers.

Still, most U.S. managers are having difficulty reaping these advantages. For years, manufacturers have acquired new equipment much in the way a family buys a new car. Drive out the old, drive in the new, enjoy the faster, smoother, more economical ride—and go on with life as before. With the new technology, however, "as before" can mean disaster. Executives are discovering that acquiring an FMS or any of the other advanced manufacturing systems is more like replacing that old car with a helicopter. If you fail to understand and prepare for the revolutionary capabilities of these systems, they will become as much an inconvenience as a benefit—and a lot more expensive.

Buy a helicopter and you can engage in new professional and recreational activities, live in some remote place, develop new work methods, get a new perspective on the lay of the land. If you don't do these things, you waste the small fortune you paid for the machine and for acquiring new skills and logistical support. In short, you don't buy a helicopter unless you're committed to getting the most out of it. You have to organize for it.

Managing Precision

The new manufacturing technologies can shock a business organization—as a helicopter would disrupt one's home life—because they require a quantum jump in a manufacturing organization's precision and integration. Automated machine tools can produce parts to more exacting specifications than can the most skilled human machinist, but to do so they need explicit, unambiguous instructions in the form of computer programs.

The new hardware provides added freedom, but it also makes possible more ways to succeed or fail. It therefore requires new skills on the part of managers—an integrative imagination, a passion for detail. To prevent process contamination, for example, it is no longer possible to rely on people who have a "feel" for their machines, or just to note on a blueprint that operators should "remove iron filings from the part." When using the new automated machine tools, everything must be stated with mathematical precision: Where is the blower that removes the filings, and what's the orientation of the part during operation of the blower?

Moreover, the tightness of the procedures that govern automated machine operation magnifies the harmful effects that faulty upstream processes have on downstream processes. Without machine operators physically handling parts, there is no one to realign them in a fixture, tweak cutting tools, or compensate for small machining or operational errors, and nobody to inspect parts for holes, cracks, or other materials defects. To replicate a machinist's talent for recognizing errors, engineers and supervisors of an automated system need either an elaborate data base incorporating, say, an expert system incorporating the implicit rules of the skilled machinist, or a scientific understanding of the technology itself. Process engineers must provide the system sensors to detect errors and programmed controllers to interpret the sensors' signals and initiate corrective actions or shut down the machine.

Indeed, production-control data will increasingly become useless to human operators in real time as batches of materials move down the line. It is the computer that analyzes the microstructure of processing from one microsecond to the next and that takes action against a badly made part. In the new manufacturing era, therefore, the manager's job is mainly taken up with making pieces fit together, both the equipment hardware and the programmed software. To maximize the capabilities of the new technologies, managers must learn to think more like computer programmers—people who break down production into a sequence of microsteps.

In this sense, a manager's task may be compared to a movie director's. Viewed continuously and from a certain distance, the film appears seamless. Apparently the director's only challenge is to inspire the actors. But stage directors who become film directors learn that gestures that look subtle on the stage seem rather gross in the cutting room. Once stage directors move to film, they have to think more like film editors. To control and integrate their product they have to understand the nuances of action, frame by frame.

Like film directors who master editing, manufacturing managers have to learn how to cut and splice small, discrete "frames" of information, then build them up in more elegant, internally consistent ways. A manager who doesn't understand one part of a factory process as well as the other parts finds it impossible to make the necessary trade-offs—between cost and smoothness, say, or speed and robustness. Managers need to develop procedures in advance, even before starting up a plant, to take into consideration all possible consequences from design to assembly.

Clearly, the new manufacturing hardware will work best in an organization geared for the tight integration of design, engineering, and plant control. The managers who preside over advanced manufacturing tasks must think more like cross-disciplinary generalists, people with a deep understanding of machine design, software engineering, and manufacturing processes. They must learn to direct highly educated people working in small, tightly knit groups. They must encourage corporate learning, harmonize the efforts of specialists. Why aren't U.S. corporations making the changes necessary to put the new technology to work?

The real impediment lies not in the inherent demands of the hardware but in the managerial infrastructure that has become embedded in most U.S. companies over the past 50 years. This includes the attitudes, policies, systems, and habits of mind that are so ingrained and pervasive within companies that they are almost invisible to those within them. (It is said the last thing a fish discovers is water.)

Traditional managerial attitudes, manifested in top-down decision making, piecemeal changes, and a "bottom-line" mentality, are incompatible with the requirements and unique capabilities of advanced manufacturing systems. Until their attitudes change, companies will be slow to adopt the new technologies, and those that do will run a high risk of failure.

Such attitudes cannot change without profound reform in the modern corporation. At one level, reform means changes in cost accounting and performance measurement procedures, human resource management, and capital budgeting. At the next level, it means new organizational structures that can accommodate more interactive and cooperative working relationships. At a still higher level, reform means that top officers must cultivate new skills and managerial styles. It may well require a new generation of executives.

Corporate Divisions: My Gain, Your Loss

Underlying many of the problems in the modern manufacturing corporation is its organizational structure, which divides key people into separate functional responsibilities and measures their performance using different yardsticks (see diagram). In a typical facility, the purchasing group acquires raw materials, and senior management measures the purchasing group's performance by examining the cost and quality of the materials it buys and the timeliness of its activity. Materials managers are measured by how quickly they deliver the finished goods and how large an inventory they keep. The production group usually is judged by the cost, quality, and timeliness of the conversion from raw materials into finished goods.

Similarly, the quality group is evaluated according to how well it prevents defective parts from entering the conversion process and defective goods from leaving it. The maintenance or manufacturing-engineering group, or both, is measured by the cost of maintaining and upgrading equipment and by mishaps like machine downtime.

A basic principle behind this design is that administrators' responsibilities equal their authority. That is, a group overseeing a certain job should be accountable for the steps it takes to carry it out. The performance of that task should be measurable, moreover. Since it would be unfair to measure the group's activities in dimensions that its management has little control over, customized performance measures have been developed. The narrower the task, the narrower the measure.

A factory divided into these functions and evaluated by these measures may operate well in a stable environment like that in which U.S. companies thrived for 30 years after World War II. Pressures on any one of these subgroups to make marginal improvements in performance—like improving quality, reducing inventory, shortening delivery times, and introducing new products at a faster rate—can be handled largely within itself. Where minor improvements are the goal, one group might ask another to cooperate by adjusting its behavior slightly, as long as such an adjustment does not much affect its own performance rating.

Problems do arise, however, when *major* improvements are called for

The Traditional Plant

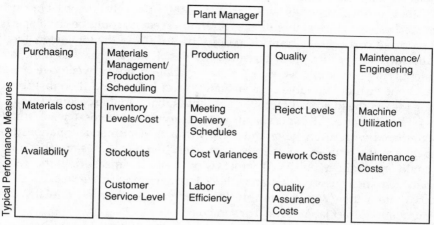

simultaneously along several dimensions, as is the case with the new manufacturing. When they operate independently, subgroups simply cannot make dramatic improvements. Yet the help one subgroup gives another may damage its own performance.

In trying to slash inventories, for example, many companies have adopted some form of a just-in-time (JIT) system. Instead of accepting large quantities of purchased materials weekly or monthly, they demand daily or even more frequent deliveries of smaller quantities. But JIT works best if the company deals with only a few suppliers that, because of their flexibility or their location or both, can respond quickly. Yet the most responsive suppliers may be unable to match the prices of the low-cost suppliers who specialize in large quantities. The materials manager's gain, therefore, is the purchasing manager's loss.

To make sure they can meet delivery schedules, production supervisors often maintain backup inventories of parts and partially completed products. At first, reducing these inventories raises the chances that the production group will miss its schedules. People work at cross-purposes also when a company tries to improve quality, compress product development time, or introduce process control technology. When reject rates go down, quality managers look good, but production workers may look less productive purely in terms of output. So it's not surprising to see infighting among managers and resistance from the workforce when a company embarks on an ambitious improvement program.

The efforts of financial officers to measure performance further confound the manufacturing organization. Accountants often lack the information necessary to show manufacturing how well (or how badly) it is doing.

When cost accounting was in its infancy, it was easy to allocate the fixed costs of production to particular work centers or products. The bulk of total production costs was variable costs, primarily direct labor and materials, for which elaborate measurement systems could be developed. Overhead costs, which comprised only 10% to 20% of the total, were then allocated to specific products and activities. Usually this was done by identifying (or simply asserting) a strong relationship between overhead and one or more variable cost—usually direct labor—and then distributing the overhead according to the amount of that variable cost incurred.

For instance, if supervision and factory support costs were small compared with direct labor, but there was a clear numerical relationship between the two—one supervisor for every ten workers, say—then one could ascertain a product's supervision costs by measuring the ratio between supervisory costs and direct labor hours *over all products*. The accountant then would multiply that "supervisory burden rate" by the number of direct labor hours consumed.

Today, however, the cost of direct labor in a typical high-technology company seldom exceeds 10% of total costs; increasingly it is under 5%, about the same as depreciation. Indirect factory costs—particularly materials control, quality assurance, maintenance and process engineering, and software development—have been growing rapidly. In many companies these now equal from five to ten times their direct labor costs. Therefore, viewing labor costs as a benchmark by which to distribute all other costs is misguided. Companies often devote three-quarters or more of their energy to measuring costs that are likely to account for less than 15% of the total.

By focusing attention on less important factors in today's production environment, traditional cost accounting systems also distract managers from more critical issues. We know of one high-tech company whose overhead costs are almost nine times its direct hourly labor cost of $10. Managers in this company are eager to buy parts from vendors instead of making them. If they buy parts, they reduce their costs (including allocated costs) by $(1 + 9) \times \$10$, or $100, for each direct labor hour saved.

Overseeing an increasing number of vendors, however, requires extra staff. This company therefore found its direct labor costs falling while overhead costs rose—driving up its overhead allocation rate for the remaining products and encouraging managers to contract out even more. This may be an extreme case. But it is not atypical of many companies today driven in unanticipated directions by the apparently innocuous mandates of their accounting systems.

Irrational Incrementalism

To reduce the risk that comes with change, companies often seek piecemeal improvement via "islands of automation." Their approach to factory automation is similar to how most transportation companies build their route structures: they find two cities they can connect and serve at a profit, then gradually add cities and routes that are comparably profitable. Sometimes one part of the system grows faster than others, but eventually it usually can be linked profitably with the rest of the system. In the same way, factories are often modernized through a series of independent projects, each justifiable in its own dollar terms until, eventually, a way is found to link these individual islands of automation into a profitable whole.

Unfortunately this approach is often not appropriate when moving toward computerized automation. No one component of a CIM network—a parts rationalization system, a CAD system, an FMS, a plant-floor data collection and information system, or a customer communication system—may be able to meet a company's profitability requirements. The desired returns materialize only when all these advances are in place.

For this reason, a CIM system should be built the way Federal Express built its famous hub-and-spoke system, which revolutionized the overnight-mail delivery business. No part of Federal Express's system could work effectively until all its parts were in place: the materials handling and sorting depot in Memphis; the planes to fly the route spokes radiating from there; and the pickup and delivery systems at each node. Building such a system requires a strategic vision, lots of money up front, and a tremendous amount of patience.

Paradoxically, even as this new hardware encourages more information sharing across the company, it enables different parts of the manufacturing organization to become more independent of one another. In fact, the new hardware encourages factories to break up into smaller units—plants-within-the-plant—of cells dedicated to making families of products. These minifactories tend to be tightly integrated, organizationally flat, almost entirely self-managing, and highly responsive to evolving market needs. The net result is reduced labor, reduced overhead, and increased capacity utilization. The factory that emerges from such changes is likely to be smaller—between a third and a fifth of the size of the traditional factories that generate similar volumes of products.

Incidentally, the new technology can also mean a revolution in relations between the company and the customer or—what is often the same thing—between OEM suppliers and procurement officers. Before the industrial revolution, people sought out craftsmen or small workshops to supply their garments, wagons, arms, and ornaments. Customers described what they wanted and the craftsmen gave them options for tailoring the product according to their wishes. The service was as important as the product.

Mass production profoundly changed the relationship between customer and producer. It shifted the emphasis of commerce away from service; products had to be designed to meet the generalized needs of large markets. With mass production, the designer, producer, and salesperson became three different people belonging to different parts of the organization. Similarly, the separation of customers from suppliers meant that customer preferences were revealed mainly through their purchasing decisions.

The new manufacturing technologies shift the focus from product features back to service, to customers. Correspondingly, they reestablish close ties between producers and suppliers. CAD and CAE allow small organizations to design prototypes faster and more economically than before. Components can be produced efficiently in relatively small batches, essentially to order, through CAM and FMS.

Command out of Control?

Some executives have argued that because the new manufacturing technologies are evolving so rapidly, they should hold off investing in them until the rate of technical progress slows. If they had similarly delayed buying a computer until computer technology had stabilized, they would be waiting still.

What those who resist the new technology fear, perhaps, is not its instability but its tendency to destabilize the chain of command. The interfunctionality engendered by the new manufacturing can mean much more informal cooperation at low levels in the organization—between engineers and market analysts, designers and manufacturers. This kind of teamwork is unnatural behavior for companies whose structures, staffing policies, and performance measures operate according to a command-and-control mentality.

Proponents of command and control expect senior management to make the major resource allocation decisions, with the help of staff and external experts whenever necessary. Their view of the line organization's role is simply to operate the established facilities, systems, and personnel according to senior management's targets.

Command-and-control managers assume that whatever specialties an organization lacks can be brought in from outside. They see management's primary task as the orderly assimilation, exploitation, and coordination of separate sources of expertise. Moreover, they thrive in hierarchical organizations in which the primary relationships between people are vertical. Decisions, rewards, and punishments flow down. Information flows back up.

None of these assumptions works well in the new manufacturing environment. Especially vulnerable are companies that have separated brute effort from intelligence by splitting them up—the engineering staff supplying the intelligence, presumably, the manufacturing-line organization, the effort. The advent of the new manufacturing technologies makes it necessary to recombine effort and intelligence, to make them more interactive. In one advanced company, a large engineering group has *become* the line organization—actually in charge of production and responsible for a factory's bottom line—while a small manufacturing group simply provides staff support, ensuring that the necessary material and information are available when needed.

As noted earlier, the companies that have mastered the new manufacturing technologies prize generalists. They strive to build close horizontal relationships throughout the company, so that product designers work directly with manufacturing process designers, vendor managers with production schedulers and quality controllers. Decisions are pushed down to operating level, and the experimentation taking place on the shop floor is no more controlled from above than that taking place in the R&D lab.

Moreover, these companies tend to dislike dependence on outside organizations or vendors for expertise. They respect the capabilities of others, but they want to develop their own people, equipment, and systems. Well-run companies like Lincoln Electric, Procter & Gamble, IBM, and Hewlett-Packard put great effort into recruiting, training, and retaining highly skilled people at the operating level.

The Biases of Capital Budgeting

Nowhere do the prejudices and inefficiencies of old, functionally separated manufacturing organizations show up more strikingly than in the capital-budgeting process. Imagine a company that is contemplating expanding its production capacity by buying standard equipment—another hundred looms, say, to supplement several thousand others that have been operating for several years. The cost of operating those looms is understood, the revenues expected from their operation are based on considerable market experience, and the capabilities needed to operate them are already in place. Buying looms is unlikely to require anything from the company beyond the money they cost, and their operation is unlikely to provide it with anything beyond the revenues they generate.

Now, suppose also that the company is considering spending an equal sum on an R&D project, perhaps on experiments with a new synthetic fiber, whose technical and commercial potential is promising but also highly uncertain. At the same time, the company is deciding whether or not it should expand its parking lot—just an added cost, but essential for its growing number of employees, suppliers, and customers.

These three investments clearly entail different demands on the organization. They generate very different business opportunities and create value in distinctive ways. The new looms merely replicate existing operations and provide an increment of capacity in a well-established business. The loom outlay fits the standard capital budgeting assumptions almost perfectly. But what about the R&D project and the parking lot? The former can create new knowledge, though it is hardly clear what this knowledge will be or how it could be employed. The R&D project's ultimate outcome may depend on future investments. The parking lot is valuable for carrying out the day-to-day work of the company, but it is just overhead. The

returns from either investment are unpredictable. Neither has clearly identifiable future cash flows, and the degree of interaction with other projects
and the nature of the risks incurred are almost impossible to estimate.

Most companies, of course, discern the differences among looms,
pure R&D, and a parking lot. Unfortunately, they often fail to realize that
most investment proposals fall somewhere between these three extremes
and contain elements of each.

One metal products company faced a capacity shortage in its heat-
treating operation. After a study by engineering staff and meetings with
marketing and manufacturing and plant groups, the vice president of
manufacturing directed the staff to draft a capital authorization request
(CAR) for a new continuous-heat treating line. The line would combine
two advanced technologies: a continuous-flow process and a computerized control system.

The CAR was based on a discounted cash flow analysis of the project
using standard forms and computer programs under guidelines set by the
corporate staff. But as the work proceeded, projections of sales volumes
and profit margins seemed uncertain. The new line was designed to
produce materials with higher strength and greater consistency, but it was
doubtful whether customers would pay a premium for these qualities. So
the CAR included conservative estimates from marketing, manufacturing,
and engineering to calculate the project's annual cash flows.

Moreover, the equipment life was 20 years, but since marketing was
willing to commit only to a four-year sales projection, the CAR simply
extended the fourth year's sales and margin numbers through the remaining 16 years. It also excluded any benefits from the new line's increased
operating flexibility, the novel products that it might facilitate, or the
knowledge that the computerized systems would generate—i.e., "soft"
benefits.

Here there was an obvious misfit between the standard capital-
budgeting process and the new technology's power. The executive
committee was trying to decide about the new processes as if it was
buying something like a slightly more efficient loom whose costs and
benefits were well known. In fact, it was buying table stakes in a new
manufacturing technology—one that provided both traditional output
and new capabilities.

In visits to dozens of U.S. factories, we have seen an astonishing
number of 20-year-old or older machines in operation. Indeed, more than
a third of U.S. machine tools fall into this category. Have these companies
adopted a conscious strategy of competing with equipment that is obsolete, breaks down, and can't hold required tolerances?

After all, it takes 20 years to create a 20-year-old machine. Over that
period, a number of investment proposals must have been studied, and
well-meaning managers at various levels decided not to replace the equipment. For many companies, the cumulative effect of these decisions has

been devastating. Such series of decisions—each no doubt justifiable but collectively suicidal—are an outgrowth less of a strategic plan than the normal functioning of the companies' capital-budgeting systems.

Once they recognize what is going on, many companies simply force new investment by short-circuiting their standard capital-budgeting process; for example, top management steps in to take responsibility for making decisions about major capital-equipment acquisitions. But this top-down approach keeps the organization's lower levels from understanding how strategic issues may affect them. It is also vulnerable to the preselection process that separates strategic from nonstrategic investments. Unfortunately, most companies regard a manufacturing equipment choice as nonstrategic even though it may change the company's cost structure, improve its ability to introduce new products, and affect the way it interacts with its customers.

Moreover, a company does not learn to exploit the full potential of advanced equipment unless it is organized to do so. Too often, the operation of new manufacturing equipment is delegated to specialists, and equipment performance is tracked through the standard staffing, utilization, and downtime reports. New equipment is thus kept apart from the rest of the organization and has little impact on how engineers design new products, how the personnel office hires and trains people, how marketing deals with customers, or how controllers monitor the manufacturing organization's performance.

Physical Assets or Intellectual Assets

Radical changes in manufacturing technology—like the invention of the first machine tool, the development of interchangeable parts, or the moving assembly line—come along only once every generation or so. When one appears, there is little expertise that managers can draw on; long experience may provide little guidance for the immediate future.

The mistake most companies make is to treat new manufacturing equipment simply as *physical* assets. Programmable automation demands a much more interactive decision-making process and tight integration among corporate functions. It also demands attention to nonfinancial, long-term considerations, particularly its impact on the company's *intellectual* assets.

Again, the new manufacturing technology not only creates and processes materials, it also creates and processes information—information linked through computer networks and available to each workstation. If workers are trained and encouraged to use this information, the new hardware becomes a powerful means for enhancing knowledge—making nonexperts expert and experts more expert.

In the early 1980s, Deere & Company began rapidly modernizing its manufacturing facilities. It set up a "Computer-Aided Manufacturing

Services" division, whose purpose was to develop a variety of software packages and to assist operating groups in implementing the new manufacturing technologies. As a result of these software development and internal consulting projects, the division developed considerable expertise in group technology, computerized process planning, flexible manufacturing systems, and computer-integrated manufacturing. By 1986, the group was confident enough to propose marketing its software and consulting skills externally. This new business has been quite successful, and it has opened up new markets for Deere's manufactured products.

Ideally, the manufacturing organization is made up of multidisciplinary engineering groups working with powerful computational tools and is evolving in new ways. Such *intelligent* organizations are ephemeral, formed when problems surface, disbanded when they are solved; they often include suppliers and other people from the outside. The structure they assume is based on how the problem is posed. If it's noise in a motor, management would create a team of mechanical engineers; if it's faulty sensory feedback to a motor, a team of electrical engineers. Exploiting the potential of these dynamic coalitions becomes the new managerial challenge.

A company's ultimate success, therefore, depends on how effectively it can shift from measuring and controlling costs to choosing and managing projects that enhance its organizational capabilities. New measures of performance and new approaches to capital investment are needed in companies whose costs are mostly fixed, related not to the manufacture of certain products but to the creation of new capabilities. Continual improvement in production science is the ultimate measure of world-class manufacturers. They push at the margins of their expertise, trying on every front to be better than before. They strive to be dynamic, *learning* organizations.

Incidentally, not only does programmable automation make manufacturing support costs go up but the direct labor that remains becomes much less "variable." Worker skills are critical to a company's success; a layoff could mean permanent loss of that resource. At the same time, companies need to encourage cooperation among workers, to reinforce the value of long-term employment. People work best with people they know. The most important variable costs for an advanced manufacturing company may well be the costs of training and retraining people.

Just a few years ago, we used to hear this complaint from manufacturing managers: "Top management doesn't understand us. They don't understand the pressures we're under, the constraints we have to deal with, or the limited resources we can draw on. If only they would give us the authority and resources we need, we could achieve the goals they set for us."

Today it's top managers who are complaining: "Our manufacturing managers don't understand us. They don't understand the seriousness of the competitive situation we're facing or the magnitude of the improvements we must make if we're going to survive. We tell them, 'Let us know what your ideas are, and what new resources you need.' But all they come back with is more of the same. They don't seem to see that this new environment requires new approaches."

This change in the source of complaints reveals perhaps the most daunting problem of all. Over the past 30 years or so, top executives have tended to choose a certain kind of person to manage their manufacturing organizations. They assumed that if the manufacturing process was carefully set up, staffed, and equipped, all they needed to keep things running smoothly was a group of caretakers. Worse, they favored highly specialized caretakers, to the point where many factories today resemble the academic institutions that Ralph Waldo Emerson railed against 150 years ago, staffed by people who "strut about like so many walking monsters—a good finger, a good neck, a stomach, an elbow, but never a man."

Today, however, companies are beginning to realize that they need something more than caretakers and specialists. They need generalists—people with an architect's skill, who can pull out a fresh sheet of paper and design something new.

It is not easy, however, to convert caretakers into architects. It takes a long period of training, of trial and error—new expectations and new rewards. It probably will also require new people, people like the giants of the first half of this century who established most of the perfectly reasonable—but now failing—manufacturing infrastructure common today.

CHAPTER 14

A Measure of Delight

The Pursuit of Quality at AT&T Universal Card Services (A)

*I*N THE LOBBY OF the headquarters building of AT&T Universal Card Services Corp., a crystal Malcolm Baldrige National Quality Award rotates silently on a pedestal within a glass case. On one marble wall, above a sheet of flowing water, are the words, "Customers are the center of our universe." The inscription on the opposite wall reads, "One world, one card." Despite a steady stream of visitors and employees, the lobby has the hushed and serene atmosphere of a shrine.

But on the upper floors of the building—in the heart of the operation that brought home the nation's top quality award—it is never silent. In a honeycomb of open and brightly lit cubicles, about 300 men and women are speaking intently but pleasantly into telephone headsets while deftly keying information and instructions into the computer terminals before them. In all directions, one phrase is repeated so often that it seems to hang in the air: "AT&T Universal Card, how may I help you?"

The workers appear private and autonomous, connected only to their customers on the other end of the line. Yet at any moment, day or night, there may be someone else listening. It may be a co-worker, monitoring the call in order to suggest how a request might be handled differently. It may be a team leader, gathering the information that will figure in next year's raises. It may be a senior manager, putting on a headset to listen to calls while working out in the company gym. Or it may be a quality monitor in another building, scribbling ratings and comments on a one-page sheet that will help determine whether everyone in the company gets a bonus for that day. And all the while, as the pleasant voices talk on, a computer tracks every call that comes in, continually measuring how long it takes to answer each call, how many seconds are spent on each conversation, and

This case was written by Research Associate Susan Rosegrant as part of a joint effort between the Kennedy School of Government and the Harvard Business School. The case was prepared as the basis for class discussion rather than to illustrate either effective or ineffective handling of an administrative situation.

whether any customers hang up before their calls are answered. In the eyes of the executives who designed the company's operating philosophy and strategic plan, the monitored calls were an indispensable component in boosting AT&T Universal Card over its competitors, and making it a true quality company.

The Challenge

In the summer of 1993, Universal Card Services (UCS) was, by most standards, in an enviable position. The wholly owned AT&T subsidiary had broken into the highly competitive credit card business in 1990, determined to build on the AT&T name with a philosophy of "delighting" customers with unparalleled service. To help do that, the company had created an innovative measurement and compensation system to drive the pursuit of quality and customer satisfaction. Now just three years later, UCS, with nearly 12 million accounts, was the number two credit card issuer in the industry. Not only that; in 1992 UCS was the youngest company ever—and one of just three service firms—to win the coveted Malcolm Baldrige National Quality Award.

But despite these successes, there was a sense within the Jacksonville, Florida-based company that some fundamental changes were in order. In particular, Rob Davis, vice president of Quality, was searching for ways to push UCS's quest for quality one step further. A number of factors triggered this critical self-examination. Competitors had begun to close the gap opened by UCS when it pioneered its innovative policies and practices three years earlier. The departure of two key architects of company policy underscored the fact that now, with more than 2,700 employees and three new sites across the country, UCS was no longer in a startup, entrepreneurial phase. Finally, Davis and other senior managers were questioning many of the basic concepts underlying the measurement system that had helped the company achieve so much. Nearly everyone agreed that changes were needed in what the company measured, how it measured, and what it did with the information. There was no consensus, however, on exactly what to do.

The Founding

When AT&T recruited Paul Kahn in 1989 to lead its foray into the credit card business as UCS's president and CEO, the information technology giant had two main goals. It wanted to offer a combined credit card and calling card that would bolster its long-distance calling revenues. Perhaps more important, it wanted to regain the direct link to the customer that it had lost in 1984 when a court decision forced the spin-off of its regional Bell operating companies. With the backing of AT&T, Kahn, a 10-year veteran of First National Bank of Chicago and Wells Fargo Bank, developed a bold plan for breaking into the market, where unchallenged pricing practices and highly profitable operations were the norm. First, the new company did away with the annual membership fee, saving cardholders who signed up during the first year the $25 or more typically charged by issuing banks. Second, UCS set its interest rate on unpaid balances below what most bank issuers were charging, pegging it to the banking industry's prime lending rate.

In addition to such pricing strategies, AT&T and Kahn shared a vision of the kind of company they wanted to create: an organization where motivated and empowered employees would set new standards for quality in customer service. To achieve this ambitious goal, the new company set out to measure almost every process in sight. "We decided that we had to create an environment where the net takeaway to both the parent company and to the consumer was an experience superior to anything they'd had before," explained Kahn.

On March 26, 1990, during the Academy Awards, UCS aired its first ad. The combination of the AT&T name and the waived annual fee proved more potent than anyone had imagined. In the first 24 hours, UCS's 185 employees received 270,000 requests for applications or information. The company opened its one millionth account 78 days after launch.

Pillars of Quality

In contrast to many established companies that have struggled to superimpose "quality" on an existing corporate culture, UCS had the luxury of establishing quality as an overarching goal from the start. In fact, quality was less a goal than an obsession. The seven core company values—customer delight, continuous improvement, sense of urgency, commitment, trust and integrity, mutual respect, and team work—were emblazoned on everything from wall plaques to T-shirts and coasters. Senior management was convinced that quality processes—with the end result of superior customer service and efficiency—would give UCS a key competitive advantage in the crowded credit card marketplace. As a company brochure noted:

> Each time a customer contacts UCS, it's a moment of truth that can either strengthen our relationship with them or destroy it. Each call or letter is an opportunity to create a person-to-person contact that makes the Universal Card, and AT&T, something more than another anonymous piece of plastic lost in a billfold.

In order to provide such unprecedented customer service, the Business Team, an executive committee of a dozen top vice presidents headed by Kahn, took a number of steps (see organization chart, Exhibit 14.1).

Exhibit 14.1   UCS Organization Chart, August 1992

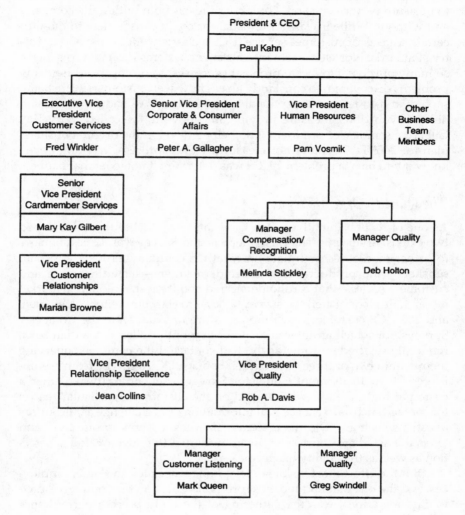

They made sure that the telephone associates—Universal's designation for its customer service representatives—were carefully selected, and then trained to "delight" customers. They set up benchmarking studies, comparing UCS both to direct competitors and to other high-performing service companies. They conducted a Baldrige-based quality assessment in the very first year, as well as each successive year, and used the results as the basis for a companywide strategic improvement process.

But the most unusual mechanism built into the organizational pursuit of quality was a unique and multi-faceted measurement system, designed to measure performance on a number of levels both within the company and without. While it was not unusual for credit card issuers to monitor certain aspects of customer service, UCS's efforts went far beyond industry standards. Nor were most measurement systems designed to achieve so many purposes: to locate problem processes; to promptly address any problems discovered; to constantly assess how well customers were being served; and to reward exceptional performance. "We had an expression here, 'If you don't measure it, you can't move it,'" recalled Mary Kay Gilbert, a senior vice president who helped develop the original business plan for AT&T. "If you're not measuring a key process, you don't even know if you have a problem." UCS was determined not to let that happen.

The Quality Organization

As one of its first initiatives, Rob Davis and his Quality team developed two extensive surveys. The Customer Satisfier Survey was a questionnaire to gather market research data on what the company termed "customer satisfiers," the products, services, and treatment—including price and customer service—that cardholders cared about most. An outside market research firm conducted the survey, talking to 400 competitors' customers and 200 UCS customers each month. More unusual were the Contactor Surveys, for which an internal team each month polled more than 3,000 randomly selected customers who had contacted the company, querying them within two or three days of their contact. UCS's survey team administered 10 to 15 different Contactor Surveys, depending on whether a customer had called or written, and on the customer's particular reason for contact, such as to get account information or to challenge a bill. Survey questions such as, "Did the associate answer the phone promptly?" and "Was the associate courteous?" were designed to gauge overall satisfaction as well as the quality of specific services.

But the effort most visible to telephone associates and other employees, and the one that had the most profound effect on the company's day-to-day operations, was the gathering of the daily process performance measures. Senior managers had debated every aspect of this so-called "bucket of measures" at the company's formation, and it was at the heart of how UCS operated.

The Business Team had agreed that the best way to drive quality service and continuous improvement was to measure the key processes that went into satisfying the consumer—*every single day*. Building on the experience of credit card industry veterans recruited at startup, such as Fred Winkler, executive vice president for Customer Services, and adding information gleaned from the Customer Satisfier and Contactor Surveys as well as additional benchmarking studies, the Business Team assembled a list of more than 100 internal and supplier measures it felt had a critical

Exhibit 14.2 Internal Process Measurement Linkages to Customer Satisfiers

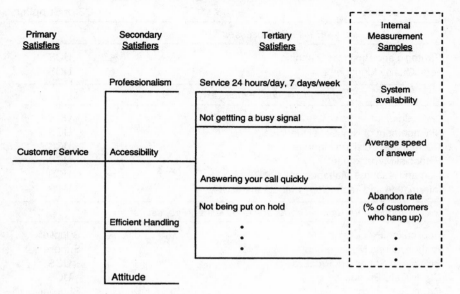

Source: Universal Card Services

impact on performance (see Exhibit 14.2 for an example of how UCS linked internal process measures with key satisfiers).

The original list was top-heavy with actions directly affecting cardholders—such as how soon customers received their credit cards after applying, and whether billing statements were accurate. But the list gradually expanded to include key production, service, and support processes from every functional area of the company, many of which were invisible to customers but which ultimately impacted them (see Exhibit 14.3 for a list of such processes). By the middle of 1991, Vice President Jean Collins and her Relationship Excellence team, the independent monitoring group within UCS charged with collecting the measures, were tracking about 120 process measures, many considered confidential. Indicators ranged from the quality of the plastic used in the credit cards to how quickly Human Resources responded to job resumes and issued employee paychecks, and to how often the computer system went down.

UCS did more than measure, though; it set specific standards for each measure and rewarded every employee in the entire company when those standards were met on a daily basis. To make clear the importance of quality, the bucket of measures was linked directly to the company's compensation system: If the company as a whole achieved the quality standards on 95 percent of the indicators on a particular day, all the associates—or non-managerial employees—"earned quality" for the day, and each "quality

Exhibit 14.3   Key UCS and Supplier Processes

Key Processes	UCS or Supplier
Business Processes	
Strategic and Business Planning	UCS
Total Quality Management	UCS
Support Services Processes	
Collections	UCS
Management of Key Constituencies	UCS
Customer Acquisition Management	UCS
Financial Management	UCS
Human Resource Management	UCS
Information and Technology Management	UCS
Product and Service Production and Delivery Processes	
Application Processing	Supplier
Authorizations Management	Supplier
Billing and Statement Processing	UCS
Credit Card Production	UCS
Credit Screening	Supplier
Customer Acquisition Process Management (Prospective Customer List Development and Management)	Supplier
Customer Inquiry Management	UCS
Payment Processing	UCS
Relationship Management (Service Management, Communications Management, Programs and Promotions, Brand Management)	UCS
Transaction Processing	Supplier

Source: Universal Card Services

day" meant a cash bonus, paid out on a quarterly basis.[1] Although some top managers questioned the compensation/quality link, arguing that, in essence, the achievement of quality should be its own reward, Kahn felt the tie to compensation was essential. "I think we ought to put our money where our mouth is," he declared. "We wanted quality, and we ought to pay for it." The financial incentives were not insignificant: The bonus system gave associates the ability to add more than $500 to their paycheck every quarter, and managers could earn 20 percent above base salary.

The daily push to earn quality—and to earn a bonus—was an omnipresent goal. Video monitors scattered around the building declared

---

[1]For managers to earn quality, they also had to meet standards on a separate set of indicators tied to vendors' products and services. Managers' bonuses were then based on three components: quality days, individual performance, and the company's financial performance.

Exhibit 14.4 Sample Daily Reliability Report—Telephone Associate Performance

		Wednesday 06/30/93		Month-to-Date	
Measure	*Standard*	*Sampled*	*Performance*	*Sampled*	*Performance*
Average Speed of Answer (ASA)	20 seconds	39,278	12.42 seconds	1,114,722	11.70 sec
Abandoned Rate	3%	39,278	1.24%	1,114,722	1.25%
Accuracy	96%	100	100%	2,400	98.58%
Professionalism	100%	100	100%	2,350	99.91%

Source: Universal Card Services

the previous day's quality results. Every morning at 8:00, Fred Winkler, in charge of operations, presided over a one-hour meeting of about a dozen senior managers to discuss the latest measures, identifying possible problems and proposing solutions. A summary of the "Fred meeting," as one manager dubbed it, could be dialed up on the phone later that morning. In each functional area, managers convened a similar quality meeting during the day, examining the measures for which they were responsible and, if they had failed to meet a particular indicator, trying to figure out what went wrong (see Exhibit 14.4 for a sample report showing telephone associate performance). Furthermore, the bucket of measures figured prominently in monthly business meetings, the Baldrige assessments, focus groups, and other regular process improvement meetings. According to Deb Holton, manager of Quality, the daily measures were on everyone's minds: "It is virtually impossible to be in this building for 10 minutes without knowing how you did the day before."

The Empowered Employee

At UCS, customers were referred to as "the center of our universe." At the center of the business, however, were the telephone associates who, although entry-level workers, had the highest pay and status among nonmanagerial employees. They, after all, were the front-line representatives who determined what impression customers took away from their dealings with UCS. Indeed, telephone associates were responsible for almost all customer contact—answering phones, taking applications, handling correspondence, and even collecting from overspenders and trying to intercept fraudulent card users.

To make sure that it had the right people for the job, UCS put applicants through a grueling hiring process: Only one in 10 applicants won an offer of employment after the two-part aptitude test, customer service role-playing, handling of simulated incoming and outgoing calls, credit check, and drug testing. Once hired, telephone associates received training for six weeks and two more weeks on the job. Instruction began with a two-day cultural indoctrination dubbed "Passport to Excellence," introducing concepts such as mission, vision, quality objectives, and empowerment. But the main purpose of the lengthy training was to give associates detailed coaching in telephone skills and the management of all phases of a customer inquiry, from initiation to conclusion.

UCS did not expect to get commitment and excellent customer service from the telephone associates, however, without giving them something in return. In fact, the company's vision of "delighting" customers rested on having "delighted" associates. Much of what the rest of the organization did—from Human Resources management to information support systems design and the measurement system itself—revolved around ensuring that telephone associates were able and motivated to provide the quality service that was the company's stated goal.

The Information Services group, for example, developed and continually upgraded U-WIN, an information management system tailored to the specific needs of the telephone associates. Drawing in part on the company's U-KNOW system—which gave managers on-line access to the customer, operational, and financial information in UCS's database, known as UNIVERSE—the U-WIN system allowed associates to pull up on their workstation screens information ranging from cardmember files, to form letters, to special product offers (see Exhibit 14.5 for an overview of the information management system). U-WIN even gave associates a head start on serving customers by automatically calling up cardmembers' accounts as their calls were being connected. "We're high touch, high tech," explained Marian Browne, vice president of Customer Relationships, the service area in which telephone associates handled general correspondence and responded to customer calls. "That means we work with our people and focus on our customers, but we can't do either unless we have leading-edge technology."

UCS top management was also determined to involve associates, listen to their ideas and concerns, and draw them into most facets of the business. Associates served side by side with senior managers on teams deciding issues ranging from what awards the company should bestow to how computer screens should be designed for maximum efficiency. They were encouraged to ask questions at monthly business reviews and at "Lakeside Chats"—quarterly question-and-answer sessions with Winkler held in the company cafeteria. And the UCS employee suggestion program, "Your Ideas . . . Your Universe," was broadly publicized, with impressive results: in 1991, more than half the workforce participated, and management accepted and acted on almost half of the more than 5,000 suggestions.

In addition to these "empowerment" oriented activities, the company looked for concrete ways to please associates. UCS provided generous fringe benefits, for example, including a free on-site fitness center for

Exhibit 14.5   UCS's Integrated Data and Information Systems

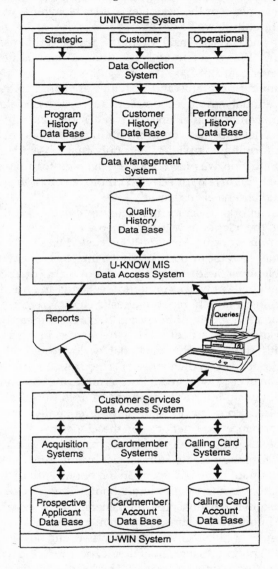

employees and their spouses, and reimbursement for undergraduate and graduate courses. The company supported a substantial reward and recognition program, sponsoring 6 companywide awards, 3 companywide recognition programs, and more than 30 departmental awards. And the Business Team encouraged managers to look for reasons to celebrate.

Indeed, boisterous ceremonies in the cafeteria marking such events as all-company achievements or the bestowal of specific awards were a regular occurrence. "The culture we've developed is very focused around rewards and celebration and success," said Melinda Stickley, compensation/recognition manager. "We've got more recognition programs here than any company I've ever heard of."

The far-ranging programs and activities appeared to be paying off. According to annual employee opinion surveys, associates rated the company significantly higher in such categories as job satisfaction, management leadership, and communication than the norm for employees at high-performing companies. Not only that, absenteeism was low, and employee attrition was far below the average for financial services companies (see Exhibit 14.6 for selected employee opinion survey results and attrition and absenteeism rates).

Despite the efforts of senior managers to create a positive environment, however, the telephone associate's job was not easy. Many stresses arose simply from working for a 24-hour customer service operation—stresses that may have been particularly trying for UCS's well educated employees.[2] Telephone associates, organized in teams of about 20, spent long days and nights—as well as periodic weekends and holidays—on the phone, performing a largely repetitive task. There was often mandatory overtime, particularly during unexpectedly successful card promotions, and associates knew their schedules only two weeks in advance.

Along with these largely unavoidable downsides, the particular culture of UCS imposed its own stresses. The pressure to achieve quality every day was an ever-present goad. Furthermore, the company's determination to continuously improve—captured in an oft-used phrase of Fred Winkler, "pleased, but never satisfied"—frequently translated into increased performance expectations for the associates. As the telephone technology systems got better, for example, managers expected associates to take advantage of the increased efficiencies by lowering their "talk time," the average amount of time they spent on the phone with each customer.

Finally, there was the monitoring. About 17 process measures were gathered in Customer Relationships, the general customer service area. To begin with, the information technology system tracked the average speed of answer, the number of calls each associate handled, and how long each associate spent on the phone. As a result of their exposure to the daily printouts detailing these statistics, most associates could rattle off with deadly accuracy how many calls they handled in a day—typically about 120—as well as how many seconds they spent on an average call—in the range of 140 to 160.

Perhaps more daunting, telephone associates were directly monitored

---

[2]Because of underemployment in the Jacksonville area, and the desirability of working for AT&T, UCS had been able to recruit a highly qualified workforce: Sixty-five percent of telephone associates had college degrees.

Exhibit 14.6 Employee Satisfaction Data

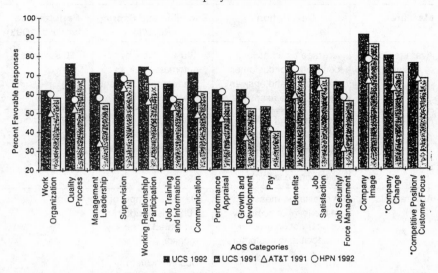

Note: 1992 data for AT&T unavailable; AT&T conducts its AOS biannually.   *HPN not available.

Note:
AOS = Annual Opinion Survey
HPN = High-Performing Norm (average response for a group of high performing organizations that use the same survey)

Adverse Indicators	1990	1991	1992	Benchmark
Employee Turnover				
UCS Total	9.7%	10.1%	12.3%	N/A
Managers	8.7%	9.0%	7.2%`	14%
Associates	10.1%	10.5%	14.1%	23%
Customer Contact Associates	10.2%	10.7%	13.5%	23%
*Absenteeism Rate**				
Managers	N/A	1.3%	1.1%	1.3%
Associates	N/A	2.2%	3.3%	1.9%
* includes pregnancy and disability				

Source: Universal Card Services.

by a number of people both inside and outside of Customer Relationships. As part of the gathering of the daily measures, specially trained monitors in both the Relationship Excellence group and an internal quality group listened in on a total of 100 customer calls a day.[3] The monitors—or quality associates—rated telephone associates on accuracy, efficiency, and profes-

[3]Relationship Excellence originally did the entire 100-call sample, but Customer Relationships began cosampling when it created its internal quality department in November 1990.

Exhibit 14.7   Telephone Associates Measurement Regime

Measure	Description	Sampling and Scoring Regime	Performance Standard (1Q93)
Average Speed of Answer (ASA)	Average time between completion of customer connection and answer by telephone associate	100% sample by automated call management system (CMS)	20 seconds
Abandon Rate	Percentage of calls initiated by customers, but abandoned prior to being answered by telephone associate	100% sample by automated call management system (CMS)	3% of incoming calls
Accuracy	A qualitative measure of the level of accuracy of information given by associates to customers	Random sample of 100 calls per day evaluated by quality monitor Scoring system includes predefined criteria for evaluating customer impacting errors, business impacting errors, and non-impacting errors	96%
Professionalism	Professionalism (courtesy, responsiveness) shown by telephone associate	Random sample of 100 calls per day evaluated by quality monitor Scoring system includes predefined criteria for evaluating customer impacting errors, business impacting errors, and non-impacting errors	100%

Source: Universal Card Services.

sionalism, recording their comments on a one-page observation sheet (see Exhibit 14.7 for a description of these measures and how they were gathered).

Any "impacts"—UCS's term for a negative effect on a customer or the business—were reported at Customer Relationships's daily quality meeting, attended by representatives from both Relationship Excellence and the internal quality group.[4] Negative reports were then passed on to the team leaders of the associates involved to discuss and keep on file for performance reviews.

Other parts of the organization monitored calls as well, each with a slightly different purpose. Team leaders listened to 10 calls a month for each of the approximately 20 associates in their groups, using the observations to review and "develop" the associates. And *all* managers at UCS, regardless of their function, were encouraged to monitor at least two hours of calls a month to stay in touch with services and practices. Rob Davis, vice president of Quality, for example, held a regular monthly listening session with all his staff, followed by a discussion period to analyze the quality implications of what they had heard. Finally, the results of the Customer Contactor Surveys, including verbatim remarks from cardholders about how associates treated them, were turned over to managers in Customer Relationships who could easily identify which associate handled a particular call if there was an "impact" or other problem to resolve.

The combination of high corporate expectations and these multiple forms of monitoring and feedback created considerable pressure at UCS not only to perform well, but to do so under intense scrutiny, at least for telephone associates. Some managers felt this took a toll. "The quality process, daily sampling, and feedback were not without pain," claimed Mary Kay Gilbert, who as senior vice president of Cardmember Services oversaw the Customer Relationships operation. "I had to stop people and say, 'Wait, we're here to make sure we're delivering the right service to customers. This isn't personal.'"

But others argued that the way the associates were monitored, and the way team leaders and managers delivered feedback, kept it from being a negative or stressful experience. Company policy dictated that all supervisors and managers were to treat associates with respect and to view mistakes as a learning opportunity. If an associate were overheard giving inaccurate information to a customer, for example, the team leader was not to rebuke the associate, but to explain the error and provide additional training, if necessary, so that the mistake would not occur again. "The positive stress for workers here is high risk, high demand, high reward," asserted Deb Holton, manager of Quality. "It is not the stress of coming in in the morning and checking their brains at the door."

Raising the Bar

Thanks in large part to the customer-pleasing work of the telephone associates, by the close of 1991 financial analysts had declared UCS a major

---

[4]The ten areas in which impacts could occur had been identified as (1) telephone contact, (2) correspondence contact, (3) application contact, (4) change of address, (5) claims, (6) credit line increase, (7) payment receipt, (8) statements, (9) plastic card production accuracy/timeliness, and (10) authorization availability/accuracy.

success for AT&T. During that year, holders of the UCS card had dramatically increased AT&T calling-card usage. And after less than two years in business, UCS ranked a stunning third in the dollar volume of charges on its card, with $3.8 billion in receivables, $17.2 billion in total sales volume, and 7.6 million accounts. Industry kudos included a "Top Banking Innovation" award from American Banker and "Best Product of 1990" from *Business Week*.

Despite this stellar performance, the Business Team was convinced that it was time to shake things up—that everyone could do better. Although some executives initially balked at the prospect of a change, after a series of debates the Business Team agreed to "raise the bar" on the number of indicators the company had to achieve to earn quality. A compelling argument for the increase was the fact that associates were meeting or exceeding standards so consistently. During 1991, associates had made quality at least 25 days out of every month, and in August they had earned quality every day, often achieving 97 percent or more of the indicators. Managers, too, were doing well. "We wanted to take it up," explained Davis, "because of our strong commitment to continuous improvement."[5] Added Marian Browne, vice president of Customer Relationships, "Everything was going fine, but if you look at perfect service every day, we weren't giving perfect service every day."

With the Business Team's blessing, Kahn sent the following letter to all employees on December 26, just five days before the change was to take effect:

Dear UCS Colleague,

In the spirit of continuous improvement, UCS will take another step in our never-ending commitment to customer delight. Beginning Jan. 1, 1992, the quality objective for associates will move from 95 percent to 96 percent. The quality objective for managers will move to 96 percent for the target goal and 97 percent to 100 percent for the maximum goal. UCS' Excellence Award program will continue to reward quality as it has in the past—the only difference will be that the objective will be moved up for both managers and associates.

UCS people have demonstrated our value of customer delight since "day one." As we continue to improve our ability to delight customers, we'll also continue to evaluate and revise our quality standards and measurements. I'm extremely proud of the work each of you performs. Your dedication to our seven values continues to make UCS a leader in the industry.

---

[5]In fact, the threshold for managers had already changed: Since January 1991, managers had to achieve 96 percent of their quality indicators for full compensation, receiving only three-quarters of the bonus for 95 percent.

What the letter didn't mention was that the raising of the bar was actually a double challenge: Not only did employees have to achieve a higher percentage of measures, but individual standards had been raised on 47 of the indicators, making each of them harder to earn. In addition, Collins and her Relationship Excellence team took advantage of the start of the calendar year and the relative lull after the holiday season to retire and replace a substantial chunk of the measures. While only 15 indicators had been dropped in all of 1991 and 26 added, the monitoring group abruptly cut out 48 indicators, many of them among the most consistently achieved, and replaced them with 46 new ones. In effect, this meant that close to half of the measures by which associates judged their daily performance—and were judged—were now different.

The reaction to the change was immediate. Associates earned only 13 quality days in January and 16 in February, and managers fared even worse. Not only was the company failing to make the new goal of 96 percent, it was missing quality by as much as six percentage points on a given day, well below the worst daily performance of the previous month. "We fell flat on our faces as far as the number of days we were paying out as a business," Davis recalled. Added Collins, "For most of the days we were well below even the old standard."

The abrupt dropoff took management by surprise. According to Robert Inks, who started as a telephone associate in May 1990, associates weren't so much mad as they were concerned—concerned that higher standards of efficiency might make it harder to deliver quality service, and concerned that regular bonuses might be a thing of the past. "The associates looked at it as, well, this is my money," explained Inks, "I'm not going to be getting my money." Added Pam Vosmik, vice president of Human Resources: "There was probably some grousing in the hallways."

It was no consolation that UCS was on the verge of logging its first profit. In fact, at a business meeting open to all employees, associates accused management of having raised the bar as a cost-cutting measure to avoid paying compensation. Nor was the timing of the slump propitious. UCS was ready to make an all-out push to win the Baldrige award, and although the site examiners would not arrive until September, it was critical that employees be motivated and on board. "I went to the Business Team," recalled Gilbert, "and I said, 'Look, we raised all these indicators and measures and I don't think the people around this table understand the impact. But if we start beating people up as a result of this, you can kiss the Baldrige good-bye.'"

Senior managers took the performance plunge to heart. In fact, according to Davis, some managers were so concerned by the apparent associate disaffection that they were ready to lower the bar to its previous level. Instead of backing down, however, the Business Team concocted an alternate scheme to reignite associate enthusiasm. In March, the same month that UCS submitted its Baldrige application, the company announced the "Triple Quality Team Challenge." The special incentive program allowed associates and managers to earn triple bonuses that month for each quality day they achieved beyond a base of 20 quality days. If employees earned 22 quality days, for example, they would get credit for 26. A four-foot by 16-foot calendar board mounted in the cafeteria and small boards in each functional area displayed daily progress toward the goal. In explaining the incentive program, *HOTnews*, an internal publication reserved for important communiqués, noted:

> . . . quality results in January and through February 26 show UCS not doing as well as it did even before we raised our quality standards in 1992. Many of the current problems have nothing to do with our new standards or indicators, but are failures of basic courtesy and accuracy. "I know we can do better," says Kahn. "The results concern me and I know they concern you. It's important that we work together to meet our quality goals and delight our customers. The 'Triple Quality Team Challenge' must be a team effort—we need to help each other achieve our indicators, not look around for who's not making theirs and punish them."

Softening the System

The Triple Quality Challenge was a rousing success. Associates' quality days spiked back up to 25 in March, and managers earned 19 days (see Exhibit 14.8 for an overview of quality days achieved over time). But the organizational upset engendered by the raising of the bar, along with fears that telephone associates—on whose dedication the company's success depended—could become disillusioned, prompted a harder look at making both measures and feedback more participatory and more palatable. In the months that followed, UCS even abandoned the "pleased but never satisfied" expression because it gave associates a sense of inadequacy and futility.

Efforts to reach out to associates took a number of forms. Managers in Customer Relationships continued to coach team leaders, one-third of whom had been promoted from the associate level, to make sure they were comfortable and skilled at giving feedback. "We've got a lot of young, inexperienced team leaders, and what you have to teach your team leaders is that you can't use feedback as a club," noted Marian Browne. "You use it as a development tool. You don't do it to beat people up, or to catch people." Customer Relationships also began to experiment with peer monitoring, having telephone associates critique each other rather than relying solely on team leaders for developmental review.

Relationship Excellence, which had already been sharing the gathering of the daily measures with Customer Relationships since the end of 1990, helped other functional areas set up internal quality departments to

Exhibit 14.8 Quality Days Performance and Bonuses

Associate Quality Days and Bonus Performance

Quarter	# Quality Days as % of Total	Bonus as % of Salary
4Q90	76.1%	6.4%
1Q91	87.8%	11.4%
2Q91	92.3%	9.9%
3Q91	96.7%	12.0%
4Q91	95.7%	11.6%
1Q92	70.3%	10.6%
2Q92	75.8%	7.5%
3Q92	76.1%	7.9%
4Q92	95.7%	10.8%
1Q93	84.4%	9.4%

Management Quality Days and Bonus Performance

Period	# Quality Days as % of Total	Bonus as % of Salary
1991	87.9%	5.6%
1992	66.1%	4.7%
1Q93	76.7%	5.6%

Source: Universal Card Services

co-sample, with the plan that they might eventually take over the measures entirely. Although some executives were concerned that this shift might hurt the integrity of the sample, Ron Shinall, a Relationship Excellence team leader, insisted it was a necessary evolution. "There's going to be a natural aversion to someone telling you how to make your process better if that person hasn't worked with you or been in that process," he declared.

Relationship Excellence also changed what it did with call observations. The daily Customer Relationships quality meeting, which had served largely as a chance for quality associates to report the mistakes they had caught, became, instead, a forum for discussion and learning. Telephone associates from the floor were invited to join the internal and external quality representatives, and the entire group debated whether negative impacts had occurred without ever identifying those who had handled the questionable calls. "It's helped get a lot of buy-in from the associates," remarked Darrin Graham, who had led Customer Relationships's internal quality department. "Back at the beginning, when you would hear that there is this group out there listening to my calls, you just naturally started to get an us/them mentality, and they're out to get us. Now that mentality is going away."

As part of this overhaul, Relationship Excellence experimented with no longer giving associates—or their team leaders—feedback on calls monitored for the daily measures. But although the experiment had been urged by an associate focus group, the so-called Nameless/Blameless program lasted only a few weeks. "The majority of the people wanted to know if they'd made a mistake," Browne explained. Feedback resumed, but with two important differences: negative impacts no longer went into associates' files, and team leaders received, and handed on, both good news and bad. The internal quality group also worked harder to stress the positive. "We used to walk up to people's desks and we'd have a piece of paper in our hand, and they'd be like, 'Oh no, here they come,'" recalled Paul Ferrando, team leader of Customer Relationships's first internal quality group. "And I'd say, 'Someone on your team had an excellent call.' When you bring good news, they don't grimace when you walk up to them anymore. People aren't afraid of quality, and they aren't afraid of this monitoring anymore."

The steady evolution of the system appeared to have increased associate acceptance of the measures. There would always, of course, be some employees who balked at being measured, as the following response to the June 1992 employee survey indicated:

> A big handicap is being monitored constantly. The people are not relaxed. They are under so much stress that they will get a variance, that they don't do their job as well as they could. Monitoring should be used as a learning tool—we're all human and sometimes forget things.

But most telephone associates professed their support. "The reason that we're measuring is to find out what we're capable of, and what we're doing right, and what we can improve on, and what we don't need to improve," declared Cheryl Bowie, who took a large paycut from her former managerial position to become a telephone associate in 1992. "There is no problem here with the feedback. You're not branded or anything. It's just a learning experience."

On October 14, 1992, near the end of a challenging year of growth and change, Universal Card was awarded a Malcolm Baldrige National Quality Award. At a black-tie celebration party recognizing employees' part in the companywide effort, associates received a $250 after-tax bonus and a Tiffany pin, and a small group of associates, selected by lottery, traveled to Washington, D.C., for the actual Baldrige presentation. But the award did not lessen the sense of urgency at UCS. "When we learned we had won the Baldrige," recalled Quality manager Deb Holton, "our second breath was, 'But we will not be complacent.'"

In truth, UCS would have had to change, whether it sought to or not. Paul Kahn announced his resignation in February 1993 over differences within the company as to whether UCS should expand into new financial products, and Fred Winkler defected for archrival First Union Corp. in April. Although David Hunt, the banking industry executive who replaced Kahn, and Winkler's successor, AT&T veteran Gerald Hines, quickly won widespread acceptance, the departure of these two critical and charismatic leaders created anxiety about the company's future direction.

The competitive landscape within which UCS operated was also changing. Although by early 1993, the company had captured the number two ranking among the 6,000 issuers of credit cards, with almost 12 million accounts and 18 million cardholders, it was becoming increasingly diffi-cult for UCS to make its product stand out. Competitors such as General Motors Corp. had introduced their own no-fee cards, and the variable interest rates pioneered by UCS had become common. "The sad part is, our competition is catching up with us," lamented Mark Queen, manager of Customer Listening, and overseer of the Customer Contactor Surveys. "Where we need to continue to distinguish ourselves is in service."

But continuous improvement—finding ways to motivate associates beyond what they had already accomplished—was not an easy task. For one thing, with the company's growth slowing, it would no longer be possible for as many associates to quickly ascend the corporate ladder to team leader and other managerial positions. Moreover, the current measurements no longer seemed to be driving the quest for improvement, and Davis and others had become convinced that it was time to retool a system that no longer fit the needs of the company. Ironically, considering how much Universal Card had already done to create meaningful and effective measures, among the Business Team's top 10 goals for 1993 was the development of a world-class measurement system.

Weighing the Options

By the summer of 1993, Davis's Quality organization was assessing a range of new approaches to measuring. In particular, a specially convened Measures Review Committee under Thedas Dukes, a senior manager now responsible for the daily measures, was taking a hard look at what to change.

Customer-Centered Measures

A project of particular interest to Davis was the company's early experi-mentation with customer-centered measures (CCM). While CCM might not change what UCS was measuring, advocates argued it would more concretely and powerfully express how the company was serving card-holders by stating this performance in terms of customer impacts.

Instead of reporting that 98 percent of cardholder bills were accurate on a given day, for example, a CCM report might state that 613 customers did *not* get a correct bill. "We are trying to change the language away from percentages and indexes to a language of customers," explained Davis. Added Ron Shinall, quality team leader, "It's hard to tell the difference between 99.8 percent and 99.9 percent, but in some of the high-volume areas, that can mean a tremendous number of people are actually impacted. Fractions of a percent mean a lot when you're talking about 40,000 daily calls."

UCS had been considering customer-centered measures since visiting early Baldrige winner Federal Express Corp. in the summer of 1991. Unlike UCS, with its 100-plus measures, Federal Express had selected just 12 processes it deemed critical to serving customers, and had based its reward system on that 12-component CCM index. In January 1993, Universal began a six-month test of CCM, reporting customer impacts on 13 existing process indicators that measured different aspects of accuracy and professionalism. The now 30-member Relationship Excellence group, which had changed its name to Quality Applications in December, sent out its first CCM report in March.

But the jury was still out on what impact CCM would have. Linda Plummer, a senior manager in Customer Relationships, applauded the idea of expressing error in human terms. Yet she found the initial reports, which simply listed the number of customers impacted in each category along with the effects per thousand contacts, to be meaningless. "Someone needs to tell me at what point I have a concern," she complained. "Is it when 100 customers are impacted, or 2,000 customers are impacted? I don't even look at them anymore because I don't know how to interpret them." Jean Wentzel, another senior manager in Customer Relationships, agreed: "Until we've really communicated it effectively and tied it back to the compensation system, it's not going to have the same buy-in or impact."

But increasing the relevance of CCM by tying it to the compensation system would not be easy. In fact, the cross-functional CCM group responsible for the pilot project had recently agreed to shelve temporarily the issue of whether to create a compensation link, concluding that the points raised were too complicated to tackle all at once. Unresolved questions included how to set standards for customer impacts; whether the compensation system should include both business-centered measures reported the old way and customer-centered measures reported the new way; and whether UCS should retire its bucket of measures and move instead to a system more similar to that at Federal Express, with compensation based on just a dozen or so service measures, rather than on a broad range of company functions. This last possibility, which would result in many people and processes no longer being measured, fundamentally challenged the company's founding philosophy of having all employees work together, be measured together, and earn quality together.

Statistical Process Control

Statistical process control was another tool Quality Applications was examining. There was a growing conviction within UCS that the company needed to adopt a more long-term outlook in quality measurement. This belief was further fueled by feedback, late in 1992, from a committee that had evaluated UCS for AT&T's prestigious Chairman's Quality Award, noting that "there is no evidence of a statistical approach to data analysis, including determining out-of-control processes, identifying special and/or common causes, and the approach to prioritizing improvement opportunities."

In fact, the gathering of measures on a daily basis, as well as UCS's commitment to a "sense of urgency"—one of its seven values—had contributed to the focus on the short term. Only recently had Universal switched from monthly to quarterly business reviews, and the group that met every morning to discuss the daily measures, now headed by Fred Winkler's replacement, Jerry Hines, was for the first time adding a quarterly quality review. Remarked Davis, "With our daily focus on measurements and our fix-it-today mentality, the thing that sometimes suffers is looking at the long-term trends in the data."

Statistical process control (SPC) seemed to provide at least a partial answer to this shortcoming. The quality improvement methodology, developed at Bell Laboratories in the 1920s to chart manufacturing processes and identify events that affect product output, had been broadly defined in recent years to include such tools as cause and effect diagrams and Pareto charts, as well as control charts to statistically examine process capability and variation. But SPC had only rarely been applied in a service environment. The challenge at UCS, therefore, was to adapt the manufacturing tool to its customer service business.

Pete Ward, a process engineer within Quality Applications, was confident this could be done. He had already begun to prepare individualized reports for associates, allowing them to use SPC to chart and trend such daily productivity measures as talk time and number of calls handled. In contrast to mere daily statistics, Ward explained, the SPC charts would help telephone associates see the impact that one action—such as spending too much time on the phone with customers—had on another, as well as aid them in spotting cyclical patterns in their own performances.

But SPC, like CCM, raised questions about the existing measurement system. It was unclear, for example, whether it was valuable to apply statistical tools to something as ambiguous and subjective as deciding whether an associate had been courteous enough or had spent too much time with a customer. In addition, SPC charts, which allowed a more meaningful and long-term look at performance than the daily measures, presented ammunition for the argument that it was time for Universal Card to switch from its obsession with daily goals and rewards to a reliance on more statistically significant trends.

A Link to External Results

These and other questions had revived old complaints that the measures did not accurately reflect how customers actually viewed Universal, nor how the company was performing. Mark Queen, manager of Customer Listening and overseer of the Customer Contactor Surveys, acknowledged that although the internal measures were designed to measure processes important to customers, missing quality days internally didn't necessarily show up in dissatisfied customers. When internal quality results took a nosedive after the bar was raised in early 1992, for example, the Customer Contactor Surveys indicated only a slight blip in customer satisfaction—a fact, Queen says, that "was driving everybody crazy."

Similarly, Queen noted that although recent customer feedback indicated that cardholders viewed associates as somewhat less courteous than before, the internal quality monitors listening in on phone calls had not logged an increase in negative impacts. "There is not a clear enough linkage," Davis admitted. "What people would really like would be for me to say, 'OK, if you can take this internal customer measure and raise it from 96 percent to 99 percent, I guarantee it will take customer satisfaction up by X amount.' But we can't say that, yet."

Linkage aside, on occasion, the internal measures seemed to be at cross purposes with the company's financial goals. Greg Swindell, who in late 1992 became vice president of Customer Focused Quality Improvement, for example, described an unexpectedly successful marketing promotion for a new credit card product that left understaffed telephone associates unable to keep up with the rush of calls. Although the surge of new business was good for the company, the telephone associates were, in effect, doubly punished: first by having to frantically field additional calls, and second by missing their quality indicators and losing compensation. "The question is, is that high response rate a bad thing?" Swindell asked. "And my answer is no. We're here to bring on more customers, to become more profitable. So how do we balance this focus on these metrics and our business and strategic objectives? For me, this offers a very perplexing problem."

A New Look at the Measures

Spurred by these and other questions, there was talk at UCS of a radical rearrangement of the bucket of measures. Although it was not clear what would take the bucket's place, more and more managers were beginning to feel that UCS's drive for continuous improvement was being held hostage by the relentless and short-term push to bring home the daily bonus. What had originally been designed as a means for identifying and improving processes and as a motivational tool, critics charged, was now holding the company back rather than driving it forward.

Greg Swindell was one who questioned the status quo: "Perhaps it is a very good tool to help us *maintain* our performance, but I'm not sure it's the kind of tool that will help take us into the next century and really get a lot better at what we're doing." Swindell was particularly concerned about how inflexible the system had become in the wake of associates' intense reaction to the raising of the bar. Managers rarely suggested adding new measures, even when they spotted an area in need of improvement, he remarked, because they did not want to make the goals too challenging and jeopardize the all-important bonus. Mary Kay Gilbert agreed: "The more focus and pressure you put on your quality standards, the less people are willing to raise their hand and say, 'I think this process should be measured,'" she declared. "Tying compensation to it just kind of throws that out the window."

Similarly, associates had grown to resist having measures retired, not only because that usually meant the loss of an "easy win," but also because it required workers to realign their priorities and goals (see Exhibit 14.9 for charts illustrating the decline in measurement system changes after 1992). In part to address the issue of stagnation in the system, Quality Applications, in a just-released draft on measurement methodology, urged managers to regularly review old measures and create new ones, noting particularly that "danger lies when the primary reason for a measurement is to adapt to the [compensation program] rather than to improve the performance of the team or process. . . . Our measures should be used to aid in our continuous improvement programs."

To keep the measures flexible, Davis was considering a "sunset law" on measures that required all indicators to be retired and replaced after one year. But although he had heard the compensation plan referred to as "an entitlement," he remained a supporter of the basic concept. "Some people in our business believe that if we didn't have measurements tied to compensation, then people would be more willing to measure the right things," he mused. "My feeling, though, is that I'll take all the negatives that go with it any day in order to get the attention." Telephone associate Robert Inks agreed: "I don't think we would have gotten as far as we have today without it, because people can look at our monitors and say, 'We didn't do too good yesterday, we're not getting that money.' And then they look at the future and say, 'Well, we have eight more days in the quarter. We're going to really focus on quality and make it, because if we don't get those eight days, that's $100 I lose.'"

Although Davis was well aware of the measurement debates, he doubted that Universal would abandon its daily measures any time soon. In fact, he had more down-to-earth concerns: In January 1994, UCS was planning to raise the bar again, and Davis was already planning how to make the transition smoother this time around. Although he anticipated some resistance, Davis was convinced that the ongoing quest for continu-

Exhibit 14.9   Changes in Standards and Measures

Number of Increases in Standards for Existing Measures

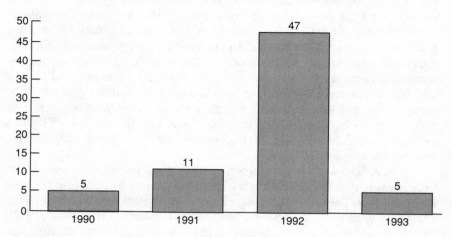

Note: Data for 1993 is Year-to-Date through June 30, 1993.

Number of Additions and Deletion of Measures

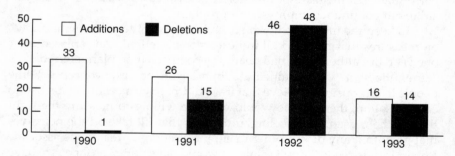

Note: Data for 1993 is Year-to-Date through June 30, 1993.
Source: Universal Card Services

ous improvement was necessary. "We'll have to hit hard on the fact that we're going to keep raising the standards, it's not going to stop," he declared. "And if we think it is, we're just fooling ourselves."

But Pam Vosmik, vice president of Human Resources, voiced a separate concern. Recalling Winkler's "pleased but never satisfied" expression, she made a plea for balance. "You need to keep people focused," Vosmik asserted, "but by the same token, in the worst case scenario, you can make an organization dysfunctional if there is never a hope that you're going to be satisfied."

CHAPTER 15

Philips Taiwan

"*I*T IS NOT EASY being one of the first companies in your country to try out a new approach to management. You have no role models to guide you, and no comparison that will help you see how much there is to gain from doing things in a different way." A senior manager of Philips Taiwan was reflecting in mid-1988 on the program of improvements in which his company had been engaged since 1985, and speculating about the steps that ought to be taken next. "We know that this approach appears to work in Japan, but it is not easy to convince the managers and workers throughout our whole organization of this, or that a similar approach will work just as effectively in our totally different environment. And, surprisingly, it is just as difficult to keep our people motivated to continue along this path now—when we have made substantial progress in a number of areas—than it was when we started. The attitude of many people is that we have gotten to the point now where the costs required to achieve further improvements are greater than the likely benefits." He continued:

> For example, consider the development of our new CM [Color Monitor] 9000 product, which we introduced just last February. By almost any measure it is the best designed product we have ever produced, and it looks as though it is also going to be our most successful product, commercially. Moreover, its development went quite smoothly, compared with previous products. We hit our target cost, even though it was an ambitious one, and missed our target introduction date by just a few weeks. The number of engineering changes required has been much lower than for previous products, and quality problems are also much less. But now, rather than taking a moment to enjoy our success, we are asking our people to reevaluate our whole approach to product

Professor Robert H. Hayes prepared this case as the basis for class discussion rather than to illustrate either effective or ineffective handling of an administrative situation.

development and suggest improvements. We want to do even
better when we begin developing a successor product to the
CM9000 later this year. "Wouldn't we use our time more productively," they ask, "if we worked on improving our products and
technical abilities, rather than on refining our management
processes?" That is not always an easy question to answer.

Company Background

Philips Taiwan was a wholly-owned subsidiary of Philips Electronics N.V.,
a multinational company headquartered in Holland; it had operations in
over 60 countries. In 1988, Philips' sales were running at an annual rate of
about US$30 billion, the bulk of which came from its lighting and
consumer electronics businesses. It was the largest producer of television
sets in the world. For well over a decade Philips had operated under a
matrix management system, composed of National Organizations (which
managed all the operations within a country), and Product Divisions
(which were responsible for coordinating worldwide strategy for their
assigned products and technologies).

Philips Taiwan was one of these National Organizations, with annual
sales of over US$1 billion. It comprised five separate businesses, operating
out of ten different factories in four separate locations within Taiwan. The
largest of these businesses was its Consumer Electronics Division located
at Chungli, about 40 km. south of Taipei. Chungli was one of three locations within Philips' worldwide network that produced monochrome and
color computer monitors for both personal and professional use. The other
two factories, in Canada and Italy, were much smaller and concentrated on
specialized markets. With production running at a rate of over 30,000 units
a week in mid-1988, and total annual sales of over US$200 million, Philips
Taiwan was one of the largest producers of computer monitors in the
world. Its world market share was estimated at about 8%.

Philips' corporate management had been encouraging its National
Organizations to improve their quality and product development for
several years. In early 1985, Philips Taiwan organized a "Company-Wide
Quality Improvement" (CWQI) seminar for all its managers, during which
it was agreed that major efforts were required both to improve the quality
of all aspects of their company's activities, and to become more attentive to
their customers' needs.

To guide this effort, Philips Taiwan adopted a process known as
"Policy Deployment." By then in widespread use among the top Japanese
companies, in essence Policy Deployment was a systematic approach for
identifying and resolving the most critical problems facing a company. It
began at the top management level with a careful analysis of different

problem areas and—based on the company's long term plan and business environment—their relative importance to the company's success. Then department heads and staff engineers at every location were asked to develop a number of Improvement Plans for dealing with these problems. This was referred to as the "top down" part of the process.

Proper implementation, however, required a "bottom-up" involvement of people throughout the organization, both through individual suggestions and group projects. The teams assigned to various projects were required to follow a detailed "Plan-Do-Check-Adjust" (P-D-C-A) process, requiring extensive documentation, as they identified and solved successive problems and then modified procedures so the same problems would not reoccur. This process forced everybody into a cycle of continual improvement.

To guide and facilitate its CWQI program, Philips Taiwan announced ambitious new quality goals, set up CWQI Steering Committees in each of its four locations, and introduced systems to strengthen the Quality Assurance function and encourage employee suggestions. A massive education program was set up to provide training in Policy Deployment, quality improvement, and problem-solving techniques. Each division was challenged to develop its own improvement program, and consultants from Japan were invited to visit Taiwan occasionally to evaluate progress and offer suggestions.

Although "quality" is usually thought of in terms of *product* quality, Philips Taiwan managers believed that quality problems existed in all aspects of their operations. For example, Quality Improvement methods were being applied by the Human Resource Function to deal with problems in the areas of recruiting, training, compensation, and staff turnover. Such turnover, the result of employee decisions—usually quite sudden and often apparently unprovoked—to leave the company and look for another job, had become a serious problem throughout Taiwanese industry. Turnover was running at a rate of between three and four percent per month at Chungli in mid-1988, somewhat less than the average rate in its local area. Over half of those resigning had worked at the factory less than three months, and 75% less than one year. Only about 15% had worked for more than two years.

A number of explanations had been offered for this high turnover rate. Most prominent was the unusually low rate of unemployment (about 1%) during this period of booming economic growth. The difficulty of getting qualified people, in turn, had led to rapid inflation in wages, inducing people—particularly younger workers who had not developed strong loyalty to their companies—to move from job to job chasing the best salaries. The rapid growth of the service sector, particularly financial services, which was desperately trying to attract people and was unconstrained by the compensation practices of traditional Taiwanese companies, made it particularly difficult for manufacturing companies to attract and retain people. Despite these external causes, Philips Taiwan felt that some of the causes of personnel turnover were within its control and set out to identify and eliminate them.

Different groups identified a variety of possible causes. These included both inadequate and improper communication between employees and their immediate supervisors, unfair work assignments and employee appraisals, and inadequate social opportunities. Problem solving groups were assigned to propose ways to address all these possible causes, and over the next year the turnover rate steadily decreased.

The success of such efforts encouraged Philips Taiwan to set for itself the goal of becoming the first Asian company outside of Japan to win the Deming Prize—given each year by JUSE (the Union of Japanese Scientists and Engineers) to a few Japanese companies that had achieved the most impressive improvements in quality and productivity.

"We have the opportunity to develop an entirely new approach to management, one that combines the Western approach, which is results-oriented and emphasizes business planning, with the Japanese approach, which is process-oriented and emphasizes continual improvement," stated Mr. Y. C. Lo, who had recently been selected to be the new President of Philips Taiwan. He had been with the company for many years, most recently as its Executive V.P. for Quality Management. Mr. Lo continued:

> Until fairly recently, unfortunately, planning within Philips has tended to be confined to generating rather general sales and financial projections—and these plans were seldom translated into specific action. We have to focus now on making very detailed plans for improvements in operations, and then translating those improvement plans into specific assignments for people and groups. These plans don't have to be very elaborate, but they must be very clear. And they must be implemented. Moreover, everybody in the organization has to be involved, not just in implementing the plans, but in developing them as well. And top management has to be personally committed to making the process work—by selecting team members, establishing clear, precise targets, and then following up to make sure things get done.

The Chungli Factory Complex

The original factory at Chungli had been built by the Bendix Corporation in the late 1960s to produce car radios. It was bought by Philips in 1975, and initially assigned to produce black and white television receivers. Over the next few years new factory buildings were added, production volume increased dramatically, and additional products were introduced. Little investment was made in improving the plant's equipment and human resources, however, because of the low profit margins in B&W television. In 1983, in an attempt to build its future on a more secure base, Chungli began producing low-end monochrome monitors for home computers, while phasing out B&W television receivers. Initially it utilized corporate designs, but gradually began designing more and more of its own products. Whereas in 1980 its design group consisted of only six engineers, by mid-1988 over 100 people were engaged in product design, and another 50 worked on process design. These people had the capabilities required to carry out all phases of product development except for the original concept development.

In 1985 Chungli began producing both color television sets and color monitors, and was designated by Philips' VDP (Video Display Products) Business Unit as an International Production Center. As such, it now became the primary source of Philips' high volume computer monitors. Moreover, it was now responsible for designing them, operating within specifications established by the product planning group at Product Division headquarters in Holland. Being designated as an IPC not only signified a long-term commitment to Chungli on the part of Philips, but also implied a willingness to invest in upgrading its technological capabilities.

In mid-1988 Chungli was increasing the production of video monitors while phasing out color television sets. Eighty percent of its 2200 employees were assigned to monitors, of whom about two-thirds were involved in direct production activities; the other third worked in a variety of support activities. Factory workers, most of them young women, took home about NT$9000 a month[1] and also received annual bonuses amounting to 2 to 3 months' salary. The company paid an additional 15% of total wages for employee-related taxes and fringe benefits, including insurance, free meals, and transportation to and from work. The wages of engineers and management personnel averaged somewhat over three times as much. Purchased materials accounted for almost 85% of the total manufacturing cost of a monitor, while direct labor came to somewhat over 2%.

A manufacturing facility's ability to reduce its costs during business downturns was limited by Taiwanese restrictions on laying off workers. Any substantial lay-off had to be approved by the government, and severance payments awarded amounting to one month's pay for each year of service. Despite such penalties, U.S.-owned factories in Taiwan routinely added or eliminated workers to adjust to business fluctuations. Philips Taiwan, however, chose to avoid lay-offs under any circumstances, both because of Philips' policy and a Chinese sense of responsibility to its corporate "family."

Chungli had been particularly aggressive in implementing the company's CWQI program; in late 1986 it won a Quality Award for its efforts from Philips' headquarters. Over the next two years it continued to

---

[1]NT$ stands for "New Taiwan Dollar." At the time of this case. NT$28 = US$1, approximately.

show remarkable improvement. For example, between early 1986 and mid-1988 it was able to reduce the number of defects identified during production by 75%, the outgoing defect rate by almost 90%, and labor hours per unit by 20%. The manufacturing cost of an average unit was also reduced by over 20%, and sales per employee rose to almost US$140,000, well above the average for Taiwanese companies.

It was also working to improve its product development process. Although CAD/CAM had been introduced in 1987, Chungli's top management still felt that new products too often were introduced behind schedule, did not incorporate the most advanced technologies, and generated too many customer complaints after introduction. Just as disturbing, little improvement had been observed for several years. The same problems arose again and again, were solved in an ad hoc manner by a new group of people, and little of the knowledge they gained was passed on to the next design group.

Video Monitor Technology and Markets

Like most computer-related technologies, the technical specifications for video monitors had been undergoing rapid improvement. In 1980, for example, the standard resolution of a 14-inch monochrome (black and white) television receiver was 420 by 315 pixels. (In simplest terms, a pixel is a point on the video screen that can be lighted up by an electron beam emitted from the base of the picture tube; this beam sweeps across each pixel several thousand times a second in most video displays.)

The monochrome monitor that Chungli began producing in 1983 for the home computer market, however, had a resolution of 640 by 348 pixels, an increase of over 70%. This necessitated much more precise placement of the fluorescent dots on the screen, as well as greater precision in the manufacture and alignment of the mask through which the electron beam had to pass on its way to the screen. Both added to the complexity of making the picture tubes that Philips Taiwan's Chupei factory supplied Chungli. It also required that Chungli incorporate much more complex electronics into its monitors.

The CM8000 that had been introduced in 1985 contained somewhat fewer pixels (640 by 200), but each was composed of three colors that had to be individually stimulated. In early 1988 Chungli introduced a new 14-inch color monitor, the CM9000, which offered more than twice the resolution of the CM8000 (640 by 480 pixels). Its factory price of about US$250, however, was only 30% greater. While the CM9000 was designed to be used with the latest generation of powerful personal computers, the next color monitor Chungli was proposing to develop would be targeted for the even more demanding requirements of desktop publishing. Although its specifications had not been formally established in mid-1988, it was likely to require at least another doubling of resolution, as well as an increase in size—and the CAD/CAM terminal that soon would follow it into the marketplace would require yet another.

The market for video monitors was also growing rapidly. It was estimated that over 10 million color, and 8 million monochrome, video monitors would be sold around the world in 1988. Philips Taiwan expected to produce 900,000 and 600,000, respectively, worth over US$250 million. Almost 60% of these were sold under its own brand name, and the rest under other labels. Over 15 companies competed for a share of this increasingly competitive market; seven of these were Japanese and five Korean. Korea's Samsung was believed to account for the largest number of units sold, while Philips, NEC, Sony, and Mitsubishi were generally acknowledged to offer the highest quality—for which they charged premium prices.

"Our Japanese competitors are starting to take us seriously now, both because of our market success and our improvements in quality," commented Mr. Jett Chen, the Regional Marketing/Sales Manager for monitors. "Unfortunately, we rely on some of these same competitors to supply us with critical parts. We are concerned that they may become less willing to supply us with the most advanced components, so are trying to develop alternative sources, both within Taiwan and at non-competing Japanese suppliers."

The Product Development Process

"Product development requires three things," observed Mr. L. P. Hsu, the General Manager of the Chungli IPC. "First, of course, is technological capability, which has to be built carefully and continuously. Second, there must be involvement by end users, which makes it possible to translate customer needs into technical specifications. Finally, and this is too often overlooked, there must be a parallel development of the methods used in development. We are working to improve ourselves along all three fronts."

For many years Philips had followed a seven step process for product development (see Exhibit 15.1 for a summary). Although this process informally started much earlier, with preliminary evaluations of potential markets and appropriate product features by the Product Group's marketing and product planning departments, its formal beginning was a top management meeting in Holland. During this meeting these analyses and proposals were reviewed, a decision was made to initiate a "Product Range Start" (PRS), and a project team was selected. The new team began developing the new product's detailed specifications and the design of its basic architecture. Once an "Approved Functional Model" was in hand (the second step), work could begin on building an actual prototype. The working model was approved at a "Commitment Date" (CD) meeting—the third step.

While the product team continued to improve the initial model, 150

Exhibit 15.1　Main Product Development Activities Monitors (mid-19880

Milestones	Activities After Each Milestone	Number of Weeks	End Product (of foregoing activities)
P.R.S.—Product Range Start	• Start development project	16	Functional Model
A.F.M.—Approved Functional Model	• Improvement of functional model • Ten models made	9	Commitment Date (C.D.) Model
C.D.—Commitment Date	• Improvement of C.D. model • 150 models made • Evaluation of model • Design Quality evaluation	10	Final Design Model
D.R.—Design Release	• Coding components • Bill of Materials • Trial run by Factory	12	Trial Run Model
I.R.—Industrial Release	• Prepare pilot run material • Process adaptation • Production line debug • Pilot run • Production QA check	5	Pilot Run Model
C.R.-Commercial Release	• Attain production rate • Attain fall-off target	6	Commercial Products
Mass Production Release	• Mass production		Competitive Products

working models were produced by hand by the Development Department and work began on developing the production process that would be used to produce the product. After a design quality evaluation of the second (improved) model, a decision was made to give the project its "Design Release," the fourth step. At this point the marketing department began making formal plans for introducing and marketing the product, and manufacturing began preparing a bill of materials and detailed specifications for components, leading up to a trial run in the factory. This triggered the trial production of a few units, and a final evaluation of both product and process.

The product's "Industrial Release" (IR), the fifth step, authorized preparations for a pilot production run of several hundred units. After careful evaluation of the results of this pilot run, and modifications of the production line, another meeting granted the project its "Commercial Release" (CR). This triggered the new product's commercial rollout and the beginning of mass production. Exhibit 15.2 diagrams the steps followed in developing the CM9000.

Although the seven steps were standard throughout Philips' worldwide organization, the specific actions that took place at each stage, the amount and kind of documentation required, and the amount of time that was allotted for it differed according to the nature of the product being introduced. As a rule of thumb, however, the total development cycle—the time elapsing between the PRS meeting and the product's commercial rollout—was a little over a year for video monitors.

Exhibit 15.2 New Product Development System Diagram for the CM9000

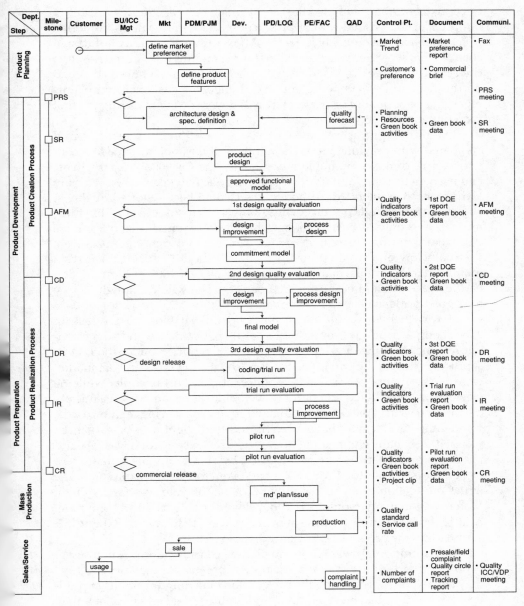

A number of measures were used to evaluate the success of a new product development project. Most important, of course, was whether it achieved its technical and cost specifications, and met its targeted introduction date. Others included the rate at which manufacturing was able to ramp up to the desired rate of production, the initial "fall-off" (internal reject rate) and how quickly it decreased over time, the number of design changes that were necessary in the first three months after introduction to correct errors in the original design or to adjust for market needs that had not been identified properly, and the number of customer complaints regarding poor quality or performance that were received during the first six months.

On all these measures, the CM9000 had performed unusually well compared with previous products (although it was not possible to reconstruct some of the comparable measures for the CM8000). Its target cost had been met exactly, and its development cycle had taken 60 weeks, only eight more than intended. Although defects had been detected in almost 60% of the initial units produced, this number fell to under 5% within three months, and only 12 design changes had been required to correct errors discovered during this same period. Customer complaints also were unusually low, and would probably total only about 15 during the first six months. On top of this, market acceptance was very high and production had increased to a rate of over 3000 per day. The whole Chungli factory took quiet pride in its accomplishment.

It was therefore with some reluctance that it took up the task of conducting a critical self-examination of its performance and suggesting improvements in the development process, as required under the P-D-C-A process. Most of the criticisms that surfaced during this self-examination were in the nature of "not quite good enough." For example, while 60 weeks was considered good for developing a product as technically demanding as the CM9000, it could have gotten an even bigger jump on its competitors if it could have been introduced eight weeks earlier, as planned. Too many engineering hours had been expended, it was felt, and too many tooling errors uncovered. Also, by almost any measure (except by comparison with the CM8000), it had taken too long to ramp up to the target production rate and the initial 60% fall-off rate was far too high. Moreover, too many monitors had developed problems during shipping. And 12 design changes because of mistakes were 12 too many. Exhibit 15.3 summarizes the problems experienced.

Just as important were more qualitative considerations. A number of people, for example, expressed frustration because of the "uncertainty" they had experienced during the project. Too many modifications in product specifications had been required, and problems had surfaced later than they should have. "The product planning department doesn't have enough time to develop the specs for a new product, because it has to wait for direction from the Product Division. Preliminary planning for the CM9000 should have begun long before we got to the PRS stage, not a few months before. Moreover, even though some of those involved in product planning have moved here over the past couple of years, all the initial decisions were made in Holland. In fact, the Senior Product Manager for our products still has his office there, totally separated from the market and factory realities that we have to contend with every day. As a result, he simply isn't able to develop the closeness that should underlie the initial planning of a new product," one manager commented. "We ought to move him, and all major product decisions here, where the people and expertise are, and where their attention isn't distracted by what is going on elsewhere."

"If we do that, we lose all the advantages of belonging to a large company that is marketing products in many countries and working with a number of related technologies," countered another. "The advantage of doing this preliminary work at corporate headquarters is that the product planners have much better access to what is going on in the research laboratories in Eindhoven, and can integrate what we are doing more closely with

Exhibit 15.3 Problems Encountered During Development of the CM9000

A. Unacceptable number of customer complaints during post-introduction period.

1. Inconsistent color (4 complaints) (Note: appears to be largely due to differences in characteristics of broadcast transmission between northern and southern hemispheres)

2. Not compatible with different characteristics of the electrical power supply in different countries (3)

3. Poor picture resolution (2)

4. Text in picture not sharp (2)

5. Poor contrast control (1)

B. Unacceptable number of internal problems that delayed development.

1. Set performance (6)

2. Component quality and availability (4)

3. Electrical/Mechanical Interference (2)

4. Drop test failure (2)

5. High defect rate during initial production (1)

the development projects at other business units." A third observed, however, that sometimes there were undesirable effects from close interaction among product planning groups. "The thinking of the top people in our Product Division is still dominated by their experience with the television display market, where technical specifications are much different. Our products, for example, are used to enhance personal productivity rather than to entertain. And 95% of them are used in air-conditioned environments. For those reasons, Product Division engineers tend to overdesign products for the personal computer market, just like Hewlett-Packard does."

Others focused more on the problems that arose during the detailed engineering and initial production of the CM9000. "The PRS decision was made on the basis of a lot of paper and a breadboard model of the product," observed one engineer. "It was only after we built an actual working model that we discovered the need to make substantial changes in some of the product specifications. That forced us to go back and redefine some of our component requirements with our suppliers, as well as make changes in our proposed production process. This alone added several weeks to the project. Why can't we build a prototype and work out the obvious problems before the PRS meeting?"

The major objection to this proposal was that building a prototype working model usually took roughly three months and cost in the neighborhood of NT$5 million. "Delaying the PRS, which is really a signal to the marketing and production people to start taking a proposed product seriously, simply compresses the time they have available to get ready for it," stated one. "Investing that much money before we get top management commitment to the project is risky," agreed another. As an example of where going ahead and building a prototype model would have wasted a lot of time and money, he pointed to a recent proposal to design a new computer workstation, which had failed to receive management approval during the PRS meeting.

Discussion also surrounded a third recommendation that had been made for improving the product development process: applying an approach called "Quality Function Deployment."

Quality Function Deployment

When applied to new product development, the Policy Deployment approach had been elaborated into what was called Quality Function Deployment (QFD). The essential idea of QFD was to begin by talking directly with customers to identify the aspects of a product's performance and appearance that they considered to be important, and then working through the design and production process to insure that those aspects received appropriate attention and support (that is, were "deployed") at every stage. The goal was not only to match user requirements with engineering specifications in a systematic, integrated fashion, but also to facilitate decisions involving tradeoffs if two or more user requirements conflicted either with each other or with various design specifications. A simplified example of the QFD approach is provided in the Appendix.

"The great value of QFD is that it allows an organization to work systematically on little parts of the whole problem, while never losing sight of how they fit together," commented L.P. Hsu. "Western thinking stresses reductionism—dividing up a big problem into pieces. But sometimes it places too little emphasis on holism—integrating all the pieces back into the whole. QFD makes it possible for people to see what other people are doing, and how the activities of each contribute to the total."

In one sense, applying the methodology of QFD and the P-D-C-A approach to the Product Development Process was a natural extension of the Quality Improvement activities being conducted throughout Philips Taiwan. "Product Development is a process involving people, products, and customers, just like all other important aspects of business," argued Mr. S. C. Wu, the Manager of the Chungli's Development Department. "It generates data from customer complaints and repair statistics. QFD will work here just as it has worked elsewhere. Moreover, it will force us to become more formal and specific. For example, we will have to conduct much more detailed discussions with our customers about proposed products and alternative specifications than we have in the past. And it will drive us away from our traditional engineering-driven, cost-based mentality to one that focuses on prices, like the people who buy our products. This is something we should have been doing long ago."

Others were not convinced. "We have seen the power of the QFD approach in certain areas," remarked one engineer, "but we have also seen its drawbacks. For example, it is highly time-consuming and requires the preparation of numerous reports. As we try to cope with faster and faster product cycles, we can't allow ourselves to get bogged down in endless meetings in which we examine and document every little thing. We would do much better at this point, in my opinion, if we just concentrated on simplifying and compressing the traditional seven-stage process."

Another agreed: "I don't believe that sort of detailed examination is appropriate for every kind of activity. Is it, for example, as appropriate for assembly operations as it is for machining or chemical processing—the kind of thing for which it was developed initially? Is it as appropriate for development projects, which are essentially one-of-a-kind, as it is for repetitive activities? Will it work as effectively with Chinese people as it does with the Japanese, who seem to be much more willing to follow direction? A lot of people here find it difficult to understand, and therefore frustrating. To them, it is just a lot of added paperwork and time in meetings. After all, we are in business to make money, not to demonstrate our mastery of the latest management techniques."

Appendix

To illustrate how QFD might be applied to the development of a new computer monitor, Mr. S. C. Wu listed a few of the important characteristics of a monitor, from the user's point of view, and arrayed them against representative technical considerations that could affect those characteristics. To the right of this matrix, he added columns for Customer Complaints, Comparative Competitor Analysis, Planned Quality, and Major Features (or Selling Points). "Planned Quality" referred to the visual, tactile, and operating performance of the monitor as perceived by the customer rather than the design engineer. Those aspects of performance whose Planned Quality was targeted to be much superior to competitors' products were characterized as Major Features/Selling Points.

Finally, along the bottom of the matrix he listed the target values for each of the Technical Specifications, and compared them with those available in competitors' products. He cautioned that the actual matrix might

Simplified Example of QFD for the Development of Monitors

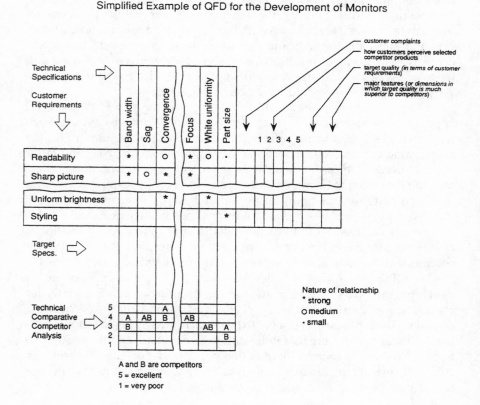

Nature of relationship
* strong
O medium
· small

A and B are competitors
5 = excellent
1 = very poor

contain over 70 different User Requirements and over 100 different Technical Specifications.

Once User Requirements had been mapped onto Technical Specifications, and the appropriate tradeoffs made, the task for the development team was to make sure that those specifications were incorporated in the specifications for each of the components that went into the monitor. To show how this might be done, Wu sketched out another matrix in which the monitor's overall Technical Specifications were arrayed against the Component Characteristics (both electrical and mechanical) for each part.

Given the technical specifications of these components, the next task was to ensure that the production process to be used was capable of assembling them properly and achieving the desired overall performance characteristics. Wu sketched out another matrix depicting the Component Characteristics along one side and a number of Critical Process Parameters (such as vacuum pressure, curing temperature, clearance of punch & die, air pressure, magnetic flux, and equipment accuracy) along the other.

In a final matrix the Critical Process Parameters were mapped against actual production steps or requirements: quality control, preventive maintenance, mistake-proofing, operator training, cycle time, and so forth. Once this step was completed, it was possible to trace each user requirement (or desired attribute) back through the four matrices to see its impact on component design and sourcing, process requirements, and the demands on each factory worker and support group.

CHAPTER 16

What Really Makes Factories Flexible?

David M. Upton

MANUFACTURING MANAGERS in a broad array of industries agree that achieving low cost and high quality is no longer enough to guarantee success. In the face of fierce, low-cost competition and an army of high-quality suppliers, companies are increasingly concentrating on flexibility as a way to achieve new forms of competitive advantage. The flexible factory, they hope, will enable them to respond to customer orders quickly, provide a broad product range, or introduce new products to the range effortlessly. The push to make factories more flexible has been spreading throughout manufacturing and currently is even permeating industries such as chemicals and paper, in which the assumption for decades has been that the plants with the longest production runs are typically the most competitive.

Having acknowledged the importance of flexibility, managers in industry after industry are finding it frustratingly difficult to improve. Some have organized cross-functional teams in the hope that new ways of working will generate greater agility. Many have collectively invested tens of billions of dollars in hardware and software in the hope that computer-integrated manufacturing (CIM) will transform their factories into highly flexible operations. Time and time again, managers have been disappointed and frustrated because they have not understood exactly why enhanced flexibility has eluded them. Was it the degree to which they automated their operations? Was it the software, whose complexity and cost they had underestimated? Or was it the inability of employees to take advantage of the new technologies?

In a quest to help manufacturing managers understand why the

David M. Upton is an Associate Professor at the Harvard Business School in Boston, Massachusetts.

Reprinted from the *Harvard Business Review*, July–August 1995.

improvement of flexibility has been so elusive, I embarked on a study of 61 factories in North America that manufacture fine paper. At first glance, the paper industry may seem like an unusual starting point for the study of flexibility. It is rarely characterized as flexible and has not, until recently, given high priority to improving flexibility. However, there are some less obvious characteristics that make the paper industry an ideal place to begin.

Unlike most industries in which different plants make different products—and, indeed, in which the same plant may make different products—the paper industry's products are comparable across plants and are always manufactured by the same fundamental process. There are only a small number of ways in which one type of paper differs from another type—the most fundamental being the basis weight, or area density, of the paper. These characteristics, or grades (each particular pulp and weight combination is a grade), are straightforward to measure. Those facts enabled me to develop concrete measures of both the range of products that a given plant could produce and the time it took a plant to switch from making one product to making another product.

My findings turn much of the conventional wisdom on its head. In the plants I studied, there was little direct correlation between the degree of computer integration and the degree of operational flexibility. I found that large plants were not inherently less flexible than small plants. Contrary to what many believe, newer, bigger processes were typically better able to perform quick changeovers than older, smaller machines. And although experienced workers provided powerful advantages in some situations, they impeded a plant's ability to be flexible in others.

The primary revelation of my research concerns the role of people—both managers and operators. The flexibility of the plants depended much more on people than on any technical factor. Although high levels of computer integration can provide critically needed advantages in quality and cost competitiveness, all the data in my study point to one conclusion: Operational flexibility is determined primarily by a plant's operators and the extent to which managers cultivate, measure, and communicate with them. Equipment and computer integration are secondary.

At many of the plants in my study, however, managers embraced computer integration as the solution to the growing need to forge new capabilities. In reality, computer systems were often a quick fix that helped managers avoid the tremendously difficult task of defining precisely what kind of flexibility they required from a plant and then setting goals, revamping measurement and compensation systems, building training programs, and overhauling work practices in order to achieve that flexibility.

To state it simply, most managers put too much faith in machines and technology, and too little faith in the day-to-day management of people.

What Is Flexibility?

Ten or 15 years ago, quality was much like flexibility is today: vague and difficult to improve yet critical to competitiveness. Since then, managers and academics have studied and experimented with ways to improve quality; as a result, there is currently an enormous variety of quality-improvement techniques and a plethora of textbooks and gurus from which to choose.

Flexibility is only beginning to be explored. If managers aim to improve a plant's flexibility, where should they start? The first problem is one of definition. Flexibility means different things to different people. At the plant level, flexibility is about the ability to adapt or change. But there are many ways to characterize such an ability. One manager might be talking about the cost of changing from one product to the next. Another might be talking about the ability to ramp production volumes up and down to fit the demand of the market. Yet another might be talking about the ability to increase the range of available products. All these abilities might be called flexibility, but they require very different courses of action to develop.

The type of flexibility a given company should emphasize should be determined by its competitive environment. Whether one is referring to products, production volumes, or manufacturing processes, flexibility is about increasing range, increasing mobility, or achieving uniform performance across a specified range.

Product range can mean different things. For example, a plant can have the ability to make a small number of products that are very different from one another, or it can have the ability to produce concurrently a large number of stock-keeping units that are only slightly different from one another.

Mobility means a plant's ability to change nimbly from making one product to making another. It is this kind of flexibility that is associated with quick response times—mobility minimizes the need for long runs and allows production to follow demand without excessive inventory.

Finally, there is uniformity of performance. Plants always have one product that they would much rather make than others because that product maximizes productivity, quality, or some other measure. When a plant moves away from its favored set of parameters, performance falls off. If it falls off steeply, many managers will label the plant inflexible. According to that definition, a flexible plant is one that can perform comparably well when making any product within a specified range. It is this capability that is most important to a full-range manufacturer; the uniformity of performance across the range, more than the size of the range, will protect a plant from cherry-picking predators. Uniformity of performance also applies to production volumes: Some plants are able to work productively over a broad range of output volumes, while others are unable to increase or decrease volumes without incurring considerable penalties.

Once managers have defined the kinds of flexibility they want to develop, they face another set of issues. First, because flexibility is not easy to measure, improvement in flexibility is also difficult to measure. For example, is a plant that can produce 200 different colors of paint 100 times more flexible than a plant that can make 2 products (say, a car and a truck) on the same line? Clearly, simply counting products won't suffice in defining flexibility because it doesn't account for the "differentness" of the products concerned.

Second, the products that a plant actually makes do not necessarily reflect its flexibility. Those products that a plant *could* make matter, too. For example, a factory can have the flexibility to machine titanium without a chip of titanium ever being cut. Unlike most other sources of manufacturing advantage, such as low cost or high quality, flexibility is sometimes about a *potential* ability rather than a demonstrated one.

Third, it is often unclear which general features of a plant must be changed in order to make its operations flexible. For instance, many management experts preach that cross-functional empowered teams and computer integration help make plants more flexible. But do they always translate into operational, competitive capabilities that the company can sell? The answer is often no. Similarly, one type of equipment may be capable of making a large range of products, while another may possess quick-changeover capabilities, and both may be called flexible. Yet the latter will be of little value if the market demands great variety. The same holds true for training programs, information systems, incentive schemes, and measurement methods. They, too, must be aligned to provide precisely the form of flexibility that is needed from the overall system. Few factories have actually aligned those elements.

Surprising Discoveries

Managers at many of the plants I studied deemed an astounding 40% of flexibility-improvement efforts to be unsuccessful or disappointing. In the vast majority of those cases, the cause could be traced to a failure to identify precisely what kind of manufacturing flexibility was needed, how to measure it, or which factors most affected it.

A paper mill usually consists of a pulp plant, which provides pulp for a group of two to ten converting plants that turn the pulp into paper. The paper-making process is essentially a water-removal procedure. Water is removed from a pulp slurry by use of gravity, squeezing, and heating. The pulp slurry is laid onto a moving fabric belt from which water drains off. The pulp web is squeezed and heated by a series of rollers until it is strong enough to support its own weight. Further heating then takes place until the paper's moisture content is just below that of the ambient atmosphere. The paper is then collected on a reel and sliced into roll sizes that are convenient for customers and sheeting machines.

By collecting production data and interviewing managers, supervisors, and operators, I was able to measure the breadth of paper grades that each plant was capable of producing and the changeover time that each plant required to switch between grades. In addition, I measured the experience of the workforce by length of service, the vintage of the technology, the level of computer integration, the scale of the plant, and the degree of emphasis that management placed at each plant on various types of flexibility. In order to assess the latter, I asked the shop-floor people responsible for running the plant how much emphasis *they* thought that managers were placing on a whole range of factors, from safety to quality to the various types of flexibility. (See the table "Plant Flexibility: Factors and Findings.")

I found large differences in the flexibility of the plants. Changeover times varied from one minute to four hours, even for similar types of change on comparable equipment. I found that the potential range of product variation in the plants differed by a factor of 20. This discrepancy is not surprising given the wide variety in the capacity and vintages of the plants in my study. What is surprising, however, is that very few of my assumptions about the reasons for such disparities—the same assumptions, incidentally, that prevail within the industry at large—turned out to be correct.

First, I found that the degree of computer integration in a plant was not in itself associated with either increased range or improved changeover times. (See the chart "Computer Integration Reduces Flexibility.") Indeed, even computer hardware and software designed specifically

Plant Flexibility: Factors and Findings

Description	Units	Mean	Minimum	Maximum
Changeover times	minutes	15.40	1	240
Range of plant	pounds	64.6	1	161.0
Change frequency	changes per month	29.02	0	500
Date of last major rebuild	year	1973	1919	1991
Width of paper web	inches	159.8	76.0	348.0
Speed	feet per minute	1,466	250	3,200
Net output	tons per day	236.8	18	1,200
Average crew service	years	17.6	1	25
Degree of computer integration (general)	scale of 0.0 to 0.8	5.16	1.83	8.0
Break frequency	breaks per week	16.0	1	60

The data are drawn from a study of 61 fine-paper plants in North America.

Computer Integration Reduces Flexibility

Plants with more CIM have less range...   and longer changeover times

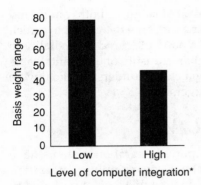
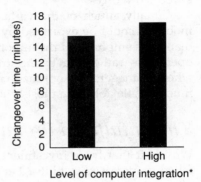

*The data have been corredted for factors other than CIM, such as scale and workforce experience.

for the purpose of improving the changeover process, such as automatic grade-change systems, did not decrease the time required to make grade changes in the plants and actually inhibited the ability of plants to produce a broad range of grades. This discovery is especially important because managers often have difficulty justifying computer-integration projects on the basis of cost savings or quality improvements and therefore justify them on the basis of the improved flexibility they will provide.

Second, I discovered that there were no de facto relationships among the various forms of flexibility. In other words, just because a factory is flexible in one way does not mean it will naturally be flexible in others. To explore whether there are generally flexible and generally inflexible plants, I looked at the relationship between two forms of flexibility in each paper plant: its mobility (measured by changeover times) and its range (the breadth of product characteristics it could produce). I found no relationship between the two types of flexibility. (See the chart "There Is Little Relationship Between Two Types of Flexibility.")

Third, while there was a clear relationship between the scale of an operation and the breadth of products it could produce (larger plants made a smaller range of product characteristics), I found no clear link between the scale of an operation and its ability to change swiftly between products. Although it is true that the cost of downtime resulting from changeovers is higher in bigger plants (because the lost output and investment involved are much larger), it is also true that the advantages of quick changeovers, which provide the ability to undertake just-in-time production, could be accrued at a proportionately larger scale.

Fourth, workforce experience, an important factor in building flexibility, affected different types of flexibility in different ways. In general, the more experience a workforce had (as measured by length of service), the greater the range of products the plant could make. Surprisingly, however, changeover times, or mobility, were worse in plants with more experienced workforces.

Finally, much of the variance in plant flexibility (both range and mobility) could be explained by managerial action—the extent to which managers emphasized the importance of a particular kind of flexibility to operators—rather than by the structural characteristics of the plant. Plants whose managers had not made flexibility a clearly understood goal were much less flexible than those whose managers had.

The Unfulfilled Promise of CIM

Why is it that huge investments in computer-integration systems have failed to increase flexibility? Let's think about how computer integration affects the range of work that a plant can do. Imagine a plant designed to manufacture a range of products. When the process is computerized, any competent engineer will ask, Over what range of conditions should this system work? After the possible operating range has been identified, the engineer will come up with a dollar figure for the computer systems needed to coordinate the process. When the company's manager is taken aback by the price, the engineer will point out that the extremes of the range are pushing up the price. The manager will then decide to sacrifice the extremes on the grounds that they are seldom needed.

But look at what has been given up. Although handling the extremes was difficult when the plant was being operated manually, an experienced and skilled crew could coax a plant to make those products. With the processes computer integrated, the plant runs into the "there isn't a button for that" problem. At such plants, the range of products often fell by 20% to 30% after the mill made a major investment in CIM. What's more, the operator skills required to perform such acrobatics typically atrophied from lack of use.

Some of these problems were recognized 30 years ago when "hard" automation reigned supreme. The hope was that software-based CIM would solve such problems. Although it is true that computer integration may be changed to accommodate new requirements, many companies have been misled by the *soft* in *software*. *Soft* implies easily changeable or malleable. Experience shows that manufacturing-integration software is often anything but. As one manager pointed out, "I'd be better off with a flame cutter and a hacksaw than I would with a team of software engineers. At least I'd be able to see what was taking so long to change."

One of my more surprising findings was that computer integration did not decrease the time needed to switch from making one product to making another one. While the worst manual-change system took much longer than the slowest computer-integrated system, the best manual-change teams were much faster than the computer. Many teams of operators had developed routines and tricks that enabled them to change the plant over efficiently, and the best teams took great pride in the fact that they could beat the computer. "The computer is really slow; it gets kind of boring sitting and watching the plant run, so we figured out a better way to change manually," one young operator in the Midwest said, echoing a sentiment expressed by many people in other plants. "We all practiced and worked out who should do what and when, and now we can always beat the computer and do changeovers more quickly than we used to do them with the computer."

The operators' ability to outperform computers can be explained as follows: One of the primary risks in making any change is that of catastrophic failure, such as a paper break, which is akin to a tool breakage in machining. When the paper running in the machine breaks, it must be rethreaded, which is always time-consuming and expensive. To avoid downtime, the methods for changing between products under computer coordination are conservative. People, however, may be a little more daring. They have access to sensors that are unavailable to computerized systems, such as the sound of the process or the feel of the pulp. Some managers might fear that such practices will result in higher breakage rates and more downtime. My data show that, to the contrary, the computer-integrated systems not only were slower than the manual systems but also resulted in a higher breakage rate in the average plant.

Why would managers invest in such equipment if it is not particularly effective in boosting flexibility? The answer is that they often do not know how effective—or ineffective—it is. In most traditional industries, managers do not routinely benchmark flexibility. While flexibility can provide a powerful means for increasing revenues, most managers still focus on comparing cost figures—if they make any comparisons at all. Even those paper-plant managers who did routinely benchmark flexibility were unable to collect data from a sufficiently large sample of plants; as a result, they were unable to see that computer integration was failing to generate a clear advantage in process flexibility.

It is important to point out that many computerized systems have been installed for reasons other than increasing plant flexibility. Those reasons include facilitating the tracking and delivery of information and improving the quality of the process. And computerized systems used to those ends have succeeded. Judicious use of computer integration can provide valuable new sources of competitive advantage when closely aligned with the competitive needs of the business.

Still, when I have shown my study to managers in a variety of industries, particularly in process industries such as glass, chemicals, and steel, they have sighed. They, too, have discovered that computer integration does not necessarily guarantee greater flexibility. In many cases, the additional complexity resulting from computer integration has been a competitive millstone around their companies' necks, demanding new and expensive skills that have not translated into clear advantages in the

There Is Little Relationship Between Two Types of Flexibility

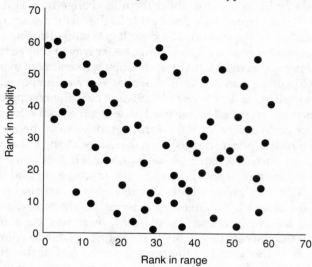

• Relationship between range (breadth of product characteristics) and mobility (changeover times) at each paper plant

market. More data is not the same as more information. Systems often sidetrack manufacturing organizations from the tasks they should be doing well. Many continue to hail computer-integrated manufacturing as a panacea. But unless it is treated as a tool rather than as an end in itself, CIM may exclude most people in an organization from the process of shaping and improving the way the operation runs.

The approach of "investing one's way to flexibility" through computer integration can be damaging in two ways. Not only is computer integration not the panacea for flexibility problems but it also comforts managers with the thought that they are doing *something,* when all along they should have been doing something *else.* The implication for managers, as Robert S. Kaplan pointed out in "Must CIM Be Justified by Faith Alone?" (HBR, March–April 1986), is that the blanket acceptance of computer-integration projects on the grounds that they will improve flexibility must be replaced with a healthy skepticism.

Building the Right Workforce

It is not a revelation that people can often become less flexible in their work patterns as they become more accustomed to a particular way of doing their jobs. But my research raises a more complex question. Setting aside work practices, how does experience affect those capabilities that can more directly contribute to a company's success? How does experience affect operational flexibility? While my research shows that a workforce's experience is an important factor in determining the flexibility of an operation, it also shows that experience affects different types of flexibility in different ways: Long service had a positive effect on the range of manufacturable products and a negative effect on the ease with which the plant could switch between those products. This finding makes sense. In order to work on unusual jobs at the extremes of a plant's range, people need experience to know how to get the job done. Experienced people know how to run the plant without breaks when making very thin paper or how to get the paper dry without burning it when making very thick paper.

A few theories could explain why plants with more experienced workforces were less mobile. First, many of the more experienced crews held the view that each individual plant was made to do one thing well and that changeovers that went beyond those established parameters were making improper demands on the plants. Less experienced crews, however, had learned papermaking at a time when flexibility had started to become critical. Many of these crews had developed their own novel ways of making changeovers and saw them as a welcome switch from the tedium of machine tending. In particular, they often viewed change as a defining part of their jobs. I don't think that it is a coincidence that one outstandingly mobile plant had the following rule when selecting its operators (although not its supervisors): You must never have worked in this industry before.

Pursuing Flexibility

How, then, should managers approach the challenge of making their manufacturing operation more flexible? The first step is to ask, What form of flexibility does the company need from its plants? For example, a manufacturer that wanted to excel at customizing products would need to develop the ability to carry out a large range of jobs in the plant, while one that wanted to use quick response as its primary competitive weapon would need to focus on building quick changeovers into the manufacturing process.

Once they have identified those capabilities, managers must determine the type of workforce or equipment they need to enhance flexibility. For example, the manufacturer emphasizing customized products would require an experienced workforce that could make even the most difficult products. The company hoping to be flexible through quick response would be better off with a workforce less steeped in the traditional ways of operating, a workforce that is ready to adapt to an environment of continuous change.

Next, managers should find ways to measure the type of flexibility sought and should emphasize the importance of those measures to the workforce, letting them make industry comparisons and providing them with incentives to underscore the point. Most managers at the plants I studied were still clinging to measures that had no connection to flexibility. For example, plant managers and their superiors tended to focus on measures that made sense when their plants were big enough to be able to compete on cost: capacity utilization and tons of output per hour. To expect a plant both to be flexible and to continue to focus solely on the utilization of its equipment and the cost of production makes no sense. The plants that were flexible in terms of range and mobility tended to have clear, nonfinancial measures of the flexibility they were trying to develop—changeover times, lead times, or process range.

Training is an important mechanism for building operational flexibility. On the surface, training simply provides the skills people need to carry out new tasks. Its ancillary roles, however, are much more critical. First, training plays an important part in moving people beyond a "this is the way we've always done it" mentality. In industries in which people are trained primarily by serving as understudies to those with more experience, the new mind-set is particularly critical. Second, training builds confidence: Many people in manufacturing are reluctant to try new approaches or techniques because they are afraid of exposing their ignorance. Third, it builds an esprit de corps and helps emphasize the growing competitive need for the right kind of flexible operation—providing a sense of common purpose from a common experience.

Increasing flexibility may be costly in the short run, but it gets easier over time. Plants become more flexible because their managers emphasize the importance of flexibility and because they *practice* being flexible. A self-reinforcing process then begins. Because such plants are flexible, they are assigned varied and quick-response work, which in turn makes them still more flexible. And just as a plant with mediocre quality can be stretched by challenging it to produce higher-quality goods, previously inflexible plants can be made more flexible by changing the work assigned to them.

Once manufacturing managers have determined the type of flexibility they need, they have to give careful thought to how they will develop that capability. Designing the right mix of machines, computer systems, and people, and figuring out the most effective way to orchestrate them are hard work. But turning only to machines, hardware, and software as the solution will not suffice. People count more than machines.

Combining Computers and People to Build Flexibility

Managers and engineers have long preached that computer systems should complement, rather than replace, the skills of operators. In the end, however, most have embarked on a path to computer integration that caused them to place machine over man and resulted in less flexible rather than more flexible factories.

What accounts for the disparity between idea and execution? The problem rests with how—or whether—managers define the type of flexibility to pursue and then choose the appropriate computer systems, work practices, training programs, incentives, and measures. To create a highly flexible computer-and-people-integrated manufacturing system, managers of each individual factory have to come up with their own unique formula. The managers of Mead Corporation's Escanaba Mill, in Escanaba, Michigan, which makes coated fine paper and employs 1,300 people, did just that.

In the early 1990s, the Escanaba complex, like the paper industry in general, was struggling: The market was in a deep slump, there was a glut of capacity, and price cutting was rampant. To make matters worse, the mill was facing intensifying competition from a growing number of competing mills with bigger and newer machines. Finally, a spurt of imports from Europe raised concerns that foreign producers, which had never posed a threat, might be planning a major assault on the North American market.

Like most of their peers in the paper industry, Escanaba's managers had long believed that the key to competitiveness was to achieve the lowest possible costs through long production runs and few product changeovers. But suddenly many in the industry were forced to rethink those assumptions and look for new ways to distinguish themselves from competitors.

The answer for Escanaba, its managers decided, was to be more responsive to customers than their competitors were. They would accomplish that goal by being highly mobile—able to change production schedules quickly so that they could fill orders much faster than competitors could. At that point, the industry's customers might have to wait as long as two weeks to receive an order, even in slack times. Escanaba's managers set out to slash that time to one or two days.

The new strategy of emphasizing responsiveness demanded a new way of working in the mill: It required faster product changeovers and nimble decision making. When managers analyzed how the mill had been operating, they came to a sober conclusion: The plant was slow in switching from one product to another and in changing schedules to accommodate new customers' requirements. It took too long to execute a production-schedule change, and grade changes often generated product-quality problems or mistakes. They also realized that the plant was not inherently capable of quick changeovers; changeovers hadn't improved, because improving them had not been a high priority. Managers had been judged primarily on their success in maximizing the mill's capacity utilization and product quality, and they simply focused on long production runs to achieve their performance targets. The long runs meant that operators did not have to learn how to improve changeovers. They also produced a culture that placed very little value on responsiveness to customers. "We make it; you [the sales force] sell it—that's the way the manufacturing people used to see things in this mill," recalled Henry Swanson, the mill's manager of process control and information.

The mill's managers also realized that computerization in itself was no panacea. Some of the machines in the mill were relatively highly computer integrated. "Even though we had a lot of computers on the plant, sometimes we'd make a couple of hours' worth of production before someone realized

(continued)

that something was wrong," Swanson said. "It was just too easy to trust that the computers had got it right." In addition, the opaque computerized system prevented workers from learning how they might improve operations.

So one of the first steps that managers took to transform Escanaba was to rip out the old millwide computer systems. They replaced them with a new system called QUPID (for Quality and Information for Decisions). Unlike the turnkey systems that previously coordinated manufacturing processes, QUPID was custom designed to support operators in each operation; the operators controlled the manufacturing process and would be free to make changes, depending on what they saw happening on the production line. In other words, the system was designed from the outset to help workers make better decisions rather than to cut them out of the decision-making process.

To that end, the mill's managers insisted that operators be intimately involved in the system's design and development. "If the previous system taught us anything, it taught us that we didn't want black-box computer integration that only the vendor really understood," said Glendon Brown, the mill's vice president of production technology. "We needed an architecture that we were part of and that was much more open and easy to change."

Rather than depending on a single supplier, the mill bought the system's building blocks from several different sources. There were two fundamental criteria for choosing those sources: Each had to be a leader in its area of expertise and be willing to customize the system for Escanaba.

Significantly, Escanaba designed the system's interfaces in-house. Each function designed its own interface to ensure that its people got the information they felt they needed to do their jobs and in the format that was easiest for them to understand. "If we were going to succeed in the longer term, we needed the ability to make changes 24 hours a day, seven days a week— times when most managers aren't around," Brown said. "We needed to provide useful information to our operators at the lowest level in the organization, so that *they* could make decisions."

The mill also overhauled its training programs. But it took several attempts before managers hit on the right approach. First, Mead made a common mistake: It used technical people to explain to the operators how the new computer systems worked. "It was a disaster," Swanson said. "The technical guys knew too much about the systems and told people more than they needed to know about technical issues and not enough about the business issues and why we needed to work differently."

The mill's managers dropped that program. In its place, they created one designed to help workers understand what they had to do to satisfy customers. The program explained why quick changeovers were critical to the mill's long-term success. And it emphasized that the systems were only a tool to help them perform their jobs better. Operators who had long assumed that keeping the machines running was all that mattered began to look at their work differently.

That program has since evolved. Originally, a professional trainer conducted classes in a seminar-like setting. However, managers came to believe that learning and training should be part of all their employees' jobs. With that goal in mind, managers trained a team of the mill's supervisors and operators to teach others on the floor and in classrooms.

The result of the training program is a plant that now excels at learning. Armed with an intimate knowledge of different jobs and their challenges, the new trainers have played an instrumental role in helping operators become increasingly adept at carrying out quick changeovers and responding to the demands of new customers. Operators are no longer mere machine tenders.

Managers also wisely realized that the mill's measurement and incentive systems had to bolster its new strategy. Accordingly, measures and incentives aimed at maximizing capacity utilization and output and minimizing costs have given way to measures and incentives aimed at maximizing responsiveness and customer satisfaction.

Each year, the mill surveys customers to identify what it is doing well and how it needs to improve. Using the survey, a team drawn from managers and employees throughout the mill then generates specific operating goals. For example, the team might challenge Escanaba to reduce changeover losses by 25% within six months. (This kind of focused goal is much more effective than simply declaring, like managers at all too many factories still do, "We should strive to improve flexibility.") The compensation of managers and superintendents is based on the mill's success in achieving those goals.

The results have been astonishing. The mill's responsiveness and customer satisfaction have increased dramatically. In 1993, it sold the most paper in its history. Escanaba is now the most productive mill in Mead's fine-paper group and has dramatically increased its market share. By emphasizing what workers need to do and providing them with the information they need to do it, Mead has proved that a factory can increase flexibility and, at the same time, boost productivity and lower costs. It's just a question of figuring out precisely what kind of flexibility one wants to achieve and giving people the support they need to achieve it.

Building Flexibility You Can't Sell

When factory managers don't carefully assess their strategies before embarking on a flexibility program, the results can be competitively destructive. One U.S. mill, which I'll call Kildare, had just such an experience. A complex equipped with medium-size paper machines, Kildare made relatively high-volume fine papers and employed about 1,500 people.

In the early 1990s, Kildare's markets were in the grip of a severe slump, and mills with giant, lower-cost machines had come to dominate the business. With Kildare losing market share and struggling to stay in the black, its

(continued)

managers soberly concluded that they could not stand still and wait for the market to rebound. Several competitors had launched reengineering programs aimed at improving their responsiveness, that is, their ability to fill customers' orders quickly. Deeply worried, Kildare's managers decided that they had better follow suit and began to reengineer the order-to-delivery process to make the mill even more responsive than the competition.

To that end, the mill created a training program to teach operators the skills that would enable them to make the swift product changeovers required by the new strategy. In addition, the computerized recipes and other procedures used to produce each grade of paper were carefully documented and routinized. The only aspect that management overlooked was the measurement and reward system, which continued to focus on the plant's capacity-utilization rate. Delivered in the form of praise and criticism as well as pay, the message to supervisors was to keep utilization high. With its emphasis on fewer and longer production runs, that message flew in the face of management's contention that responsiveness was now what mattered most.

Nevertheless, by mid-1993, after an intense, year-long effort, Kildare had cut its lead times in half and had achieved its target of becoming world class in responsiveness. But managers then made a painful discovery. The mill's vastly improved responsiveness had enabled it to hold on to existing customers, who were delighted by Kildare's ability to fill their orders more quickly. But for two reasons the mill had not been able to increase its market share or sales significantly. First, competing mills had made similar strides, and many of them had the advantage of bigger machines. Second, there was simply not enough business in Kildare's particular market.

Kildare's managers realized that they would have been better off had they focused on expanding the range of products that the mill made. A series of opportunities to make a challenging array of relatively high-volume products that were outside the mill's traditional product range sparked the epiphany. The main opportunity was a chance to supply papers to be used to make lottery tickets sold in Central America. The papers had to be difficult for would-be counterfeiters to forge, yet cheap and sturdy.

Kildare's experienced crews were able to manufacture these difficult products. But they found that the systems and procedures installed to improve responsiveness, which assumed a core set of standard, unchanging papers, were a hindrance. For example, the emphasis on perfecting a routine and documenting the procedures and computerized programs for making each paper grade was counterproductive when no two orders were exactly alike and when success depended on excelling at figuring out how to make a particular order during trial runs rather than on delivering that order quickly. In other words, the systems and procedures designed to make the plant more responsive discouraged the development of the skills required to excel at experimentation. Conversely, the trial runs, whose duration was impossible to predict, produced the kind of constant scheduling headaches that one tries to minimize or eliminate if responsiveness is the top priority.

About six months after managers had targeted the new markets, they finally recognized the problem and dismantled many of the changes they had instituted to increase the mill's responsiveness. For example, operators no longer have to enter the programs for making every paper grade into the computer that controls production. Other practices introduced to improve responsiveness—for example, a streamlined order-processing system—did not have to be dismantled. In addition, the mill changed its measurement and reward system to relax pressure on operators to keep the machines running and make fast changeovers. As a result, although responsiveness is no longer the top priority, Kildare has been able to hang on to its traditional customers and win new ones. The mill's sales and profits are soaring. Admittedly, the end of the industry's recession is one reason for its success. But, more important, the mill now excels at a type of flexibility that it can sell.

CHAPTER 17

Stermon Mills Incorporated

A S HE SAT AT HIS DESK, waiting for the improvement team to arrive, Stan Kiefner, President and CEO of Stermon Mills, stared blankly at the letter in front of him. The letter was from Pete Cushing of the Renfield Consulting Group:

10/1/92

Dear Stan:

I have given a lot of thought to our conversation of last Friday. Having looked at the latest price figures and the projections for the next five years, I would say that I have to agree with you: Stermon is unlikely to be competitive on the basis of cost without an investment in a new, state-of-the-art paper machine. Given the over-capacity projected for the industry, and the $500m cost—I'd say you have to find an alternative! Stermon just can't keep chiselling on price. In my opinion, the only way to maintain and grow your customer base is to offer something the bigger companies can't—you have to become more flexible than the competition.

The letter confirmed what Kiefner already knew. It was no longer possible for Stermon to match the price being offered by the large mills for commodity grade paper (see Exhibit 17.1). With the huge economic rewards available to large scale technology in paper-making, Stermon's small machines simply cost too much to run for the output they produced. Since he left Boise Cascade in 1990, Kiefner had known Stermon was headed for trouble without some dramatic changes. But it was only recently, as the real price of Xerox grade paper hit a twenty year low, that the urgency of the situation had become clear.

This case was prepared by Professor David Upton as the basis for class discussion rather than an illustration of either effective or ineffective handling of an administrative situation. Names and data have been disguised.

Exhibit 17.1 Monthly Statement of Income for
Machine 4: September 1992

Item	$ PER TON
Gross Sales-Paper	**769**
Freight & Other	(79)
Net Sales-Paper	**690**
Variable Costs	
Wood	58
Purchased Pulp	125
Chemicals and Additives	94
Electricity	28
Fuel	54
Other Materials	29
Total Variable Cost	**390**
Variable Contribution	300
Fixed Costs	
Mill Operating Labor	99
Mill Maintenance Labor	36
Contractor Maintenance	22
Maintenance Materials	27
Operating Supplies	19
Mill Supervision	17
Mill G & A-Salaries	6
Mill G & A-Other	16
Depreciation/Amortization	78
Insurance and Taxes	12
Total Fixed Cost	**332**
Total cost of goods sold	722
Income-Paper operations	(32)
Non operating income (expense)	(2)
Net Income	**(34)**

If it was to continue to be viable, in both the short-term and the long-term, Stermon had to become more flexible. Kiefner had put together a team of his best managers to look at the problem. He had asked the head of the team, Bill Saugoe, to put together a two-year flexibility improvement plan, which would specifically address the competitive problems facing Stermon, and detail the steps which needed to be taken in order to make Stermon flexible.

Kiefner was unsure about the whole business. It was a lot easier to work on costs, he thought. You could count dollars after all. But flexibility was a different matter. How could they improve something if they weren't really clear what it was? How could they measure their competitors' performance? How would they even know if they had improved? This was not going to be easy.

Kiefner sat back, and waited for Saugoe's knock at the door.

The Stermon Story

Stermon Mills Incorporated was a small, independent fine-paper producer. It was founded by Tom Brasker, a second-generation Scot, in 1910. Located in the town of Fond du Lac, in Northern Minnesota, Stermon's (single) paper mill was a collection of some twenty buildings, housing one pulping plant and four paper machines of varying vintages (See Exhibit 17.2). The oldest (#1) was the original machine installed when the company was founded. Though a giant in its time, it was now the smallest machine in the plant and was affectionately known as "Little Jack."

Stermon had added two additional machines in the 1950s—#2 and #3 machine were also the giants of their day. The #4 machine had been added in 1976 and was the largest machine on site: 186" wide, it ran at a speed of 1700 feet per minute (about 20 miles per hour). Total output from the site was 570 tons of paper a day, with 280 tons of that being produced on machine #4 (see Exhibit 17.3).

Exhibit 17.2   The Stermon Plant in Fond du Lac

Exhibit 17.3 Schematic of Fond du Lac Plant

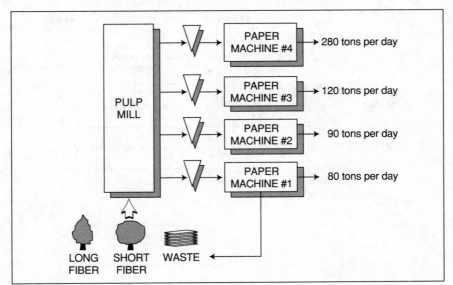

The company's major products had always been uncoated wood-free papers (see Exhibit 17.4). This market was dominated by the demand for Xerographic paper, although many other papers were produced in the general category of uncoated fine paper. For example, Stermon also made book paper and paper for writing tablets. Coated papers required extensive additional coating equipment, while mechanical papers could not be produced in Stermon's pulping plant. For this reason, Stermon restricted itself to the production of uncoated fine papers.

Uncoated fine paper was differentiated from other types of papers by both its end uses and its manufacturing process. The primary end uses were printing and writing, and included, for example, the paper on which this case was printed. The end uses could be categorized into four segments: publishing (books), commercial printing, office/business (computer printers and copiers), and writing. Such papers varied from each other in a number of ways. First, and most important, was the basis weight of the paper. Paper could vary in area density from 15 lbs per unit area to 100 lbs per unit area in Stermon's plant. Xerox paper weighed 20 lbs per unit area. Second, paper could include different proportions of chemicals in the pulp that was used. This was called the furnish. Third, paper could be dyed in order to produce different colors of paper. Colored paper was made only on the smaller machines. The machines required a lengthy wash down after each run of paper and few companies could afford to keep their larger machines idle for this task—Stermon was no exception.

Exhibit 17.4 Types of Paper and Pulping Processes

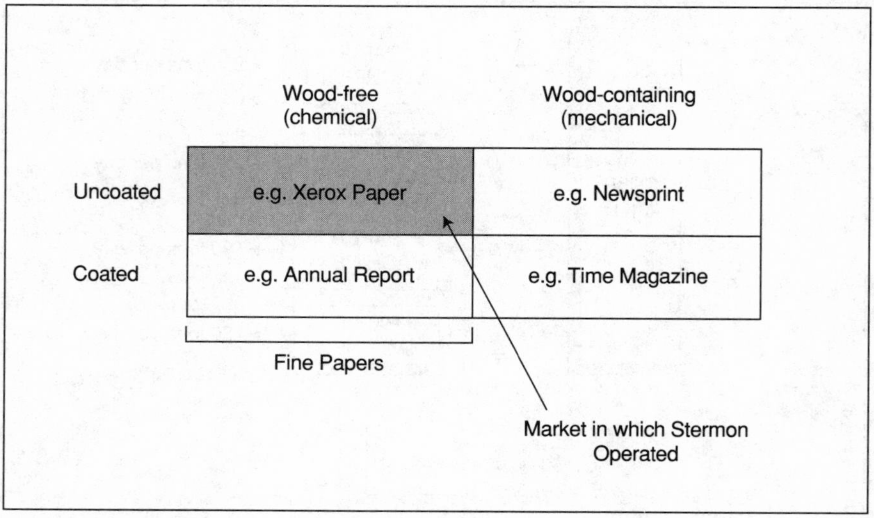

	Wood-free (chemical)	Wood-containing (mechanical)
Uncoated	e.g. Xerox Paper	e.g. Newsprint
Coated	e.g. Annual Report	e.g. Time Magazine

Fine Papers

Market in which Stermon Operated

Making Paper

The first step in making paper and paperboard, after the wood was cut, involved "pulping." This process refined the wood so that only the cellulose, the substance required in paper, remained. Wood consisted of approximately 50% fiber, 30% lignin, a tough, resinous adhesive that gave structural support to the tree, and 20% extractable oils and carbohydrates. During pulping, the cellulose fiber was separated from the other components so it could be processed further; pulping could be done either mechanically, by grinding the wood, or chemically, by boiling the wood with chemicals. Although newsprint manufacturers relied on mechanical pulping, the grinding process broke the cellulose into shorter fibers when tearing them apart and left some lignin in the resulting pulp. This created a weaker paper that turned yellow more quickly. Only products with less rigid quality requirements—newspapers and telephone books, for example—used mechanical pulp. Unlike mechanical pulping, which used 90–95% of the wood harvested, chemical pulping used 45–50%. Chemical pulp yielded 1.25 tons of paper per ton of pulp because inert "fillers" were added in the process (see Exhibit 17.6, p. 365).

When transformed into fine paper—the bright white type used in business and printing—chemical pulp went through an intermediate step: bleaching. Bleached pulp allowed producers to make a strong, bright paper that did not discolor during storage or when exposed to sunlight. It thereby satisfied the needs of paper products with high demands for purity, brightness, and permanence. Once the pulp was bleached, it was processed into "stock": a suspension of fibers and additives in water. Individual fibers of pulp were suspended in water and then "beaten" and refined to produce fibers with the proper characteristics of length, flexibility, surface area, and density. Chemicals could then be added to the stock: rosin, aluminum sulphate, or synthetics to reduce absorbency for writing papers; starch to add strength; dyes for colored paper. At the end of this process, stock could be made into a sheet of paper.

To produce a finished sheet of paper, a paper machine had to remove water from the stock—between 100 and 500 tons of water for every ton of pulp. Water was removed by three methods in sequence: first by gravity, second by squeezing, and finally by heating. In the "wet" end of the paper machine, the stock was deposited on a "wire"—a continuous belt of mesh material—with inclined blades of metal or plastic ("foils") underneath it, the wire drained the water from the stock. From the end of the wire, what was now a fragile paper web moved into the presses. Protected from above and below by continuous belts of felt, the paper moved through rollers, which pressed the sheet and drained water into catch basins (so the water could be used again). The paper web then travelled to the "dry" end of the paper machine. There the paper crossed double rows of steam-heated, cast-iron cylinders, again held by felt belts.

In the calender section, the paper was pressed further, as a set of hardened cast-iron rollers improved the surface-finish of the paper. From there the paper was wound onto a steel spool. In the final step of making paper, broadly called "finishing," large reels of paper were rewound into smaller reels, some were made into stacks of sheets (reams), and the paper was inspected. Fine paper, once inspected and packaged, was sold to merchants, who supplied end-users, or directly to the users themselves.

The North American Fine Paper Industry
Land of the Giants

The North American market was the world's largest consumer and producer of uncoated fine paper. In 1989, the North American market accounted for an estimated 45% of the world's uncoated fine paper capacity, and 44% of the world's consumption. Almost all of the demand for uncoated fine paper in North America was met by domestic (US and Canada) production. Exports and imports were not significant (around 5%) but had been growing spasmodically in recent years in top-end (high quality coated) and bottom-end (commodity uncoated) fine papers.

Despite industry fears to the contrary in the late 1970s, growth in demand for uncoated fine paper increased (rather than abated) because of information processing in the office/business segment. Since 1982, U.S. uncoated fine paper shipments had increased at 4.7% per year compared to 3.8% per year for the other three paper classifications. However, the strong growth in demand for uncoated fine paper during the 1980s had contributed to the industry's reduced profitability in the early 1990s. Significant capacity expansions to meet projected long-term demand, combined with the softening of demand during the 1989–92 recession, had led to excess capacity and depressed prices. It was generally agreed that real prices for fine paper were currently the worst the industry had seen for many years.

International Paper was the world's largest paper company with sales totalling $12.96 billion in 1990. Uncoated fine paper accounted for about 18% of International Paper's total sales. The company was a full line producer of uncoated fine paper, possessing well known brands such as Hammermill and Springhill reprographic, printing, envelope and tablet papers. A survey among users of laser paper showed that Hammermill had a 30% brand preference compared to 12% for the next leading competitive brand. Georgia-Pacific was the world's second largest paper company after its acquisition of Great Northern Nekoosa (GNN) for $3.7 billion in March, 1990. In 1990, Georgia-Pacific had sales totalling $12.67 billion. The GNN acquisition not only strengthened Georgia-Pacific's full line of uncoated fine papers, but also added paper distribution and envelope converting businesses. With the mid-1991 start up of a new 290,000 metric tons per year machine at Ashdown, Arkansas, Georgia-Pacific matched International Paper's uncoated fine paper capacity of 1,905,000 metric tons per year.

For the other top ten producers of uncoated fine paper, the production and distribution of printing and writing papers (including uncoated fine paper) accounted for a significant percentage of their total sales. For example, the proportions for Champion International and Boise Cascade in 1990 were 40% and 53% respectively. The other producers competed primarily on the basis of having focused product lines, providing product and service flexibility, and/or owning channels of distribution. For example, Domtar, Canada's leading producer of fine papers, had its own distribution company and was developing a niche in the recycling and brokerage of waste paper. Paper companies that had a distribution company often needed to complement their limited product lines by carrying products made by other paper manufacturers (see Exhibit 17.5).

Recycling

The most important change in the market for fine papers had been the growing emphasis on recycling. The very visible problem of the disposal of solid waste, of which, in the United States, 41% is paper and paperboard, had spurred businesses and governments to demand fine papers that contained significant amounts of recycled fiber. Unfortunately, the demand for recycled fine papers was not being adequately met because of a limited supply of suitable waste paper. The traditional sources of suit-

Exhibit 17.5   The Top Ten North American Producers of Uncoated Fine Paper

Company	Annual Capacity (000 Metric Tons)	Market Share (%)
1. International Paper (U.S.)	1,905	14.6
2. Georgia-Pacific (U.S.)a	1,905	14.5
3. Champion International (U.S.)b	1,112	8.5
4. Boise Cascade (U.S.)	1,093	8.3
5. Union Camp (U.S.)c	816	6.2
6. Weyerhaeuser (U.S.)d	694	5.3
7. James River (U.S.)e	662	5.0
8. Domtar (Canada)	590	4.5
9. Mead (U.S.)	472	3.6
10. Williamette (U.S.)	435	3.3

a New 290,300 metric ton per year machine at Ashdown, AR, started up mid-1991
b Year-end 1990 capacity
c New 226,800 metric ton per year machine starts up at Eastover, SC, mid-1991
d Includes Prince Albert, Saskatchewan
e Includes carbonless base stock

Market share of top five companies	62.3%
Market share of top ten companies	77.0%
Total 1991 North American capacitya	13,149 million tons

a Includes all other companies

able, or high grade de-inking waste paper, such as printing and converting waste, were already being heavily exploited. The current North American recovery rate for these pre-consumer waste sources was about 85%. The largest untapped source of high grade de-inking waste paper was office/business waste. However, this source was limited due to logistical and technical difficulties. The logistical challenge involved the setting up of efficient and low cost collection programs for offices and businesses. The technical challenge was twofold. The first was controlling the variety of contaminants in the office waste. The second difficulty was the inability of current de-inking technology to remove key contaminants such as xerox and laser print.

These challenges had major implications for both consumers and paper companies. Consumers would assume a critical role in shaping not only the demand, but also the supply for recycled fine papers, since they would be generating and sorting the raw material to be used in the manufacture of the product. For paper companies, it was clear that the distribution of fine papers to businesses might become increasingly tied to the collection of high grade de-inking waste from those businesses.

Stermon's Integrated Mill

Plants in the industry were either "integrated" or "paper only." Integrated mills, like the one in Fond du Lac, had a pulp plant on site, while "paper only" mills had to ship in dried pulp from outside. Because of the cost of drying and transporting pulp, modern mills tended to be integrated, and only a few specialty mills now ran without pulping capacity on site. Larger pulp facilities were very much more efficient than smaller ones and the output of even a modest modern pulping plant exceeded the requirements of the world's largest machines. Because of the disparity in minimum efficient scale between pulp plants and paper machines, integrated mills usually included a central pulp plant feeding three to six paper machines on the same site (see Exhibit 17.3). Plants were almost always located near a plentiful supply of both water and trees. Two types of tree were used to make fine paper. Pine trees supplied long-fiber pulp for strength, while deciduous trees supplied short fiber pulp for smoothness and consistency. For this reason, there were paper plants in both the North and South of the USA. Plants in the North shipped in short fiber pulp, while southern plants shipped in the faster growing long-fiber. The ideal recipe for paper was around 50% of each type of pulp.

Plants within Plants

The four paper machines at Fond du Lac were like factories within factories. Each was housed in its own building, and was supplied with pulp through pipelines from the pulping plant. The huge buildings were old and splattered with dried pulp, particularly those housing the older machines. Each machine operated three shifts a day, seven days a week, with a two-week shutdown in the summer for maintenance. About 30% of the hourly workers in the plant worked in maintenance. The remaining direct operators worked in the pulping, paper-making, reeling/winding and shipping areas.

Each machine required between four and six operators to run. Operators' tasks were ranked: from machine tender (the highest rank) to spare hand (the lowest). Movement through the ranks was strictly by seniority, and a bright young addition to the shop floor staff at Stermon could look forward to being a machine tender after about fifteen years of service. The average length of service of the machine tenders in the plant was 24 years. While there were often disagreements within a shift on any machine, a shift formed a tight cluster of people who knew each other well, and had to solve problems arising on their machine, day and night. In keeping with the tradition of the paper industry, the key measure by which operators were judged was the utilization of the machines. Lew Frowe was a back-tender on #4 machine:

Exhibit 17.6 The Paper Making Process

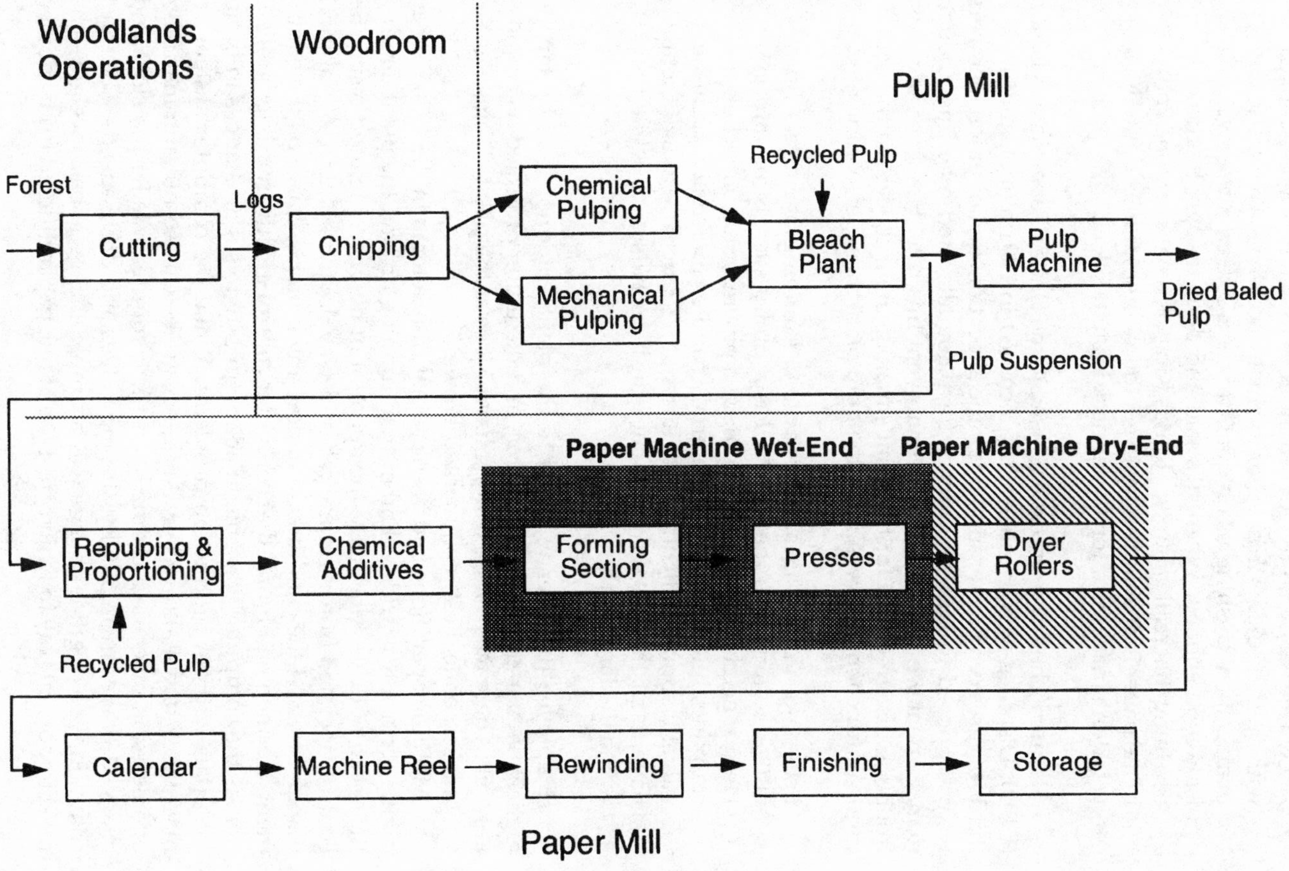

There has been a big push recently on improving safety in the plant. A few weeks ago, a guy got caught in a storage tank when it filled with pulp: he died. We have far too many accidents. We've also had management pushing us on quality. Seems like whatever we do it isn't good enough. When all's said and done though, there's only one thing that really counts: "Tons is King" is what everyone knows in the paper industry. You try to get lots of other things right, but if you don't make your tons, your neck is on the block.

Stermon's hourly workers belonged to the United Papermakers Union (UPU). Disputes were frequent (274 recorded in 1991 alone), and in two-thirds of cases centered around overtime allocation. Senior union members were supposed to take precedence for being allocated overtime, though management would often try to circumvent this rule. However, the most troubling disagreement for the plant's management concerned the demarcation of functions. Dave Yarrow, the pulp plant manager, commented:

Let's take unloading as an example. Pumping chemicals off a tanker coming into the rail yard is a pretty straightforward job. Here, it needs two people. You need a pipefitter to connect up the coupling, but you need a materials handler to actually turn the valve! It sounds ridiculous and it is, but it's true! The two of them have to sit there like twenty buck an hour hatstands while they watch the tanker empty.

Employee turnover was low in the plant—Stermon was by far the highest paying employer in the area, and the union protected its employees well. There was a long waiting list for jobs at the plant. "You've got to wait till someone dies!" commented Frowe.

Machine operations had been dramatically altered in the 1980's when digital control was added. Rather than running around the plant altering the speed of drives manually, the operator of the machine used computer control, operated from a central cab mid-way down its length. A graphical display showed the condition of almost any motor or valve on the equipment. Stermon had found that computer control greatly improved utilization as the computer was able to adapt quickly to slight changes in input materials without production problems. While the computer system on machines 3 and 4 allowed grade changes to be carried out automatically, operators on machine 3 claimed that the computer was far too slow, and changed grades manually by altering valves and drive speeds. The most common type of grade change was a simple change in basis weight—the most important way in which one type of fine paper differed from another.

"The computer never quite does it right—but it never messes up too bad either. We just let it take the reins in the middle of a run.

For grade changes though, we prefer to do it on our own." (Back-tender, machine 3)

The smaller machines carried out four or five grade changes within a day, but machine 4 averaged one grade change a day, because of the high cost of having it not producing paper. Each machine ran on a two week cycle, and progressed up and then down the basis weight range for the machine, changing furnishes as it went. The order was important, since gradual grade changes kept the paper-making process more stable than large shifts. The machines stayed on each grade for a varying length of time depending on the orders for that particular grade.

Selling the Sheet

Sylvia Tannar had worked in the sales department at Stermon for almost fifteen years. "We've seen slumps before," said Tannar, "but never one as bad as this. We've got guys in this plant who say their fathers don't even remember it being this tough. Paper prices are through the floor. 20 lb Xerox paper has been selling as low as 650 bucks a ton. We can't even get close to that!"

In 1991, three new uncoated fine paper machines came on line in the Unites States. Georgia Pacific, Union Camp and Boise Cascade all introduced state-of-the-art machines running at 4000 fpm, producing 850 tons per machine each day. All three were focussed on 20 lb Xerox paper, with occasional runs of 18 lb or 24 lb. These gargantuan new machines took advantage of the tremendous economies of scale in the technology. Paper machines had consistently grown in size and speed since the early twenties. With each new machine introduced into the industry, its owner hoped to grab greater economies than competitors, and win out on price or margins. Each of the 1991 machines cost $500m. Historically, the big companies had often invested in new capacity at about the same time, each seeing the same window of opportunity. This magnified the already cyclical nature of the paper industry and 1991 saw the biggest capacity glut the world had ever seen. Fine paper prices fell from $950 per ton in 1988 to $650 per ton for comparable grades of paper in October, 1992.

While such prices were hurting Georgia Pacific, Boise Cascade, and Union Camp, they were devastating to a small company like Stermon, that lacked the scale economies of the bigger machines. "We've had to find new ways to win orders," noted Tannar. One way Stermon had kept machine 4 busy was to begin making grades which were lighter and heavier than were usually made on the machine. " We might not be able to run flat out on one grade," said Tannar "but we can try to keep busy by selling some cats and dogs at the ends of the range. People can come to us for stuff they can't buy elsewhere."

Forty-two percent of Stermon's paper went to paper merchants, who sold their paper to converters. Converters turned the paper into envelopes and forms. In the last two years, merchants and other customers alike had shown an increasing reluctance to carry inventory, pushing the inventory back into the struggling paper plants. "They want it Just-In-Time or not at all," complained Tannar. "I never thought I'd see the day when this JIT business would hit a process industry, but its here. If we don't deliver in bits and pieces, we lose the business. It either ends up with us carrying the inventory, or pushing really short runs onto the machines. The manufacturing guys hate it—but what can we do?"

Are We a Cessna or a 747?

Together with the other five members of his crew, Charley Jonn was responsible for keeping #4 machine running. Jonn had worked the night shift tending machine 4 for 21 years.

> "There's been a lot of pressure around here lately. I usually get in around 10ish, and deal with whatever problems the late shift has left me with. I set the machine back in trim: Hank on the last shift never does set it on its sweet-spot. Then, I start to take a look at any changes coming up in the schedule."

The paper machine operator's job was essentially one of monitoring the machine, keeping an eye open for equipment problems and making changes in paper grade from the control booth at the center of the machine. Operators generally liked to keep a machine stable, running on one grade. This gave the process stability and avoided a common but catastrophic source of failure—a paper break. As the name suggested, a paper break occurred when an instability in the process or some impurity in the web caused the paper running in the machine to tear. Paper tangled everywhere and the machine would shut down while the web was re-threaded. This meant having the whole crew clamber over the machine, tearing out paper. One intrepid member would throw the leading edge of a new web into the machine while precariously balanced between two rollers. It took anything from 10 minutes to 8 hours to repair a break, during which time production was at a standstill. Breaks were much more likely with thin papers and unfamiliar grades. Curiously, they seemed to occur much more often at the beginning of a shift than any other time.

Jonn threw his hands up in despair at the increasing frequency of grade changes the crew was being asked to make.

> "A big paper machine is like an airliner. It takes time to get up in the air and time to come down. If you want to do small hops, you go in a Cessna not in a 747. This paper machine was made to stay in one spot. We lose 30 minutes of production time every time we change grades. That might be OK on machines 1, 2 and 3 but this

is a high output machine and we lose a lot of output in 30 minutes. I know that times are hard, but if you're always changing over, you never have time to make paper.

We're all measured on output. The bottom line is and always has been tons per day. You don't make your tons—you've got problems, so we're really careful when we change grade. We're careful and we try to get it right.

Even so, time lost due to grade changes had almost doubled from 6% in the early 1970s to 10% in 1992. On average, #4 machine was making twice as many changes as it had in 1990, and productivity was suffering. "It's bad enough as it is, without losing all this time and making all this broke[1] changing grades."

Quality

"We've always prided ourselves on making a real quality product," noted Lars Robikoff, superintendent of machine 4, "but some of the problems we've been having recently have really taken us by surprise." A large piece of holed paper pinned to the wall was testament to this. "This hole cost us $5,981.28" said the felt-penned inscription.

It's only in the newer grades—we're so used to making 20 lb, that we make a mistake here and there on the heavy stuff and the light stuff. Customers are coming back screaming at us—you can't blame a printer for crying out when he's got a web with holes the size of lumberjack's thumbs breaking in his press.

Stermon relied heavily on sampling inspection to ensure the quality of the product shipped. Inspectors would check for moisture content, ash content, color and a host of other features. Any discrepancies would be reported back to machine operators, who would take the appropriate action. Product quality was also monitored continuously by computer on machine 4—even so, the occasional problem slipped through the net.

Robikoff attributed the quality problems to the instability in the paper making process, due to the higher frequency of changes and the "odd" papers which were becoming more common. He was nevertheless optimistic.

"All of these changes have to end soon. Once business picks up again we'll be back making one or two grades I'm sure—it'll be the same as it was before."

---

[1]Broke was the term used for off-standard paper. Between runs, the off specification paper made was repulped and cycled back through the plant.

No Paper Tiger

"I don't think it's ever going to be the same as it was before," said Kiefner. "No matter what happens, we can't compete with the likes of Boise Cascade and Union Camp. We just can't hit those kind of costs in this plant. We'll always be marginal. But you know we're small—and we can do one thing those guys can't—we can be flexible." It was the only way to continue to compete. "Even if things pick up," he said "we'll still need something we can be really good at—we need to become excellent at being flexible."

Kiefner had charged Saugoe with the job of developing an improvement program to set Stermon on a path which would make it once again a world-class plant. But now it would be world-class in terms of its flexibility rather than its cost. The improvement scheme would begin on November 10th, 1992 and was to set clear goals and milestones. The initial focus of the plan would be machine #4, the largest machine in the plant, and the one considered the most important and the least flexible.

Saugoe had been included in a number of improvement schemes in the past. In August, 1977, he had set up a real-time cost analysis system in the plant. In March 1983, he had led the Total Quality Initiative (TQI), with the specific aim of reducing defects in the paper. Saugoe had looked at a number of Quality Improvement Programs in the process industry before the team finally agreed on a scheme developed by Manzax Chemical in the UK, based on Philip Crosby's methods. Both schemes had been considered a success by management. But flexibility seemed different. What did it mean to "get flexible?" Saugoe didn't know, so pulled together a team to find out.

Flexibility in Manufacturing

On September 12th, Saugoe's team of manufacturing specialists discussed the flexibility improvement scheme. A handful of worried people crowded into his office. He had asked each of them to come up with ideas on how to improve flexibility.

Davie Pemthrall was superintendent on machine 3.

> "We should figure out how to push this machine a little more. If we improved some of the process control systems, and put in higher powered dryers on machine 4, we'd really be flexible. We'd be able to dry real heavy papers, but still be able to control the process well enough to make light papers. We'd be able to make almost anything if we did that, then we'd really be flexible."

Peter Lohresich (Machine 2 superintendent) differed:

> "I don't know Pem, I saw it a little differently. I think we need to improve the changeover times so we can switch between the

grades a little more easily. Grade change time and paper breaks are really starting to eat into the efficiency on machine #4. Some of the guys on 3 have got together a fire-brigade. They figured out a way to beat the computer every time on grade changes. They run around like crazy when it comes to changing the machine. The computer does it in ten minutes. These guys are incredible! They do it in two or three."

"Yes Pete, but number 3 is a little machine, you can play around with that kind of thing there. Machine 4 is making almost 300 tons a day. You need to be safe when you change grades."

"I still think we should work on speeding up grade changes on 4. I don't see any reason why it can't start getting really flexible, just like number 3."

Lars Robikoff (Superintendent, Machine 4) disagreed:

"No, I don't think either of these things really makes us flexible. It's all very well saying we should work on getting machine 4 to make a large range of weights or to changeover quickly, but you'll never be really flexible until you fix the fundamental problem: the machine was built for 20 lb Xerox paper. It likes to run there—that's where it's most efficient. You should forget about getting it to do real heavy, light and all those other weird papers. Let's get it to be efficient across the range of papers we make *now*—on 15 lb, 18 lb and 24 lb—get the yields up there. Then we won't care which we produce—we'll really start to be flexible."

Pemthrall agreed:

We have really patchy quality across the grades we make now on 4. Customers shouldn't have to put up with holes in the web just because we're making stuff our machine doesn't like. As well as that, there are folks out there who've got machines that *are* set up specifically for 15 lb or 24 lb. We better learn to be as good as them, or they'll win every time.

Flexibility in Sales

"It means doing what the customer wants," said Elly Ryesham in the sales department. "Flexibility means being all things to all people—of course, you can never do it; but you do your best. It means giving the customer exactly what they want, when they want it, I suppose."

Saugoe wasn't sure that helped. What kinds of things did the customers want, and what exactly did they mean by flexibility? Saugoe set Ryesham a task. "Go back to your salespeople, and see if you can put together a list of things we need to do, to be what our customers call 'being flexible.' Break them into categories, and see which kind of request comes up the most."

Two days later, Ryesham returned.

Well, it wasn't real clear, but I guess we came up with three things. The first need is for customized paper—one-offs and specials— that kind of thing. Some of our customers would really like us to be able to make paper tailored to their specific needs, even real lights and heavies. Second, customers want us to deliver just-in- time frequently rather than pushing a whole run onto them. Finally, I guess they like the fact they can do one stop shopping here; we've got a lot of product lines. I have my own opinions about which of these is most important, but I also asked the sales- people.

Ryesham had taken a straw poll of the sales force, asking which of these were most important. "They all are!" replied one saleswoman. Eventually the committee ended up with a list, grading each type of flexibility from A (important) to E (unimportant) (see Exhibit 17.7) Unfortunately, some sales- people had added more "flexibility" items to the list.

"There are all types of flexibility," said Saugoe, "but now we have a better idea of what's really important to the customer. Saugoe still wasn't sure how this translated into a flexibility plan for the plant. One compli- cating problem was that there was already a flexibility improvement program in operation. For the past two years, HRM people had been nego- tiating a flexibility scheme with the union. Union officials had agreed to begin to relax the traditional constraints on workers taking each others' jobs. Aidan Waine, UPU representative in the pulp plant, commented on the rumors he had heard:

We've been negotiating this deal for three years and now they're saying we've got to be even more flexible! Sounds to me like another way of getting something for nothing.

Exhibit 17.7 Survey of Sales force

Requirement	Andy Newland	Liz Foxell	Jimmy Mellor	Tracy Shaw	Nick Walker
Customization	A–	A–	B–	D	B–
Responsiveness in delivery/JIT	A	A+	A+	B+	A
Having a broad product line	B	A	B	B	B–
Having flexible, helpful salespeople	B	A	C	C	B
Bring in new products frequently	D	E	B	E	C

Flexing the Factory

Saugoe sat in his office putting together his presentation on overhead foils for Kiefner. He felt that Kiefner had been losing some patience with the team recently. It took them two weeks just to work out what a flexibility improvement program meant! Kiefner was a man with a cold, steely heart for warm, fuzzy ideas. Two weeks ago, the team had come up with some comparatively vague suggestions for an improvement program. Kiefner had insisted that nothing would ever happen if the results could not be measured. Besides, he was concerned that Saugoe had no idea how to rank the various schemes in terms of their importance. Saugoe had remade a list of the flexibility improvement options, and was now working on which of these should be carried out.

First, Stermon could upgrade machine 4 with computer control, extra dryer capacity, and better training, so that it could make a much broader range of basic weights. With better control, the number of "recipes" the machine could make would also be increased. This would clearly improve the flexibility of the machine. If the machine were able to make heavier weights as well as slightly lighter weights than it could now, Stermon could make money by tailoring paper to customers' specific requirements both within the existing range of the machine, and outside it. Marketing estimated that a 7% premium (before freight) could be charged for such a service on these grades, though the machine would only produce such specialty jobs for 30% of the time. The capital cost of improving the flexibility of the machine in this way was $3.1 million.

The second option relied much more on the people in the plant being able to adopt new ways of working. It would mean completely breaking with paper industry tradition. Machine 4 could be taken to a one week cycle, and run through the existing grades every week instead of every two weeks. This would certainly save on inventory costs—but even if inventory stayed the same, marketing estimated that Stermon could charge a 5% pre-freight premium for the ability to make weekly "JIT" production runs. This was not at all straightforward though. If changeover times remained the same, it would mean a lot more time lost due to grade changes on machine 4. Ten percent of available machine time was currently lost due to changeovers. Would the machine operators be able to learn to change over faster? Perhaps some of the machine tenders from machine #3 could help the crew on #4 to become more flexible among the grades.

The third option was to improve the yield on machine 4 on the less frequently produced grades. In general, paper produced on the machine split into four categories, as shown in Exhibit 17.8. Machine 4 was strongly focussed on 20 lb Xerox paper. Over the past year however, demand had been very soft for this paper because of the new capacity in the industry. For 28% of the past year's two-week machine cycles, there had been no demand for 20 lb paper, and the capacity of the machine was shared among

Exhibit 17.8	Yields and Proportions of Output on Machine 4

Grade	< 15lb	18lb	20lb	24lb+
Yield[a]	78%	86%	95%	89%
Usual proportion of production	14%	16%	62%	8%
Proportion when no 20lb demand	37%	42%		21%

a. Yield figures are net of grade changes. These are the yields once the machine is running the grade.

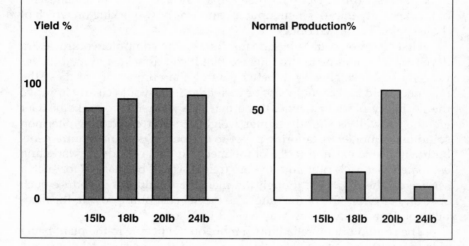

the other grades in their "normal" proportions to each other. This situation was expected to continue for at least two more years. These abnormal weeks were very unpopular on the floor, since it meant spending two weeks without running the machine on its sweet spot. The machine was not sufficiently flexible to produce all grades well. To improve this flexibility among the grades, a new expert system for process control could be installed. This system promised to raise the yields for 15 lb to 24 lb paper made on the machine so that they would be comparable to that for 20 lb, providing the machine with much more flexibility across its grade range. The machine would then be much more tolerant of a lack of demand for its "favorite" grade. In addition, quality would become more consistent across the grade range. The cost of this system and the associated actuator network was $5.05 million.

Finally, Saugoe could recommend accelerating the flexibility program which was being worked out with the Union. There had been other fires to fight in recent months, and a lot of the original impetus in the program had drained away. This program had the advantage that it was already under

Exhibit 17.9 Employee Satisfaction Data

	Increase Range	One week cycle	Uniform Yields
One week cycle	Might be difficult just to make new grades <u>without</u> trying to change between them quickly. Combination of unfamiliar grades and process instability might cause paper breaks and/or quality problems.		
Uniform Yields	Would be too difficult to improve yields at the same time as stretching the machine. With the new grades being anticipated, would not expect any yield improvement on existing grades.	In order to improve yields, would probably need to stay on grades for at least as long as current run lengths. Unlikely to get process stable enough to improve yields if more changes. Could do it—but results would be to raise non-20 lb. yields only about 3%.	
Labor Multi Skilling	Could use existing skill base and use this as an opportunity to cut across functional lines. People generally enthusiastic about "difficult" papers. Would need to relax "output" pressure.	Might cause a lot of discontent if people were being asked to change over faster/more often, as well as performing multiple functions. Not likely to work well.	This would already be seen as a way of improving output rather than improving flexibility. Hard to combine with a push on multi-tasking.

way, and was important in improving the effectiveness of the labor in the plant. Seeing people sitting around waiting for the "right" job to show up was getting to be really demoralizing for everyone in the plant.

While Stermon could go ahead with all four plans, Saugoe knew from his experiences with other improvement schemes that it would be much better to focus attention on one or two. In addition, he was concerned that some combinations of the flexibility improvement plans would conflict. He sketched out some notes to himself on how the plans might interact (see Exhibit 17.9). Saugoe wondered if there might be another way out. "Maybe we should work on having enough flexibility to get out of this business altogether!" thought Saugoe, half- cynically, half-seriously, as he put together the slides for his presentation to Kiefner.

As he checked his recommendation in indelible pen on the slide, Saugoe thought, "No changing my mind now I guess." With no flexibility left, he knocked on Kiefner's door.

CHAPTER 18

Kanebo Ltd.

Introduction

*I*N EARLY 1988, senior managers of the Cosmetics Division of Kanebo Ltd. were preparing to implement a strategy for improving their responsiveness to consumer demand. The strategy consisted of two parts. First, they proposed to introduce a new POS (point of sale) information system that they hoped would both stimulate demand for Kanebo products and eventually make it possible to obtain accurate, up-to-date sales information from the division's 30,000 retail outlets around Japan. This would enable them to identify products that were selling much better or worse than expected, so they could make changes in both their production schedules and their marketing approaches.

But the equipment and workforce policies in use at their Odawara factory prevented it from being able to respond as quickly as the new market information required. Therefore, the second part of the new strategy was to invest as much as ¥2 billion[1] at Odawara in new "FMS" flexible manufacturing lines. These lines not only would require fewer workers and be able to change from one product to another much faster than could the existing lines, but they could also be run with a skeleton crew at nights and on weekends, when the factory normally was shut down. The ultimate goal of this combination of POS and FMS was to be able to respond promptly—and, in fact, automatically—to unexpected changes in the demand for any of Kanebo's products.

Recently, however, a number of people had begun to express concerns about both projects. One group was uneasy about basing the new POS system on NTT's (Nippon Telephone and Telegraph's) new nationwide video-text system. The NTT system allowed users to gain instantaneous

---

[1]¥127 = U.S.$1.00, approximately, at the time of this case. At this rate of exchange, a simple way to estimate the dollar equivalent of a Yen amount is by dividing it by 1000 and then multiplying the result by 8.

Professors Robert Hayes and Hirokazu Kono prepared this case as the basis for class discussion rather than to illustrate either effective or ineffective handling of an administrative situation. Certain information has been disguised.

access to a large central information bank through a simple video terminal. Kanebo had modified and expanded this system so that the stores could also gain access to information about specific Kanebo products and advice about how to deal with typical skin or beauty problems. Even more important, the Kanebo system was equipped with a bar code detector that made it possible for store managers to record automatically information about customer purchases onto a memory card. At the end of each day, the contents of this memory card could be transmitted back to Cosmetics Division headquarters for analysis. This would make it possible both to institute corrective action, if necessary, and to compare the performance of different stores.

Unfortunately, NTT had recently run a test of its new system in one small region in Japan and had experienced disappointing results. Not enough people had signed up to use the system, even at a heavily discounted leasing price, and many of those who did had experienced difficulties with it. Few had renewed their subscriptions to the system after the trial period. Rather than attach Kanebo's POS system to an NTT system that had lost much of its credibility, some Cosmetics Division managers argued for a whole new approach. They recommended Kanebo develop a system based on low-cost personal computers, which could transmit data periodically to headquarters through standard telephone lines.

Concerns were also being expressed about the factory automation project. While the pilot model of the new FMS packaging line required much fewer workers than existing lines, and less time to make changeovers between products, some managers felt that the degree of improvement still was not sufficient to justify its cost. "The goal was to reduce the number of workers to at most one or two, and to make a changeover in less than 10 minutes," explained one. "But at present it looks as though at least three people will be required, and the changeover time is closer to an hour than 10 minutes. Moreover, small bottles still can not be produced efficiently on the FMS. Perhaps we should wait until the system is operating closer to its goals before putting it into our factory."

These concerns and suggestions for alternative approaches were reported to Mr. Kazutomo Ishizawa, Kanebo's president and one of the early advocates of such a system. Although he still felt that the Cosmetics Division needed to become more responsive to market changes, it no longer was clear to him that the approach being proposed was the best one for Kanebo. On the other hand, he felt it was important for the organization to improve its flexibility, and was concerned that waiting for the development of a whole new approach might cause an unacceptable delay in making this improvement.

Company Background

Kanebo celebrated its 100th birthday in 1987, making it one of Japan's oldest companies. At one point in the 1930s it was also the largest, in terms of sales, privately-owned company in Japan. Its corporate symbol—a ring-ing bell (the Japanese word "kane" means "bell")—was well known throughout the country because of the company's age and size, as well as its penetration into a number of consumer markets. In 1987 its nearly 9,000 employees generated sales of over ¥380 billion, and a profit after tax of ¥2.3 billion. Additional financial information is contained in Exhibit 18.1.

Kanebo limited its activities to the textile and related industries for most of its first 75 years, but in 1961 it began a broad program of diversifi-cation. Beginning with toiletries and cosmetics, it gradually added specialty foods, pharmaceuticals, housing and environmental products, industrial materials, electronics (including the production of integrated circuits), and information systems. In 1981 it announced that in the future it would place top priority on its fashion, cosmetics, and pharmaceutical businesses, while deemphasizing standard textile products.

By 1988, textiles and fashion products still represented almost 50% of

Exhibit 18.1 Financial Summary (in ¥ billion)[a]

	1987	1986	1985	1984
Net sales[b]	381.8[(29.0)]	352.5[(33.8)]	330.8[(35.3)]	326.5[(34.8)]
Cost of goods sold	266.9	249.7	236.3	236.0
Sales and administrative costs	90.5	83.7	74.4	70.9
Operating Earnings	24.4	19.1	20.1	19.6
Nonoperating expenses (including net interest)	17.2	13.0	12.0	12.3
Ordinary earnings	7.2	6.1	8.1	7.3
Earnings before taxes (after extraordinary earnings and expenses)	5.2	5.2	5.0	5.7
Net earnings	2.3	2.8	2.8	2.4
Assets:				
Current	299.9	268.0	235.3	236.5
Fixed	171.5	159.2	107.1	111.8
Total assets (including deferred assets)	478.5	434.5	349.1	354.4
Liabilities:				
Current	355.4	314.0	241.9	250.7
Long-term	73.9	72.0	62.5	60.3
Stockholders' Equity	49.2	48.5	44.7	43.3

[a] Fiscal years ending March 31 in 1988, and April 30 in other years.
[b] Cosmetic sales, as percent of total, are contained in parentheses.

total sales, while cosmetics and toiletries accounted for about 30%. Most of these sales occurred within Japan, but international sales—particularly of cosmetics—were becoming more important. Some of Kanebo's production of textiles was carried out by affiliated companies in other countries. Aside from a small cosmetics factory in Taiwan and a small independent joint venture in Europe, however, the production of all other products took place in Japan. The increasing value of the Yen relative to most other currencies therefore was making it more and more difficult for Kanebo to compete in foreign markets.

Although corporate headquarters was in Osaka, Kanebo's fashion, cosmetics, pharmaceuticals, and foodstuffs divisions all had their headquarters in Tokyo. Each division was given considerable autonomy, and conducted its own R&D. The company also had a central R&D Laboratory that focused on three fields having broad application across the different divisions: biotechnology, electronics/information systems, and new materials/polymer chemistry. Its goal was to identify technological synergies among the various divisions, and ensure that technological developments in one part of the company could be exploited by others.

The Cosmetics Division: Marketing

After growing rapidly in the 1960s and early 1970s, Japan's cosmetics industry appeared to have matured by the mid-1980s. The industry growth rate fell below 10% in 1977 and to less than 1% in 1987. As the growth rate fell, competition intensified among the many companies competing for a share of this market. Shiseido, the largest of these companies, held about 28% of the market while Kanebo, the second largest, held about 13%. Other companies, such as Clinique and Estee Lauder, tended to specialize in particular market niches. Giant Kao, sometimes called the "Procter & Gamble of Japan," focused primarily on low-cost, high-volume cosmetics and toiletries. It held only about 3% of the market for major cosmetic products.

In the face of this stiffening competition, which both reduced its gross margins and caused its growth to stagnate, Kanebo put increasing emphasis on innovation and customer service. Introducing new products at a rapid rate, its product line grew from about 1,100 to almost 2,500 items between 1980 and 1988; this included over 200 shades of lipstick alone. (Exhibit 18.2 depicts a representative sample of these products.) Many of these new products were seasonal, in that their colors and scents were tailored to a specific time of the year.

Periodic conferences, which included sales managers, store managers, beauty consultants, and Cosmetics Division personnel, were held to choose the products that were to be made the focus of new promotional campaigns. These campaigns generally lasted two to three months, and

Exhibit 18.2   Kanebo Cosmetics Products

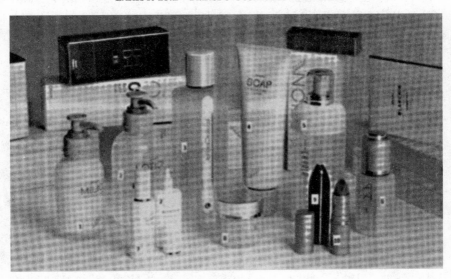

¹*Alga Milky Lotion (Skin Moisturizer: 80 ml., ¥ 2500)*
²*Alga Lotion (Skin Conditioner: 150 ml., ¥ 2500)*
³*Faircrea Whitening Lotion (Skin care for sun exposure: 150 ml., ¥ 3800)*
⁴*Alga Soap (Scrubbing Facial Soap: 120 gr., ¥ 2500)*
⁵*Chyria Milky Water (Skin Moisturizer: 170 ml., ¥ 4000)*
⁶*DaDa Essence (Medicated Skin Conditioner: 30 ml., ¥ 10,000)*
⁷*Blanchir Whitening Spots (Sun Shield and Conditioner: 2 @ 15 ml., ¥ 10,000)*
⁸*Affinique Summer Foundation (Cream Foundation with special applicator: 35 gr., ¥ 15 ml., ¥ 10,000)*
⁹*RS-102 Lipstick (¥ 3500)*
¹⁰*Raphaie RS-75 Lipstick (¥ 4500)*

featured catchy songs, pretty "campaign girls," and heavy advertising. In 1988, products promoted in this way accounted for about 20% of Kanebo's units sold, and 40% of its total sales revenue.

As a result, cosmetics products increasingly displayed the characteristics of fashion items, making it difficult to predict the likely demand for individual items. The demand for the most popular shade of lipstick, for example, was often more than 100 times that of the least popular. By the time Kanebo became aware that one of its newer products was selling much better than expected, it was often too late to increase production before that item's selling season was over. The Cosmetic Division estimated it had lost over ¥1 billion in sales because of stockouts during 1987 alone.

Different competitors chose different approaches to distributing their products. Shiseido and Kanebo, among others, used the "Seido-hin" system, in which wholly owned sales companies were responsible for all sales within specific geographic regions. Each sales company purchased products from its parent company and distributed them through a large number of independent retail outlets in its territory. Kanebo, for example, owned 72 sales companies, which served 30,000 retail outlets throughout Japan with a sales force of about 1,100 salesmen (called Area Managers). Almost 80% of these outlets were chain stores, while supermarkets, department and convenience stores accounted for the rest.

Most of these retail shops were quite small in size; only about 13% of them sold more than ¥1.5 million worth of Kanebo products a month, while almost half sold less than ¥450,000. Their average monthly sales was about ¥600,000. Slightly more than half of them handled Kanebo products exclusively, and they accounted for about 45% of total Kanebo sales. The others offered competing products as well, which made them somewhat difficult to control. Much of a salesman's time, therefore, was devoted to cultivating relationships with store owners and motivating them to sell his products rather than those of other companies.

Moreover, these small stores usually were managed in a very informal way, and decisions were made in an ad hoc manner. They seldom carried enough inventory of all products, and therefore expected delivery of items ordered from the sales company within a day or two.

Salesmen were hired by Kanebo itself, and underwent one year of training at one of the sales companies. A typical salesman was responsible for about 26 stores, and visited 8 to 10 per day. During their periodic visits to stores they confirmed the delivery of previously-ordered items, checked the stock of Kanebo products (which was the only way to get an accurate estimate of actual sales), took orders for additional items, informed store personnel about new products, and answered whatever consumer questions had arisen.

The store, in turn, could ask the salesman to return unsold stock to the sales company for credit. One of a salesman's most important tasks, therefore, was to limit the amount of returned merchandise by maintaining good communication with store managers. Salesmen prided themselves on their knowledge of local market conditions and trends, as well as the situation at each of their retail stores. They were paid a monthly salary, plus incentives based on actual sales.

Other companies, particularly those specializing in very high priced items, had adopted a much different system in which the sales companies that distributed their products were independently owned. Moreover, the sales forces of these sales companies sold their products directly to customers through personal visits to their homes or offices. Finally, Kao and other companies that emphasized lower priced items used still another approach—the so-called "Ippan-hin" system—in which they distributed their products through huge independent wholesalers. These wholesalers serviced the whole range of retail outlets, from small specialty and grocery stores to large department stores. Kanebo itself increasingly was using an Ippan-hin system for distributing its line of toiletries.

In 1988, companies using the Seido-hin system accounted for just under 40% of cosmetics sales in Japan, whereas those using the Ippan-hin system accounted for just under 30%. There was evidence, however, that the latter companies were slowly gaining market share from those that used other systems. It was suspected that this was largely due to the growing acceptance of lower priced items, particularly among young people.

Despite the recent slowdown in the growth of cosmetics sales in Japan, some industry observers predicted renewed growth during the 1990s. This resurgence would be based, they felt, on both Japan's growing affluence and its changing demographics and behavior patterns. Not only were younger women increasingly using cosmetics, but so were women over 40—and the number of people in this latter category was increasing rapidly as Japan's population aged. These trends were expected not only to encourage growth in the cosmetics market, but to cause it to fragment as well. As Japanese women broadened the range of activities they engaged in, to include travel, sports, and cultural pursuits, they demanded a broader range of colors and styles.

They also wanted more and better information to guide them when buying cosmetics. Kanebo's marketing department estimated that only about 30% of its products were "self-selling," in that customers did not request any advice or other assistance from a sales person when making the purchase decision. Partly because of this, small retail stores (which had limited product lines and expertise) were expected to lose their attractiveness, relative to the larger department and retail stores, to this new breed of consumers.

Cosmetics Division: Manufacturing

Just over 50% of the bottling and packaging of Kanebo's cosmetics took place at its factory in Odawara, Japan, about 40 miles southwest of Tokyo. Lower cost, less fashionable items tended to be sourced from subcontractors in Japan, who primarily packaged formulations that were produced in bulk at Odawara. Shipping costs and legal restrictions combined to make it impractical to supply Kanebo's Japanese customers with products packaged at its factory in Taiwan.

The Odawara complex consisted of the factory itself, an administration building, two technology centers (one specializing in biotech research), a raw material warehouse, and separate dormitories for unmarried men and women. It employed about 350 people, of whom over two-thirds were women and 15% worked part-time. The factory usually operated one 7.5 hour shift each weekday, and one every other Saturday. Under Japanese law, women were not allowed to work after 10 o'clock at night. Because of the tight labor market in Japan, it was becoming increasingly difficult to recruit people to do factory work—much less at night or on weekends.

A typical factory worker at Odawara earned about ¥1.6 million per year in salary and another ¥750,000 in bonuses. In addition, Kanebo paid roughly ¥150,000 for social benefits. Workers received a 20% premium for working beyond the usual quitting time; such overtime, however, was limited for women workers to three hours a day, six hours per week, and 150 hours per year. Workers also received a 50% premium for working after midnight or on holidays.

The factory produced three major types of products; skin care (largely creams and lotions), makeup (lipsticks and face powder), and fragrances (perfumes and toilet water). Most used the same batch production process, which involved four separate stages. First, ingredients were measured into a stainless steel vat, following the directions of a recipe stored in the factory's computer. Liquid ingredients were introduced directly, under computer control, while operators measured dry ingredients on an electronic scale following directions displayed on a computer video terminal. The capacity of these vats ranged from 2,400 to 5,000 kilograms. The batch sizes of emulsified products could be as low as 200 kg. or as high as 5,000, and averaged about 1,300.

Next, these materials were heated and mixed. In the latter stages of this emulsifying process, a semi-vacuum was introduced into the vat to facilitate the removal of air in the mixture as it was gradually cooled back to room temperature. The mixing/degassing/cooling stage required about two hours, most of which time was consumed by the cooling process. After cooling, the mixture was inspected and held in storage vats for several hours (or several weeks, in the case of perfumes) so that it could stabilize.

After this stabilization period the mixture was transferred through glass tubes to one of the plant's 23 bottling/packaging lines. Four of these lines were dedicated to lipsticks and three to foundation powders. A typical bottling/packaging line was staffed by nearly 20 workers, and operated at a rate of between 1,500 and 7,500 units per hour (averaging about 5,000 per hour for bottled products and 1,500 per hour for lipsticks). A nonstandard item requiring special packaging might need as many as 25 workers, however. After packaging, the finished item was again inspected and shipped immediately to the Division's nearby central warehouse. From there it was sent to one of nine distribution centers around the country. It took three days, on average, for a product to proceed from unmeasured raw material to finished goods. Once packaged, it could be delivered to a retail store within 5 days.

The containers used for skin care products, which consumed the bulk of the bottling activity at Odawara, consisted of three basic types: bottles, tubes, and jars. Each of these, in turn, came in three basic sizes: small, medium, and large. Additional complications were introduced by the fact that some bottles were of the "pour" type, while others were of the "pump" type. Because of the difficulty of changing over a bottling line from one of these type-size combinations to another, each line was dedicated to one such combination. As a result, on any given day some of

Odawara's lines would be operating at capacity while others would be idle—but the lines falling into each category were constantly changing.

This made it difficult to calculate the factory's capacity, particularly for skin care products. Because it involved fewer lines and container shapes, the packaging capacity for lipsticks was somewhat easier to determine. It was estimated to be about 1.2 million units per month, somewhat greater than the average lipstick demand of about 935,000 units per month. Demand had risen to almost 2.5 million units a month during peak selling periods, however.

The cost structure for cosmetics varied by item and price level, but the usual practice of companies using the Seido-hin system was for a sales company to sell products to its retail stores for about 20% more than the price it paid its parent company. The retail store, in turn, priced the product so as to receive a margin of somewhat over 50%. The factory's total manufacturing cost was usually about 30% of its selling price, and raw materials (including packaging materials) accounted for about 75% of this. Direct and indirect labor, depreciation, and light and power costs accounted for the other 25%.

The factory had been continually examining and improving its performance, concentrating in recent years on reducing costs and improving its ability to produce small lots economically. For example, cleaning out the glass transfer tubes between batches had been reduced from 90 to 30 minutes in 1984, when a steam cleaning process had been introduced. Changing over a packaging line to a new container shape or size used to take two skilled workers about half a shift. Recently, however, the changeover time had been reduced to about 1.5 hours on average (and, in some cases, to less than one hour), and could be carried out by one unskilled worker. Similarly, the factory's production lead time—from ordering materials to final shipment—had been reduced from 75 to 45 days, largely through improvements in its raw material ordering process and production scheduling system. It was now limited primarily by the time required to obtain packaging materials.

Despite such improvements, increasing the number of different products produced at the factory had dramatically reduced its effective capacity. In an effort to reduce the time lost through changeovers, Kanebo had worked to rationalize its product line. For example, it had redesigned its lipstick products so that three basic holders (which could be embellished in a variety of ways) replaced the 30 holders offered previously.

Scheduling production for the factory took place through a hierarchical process. First, the 72 sales companies estimated the demand a year ahead for each of Kanebo's products. These estimates were combined and used as input to a computerized demand forecasting system that incorporated each item's demand history (if such historical data were available). From the resulting forecast an aggregate production schedule was prepared for the next three months and used as the basis for ordering raw materials from suppliers. A detailed production schedule, divided up into three 10-day periods, was prepared a month in advance and "rolled forward" every 10 days. This schedule indicated when a given product could be delivered to retail stores. Factory management had some freedom to revise daily production schedules to reflect the availability of specific equipment and raw materials. Preparing and implementing new production schedules was not an easy task, both because the number of workers assigned to a given packaging line could vary according to the product and line specifications, and because the difficulty of hiring new factory workers required that the existing labor force be fully utilized.

Because the total capacity of the factory's skin care packaging lines exceeded the average demand rate, each line was in operation only about half the time. When operating, a line typically produced two different products during each shift; the average run length was roughly one month's estimated sales. About two weeks' worth of raw materials were held at Odawara, which facilitated changes in the production schedule if they became necessary. The factory's ability to change production volumes was limited, however, by the fact that it usually took over a month to obtain packaging materials from suppliers.

In addition, nearly two months' worth of packaged products, on average, were held in Kanebo's distribution system. Because of the extreme seasonal nature of demand, production of most items had to begin well in advance of the target selling period. Kanebo was willing to hold as much as three months' supply of an item if it was sure it could be sold. Nevertheless, sales companies quickly ran out of products that sold much better than forecasted, while they had to take back products whose sales were well below forecast. The value of such returned products had been somewhat over ¥2 billion in 1987.

Improving the Flow of Information from Retail Stores

Relying on salesmen to transmit information, recorded by hand, about estimated sales at the stores they visited made it difficult for Cosmetics Division managers to get accurate, timely data about retail sales trends. The variation in total demand from month to month made it even more difficult to predict the demand for individual items accurately enough to ensure adequate supplies from the factory. Therefore, the Cosmetic Division had been working for several years to develop better methods for obtaining data about product sales from its retail stores.

Its first attempt was the so-called "Sellable Store" system, which was introduced in 1983. This system combined a POS terminal with a personal computer, and was designed for large retail stores. Such stores not only wanted to keep accurate records of the sales and inventories of different items, but also needed to maintain background information and purchase histories for individual "Member Customers." These were repeat buyers whose business was cultivated through individualized attention, including telephone calls and frequent mailings providing information about new products, skin problems, or beauty tips. The Sellable Stores system maintained these customer files, and also could generate product reorders and promotional letters automatically.

The number of stores that were potential users of this system was limited, however, by the system's monthly leasing cost of ¥30,000 to ¥50,000 and the burden of maintaining up-to-date information about customers' changing needs and preferences. The 500 or so stores that kept records for over 1,000 Member Customers each were potential users; they accounted for over 700,000 Kanebo customers. A sample of this size was expected to provide a useful indication of the purchasing behavior of the other six million or so regular buyers of Kanebo cosmetics. By early 1988 about 150 stores had adopted the system.

By 1985, with the Sellable Store system launched, Kanebo's attention turned to the development of a simpler, lower cost system that would be more appropriate for servicing its smaller retail stores. In 1987 it began experimenting with an "Electronic Diary," a hand-held computer with a removable IC Memory card that salesmen used to record the stocks of various Kanebo products in the stores they called on. Periodically the information on this memory card was transmitted to Division headquarters, and used in estimating sales rates. The capability of this simple device was limited, however, by the frequency with which the salesman could call upon a store and count its stocks.

Dissatisfaction with this approach led Kanebo to begin designing a simpler version of the Sellable Stores system. This new system would not be required to maintain individual customer files, so it would not have to accept information from a keyboard, but would provide information about the daily sales of each product. This would both facilitate the reordering process and provide more accurate information about demand patterns for diagnostic purposes. It was known that both Shiseido and Kao were developing such systems.

There was debate among Kanebo managers about the relative merits of a system based on a low-cost personal computer, which could both provide promotional information at the store level and collect sales data for periodic transmission to headquarters, or one based on a large telecommunications network. The second type of system could provide a wider range of more sophisticated information through a powerful central computer. The systems being designed by Shiseido and Kao were of the first type, but Kanebo was leaning toward adopting the second. Personal computers with sufficient capabilities cost around 800,000 yen without a printer. Although they could transmit 80 to 100 characters per second, transmission of graphic material took much longer, and retail stores were required to input information through a typewriter keyboard. Kanebo proposed to build a system around NTT's newly developed CAPTAIN (**C**haracter **A**nd **P**attern **T**elephone **A**ccess **I**nformation **N**etwork) system, which was expected to have about 80,000 subscribers by the end of 1988 and 110,000 by the end of 1990. If it went ahead with this approach, Kanebo would be the first company in Japan to base a nationwide retail store information system on the CAPTAIN system.

The proposed "BellCap" (a combination of Kanebo's familiar symbol and CAPTAIN) system was composed of a POS register, equipped with a wand capable of reading bar-coded information that could then be stored on a removable IC memory card, and a low-cost color terminal attached to a telephone outlet. Kanebo was in the process of designing the POS register with Mitsubishi Electric, which would then manufacture them, while NTT would provide the terminal. Kanebo was modifying this terminal so that it could accept information from the removable memory card and transmit its contents periodically to division headquarters. It also proposed to design a low-cost printer to attach to the terminal; this would enable the store to obtain a hard copy of information displayed on the terminal. The terminal did not contain a keyboard, but the operator could request assistance and certain kinds of information by using the wand to select from among a number of bar-coded instructions. The system was designed to be simple enough that an eight-year-old child could operate it.

Data could be transmitted to the store's video terminal very rapidly, enabling "snapshot" images to be displayed (transmission took around 1 minute per single shot, about 4 times faster than if a personal computer were used). Sequences of such images could be used to promote selected products or assist in beauty consultation. The store could also use the system to keep track of inventories and transmit replenishment orders to its sales company, thereby speeding up the delivery of high selling items. Moreover, store managers and customers would have access to all the data in the CAPTAIN data bank. This enabled them to order tickets to various events, make hotel reservations, and obtain information about what nearby stores were having sales, where child care facilities were located, the weather forecast for different parts of Japan, etc. Finally, store managers could use the system to assist them in evaluating their store's performance and in guiding changes. For example, they could ask the system to provide graphs comparing their sales with those of the average store in Japan or their local area.

The great advantage of this system over a PC-based system was its very low telecommunication cost. The usual telephone charge for a local call in Japan was only ¥10 for three minutes, but this rate rose rapidly as the distance increased. For example, the same amount would pay for only

10 seconds of a call at night between Tokyo and Osaka, a distance of 300 miles. The cost of communicating anywhere in Japan over the CAPTAIN system, however, was ¥10 per minute during the day and ¥6 per minute at night. Large blocks of information could be transmitted very quickly to a BellCap terminal, which could then store this information in its memory for repeated play. As a result, it was anticipated that the store would only have to be connected to the system ten to twenty minutes each day.

The participation of Mitsubishi Electric, NTT, and NTS (the company providing the video-text network) in developing the BellCap system reduced Kanebo's development cost to about ¥35 million. Mitsubishi was not a market leader in the POS register business, and regarded the BellCap project as a way to acquire advanced technology and experience. Kanebo proposed to lease the BellCap system to stores at ¥12,000 per month, ¥5,000 less than its actual cost. Alternatively, stores could purchase the system for about ¥1 million, about 30% of which was for the CAPTAIN terminal. In either case the stores would pay their own transmission cost.

Through this system Kanebo hoped to achieve four goals. First, by establishing closer linkages with its stores and enabling them to provide better service to their customers, it hoped to build stronger loyalty to Kanebo products among store managers. This was particularly critical in the case of stores selling competitors' products as well as Kanebo's. Second, it hoped that store customers would be so pleased by the additional information the system made available to them that they would buy more Kanebo products. Third, Kanebo expected that the daily information provided by the system would help it in identifying emerging consumer trends. This would be useful in crafting promotional campaigns and guiding new product development.

Finally, access to daily information would help Kanebo improve the efficiency of both its marketing and manufacturing operations. Analysis of each store's sales would enable marketing to identify those stores that were selling certain products at more than the average rate (so that the approaches they were using could be studied and applied to other stores) or less (in which case they might benefit from a salesman's assistance). Just as important, information about daily sales would improve production scheduling, and enable the factory to make better use of its limited capacity. Such information was particularly valuable early in a selling season, as Kanebo's marketing people believed the ultimate success of a newly-introduced product was largely determined during the first couple of weeks after its introduction.

Kanebo proposed to introduce the BellCap system, on an experimental basis, to 30 of its larger stores in late-1988. If it worked satisfactorily, another 400 stores would be added to the network. Assuming that enough stores volunteered to adopt BellCap, Kanebo hoped that 3,000 stores would be involved by 1993, and 7,000 by 1995. Moreover, direct transmission of orders would allow Kanebo to reduce from 250 to 100 the number of people currently occupied with receiving and summarizing the daily barrage of orders received by telephone and fax.

The Internal Debate

The critics of the proposed BellCap system were uneasy both about basing it on the CAPTAIN system and whether it would be accepted by the retail stores. Some argued against BellCap on technological grounds. "Already over two million people in Japan are using PC's," one person stated, "but only a few thousand have ever used the CAPTAIN system. Moreover, given the way computer technology is evolving it is reasonable to expect that soon we could install a very powerful PC, having much broader uses, in a store for less than the leasing cost of the BellCap system." Another pointed out that, while stores could receive information very quickly through the BellCap system, they could only transmit at a rate of 8 characters per second. "Transmitting sales information back to Division headquarters could turn out to be very expensive for them," he observed.

Others based their criticism on the effect the proposed system would have on store managers and Kanebo salesmen. "The stores will not adopt this system, even if we reduced its cost to nothing, unless they feel it will improve their sales and simplify their jobs," stated one person. "Instead, it appears to complicate their jobs, and it is not clear that it will improve their sales. Moreover, they will resist being monitored so closely."

Another talked about the reaction of Kanebo's salesmen. "The BellCap system will have to be sold to our retail stores and their managers trained to use it effectively. This will simply add to the burden on our salesmen, who already work very hard. And what will be their reward for this added work? If the computer becomes the source of all important information, and the main communication link with the company, what is there left for the salesman to do?" he asked. "And what pride can he take in his job?"

Still others observed that stores selling other companies' cosmetics (as well as Kanebo's) would probably be reluctant to use the BellCap system to record the sale of competitors' products, as this would transmit competitive information to Kanebo. This implied that they would have to use different methods for recording sales, depending on whose product was being purchased. Worse, when Shiseido came out with a competing system, the store might have to lease both systems—in addition to the electronic cash registers that many of them were already leasing.

Others pointed to the problems the BellCap system would create for manufacturing. "It will provide more data than the factory can use," argued one. "Our purchasing/manufacturing system is basically not very flexible, and continual changes in the production schedule will simply cause confusion and inefficiency." Another was concerned that faster feedback from the retail stores would simply relieve the sales organization of the pressure to develop good forecasts. "This just gives them an excuse to dump their mistakes on the factory more frequently, and expect it to solve their problems for them. Besides, getting more accurate forecasts requires that several thousand stores adopt BellCap, and even under the most optimistic projections we won't have that many stores on the system for at least five years."

Improving the factory's flexibility, of course, was the goal of the proposed FMS bottling line. Developing a prototype of this line had taken Kanebo engineers several years. It had been improved to the point where it could now change from one shaped bottle to another, under computer control, in less than one hour. At least three people were needed to operate the line, which bottled at the same rate as Kanebo's standard lines. The high cost of the FMS, combined with uncertainty about whether and when it would achieve its goals of single-digit (less than 10 minutes) changeover times and a single operator had delayed its introduction. Also, it was still not possible to handle very small (50 milliliter or less) bottles, which Kanebo used for its most expensive skin lotions. Finally, it was not known how much of the potential capacity of the FMS lines could be utilized. It was becoming so difficult to persuade workers to work outside of normal hours, many people felt it was unlikely the lines could be operated more than two shifts (90 hours) a week.

Converting an existing skin care bottling line to one that was both automated and could fill different sized bottles was estimated to cost about ¥270 million, while converting a lipstick line would cost over ¥120 million. These estimates were for hardware costs alone; the cost of the software that had been created by Kanebo personnel was not included. These costs were somewhat over twice the cost of one of the semi-automated bottling lines that Kanebo had purchased in the early 1980s.

"Clearly, it is difficult to justify such an expenditure on the basis of labor savings alone," commented Mr. Ishizawa. "But can we justify it on the basis of the additional flexibility it will give us? And how many new lines will we have to install in order to make a significant improvement in the ability of the factory to respond to large changes in sales forecasts?"

CHAPTER 19

Daewoo Shipbuilding and Heavy Machinery

W ITH THE SOUND OF THE WAVES of the East China Sea kissing the shore of Kŏje island, Park Dong-Kyu, executive vice-president and General Manager of Daewoo Shipbuilding and Heavy Machinery (DSHM), Ltd. looked out over the ocean and considered the course that lay ahead.

By 1994, DSHM had become one of the most efficient shipbuilding companies in the world. Probably more important, DSHM had recently benchmarked itself, and found its Okpo shipyard to be the fastest improving. Over the seven years between 1987 and 1994, Daewoo had built what many companies were still striving for: a plant that had learned how to learn—and was becoming better at it every day.

Despite DSHM's meteoric improvement path, there remained two driving goals which had eluded even the most inventive shipbuilding companies: speed and productivity. Construction lead time was becoming one of the key competitive elements in the industry. Daewoo's major competitors had each announced a major capital investment project to speed up their manufacturing process, and become more productive. Daewoo had no such plans, relying instead on the promise of continued gains from its unique improvement methods, rather than further capital investment to maintain its targeted 10% share of the world shipbuilding industry.

It was a gamble. Could the shipyard continue to improve as it had over the past five years, and would this incremental path provide the needed capacity?

DSHM

Daewoo's Okpo shipyard made a wide variety of vessel types, including crude oil carriers, gas carriers, chemical tankers and container ships. In

This case was prepared by Professor David Upton and Doctoral Student Bowon Kim as the basis for class discussion rather than an illustration of either effective or ineffective handling of an administrative situation. Names and data have been disguised.

1992, DSHM built 1.7 million gross tonnes (GT)—about 10% of total world production of 18 million GT—and made a net profit of $280m. DSHM's quality and productivity were, by 1994, among the best in the world. Order books were full until 1995 and the yard was held up throughout Korea as a paragon of manufacturing performance.

Upheaval in 1987

Things had not always been so bright. Daewoo acquired the shipyard from the near-bankrupt Okpo Shipbuilding Company in 1978—primarily as a result of some government arm-twisting, as part of South Korea's industrial restructuring policy. At the time, the shipyard was only 25% complete. Daewoo completed construction of the yard and its first vessel floated into the East China Sea in 1982.

It was not an easy year. In its first full year of operation, DSHM suffered a loss of $9 million on sales of $485 million, and for the next few years, Daewoo struggled with the challenges of building a new business in the face of a continuing world recession in shipbuilding.

As if these troubles were not enough, 1987 saw South Korea gripped by political unrest, and DSHM soon became part of a political firestorm that pulled even the healthiest Korean firms close to the flames. Throughout Korea, the democratic movement swept through workplaces, and newly organized labor unions demanded radical changes in the distribution of wealth and social status. The dispute at the Okpo shipyard was particularly harsh.

The labor dispute hewed deep wounds in the isolated community on the island of Kŏje. DSHM came close to total collapse, and many were concerned that the vitriolic battle was destroying any future chance the fledgling shipyard might have had to compete in the world market. Kim Woo-Choong, Chairman of the Daewoo group, was determined that the plant be saved, and in 1987 flew onto Kŏje island to personally supervise DSHM's rebirth.

DSHM: Tragic End to Violent Labor Demonstration: one man dead and 20 injured

Chasun Ilbo, August 23, 1987.

The bitter labor dispute between DSHM workers and management reached new depths yesterday, when workers responded to management's decision to close the yard by laying siege to the plant and its president. One worker died and 20 others were injured during the clash with riot police guarding the Okpo Tourist Hotel, where DSHM President Yoon was staying. Twelve companies of riot police blocked the road to the hotel firing tear gas into the crowds of angry workers hurling stones. In the melee, Lee Suk-Kyu, an assembly worker, was hit in the chest by a tear-gas canister and was taken to hospital, where he died at 3.45 pm yesterday afternoon.

The Shipbuilding Industry

The locus of power in the Shipbuilding industry had traditionally been moved from region to region—as each region took advantage of particular skills or materials (see inset). By 1992, Japan and Korea had emerged as the world's shipbuilding giants, accounting for close to 42% and 25% of global production respectively (see Exhibit 19.1). Despite Japan's continued dominance, it was in Korea that the most dramatic changes had taken place. The 1980s saw explosive growth in Korean shipbuilding: In 1980, Korean companies had accounted for less than 4% of the world's output (versus the 47% for Japanese companies at that time). While the focus of the competitive war was Japan, Koreans were keenly aware of the possibility of new

Exhibit 19.1   Ship Construction by Country (Unit: 1,000 GT)

YEAR	DSHM PROFIT % OF SALES	GT	JAPAN	KOREA	GERMANY[a]	U.K.	CHINA	FRANCE	DENMARK	U.S.A.	WORLD[b]
1980	10	1	6094	522	722	427	-	283	208	240	13101
1981	-1.7	80	8400	929	1061	213	30	502	352	311	16932
1982	10	400	8163	1401	958	435	135	265	451	459	16820
1983	10	350	6670	1539	1135	497	259	308	444	345	15911
1984	12	890	9711	1473	884	445	329	327	474	822	18434
1985	25	840	9503	2620	920	172	166	200	458	278	18157
1986	25	720	8178	3642	877	99	258	158	361	383	16845
1987	25	780	5708	2091	633	194	286	167	243	342	12259
1988	-42	300	4040	3174	813	60	254	72	377	453	10909
1989	-20	1000	5365	3102	718	102	325	160	343	405	13236
1990	10	980	6824	3460	857	131	367	60	395	15	15885
1991	20	1550	7193	3491	803	180	292	107	430	-	18254
1992	30	1668	7569	4502	882	228	346	131	534	54	18198
1993	35	920	7850	3382	NA	NA	NA	NA	NA	NA	17831
1994	35	1870	7106	5480	NA	NA	NA	NA	NA	NA	18700

[a]German data include West and East Germanies before 1990.
[b]The world total figures from 1976 to 1979 are 33906, 27532, 17594, and 13727, respectively.

entrants from developing countries, such as China, who might achieve the same kinds of success as they themselves had in the previous decade.

As well as fierce international competition with Japan, the Korean industry was also characterized by intense domestic competition from five Korean companies: Hyundai, Daewoo, Samsung, Hanjin, and Halla (see Exhibit 19.2). Domestic competition was becoming more of a concern for

Exhibit 19.2   Shipbuilding Facilities and Ship Construction of Korean Companies in 1992

COMPANIES	# OF BUILDING DRY DOCKS	TOTAL CAPACITY (DWT[a])	CONSTRUCTION IN '92 (GT)
Hyundai	7	3,015,000	1,863,200
Daewoo	2	1,362,000	1,668,425
Samsung	2	315,000	712,417
Hanjin	2	210,000	104,220
Halla	-	-	141,000

[a]DWT stands for Dead Weight Tonnage, a vessel's carrying capacity.

"Until the first half of the nineteenth century, at a time when 90 percent of the world's merchant vessels were still made of wood, the United States was an undisputed leader in the shipbuilding industry with its abundant supply of cheap timber. With the advent of the steam-powered steel ship, however, the supremacy of the U.S. shipwright was quickly eroded by the British shipbuilders, who by 1882 captured 80 percent of the world's ship-building market. In the post-World War II period, the British shipbuilders succumbed to the other Western European shipbuilders who by then commanded the most sophisticated technologies. Before long, however, these Western European shipbuilders lost their market share leadership to the Japanese. By 1965, Japan firmly established its leadership and held on to it with about 50 percent of the world market. Today, a potent challenge to the indomitable Japanese shipbuilders is coming from Korea, and its prospect for overtaking the Japanese seems to be within reach. Toward the end of the twentieth century, however, China may well emerge as the industry leader"

Dong Sung Cho and Michael E. Porter in "Competition in Global Industries" p. 539 HBS Press 1986

Daewoo, since it appeared that, despite industry over-capacity, a number of firms planned to increase their shipbuilding capacity in the near future. While Daewoo had decided not to make such an expansion, it was not entering the fray unarmed. Its weapons were buried deep in the heart of its manufacturing process.

Building Ships at Daewoo SHM

The process of building a ship was primarily characterized by the huge scale on which manufacturing operations were carried out. The production process at DSHM is shown in Figure 19.1. First, raw materials (mainly steel sheet) transported by sea were discharged onto the Unloading Quay. The incoming pieces of raw material then passed through the Treatment Line where they were blast-treated and physically re-arranged before passing to the Cutting Shop. While a small stamping shop might be able to juggle pieces of sheet steel in a simple stockroom, the sheer size of the slabs of steel coming into DSHM demanded careful thought about which sheet of steel should lie at the top of the pile to await cutting.

In the Cutting Shop, the steel was cut by Computer Numerical Control (CNC) into appropriate shapes and sizes for the subsequent production steps. After preliminary assembly, flat steel components were sent to the Panel Block Shop—(a 300m long production line, with side wings for sub-assembly), while other components passed into the 3-Dimensional Shop. In the Panel Block shop (PBS), the large rectangular-shaped body parts of the ship were built. These blocks weighed between 200 and 400 tonnes. Steel stock passed through a frame planer (where

Figure 19.1   Ship Construction at Daewoo SHM

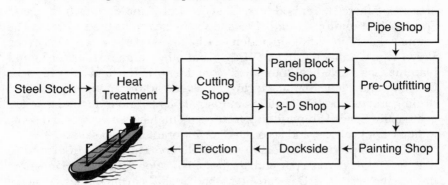

additional surface treatment was applied), then through initial welding stages, sub-assembly and fitting through to final welding and outfitting. In the 3-D shop, plates and components needing complex curvature were bent, line-heated, sub-assembled and eventually welded together as a module. Blocks from the Panel Block Shop as well as modules from the 3-D Shop moved to the pre-outfitting Shop where unit and block outfitting was done (installing such parts as pipes, machinery and electric cables), and subsequently to the Painting Shop. These completed large blocks and curved modules were then put together to build gigantic pre-erection blocks. The use of these *superblocks* made DSHM unique.

A ship was usually built by laying a keel in a dry dock, and progressively building the ship from the keel up, using comparatively small and light pre-built subassemblies. DSHM's process was completely different. DSHM pre-erected enormous superblocks at the side of the dry dock which were then assembled in the dock like a giant Lego™ kit. Pre-erection was difficult: it required tremendous accuracy in manufacturing. Each of the blocks was a whole section through the ship, replete with pipes, wiring conduits, and occasionally half a room! These components had to fit perfectly together once built. While this would have been difficult even in a smaller scale assembly process, it was made much more challenging by the fact that many of the blocks were the size of office buildings. However, the advantages of overcoming this problem were also great. First, pre-erection required much less labor than dry-dock erection since welding and outfitting could be carried out at convenient angles and away from restrictive, inaccessible places. Second, a shipyard's primary bottleneck was usually its dry-dock, and pre-erection essentially rebalanced the line, and improved the output of the yard. Daewoo SHM also had the advantage of the world's largest dry-dock and—a necessity for building with the world's largest Lego set—the largest crane in the world.

By early 1994, DSHM was on track to achieve the annual sales goal of $2 billion by building 1.9 million Gross Tonnes, and had already filled

1995's order book. With 11,000 workers, DSHM operated in three major areas: Commercial Shipbuilding, Offshore and Plant Manufacturing, and Special Shipbuilding. Exhibit 19.3 shows the layout of the shipyard. The commercial shipbuilding operation was hallmarked by vessels such as the Very Large Crude-oil Carrier (VLCC), and other large carriers for Liquid Natural Gas (LNG), automobiles, containers, and chemical products. Offshore and Plant Manufacturing involved the production of offshore drilling and exploration facilities, industrial plants, and industrial machinery. Finally, Special Shipbuilding focused on high-speed vessels and some military applications, and accounted for 7% of total dollar sales.

DSHM's productivity, quality, and delivery time had all improved so that by 1994 it was on a par with the best in the global industry. Even more impressive was that Daewoo SHM had made startling improvements without heavy capital outlay (see Exhibit 19.7). The number of labor-hours (LH) needed to build a VLCC had, for example, been reduced from 1.3 million in 1990 to about 0.65 million LH in 1993. The leadtime to build a VLCC had come down from 14 months in 1990 to 9 months in 1993.

Exhibit 19.3   Shipyard Layout

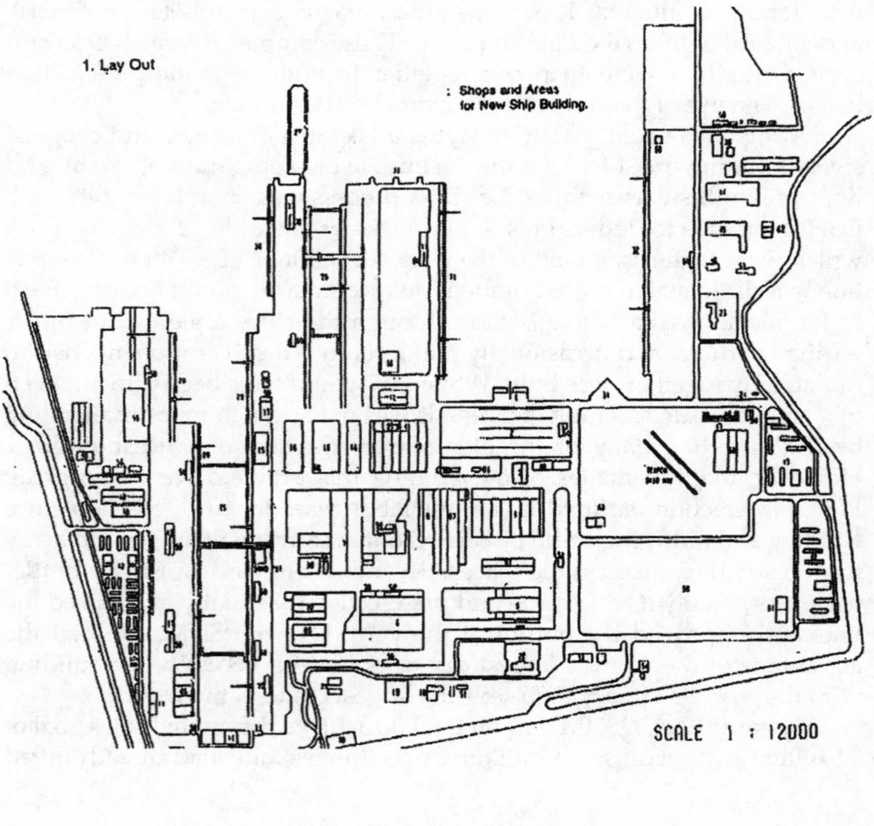

1. Lay Out

: Shops and Areas for New Ship Building.

SCALE   1 : 12000

During the same period, the defect rate had shrunk from 20% to virtually 0.5%, and the accident rate from around 10% of the workforce per year to less than 1%. Not only had Daewoo SHM been saved from disaster in 1987, it had been set on a path which improved its performance—and for a number of years had improved the *rate* at which performance improvements were gained. While everyone remembered the bad times back in 1987, most often remembered were the experiences and actions that brought the plant back from the edge of the abyss.

Back from the Brink
Family Values

Korea had historically been culturally distinct from neighboring countries such as China and Japan, and these roots, along with many periods of adversity, had fuelled a strong sense of collective identity among Koreans. The influence of Confucianism had contributed to the view that the family was the backbone of the nation as well as society as a whole.

The 1987 dispute had been painful and divisive for everyone and both management and the union knew that neither was likely to benefit from continued disruption. Yet resolution seemed difficult to find. Daewoo management eventually took the initiative to resolve the crisis and Chairman Kim's personal action—to go and live with the plant—sent a strong signal of Daewoo's commitment to the shipyard to both union workers and field managers.

Kim's first step was to heal the deep wounds in the relationship between management and union, and to begin to build renewed trust among them. Kim started a *'unity movement'* which played on traditional Korean values and encouraged both sides to begin to act like members of the same family. The company sponsored a family training program which also included members of the community as a whole as well as its own workers' families. It also sponsored cultural events, and a variety of education programs. Many employess were single men so Daewoo sponsored opportunities for the single men to meet single women from other Daewoo affiliated companies (for example, in electronics and textiles).

Training and Education

The most important initiative addressed the training and educational needs of the hourly staff. First, the entire workforce was divided into small groups, each comprising 10 to 15 members. This small group structure became the primary unit from which the on-going improvement endeavor was built. Education and training were based on this close-knit small group structure.

Training began with operators rather than supervisors. "A small group is like the roots of a tree. If these roots are healthy, the tree will flourish" observed Mr. Chung. The course addressed the following subjects:

1. Motivation for change and commitment
2. Technical knowledge of the job
3. Quality Improvement Techniques
4. Safety Improvement

Instructors were generally experienced Daewoo workers in the company rather than outside experts—though these new instructors attended external education centers to learn new and more efficient techniques. Having completed the external program, they came back to the company and taught their fellow workers.

Education and training were not just confined to directly applicable work skills. Daewoo was keen to use training as part of a new benchmarking process:

> We sent our employees, both field workers and managers at all ranks, to the most efficient Japanese manufacturers[1] for benchmarking as well as education and training. We sent *all* employees, not just managers or a particular group of workers. The reason was that we believed workers could do the best job of benchmarking when they saw their best competitors doing their own jobs. For instance, a welder on the line is the best person to benchmark welding. He can compare his skill against that of the best welder in the world. Likewise, the welder himself is the one who can derive most benefit from observing the benchmarked welding process.
>
> —Suh Wan-Chul, Executive Managing Director

By 1994, more than half of the workforce had been through the education and training program.

An additional benefit of the small-group-based training scheme was that the members in a small group came to know one another extremely well. A production process based on the same small group structure was then a logical and effective work unit. Moreover, since managers had participated in the education program alongside operators, trust began to be rekindled between the two parties—and common goals again became clear. Once it became clear that each group's fate was tightly intertwined, things began to change. Operators began to become active in making suggestions to improve inefficient operations or eliminate excessive

---

[1]Group level corporate relationships were leveraged to allow this close observation. Japanese manufacturers were careful, however, to keep secret those processes they considered to be core technologies (such as parts of the design process).

consumption of resources. In turn, Daewoo management devised an incentive system to encourage and reward such suggestions, and also tried to build a process for more systematic learning and experimentation for those problems requiring a higher level of engineering expertise.

Dynamic Scheduling

This new way of working demanded radical changes in other areas of operations in the plant. An important change was the move away from tight command-and-control based scheduling. The old system had demanded workers simply "do the job"—in and at the allotted time, with very little flexibility. To fit and encourage the growing atmosphere of trust, a new dynamic scheduling system was devised, building on the strengths of the small group structure.

While aggregate project scheduling was still carried out centrally (though now by a computer-based Artificial Intelligence (AI) program), an important departure from tradition was made: The recognition that the most important events in any scheduling scheme were unexpected ones. Scheduling could never be perfect since such events were inevitable. In the past, schedule slippage in one part of the process affected all subsequent processes and resulted in disproportionately long leadtime increases, low productivity, and poor quality.

The dynamic scheduling system shifted the power to allocate short-term resources from the computer system to the people on the floor. Daewoo's new planning system was based on aggregation and disaggregation (see Exhibit 19.4). At the aggregation stage, the overall schedule was constructed using the AI system. This dealt with the problems of scheduling resources for the construction of multiple ships in the yard over the course of a year or so. A good aggregate schedule was vital to the plant, since level utilization of people, materials handling devices, and capital equipment throughout the year was critical for overall performance of any shipyard. At DSHM, there were often more than 10 vessels at various stages of production. With lead times of nine months or so, scheduling was a daunting task. Even though scheduling the yard was a complex matter, and required a high-level of expertise, the harder problem had always been making the schedule happen, rather than the development of the plan.

Unless plans were effectively implemented at a detailed "blow-by-blow" level (the disaggregated level), the overall performance of the schedule would be unpredictably distant from the original projection. Such random schedule departures had been a common feature of operations in the past, and had become competitively unacceptable.

For this reason, a grand scheduling experiment was devised. Rather than trying to make a schedule happen by direct execution commands from the computer system, detailed planning at the disaggregate level was delegated to the foremen of the small groups.

Exhibit 19.4 Dynamic Scheduling

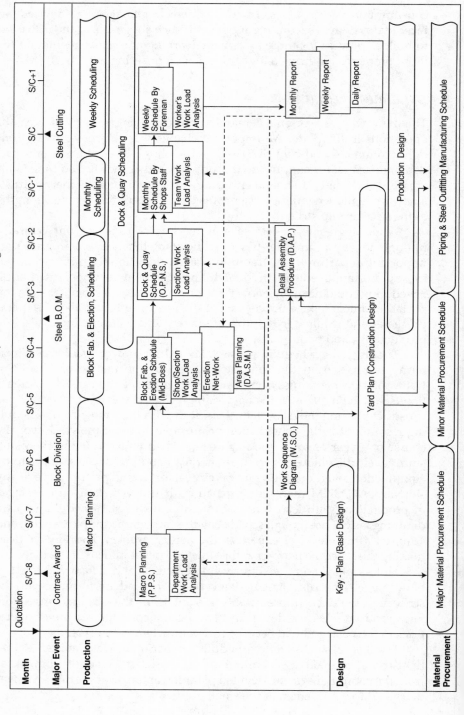

All the monthly and some of the weekly workforce allocation was carried out by the senior foremen, who were in charge of several of the small groups. These monthly and weekly plans were further refined by the foremen at the small group meetings each Monday. The product of these meetings were detailed weekly and daily plans (as well as the resolution of problems related to productivity, safety, quality and morale). On the Friday morning of the same week, the foreman had to evaluate the progress made during the week and determined whether the goal set up on Monday had been met or not. If the week's target had been met, then the following week's plan could be implemented according to the aggregate schedule. Otherwise, it had to be revised by the group to incorporate the remaining portion of the week's work into the following week's workload. Slippage problems thus became the group's problems.

In most cases, the single small group could adjust its weekly workload to accommodate any minor scheduling slippage. Should it not be able to cope with a particularly severe or serious slippage, then the senior foreman in charge of that group could reallocate people among the groups he oversaw. If things became so difficult that even the senior foreman could not resolve things, then, and only then, did it become his responsibility to inform the management of the yard. Managers might then readjust the workload allocation among senior foremen, and (if absolutely necessary) revise the overall scheduling plan for the shipyard as a whole and promulgate it. Information thus flowed continuously in both directions: from the aggregate to the disaggregate level, and from the disaggregate to the aggregate.

Cutting Waste and Lost Time from the Manufacturing System

Over the next few years, as part of an ongoing policy of identifying opportunities for improvement without investing large sums of capital, Daewoo SHM began to develop methods for systematically reducing waste in materials and time from the plant. These methods again relied strongly on the educational foundations that had been laid, and encouraged people to recognize that the greatest gains were likely to result in a series of small improvements over time—each of which provided a platform for more improvement—rather than one or two immediate big hits. As the number of improvements made increased, people learned to look for prospective sources of waste reduction as a matter of course.

Cells in the Cutting Shop A typical example of this philosophy translated into action was the layout change in the Cutting Shop. The Cutting Shop comprised seven bays, each of which operated as separate processing lines.

Before improvement, each bay was dedicated to a few particular types of steel stock, or particular processes. The components for each block were therefore cut in different bays, and considerable time was wasted in collecting together the exact set of components for a block. Moreover, the fact that each block made different demands on each of the processing bays meant that the allocation of work between them was often uneven. To address this problem, the cutting shop layout was changed so that each bay could cut a variety of shapes of steel stock, and be temporarily dedicated to the production of a particular module. In order to accommodate this, each bay had to be made much more flexible. However, this flexibility required little additional capital investment—though it did demand more careful sorting of raw materials before the Cutting Shop stage, more understanding of the production process by the operators, and dynamic allocation of labor.

Daewoo Specific Improvement

Although improvement programs like these were frequently seen in other manufacturing firms, and seemed straightforward enough for other companies to emulate, most improvement steps were devised in a way that was unique and specific to DSHM's particular structure. Indeed, even those structural features which would have caused many firms to look to reconfiguring the system with new capital investment, were turned to DSHM's advantage.

For example, the value of the huge investments in the Goliath crane and the Dry Dock hinged on Daewoo's ability to schedule these hungry overhead monsters effectively. As time went on, many shipbuilders had become skeptical about these investments, and saw them as albatrosses around Daewoo's neck, which they may well have become without some clever maneuvering in operations. Thus, a number of initiatives grew out of turning seemingly handicapping features to great advantage. Two such initiatives were *pre-erection* and the *dock operating system*.

Goliath and Pre-Erection The shipyard had two dry docks. Dock 1 was 530m × 131m, and was served by the Goliath gantry crane—the largest in the world. Goliath was designed by Krupp with a width of 200m, and a capacity of 900 tonnes. Since Goliath spanned Dock 1, the difference between the width of the crane and the dry-dock, about 70m, was available for use as a pre-erection area. As described above, there were great advantages in completing as much assembly as possible before the erection in the Dry Dock (provided, of course, that the work could be done with sufficient accuracy). However, in most shipyards, the proportion of work that could be done in pre-erection was limited by the capacity of the crane. For the Daewoo shipyard—with its huge crane—this was not a problem. DSHM could use Goliath for both pre-erection and erection in the dock. To build a VLCC, over 200 super blocks were needed. Without

Exhibit 19.5   Goliath Crane

Goliath, most of the 200 blocks would have to be assembled in the Dry Dock. By using Goliath, Daewoo could assemble super blocks in the Pre-Erection area, so that by 1992, only 80 super blocks were being assembled in the Dry Dock. DSHM could complete more than 85% of the shipbuilding operation before the Dry Dock (compared with 50% in 1990). The benefit of the increased pre-erection operation was dramatically reduced leadtime because of the simplicity of pre-erection compared to Dry Dock erection.

The Dock Operating System In the past, the shipyard built several vessels in the Dry Dock simultaneously (Figure 19.2). The result was a poorly balanced workload. Sometimes, everyone in the yard would be busy, at others, people would be waiting around. The busy, labor-constrained times resulted in poor dock utilization. To rectify the problem, DSHM changed the dock operating system so that Dock 1 was devoted to building only VLCCs.

After the change, Dock 1 built two full-VLCCs and 2 half-VLCCs concurrently. Once the two full-vessels were completed, the dock was filled with sea water to float them out of the dock, and the two half-sized VLCCs were moved to the dock door so that they could be built up to full-size. The result of this change was a well-balanced workload in the Dry Dock over the whole production cycle and an increase in dry dock utilization.

Figure 19.2   New Dry-Dock Operating System

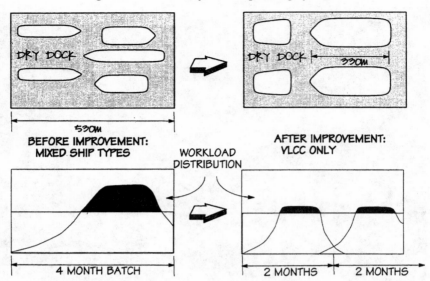

Continuous Improvement and Discrete Leaps

Paradoxically, the primary advantage of continuous improvement in quality for Daewoo was that it provided opportunities for step-improvement in lead times. Two conspicuous examples of this were the change from *rigid matrix* to *in-line construction* in the panel block shop and *propeller installation*. Both operations required extremely accurate welding. The new levels of accuracy ultimately allowed DSHM to make step changes in the overall manufacturing process.

Step Change in the Panel Block Shop Environmental concerns had meant that most new super-tankers (VLCC) were double-hulled. If the outer hull became punctured, an inner hull would retain the contents of the vessel. A double hull was constructed from a criss-cross arrangement of T-beams sandwiched between two skin plates. The fabrication of these structures gave rise to one of the primary bottleneck operations. With the traditional levels of welding and marking accuracy, the design of the matrix structure had to provide large slack spaces when assembling T-bar frames onto the skin plates and accompanying web structures (see Figure 19.3).

In order to close the slack space accommodating jigging & cutting errors, operators had to patch it with a small collar plate. The need for this time-consuming operation was eventually removed by using a direct insertion method, which relied on making web-structures accurately enough to be inserted through the T-bar frames *without* any slack. This

Figure 19.3 Collar Plate and Insertion

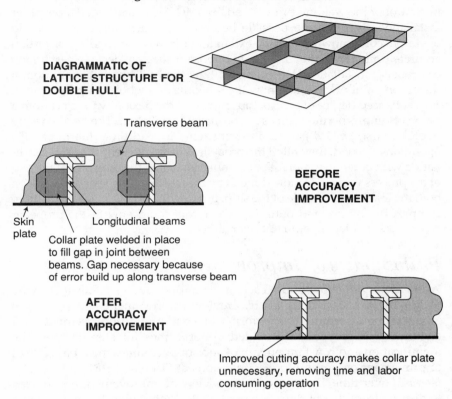

DIAGRAMMATIC OF
LATTICE STRUCTURE FOR
DOUBLE HULL

Transverse beam

BEFORE
ACCURACY
IMPROVEMENT

Skin
plate

Longitudinal beams

Collar plate welded in place
to fill gap in joint between
beams. Gap necessary because
of error build up along transverse beam

AFTER
ACCURACY
IMPROVEMENT

Improved cutting accuracy makes collar plate
unnecessary, removing time and labor
consuming operation

became possible only because of progressive improvement in accuracy of welding and marking, and completely eliminated a severe bottleneck in the shipbuilding process.

Propeller Installation Another example of continuous improvement leading to step change was in propeller installation (see Figure 19.3). Generally, the propeller was installed in the last stages building a ship. Conventional wisdom held that this had to be so since the installation of a propeller required a very high level of accuracy—the propeller had to be exactly centered with the rest of the ship. Unfortunately, the distortion of the hull caused by welding meant that it was unwise to install a propeller too soon—all relevant welding distortion had to be undergone before installing the propeller.

Because distortion precluded the parallel installation of a propeller with other parts of the ship, propeller installation time translated directly into lead time. It was also an unpredictable process and it could therefore prolong completion time without warning. However, the progressive improvement in control of the welding process had, by 1992, facilitated parallel propeller installation. This became possible because manufacturing engineers and operators could now predict the extent and direction of welding distortion accurately enough so that they could opportunistically select the best timing of propeller installation depending on how the hull was behaving from a distortion point of view, and how the schedule as a whole was playing out. This enhanced degree of control thus provided the flexibility to select from a range of (unprespecified) times for propeller installation. The benefits were twofold. First, DSHM gained a direct saving in lead time due to parallel operations. Second, they fitted the propeller at a convenient time for coordination with other operations. For example, installing the propeller at the end of the process was made more difficult by the fact that people had to work on both the inside and outside of the ship, in an awkward 3D space made more complex by fixtures and outfitting. Operators could now fit the propeller before such spatial impediments were fitted.

Philosophies of Improvement

As the examples above show, each of the improvements made at Daewoo SHM built on foundations laid by previous improvements—step changes in operations permitted new forms of continuous improvement, and continuous improvement provided opportunities for step change. The identification and constant pursuit of such opportunities meant the rate of improvement on a number of dimensions at Daewoo SHM had initially *increased* over time. Daewoo operators' view of improvement had started to diverge from that of their Japanese rivals. Rather than seeing improvement as a process of slowly exhausting a static pool of possibilities (as a European competitor might see things), or even of continually drawing from vast, an apparently inexhaustible pool of improvement opportunities (as a Japanese firm might see things), Daewoo SHM began to see improvement as a *way of providing opportunities for more improvement*, and selected improvement projects by the same criterion.

At the core of this explosive improvement mentality had been a relentless learning capability nurtured and systematized by the education and training programs begun in 1988. At a deeper level, many saw the change of mindset as a result of a "spiritual endeavor" which bonded both management and workers. This spiritual unity (described by many people in the plant) powered the incessant drive for small improvements—which became the purpose of the plant. After a year or two, these improvements were flooding from virtually everywhere in the shipyard, as if the energy spent in conflict had only one place to go. Improvement and more improvement. Great pains were taken to harness this work, through careful integration and channeling of improvement, and the forging of new links between management and operators.

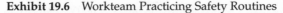

Exhibit 19.6   Workteam Practicing Safety Routines

The View from the Bridge

Our biggest challenge for the coming years will be coping with the inherent uncertainty in the market for shipbuilding.

While the recent focus has been speed, we cannot predict what the most important competitive dimensions will be *in general*, they will differ from customer to customer. We must manage the uncertainty by focusing on several strategic dimensions for improvement at once. Quality, productivity, lead-time, and product line mix may *all* need to be improved.

—Park Dong-Kyu, Executive Vice President and General Manager of the
Daewoo SHM shipyard.

Although the outlook for the world shipbuilding industry as a whole had begun to look brighter by 1994, domestic competition among Korean shipbuilding companies was becoming fiercer. Some of the big players planned to further expand capacity, despite the prevailing excess (Exhibit 19.8). With regard to the escalating domestic and international competition, Chung Uee-Dong, Director of the Management Strategy Center, pointed out:

We do not have to meet the capacity increase in the industry by increasing capacity ourselves. Improvements in productivity have almost the same effect as increasing capacity. Moreover, we have options to utilize the increased productivity in ways our competitors don't. First, we may want to use the increased productivity [and thus capacity] in the shipbuilding operation. The second option is to shift the increased capacity to our other operations such as industrial machinery or heavy equipment. This option is based on the assumption that we do not grow our 10% target market share in the world shipbuilding industry, and will be necessary in any case when the industry dives into another cycle of recession.

Although we believe we are among the best shipbuilders in the world, we know there is still ample opportunity to improve more. Recently, we completed an internal study to measure all of our processes to establish new standards. This helps us to re-benchmark. We know that we are achieving only 70% of the output that is theoretically possible from the way our current operations are configured. We will try to reach the 80% level early this year by eliminating all the losses that this new study helped us see. We believe we can achieve 100% level only if we can eliminate the less visible losses completely. In order to stay ahead, we have to reach that 100% target within a few years. However, the worrying thing is that we estimate the very best Japanese shipbuilding company would run at 120% *in our configuration.*

Now admittedly, we have built this configuration as a result of our improvement program, and it's not clear that it could be emulated, but the difference in raw productivity is a concern. Our goal is to surpass their performance level by incrementally improving our productivity standards. Continuous improvement in the standards will lead us to a much stronger competitive position. We know from bitter experience that such improvement cannot be accomplished simply by pouring more money into the hardware. That is partly why we do not want to match our competitors' capacity expansion spree. Rather, we plan to spend efficiently in softer features which we know we can build on, using techniques we have proven will work.

This was a critical gamble for Daewoo. To eschew investment in capital equipment and rely on continued internal productivity improvement meant entrusting the future of the company to the culture that had been built since the 1987 conflagration. Echoes still resounded on the shop floor. A foreman voiced his concerns:

This year will be a crucial one. Ever since the big labor dispute back in 1987, management and union have been working together.

But, now we face an even more intense environment and we need to reinforce our mutual trust firmly. Managers should spend more time on the shop floor, to communicate with the line workers, and get rid of any of the remaining barriers. They should not rely so much on the operators to look for improvements by themselves.

In the long run, Suh, Executive Managing Director, predicted:

Ten years from now, there will probably be very little change in the physical facilities in the shipyard. It will, however, become critical to speed up the entire shipbuilding process. This is the only way to continue to be superlatively productive and flexible, without committing ourselves to more capital investment. The key is building even more integration between functions and processes in the yard.

However, two mid-level managers were less sure of DSHM's strategy. Choi Dae-Soon, Deputy Manager of the NSC (New Shipbuilding Concept) Office made the following point:

I am convinced that the primary, untapped key to making the most of what we have is the progressive elimination of stochastic losses in the production process. For example, suppose the time needed to produce a panel block fluctuates between 30 and 40 days. The current scheduling mechanism would use 35 days as a standard for the formal production schedule. To be competitive, we want to move that standard towards 30 days, rather than leave it at 35. However, unless the new target is formally included in the schedule, line workers will not recognize the need to speed things up. It is up to us to find a solution to this problem—its not easy when you look at how difficult it is to schedule in the first place. The speed up must also be carried out in a consistent way across the whole of the process, not just part of it. A lot of the advantages we've achieved come from our ability to schedule our equipment better than our competitors. But we are also improving faster than they are, and want to improve even faster. This makes the whole scheduling issue even more complex.

Jang Se-Jin was another Deputy Manager in the NSC Office. He sounded a related concern:

Although the engine of our improvement has been the workers on the floor, we are now faced with the limitations of that force. In other words—we have to acknowledge that we cannot continue to improve simply by relying on more and more hard work from the

Exhibit 19.7 Improvement Results

	1990	1991	Δ	1992	Δ	1993	Δ
Total Sales (billion Won)	700	945	+35%	1195	+26%	1295	+8%
PRODUCTION (000 GROSS TONS)							
Commercial Shipbuilding	450	522	+16%	581	+11%	482	-17%
Offshore Plant	30	29	-3%	41	+41%	74	+80%
Ship Repair (billion Won)	3.8	12.5	+229%	23.9	+91%	91.5	+283%
Number of Employees	12000	11800	-2%	11300	-4%	10900	-4%
Overall Leadtime (months)	14	12.5	-11%	10.5	-16%	9	-14%
Labor Hours per ship (million)	1.3	1	-23%	0.9	-10%	0.65	-28%
Overall First-Pass Defect Rate (%)	20	10	-50%	5	-50%	1	-80%
PANEL BLOCK ASSEMBLY							
Leadtime (Days)	24	19	-21%	14	-26%	11.3	-19%
Work-in-Progress (000 pieces)	100	40	-60%	25	-38%	18	-28%
First Pass Defect Rate (%)	28	10.1	-64%	2.52	-75%	1.4	-44%
(PRE) ERECTION TIMING (DAYS RELATIVE TO LAUNCH)							
Main Engine	-15	-20	-33%	-40	-100%	-55	-38%
Painting of Wing Water Ballast Tank	50	40	-20%	20	-50%	-10	-150%
Anchor Erection	50	35	-30%	-4	-111%	-10	-150%
Forebody Final Block Erection	-7	-10	-43%	-20	-100%	-35	-75%
MAINTENANCE							
Mean Time Between Machine Breakdowns (hours)	54.7	65.2	19%	72.5	11%	83.4	15%
SUGGESTIONS							
Employee Suggestions (#/yr.)	10000	17700	77%	26700	51%	32000	20%

floor. This is why we have instituted this new project to better integrate the whole of shipbuilding procedure—from design to float-out. The project started three years ago, and we are now beginning implementation. We are trying to build a computer-integration system which builds on the expertise of our operators, rather than tries to automate it away. For example, we are currently trying to implement Computer Aided Process Planning at the production line level—which is an unheard of idea. However, if we can pull it off, we will get a big advantage over the competition, who have just started to recognize the importance of integration.

Exhibit 19.8   Planned Capacity Increase among Korean Companies (as of late 1993)

INVESTMENT	HYUNDAI	DAEWOO	SAMSUNG	HANJIN	HALLA
New Dock Size (LxW; meter)	#8 360 x 70 #9 366 x 70		650 x 97.5		#1 500 x 100 #2 400 x 65
New Crane	#8 900 (tons) #9 900 (tons)		700 (tons)		#1 600(tons) #2 600(tons)
Capacity Increase (#V.L.C.C. / yr.)	6 units	?	6 units	?	6 units
Capacity Increase (GT / yr.)	1.5 Million	?	1.0 Million	?	0.5 Million
Construction Cost ($M)	500		500		440
# Employee Increase	2400		2200		2700
Other Investments in 1993	• Factory Building Renovation • Dry Dock Maintenance • Several Shops being Renovated	• Erection Painting Specialty Shop Building • Two 500t Transporter Purchase • Cutting Tools Change • CAD System Purchase	• Shop Blasting Expansion • Design Building Construction • 2000t Press Purchase	• LNG Factory Construction • Blasting Shop Construction • N/C Cutting Machine Purchase	• 2000t Roll Press Purchase • Panel Line Expansion • Block Stock and Pre-Erection Space Expansion

Park Dong-Kyu agreed with many of these sentiments. Although the shop floor had indeed been the primary source of performance improvement over the previous few years, it was becoming clear that new paths for improvement also had to be found. Indeed, DSHM was relying on such improvement to carry the day in the face of daunting investment by competitors. Further manufacturing integration was a promising new source of opportunity.

First, Park wanted to know if productivity improvement effort would be enough to satisfy Daewoo's goal of maintaining 10% market share over the next five years. Park wondered how much of the wind was emptying from the sails of the shop floor improvement effort. While DSHM's improvements had originally been increasing in pace, recent results were more mixed (see Exhibit 19.7). What should be done to ensure its continued vitality and what dangers lay ahead? Second, what should 'integration' mean for DSHM and should integration projects be selected on the same basis as shop-floor projects? Finally, could DSHM continue to rely on generalized improvement, on multiple dimensions or was it now time to pick a more focused direction for improvement? While this would clearly focus attention and resources, the market was increasingly capricious, and there was great disparity between individual customers' requirements. In addition, there were many spillovers from one path to the next (say, in improved quality to improved lead times), many of which were not anticipated at the start of a project. Park also worried that constraining the plant to improve on one particular competitive dimension would itself begin to becalm the plant on its journey of improvement.

The questions ebbed and flowed from Park's mind as he watched the light flicking over the waves, as they kissed the shore of the East China Sea.

PART III

SELECTING, DEVELOPING, AND EXPLOITING OPERATING CAPABILITIES

Selecting Capabilities and Drawing Organizational Boundaries

*O*rganizations succeed in a competitive marketplace over the long run because they can *do* certain things that their customers value better than can their competitors. Throughout this volume we have emphasized that a company's operations, if properly designed, managed, and nurtured, can be a source of such strategic capabilities. We have already seen examples of companies (such as DJC, McDonald's, John Crane, and Daewoo) that achieved strong competitive positions on the strengths of their exceptional operating capabilities. We also have seen examples where a lack of certain operating capabilities created strategic vulnerability. For example, although BMW was historically able to dominate the luxury car market through its distinctive design and engineering capabilities, it came under intensifying competitive pressures in the late 1980s from Japanese entrants who were able to provide both lower costs and high *conformance* quality. American Connector provides an example of an organization whose operations, after years of neglect, could not contribute any distinctive competitive capabilities, and which was facing serious competitive threats as a result.

Nurturing an appropriate set of operations capabilities should therefore be a top priority of operating managers, but they also need to recognize that developing capabilities requires trade-offs. Although companies can improve across a broad front, they generally need to focus their efforts (and organizational resources) on a few selected areas. Thus, one often hears that a company should focus on developing its "distinctive" or "core" capabilities. This advice clearly has a certain appeal: it is hard to come up with examples of companies that are "world-class" at *everything* they do. Indeed, the historical success of companies such as BMW, Eli Lilly, and McDonald's can usually be traced to their enduring emphasis on developing very distinctive sets of capabilities. At the same time, however, advising an organization to focus its efforts narrowly leaves unanswered the critical question: *which* capabilities should it seek to develop? Although some companies have been able to develop powerful capabilities almost unconsciously—even by accident—building them purposefully requires a conscious selection.

This module, Part III, explores this first requisite step in building strategic operating capabilities: *identifying* and *selecting* them. The next module, Part IV, will turn to approaches for *building* those capabilities. We use the issue of vertical integration and sourcing decisions as the window for examining the selection of strategic operating capabilities. When companies make sourcing decisions, they are doing more than deciding simply which products or services to produce themselves and which to buy. They are also deciding what *capabilities* they want their organization to develop and control internally, and which ones they will access through some alternative arrangement. In deciding whether to outsource a particular part or whether to perform a particular operation in-house, managers need to analyze the broader implications of that decision on their company's capabilities.

Background

Any product or service is normally the result of a series of processes, often called the "value chain" (Porter 1985). The value chain for a car, for example, would include everything from processing raw materials (such as steel, aluminum, and plastic) and fabricating literally thousands of components, through the assembly, distribution, and servicing of the finished automobile. The major components of the value chain for a mutual fund, on the other hand, might include taking in cash (from investors), conducting research on investment opportunities, buying and trading securities, preparing financial reports, and distributing proceeds back to investors. *Access* to all of the capabilities in a value chain is required in order to compete over the long term in that business. However, an organization can gain this access in a variety of different ways. In certain situations it might want to undertake an activity in-house (vertical integration); in others, it might seek access through relationships with suppliers or customers. One of the fundamental issues in developing an operations strategy (and, for that matter, a competitive strategy) is which activities should be performed internally, and which should be left to others—such as suppliers, customers, or partners.

Beginning around the middle of the nineteenth century, American companies began to expand the scope of activities they performed in-house (Chandler, 1977). Despite this trend, however, different industries typically exhibit a great deal of variation in the extent of their vertical integration. For example, industries like aluminum have always maintained a relatively high degree of vertical integration, from the mining of ore and the processing of ingots through the fabrication of semifinished aluminum parts. At the opposite extreme are industries like publishing. Take this book as an example. The key activities required to create this book and deliver it to you, the reader, are largely performed by independent entities who deal with each other through contracts. We have written the book, but Simon & Schuster is publishing it. The publisher uses its own staff for editing, but may subcontract other functions (such as designing the jacket cover, printing, and binding). Finally, the book is sold at the retail level by stores that are not owned by the publisher. It is not necessary for writers to develop the capabilities to publish or sell their own books; they gain access to those capabilities through contracts with publishers.

There are also significant differences in how firms within an industry go about achieving the access to the capabilities they desire. In automobiles, for example, General Motors has historically chosen to control much more of the total design and production capabilities in-house than have Ford and Chrysler. At the other extreme, Japanese auto companies have generally relied on suppliers for a much more significant share of component design than have American and European companies. In lieu of vertical integration, however, the Japanese companies have forged closer, longer-term relationships with their suppliers.

Such divergence reflects both the histories and traditions of each company and the fact that companies having different competitive priorities might be expected to focus on different sets of in-house capabilities. In the personal computer business, for example, Compaq has competed primarily through low-cost, relatively standardized products sold through mass distribution channels. Therefore it has pursued a much higher degree of vertical integration into component fabrication than has Dell. For Dell, which sells made-to-order systems to customers who buy directly over the telephone, it is much more important to couple final assembly tightly with their order fulfillment process.

New Approaches to Accessing Capabilities

Like so many other aspects of operations strategy, companies' vertical integration decisions and supplier relationships have been undergoing significant transformations over the past several years. Beginning in the early 1980s, there has been a marked shift away from vertical integration in a wide range of U.S. industries. This trend extends beyond component production to complete products and, indeed, whole functions. Companies increasingly are making use of third-party "contract manufacturers" that provide high level production capabilities. A few, in fact, have decided to divest themselves completely of all manufacturing activities. Vertical disintegration has also spread to service and support activities. Outsourcing of data processing, accounting, and other administrative support activities has become commonplace and, analogous to contract manufacturers, there are now companies that specialize in providing these services.

Even more interesting is the increased tendency of companies to collaborate with outsiders in developing and commercializing technology. Historically, firms have preferred to develop technology largely through in-house R&D programs and to commercialize it themselves. Now, in industries ranging from aircraft and computers to semiconductors and biotechnology, firms routinely use R&D contracts, R&D joint ventures, technology licensing agreements, and other forms of collaborative development to either acquire or commercialize new technologies.

A second, perhaps related, trend has been the tendency to forge closer, longer-term relationships with suppliers and customers. Historically, companies' relationships with outside suppliers were of a short-term, "arm's-length" nature. Such relationships were governed by detailed contracts that specified all the relevant terms (e.g., prices, volumes, delivery dates, etc.). Although a company might engage the same supplier repeatedly over time, there was no explicit or even implicit expectation that this would be the case. Price was usually the determining factor for which supplier got a contract, and companies sought to gain the maximum leverage possible over their suppliers in order to ensure the lowest possible prices. The threat of switching suppliers was their primary weapon. To make this threat credible, short-term contracts (with multiple suppliers) were preferred to long-term ones (with single sources) in order to ensure continual supplier competition.

In this context, vertical integration can be viewed as placing a particular transaction within the hierarchical boundaries of an enterprise, while arm's-length contracts expose it to the cold winds of the marketplace. While intermediate forms of exchange between the two extremes of "markets" and "hierarchies" (such as joint ventures) have always existed, there appears to have been a noticeable increase in their use since the early 1980s. These go by various names, including "partnerships," "strategic alliances," and "hybrid governance structures." Many companies have embarked on explicit strategies of reducing the number of their suppliers, and viewing and treating the remaining ones more as "partners." Joint ventures, equity investments, long-term technology-sharing agreements, and other types of strategic alliances blossomed, in high technology as well as in more mature industries.

The popularity of such "intermediate" relationships seems to have come from two directions. On the one hand, many companies have chosen to outsource certain activities that they had traditionally performed in-house, often deciding that the internal environment of the firm was perhaps too comfortable and too far removed from competitive forces to stimulate the requisite performance incentives. In the automobile industry, for example, Chrysler spun off its parts-supplying operations into a separate entity called Acustar. On the other hand, in situations where activities (like technology development) required a high degree of coordination with internal operations, or required long-term commitments on the part of suppliers, an arm's-length relationship might impede close coordination. Thus, in some instances companies that traditionally had used arm's-length relationships with suppliers began to forge longer-term relationships with them in order to facilitate coordination and cooperation. We saw an example of this in the "BMW" case, where the company was contemplating asking a supplier to participate, for the first time, in the design and production of prototype parts.

The growing popularity of such intermediate structures is understandable. They seem to strike a nice balance between the security of an organization and the unforgiving jungle of the market. When successful, they provide the coordination and cooperation of vertical integration without sacrificing the incentives and flexibility provided by markets. Some go so far as to proclaim that these intermediate forms are a new "dominant design" for organizing operations. Although we see their virtues, we do not subscribe to this view. Like all other aspects of operations strategy, there is no one unconditionally best "solution" to vertical integration/sourcing decisions. Choices about when and what to produce internally, when to use arm's-length relationships, and when to structure some type of more complex intermediate relationship need to be based on the specific situation confronting a company. The goal of this module is to provide a framework for helping to make these choices.

Issues and Themes

Core Capabilities

Three of the cases in this module describe companies that, in the pursuit of a given competitive strategy, are grappling with whether to develop or retain a particular type of capability in-house. Whistler, a small electronics company, is deciding whether to continue manufacturing its products or to follow its competitors in outsourcing them from off-shore suppliers. Nucleon is a small, young biotechnology company that has restricted itself to product R&D since its birth, but now is contemplating integrating vertically into manufacturing as its first potential product approaches commercialization. Alternatives to vertical integration include licensing or a joint venture agreement with more established pharmaceutical companies. Crown Equipment is a manufacturer of forklift trucks and other materials handling equipment. For 30 years it has successfully procured industrial design services from an outside design house. Given changes in its competitive situation, it is now considering creating an in-house design group. In both the "Nucleon" and "Crown" cases, the issue is complicated by the question of whether those companies can successfully develop the requisite new capabilities if they choose to vertically integrate, while one of the questions raised by the "Whistler" case is whether the capabilities the company wants to retain in-house will be impaired by the decision to drastically cut back its manufacturing capability. In all three cases, managers have to decide: Which capabilities are key to their success and which can be safely delegated to others?

Complementary Skills and Assets

Once an organization understands and defines the specific set of capabilities that make it truly distinct, does this mean that it should outsource everything else? Does a strong focus on core capabilities imply that organizations will become highly vertically dis-integrated? There are many who have argued in recent years that a new organizational structure is emerging in which the companies of the future will be relatively small, specialized firms that develop long-term relationships with one another along value chains (see, e.g., Piore and Sabel, 1986). The textile-apparel industry located around Prato, Italy has become the classic example for proponents of this vision. While we do not disagree with the possible advantages of this kind of extreme focus in certain situations, managers have to pay careful attention to two kinds of complications. First, in order to extract the full potential of certain capabilities, organizations often need to have close access to complementary assets, resources, and skills. For example, even though a company may decide that product R&D is the capability that makes it distinctive, it may still benefit from access to manufacturing and marketing skills and resources in order to facilitate product design and development. Where markets for these complementary capabilities do not exist or where they require very complex and unstable contractual relationships, companies may need to develop them in-house as well. In this module, we examine the conditions under which organizations may well want to expand their scope beyond their narrow band of core capabilities.

A second issue is that making extensive use of the capabilities of outside organizations usually requires the development of complementary internal capabilities. Crown Equipment, for example, had become very good at integrating the efforts of its external industrial-design consultants with its internal engineering department. In the "Intel-PED" case, in contrast, the company is considering going from a single-supplier to a dual-supplier sourcing policy for certain production equipment. Because the adoption of two suppliers would require different plants—or possibly even the same plant—to utilize different makes of the same equipment, Intel's IC plants will have to develop new capabilities in equipment selection, maintenance, and improvement. In "Whistler," a decision to outsource all production would require the company to develop capabilities to manage OEM suppliers located almost 10,000 miles away from its design center.

Multiple Channels of Access

Traditionally, corporate boundary decisions were viewed in simple make-versus-buy terms. A company could perform an activity in-house ("make" it) or it could buy the output of that activity from an outsider. As noted earlier, however, this dichotomy grossly oversimplifies the broad range of choices that firms actually face. Access to the capabilities of an outside source can be accomplished in various ways. Firms can craft relationships with outsiders that vary according to the number of competitive suppliers (e.g., single sourcing), the length of the relationship, the degree of operational integration and information sharing, and the distribution of rewards and costs. In all the cases in this module, managers are being asked to reconcile these conflicts, and to evaluate alternative approaches to structuring and coordinating their internal and external activities.

References

Chandler, Alfred D., Jr. (1977). *The Visible Hand.* Cambridge, Massachusetts: The Belknap Press of Harvard University Press.
Piore, Michael J. and Charles F. Sabel. (1984). *The Second Industrial Divide.* New York: Basic Books, Inc.
Porter, M. (1985). *Competitive Advantage,* New York: Free Press.

CHAPTER 20

Whistler Corporation (A)¹

I n the summer of 1987, Charles Stott, the recently appointed President of the Whistler Corporation, realized that the company had reached a critical juncture—the once profitable maker of radar detectors was losing $500,000 per month. Stott had been brought in by Whistler's corporate parent, the Dynatech Corporation, to return the company to profitability. Within the next few weeks, Stott was to present a decision to Dynatech regarding the future of Whistler's manufacturing operations.

Stott was considering radically restructuring Whistler's domestic manufacturing operations in an attempt to become cost competitive with off-shore manufacturers. A pilot "just-in-time" (JIT) synchronized production line that had been in operation for less than three months would be the model for the new manufacturing system. If the synchronized production system could be successfully scaled up, Whistler could expect significant cost savings from reduced work-in-process inventory, better quality, higher labor productivity, and more efficient utilization of floor space. Major savings in fixed costs would also come from being able to close the company's plant in Fitchburg, Massachusetts.

A second option being contemplated was instead to expand the company's long standing and successful relationship with a Korean consumer electronics company. This company was already supplying complete "low-end"² radar detectors to Whistler at very attractive prices. Turning over additional low-end products to this Korean supplier would allow Whistler to be more cost competitive in this segment of the market. It would also alleviate some of the capacity problems the company was experiencing in its two domestic plants (in Westford and Fitchburg, Massachusetts). A third, and more extreme, option was also being given serious consideration: Move all production off-shore and shut down the

---

¹Some proprietary data have been disguised.

²In the radar detector market, "low-end" indicates a product with basic features, relatively low engineering costs, and modest performance specifications.

Professor Gary Pisano prepared this case as a basis for class discussion rather than to illustrate either the effective or ineffective handling of an administrative situation.

company's two domestic plants. This route had been taken by all but one of Whistler's competitors in the radar-detection market.

Background

Radar detectors, known in the vernacular as "Fuzz- busters"[TM3], are small electronic devices which alert drivers to the presence of police band radar used to track vehicle speeds (Exhibit 20.1). The device contains three basic functional (internal) parts. The *microwave assembly* is an antenna which picks up microwave signals (emitted by police "radar guns") and converts them into lower frequency radio signals. These signals are then processed and interpreted by the *radio frequency assembly*. If police band radar signals are detected, the *control assembly* alerts the driver through flashing lights, a beep, or some combination of visual and audio cues.

The first radar detectors were introduced in 1972. Truck drivers were then the overwhelmingly dominant users of radar detectors. In the late 1970's, the use of radar detectors began to spread to automobile "enthusiasts," salespeople, and others who frequently drove long distances on highways. It was still a small, specialized niche market when the Whistler Corporation decided to enter the business in 1978.

Whistler was founded by Dodge Morgan in the early 1970's. In its

Exhibit 20.1   Representative Products of Whistler Corporation

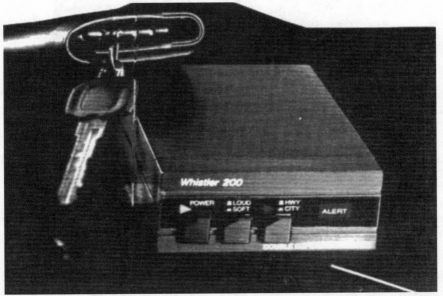

(continued)

3"Fuzz-buster" is a registered trademark of Electrolert, one of Whistler's major U.S. competitors.

Exhibit 20.1 *(continued)*

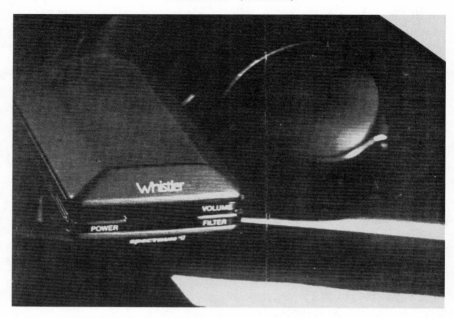

earliest days, the company designed and manufactured electronic specialty products (voice scramblers, marine radars, and gas leak detectors) in the founder's garage. As revenues began to grow, the company relocated first to an old mill and then to a larger, more modern facility in Westford, Massachusetts.

Because of the company's strong design and engineering capabilities, it quickly became a dominant and profitable player in the small, but growing market for radar detectors. Its first radar detector, designed in 1978, became a leading seller. In 1982, Whistler introduced two more models. In 1983, Whistler was one of six companies competing in what was still a rather specialized, but profitable, niche market. In this same year, Whistler was acquired by Dynatech, a Burlington, Massachusetts company whose strategy was to purchase small to medium sized companies with dominant positions in niche markets.

Explosive Growth: 1983–1987

Shortly after Dynatech acquired Whistler, a number of interrelated changes occurred in the market for radar detection devices. As indicated in Exhibit 20.2, unit aggregate demand exploded. Between 1982 and 1987, the total number of radar detectors sold in the United States increased by more than 450%. Annual rates of market growth during this period averaged 35.6%.

This growth was associated with a fundamental change in the composition of demand. "Mass" consumers became the dominant buyer segment. The market became segmented according to price, quality, performance, and purchasing convenience. Distribution expanded from specialty auto and truck shops to a variety of general retail outlets (electronics shops, mass merchandisers, and mail-order catalogues). To serve as many segments

Exhibit 20.2   U.S. Market for Radar Detectors (Units)

Year	Number of Units	% Increase	Average Retail Price
1980	473,000		
1981	583,000	23%	
1982	618,000	6	
1983	985,000	59	$150
1984	1,458,000	48	136
1985	1,910,000	31	125
1986	2,505,000	31	115
1987	2,840,000	13	95
1988*	2,982,000	5	90
1989*	2,684,000	-10	88
1990*	2,415,000	-10	85
1991*	2,295,000	- 5	80

* Projected

of the rapidly growing consumer market as possible, Whistler introduced nine new models between 1982–1987.

As could be expected, demand growth attracted new competition. By 1987, Whistler had 19 competitors. While many of these were American companies, virtually all of them sold radar detectors which were manufactured under subcontracting arrangements with Asian suppliers. The majority sourced exclusively from Asia. In the wake of intense competition and access to low-cost off-shore producers, the average price of radar detectors declined steadily (Exhibit 20.2).

It was during this period of rapid growth that Whistler experienced severe problems in its manufacturing operations.

Manufacturing Operations

Manufacturing at Whistler was divided into two sets of operations: subassembly production and final assembly. Before 1985, both subassembly and final assembly operations were done in Whistler's 40,000 square foot plant in Westford. In 1985, Whistler moved final assembly operations to a new 20,000 square foot plant in Fitchburg, Massachusetts (approximately 25 miles from its Westford plant).

Subassembly

As indicated earlier, radar detectors consist of three internal major subassemblies: (1) a microwave subassembly, (2) a radio frequency (RF) subassembly, and (3) a control subassembly. Whistler designed and built all three of these subassemblies in-house. Both the RF and control subassemblies consisted of printed circuit boards containing through-hole soldered, as well as surface mounted, electronic components. The RF and control boards were assembled from electronic components and bare printed circuit boards purchased from outside vendors. The microwave subassembly was manufactured using zinc die castings supplied by an outside vendor. Normally, these subassemblies were produced in batch sizes large enough to meet the requirements of one month of final assembly.

Circuit board production required a number of steps. First, all of the components required to produce a batch of a particular circuit board were brought from the stockroom to the circuit board production area. Then, electronic components were automatically mounted onto the surface of the bare panels. After this "surface mounting," the batch was inspected to ensure that all of the appropriate components were correctly placed. The entire batch then moved to the "hand stuffing" work area where components that could not be automatically mounted were manually inserted into the board. These "hand-stuffed" components were then soldered into place on an automated wave solderer.

The entire batch of boards was then tested; boards which failed the test were marked. All panels were then sent to the "waterknife" which used a high-pressure stream of water to cut the panel into individual circuit boards, a process known as "depalletization." After depalletization, any defective boards were sent to the printed circuit board re-work area. The boards which had passed the first step were sent to another work station for RF tuning and functional testing. Boards which failed this second test were also sent to the re-work area. Finally, the entire batch went through a final quality control audit to ensure that only good boards would be sent to the board inventory in the stockroom[4] and ultimately on to final assembly.

Microwave assemblies were assembled in a separate part of the factory. Like the RF and control boards, the microwave assemblies were produced in batches large enough to meet one month's final assembly requirements.

Final Assembly

Final assembly consisted of six steps. First, the three major internal subassemblies were wired together. Second, a "quick test" of the integrated electronic system was done. Defective units were sent to a final assembly rework area. Third, the now-integrated electronic systems were attached to the bottom half of the unit's plastic molded shell. Fourth, the top half of the exterior shell was fastened onto the bottom half (now containing the electronic system). Fifth, the entire unit was tested (defective units were sent to the re-work area). Finally, the unit was packaged with instructions and sent to the finished goods storage area.

Production Control

The flow of materials was controlled by what is commonly referred to as a "batch-and-kit" method. In a batch-and-kit operation, all subassemblies and final assemblies are produced in batches—at Whistler, normally monthly batches. For example, if 5000 Spectrum 1 radar detectors were scheduled for production in a month, all 5000 would be assembled in one batch.

Before the final assembly of a batch could begin, all requisite subassemblies and parts had to be ready. Several weeks before final assembly of a batch of Spectrum 1s was scheduled to begin, the subassembly area produced 5000 of the appropriate RF boards, 5000 of the appropriate control boards, and 5000 of the appropriate microwave assemblies. The finished batches were then sent to the stockroom. Just prior to the time at which final assembly was scheduled, all the required subassemblies were picked from the stockroom and organized into a "kit"—all those parts

---

[4]It was not unusual for there to be no room in the stockroom for finished boards. In these instances, finished boards were stored on the factory floor until the batch was needed in final assembly.

required for the final assembly of one batch of finished product of that model. The kit was then sent to final assembly.

Most of the small electronic components used by Whistler were supplied by vendors located in Asia. For these components, the lead time from order to delivery was about ten weeks. Due to these long lead times, and because of the relatively low cost of these components, Whistler generally stocked enough raw materials to satisfy the next two months of scheduled production.

Strains in Manufacturing

As production volume began to increase rapidly after 1983, manufacturing operations experienced a number of problems. When Whistler had been producing four models in relatively low volumes, the number and size of production batches were manageable. However, increases in both total production volume and the number of models meant an increase in the number and size of batches. With a total of 13 models in production, the factory often found itself with several batches of in-process units lined up and waiting between work areas. With available stockroom space full, the floor of the Westford factory quickly became cluttered with work-in-process.

Floor space was not the only constraint in the Westford plant. There were many electronics companies in the Westford-Lowell area. Because of defense spending and a general expansion in the economy, these companies were experiencing a boom in business. Demand for semiskilled assembly workers was extremely high. Whistler, competing for labor with such companies as Digital Equipment Corporation (DEC) and Wang, found it difficult to staff its production operations at the wages it could pay.

A decision was made to lease a factory in Fitchburg, Massachusetts where both labor and space were more economically available. Management viewed the Fitchburg plant as a way to quickly add capacity and capture some of the business Whistler had been losing. In 1985, the Fitchburg plant was opened. All final assembly and test operations were moved to Fitchburg. Subassembly operations and packaging remained in Westford. Thus, the process flow was altered as follows: RF boards, control boards, and microwave subassemblies were produced and tested in Westford. These subassemblies and all the other parts required to make a batch of a particular model were "kitted" and then trucked to Fitchburg. In Fitchburg, the kits were assembled into final products and tested. The entire batch (or multiple batches) were then trucked back to Westford where finished product was packaged and stored.

During this time period, Whistler began to experience quality problems in the subassembly of RF and control boards. Some of these problems were due to defects in components sourced from outside vendors. However, a major part of the problem was caused by the new surface mount technology (SMT). Components which are surface mounted take up less space on the circuit board than those that must be inserted and soldered into holes. As a result, surface mounting allows more components to be packed onto a smaller circuit board. The trend toward smaller radar detectors made this technology desirable. When automated, the surface mounting process reduced cycle time dramatically. Given the need to increase production volume to keep up with demand as well as the increased demand for smaller detectors, SMT was a natural technology to adopt, even though it was a far more complex process than traditional methods.

The first SMT equipment was installed in 1986. The yields on the SMT process were quite low while operators, designers, and process engineers learned about and adjusted to the subtleties of the new process. By early 1987, the first-pass yield (the percentage of "good" output the first time through, before rework) had climbed to 75%. Through diligent inspection and extensive rework[5], the quality of products reaching customers remained extremely high. However, ensuring that reliability in the field was quite costly. For example, at the end of 1986, 100 of the company's 250 production workers were deployed to fix defective boards. About 30% of the Westford plant's floor space was taken up with in-process rework. Rework accounted for approximately $600,000 of the company's $2 million of work-in-process inventories.

Defective boards also hampered smooth material flow. A strict batch-oriented material flow discipline requires that an adequate number of subassemblies of each type be available to complete a kit. High rates of defective subassemblies created problems in matching subassemblies to create final assembly kits. In final assembly, incomplete kits could sit for weeks waiting for defective subassemblies to be reworked. The pressure to ship products was so great that common parts from other batches in process would sometimes be used as replacements. Unfortunately, this "borrowing" of components often went unrecorded. As a result, the missing parts were not available when the other batch was ready for final assembly. High defect rates became so normal that they were built into the production schedule. For example, as a matter of policy, the Production and Control Department ordered 20% more subassemblies than the final assembly production schedule called for.

Work-in-process piled up because of frequent unexpected schedule changes. When Whistler had been producing only four models for a rather narrow market, the schedule could be set well in advance. The "mass" market, however, was far more volatile. As one production scheduler put it:

Out of the blue we could get an order for 5000 Spectrum 2's from a big retailer running a weekend promotion. If we had the products to ship, we had the order. If not, we lost it. This was something we just weren't used to. Truckers don't go out and buy a radar detector just because it's George Washington's birthday.

Production schedule changes often meant stopping work on one batch of products to free up resources to start another. In early 1987, work-in-process inventory had reached $2 million. A production controller who had worked on the production line described the scene: "The place was a total zoo. Boards and half-assembled units were piled up from floor to ceiling. We even had to rent three trailers to handle the overflow."

Work-in-process had also become a materials-handling nightmare. The longer kits remained on the factory floor and the more they were reshuffled (to make room for other work-in-process), the greater the likelihood of damage to delicate electronic parts and further problems in final assembly. In 1987, by the time a unit had completed final assembly, it had spent an average of 23 days in process, although actual production time was only eight hours.

Performance

Until late 1986, manufacturing was of little concern to the Whistler management. Innovative design and good marketing were, as one executive put it, "the name of the game." Sales had been growing rapidly and manufacturing, despite its internal problems, had managed to keep up. In 1985, profits before taxes were 20% of sales; the company had a pretax return on assets of 40%. In that year, the company was the market share leader with 21% of the domestic radar detector market (units). The "build as many as you can, any way you can" strategy seemed to be working.

In 1986, however, financial performance deteriorated rapidly. High manufacturing costs were making it difficult to compete with off-shore manufacturers. The manufacturing costs of Asian subcontractors were substantially lower than those of Whistler (Exhibit 20.3). A marketing analysis suggested that, due to their performance, quality, reputation, and brand image, Whistler's products could support a 10% price premium, but not much more. By the end of 1986, Whistler's market share had fallen to 12%. By the end of the summer of 1986, the company began to lose money for the first time in its history, at the rate of almost $500,000 per month. The problems in manufacturing began to draw notice.

According to Jack Turner, Vice President of design and engineering, who headed manufacturing at the time: "We knew manufacturing was sick. We knew something had to be done. We just didn't know what it was."

In September 1986, a consulting firm was hired to study Whistler's manufacturing process and to make suggestions for change.

Exhibit 20.3 Off-Shore Sourcing Alternatives: U.S vs. Far East Manufacturing (Spectrum 1)

	United States Current (1/87)[1]	Far East (in $ U.S.)
Material	$31.90	$30.48
Scrap	3.83	0.92
Direct labor	9.00	1.88
Variable overhead	6.30	7.46[2]
Shipping	—	0.30
Duty	—	2.40
U.S. coordination costs	—	1.00
Fixed overhead		
Westford(HQ)	3.38	3.38
Westford plant	9.28	—
Fitchburg plant	8.14	
	$20.80	$3.38
Total	$71.83	$47.82

[1] Data for traditional manufacturing system; does not include estimated results from MPL.
[2] Includes the subcontractor's fixed overhead, variable overhead, and profit margin.

The RACE-ME Program

The consulting firm suggested a comprehensive program to reform manufacturing operations. The program was dubbed RACE-ME (Restoring A Competitive Edge Through Manufacturing Excellence). Its goal was to make Whistler's manufacturing as efficient as its Far Eastern competitors within 24 months.

The RACE-ME program included reforms in materials handling practices, operator training, process lay-out, inspection and quality control, tooling, and production flow. A model (pilot) production line (MPL) was set up in a corner of the Westford plant to implement, evaluate, and demonstrate various reforms. The line consisted of a series of connected work benches. For symbolism, the benches were a different style and different color than those found in the main manufacturing operations. The relatively high-volume Spectrum 1 was chosen to be produced on the MPL.

The MPL was designed to change the flow of materials and work-in-process. Rather than a batch flow, the MPL would operate as a "repetitive" or a synchronous line-flow manufacturing process with only very small buffer stocks between adjacent stages of production. In the traditional system, a work station received large batches of components and subassemblies as scheduled, whether or not it was ready to start working on them. On the MPL, a work station would receive materials or work-in-process only when it requested them. The second major change was in the production schedule. The MPL was scheduled to produce the same quantity of detectors day after day.

After some trial-and-error, the MPL process evolved as follows: RF boards, control boards, and microwave subassemblies were produced with the same equipment and through the same process as before. However, separate inspection points were eliminated. Each work station was made responsible for identifying and correcting its own quality problems.

Batch sizes and production flow were dramatically different. Rather than produce boards in one-month batches, the SMT operation ran only enough boards to supply one day of final assembly. The batch sizes were only 2 hours in the board assembly operations after SMT (hand stuffing, wave soldering, and depalletization).

The production flow was controlled by "kanban"[6] racks between each work station. Workers at any particular work station were instructed to work on a particular batch of boards only when an empty tray appeared in the rack between it and the next work station. When a specific work station needed more of a certain type of board, a worker would place an empty tray (with a production control card indicating the type and number of boards required) in the rack. This would signal a worker in the preceding work station to begin making a batch of those boards. The worker receiving the "produce" signal first checked the inventory in the rack between it and the station preceding it. If the appropriate work-in-process or components were there, the worker could begin processing immediately. If not, he or she would order them from the preceding station by putting an empty tray with the appropriate production control card on the rack. Through this kanban chain, materials and work-in-process were pulled as needed by downstream stations.

The flow of materials through subassembly was similarly controlled by the final assembly line. When required, final assembly would pull small lots of boards (a 15- to 30-minute supply) from the kanban rack located after the depalletization area. The small lot would then be tested. Boards that failed were sent to a rework area assigned especially for the MPL. A limit had been set on the maximum number of boards permitted in the board rework station. Once the limit was reached, the board subassembly operation would be shut down until the cause of the quality problem could be identified and corrected. It was hoped that this line shut-down procedure would help keep the process under control by drawing attention to defects and by forcing shop management to deal with their causes.

The boards were then passed along to the unit integration station

---

[6]"Kanban" is a Japanese word meaning "sign." It refers to the cards or signs attached to the containers holding work-in-process in some Japanese factories using the just-in-time approach.

where the three major subassemblies were joined. The MPL operated as a worker-paced assembly line. After completing a particular assembly step, the operator would pass the work piece a few feet down the bench to the next station's incoming work tray. These trays could hold a maximum of six work pieces. Once the tray was filled to capacity, the operator at the preceding station was instructed to stop working. He or she could resume assembly only when the tray contained fewer than six in-process work pieces. At the end of the MPL, an enclosed work station[7] performed the final test. Any unit failing this final test was sent to another rework station. The entire production line would be shut down if one day of inventory accumulated in this rework area.

Each worker on the MPL received 15 hours of training in work methods, quality inspection, and statistical process control.

MPL Results: April–June 1987

The MPL began producing Spectrum 1's on April 7, 1987. By late June, a study of the pilot line was completed. The data (summarized in Exhibit 20.4) suggested that it might be possible for Whistler to achieve substantial improvements in the productivity of people, equipment, and space if the manufacturing methods used on the MPL were used to produce all of Whistler's radar detectors. In addition, the MPL enabled Whistler to produce a Spectrum 1 from start to finish in 1.5 days, as compared to the 23 days required in the traditional system.

One option was to implement MPL concepts throughout the Westford plant. The expected gains in productivity were expected to allow Whistler to close the Fitchburg plant and reduce its total labor force. However, several questions remained.

Some managers in the company wondered whether the results of the pilot project could be replicated on a plant-wide basis. Which product lines might be best suited to the repetitive manufacturing process? Ed Johnson, the Director of Marketing, argued:

> This is extremely risky. You're talking about changing the entire manufacturing system and maybe shutting down one of our plants. Frankly, the possibilities scare me to death. Any kind of major disruption in output could really hurt us. I know things aren't very good now, but, at least we are getting product out the door. I think we should make changes in manufacturing, but let's phase them in more slowly.

Larry Santos, the plant manager at the Fitchburg plant, was also concerned:

---

[7]This testing station was enclosed to prevent stray microwave interference from invalidating the test.

Exhibit 20.4 Pilot Results of RACE-ME (two months of operation)

Category	January 1987*	June 1987
Output (units) per direct employee	100	237
Output (units) per sq. ft.	100	146
Work-in-process (units)	100	46
RF board: 1st pass yield	100	114
Variable Overhead++	100	68
Scrap	100	17

* Note: 100 = index for each category
++ Indirect labor (materials handlers, stockroom employees) accounted for virtually all of variable overhead.

I know this sounds like I am just looking after my own job, but I have to say I am not sure closing Fitchburg is the best decision. First, the plant has only been open for two years. The people there have been showing some real commitment. In fact, most of the quality and scheduling problems have originated in Westford.

The Director of Operations Planning, Sharon Katz, was also concerned about closing Fitchburg:

I'd have to agree with Larry about closing Fitchburg, but for a different reason. If we plan to grow, we're eventually going to need the extra capacity Fitchburg gives us. It's going to be very expensive to start up a new plant in a few years.

The Executive Vice President of Finance, Margaret Curry, had a more extreme viewpoint:

I am very impressed by the results of the MPL experiment, but I just don't think the cost savings will be enough. I just don't believe we can compete by manufacturing our products domestically.

The offshore option buys us tremendous sourcing flexibility. We can shop around for the best suppliers in cost, quality, and delivery. If one isn't working out, there are plenty of other potential suppliers throughout Asia we can go to. We can take care of the foreign exchange risks with appropriate hedging positions, so that needn't cloud our analysis.

Some within the company believed that despite the success of the MPL pilot project, manufacturing was not what Whistler should be worrying about. One executive, who had been with the company eight years, argued:

I agree with Margaret. We should be focusing on what we do best, perhaps better than any of our competitors—design and engineering. Our competitive edge is high performance in a small package. But, Cobra, Bel, and other competitors are really putting the heat on our technological lead. If we try to do everything, we'll lose our edge in technology. Manufacturing, while obviously an important part of the value chain, can be efficiently handled by our Korean partner or other overseas suppliers, if necessary. Every dollar we save by manufacturing offshore is another dollar we can invest in product development.

Ed Johnson added: "Or it's another dollar for advertising and market research!"

Richard Packer, a member of the outside consulting team, raised another issue: "I think there's a benefit of MPL that's been overlooked. By shrinking the throughput time from 23 to 1.5 days, the new system gives you the flexibility to respond quickly to changes in the market."

Charles Stott was worried about larger issues. Growth in the market for radar detectors had essentially stopped. In addition, two states had recently banned radar detectors; several more states had such legislation under consideration. The domestic market could evaporate quickly; expanding overseas sales into Europe, the next biggest potential market, was not a realistic option because most European countries had legislation already banning detectors. In Stott's view, diversifying out of radar detectors might soon be a strategic imperative. The marketing group was already looking at potential product lines which could be sold through the same channels of distribution under the Whistler brand name. The design engineering group had commenced early development projects in several new product areas—CB radios, battery chargers, anti-theft devices, FM antenna boosters, emergency lights, breath analyzers, collision avoidance radar, scanners, and marine UHF radios. In view of these changes in Whistler's business, Stott contemplated the role that manufacturing would play in its future.

CHAPTER 21

Crown Equipment Corporation

Design Services Strategy

*A*S HE DROVE TO WORK on the morning of January 24, 1989, Tom
Bidwell, executive vice president of Crown Equipment Corporation, could see the company's large manufacturing complex
across the frozen cornfields around New Bremen, Ohio. He remembered a
time when the company had manufactured its products in a building not
much bigger than a garage. The past thirty years had been extraordinarily
successful for Crown; it had grown from a niche producer of small,
manual forklifts to one of the world's leading manufacturers of industrial
materials handling equipment.

Bidwell was well aware that the company's emphasis on excellent
industrial design and its longstanding relationship with the design consultancy of RichardsonSmith (RS) had played a key role in its success. This
morning Bidwell would meet with Jim Moran, Crown's vice president of
marketing, and Dave Smith, cofounder of RS and a longtime friend, to
discuss Crown's proposed new design strategy. For some time now, Bidwell
had wondered whether changes in the competitive environment called for a
new course, and, in particular, the establishment of an in-house design
group at Crown. The decision would not be an easy one. For the past thirty
years, all of Crown's industrial design requirements had been contracted to
RS. Over this period, both companies had literally grown up together.

Background: From Antennae to Lift Trucks

Crown Equipment Corporation was a privately held business that began
operations shortly after World War II as a manufacturer of temperature
controls for coal-burning furnaces. Over the years, Crown had successfully
diversified into several industries. In 1949, James Dicke, the company's
president and co-founder, responded to the emerging television market by

This case was prepared by Dr. Karen Freeze, Director of Research of the Design Management Institute, and
Professor Gary Pisano of the Harvard Business School, as a basis for class discussion rather than to illustrate either effective or ineffective handling of an administrative situation.

moving the company into the production of antenna rotators, a business that grew rapidly during the 1950s and 1960s.[1] In 1951 the company began manufacturing and repairing mechanical and electronic components for private industry, government, and its own operations.

A Materials Handling Niche

One day in 1957, Tom Bidwell, a recently hired engineer, was watching some Crown people put together a hydraulic jack for Jim Dicke's father-in-law.[2] It occurred to Bidwell that Crown was making the hardest part of what could be a series of useful tools. "The rest is just welding." So Tom, a frustrated artist who had turned down an art scholarship in favor of a manufacturing career, started sketching. His sketches of, as he put it, "packaging" for hydraulic jacks, resulted in Crown's first "walkie" forklift, which hit the market in 1957. (See Exhibit 21.1.) Its success pointed to the need in industry for small, high-quality lift trucks for intermediate-duty use in materials handling. At that time, the company had 150 employees and $1 million in sales.

Industrial Design at Crown

After the success of his first attempt at designing a forklift, Tom Bidwell continued to sketch out various kinds of forklifts and other lift mechanisms with clean lines and simplified assembly. Thirty years later Tom reflected,

> Back in the early 1960s, we were a new and relatively small company in a mature market. We needed an edge, something to distinguish our products. We couldn't compete on cost alone. At that time, everyone in the business had comparable capabilities in mechanical, hydraulic, and electrical engineering. Everyone could achieve roughly the same functional performance. All that was left was how you packaged the technology.
>
> But as I looked around, I could see that nobody was giving any thought to design in lift trucks. There was a fallacy that these are industrial products and the people who buy them don't care about design. Why not? These people have design preferences when they buy things for their houses; why should they leave them at the door when they go to work? I've always believed that it's important for things to look good regardless of what they are or what they're used for. Over the years, though, we've gotten

---

[1]Crown's antenna rotators were marketed and distributed by Channel Master Corporation.

[2]A jack (e.g. an automobile jack used to change tires) is a mechanical device used to lift heavy weights a short distance. Hydraulic jacks use the force created by liquid under pressure to augment greatly the mechanical force exerted by an operator or a motor. Most lift trucks are based on the principles of the hydraulic jack.

Exhibit 21.1   Tom Bidwell's First Forklift, 1957

more than good looks for our money. Good design actually lowers your manufacturing costs, and we can prove it.

The RichardsonSmith Relationship

About the same time Crown began manufacturing forklifts, two industrial designers, Deane Richardson and David Smith, teamed up to form a design consultancy in Columbus, Ohio, one hundred miles from New Bremen. They christened the firm RichardsonSmith—soon to be known in the design business as RS. They opened their doors in 1959 and immediately began to hustle for business.

"We started with lists of businesses from the Chambers of Commerce in every town in Ohio," recalled Dave Smith. "Then one of us would go to a town and make 'house calls'—cold. Hopefully that would result in proposals and second visits." Another tactic was the trade show: "We'd go to trade shows—say, a boat show—and follow up with visits to all the manufacturers in the area. By the time we'd talked to ten of them, we'd sound like we really had something to offer. It was a great way of learning about an industry."

On a house call trip to New Bremen in 1960, Deane Richardson dropped in on Tom Bidwell, who by then had become Crown's director of engineering and manufacturing. "Deane was out trying to drum up some business for his struggling new design firm, and wanted to do a project for us. I was the easiest sell going—we had a new forklift in mind, but I had only $750 available. Fortunately, Deane agreed to do it anyway."

RS made the most of their opportunity. They took on the account and designed a medium-duty, hand-controlled pallet truck for Crown that won a design excellence award from the Industrial Designers Institute in 1963 and gained rapid market acceptance. (See Exhibit 21.2.) More importantly, the product attracted attention for Crown and was a critical starting point in building its brand image.

The success of the pallet truck reinforced Bidwell's belief in the value of excellent design. It also became the foundation for a long-term, mutually beneficial relationship between Crown and RS. Crown continued to hire RS exclusively to do the industrial design work on every new product development project, and did not employ any internal industrial designers.

Crown also turned its corporate identity needs over to RS. The designers developed an inclusive program, including the Crown logo and color system, in 1961–62. The program was redone in 1965, and again in 1973.

As Crown grew rapidly, so did RS, becoming one of the world's largest and most respected industrial design consultancies. The companies managed to maintain a close relationship, however; despite a growing list of clients, RS always treated Crown as a key account. Although other RS

Exhibit 21.2 RichardsonSmith's First Lift Truck, 1963

people were primary designers for Crown during various periods, Dave Smith provided the continuity and remained intimately involved in most Crown projects. As Tom Bidwell described it: "Dave Smith was so closely involved with our product development efforts that he was more like a Crown employee than a consultant." Indeed, all the RS industrial designers who worked on Crown products were viewed by the Crown engineering group more as partners than as outside consultants. The feeling was mutual. According to Dave Tompkins of RS, who headed the Crown account from 1963 until he left RS in 1977 to start his own firm,

> The thing that was so wonderful about Crown is that they cared passionately about how these things looked. The engineers would call us up if they had to make the slightest change. The difference between them and many of our other clients was like night and day.

In particular Tompkins admired Harold Stammen, the senior engineer in product development. "Talk about patience and attention to detail!" Dave Smith called Stammen the "brightest, most creative engineer you'd ever want to know. And completely self-taught." Like Bidwell, Stammen, who had been with the company since its beginnings, enjoyed the challenge of "out-designing the designers." Dave Smith viewed his role and Bidwell's as essential: "They are the reason we can do what we do. All the Crown engineers care about design, but Bidwell and Stammen are the design conscience of the company." Bidwell was particularly conscious of this role and frequently contemplated who would take it over after he retired. "I'm usually the one who walks around the plants and notices something, like an old nameplate, that needs to be changed. How do you define a system that takes the place of *me*? And then what do you *do* about it?"

Crown's approach to industrial design stood in stark contrast to that of most other industrial companies, who typically hired design consultants to style a product after all the internal engineering was completed. Often design consultants had little say in defining the product concept and were seldom in a position to influence the engineering. With Crown, the situation was quite different. They would call in the RS team as soon as they had a clear idea of a new product target. Both RS's industrial designers and Crown's engineers would assess the user's needs and the competitors' products, from different points of view. Then RS would develop a proposal and work with Crown engineers during product development. According to Don Luebrecht, a senior project engineer who had been with Crown since 1978, this was the secret to Crown design:

> We work together very well. They always listen carefully to us and we always listen carefully to them. Sometimes we have to re-do some of our engineering to accommodate their designs; sometimes they have to change their design recommendations to

accommodate our engineering. Sure, there are minor conflicts, but we always manage to work these out. There is always a lot of give-and-take. Of course, they always go home at the end of the day.

Dave Smith had similar views. "For example, many capital goods people, when they get a prototype, don't want you to touch it at all. But at Crown that's no problem. They will do three or four major iterations, because they see the prototype as a three-dimensional drawing to be refined and made better. Only with a prototype can you go through such things as service procedures, testing, careful operator analysis, and project evaluation, and Crown really understands that." (See a list of Crown's major design awards in Exhibit 21.3.)

The "Pretty Truck" Company

In the late 1960s and 1970s Crown expanded its line of lift-trucks by introducing a series of new products, all of which were distinguished by innovative design and an unusual level of attention to details. Everything from the shape and color of control levers to the placement of light was carefully considered and designed to enhance the operator's safety, comfort, and efficiency and to improve the truck's appearance as well. (See Exhibit 21.4 for an advertisement reflecting these principles.) Because these features promoted operator productivity and reduced the risks of costly accidents, customers were willing to pay a 10% price premium for Crown products.

A key part of Crown's marketing strategy during this period was to enter segments where the dominant design left something to be desired, or where a niche in the market waited to be filled. In these segments, Crown believed that it could capture market share by being the company that offered a logical and preferred alternative to the competition. In one segment after the other, Crown used this strategy successfully.

By 1972, Crown was making over 100 different models of lift trucks, all in the lighter, 1,500–3,000 pound capacity range, which it sold in 80 countries. Most of its manufacturing was located in Ohio (including its own components' manufacture), but it also had plants in Australia and Ireland. Crown's niche was smaller trucks "that looked nice and won design awards." Other forklift truck companies, most of which competed in the upper range of trucks above 4,000 pounds, ignored Crown, referring to it as the "pretty truck" company.

The First Real Choice

In the early seventies Crown's management decided to take on the big companies by developing a new design for a counterbalanced "rider truck," a product segment dominated in the U.S. by Raymond Corporation, which held a 75% market share. A standard product in the industry, counterbal-

Exhibit 21.3   Crown Equipment Corporation Design Awards

Year	Product	Award
1987	Series SP Stockpicker, Operator's Platform	Selection, Equipment Category Annual Design Review *ID* Magazine of International Design
1985	Walkie Trucks, Control Handle	Selection, Equipment Category Annual Design Review *ID* Magazine of International Design
1980	Series RR Rider Reach Truck	Industrial Design Excellence Award Industrial Designers Society of America (IDSA)
1975	Series SC Sit-Down Counterbalanced Rider	Industrial Products and Equipment Design in Steel Award American Iron & Steel Institute (AISI)
1973	Series RC Stand-Up Counterbalanced Rider	Industrial Products and Equipment Design in Steel Citation American Iron & Steel Institute (AISI)
	Series WPT Walkie Pallet Truck; Series W, EW, 30 W Walkie Stacker; Series TWR Walkie Rider Tow Tractor; Series RC Stand-Up Counterbalanced Rider	Industry Form (IF) Award Excellence in Industrial Design Hannover Messe [Industry Fair]
1972	Series RC Stand-Up Counterbalanced Rider	Selection, Equipment and Instrumentation Category Annual Design Review *ID* Magazine of International Design
1969	Series SP Stockpicker Series 30W Walkie Stacker	Industry Form (IF) Award Outstanding Design of an Industrial Product Hannover Messe
1965	Tow Tractor/Personnel Carrier Pallet Truck W227	Industrial Products Design In Steel Citation American Iron & Steel Institute (AISI)
1963	First W series pallet truck	Design Excellence Award Industrial Designers Institute

anced trucks, quite simply, have a mass of pig iron in the base that keeps them stable when lifting loads of several tons. This truck was bigger than any Crown product yet, having a lift capacity of 4,500 pounds. Dave Tompkins of RichardsonSmith, who had been working with the Crown account for over ten years, headed the RS contingent. "As with all new products, Tompkins recalled, "Crown began with analyzing everyone else and coming up with what the new truck would have to be. It was like a dot-to-dot drawing, with this information (like head length, turning radius, lift capacity) being the dots." Tompkins and his RS colleagues carried the research further.

At this time, every other truck had this bizarre condition that, when travelling in reverse, the operator had to turn around and

Exhibit 21.4

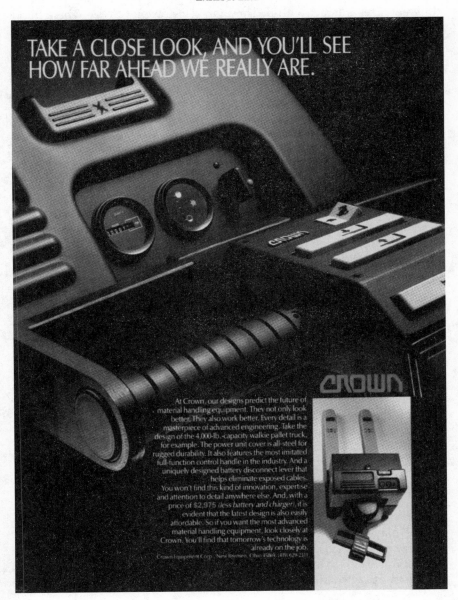

operate the controls from behind his back. We tossed around all sorts of ideas as to what to do about that problem. Then we said, 'in theory, you could stand sideways, and see both forwards and backwards, just by moving your head. But then how would you operate the controls?

Tompkins's team then built a full-scale mock-up and had people of different sizes interact with it. They ran a vision plot to see where blind spots were, and they tested various configurations of a multi-function control system. To accommodate nearly a dozen functions, they developed two controls. The main control lever, for the right hand, moved the forklift forward and backward, up and down. It had two buttons—one for the horn and the other for the tilt mechanism. Steering was controlled by the left hand. When Tompkins offered this radical proposal to Crown, "it took a while to convince them." Bidwell made the final decision to go with it.

The mock-up was moved to New Bremen, and Crown's engineers set to work on the new truck. Eighteen months of engineering and design work followed. For the multi-function control, they first looked at aircraft pistol-grip controls. But when they found out that such controls would cost $250 per unit, RS decided to design it themselves. The result was a sandcast aluminum part. "We got a finished appearance without a big investment in tooling," noted Tompkins. Several other details completed the revolutionary look of the new truck. One was the "dashboard," made of vacuum-molded 1/4" ABS plastic, rather than welded steel. This created a softness and high durability.

The new RC (Rider Counterbalanced) truck, bombarded with criticism by the competition, offered customers their first "real choice" in lift trucks. Within four years, the truck captured a 40% market share. (See Exhibit 21.5.) Spurred by this success, Crown developed a follow-on rider reach (RR) truck, designed for the narrow aisles that increasingly characterized warehouses and distribution centers. Unlike the counterbalanced trucks, the rider reach had "feet" in the front that kept it in balance. Using the principles developed in the RC, the RR became Crown's showpiece. It won a design award from the Industrial Designers Society of America in 1980, and in 1989 was expected to be in the running for a "Design of the Decade" award. (See Exhibit 21.6.)

The TSP Project

With the RR series and other products that followed, Crown evolved from a niche-player and follower to an industry leader with a full product line. Capping off the 1980s, was the recently introduced TSP Turret Stockpicker (see Exhibit 21.7). In just a few months, the TSP, the first of its kind in the U.S., had attracted much attention in the industry. It could operate in

Exhibit 21.5   The First Real Choice

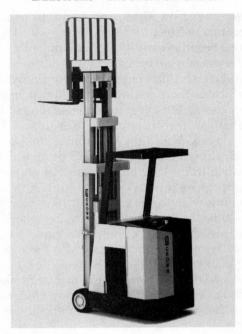

Exhibit 21.6   The First Series RR Truck

warehouses with very narrow aisles, and could lift pallet loads of 3,000 pounds up to a height of 40 feet.

The TSP project began in early 1983. (See Appendix 1 for a timeline of the project.) RS designers were brought in within the first few months to assist Crown's product development group with product criteria, appearance, and human factors. Early on it was decided that operator functionality would be a key design objective; since material handling productivity is largely dependent on the operator, the design had to be "operator-friendly." To learn more about how to improve the operator's comfort, safety, and control, Crown engineers and RS designers studied existing European turret-style trucks and other industrial equipment. The team also visited the facilities of key customers to study how current products were used and to interview operators about how they performed their jobs. Ergonomic studies were also conducted. Designers used this information to make preliminary sketches that explored all key design features—e.g., the layout of controls. They also built three-dimensional foam models to investigate alternative designs.

These sketches and three-dimensional foam models allowed the team to explore various design concepts relatively quickly. Once the field of choice was narrowed, the Crown-RS team began the difficult task of making firm

Exhibit 21.7   The TSP Turret Stockpicker

commitments to specific design details. They had to consider everything from the shape of the control levers to the location of the transmission and drive motor, and to evaluate their collective impact on the overall product.

Don Luebrecht recalled, "We sweated every detail. Nothing was considered 'too minor' to ignore." Design, engineering, manufacturing, service, and marketing were all involved in these choices. After an initial set of design commitments were made, a working prototype was built and tested. The process of revising and refining the design required three more prototype iterations.

In order to ensure that this attention to detail would be matched in final product quality, Crown custom-designed a very large proportion of the TSP's components for manufacture in-house; relatively few off-the-shelf components were used.

Finally, four and a half years after beginning the project, the design was finalized and ready for field testing and manufacturing start-up. The TSP entered the market in late 1988 and was soon in the running for several design awards.

Crown People

Design was not the only factor in Crown's success. Crown's technology too was state-of-the-art, but Crown's top management believed that people were the real key to the company's success.

Crown's talent came not from MBA programs or prestigious engineering schools, but from the villages and farms of the surrounding countryside. Half of Crown employees lived in New Bremen, a town of some 3,000 people situated about 75 miles northwest of Dayton, a city of 200,000 people with a metropolitan area of 800,000 and the nearest major airport. The rest lived within a forty-mile radius, in the small- and medium-sized towns of central Ohio. New Bremen itself housed the county airport. Most of Crown's senior managers had been with the company since its beginnings or shortly thereafter, and most of its employees had spent their working lives at Crown. Many had grown up on family farms. As Don Luebrecht, one of the company's leading project engineers (himself still a practicing farmer), put it: "Farming helps keep your sense—as a user and a fixer—of what's real and what's not."

Many employees had left the area for their education, but then returned to be near their families, or to have "a good place to raise kids." The rural background of the workforce resulted in a stability, a distinctive work ethic, and an individualism that contributed substantially to Crown's culture and the quality of its products. That individualism could be a problem, however, when introducing something so new as a computer-based scheduling system, noted Bidwell with a grin. "We didn't realize that we had an informal communications system that beat our computer. So many people in the company are related to each other that they all think they know what's going on. So they assume they know better than the computer." Eventually management did convince people to start using the computer system, and within a few months it began to take hold.

Good communication among departments and disciplines was an evident characteristic of the company. With most operations located within walking distance of one another, that communication network had developed almost effortlessly. As for the future, there was some concern as to how the communication would operate and how the culture would look when the company doubled in size—management's goal for the next decade.

Manufacturing at Crown

Australian and German facilities aside, the vast majority of Crown's manufacturing activities were concentrated in the company's enormous New Bremen complex. Located just across the street from the engineering center, the complex consisted of several component fabrication facilities and assembly plants. Within these facilities, the company undertook everything from plastic injection molding and precision machining to chassis welding and body painting. In early 1989 Crown was manufacturing about 80% of the components for its products, and was building a plant that would begin manufacturing lift-truck motors before the end of the year. Crown's manufacturing engineers were "can-do" people: "Whatever you guys want, we'll make."

Typically, components were fabricated in batches (usually about two weeks' worth at a time) and transported (via Crown lift truck, of course) to the appropriate assembly plant. The need to coordinate the flow of this massive variety of parts was a major challenge for Crown's manufacturing operations. This challenge was augmented by the wide variety of product families and models Crown offered, each of which could be ordered with any number of customized options. Moreover, the cost and size of a finished truck mandated that finished-goods inventories be kept as low as possible. Therefore it was imperative that the assembly operations accommodate a high degree of flexibility. The trucks were generally assembled according to marketing forecast, but customized options were added only after an order commitment was received. Delivery lead time generally averaged around three weeks. To help meet the challenges of coordinating the production of a wide variety of finished models, the company had recently implemented a computerized materials resource planning (MRP) system.

The low volumes and high product variety at Crown made fully automated assembly operations infeasible. Unlike an automobile plant, where each assembly step occurs at a fixed point along a moving assembly line, Crown's assembly operations were designed to accommodate a maximum variety of product and process flow. Trucks were typically assembled in batches of varying size. Each assembly operation (such as installing the seats) took place more or less at the same time for all trucks in a given batch.

After a given assembly operation was complete, another operation would begin in the same general work area. At certain points the batch of trucks would be moved to a new work area, but in general, the trucks (especially the largest ones) were moved very little during assembly operations. The sequence of assembly steps was organized so that standard components and sub-assemblies were attached first, and customizing options were put on later. One of the chief advantages of this production process (over the assembly line) was its flexibility, which made it possible to alter the sequence of products being assembled. For example, if optional parts for a particular order were not ready, the truck or trucks could be set aside (without holding up production of other trucks) until those parts arrived on the line.

The Lift Truck Industry

The materials handling industry was born when people started to think of ways to enhance the productivity of the hired hand who lifted stones and bricks, stacked cotton bales or iron pigs, loaded milk cans or flour bags. Various devices using pulleys and levers were invented to assist in the lifting and moving of raw materials, products, and parts. From the simple "dolly," which enabled people to move relatively small but heavy loads around easily, through the highly sophisticated and varied lift trucks that populate late 20th century factories and warehouses, the industry has followed changing needs and technology.

Lift trucks were powered by gas or electricity—the latter from huge batteries. Gas trucks were used outdoors and in well-ventilated factory areas. Electric trucks, somewhat more expensive than gas, were needed indoors, or wherever air pollution was a problem.

Developments in Warehousing

As the price of land in urban areas became increasingly expensive, warehouses tended to grow up, rather than out. This development required equipment that could help people stack goods on multiple levels of shelves, which might reach up several stories. In the 1950s, the pallet system evolved, which made it possible to store an indefinite number of items in or on large, uniformly sized pallets. This system called for careful tracking, but reduced the handling time of individual parts or materials. It also made possible clear parameters for the designers of materials handling equipment.

As developments in structural materials permitted pallets safely to be stacked ever higher, and space limits resulted in ever narrower aisles, lift truck manufacturers were challenged to provide equipment—like Crown's new TSP—that could maneuver and perform under these conditions.

Because warehouses were no longer predominantly storage areas, but rather distribution centers, this equipment had to be especially flexible, efficient, easy to operate, and reliable.

Little Chips and Big Machines

The manufacturers were also challenged—and had been for many years—by the computer. Some warehouses were fully automated, reducing the need for operators, and mandating the need for robot-operated equipment. In many industries, such as food, bar-codes were becoming ubiquitous, simplifying the work of the operator. Factory applications of lift trucks had changed too, in large part because of automation. In high-labor-cost countries, manufacturers turned to capital-intensive machines to do much of the work previously accomplished by men and women. These machines were often fed by automatic materials handling equipment, from one end of the process to the other. Despite the efforts of industry analysts to predict how the computer would continue to influence and change the industry, long-range product planning was no easy task.

Safety Issues

Another factor was pressing upon Crown and its competitors as the 1980s drew to a close: safety issues. This was especially true in the U.S., where the Office of Occupation Safety Hazards had ever-increasing powers and where product liability suits were a major concern. For Crown, the emphasis on operator-safety and comfort was welcome: "We love it!" exclaimed Tom Bidwell, "We've been doing it for thirty years."

Competition and the Marketplace in 1989

At the end of the 1980s, the lift truck industry consisted of some 250 manufacturers worldwide, 25 of which competed directly with Crown. Crown's strongest U.S. competitors were Hyster, Yale, Clark, and Raymond (depending on the type of truck), while Linde of Germany was its chief European competitor. Crown ranked third in sales (all types of trucks included) in the U.S., and tenth in the world. Japanese companies such as Toyota, Nissan, and Komatsu, though major players in the global market, tended to be stronger in gas and diesel trucks than in Crown's segment, electric trucks. (See Exhibit 21.8 for selected market share information, and Exhibit 21.9 for list of international competitors.)

By the end of 1988 Crown was a full-line producer of lift trucks, ranging from the small pallet hand truck (selling for around $500) to the enormous turret stock picker (price tag around $85,000). Within nine product categories the company offered some 66 different trucks. Crown employed 3,800 people worldwide and had annual sales of over $450 million. It held 30% of the U.S. market share in lift trucks, and worldwide it ranked tenth among all lift truck manufacturers, both gas- and electric-powered, even though it produced only electric trucks.

In each of its market segments in the U.S., Crown enjoyed a leading position in terms of sales revenues. In several product categories (e.g.,

Exhibit 21.8 U.S. Market Shares in Selected Product Categories

	1987	1988	1989
Class 1: Electric Motor Rider Trucks[1]			
Clark	17.0%	16.0%	16.2%
Hyster	14.0	14.4	17.4
Caterpillar	12.3	12.6	13.4
Crown	11.6	11.4	11.5
Toyota	5.7	5.1	5.0
Kalmar AC	4.0	3.2	2.4
Linde/Baker	3.5	4.7	4.5
Nissan	3.1	5.0	5.0
Komatsu	2.3	0.2	2.0
TCM	2.1	1.5	1.2
Schaeff	2.0	2.7	1.0
Drexel	1.8	1.2	1.2
Raymond	1.5	1.4	1.2
Mitsubishi	1.5	1.4	1.4
Class 2: Electric Motor Narrow Aisle Trucks[2]			
Crown	37.4%	31.0%	30.5%
Raymond	22.8	27.7	26.4
Hyster	7.0	5.8	5.2
Yale	7.0	6.1	6.0
Clark	6.1	6.1	6.3
Linde/Baker	2.8	4.0	4.4
Blue Giant	2.6	3.9	2.6
Lancer Boss	2.2	1.2	1.6
Prime Mover/B.T.	1.8	3.3	4.5
Mitsubishi	1.5	0.7	0.7
Toyota	1.3	0.8	1.0
Big Joe	1.1	1.5	1.9
Drexel	NA	2.3	2.6
Barrett	NA	1.8	2.4
Class 3: Electric Motor Hand Trucks[3]			
Crown	20.4%	21.3%	34.2%
Yale	1.39	15.9	16.4
Clark	8.1	6.8	6.8
Prime Mover	6.9	6.8	7.4
Blue Giant	6.8	6.2	4.1
Linde/Baker	5.8	6.5	5.7
Big Joe	4.7	4.7	5.0
Barrett	4.6	4.9	5.3
Hyster	3.5	0.8	2.1
Multiton	3.5	3.8	2.8
B.T. Lift	1.4	1.8	2.4
Kalmar AC	1.4	0.9	1.1
Raymond	1.4	3.1	3.4

Source: *Dataquest*
1 Counter-balanced riding forklifts
2 RC, RR, TS, TSP models from Crown.
3 Low Lift pallet trucks - GPW, PW, PE, PC models from Crown.

Exhibit 21.9   The Ten Largest Lift Truck Manufacturers
Worldwide, 1988

1. Balkancar (Bulgaria)
2. Linde-Stihl-Gruppe (West Germany)
3. Toyota (Japan)
4. Hyster (USA)
5. Komatsu (Japan)
6. Clark (USA)
7. Jungheinrich (West Germany)
8. Lansing (Great Britain)
9. BT (Sweden)
10. Crown (USA)

high-lift stockpickers, walkie stackers), its market share was consistently well over 50%. The company had also begun to increase its emphasis on foreign markets. In 1986 it made a major commitment to the European market by opening a subsidiary in Germany, the home of its leading worldwide competitor, Linde-Stihl GmbH. As 1992 and European economic unification loomed nearer, it was clear that the decision was a good one, despite start-up problems. "We wanted the German operation to be *European*," Tom Bidwell explained, "not American. But it is no simple matter to get all of us thinking on the same wavelength."

Success in the marketplace, which transformed Crown from a small, niche-producer of hand trucks to a multinational producer of a full line of lift trucks, created its own set of challenges for top management. As Jim Moran noted,

> The key challenge in this industry is to stay on top. If you look at lift trucks historically, you see that no one has ever sustained market leadership over time. The leaders have always been toppled by someone trying a new approach. For years, we had the luxury of being able to sneak up on market leaders who had become lulled by their own success. Now we've become the market leader that others are gunning for.

Crown's management was particularly concerned that its traditional competitive edge—superior design—would no longer be its exclusive domain. Tom Bidwell noted,

> For years, we have not had to worry. So few companies took design seriously. Unfortunately, our success has shown people just how important good design is. Sooner or later, they're going to start getting serious about design.

This was already beginning to happen. Linde, for example, had recently hired the internationally renowned design firm, Porsche Design Group. Competitors were also beginning, with some success, to copy design features of Crown's products.[3] In one instance, Crown spent three years redesigning the steering-wheel console of one of their older trucks. Within six months of introducing the trucks with the newly designed console, several competitors introduced their own versions. Jim Moran recalled,

> This was a major blow. The new console was supposed to be a critical distinguishing feature on one of our major product lines. The sales force was really excited about it. When competitors began introducing their own versions, it took all the momentum out of sales. It really hurt the morale of our sales force.

The console incident was particularly disturbing given top management's belief that similar design refinements—expeditiously implemented—would become an increasingly important competitive necessity for Crown. For years, the company had emphasized new product development over refinement of existing products. As a result, several of Crown's key products were beginning to age. For example, three of Crown's best-selling W-series High Lift Walkie Trucks, introduced between 1967 and 1971, had essentially remained the same ever since. One of its first walkie stackers had last been upgraded in 1973. The SC Sit-Down Counter Balance truck introduced in 1974 had not been upgraded. From projected orders for 1989, the marketing people sensed that this lack of upgrades on older products was starting to cost them share in some key markets. There were occasional exceptions, however: the SP Stockpickers introduced in the mid-1960s, for example, had received upgrades every five years or so, most recently in the mid-1980s.

These exceptions were neither often nor fast enough for Tom Bidwell. He was frustrated by Crown's inability to do even minor product upgrades in a relatively rapid fashion.

> The minute we talk about a small design change, it seems to turn into a major project. For example, one day while I was walking through the factory, it occurred to me that the nameplate carrying the Crown logo was really getting out of date. It looked fifty years old! I asked RS about redesigning the nameplate. A few months later, I checked back and found out that they were exploring changes in the location of the nameplate. This prompted our engineering department to look at how the nameplate was mounted. Now, RS and our engineering group are exploring a complete redesign of the entire back of the forklift. It's been three years and we still don't have an updated nameplate!

---

[3]Design innovations are notoriously difficult to protect with patents.

Although Bidwell and Moran believed that Crown had to put greater emphasis on upgrading existing products, they also knew it could not ignore major new product development activities. Indeed, as competitors took aim at Crown, and as Crown expanded into growing international markets with different design requirements, it seemed likely that the need for new products would only increase. Bidwell believed that Crown was going to have to become much faster at product development than it had been. In the last decade, Crown had developed only two major new products—the recently introduced TSP stockpicker, and a four-wheel sit-down that was still being tested. The TSP had taken about five years from concept to market, and the four-wheeler was taking just as long. Bidwell was concerned that such long product development lead times would not be acceptable in the future competitive environment. "We need to be able to update our products every one to one and a half years and to introduce a new product every two years."

Re-evaluating the Design Strategy

In addition to the changes in the competitive environment that demanded faster new product development and continuing refinement of existing products, another factor weighed heavily on Bidwell's mind. RichardsonSmith had recently been purchased by Fitch, a highly regarded, British-based design consultancy; after the purchase, the company was renamed Fitch RS. Bidwell wondered whether the new owners understood the special relationship between Crown and its design partner. He was concerned whether FRS, suddenly a very large firm of 500 employees, would be willing or able to do small-scale projects for Crown. He was also concerned about the cost of the consultancy's new prestige: would FRS's services inevitably be much more expensive? Some project engineers also noted that after the acquisition, interaction between the firms had become much more formal. Still, many of the same designers remained at the firm and, most importantly, Dave Smith, although no longer an owner of the firm, was expected to remain at Fitch for at least a few more years.

Several options were considered at this point. To be sure, RS had been Crown's sole design consultant, but there were dozens of other industrial design firms in the U.S. Crown could easily find another design consultant. (See Exhibit 21.10 for the largest U.S. design consultants, with locations.) Crown's reputation for design consciousness, and its $1 million annual design budget, made it an extremely attractive client to many top-notch design houses. Another approach would be to expand the number of design consultants with whom Crown worked. Indeed, many industrial firms preferred relationships with several design consultancies in order to maximize their exposure to different viewpoints and new ideas. Moreover, outside designers could often provide a broad, objective perspective to the problem at hand, unhindered by company traditions and turf issues.

Another option being given serious consideration was the establish-

Exhibit 21.10 The Ten Largest Product Design Firms in the U.S. 1989
(Annual Fee Income in Millions)

Walter Dorwin Teague Associates, New York, Seattle, Los Angeles, Washington, D.C.	$7.0
Fitch RichardsonSmith, Worthington (Ohio), Boston	$4.8
Designworks/USA, Newbury Park (Calif.), Troy (Michigan)	$3.5
Design Continuum, Boston	$3.3
Henry Dreyfuss Associates, New York	*
GVO, Inc., Palo Alto (Calif.), Minneapolis	$2.8
frogdesign hartmut esslinger, inc., Menlo Park (Calif.)	$2.5
Herbst LaZar Bell Inc., Chicago, Wellesley (Mass.)	$2.5
David O. Chase Design, Inc., Skaneateles (New York)	$2.4
Design West, Mission Viejo (Calif.)	$2.2

*Ranked by W&A estimate.
Source: Based on a study by Wefler & Associates, Inc., Chicago, IL

ment of an in-house design group at Crown. Crown had become large enough and required enough industrial design services to make this option viable. This would entail, according to Bidwell, a group of six to eight designers, the critical mass for this type of endeavor. The internal design group option was attractive for several reasons.

First, communication between industrial design and engineering would likely improve. Rather than having to travel 100 miles between New Bremen and Columbus (the home of Fitch RS), in-house designers and engineers could easily see each other on a daily basis. In addition, an in-house design group could conceivably be integrated more effectively into the entire product development process. With better communication and with tighter integration, product development would presumably proceed faster. And, as the designers gained experience within Crown, their in-depth knowledge of every detail of the company's process and product technology would be increasingly valuable. Moreover, an in-house group could efficiently give attention to the smaller tasks involved in the upgrading of existing products.

The in-house design option also contained a number of risks. Maintaining creativity was perhaps the greatest concern. One advantage outside consultants had was their broad exposure to different types of products. Design consultants tended to believe that their creativity was best stimulated by working on diverse projects, and did not specialize by industry. It was not uncommon for a top design house to work on products as different as medical instruments and athletic shoes. The working environment of such a firm fostered cross-fertilization and was an ongoing source of new ideas. A critical question was whether Crown, a medium-sized manufacturer of heavy equipment in the Ohio farm country, could create an equivalent environment in an in-house design group. Because

Exhibit 21.11   Timeline of the TSP Project

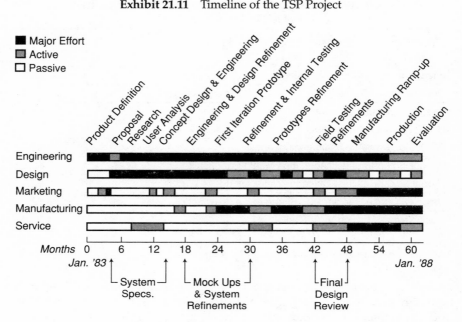

they would be working on only one type of product, in-house designers could run the risk of becoming stale.

Providing an attractive environment for an in-house design group would involve gutting and redoing a historic building in the center of New Bremen, about five blocks from the engineering staff. Bidwell estimated the renovation costs at about $120,000. Equipping the studio and model shop with state-of-the art equipment for designers and model builders would cost another $110,000. Crown's tool shop had a surplus of small machines that would be suitable for the model shop. Each designer, fully burdened, would run about $100,000 annually. Bidwell and Moran had also been discussing the issue of where to locate the group organizationally. If they did decide on an in-house group, should it be under engineering? Marketing? Or should it report directly to Bidwell?

As he pulled into the parking lot of Crown's headquarters, Tom Bidwell recalled his first meeting with Dave Smith, some thirty years ago. In retrospect, that meeting had radically altered the course of Crown's history. This morning's meeting with Dave Smith could mark another turning point. Bidwell hoped that his instincts would serve him as well today as they had at the meeting thirty years ago.

CHAPTER 22

Nucleon, Inc.

*R*OBERT MOORE, A RECENT GRADUATE of a top-ranked M.B.A. program, now realized what it was like to be on the other side of a case study. It was December 1990 and Nucleon, the young biotechnology start-up at which he had recently become project manager, faced critical manufacturing choices. Moore and Jeff Hurst, the firm's CEO, had met to discuss the situation, and within the next few weeks, Hurst needed to present the company's manufacturing strategy to the board of directors. In the meantime, he asked Moore to evaluate in detail Nucleon's options and give his own recommendation.

Nucleon's first potential product, "cell regulating protein-1" (CRP-1), had been undergoing extensive experimentation and analysis in the company's R&D laboratories for several years. The next major hurdle was human clinical trials, which also typically took place over several years. However, before Nucleon could launch clinical trials, it had to decide how and where CRP-1 would be manufactured. To ensure participants' safety, the U.S. Food and Drug Administration (FDA) imposed strict guidelines; products being tested in humans had to be made in facilities certified for "clinical grade" production.[1]

Since CRP-1 was the company's first product to go into the clinic, Nucleon had no manufacturing facilities which met FDA requirements. It was faced with three options for supplying CRP-1 to the clinic: The first was to build a new 5000 square-foot pilot plant with enough capacity to supply all the CRP-1 needed for Phases I and II of clinical trials. The second option was to contract clinical manufacturing to an outside firm. And a third option was to license the manufacturing to another biotechnology company or to a pharmaceutical firm. Under this third option, the licensee would be responsible for all manufacturing, clinical development, and eventual marketing of CRP-1.

---

[1]"Clinical grade" indicates the minimum conditions under which drugs must be produced for use in human clinical trials.

Professor Gary Pisano wrote this case as the basis for class discussion rather than to illustrate either effective or ineffective handling of an administrative situation.

Data and names have been altered for purposes of confidentiality.

Definite risks and rewards were attached to each option, and Moore knew that the one ultimately chosen by Hurst would have long-term consequences for Nucleon's survival in the intensively competitive and high-stakes drug industry.

Background

Nucleon was founded in 1985 by Dr. Alan Ball, an internationally respected researcher at the Children's Hospital and an Associate Professor of Clinical Medicine at the Greaves Medical Center, to develop pharmaceutical products based on a class of proteins known as cell regulating factors. From 1985 to 1988, Dr. Ball and a small group of scientists who joined Nucleon researched ways of producing CRP-1 outside the human body. Although CRP-1 was a naturally occurring protein contained in human blood plasma, the amount that could be extracted was far too small to be of any commercial use.

Scientists first isolated a small amount of naturally occurring CRP-1 and determined the gene that instructed human cells how to produce CRP-1. The gene was then cloned. While this laboratory process for producing CRP-1 was still very small scale, it generated enough material to send to academic collaborators who were exploring the potential therapeutic uses of CRP-1. Although an actual product was still several years and millions of dollars away, early research indicated that CRP-1 had potential as a treatment for burns and kidney failure.

Strategy and Competition

Nucleon was one of over 200 firms founded since the mid-1970s to develop pharmaceutical technologies based on recent advances in molecular biology and immunology. This new field of R&D, commonly called "biotechnology," also attracted the attention of established companies. By 1989, most of the world's largest pharmaceutical enterprises, like Eli Lilly, Merck, and Hoffman LaRoche, had extensive in-house biotechnology R&D programs as well as collaborative ties with many of the new entrants.

Competition was intense. Scientists at both start-up and established companies were racing to be the first to clone certain genes and establish proprietary positions for their firms in emerging areas like cell regulating factors. Establishing a strong patent position was particularly important for small companies like Nucleon. Moore explained: "Given the enormous costs of developing and commercializing a new drug, potential investors want to see a strong proprietary position before they commit serious capital. Just one strong patent on the right molecule can ensure survival for years by allowing you to attract capital."

Biotechnology patent law, however, was as new and uncertain as the technology itself. Indeed, the legality of patenting a genetically engineered microorganism was only established in 1980 by a landmark United States Supreme Court decision, and the ensuing decade saw many legal battles over the scope and efficacy of specific patents. In some cases, two or more companies had claims on different proprietary elements of the same molecule. For example, one company might claim ownership of the molecule itself while another of the genetic sequence used to synthesize the molecule. Further, it was extremely difficult to patent the process technology used to obtain a biologically important molecule, even though the starting material and the resulting molecule were considered original enough to be patented. Given the lack of precedent, it was always difficult to predict how the courts would rule in any given situation.

Moreover, the United States Patent Office might take several years to process an application. And while few companies could afford to wait until a patent was granted before continuing development, there were big risks in going ahead with development before the granting of a patent. A company could spend tens of millions of dollars in clinical trials and manufacturing facilities yet wind up not having a proprietary position if the patent office denied the application. Even if patents were granted, it was always possible for a competitor to challenge them in court. While Nucleon believed it had a strong patent position on the CRP-1 molecule, its rights to other necessary proprietary components (such as the genetic sequence) were less certain.

Nucleon management believed that several factors, were critical to the company's survival. As Hurst commented:

> Given how small we are, it's absolutely essential that we pick the right projects. We can't hedge our bets with a big portfolio of projects, like the big pharmaceutical companies can. We've got to pick winners the first time.

Gordon Banks, Nucleon's vice president of R&D, and one of the leading scientists in the field of cell regulating factors, added:

> That's why it's so important for us to be at the leading edge of scientific research. This means not only attracting the best in-house scientists, but also maintaining close contact with universities. If someone at a university clones the genes for a new cell regulating factor, we want to know about it.

Nucleon management believed that it had found an attractive niche: relatively few firms were working on cell regulating proteins. Banks believed that the company's distinctive technical capability lay in its ability to identify potentially therapeutic cell regulating factors. Although Nucleon was a leader in cell regulating factors, the company was not free from competition. Other companies were developing drugs using some-what similar technology. Also, many companies were using alternative technologies to develop drugs for some of the same diseases for which cell regulating factors were being developed. As Hurst commented, "We're a leader, but we're not alone. It's important for us to get our products into the clinic before others do."

Biotechnology firms were using different strategies for developing and commercializing their technologies. Virtually all the biotechnology companies started, like Nucleon, as specialized R&D laboratories. Over time, some vertically integrated into production, and a few of the oldest companies, like Genentech, were even vertically integrating into market-ing. Nucleon was presently contemplating its manufacturing strategy. Its marketing strategy, however, was clear. Nucleon management believed that the company could not afford to market its products on its own. Instead, it planned to link up with established pharmaceutical companies, with strong distribution capabilities, to market its products. Hurst, who once worked in marketing for a large pharmaceutical company, noted:

> Companies like Merck have hundreds of salespeople. They can reach every doctor's office in the country within one week. It would be crazy for a company like us to go up against them in marketing. Besides, our products are likely to be targeted at a vari-ety of therapeutic markets. We would need a few hundred sales-people to market all these products directly. We're much better off linking up with the best company in each therapeutic market.

By December 1990, the privately held company had grown to 22 employees, 18 of whom were engaged in R&D; of these about one-third had PhDs from scientific disciplines such as biochemistry, molecular biol-ogy, protein chemistry, and immunology. Most of the R&D staff had been recruited from leading university research laboratories and were strongly attracted to cutting-edge, product-oriented research. Nucleon's size and entrepreneurial spirit created an academic atmosphere in R&D and tight links to the academic/scientific community.

Since its founding, Nucleon had raised approximately $6 million in venture capital and received research grants from the U.S. Department of Agriculture totaling $600,000.

Drug Development: From Research to Market

Establishing the safety and efficacy of products like CRP-1 that were based upon novel genetic engineering technology was enormously complex, time-consuming, and expensive. Nucleon's drug development process, divided into several distinct phases, is discussed below.

Research

Before launching a research project to develop a new drug, Nucleon management considered several factors in evaluating a project's profit potential. First, there had to be a chance of achieving a dominant proprietary position. Second, the market had to be large enough to justify the R&D investment. Finally, Nucleon wanted to develop drugs where no alternative treatments were available. During the research phase, Nucleon's scientists sought to identify and purify from human plasma minute quantities of cell regulating proteins that might have therapeutic value. Some critical information to pursue this research was obtained by perusing scientific literature or by consulting with leading academic researchers. Much necessary information, however, was still undiscovered and came only from in-house research and experimentation, which seldom moved in a straight-forward, logical manner but from one obstacle to the next. This could entail abandoning one strategy and starting over again.

Cloning and Purification

Products like CRP-1 and others that Nucleon intended to develop were fundamentally different from most drugs developed by pharmaceutical companies, which traditionally were synthetic chemicals. Chemical synthesis was effective for relatively small and simple molecules, but proteins like CRP-1 were simply too big and complex to be synthesized that way and instead were produced by genetic engineering.

Through genetic engineering, the scientist created a microscopic protein factory. The gene for the protein was identified, isolated, and cloned, then inserted into different strains of the bacterium E. coli. In theory, the genetically engineered bacteria could then produce the protein in a test tube or shake flask. However, since genetic engineering was still a relatively new scientific discipline, it was not always easy to either identify the relevant genes or to get "host" (genetically altered) bacteria to produce a specific protein. In practice, it was usually necessary to try different types of host cells to find one or more capable of producing the protein in quantities that could be scaled-up to an economically feasible process.

Only a few milligrams of protein could be produced from genetically engineered cells grown in shake flasks. Thus, an extensive amount of work then had to go into developing the processes for making each of these proteins in large quantity.

Pre-Clinical Research

Before a pharmaceutical was tested in humans it underwent pre-clinical evaluation, consisting of experiments in animals to evaluate its efficacy. Over six to eight months, increasing doses were administered to animals with and without the simulated disease. Another six months might be needed to evaluate the data.

By this point, the company might have spent $6 to $10 million in R&D and preparation of regulatory documents. Only after completing all the requisite animal tests, and having a suitable production process, could the company file for permission with the FDA to commence clinical trials in humans. Though Nucleon had not begun human clinical trials, management expected to file an application with the FDA to begin human trials for CRP-1 as a burn wound treatment in 1992. The company was also doing research to determine if CRP-1 might have other therapeutic applications. There was some preliminary data suggesting that it might treat kidney failure. Moore estimated that about another two years and $3 million of work were needed before the kidney failure application could be tested in the clinic.

Human Clinical Trials

Most governments required every new pharmaceutical product to undergo extensive clinical testing before it could be marketed widely, and the FDA regulations were considered the most stringent in the world. To meet them, any new drug, or any approved drug being modified for a different thera-peutic application, had to undergo three phases of clinical trials.

Phase I trials assessed basic safety. During these trials, the drug was administered to a small group of healthy volunteers and any adverse reactions (such as fevers, dizziness, or nausea) were noted.[2] This phase usually required between 6 and 12 months. As long as there were no serious side effects, the product moved to Phase II trials where it was administered to a small group of patients having the disease the drug was presumed to treat. The patients were monitored to determine whether their condition improved as a result of the drug and whether they suffered any adverse side effects. It was during Phase II trials that appropriate dosages were deter-mined. This phase typically required between one to two years to complete. If Phase II trials succeeded, the product then moved to Phase III trials.

Phase III trials assessed the product's efficacy with a relatively large sample of patients on a statistically rigorous basis. Typically, these trials involved multiple hospitals and could require from two to five years to complete. Because of the large number of patients, doctors, and hospitals involved, this stage was by far the most expensive. The costs of manufac-turing the drug, administering it to patients, monitoring results, analyzing data, and preparing the requisite regulatory paperwork could run between $30–$100 million. It was imperative for regulatory reasons to manufacture the product with the same process that would be used when the product was marketed commercially. Any change in manufacturing would mean repeating human clinical trials to prove that the deviation did

[2]For some very serious diseases, Phase I trials were performed on afflicted patients.

not alter the product's safety and efficacy. This also added significantly to the costs of running Phase III clinical trials.

The CRP-1 Project: Current Applications

Since Nucleon's founding, its main development project had been CRP-1 and most of the company's R&D resources had been focused on the CRP-1 projects. While CRP-1's commercialization was still a few years away, Nucleon's scientists and investors were optimistic about its potential. Exhibit 22.1 depicts the expected time to FDA approval. Initial research focused on developing two major therapeutic applications—one for topical treatment of burn wounds, the other for acute kidney failure. Both the burn wound and kidney failure markets were estimated to be similar in size. Furthermore, in 1988, the company had also begun investigating two new cell regulating factors, still in the early stages of research. Dr. Banks estimated that these could be ready for clinical trials in about four years if the company spent $10 million on each one.

One of the most critical activities currently taking place on the CRP-1 project was the development of a larger scale production process, with sufficient capacity to meet all clinical trial requirements. Every step of the process had to be carefully documented and validated to ensure that it could produce identical product from batch to batch.

Process Development and Manufacturing

CRP-1 production would require four basic process steps: 1) fermentation, 2) purification, 3) formulation, 4) filling and packaging (see Exhibit 22.2).

Fermentation. Fermentation initially focused on growing the genetically engineered *E. coli* in small laboratory flasks; the process was then scaled up to successively larger vessels. Unfortunately, the process used to grow cells in a 1-liter glass bottle might not work when attempted in a 10-liter glass chamber or a 100-liter stainless steel tank (also known as a fermentor or bioreactor), given differences in heat exchange, tank aeration, and fermentor geometry. The kinds of nutrients cells were fed, bioreactor temperature,

Exhibit 22.1 Approximate Time Frame for CRP-1 Project

April 1992	Begin Phase I Clinical Trials
December 1992	Begin Phase II Clinical Trials
December 1993	End Phase II Clinical Trials
June 1994	Begin Phase III Clinical Trials
December 1996	Complete Phase III Clinical Trials; File data with FDA
January 1998	Expected FDA approval and commencement of sales

Exhibit 22.2   Process Flow for CRP-1[1]

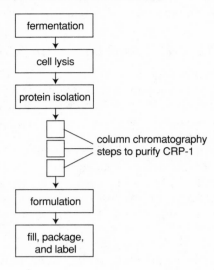

Fermentation: A process in which organisms such as bacteria or yeast are suspended in a nutrient growth medium, consisting of sugars, salts, and amino acids (protein building blocks), at an appropriate temperature and aeration level (oxygen and other gases) in order to promote these organisms' growth and metabolism. The desired products of the organisms' metabolism may be the whole organism itself, metabolic products, modified compounds, or in this case proteins.

Cell Lysis: In cases where the protein of interest is not excreted by the cell into the surrounding medium but remains inside, the cell needs to be broken open to obtain the protein. This process is known as cell lysis. Lysis can be done mechanically or chemically.

Isolation and Purification: After cells are lysed, the protein of interest must be isolated and purified from among all of the other contents of the cell. Initially, methods such as centrifugation (using centrifugal force to separate heavy and light debris) and chemical precipitation can be used to concentrate the mixture.

After a series of initial separation steps have been performed, finer, more precise separation techniques can be employed to isolate the protein of interest from other similar protein molecules. For example, chromatography isolated substances based upon their ability to separate between a liquid and a solid.

Formulation: In drug formulation, the protein of interest is put into an appropriate medium for administration as a therapeutic drug. The protein may by dissolved in purified water or another pure solvent such as ethanol for injection. In some cases, a protein must be formulated to be applied in a topical form such as a cream or put in an aerosol suspension. The challenge is to ensure the drug's safety and efficacy.

Filling: The therapeutic is then placed in an appropriate container under sterile conditions and is packaged and labeled.

---

[1]Diagram does not include holding points where work-in-process is stored between operations. The diagram also does not include quality control steps which are conducted after every operation.

acidity level, oxygen flow rate into the bioreactor, and dozens of other process parameters, were all determined during fermentation process development.

While crude fermentation processes existed for over 6000 years, fermentation using genetically engineered cells dated to the early 1980s. Many biotechnology firms encountered major difficulties when trying to run pilot and commercial scale fermentation processes for the first time, as Dr. Ann Dawson, Nucleon's director of process science, explained:

> There are so many unknowns and so many things which can go wrong. If a virus gets into your bioreactor, you could be shut down for weeks. Incredibly tight process control is an absolute must, and even then, you may still run into troubles.

For regulatory reasons, it was absolutely critical to run the process exactly as specified. Such strict adherence to process specifications was necessary because even minor process deviations could impact product quality. In addition, the efficiency of the process could be severely affected by changes in any one of the key process parameters.

Because such production methods were new, process development required a great deal of trial-and-error and close collaboration between research scientists and process development scientists early on in the project. Research scientists had to design a process that worked in a test tube as well as on a larger scale, and process development scientists had to be aware of and understand the details of the product and its host cell. Some genetically-engineered cell lines, for example, were extremely difficult to grow large-scale. Dr. Dawson noted:

> Ideally, we want the research scientists to work with only those cell lines which we know can be scaled-up. While I think they agree with this in principle, they really don't want to be constrained, particularly if they're having trouble getting expression with one of our "preferred" cell lines.

While much progress had been made over the past decade, many people considered biotechnology production processes very much an art. It was not unheard of for a process to work well in one facility but fail completely when transferred to another. One Nucleon researcher who had experience with such transfers explained:

> You would be surprised at all the little things that could be done differently from one organization to another. Most of these things are so minor you would not even think of writing them down. But they make the difference between a successful and unsuccessful process.

Currently, Nucleon had scaled up the process for making CRP-1 to 10 liters, enough to supply material for its own biochemical studies, academic collaborators, and potential joint venture partners who wanted to evaluate the product. Early phase clinical trials were likely to require a 100-liter process, and commercial production a much larger scale process.

As complex as it was, bacterial fermentation was considered one of the more efficient ways of producing proteins like CRP-1. In some cases, product characteristics could be enhanced if a mammalian cell (e.g., from a mouse or human) rather than a bacterial cell was used as a host. Mammalian cell processes, while desirable from the product side, were much more complex than bacterial processes, not well understood, and much more expensive to maintain. Mammalian cells had to be fed more expensive nutrients, and they grew much more slowly than bacterial cells. They required different bioreactors, and even stricter adherence to original process specifications than bacterial cells. Dr. Dawson explained, "With bacterial cells, a one degree Centigrade temperature change can slow the growth rate and increase your costs, whereas mammalian cells might just die altogether."

Although most biotechnology companies had some experience with bacterial cell processes, many fewer had mammalian cell capabilities. Fortunately, CRP-1 could be produced using bacterial cells. The company's R&D lab, however, was already working on second generation CRP-1 molecules produced in mammalian cells. And biotechnology companies overall were unsure whether existing process development technology would be viable in the future to produce biological products.[3]

Purification. After fermentation, the cells would be broken apart and the CRP-1 protein separated from all other proteins and cell debris contained in the fermentation tank. A series of fractionation and centrifugation steps would isolate the cell protein from carbohydrates, fatty acids, and DNA. The CRP-1 containing protein mixture would then be purified in three additional steps using a filtration procedure known as column chromatography. Like fermentation, the purification process specified during process development had to be strictly followed during manufacturing. After purification, the material would be subjected to extensive quality testing to ensure that the product met the FDA's extremely high purity standards.

Formulation. Purification processes yielded nearly pure quantities of the protein of interest, for example CRP-1. At this stage, the product was made into the intended dosage form (e.g., oral, topical, injectable), and subjected

---

[3]On the horizon was a hybrid of biotechnology and synthetic chemical techniques that could alter or replace existing process technologies. These hybrid companies used molecular biology techniques to clone and produce small amounts of biologically important proteins. The protein was studied to learn the chemical and physical structure of its therapeutically active site and then, using computer-aided modelling techniques, the active site of the protein could be constructed synthetically.

to extensive quality testing. For burn treatment, CRP-1 would be formulated into a topical dosage form.

Filling and Packaging. During the final step, bulk quantities of the formulated product were put into tubes, bottles, or other vessels required for administration to patients. The sealed vessels were then inserted into packages, which were also sealed.

The Financial Environment

A critical issue affecting Nucleon was capital availability. The situation had changed dramatically since the late 1970s and early 1980s when investors lined up to provide capital to brand new biotechnology companies. By the mid- to late-1980s, private and public equity markets grew tighter, and venture capitalists, who expected investment returns of 30%, became more selective. The state of the public equity markets in 1990 made "going public" virtually impossible for a company like Nucleon; furthermore, potential corporate partners, who had been disappointed by previous biotechnology relationships, were unwilling to fund early stage projects. As Hurst described it:

> In the early 1980s, a company like ours could have gotten corporate funding with just our idea. By the mid-1980s, we probably would have needed to have started some lab work and have had some preliminary experimental data. Now, it's hard to get a large pharmaceutical company to talk to you unless you've got some solid Phase I and Phase II clinical results and can demonstrate that you've got a stable manufacturing process. And even then, they'll cut some pretty tough terms with you. When it comes to raising capital today, it's a buyers' market.

Nucleon was just about to receive another $6.0 million infusion from its venture capitalist. This funding, combined with existing cash on-hand, revenues, interest, and grants, would give Nucleon about $6.5 million. Furthermore, if CRP-1 showed promise in pre-clinical trials, Hurst felt that Nucleon could raise enough money to pursue Phase I and II clinical trials. Some analysts were predicting that by 1991 or 1992, Wall Street would once again find biotechnology stocks attractive and there would be opportunities for smaller companies to raise money by selling stock to the public. Others thought the capital situation would stay tight for at least several more years. The possibility that a long awaited "shake-out" was about to hit the biotechnology industry was making many investors cautious. One promising sign was that large corporations again seemed willing to fund some selected projects at very early stages of research. As Moore noted, "Today, some brand new start-ups in new fields, like antisense, are cutting some deals on projects which are still years away from the clinic."

Manufacturing Options for Phase I and Phase II CRP-1 Development

Nucleon management contemplated three options to produce clinical grade CRP-1: 1) build a new pilot facility, 2) contract CRP-1 production to a third-party, or 3) license manufacturing and marketing rights to another biotechnology company or pharmaceutical firm in exchange for up front cash payments and royalties on future product sales. Each option is described below.

The New Pilot Plant

Nucleon commissioned an engineering consulting firm to study the physical requirements and costs of a new pilot plant (Exhibit 22.3). The proposed 5000 square-foot plant would be fully equipped with all the state-of-the-art processing equipment and environmental controls necessary to meet clinical production standards. Planned capacity would meet Nucleon's requirements for Phase I and Phase II clinical trials. The pilot facility, however, could not be used to produce CRP-1 for Phase III trials, because it would not meet FDA manufacturing standards for those trials. It was beyond Nucleon's financial capability to build such a plant at this time.

The main advantage in building a pilot plant, as Moore saw it, was that it would enable the firm to develop the nucleus of a future larger-scale, in-house manufacturing capability. Because most of Nucleon's employees were PhD scientists engaged in R&D, it currently lacked supervisors and technicians who could carry out the maintenance, procurement,

Exhibit 22.3 Time and Cost to Obtain Phase II Data for CRP-1 (Burn Treatment) Using a New Pilot Facility for Clinical-grade Production of CRP-1. Midrange estimate. ($000)

Pilot Facility	1991	1992	1993	Total Thru 12/93
Construction and Equipment Costs	3,100	0	0	3,100
Variable Production Expenses and Overhead	0	800	1,204	2,004
Pre-Clinical Development	250	0	0	250
Clinical Trials (Phase I/II)	0	1,040	1,000	2,040
Total	3,350	1,840	2,204	7,394

quality assurance, technical support, logistics, and other functions to operate even a small manufacturing plant. Recruiting people with the appropriate skills and getting the manufacturing organization to work
effectively would take time. Supplying clinical trials would allow manufacturing time to accumulate experience dealing with many complicated
technical and regulatory issues. Moore noted:

> If Nucleon waits until Phase III trials to bring manufacturing in-
> house, we might find ourselves with a "green" manufacturing
> organization just when the stakes are highest. By starting now,
> we'll have the basic manufacturing skills in-house and ready to go
> when we are really going to need them. The second big advantage
> of the pilot facility is that it would keep control over process and
> quality procedures firmly in Nucleon's hands.

Dawson added, "Scaling up will be much easier if we have our own
pilot plant to experiment in."

Of course, building a pilot plant was risky. Moore knew that despite
its promise in laboratory experiments, it was uncertain at this point how
well CRP-1 would work when tested in humans. Indeed, if the history of
the pharmaceutical industry was any guide, most drugs that entered clinical trials never reached the market. This high risk of failure was offset
somewhat by the fact that CRP-1 had several potential therapeutic applications. If clinical trials for burn wounds were not promising, it might be
used in other applications. Nevertheless, Nucleon management had to
consider the possibility of the pilot plant being idled if CRP-1 performed
poorly in the clinic. Other products under development were still years
away from requiring pilot manufacturing capabilities.

Another major risk involved process uncertainty. The pilot plant
would be designed to produce products using bacterial fermentation; but
the company was already in the early stages of developing a version in
mammalian cells, which would require vastly different process development capabilities.

Some board members believed that Nucleon should focus all of its
financial, managerial, and technical resources on R&D. Manufacturing,
they felt, would only distract the company from its main mission of
exploiting its unique scientific capabilities in the discovery of cell regulating proteins. According to Hurst:

> Our venture capitalists are asking us where we, as a company, add
> the most value. As a small research- intensive company, we can be
> the "fastest guns on the block" when it comes to drug discovery.
> But that means funneling our limited resources into R&D. Some of
> our investors are concerned that we could get bogged down in
> manufacturing. On the other hand, it's getting to the point where

anyone can clone a gene. I keep wondering whether we can still differentiate ourselves on R&D alone.

Contract Manufacturing

Contracting manufacturing was a second option for Phase I and Phase II CRP-1 development. The biggest advantage of this option was that it required no major capital investments on Nucleon's part. If CRP-1 failed, the contract could be easily terminated. Aside from relatively small termination penalties, the company would have little else at risk. Another advantage was that companies supplying contract manufacturing services had facilities and personnel in place.

Contract production was not inexpensive (see Exhibit 22.4). There were very few U.S. companies capable and willing to contract manufacture pharmaceuticals from bacteria. Nucleon management was meeting with several potential contractors. These included other biotechnology companies who had excess capacity. In recent years, many biotechnology companies had built GMP plants in anticipation of future products. When product approvals were delayed or even rejected by the FDA, these companies found themselves with tremendous excess manufacturing capacity. Because of mounting financial pressures, some of these companies were providing contract manufacturing services. Some industry experts believed that excess manufacturing capacity would continue to accumulate during the next few years.

One of contract manufacturing's biggest risks was confidential information disclosure. It was virtually impossible for any contractor to provide reliable time and cost estimates without knowing many proprietary product details. Moreover, the complexity of the products and processes made estimates of time and cost painstaking; reaching an agreement could take many months. Even after a contract was signed, technol-

Exhibit 22.4 Time and Cost to Obtain Phase II Clinical Trial Data for CRP-1 (Burn Treatment) Using Contract Production for Clinical-grade CRP-1.

	1991	1992	1993	Total Thru 12/93
Contract Production and Related Expense	0	955	1,550	2,505
Pre-Clinical Development	250	0	0	250
Clinical Trials (Phase I/II)	0	1,040	1,000	2,040
Total	250	1,995	2,550	4,795

ogy transfer and scale-up might take another nine months. Moore noted, "It will take about as much time to negotiate an agreement and transfer and validate the process as it will for us to build a pilot plant."

Although production contracts were negotiated typically for fixed quantities (e.g., 100 g of CRP-1 over 10 months), in contract negotiations, a balance needed to be struck. On one hand, it was risky to commit to large quantities of material—which might not be required if product specifications changed or the product was pulled from the clinic. On the other hand, short-term contracts usually involved a higher price to offset fixed costs of scale-up and batch set-ups.

Under either the pilot plant or the contract manufacturing option, Nucleon would retain ownership of the product rights at least until the commencement of Phase III clinical trials. At that point, the company would enter into licensing and marketing with a large corporate partner. The options for Phase III trials and beyond are discussed later.

Licensing the Product to Another Company

Rather than waiting until Phase III trials to enter a licensing deal, Nucleon could license the product immediately in exchange for fixed payments and future royalties. Under this option, the licensed partner, not Nucleon, would make all the requisite expenditures in clinical development, clinical manufacturing, regulatory filings, and commercial manufacturing and marketing. The partner would have the right to market CRP-1 to treat burn wounds. Nucleon would retain the right to develop CRP-1 for other therapeutic applications. Nucleon also would receive an up-front, fixed licensing fee and reimbursement for any additional development work it performed on the project. If and when CRP-1 was commercialized, Nucleon would receive royalties as a percentage of sales.

This licensing option had the chief benefit of generating cash immediately; it also spared Nucleon from making large capital investments in clinical development and manufacturing, and allowed the company to concentrate all of its financial and human resources on R&D. Of course, if the product turned out to be successful, Nucleon would receive far lower revenues than if it had made all of these investments itself. Some Nucleon employees viewed this option as "mortgaging away" the company's future.

Whether this option would mortgage the company's future depended upon the exact terms of the agreement that Nucleon could negotiate. While it was virtually impossible to know for sure what kind of deal could be struck, Nucleon management had conducted preliminary discussions with several firms. From these and consultations with the company's venture capitalists, Moore determined that Nucleon could expect to reach an agreement with the following terms:

Upon signing the contract Nucleon would get a $3 million payment.

Exhibit 22.5   Estimated Gross Sales of CRP-1 (as
topical burn wound treatment)

Year	Sales ($thousands)
1998	53,700
1999	99,500
2000	125,000
2001	130,000
2002	150,000

*After the year 2000, sales of CRP-1 as a burn wound treatment
were expected to grow at approximately 5% per year, assuming no
introduction of a substitute product.

After the FDA approved CRP-1 for burn wounds, Nucleon would receive
annual royalty payments from the partner equivalent to 5% of gross sales
(Exhibit 22.5).

Manufacturing Options for Phase III and Commercialization

One of the chief advantages of either in-house pilot manufacturing or
contract manufacturing over immediate licensing was that it gave
Nucleon more options if the project survived Phase I and Phase II trials. As
noted earlier, under these two options, Nucleon intended to line up with a
partner who would be responsible for conducting Phase III trials, handling
regulatory filings and marketing the product. However, under such an
arrangement, Nucleon could either retain commercial manufacturing
responsibilities or license these to the partner. Each of these approaches are
discussed below.

Vertically Integrate into Commercial Manufacturing

Before Phase III trials began, Nucleon could invest in a full-scale commercial manufacturing facility which met the FDA guidelines for Good
Manufacturing Practice (Exhibit 22.6). The FDA required that Phase III
trials be supplied largely by the plant which would be used to supply the
commercial market. Thus it would be necessary to commence construction
in mid-1993 so that the plant could be fully validated and operational by
the scheduled commencement of Phase III trials.

Moore estimated that the costs of such a facility would be about $20
million, and another $1 million in development resources would be
required to perform scale-up. He and Nucleon's financial advisors
believed that once the project cleared Phase II trials, it would have little
difficulty raising the needed funds to build the plant. The company would

Exhibit 22.6   Good Manufacturing Practices (GMPs)

The following are some of the major concepts behind "Good Manufacturing Practices" (GMPs):

1. A facility must have an uncluttered fermentation area, precautions for fermentation spills, and surfaces that are easily cleaned.

2. Adequate air systems to prevent cross-contamination of the product from other research products or micro-organisms in the facility. Closed system fermenters. Steps must be performed in a controlled environment. (A controlled environment is defined as being adequate to control air pressure, humidity, temperature, microorganisms and particulate matter.) An environmental monitoring system is necessary for all manufacturing areas.

3. The water used in the downstream manufacturing steps should be of high quality and, again, there should be a monitoring system in place.

4. A trained Quality Assurance department is required to oversee and assure GMP manufacturing and control.

5. A documentation system is required for the process or support systems.

6. Uni-directional production flow is required.

7. Validated processes to demonstrate removal of major contaminants is required.

8. Validated cleaning procedures to demonstrate those in place are adequate for multi-use of equipment is required.

9. A uni-directional flow of raw material, product and personnel is required with product moving from less clean and controlled areas (fermentation) to very clean areas (formulation and filling). There should be positive air pressure differentials between clean and less clean areas.

10. Space should be designated for raw material and final product storage. The area should be designed to allow for separate areas for quarantined, released and rejected material and there should be adequate security.

11. Space should be designated for media/reagent preparation with a controlled environment.

12. There should be adequate space for glassware washing and autoclaving.

13. There should be gowning areas for very clean areas (formulation/filling) and possibly the fermentation area.

14. Find out now what other microorganisms are being used in the facility and keep track of any new organisms which may be used in the future.

also have to hire at least 20 people to handle such functions as procurement, quality control, maintenance, technical support, and logistics.[4]

It was difficult to know exactly what terms could be reached. If Nucleon built a commercial plant, it would be the sole supplier of CRP-1 to its marketing partner. Judging by what other firms in the industry were receiving for similar products, Nucleon management estimated that the

[4]This assumes the company already has a pilot with a staff of six.

company could negotiate a combined supply contract and royalty agreement with the following terms: Nucleon would receive a $5 million payment upon FDA approval of CRP-1 plus royalties equal to 40% of the partner's gross sales of the product. Nucleon would sell CRP-1 to the partner at cost.[5]

Licensing Out Manufacturing and Marketing Rights at Phase III

A second option at the beginning of Phase III trials would be to license out both the manufacturing and marketing rights to a partner. This option would be similar to that discussed above, except, in this case, the partner would also be responsible for Phase III and commercial manufacturing. Nucleon therefore would not have to invest the $20 million in a commercial plant. Under this option, Nucleon could expect to receive a $7 million payment if and when CRP-1 was approved by the FDA. After that, Nucleon would receive a royalty equivalent to 10% of the partner's gross sales of CRP-1.

Moore recognized that Hurst leaned towards manufacturing CRP-1 in-house. He had said, "I keep asking myself, 'How many times will we get to the plate?' If I thought that this were our only chance, I'd go for the home run and take the risks of manufacturing." For his part, Moore decided to review Nucleon's options another time before making a recommendation.

[5]All costs, except depreciation, would be reflected in the transfer price.

CHAPTER 23

Intel—PED (A)

*I*N JULY 1991, Dr. Brian Davis, head of Intel's Process Equipment Development Department (PED), was reconsidering his company's equipment strategy. PED had been established as a central department in 1986 in response to the rising costs of integrated circuit (IC) manufacturing equipment and the need to coordinate the generations of rapidly changing process technologies across multiple plants. Since then, Intel had attempted to pursue the "best of breed" in the selection and implementation of new generations of IC processing equipment. A single supplier and system was selected for each new requirement and uniformly introduced across all factories for a particular generation of technology.

Davis had just returned from a meeting of the Senior Technology Committee (STC), at which Tom Matthews, manager of PED's Thin Films Group and chairman of Intel's Thin Films/Diffusion Technology Capabilities Group (TCG), had presented a proposal to use two suppliers for a new "Back-end Process Tool" for Intel's next generation of IC technology. While the impetus for this deviation from past practice had come from Gerry Parker, senior vice president of Intel's Technology and Manufacturing Group, there were mixed reactions to the dual- supplier option. The representatives from manufacturing, in particular, were strongly opposed to the proposal.

Company History

Intel Corporation was founded in July 1968 in Mountain View, California, by Robert Noyce and Gordon Moore. Pioneers in the semiconductor industry, they had worked for William Shockley, co-inventor of the transistor, and had later co-founded Fairchild Semiconductor with six other colleagues. There Noyce had co-invented the integrated circuit, and Moore had managed the R&D team that commercialized the first ICs. At Intel

Doctoral Candidate Gita Mathur prepared this case under the supervision of Professor Robert Hayes as the basis for class discussion rather than to illustrate either effective or ineffective handling of an administrative situation. Selected names and data have been disguised.

they were joined by Andy Grove, a Hungarian emigre who had earned a doctorate in chemical engineering at U.C. Berkeley before joining Fairchild in the early 1960s.

The new company quickly acquired a reputation as an innovator, creating such new chips as the microprocessor, dynamic random access memory (DRAM), erasable programmable read only memory (EPROM), and others that revolutionized electronics by making possible small, inexpensive, powerful computing systems.

Intel originally flourished as a supplier of semiconductor memory for mainframe computers and minicomputers. After gradually losing ground to the Japanese IC manufacturers in the mid-1980s, Intel made a strategic decision in 1985 to withdraw from the DRAM business. It continued, however, to be a leader in other microcomputer components, selling its microcomputer components, modules, and systems directly as well as through electronics distributors. Its major products were microprocessors, microprocessor peripherals, microcontrollers, EPROMS, microcommunication products, computer modules and systems, and personal computer enhancement products.

Intel was the fifth largest merchant semiconductor supplier in 1990, with $2.9 billion in sales. It was the leading supplier of microprocessors, microcontrollers, and microprocessor peripherals, as well as the fastest growing ($1.7 billion in 1989 to $2.3 billion in 1990).

Intel had used second-sourcing and licensing agreements in the past to supplement its production of microprocessor chips. While these agreements had met the goals of setting industry standards and guaranteeing customers adequate supplies, they had allowed competitors to emerge. Japanese competitors had attained their position as leading producers of these chips primarily through second-sourcing or licensing of U.S.-designed products. The high margin microprocessor business (estimated gross margins of 80%) had attracted competition from reverse-engineered versions of Intel chips, as well as new products that mimicked the functions of Intel's microprocessors. Intel's market share in microprocessor chips had fallen from 100% to about 75% through the past decade. Intel had decided not to second-source or license its newer 386 and 486 families of microprocessors to other companies. It had also responded to the increased competition by accelerating the development and introduction of new chips to the market.

Intel's principal U.S. locations (administrative offices and manufacturing) were in Arizona, California, New Mexico, and Oregon. Major international sites were in England, France, Germany, Ireland, Israel, Malaysia, Philippines, Puerto Rico, and Singapore. Intel also had sales offices and electronics distributors in many other countries. Intel operated eight IC manufacturing plants (Arizona, New Mexico—three; Oregon—two; Ireland; and Israel) and two technology development plants (California and Oregon).

IC Chip Manufacturing

An individual integrated circuit, usually on the order of ½-inch square, was commonly called a "chip." Chips were produced in batches, laid out on disk-shaped silicon substrates called "wafers," and then separated and individually "packaged." Typical IC products are shown in Exhibit 23.1.

The IC chip manufacturing process flow was divided into the "front-end" (earlier part) of the process sequence, in which individual devices

Exhibit 23.1 Typical IC Products

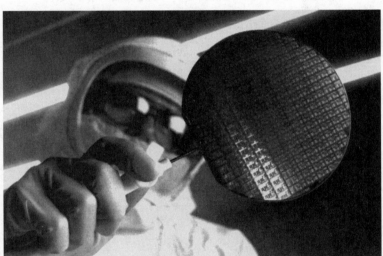

A six-inch silicon wafer

Packaged microprocessor parts

An Intel 486 microprocessor chip

(such as transistors or memory cells) were fabricated, and the "back-end" where multiple levels of interconnections were made in order to form circuits. Exhibit 23.2 illustrates a typical IC chip manufacturing process. The IC chip manufacturing sequence was also divided into several process "modules," each of which involved a number of steps performed on one or more pieces of process equipment. This segmentation specified the fabrication steps that resulted in the completion of some measurable feature of a chip.

A piece of IC fabrication equipment, such as an ion-implanter or a

Exhibit 23.2   A Typical IC Chip Manufacturing Process

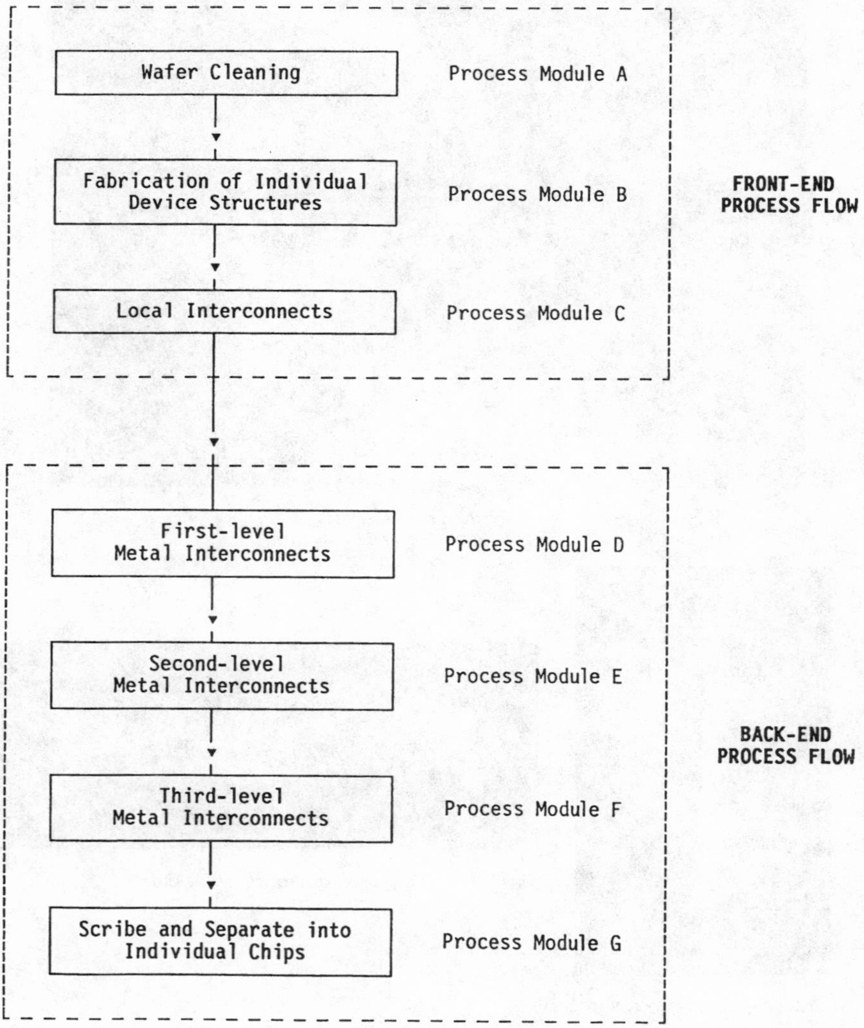

thin-film deposition system, was commonly referred to as a "tool" (see Exhibit 23.3). Most kinds of process equipment were common to more than one module, and some, such as photolithography tools, were used in almost all modules. Similar tools were usually clustered together in areas of the plant called "cells." Hence, performing the operations required

Exhibit 23.3 Typical IC Water Fabrication Tools

Technicians performing maintenance on ion-plant equipment (front-end tool)

Engineers monitoring a thin-film deposition system (back-end tool)

within a single module required several movements of a batch of wafers around the plant.

IC manufacturing plants were called "IC fabs." Each fab was designed to produce a specific set of products, and contained all the tools and process modules required to fabricate these chips. Exhibit 23.4 contains a schematic and interior view of the "clean room" area of a typical fab. In a clean room the air was continuously filtered to control the number of solid particles in the environment. The air flow was directed

Exhibit 23.4   Schematic and Interior View of the Clean Room Area of a Typical Fab

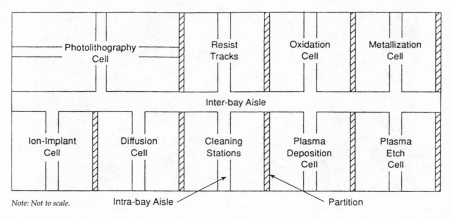

A fab operator transporting wafers through the Inter-bay aisle

from the ceiling, through holes in the floor, into a particle-filtering system. All of the air was replaced several times every minute. In a "class 100" clean room, for example, the number of solid particles whose largest dimension was more than 1 micron (one millionth of a meter) was less than 100 per cubic foot.

A typical fab had a total capital cost of $600 million, about 100 process tools in 1,000 to 5,000 square meters of clean room area, and was staffed by 100 to 500 people, working three shifts, seven days per week.

Technological Change

The IC industry had seen a progressive reduction in the interval between successive technology generations, to about three years, over the previous decade (Exhibit 23.5 illustrates the evolution of chip technology at Intel). A generation of technology was usually defined by an IC chip's minimum feature size, or "linewidth," which was the minimum dimension that could be defined on the chip (e.g., 1 micron). A "generation" was commonly associated with the DRAM product manufactured using a particular technology, since DRAMs were usually the first to implement the latest minimum feature size. The lifetime of a typical product was

Exhibit 23.5   Technological Change at Intel

DRAM Generations (megabit capacity)			
	1	**4**	**16**	**64**
Equivalent Intel micro-processor	386	486	P5	P6
Transistors per chip (million)	.275	1.2	> 3	> 5
Time of manufacturing introduction	1987	1990	1993[a]	1996[a]
Current status	peak production	ramping up	pilot production	early R&D
Minimum feature size (micron)	1	0.8	0.5	0.35
Wafer diameter (inch)	6	6	8	8
Maximum chip size (mm per side)	15	17.5	20	22
Process complexity index	1	1.2	1.7	1.9
Clock speed of processor (index)	1	1.5	2	NA
Capital investment index	1	2	4	6.0[a]

[a]Estimate.
NA = Not available.

Exhibit 23.6   Product Lifecycles for Successive Generations of Microprocessor Chips (Estimates and Projections)

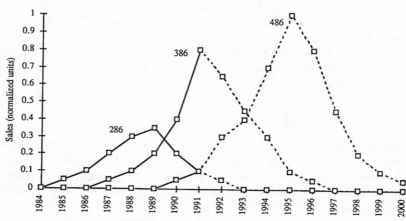

Source: Intel records.

about 10 years over the previous decade. Exhibit 23.6 shows representative product lifecycles for successive generations of microprocessor chips (estimates and projections). Product prices and manufacturing costs fell by a factor of 2 to 3 within five years of launch.

A new generation typically involved a reduction in the minimum feature size, a significant change in the process flow used in producing a chip, increased complexity in the number of metal interconnect layers and photomasking steps, and higher packing density (transistors per unit area). At Intel, the initial ("lead") product introduced with a new generation of process technology was either an entirely new product or a higher performing (faster) old product.

While the process flow was always new for a new generation of technology, the tools used were typically composed of both old and new equipment. When technological change was accompanied by an increase in the diameter of the wafer, a larger percentage of modules required changes. The ratio of new to old equipment in the transition from one generation of technology to the next at Intel was approximately 70/30.

IC Wafer Fabrication Equipment Trends

The IC industry had been characterized by very high and growing capital intensity. The capital equipment costs (industry averages) for different generations of technology are illustrated in Exhibits 23.7A and 23.7B. In 1960, the cost of a fab was about $1–$2 million, while by 1970 a plant required about $30 million in capital investment. In 1991, the cost of a single tool was typically $1–$3 million, and a state-of-the-art fab cost on average 20 times more than it did 20 years earlier. Manufacturing equipment became obsolete in only three to five years due to the rapidly changing technology. About two-thirds of the cost of a new fab was invested in equipment, with the rest in property and buildings. In 1990, and each of the preceding eight years, the semiconductor industry expenditure on wafer fabrication equipment was approximately 10% of semiconductor

Exhibit 23.7A Capital Equipment Impact on Wafer Cost by Generation

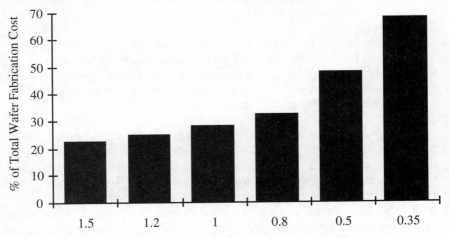

Exhibit 23.7B Distribution of Wafer Fabrication Costs for Three Generations of Technology

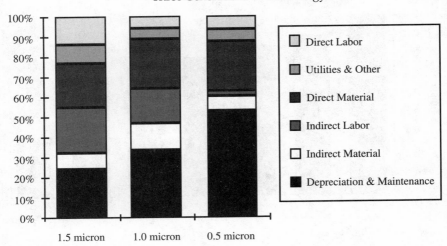

Source: Intel records.

revenue. Capital spending by leading IC manufacturers in 1990 is shown in Exhibit 23.8.

A fab that cost $600 million and was depreciated over four years incurred a depreciation cost of about $3 million a week. In addition, a delay in starting up a new fab resulted in lost potential business and the operating cost of keeping it going. As a result, the speed with which a new fab was started-up and ramped-up had become increasingly important.

Over time, U.S. IC manufacturers had become increasingly dependent on Japanese equipment suppliers, primarily due to availability (see Exhibit 23.9). Brian Davis explained:

> DRAM has been the "point technology" driving the equipment business for the past 7 to 10 years, and DRAM production is now concentrated in Japan. An analysis made in 1989 projected that Japan would have 75% of Intel's equipment business by 1993. More recent projections reduced this to 50%.

There were a number of concerns with this trend, including the possibility that Intel might gradually lose contact with the most advanced thinking in process technology, since leading equipment firms were reluctant to export tools that were not fully developed. Thus, Japanese chip manufacturers had access to the latest process technology earlier than did their U.S. competitors. There also were concerns that Japanese equipment producers might be encouraged to delay selling strategic technology or equipment to non-Japanese chip manufacturers. Geographic separation

Exhibit 23.8   Capital Spending by Leading IC Manufacturers in 1990

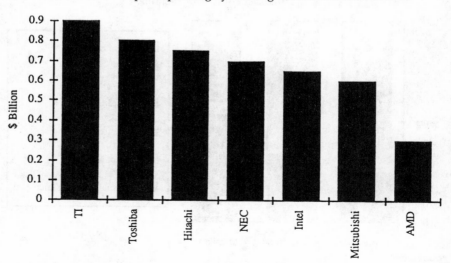

Exhibit 23.9   Worldwide Wafer Fabrication Equipment Market Share

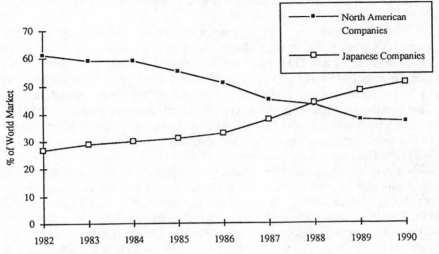

Source: Intel records.

and differences in culture further complicated doing business with foreign equipment vendors, especially when special safety, factory-specific, or process-specific requirements arose. Acting on these concerns, Intel had been a key participant in Sematech, a U.S. government/industry consortium that supported the advancement of domestic semiconductor equipment technology. Intel also increased its efforts to evaluate and support domestic suppliers. Building such close relationships did not threaten Intel's ability to protect its intellectual property, since proprietary information lay in the integration of processes, rather than in the procedures used on individual systems.

Intel's Process Equipment Strategy

Intel's process equipment strategy was formulated to reflect its concerns about rapid technological change in IC component manufacturing and the increasing complexity of the manufacturing process, given the high cost of capital and of delays in start-up and ramp-up. It favored selecting only the best available equipment suppliers and tools, and utilizing the same equipment that would be used in high volume manufacturing when developing new process modules. Brian Davis explained:

> Process and equipment are not regarded as separable at Intel. If you take away a gas stove from a chef and replace it with an electric stove, he/she will need to redesign recipes. To reduce the risk in transferring a manufacturing process from development to

manufacturing, that is, to maintain the same recipe, Intel carries the same equipment that is used for development into manufacturing.

Product development was done at one of two technology development (TD) sites, Oregon or California (near Intel's corporate headquarters at Santa Clara). Each TD group had its own fab, which allowed it both to demonstrate high yield on new products and to generate sales revenue. In order to reduce start-up and ramp-up time, Intel's strategy for introducing new products and processes involved concurrent development of the lead product (the first product offered with a new generation of technology), the new process sequence, the new manufacturing equipment, and the lead fab. The new process developed at the TD fab was cloned at the lead fab—the same equipment, methods, and material. As soon as the process on a piece of new equipment was demonstrated to be stable and within statistical control at a TD fab, the new equipment was moved into the lead fab. The only differences in the two sites were in their level of automation, data gathering, and mechanization. Hiring and training of manufacturing personnel also began as soon as the process was qualified. This approach resulted in a standardized equipment set for each generation of technology and facilitated the transfer of technology from TD fabs to manufacturing fabs.

The lead fab for a new technology typically was a new factory. Intel's growth rate usually supported this increased capacity. The more modern fabs, which contained some of the tools required for the new generation process, were usually loaded to full capacity by previous generations. The older fabs usually had a larger percentage of obsolete equipment, and clean room facilities that no longer met the particle control specifications of the new generation products. Each manufacturing fab was considered to be solely a manufacturing vehicle, and did not engage in on-site development or changes in process characteristics. Its only goals were to improve yields and increase wafer throughput. When a fab shutdown was dictated, it was usually preceded by an 18-month hiring freeze. The freeze, together with the relocation of personnel to other sites, essentially resulted in redeploying its human resources.

This strategy had some negative implications, however. Most of the managers at Intel agreed that once equipment purchasing decisions were made, a particular set of manufacturing equipment was locked in for at least three years. Intel was therefore unable to make use of new process equipment that became available during that period. As a result, its manufacturing tools typically lagged the state-of-the-art capabilities (used in DRAM production) by one to two years. This was more true for tools which were critical in the front-end (photolithography, diffusion, and ion-implantation) of the manufacturing process than those which were critical in the back-end (thin-film deposition and etching). The latter was driven more by the specific needs of microprocessor chips than those of DRAMs.

Intel's process equipment strategy was executed via a central staff group, the PED department, and had worked well over the previous five years. Approximately one tool per generation did end up being changed at the last minute, usually due to unanticipated manufacturing problems.

Evolution of the Process Equipment Development Department

The central PED group was formed in 1986, when all process equipment related activities were combined into one organization. Prior to 1986, all process development had been done at the technology development (TD) organization, and new products were transferred into manufacturing at the first sign of good parts; the fabs had been responsible for further improvements. In seeking such improvements they typically changed or modified the equipment, and redeveloped the process procedures to make them more "manufacturing worthy." Although Intel had a central equipment group, each fab conducted its own process equipment development and utilized the services of the central group only as it felt necessary. The fabs functioned autonomously, so did not necessarily use the same set of tools for a given generation of technology (with the exception of photolithography equipment, which was standardized across fabs). Often each fab interacted individually with the same equipment supplier, leading to duplication of efforts and a lot of confusion in the relationships. In addition, prior to 1986, more than one process and product were often situated in the same factory.

Increasing complexity in the IC manufacturing process created a number of problems. By 1985, it was increasingly obvious that new product introductions were being delayed by about two years, and fab yields (percentage of good chips) were lower than expected. The reputation of the TD groups suffered, because nothing worked as they claimed it would. With process/product technology cycles getting shorter, and capital costs increasing, a new approach was needed that would reduce the costs associated with start-up delays, avoid investment in poor performing equipment, shorten ramp-up time, and achieve better control over production processes.

Looking back, Paul Cheang, manager of Fab Start-Up Support, commented:

When Intel lost the DRAM war to Japan, there was a realization that change was required. It was generally accepted that Intel was not as successful at manufacturing as it had to be, and that emphasis had to shift from technology alone to technology and manufacturing. Intel's technical people had tended to be far removed from the issues of manufacturing. Moreover, it became increasingly apparent that Intel fabs needed a common purpose and a common voice. The equipment decisions needed to be data-driven, not emotional.

The PED department was conceived as a means for increasing Intel's manufacturing competitiveness. Its charter was to ensure that Intel's technology development and manufacturing were cost effective, world class, on schedule, and that there were mechanisms for continuously improving each type of equipment. It was designed to allow the technical community to take a leadership role in short- and long-term technology planning. It was also expected to facilitate the development of shared expectations, longer involvement, and closer working relationships between the TD and manufacturing groups. It was to ensure a standardized process equipment set across all fabs for the same generation of technology while getting Intel's manufacturing people involved in their suppliers' productivity improvement programs.

PED executed its charter through its coordination of a number of technical working groups and committees, which were staffed with PED members and personnel from across Intel. These groups were responsible for selecting equipment and vendors for each new generation of technology, establishing strategic roadmaps for equipment, performing accelerated equipment characterization (burn-in) for learning and predictability, supporting factory improvements, ensuring fab involvement in equipment selection and development, providing support in equipment mechanization, assisting factories in fab start-ups, and managing supplier relationships.

Intel's process equipment strategy emerged as PED developed approaches to implement its mission. Most PED managers were quick to state that PED did not make the decisions, but influenced them through its "methodologies"—a set of documented procedures that were used to guide various groups in executing their responsibilities. They described each of the PED's eight areas of responsibility, and specified procedures, committee membership, and decision processes. "Equipment selection decisions are Intel decisions, not PED decisions," emphasized one manager.

The PED Organization was headed by Dr. Brian Davis and reported to the vice president of the Technology Division at Intel (see Exhibit 23.10 for a partial organization chart). After receiving a doctorate in physics from Stanford University, and holding a number of faculty and research positions both there and elsewhere, Davis joined Intel in 1977. Prior to taking over responsibility for the newly formed PED in 1986, he held various management positions in manufacturing, technology development, and research. He was also the chairman of Sematech's Executive Technical Advisory Board. The Intel managers who reported to Davis had about 10 years of experience in the IC industry, and previously had held positions of responsibility in technology development or manufacturing.

Exhibit 23.10 Partial Organization Chart of Intel Corporation (1991)

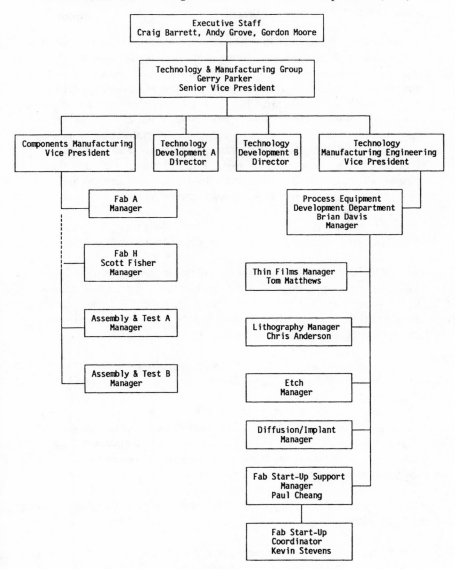

Reflections:

Scott Fisher, manager of Intel's new state-of-the-art manufacturing fab, had joined Intel in 1979 after holding a number of process development and manufacturing positions in the semiconductor industry. He had since managed several technical projects, yield improvement programs, equipment activities, and development and manufacturing fab start-ups.

Reflecting on the changes in the process equipment development activities, he commented:

> In 1980, centralization would have been considered unnecessarily restrictive. The process was more forgiving on the tool set then. The process has since become considerably more complex. Intel had actually started centralizing equipment selection even prior to the formation of PED in 1986. Today I would consider centralized process equipment development activities clearly advantageous. Given the increasing cost of capital, centralization provides a significantly better negotiating position with suppliers. Regarding disadvantages, there are really none. But a certain degree of cooperation is needed when resources are pooled, to react to the different priorities of multiple factories.

Tom Matthews, manager of PED's Thin Films Group, expressed the concerns that surrounded the decision to centralize equipment activities:

> Would it create roadblocks to the factories in getting things done? Would the central group be bureaucratic? What if the performance curve moved in the wrong direction? Today some people still feel they would be better off with more freedom, but our measures of performance show improvement.

Chris Anderson, manager of PED's Lithography group and chairman of the Lithography/ Etch TCG, felt that:

> Centralization of the equipment activities is not a problem since there is an enormous amount of information being transferred daily. Methodologies are well defined and documented, and meetings are held all the time to make sure there are no process deviations between manufacturing sites.

Fab Start-up coordinator, Kevin Stevens, weighed the pros and cons of centralization:

> A central unit eliminates individual judgments, and provides a common base for making processing decisions. Semiconductor processing is a combination of science and art. There is a need to get as much science built into it as possible. This facilitates technology transfer. However, in the event that different fab managers have varying approaches to solving a problem, it may take longer to reach an understanding on a common purpose and an action plan.

Brian Davis agreed that there were problems with centralizing process equipment activities:

> There is less factory ownership for problems that occur. However, there is now the ability to have comparative data amongst fabs due to standardization. Another disadvantage is that fabs give up the option to know how other equipment [besides the tool set of choice] functions. There is less negotiating power with suppliers, since they know that all factories will get locked into their model. They are therefore less flexible with pricing and support.

Six IC fabs had been set up since PED was formed. The previous two-year delay in new product introduction, which had led to higher costs and lost opportunities, had been considerably reduced. The time from fab start-up to peak production had also been reduced by about two years.

The Equipment Selection Process

When Intel selected a piece of equipment, it committed itself to giving the technology to its high volume fabs and to favoring future generations of technology from the technology's supplier as long as that supplier remained competitive. Intel did not like to switch suppliers between technology generations because it was helpful to use existing communication channels. However, "if the supplier does not keep us competitive, we have to look elsewhere," stated Chris Anderson. This long-term commitment carried with it a higher risk of making the wrong choice. To minimize this risk, Intel established a careful methodology for selecting process equipment.

Two Technology Capabilities Groups (TCG), one for thin film and diffusion equipment and another for photolithography and etch equipment, were established to manage the process of making equipment-related recommendations. Their membership included people from PED, the TD groups, and the manufacturing fabs (see Exhibit 23.11). Each TCG helped execute PED's charter by facilitating the sharing of information about new equipment, upgrading existing equipment, and introducing innovative manufacturing approaches across TD and Manufacturing; by providing a forum for building consensus on strategic decisions and recommendations; by serving as Intel's technical link to suppliers; and by establishing and maintaining strategic roadmaps for equipment, materials, and chemicals.

Either a TD group or a fab established a need for a new tool, and made a recommendation to the TCG. The TCG decided whether there was sufficient reason to select a new tool. It then selected a working group to perform a technical evaluation of potential suppliers and equipment, and

Exhibit 23.11   Membership of a Technology Capabilities Group

PED Area Manager 1 (Chairperson)

PED Area Manager 2

TD (California) Technologist 1

TD (California) Technologist 2

TD (Oregon) Technologist 3

TD (Oregon) Technologist 4

Manufacturing Engineering Manager (Representing Logic Fabs)

Manufacturing Engineering Manager (Representing Memory Fabs)

Components Research Representative

STC Chairperson

then to select the best possible equipment at the lowest possible cost. The
working group had members from across PED, TD groups, and the fabs.

The Senior Technology Committee (STC) was the body that reviewed
and approved the recommendations of the TCG for new process equipment, materials, and chemicals. Its members were senior management
officials from the Technology and Manufacturing organization (see Exhibit
23.12). The STC encouraged an iterative decision-making process, and
usually kept asking for more data until it was absolutely necessary to lock-
in a decision.

Tom Matthews explained the problems faced in the decision making:

> Decisions have to be made before the technology is quite ready or
> proven. The cost of a typical process tool has gone from $100,000–
> $200,000 to $1–$3 million over the last 20 years. When you spend
> one to three million on a piece of equipment, and about twice that
> on overheads, you have got to make that decision work.
> Therefore, you have to start out with the attitude that your deci-
> sion will be locked in, so you will have to live with it.
>
> The working groups look at all aspects of each decision: tech-
> nical, costs, and company background. However, their motivation
> and thinking is not the same as that of the top level of manage-
> ment. The TCG is more strategic in its thinking, but not at the same
> level as the STC. The chairman of the TCG often has to go back and
> forth between the TCG and the STC, reconciling different levels of
> concern. While PED is a neutral group, it gets caught in between
> the needs of the operations groups and the strategy groups. While
> the process is consensual and data-driven, the TD groups usually
> have the most say, since they have to deal with the problems first.

The equipment selection process usually consisted of looking at the

Exhibit 23.12   Membership of the Senior Technology Committee

---

Chairperson (Member of V.P.'s staff, Technology & Manufacturing Group)
Director of California TD
Director of Oregon TD
Manager PED (Brian Davis)
Fab Manager (Scott Fisher, representing manufacturing fabs)
Sr. V.P. Technology & Manufacturing Group (Gerry Parker)

---

total cost (capital cost and operating expense) of owning a system used to perform a specific semiconductor process step or sequence of steps. Two often used measures included "total cost per wafer through the system" and "capital cost per wafer start per week" for wafers produced over the depreciation life of the system.

The New Back-end Process Tool Requirement

Intel's latest generation of technology, a 0.5 micron linewidth that was to be implemented on an eight-inch diameter wafer, was still in the pilot stage. The previous generation, then in the process of ramp-up, was a 0.8 micron technology using six-inch diameter wafers. The new specifications required a variety of new tools for both the front- and back-ends of the manufacturing process. In January 1990, the Thin Films/Diffusion TCG put together a technical working group to evaluate prospective next-generation tools to be used in a number of the back-end modules.

The group's charter was to locate the best system, and preferably, the best U.S. supplier. Thirteen prospective suppliers were audited to evaluate process capability, hardware, reliability, automation, safety features, service and support, training and documentation, cost of ownership, and long-term viability. Initial screening and preliminary tests produced three finalists. All three tools were judged to be technically acceptable for Intel's needs, but all needed additional work (the evaluation summary for the three suppliers is given in Exhibit 23.13). The overall consensus was that Equiptek Corporation, a U.S. supplier, had the system of choice, and its open issues were resolvable. Intel already had a number of Equiptek tools in its older fabs. A close contender was a new-generation tool from NSE, a Japanese supplier. The existing generation of technology at Intel used an older NSE tool. While the technical track records of both Equiptek and NSE were good, NSE was known to have a poor reputation for service, and Equiptek had not achieved any continuing productivity improvement with its previous generation of equipment. The third tool that was potentially acceptable was manufactured by Fab-Tools, another leading U.S. equipment supplier. It had no clear technical edge over the Equiptek or

Exhibit 23.13 Supplier Evaluation Summary (For New Generation System)

Criteria	Technical Working Group Ranking				
	First	Second		Third	
Process capability	Δ— — —	Same		— — —Δ	
Uniformity (6" diameter)	Δ— — —	Same		— — —Δ	
Uniformity (8" diameter)	Equiptek	Δ— — —	Same	— — —Δ	
Defect density	Equiptek	Fab-Tools		NSE	
Hardware capability	NSE	Equiptek		Fab-Tools	
Automation	NSE	Equiptek		Fab-Tools	
Safety	Fab-Tools	Equiptek		NSE	
Cost per wafer	Equiptek	Fab-Tools		NSE	
Business evaluation	Equiptek	NSE		Fab-Tools	
Overall consensus	Equiptek	NSE		Fab-Tools	

	Other Information		
	Equiptex	NSE	Fab-Tools
Number of 8" systems shipped (ratio)	1	2	15
Ratio of Japanese to North American clients	0.54	3.0	0.5

Source: Intel records.

NSE tools. Fab-Tools had been the first-to-market with an eight-inch system, but its existing customer base was extremely dissatisfied with the company's equipment uptime. The TCG requested approval from the STC to go with Equiptek. The STC approved this recommendation on April 1991, subject to the resolution of certain issues.

After another two months of discussions, the TCG was not satisfied with Equiptek's commitment to improving the productivity of its equipment. The capital cost per wafer start per week of Equiptek systems in use had increased over the years, but the equipment-related reliability and yield had not improved over time. The fabs were dissatisfied with Equiptek's lack of responsiveness to past problems, and user groups had failed to motivate Equiptek to reduce its costs over the past five years. Brian Davis explained the emphasis on equipment productivity:

> In the 1990s we expect a 100% increase in capital cost per wafer start per week in going from one generation of technology to the next. This increase cannot be offset by yield improvement alone, even by going from a typical 80% fab yield (percentage of good chips) to 100%. We can achieve a 30% to 40% enhancement in the

number of chips per wafer by going to a larger diameter wafer. However, wafer size is not expected to evolve as rapidly as capital cost per wafer. This leaves the need to focus on other productivities, specifically run rate (wafers per hour) and utilization capability (percent time in use) of the equipment.

Gerry Parker, senior vice president of Technology and Manufacturing and a member of the STC, suggested that the TCG look into a dual-supplier strategy (two suppliers for the same requirement). It was not a popular suggestion. Even top managers tended to avoid operational risks. The fab managers were very opposed to the suggestion.

At a meeting of the STC on July 9, Tom Matthews reviewed the results of the experience with Equiptek, outlined the options Intel had for meeting the new back-end process equipment needs, and presented an analysis of the costs of a dual-supplier option (see Exhibit 23.14 for cost considerations).

Three different options were presented at the meeting:

- Commit to the Equiptek system and continue efforts, through user groups and other supplier programs, to get Equiptek to improve productivity. Based on past experience, there was no reason to be optimistic about this option.
- Select one of the other suppliers. While their tools were not technically superior on some attributes, their track records were promising.

Exhibit 23.14 Cost Considerations for the Dual-supplier Approach

Background Information

Total number of systems required	50
Capital cost per system (includes installation)	$2.0 million
Operating expense per system over four years	$6.0 million
Depreciation life	4 years
Run rate on machine	5 wafer/hour
Utilization capability	75%
Cost of each additional person per year (includes salary, benefits, and overhead)	$100 thousand
Additional resource allocation required over four years:	
Development resources	60 person years
Manufacturing resources	15 person years
Fabs are assumed to operate 24 hours a day, 7 days a week.	

Source: Intel records (numbers have been disguised).

- Pursue a dual-supplier approach to create competition and thereby motivate Equiptek and NSE to improve over time or lose the business.

While the TCG had been split between option one and two during the evaluation process, support began to grow for following a dual-supplier strategy. The STC was reluctant to commit to one supplier because this particular system was expected to require an investment of $100 million across the fabs over the next five years (see Exhibit 23.15). Most members agreed that a dual-supplier strategy would allow them to pit one supplier against the other, leading to improvement. A purchase order for 10 systems would represent from 3%–5% of each supplier's annual revenue.

Most other IC manufacturers in the United States and Japan used a dual-supplier approach, either by default or by design, in selecting their process equipment. If one piece of equipment outperformed another, they just changed the mix of purchases. Much of Intel's reluctance to do the same was due to its strategy of concurrent development and standardization across fabs within the same technology generation. This strategy, by definition, necessitated a single supplier. Unfortunately, it was also becoming apparent that its vendors were aware of, and were exploiting, this situation.

After a careful analysis of run rates, equipment utilization, cost per system, and additional headcount required to support the two-system strategy, the TCG recommended a dual-supplier strategy. A 2% increase in productivity was expected to justify the added cost of the resources required for the dual-strategy.

A Divided Response

The STC was divided in its response to the recommendation. Everyone agreed that a dual-supplier strategy would buy Intel insurance on a very critical equipment choice, and it would also create some motivation for improvement by its suppliers. Some members felt, however, that the complexity of implementing a dual-supplier strategy was not really

Exhibit 23.15 Five-year Projection for Back-end Process Tools Required

	91	92	93	94	95
TD Fabs	2	3	4	4	2
Fab H		1	5	5	4
Fab I			4	5	4
Fab J				3	4
# of systems (cumulative)	2	6	19	36	50
Capital costs ($M)	4	12	38	72	100

Source: Intel records (numbers have been disguised).

accounted for by the cost model. It would lead to an increase in the diffi-culty of process integration, training, documentation, managing spare parts and consumables inventory, and managing service contracts and relationships. The operations representatives felt that dual sourcing would also increase start-up and ramp-up time for the fabs.

Reflecting on previous equipment selection and fab start-up experi-ence at Intel, Paul Cheang (manager of Fab Start-up Support) noted:

There is often conflict arising from the different viewpoints of the operations and the strategy groups. The fabs want to stick with known equipment or suppliers for a new fab start-up, but at the same time want improved reliability and automation. The strat-egy groups are more concerned with industry trends, while oper-ations want assured spare parts and supplier service support in the short term.

According to Kevin Stevens:

For operations, a dual-supplier strategy is like having two kids versus one kid. You need to learn about two sets of people, the physical aspects of two machines, two sets of spare parts and consumables. The development of process procedures becomes twice as complex, as does subsequent training of fab personnel, process control, and the management of maintenance contracts. On the positive side, the suppliers are on their toes keeping the equipment competitive, so you have better tools in the long-term.

While acknowledging the various advantages of a dual-supplier strat-egy, Scott Fisher, manager of the lead fab (Fab H), was concerned about the problems it would create in manufacturing:

Steps in the wafer fabrication process sequence are interdepen-dent. A change in one step results in changes up and down stream. Integrating two different process tools for the same step will result in two distinctly different process flows in the fab. This is likely to result in a number of problems. On the operational side, not only will there be an incremental increase in training, but also an expec-tation that fab personnel can discern differences between the two process flows. There will be an increased probability of human error that may or may not be discernable in-line. So we will have to develop additional screening and testing procedures to avoid reliability problems. This will add to the upfront cost of develop-ment resources.

On the maintenance side, requirements of the dual-supplier strategy will also have an impact. Today, process tools are maintained by specialists not generalists, due to the complexities of the equipment. Three-fourths of the maintenance of our fab equipment is done by suppliers. A dual-supplier approach will require an additional maintenance contract. NSE, in addition, has no infrastructure in place to support Fab H, due to our geographic location. We will be required to maintain the NSE tool internally, and also have a sort of "crisis contract" for flying in the NSE service guys as required. This is not a simple change. The supplier has been the first line of defense for our equipment. Team work will also be more difficult if the service people in the fab are competitors. The spare parts' supply logistics will also be compounded with two suppliers.

The Final Decision

The STC was scheduled to meet again later in the month to make a final decision on the next-generation back-end process tool. Davis was still uncertain about what he should recommend. Based on the data that had been presented, he was inclined to support the dual-supplier decision. However, as the head of PED and a key decision-maker on the STC, he was concerned about the longer-term implications of such a deviation from strategy. Since PED's charter included the responsibility for fab start-ups, he also was worried about the lack of support for the dual-supplier strategy from the manufacturing people.

Developing Capabilities

*T*he previous module focused on an organization's *choice* of capabilities, which we looked at in terms of a series of vertical integration and sourcing decisions. The issues raised by each case study revolved around such questions as: Which capabilities are important for the organization to retain or develop internally, and which can it safely assign to outside suppliers (and what criteria should be used to select such suppliers)? What competitive advantages can be achieved by being able not only to *do* something well internally, but being able to integrate that activity with other internal activities? Conversely, as in the Intel case, under what circumstances might an organization benefit by stripping itself of a capability (e.g., the ability to manage multiple makes of equipment) in order to focus its energies on other, more important capabilities?

In the process it became apparent that if one thinks of companies as bundles of evolving capabilities, rather than as bundles of products and businesses, the traditional make/buy analysis becomes suspect. Instead of thinking in terms of "parts" (e.g., brake pistons) that get incorporated into "products" (braking systems) one should think in terms of those capabilities that are closely linked and mutually reinforcing, and of those that can safely be separated. Moreover, if a potential supplier possesses capabilities that are essential to a company's competitive success, it must either work to assimilate those capabilities or develop very close, partnership-like relations with that supplier.

Through the prism of these cases we have seen how valuable and powerful, in competitive terms, a unique or particularly effective organizational capability can be. That was our first goal in this section of our book: to draw managers' attention away from their usual preoccupation with capital investments, business plans, and specific programs for improving their company's performance in certain areas and focus it instead on the *foundation capabilities* that these investments of resources are intended to augment—and that underlie the ultimate success of their plans.

A capability is a skill, not a tool. It is the difference between owning a state-of-the-art tennis racquet and being a world-class tennis player (who can beat lesser players even using inferior racquets). As a result, it is difficult to acquire through purchase, and difficult to imitate just by watching someone else. A company may be able to acquire access to a certain technology, for example, but it cannot buy the ability to produce it in volume, sell it effectively, or improve it over time. AM International, a long-successful producer of office equipment that began to struggle as xerography and computers invaded its traditional markets, learned this lesson too late, and went bankrupt as a result. As *Business Week* editorialized:

> This company had a superb plan. It would turn to high technology to revitalize its aging product line in the fast-changing office equipment market. To implement its new strategy, it would acquire new high technology companies and new managers to run them. [But management] neglected to make sure that its production line was geared up to build quality into its products, [or] that its sales and service staff were trained to satisfy customers. (1/25/82: p120)

Such skills can only be acquired through experience and over time. The fact that they are difficult to purchase, assimilate, and develop, indeed, is what makes them so valuable. Just as important, one cannot rely on market forces to guide the development of capabilities; they often take so long to build that a company cannot wait for the market to demand a specific capability before beginning the process of developing it. For all these reasons, an organization's capabilities are both its foundation and the product of its strategic decisions. They are as critical as its buildings, equipment, and inventories, and it needs to put at least as much effort and resources into auditing and maintaining them as it does into the upkeep of its physical assets. Redirecting one's attention along these lines can have a profound impact on management thinking and organizational performance.

But simply being aware of the potential power of this alternate approach is not enough. Managers have to know *how* to go about building competitively important capabilities. How, for example, did Hitachi-Seiki build the technological skills that allowed it to emerge from obscurity in shattered postwar Japan to become one of the largest and most advanced machine-tool manufacturers in the world—in an industry dominated up to then by much larger competitors in Germany and the United States? How did Philips-Taiwan grow from a small, low-tech assembler of low-end black-and-white television receivers to become a major designer and producer of leading-edge computer monitors, the first Asian company outside Japan to win the prestigious Deming Prize? How did tiny Micom Caribe, a small factory in central Puerto Rico, isolated both geographically and psychologically from its parent company in California, develop into a world-class assembler of electronics products? Or, to use an example not included in this collection, how did Wal-Mart develop the ability to respond so rapidly to the shifting demands of its churning markets that it propelled itself ahead of such established giants as Sears and KMart?

Conversely, sometimes the most effective lessons in how to accomplish something come from analyzing an organization that has failed in the attempt. So we look also at the case of the Ex-Cell-O Corporation, which in 1979 was the second-largest manufacturer of machine tools in the world. Despite all its resources and good intentions, Ex-Cell-O was slow to develop the capabilities that would allow it to compete effectively in the growing market for computer-controlled machining systems. Only six years later, in 1985, it was contemplating whether and how to cut its losses and exit a business that many observers had predicted would be the basis for the industry's future growth. Why did a company with such a long record of success find it so difficult to develop the new capabilities required by this apparently natural evolution in technology? Similarly, why did the Medical Products Company's European operations remain unprofitable despite the company's dominance of the U.S. market and the substantial investments it had poured into Europe over the years? Why had it been unable to transfer to its European factory network the impressive capabilities it had built up in its U.S. operations, or even to transfer the operating capabilities that two of its European factories had developed to its other European factories?

The Steps in Building Capabilities

To help prepare ourselves for analyzing and understanding the contrasting experiences of these various companies, it is useful to disentangle two logical threads that tend to be naturally intertwined. First, we have to understand the progression, *over time*, of the activities and actions that build capabilities. Second, we have to separate the notions of *individual* capability and *organizational* capability.

As regards the first issue, recall that our definition of *capability* combines the notions of *ability* and *competence*. Ability simply implies feasibility; that is, an individual or organization is able to do something, however imperfectly or inefficiently. For example, as our life's experiences accumulate most of us learn to repair simple electrical fixtures, drive a car, change tires, program a VCR, use a computer, and replace a pane of glass in a window. Few of us, however, achieve a level of ability in any of these pursuits that allows us to accomplish them both efficiently and *consistently* well—so that, for example, we would be comfortable asking others to pay us for performing those services. At the point where one does get good enough to be able to charge for such services, the ability becomes a *capability*. And if you get so good that you are better than almost everybody else, that capability becomes a *distinctive* capability—for which you can charge higher prices than your competitors or from which you can extract more profit.

How does one make the progression from one extreme to the other? The beginning of an answer to this question is that one has to proceed in that same order: encourage the development of certain abilities, then select a few of these abilities and devote the time and resources necessary to develop them into capabilities, and finally polish and refine a very few capabilities to the point where they become the basis for a competitive advantage. In that sense, developing a distinctive capability is like developing a new product: one starts by encouraging a variety of product ideas, then puts them through increasingly intense scrutiny as the amount of resources necessary to take them to the next level of development increases, until a relatively small number of final products enters actual production. The front end of this "capability development funnel" is dominated by curiosity and experimentation, the center by focus and conscious development, and the end by incessant repetition. "Practice makes perfect," but perfection requires *endless* practice.

Therefore, you start developing a capability simply by trying to do something yourself instead of relying on others to do it for you, even though others may be able to do it better or less expensively. In a corporate context, this might mean making a certain part or writing a piece of software instead of automatically seeking to purchase such items from external suppliers who are acknowledged as experts in their field. Taking such an apparently illogical step sometimes comes about through a corporate directive. Top management may make a conscious decision to learn to do something internally so as to become less dependent on suppliers; or, as part of a belt-tightening program, it urges everybody to economize by making use of existing resources rather than paying money to outsiders. But such abilities sometimes arise naturally simply because a given individual or group is attempting to deal quickly with a problem and there is not enough time to seek out an outside supplier. Or they are curious to learn how something is done (it looks like fun and they want to try their hand). Or it is similar to something else they are good at, and they decide to capitalize on that similarity; we return to this idea with our concept of "hinge capabilities" in the next section.

Intel, for example, entered the microprocessor business almost by accident, by agreeing (as an adjunct to its primary business at the time: memory ICs) to produce a set of special integrated circuits for a Japanese calculator manufacturer. A small group of believers in this new chip architecture fought for the resources to develop it and gradually built a market for it. In fact, until Intel's top management was persuaded to buy it back, the Japanese customer initially owned the patent to the basic microprocessor architecture. Several years later, in the mid-1980s, Intel was forced to exit the memory business because of its plummeting profit margins and burgeoning capital requirements, and microprocessors became the lifeboat of its survival.

If a company wishes to encourage such activities, at the very least it ought not to publicize directives that forbid or discourage them. "That's not our business," or "Let's leave that to the experts" are examples of the kind of attitude that destroys employees' initiative to try to do something for the first time and thereby cultivate and test their abilities. The companies that are recognized as possessing the most competitively effective capabilities seldom start out with the intention of developing those specific ones. Usually, just as people try lots of activities until they find the ones they particularly enjoy and excel at, companies usually experiment with a variety of things until they find some that seem to fit their particular skills and market needs. Intel, for example, started out with the intention to become a world leader in DRAMs; microprocessors were a sideline that developed later. Toyota began as a producer of textile equipment. Such a process is time-consuming and inefficient—and even, until one understands the underlying logic, irrational—but it seems to work.

But at some point every individual and organization has to set priorities and focus on what it is that is really important. A few people, such as Leonardo di Vinci, Benjamin Franklin, and Thomas Jefferson, are so gifted that they can become expert at a number of different pursuits, but most of us have to choose. Converting an ability into a real capability does not happen by accident: it takes time (not just man-hours, but *elapsed* time) and consumes resources. And building such a capability into something that can become the basis of a competitive advantage requires a dedication that approaches fanaticism; the time and resources required often well exceed what one can logically justify.

Consider the amazing story of Sochiro Honda, the iconoclastic founder of what is today the Honda automobile company. Over a 20-year period Honda persistently (in fact, almost obsessively) built up his company's capability to design and manufacture very small, highly efficient gasoline engines. Although the company initially flourished making small motorcycles for the expanding Japanese market, Mr. Honda was not satisfied by commercial success alone; his real passion was racing. This led him to shift most of the young company's engineering resources into developing ever more powerful and efficient engines until by 1961 his cycles took the five top places in the "motorcycle Olympics"—the annual race around Great Britain's Isle of Man. Similarly, Xerox, Milliken, and Motorola all began corporate-wide quality improvement programs in the early 1980s—almost a decade before they were widely recognized for superior quality and were able to use that capability as a competitive weapon.

This growing expertise in developing efficient, powerful engines led first to building ever-larger motorcycles, but it also enabled Honda to develop the sporty lightweight cycles with which it successfully established a foothold in the U.S. market. Producing small cars, whose initial competitive advantage was their fuel economy and low pollution levels, was the next step. And finally Honda followed its ability to make highly efficient small engines into producing lawnmowers (almost exclusively for Western markets, as few Japanese have yards big enough to justify a powered lawnmower), snowblowers, and snowmobiles.

The second aspect of capability building that must be understood is that building organizational capabilities is much more complicated than building an individual's capabilities. Obviously, an organization's capabilities are circumscribed by the capabilities of the people within it: if nobody in a group can play a violin, the group as a whole will not be able to play a violin. Conversely, a group has a much wider set of capabilities that it can draw upon than can any individual within the group. More important, however, is that a group's capabilities are also a function of the working relationships among its individuals. So building organizational capabilities requires both building individual capabilities and building the linkages among them. As an example of the importance of such linkages, consider one manager's explanation of the way process development took place in his company:

> [it] depends on the informal system. It comes down to this person having or developing a working relationship with others who have the technologies he needs to access, and his ability to keep a door open to his supervisor so he doesn't have to go through the chain of command every time he needs something.

There are a series of means through which an effectively managed organization can develop a higher level of capability than is possible for any of the individuals composing it. *First,* the organization can consciously augment its capabilities by selecting the individuals that compose it (we individuals, unfortunately, are stuck with ourselves!). *Second,* the capability to do something that is really complex usually involves a number of component capabilities; designing an efficient 4-cycle gasoline engine, for example, requires expertise in a variety of engineering and manufacturing disciplines. Few individuals have mastered all these component capabilities to the point where they can perform the whole task with any degree of competence. But a group can divide up the various component capabilities that are required, choose and/or develop the specific capabilities of selected individuals, and organize their efforts to accomplish the whole task. *Third,* an organization can operate on a scale and develop tools that are unavailable to an individual: assembly lines, telecommunication networks, laboratories, etc. Relatedly, a group can "practice" more in a given time period than can any individual within it. If these efforts are managed properly, what is learned in the course of each person's individual practice becomes available to all (through, for example, tool development and methods improvements).

How does one systematically go about developing the working relationships among the individuals and subgroups within an organization? One approach is by consciously encouraging the expansion of the skill base of one's personnel by recruiting people who have a broad range of skills, so that they can interact with their colleagues more comfortably and on a wider range of issues. In addition, resources must be provided, and the organization's performance measures and incentive structures must be adjusted, to encourage people to take the risks and learn the new skills that are required. In addition people should be encouraged to take on a variety of assignments that bring them naturally into contact with other functional disciplines and groups. Or, they can be assigned to cross-functional teams that work together to solve problems and, in the process, teach each other new skills and approaches. Notice, in the cases that follow, the use of all these approaches by Hitachi-Seiki and their utter absence in Ex-Cell-O.

Finally, one must be aware that capabilities erode if they are not used and nurtured. Unfortunately, many of the practices that one associates with "modern management"—particularly a belief in decentralization, an overemphasis on "being close to customers" (to the point where one begins to rely on them for guidance as to which capabilities to acquire or hone), a reliance on performance measures and rewards that are primarily financial in nature, and an insistence that each step along a value chain (and each subunit within an organization) "pay its own way," abandoning those that do not—can inadvertently cripple the generation of new capabilities, or allow existing capabilities to atrophy. Ex-Cell-O in 1985 was not some hidebound anachronism, burdened down by a century or more of outdated traditions and management practices. It began as an innovative producer of state-of-the-art machine tools during World War II, and its current chairman had a long and distinguished record of success.

Case Synopses

We have already alluded to the issues raised by the cases in this module, but the following capsule descriptions may be useful.

Hitachi Seiki and **Ex-Cell-O.** These cases describe the situations and decisions faced by two companies, operating in the same industry and confronted with the same new technology—flexible machining systems— at about the same point in time. These two companies, however, have approached this technological challenge very differently. In the process of comparing their different approaches—and the vastly different outcomes they lead to—the reader is enabled to glean some lessons as to how companies can systematically build, *or destroy,* their organizational capabilities.

Philips-Taiwan. This company has grown in less than a decade from being a low-cost assembler of simple black-and-white television receivers (essentially a commodity product by 1980) to one of the world's leading producers of advanced computer monitors. Now it is attempting to simultaneously improve the quality of its new products and speed up their development—and, in a larger sense, to make the transition from being a domestic Taiwanese company to a "global player" that can assimilate best practice from around the world. The case describes three of the proposals it is considering, each of which has important implications not only for its approach to product development, but also for its role within the world-wide Philips organization.

Medical Products Company. After several years of slowing growth and disappointing profits in its European operations, MPC enters 1990 with too much production capacity and a disparate set of factories that do not form an effective network. Two of its plants have developed impressive manufacturing capabilities, but these have not been transferred to the others. How should it rationalize its plant network and how can it exploit the advantages of being part of the same large and very successful multinational parent company? Just as important, what are the managerial policies and organizational practices that have led to its current dilemma, and how should they be changed?

CHAPTER 24

Hitachi Seiki (Abridged)

B ESPECTACLED AND GIVEN to frequent contemplation and philosophizing, Yutaka Matsumura looked more like a college professor than a managing director of one of the largest machine tool companies in Japan. Yet, in his 35 years with Hitachi Seiki, mostly in research and development, Matsumura (now age 58) had succeeded in establishing that company as an innovative leader in an industry whose competitive environment was undergoing significant changes.

This change was being driven primarily by rapid and continuing evolution in machine tool technology. Matsumura believed that the greatest contribution he could make to Hitachi Seiki would be to set an example for the next generation of company managers and technologists, showing them how to cope with this "incessant change." "Medium-term planning is science fiction," Matsumura had said, "and long-term planning is religion." It was now up to him to write a book on science fiction for Hitachi Seiki.

Although he formally reported to the president, Matsumura was responsible for all engineering and operations activities. Recently he had received permission from his board of directors to hand over the reins of his 250-person engineering organization to one of his managers, gather around him a group of about seven professionals, and start a new development group. Plans had to be developed, he argued, in three areas: a reorganization of the engineering function; choices among automation projects; and long-term product development. In his mind, all of these were closely related.

In Matsumura's lifetime, engineering had come full circle. In 1947, when he enrolled in Tohoku University to study electrical engineering, an engineer needed to be a generalist. A trend toward specialization gained momentum during the 1960s and peaked in the mid-1970s. That was followed by a renewed need, occasioned by the advent of flexible manufacturing systems in the 1980s, for generalist engineers—but with an important difference. The new generalist engineer possessed not only the broad

This case was prepared as the basis for class discussion rather than to illustrte either effective or ineffective handling of an administrative situation.

knowledge of earlier generalists, but also a deep understanding of machine design, software engineering, and manufacturing processes. Matsumura's proposals for reorganizations, automation, and product development required this kind of integrated perspective. He believed that Hitachi Seiki's future competitive success would depend on its ability to develop system engineers, a resource in critical shortage throughout industry.

NC Machines: The Early Years

Matsumura had specialized in electrical engineering in technical school. He then entered college, but left after two years. Life was difficult in post-war Tokyo and he worked at odd jobs for another two years before joining Hitachi Seiki in 1951. There were not many electrical engineers in the machine tool industry at that time; Matsumura was one of the first to join Hitachi Seiki.

The development of the first NC (numerically controlled) machine at MIT in 1952 added a sense of urgency to the Japanese machine tool industry's efforts to catch up with the rest of the world. At Hitachi Seiki, Matsumura was asked to study the new development. To encourage NC development, Japan's Ministry of International Trade and Industry (MITI), made a small grant in 1957 to a consortium that included Hitachi and Hitachi Seiki. The consortium planned to collaborate on joint development of advanced components; Hitachi was responsible for hydraulic servos and Hitachi Seiki for electrical servos. Matsumura helped develop Japan's first commercial NC machine in 1959. After the group disbanded, Matsumura assumed responsibility for developing NC controllers for Hitachi Seiki.

There were many problems with the new technology, and developments in automation did not materialize as rapidly as expected. As a result, many companies stuck with traditional manufacturing processes. Matsumura sensed, however, that as transistors and computers developed it was only a matter of time until automation moved into the driver's seat.

Progress, though, was slow. An entire industry trained to think in terms of mechanical technology had to learn to develop machines with electronics in them. In 1962, Matsumura set up a separate electrical engineering group of five people, which grew to twenty people by 1967. The NC machines of the later sixties were becoming increasingly sophisticated, so Hitachi Seiki employed the machines it built in its own factories; this both demonstrated their potential benefits to customers and developed in-house technological capability.

Hitachi Seiki's experience designing both special-purpose machines and transfer lines for mass production industries provided a solid base for developing versatile, high-performance NC machines. In 1967 it deemed the new technology finally ready for commercial introduction, and demonstrated its first automated machining center (see Figure 24.1 for pictorial definitions of various technical terms) at the International Machine Tool

Figure 24.1 Comparison of Automated Activities Under Different Production Methods

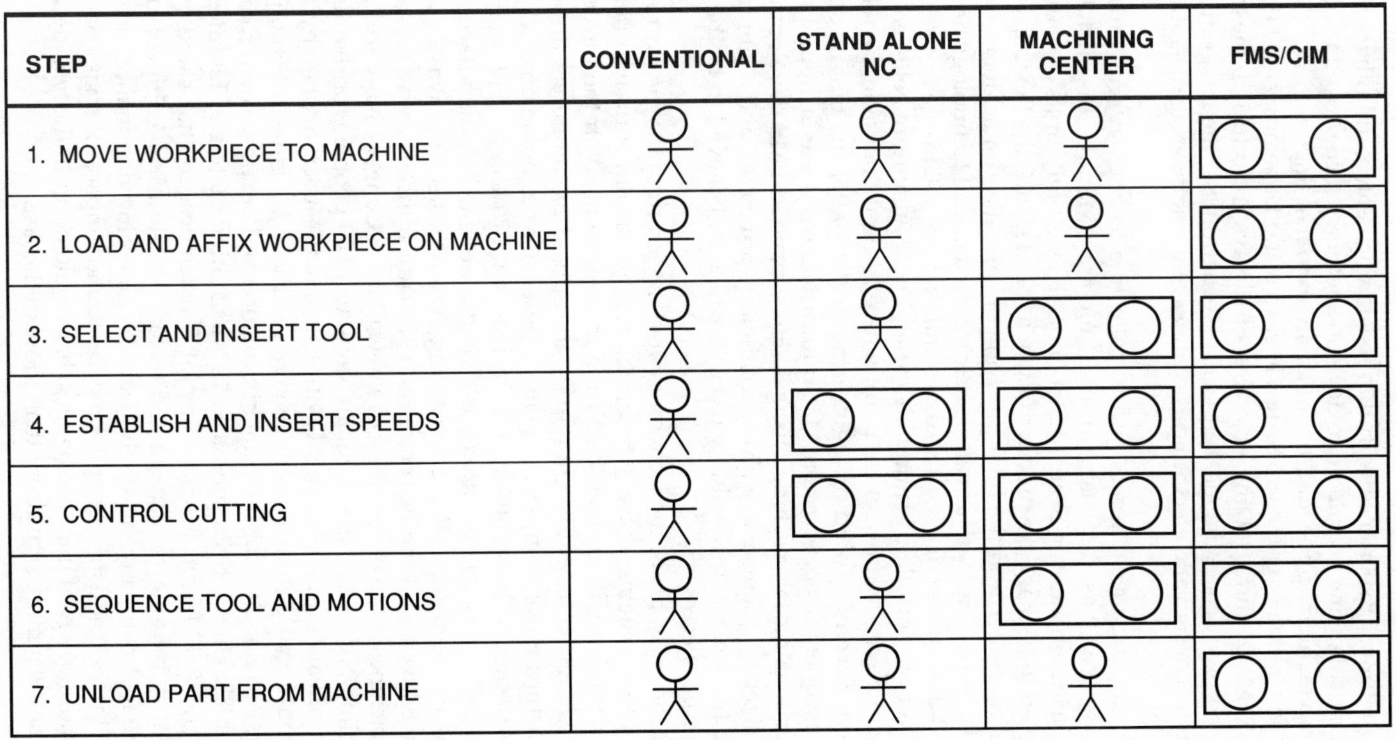

STEP	CONVENTIONAL	STAND ALONE NC	MACHINING CENTER	FMS/CIM
1. MOVE WORKPIECE TO MACHINE	Manual	Manual	Manual	Automated
2. LOAD AND AFFIX WORKPIECE ON MACHINE	Manual	Manual	Manual	Automated
3. SELECT AND INSERT TOOL	Manual	Manual	Automated	Automated
4. ESTABLISH AND INSERT SPEEDS	Manual	Automated	Automated	Automated
5. CONTROL CUTTING	Manual	Automated	Automated	Automated
6. SEQUENCE TOOL AND MOTIONS	Manual	Manual	Automated	Automated
7. UNLOAD PART FROM MACHINE	Manual	Manual	Manual	Automated

Show in Tokyo. Experience with that machining center, and others introduced the following year, led it to develop another, which proved to be the most successful machine tool sold in Japan up to that time.

Upon taking over Hitachi Seiki's Research and Development Division in 1967, Matsumura set the objective of always introducing the most advanced products in the marketplace. "Mechatronics," the integration of mechanical design and electronics, became a new engineering discipline at Hitachi Seiki.

Combining mechatronics and transfer line technology into an integrated system was the basis, in 1972, for the FMS 102, the first FMS (Flexible Manufacturing System) that Hitachi Seiki built for its own use. It attempted to package the productivity of a transfer line, the flexibility of a machining center, and the high precision of specialized machinery into a single large system. With advances in integrated circuit technology having reduced the number of circuit boards required from 100 to one or two, and the power of controllers continually expanding, Matsumura believed that NC technology was now to the point where it should pervade the whole company. Becoming head of engineering in 1975, after the first oil shock and consequent deep recession, Matsumura decided it was an appropriate time for making far-reaching changes. He expanded FMS development, rationalized his plants using group technology principles, and continually pushed to increase the flexibility of FMS, which he believed to be the key to its future success.

By the early 1980s, the technology had moved from the mechatronics phase into a systems phase, which required, yet again, entirely different ways of thinking about manufacturing management. With the introduction of computer-aided design (CAD), the spread of computers through manufacturing was complete, making it possible to combine product and process design with manufacturing. In 1984, with 20% of its sales in FMS, Hitachi Seiki was one of the largest vendors of flexible manufacturing systems in the world. Of the remaining 80% of sales, 70% was equally divided between machining centers and NC lathes, and 10% was in heavy-duty machines. With the opening of a new plant in Congers, New York, for assembling NC lathes, the company grew to 1,800 people worldwide. In 1985, it concluded an agreement with Cincinnati Milacron whereby that firm would market the turning centers produced by Hitachi Seiki. (See Exhibits 24.1 and 24.2 for financial information and organizational charts.)

In 1985, Hitachi Seiki produced 132 machining centers of 12 different types, and 8 FMSs, each consisting of 5 machines. In that same year, Matsumura became a managing director. An electrical engineer in a machine tool company, he symbolized the emerging dominance of electronics in the industry. Despite the profound impact of that change, Matsumura believed that the changes that would occur in the next decade would be even more significant than those in the last.

Exhibit 24.1   Financial Income Statement (April 1, 1984 through March 31, 1985)[a]

	Accounts	
Amount	**Expenses, Revenues, and Profits**	
Sales	$41,176,071	
Cost of sales	32,999,464	
Gross profits		$8,176,606
Postponed unrealized income from installment sales	278,399	
Reimbursement for postponed income from installment sales	265,971	12,428
Adjusted gross profits		8,164,178
Selling, general and administrative expenses	6,807,455	
Operating income		1,356,723

[a]All figures in 1,000 yen (250 yen = 1$U.S.).

Flexible Manufacturing Systems Development

Hitachi Seiki's development of flexible manufacturing systems took place in three phases: Narashino, Abiko 1 and Abiko 2. Built in 1972, the Narashino system (FMS 102) was one of the earliest flexible manufacturing systems manufactured in Japan. It consisted of nine different NC machine tools connected by a chain conveyor. The system was designed to make 16 different components in lot sizes of seven to one hundred parts. All nine machines, as well as the interconnected transport system, were under computer control. It was essentially a flexible transfer line, conceived for mass production.

The problems experienced with the Narashino FMS showed that untended parts manufacture was still a few years away. Its productivity was not much greater than that of conventional NC machinery; in fact, it was lower than that of special-purpose machines because of its frequent breakdowns and coordination problems. Yet, despite its lack of success and its high costs, both in money and development time, the Narashino FMS taught its developers a great deal about conveyors, materials handling, and the importance of work scheduling in general.

Among the twenty-four people from widely varying disciplines who were brought together to design, install, and operate the Narashino FMS were some of Hitachi Seiki's top specialists. For many of them it was their first experience in a large software project, made more difficult by the fact that NC controller technology was still in its infancy. Coordination prob-

Exhibit 24.2   Organizational Chart as of April 1, 1985 (Number of Full-Time Employees as of September 16, 1985)

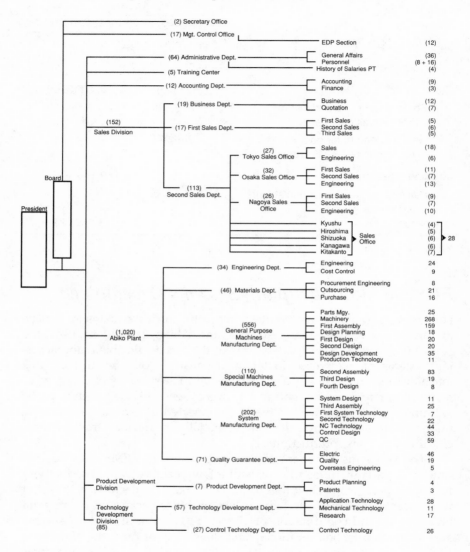

lems were experienced not only between machines, but also in problem-solving between specialists.

Forced to sell the Narashino plant during the recession in 1974, Hitachi Seiki moved FMS development to its plant at Abiko (30 miles north of Tokyo, where it had its headquarters) and undertook to rethink the entire concept. The next FMS (Abiko 1) consisted of five machining centers connected by a shuttle conveyor. Pallets were standardized and made interchangeable, and more powerful NC controllers were used. It could make more than forty different parts, in lot sizes of from five to forty. Abiko 1 still fell far short of untended operation, however, and its productivity, though higher than that of the Narashino FMS, did not provide an adequate return on investment. Productivity and flexibility were still in conflict. Different products required different tools, and the number of tools that could be held in tool magazines was limited. Tool changing still required human involvement in measuring off-sets (tool positions relative to the workpiece) every time a workpiece was set up, significantly reducing cutting time. Abiko 1, like its predecessor at Narashino, was considered a failure.

Realizing that coordination across all organizational functions was needed in order to achieve truly untended operation, in 1980 Hitachi Seiki set up a new office under Matsumura. The Engineering Administration Department brought together a variety of different functions, including machine design, software engineering, and tool design. The Narashino and Abiko 1 machines had viewed the design of an FMS as a technical problem, to be solved with technical expertise. Matsumura, observing the difficulty his engineers had making trade-offs whenever conflicts arose over design specifications or control procedures, believed that problems of coordination among people were more important impediments to systems development. Looked at as a manufacturing problem, rather than as just an engineering problem, FMS required both manufacturing and technical expertise. Consequently, the third phase, Abiko 2, presented a significant departure from the previous two.

Notwithstanding the two unsuccessful attempts at FMS design, the team put together by Matsumura for Abiko 2 came up with an audacious plan. It proposed that Hitachi Seiki build not one, but four different FMSs, all of them designed simultaneously and installed within two months of one another. It further proposed that the entire effort, including design, development, installation, and operation, be accomplished by just sixteen people. Even more ambitious, it proposed to have all four systems installed within 18 months.

Hitachi Seiki's board of directors had always required a three-year payback on all machine development projects. The development team believed that a system capable of twenty-four hour per day untended operation could achieve this. At Matsumura's urging, the board accepted three of the four systems; the fourth, an ultra-high precision system, was tabled for further refinement.

The team's confidence grew out of recent experience gained in a parallel activity. A year previously, Yukihisa Gai and two other engineers had formed a team to examine production rationalization at Hitachi Seiki's subsidiary plants, particularly the one at Sashima. The Sashima plant manufactured high volumes of small NC lathes and was extremely efficient. Gai designed and installed three different flexible manufacturing cells (FMCs) at Sashima in 1980. Each cell, which consisted of a single machine and several pallets, tried a different concept and all achieved totally untended operation. Gai's success convinced the team that Hitachi Seiki was ready to tackle larger systems.

Gai and his team were assimilated into the newly created FMS project team in 1982. Drawing on his earlier successful experience with a small, close-working team, Gai assembled a group of five people. Between April and December they designed the three systems—FMS 112, 113, and 114—that were approved by the board as part of Abiko 2.

A gregarious man with an easy laugh, and comfortable in any conversation concerning manufacturing, Gai had joined Hitachi Seiki soon after graduating from Chiba University in 1963 as a mechanical engineer. He spent his first year as a lathe operator. Subsequently, he worked for two years in tool design for Gildemeister, which had established a technical collaboration agreement with Hitachi Seiki. In fact, Gai spent the next 15 years in tool design, becoming a specialist in the field. But the close relationship between tool design and manufacturing led him also to develop a comprehensive understanding of how to solve manufacturing problems.

The experience gained in the Sashima FMCs suggested that it should be possible to manufacture a wide variety of nonrecurring parts on an FMS. In order to achieve this, the team needed to design universal fixtures similar to those in "erector" sets—capable of holding workpieces with a variety of standardized clamps and jigs. The team's short-term goal was to reduce the break-even point—between manufacturing a product in their FMS and manufacturing it with conventional machine tools—to fewer than 10 parts.

Machines, workpieces, and tools had to be coordinated so that processing would never be interrupted by the lack of one or the other. In order to achieve intended operation, it was necessary to understand not only what was required to make an item, but also (and this was, perhaps, the most difficult task) everything that could go wrong in its production. The development team had to be aware of every possible contingency, in order to build software that could avoid a system halt. All setups either had to be automated or done off-line; if processing was to take place untended at night, the necessary setup for the operation had to be done during the day. In order to compensate for slight variations in workpiece alignment and cutting tools, machine tool operators historically had to make careful measurements and perform trial cuttings using actual workpieces. These operations required time and close attention, since any miscalculation could result in dimensional defects, or even total scrap. Worse, it was possible for the tool and the workpiece to collide, resulting in tool breakage or machine shutdown. Therefore, the team needed to develop sensing devices that could gauge the positions of both the work-piece and the tool, and design control mechanisms that automated this alignment process and eliminated the need for human intervention in the event of problems.

Building FMS 112, 113, and 114 (Abiko 2)

Each of the three systems concentrated on different developmental areas: the FMS 112, on the basics of untended production; the FMS 113, on flexible fixtures and automated tool supply; and the FMS 114, on automated tool supply and turning operations (see Exhibit 24.3). The conceptual design for all three systems was carried out simultaneously by Gai and five others. More people were added later; Gai assigned four to each system for detailed design, installation, and ramp-up. The designs were completed in nine months and the systems installed and ready for operation in five more. The rapid improvement in system performance, as shown in Exhibit 24.4, proved not only that it was possible to build highly flexible systems, but that it could be done by a small team. Software problems were minimal; most were solved in the first two months of operation, and almost no subsequent difficulties were encountered.

For three months after installation the systems were operated jointly by Gai's development group and the people normally in charge of production. Subsequently, Gai's group concentrated on optimizing the performance of the systems. Process changes per month dropped from over ten to five or six. The FMSs all achieved their major design and ROI goals, including requiring minimal human involvement during a regular shift, and running untended for sixteen hours overnight. One measure of their success was the enhanced ability to produce unique workpieces in a cost-effective manner. The ratio of the machining time required to process a single item to that for making it as part of a large lot varied from 3:1 for FMS 112 down to 1:1 for FMS 114.

FMS 112 was designed to produce large-sized prismatic workpieces such as beds, columns, and saddles. It consisted of four machining centers arranged in a line beside a carrier, and a rail transfer system capable of running at sixty meters per minute. Pallets were stacked close to the rails, as were specially designed modular fixtures and a device for handling very large pieces. The use of standard components allowed any workpiece to be rapidly mounted for processing, enabling the FMS 112 to reduce its setup time to one-tenth that required by traditional systems .

FMS 113 was designed to machine small- and medium-sized prismatic parts. It, too, comprised four machine tools (two horizontal-spindle machining centers and two vertical-spindle centers) served by an automatic tool supply unit and an untended rail carrier for transporting work-pieces. The movement and storage of completed pieces was accom-

Exhibit 24.3

Abiko 2: Systems Descriptions

FMS 112		FMS 113		FMS 114	
HB4000-F Floor type machining center	1 unit	HC500 horizontal machining center	2 units	NF CNC Turning center with RE-30 robot	3 units
HB5000-F Floor type machining center	2 units	VA55 vertical machining center	2 units	Automatic tool supply device (2 tool magazines having 5 lines and 24 rows)	1 unit
12 MB horizontal machining center with pallet pool line	1 unit	Multi-shelved pallet storage — 3 shelves and 54 rows		Soft jaw turning attachment: 350kg)	unit
Track-type untended Carrier (load capacity 6 tons, CNC one axis control)	1 unit	Stacker crane (load capacity: one ton)	1 unit	Untended carrier (load capacity: 350kg)	2 units in each line
		Untended Carrier (load capacity: 750kg)	1 unit		
Pallets 2 sized		Workpiece cleaning station	1 unit	Pallet storage	1 unit
1250 x 1250mm and 1500 x 1500mm	30 pallets	Tool storage and automatic tool supply device	1 unit	Setup station	1 station
Pallet storage station	30 units	Setup station (including two fixture setup stations)	6 stations	Centralized coolant and chip disposal equipment	1 set
Chip removing equipment for pallet	1 unit				
Centralized chip disposal equipment	1 unit	Centralized coolant and chip disposal equipment		Maximum workpiece dimensions	
Large workpiece turnover device	1 unit			300mm die x 300mm long	
Setup station (including one tool setup station)	5 stations	Maximum workpiece dimensions 500mm x 500mm		Machining time	1 hour per pallet
Maximum workpiece dimension		Machining time	1 to 2 hours per pallet	System running hours a month	1600
1500mm (width) x 2500mm ((length)		System running hours a month	2000		
Machining time	3 to 4 hours per pallet				
System running hours a month	2000				

- The FMS112 is production line for large workpieces. It consists of four machining centers aligned in series and the Carrier which transports workpieces from one machining center to the other in the line.
- The setup station and large workpiece turnover device are provided.
- The centralized chip disposal equipment and chip removing equipment for pallet are provided.
- NC data, machining schedule and setup schedule

- The FMS113 is a production line for a wide variety of small and medium size workpieces. It consists of two horizontal and two vertical machining centers with peripheral equipment such as the automatic tool supply device, and track type untended Carrier which transports workpieces from one machining center to the other in the line.
- The horizontal and vertical machining centers are provided with the same pallet clamping devices not only to exchange the pallets between the machines, but also to facilitate adjusting the load for each machine and to ensure the system to be operated by separating a failing machine if a machine fails.

- The FMS114 is a production line for 468 kinds of round workpieces, lot sizes of 20 or less. It consists of three CNC turning centers with robots and one horizontal machining center with robot.
- The workpieces are transferred to each machine by Track-type Carrier and loaded to the machine by the robot provided on the machine. After machining processes on the machine have been completed on the machine, the workpieces are unloaded from the machine by the robot and placed on the Carrier.

Exhibit 24.3 (continued)
Abiko 2: Systems Descriptions

FMS 112	FMS 113	FMS 114
are transferred to Carrier and machining centers through the optical fiber data highway. • The Carrier is controlled by one axis CNC unit SEICOS-PO4 with the traverse speed of 60 m/min. • The ratio of total machining time of recurring workpieces is 3:1.	• The workpiece storage and stacker crane are provided to facilitate handling a wide variety of workpieces. • The automatic tool supply device accommodates 528 tools. The robot picks up the tool according to the command from the computer. The tool is placed in the tool fixture and transferred to the buffer storage, then it is supplied to the machine by the cart. This system supplies the required tool to an arbitrary machining center without having any additional equipment on the machining centers. • Chips are discharged from the machines and transferred to the outside of the building by the centralized coolant and centralized chip disposal equipment which commonly serves for FMS114. • The tools are grouped according to machining. The machining processes are executed according to the priority of tools, not to the machining location, i.e., machining processes which are done with the same tool are consecutively executed. • After the tools are used for machining, the tools which are likely to be worn are changed with spares earlier than the others. • The ratio of total machining time of recurring workpieces to total machining time of nonrecurring workpieces is 2:1.	The Carrier transfers the workpiece to the next machine for succeeding machining processes. The machining center is provided with the indexing chuck. • The cartridge-type pallet accommodates three to six workpieces of 50 to 300 mm in diameter in line, depending on the size of workpieces. The machining time required per pallet is one hour. The automatic jaw devices are provided to accommodate a wide range of workpiece diameters. • The data for turning the soft jaws are programmed at the top of part programs as required. • The block tool magazine having five tools on the machine is replaced with one of 48 block tool magazines having 240 tools in total by the tool loader. • RE-30 robots which load and unload the workpieces to and from the machine are controlled by the part programs stored in the CNC unit of the machines. • The ratio of total machining time of recurring workpieces to total machining time of nonrecurring workpieces is 1:1.

Exhibit 24.4 FMS Productivity

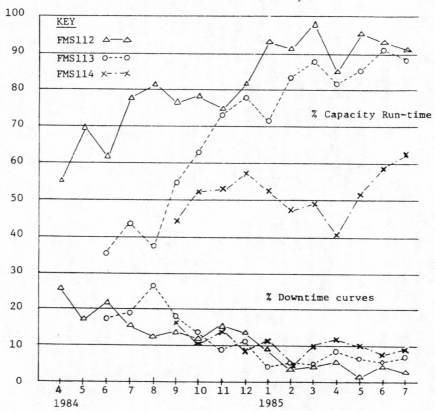

plished using a computer-controlled crane, which allowed a large overnight inventory to be built up without human attention. A key innovation
in the FMS 113 was the automatic tool supply unit. This system enabled a
robot, guided by computer software, to pick up any of 528 tools from a
storage rack and transfer them by rail to the appropriate machining
center, where they were mounted automatically. Groups of tools could be
changed at the same time, and the tool-changing process took only five or
six minutes.

The FMS 114 was designed to manufacture small- to medium-sized
round parts. It was comprised of three NC lathes and one horizontal
machining center, and could turn around one pallet load of mixed workpieces in one hour. Workpieces were transferred automatically between
the NC lathes by robots. A robot also selected and mounted tools from a
magazine that held 240 items. Removal and disposal of metal scrap was
accomplished by an automatic conveyor.

All three systems required very little human intervention—on the order of two and one-half person days per month. Additional labor costs, distributed among the three units, included one to three days per month for indirect maintenance and one to three days for scheduled maintenance. All sources of downtime were carefully tracked, and tool wear and breakage strictly accounted for. Preparation of NC tapes for each job remained a manual process, however. In fact, the time required to check NC tapes was four times longer, and programming was five times longer, than processing (run) time. (The whole tape programming, checking, and compiling system was a candidate for automation in the next stage.) Tape check time was not treated as downtime, accounting for the difference between actual utilization times versus system uptime in Exhibit 24.4.

Hitachi Seiki ran the FMS 112, 113, and 114 systems in-house both to demonstrate their usefulness to customers and as a basis for developing the next generation of automation. Perhaps the most significant operational advantage the company derived from these systems was the ability to produce its own new components within two days. A summary of the history of Hitachi Seiki's efforts in FMS development is provided in Exhibit 24.5.

Flexible Manufacturing Systems: The Next Step

The success of the three FMSs not only was highly acclaimed in technical circles in Japan, it also enhanced Hitachi Seiki's reputation as a vendor of sophisticated and versatile machine tools. Beyond helping sales, it raised the expectations of both its customers and industry observers regarding what would come next. With all kinds of ideas being discussed, it fell to Matsumura to try to strike a balance between keeping his organization's creative energy at a high level and not taking on more than it could deliver. The funding of projects, after all, was not easy; not only did every project have to meet a strict three-year payback criterion, but there were only so much investment money and skilled people to go around. The machine tool industry was notorious for its acute cyclical swings and, while it was then in a boom period, there was no telling when a downturn might begin. Because of these cycles, the imaginative management of both engineers and capital investment was crucial to the health of the company. Three specific proposals had been made to Matsumura during the spring of 1985, and others were bound to arise.

Proposal 1: Automated Material Handling for Assembly

A group of young engineers returned from a machine tool show in Chicago in October 1984 very excited about the prospects for automating the material handling for assembly processes. A team was therefore orga-

Exhibit 24.5 FMS Introduction and Progress

	1980 — 55	1981 — 56	1982 — 57	1983 — 58	1984 — 59	1985 — 60
	Current Production Methods 1980	Introduction of Cell System Line	Study/Preparation of FMS Based on Cell Systems	Actual Installation of FMS (FMS 112, 113, 114)	Operation/Improvement FMS	FMS Use Operation

Study/Anaylsis of Simulation

Increase Operating Rate Reduce Labor

Construct System with High "Unmanned" Level

Construct system with high flexibility level

Promotion of Technology for Unmanned Operation/Determining Issues

Study/Construction of FMS with High "Unmanned" level and flexibility

Test Run — On-Line

Study on Realistic Introduction of Unnamed System

| Study/Analysis of Current Status Simulation | • Start Cell System Line Development of Car-Type Pool Line • 24-Hour Operation of the Pool Line | • Objectives of System to be Developed • Study/Analysis of Processed Works • Determining Issues Analyzing Issues • System Basic Plan Preparations | • System Basic Design • System Detailed Design • Manufacturing Installation | • Test Run • On-Line Operation | • Operation/Use • Training of System Operators • Level Up System |

nized to propose a new physical layout and storage system for the main plant, and addressed the following questions:

1. How should the assembly process be organized?

Sashima had employed two-person crews at each of nine stations, served by an assembly conveyor that moved from station to station once every four hours. The conveyor had increased productivity on the line by 35% and reduced assembly time from 110 to 72 person hours. The handling of parts was still done manually, however. The team believed that automating materials handling—providing for automatic delivery of the right parts to the right stations at the right times on robot carriers—could further reduce assembly time to just 60 hours.

2. How should the automatic storage system be organized?

Materials would arrive in the storage area on pallets holding between one and ten identical components. Subsequently, they would be retrieved and "kitted," that is, arranged so that all the components required at a particular workstation would be on a single pallet. After kitting, the pallets would be returned to storage and retrieved just-in-time for assembly. Debate focused on the size of the warehouse (number of pallets required), and crane speeds.

3. How should the production control system be organized?

The team believed that with robot carriers they could synchronize all workpiece movement—between workstations, between the fabrication area and the warehouse, and between the warehouse and assembly area—thereby reducing the need for buffer inventories. Careful design would be required to achieve such synchronization, however.

The cost of such a system, in addition to the production and people time that would be lost while changes were made, was broken down as follows: $600,000 for computer systems, $400,000 for distributed terminals, and $200,000+ for robot carriers. Depending on the warehouse size and the number and size of conveyor lines, additional costs of $200,000 per assembly line and $25 per warehouse storage location were anticipated. While it was possible to estimate the "hard" costs for configuring the system, its "soft" costs (associated with issues of efficiency and flexibility) were still very uncertain, and it was difficult to be more accurate about either costs or benefits.

Proposal 2: High-Precision FMS 111

FMS 111 was one of the four original systems proposed by Gai for the Abiko 2 phase. The most controversial of the four, it had been rejected after considerable debate, primarily because of his inability to cost justify its development. The very ambitiousness of the undertaking, coming on the heels of the failures of Narashino and Abiko 1, had worked against it. Now, following the success of the other three FMSs comprising Abiko 2, the proposal had surfaced again.

The controversy around FMS 111 had stemmed from the need for extremely high-precision machining in finishing operations, a degree of precision many believed could not be achieved in unmanned operations. There were two schools of thought on the matter. One held that, although difficult and challenging, the development of such a system was possible and could yield experience that might lead to a new generation of marketable high-precision products. The other held that ultra high-precision untended processing should first be conducted in specialized machining centers and only later integrated into an FMS.

Tolerance ranges for FMSs generally were from five to ten microns (one micron equals one-thousandth of a millimeter). The most precise of the existing systems (FMS 114) operated in a tolerance range of from one to five microns. FMS 111, however, was to operate within a tolerance range of from one-tenth to half a micron. While Hitachi Seiki already produced machines capable of achieving such precision, they required lengthy and careful setup procedures that could take as long as four hours, and careful monitoring and periodic adjustment while they were operating. Convinced that Hitachi Seiki stood to reap substantial dividends if it could achieve unmanned high-precision operations, Gai personally favored development of the FMS 111, but he hadn't the numbers to substantiate his intuition.

The team working on FMS 111 selected 40 products that required precision in the submicron range. Processing times for these products ranged from two to six hours. All operations were to be done in a single, five-phase, ultra high-precision machining center, costing $700,000. Two such centers would be arranged side by side. Converting them so that they were capable of unmanned operation was estimated to be $500,000 per machine. Additional system costs were expected to add another $800,000 per machine. Yet the biggest cost to Hitachi Seiki was the commitment of significant human resources over up to two years. The benefits anticipated from this outlay of money and resources were that setups could be done off-line and reduced to one hour; processing time would be reduced by 25%; and total system utilization would increase from 80% to 95%.

Proposal 3: Full-Line FMS 112.5

FMS 112.5 was perhaps the least controversial of the proposed flexible manufacturing systems; everyone on the manufacturing floor believed it was needed to fill a gap in their capability to machine prismatic parts in the size range of 800 by 800 millimeters. Although the installation of FMS 112 and 113 had substantially reduced the lead time required for fabrication of many parts, the total lead times for products that required parts in the 800 by 800 millimeter range was not greatly affected. To extend the lead time advantage to all final products would require FMS capability for the entire line of components. This was the niche the FMS 112.5 would fill.

Technologically, the FMS 112.5 would be only a marginal improvement over the FMS 112 and 113. In addition to the advantages provided by its predecessors, FMS 112.5 was to deliver the benefit of reduced lead time for completed products. The cost of the system was estimated to be around $3 million. Enthusiasm for it was highest in the production organization, while the designers were somewhat ambivalent.

CHAPTER 25

Ex-Cell-O Corporation (B)

*I*N JANUARY 1985, Paul Casey, President and Chief Executive Officer of
Ex-Cell-O Corporation, wrestled with the problem of continuing
losses in the company's machine tool industry segment. Although
Ex-Cell-O had strengthened its position in defense/aerospace, automotive, and specialty products areas in recent years, machine tools remained
a core element of its business. Indeed, as one of the largest participants in
that industry, Ex-Cell-O had expected to benefit from the reindustrializa-
tion of America, which management felt would occur through investments in new, computer-aided manufacturing systems. Order backlogs
continued to fall for most of the Industrial Equipment Group's divisions,
however, and Casey was under increasing pressure from his board of
directors to formulate a plan for stemming the losses.

As Casey reviewed the machine tool situation and especially that of
the Manufacturing Systems Division, he wondered how much of the problem was due to management inadequacies and product line deficiencies
and how much to the condition of its markets. While most of the divisions
in the United States were doing poorly, the company's German subsidiary
was profitable, enjoyed a strong backlog, and was viewed as a technical
leader. He also wondered how a major retrenchment would be viewed by
the company's employees and customers (in particular, the automobile
manufacturers) and by the investment community.

Objectives and Outlook: 1980–1981

Ed Giblin, Chairman and Chief Executive until his retirement in December
1982, believed strongly in the virtues of a balanced manufacturing base.
The 1980 letter to the stockholders that he authored with Casey reflected
his optimism for the future. It read in part:

> Although below the record level of 1979, earnings for 1980 were
> the second best in Ex-Cell-O's history. We are pleased with this

performance, considering the adverse conditions influencing some of the markets that we serve. While the Automotive Components segment was severely affected by depressed market conditions and Ordnance earnings declined sharply because of softness in orders for wheeled armored vehicles, the Industrial Equipment and Aerospace segments were strong. This offset reinforces our belief that Ex-Cell-O's program of balanced diversification is a sound strategy.

For the longer term, Ex-Cell-O is in a good position to meet the challenges and significant opportunities facing U.S. industry. Improved productivity, energy conservation, and a strengthened free world military posture are major national priorities for the 1980s. Almost every one of Ex-Cell-O's major products helps to meet one or more of these needs. We believe that our product position combined with financial strength and an experienced management team will enable Ex-Cell-O Corporation to continue its growth and prosperity.

In 1981, under Casey's direction, the following set of long-range financial performance objectives were established as the basis for strategic planning and decision making throughout the company.

- To achieve sustainable sales and profit growth of at least 10 to 12 percent annually, assuming a moderate inflation rate.
- To increase return on sales to at least six to seven percent.
- To earn at least 18.5 percent on beginning-of-year equity.
- To maintain a target dividend payout ratio of approximately 40 percent of sustainable net earnings.
- To limit the ratio of debt to total capital to 25–30 percent.

These objectives were considered attainable at the time in light of record earnings achieved in 1981 and the market prospects for the company's five industry segments as noted below.

Industrial Equipment. Ex-Cell-O had a leadership position in certain segments of the machine tool industry such as grinding, honing, die casting, and electrical discharge machines. In addition, through its Manufacturing Systems Division the company sold transfer lines and related special purpose equipment which offered the potential for competing in the emerging field of flexible computer controlled manufacturing systems. The Industrial Equipment Group contributed 56% of total operating profits in 1980, due in part to the massive retooling efforts undertaken by the automotive companies as they downsized their lines to compete with imports and to comply with federal fuel economy regulations. Also included in the group was the Packaging Systems Division. While yielding modest, though declining, profits, this division faced the expiration of its patents in the early 1980s, and its opportunities for growth were seen as limited.

Automotive Components. Although dependent to a degree on overall North American auto sales, Ex-Cell-O management felt that Davidson Rubber Division, a supplier of lightweight flexible interior and exterior urethane components, provided the basis for growth opportunities greater than those for the industry itself. It was also hoped that Ex-Cell-O's other automotive divisions, which manufactured gaskets, radiators, and components, would benefit from the transformation of the industry.

Aerospace. The aerospace units produced precision components, such as fan blades, compression blades, and fuel nozzles, for commercial and military jet engine manufacturers. While the demand for business and commercial engines had been sluggish due to high fuel costs, a poor economy in 1980, and the unsettling effects of airline deregulation, Ex-Cell-O enjoyed a very close relationship with Pratt & Whitney, a world leader in the field, and expected to share fully in the anticipated growth in demand for air travel. In addition, the new Reagan administration in Washington was committed to significantly expanded defense expenditures.

Ordnance. The ordnance segment, through its Cadillac Gage subsidiary, produced wheeled armored vehicles and turret control and stabilization systems principally for tanks. As in the case of aerospace, Ex- Cell-O anticipated demand for its products to grow in response to increasing expenditures for conventional military forces both in the United States and abroad.

Specialty Products. The four units in this segment comprised the Greenlee Tool Division (tools and equipment for the construction industry), the Power Transmission Division (transmission and heavy gearing equipment for gas extraction, and similar applications), the Remex Division (floppy disk drives and punched paper tape readers and spoolers) and the Plastic Components Division (large structural foam parts for the computer and business machine industry). Although some of the industries served by these units were cyclical and had been hurt by high interest rates and a weak economy, others were in growth markets and looked forward to steady improvement.

Organization

Among Casey's major concerns in the months following the merger of McCord into Ex-Cell-O[1] was resolving the differences in organizational

[1]Casey had been President of the McCord Corporation, a leading producer of automotive components (1977 sales of $173 million) prior to its acquisition by Ex-Cell-O in January 1978. See Ex-Cell-O Corporation (A) 9-483-025.

philosophies that existed between the two companies. At McCord the structure had been straightforward: The divisions were conceived as decentralized profit centers and managed with limited corporate involvement. The situation was less clear at Ex-Cell-O. In a few cases, Cadillac Gage, for example, the divisions appeared to have a fairly high degree of autonomy, while in others a group vice president with responsibility for several divisions in similar businesses exercised considerable control. In addition, the Ex-Cell-O corporate staff maintained close surveillance over division activities and often participated in day-to-day operating decisions.

In 1979 and 1980, Casey clarified the organization structure by, in effect, adopting the McCord concept of free-standing decentralized operating units. A planning system was put in place during this period which called for the formulation of a strategy by the management of each division. The group vice presidents were to act as coaches for the division managers and to insure that operating decisions were coordinated with overall company goals and policies. This step was followed in 1983 by an examination of each corporate staff function and the transfer to the field of those which were in direct support of the businesses. In the process, the headquarters head count fell by 20% and central advertising, marketing, and purchasing departments were eliminated.

By 1984, however, Casey began to question certain aspects of the new Ex-Cell-O structure and in particular the role of the group vice president:

> I began to see a contradiction in the way we should manage those divisions which have long time horizons and are important to the corporation and those which are stand-alone businesses with shorter time horizons and of lesser importance. There may be a dual role for the group V.P.; in the former to be a business leader, responsible for strategic planning and profits, and in the latter a coordinator and a coach.

For example, Casey noted that the four aerospace divisions, all manufacturing precision components, and the ordnance unit, Cadillac Gage, reported to one group vice president. (See Exhibit 25.1 for an organization chart.) Should the group vice president take a more active part in directing the aerospace units while providing only general oversight for Cadillac Gage? Casey recognized that part of the price of giving autonomy to the divisions was the loss of an easy and natural way of transferring technology from one to another. It was also clear that to play both roles successfully a group vice president would have to be skilled as both a leader and a strategist.

Ex-Cell-O Performance, 1978–1984

Since the merger of Ex-Cell-O and McCord in 1978, the U.S. economy had experienced back-to-back recessions in 1980 and 1982–83, a significant

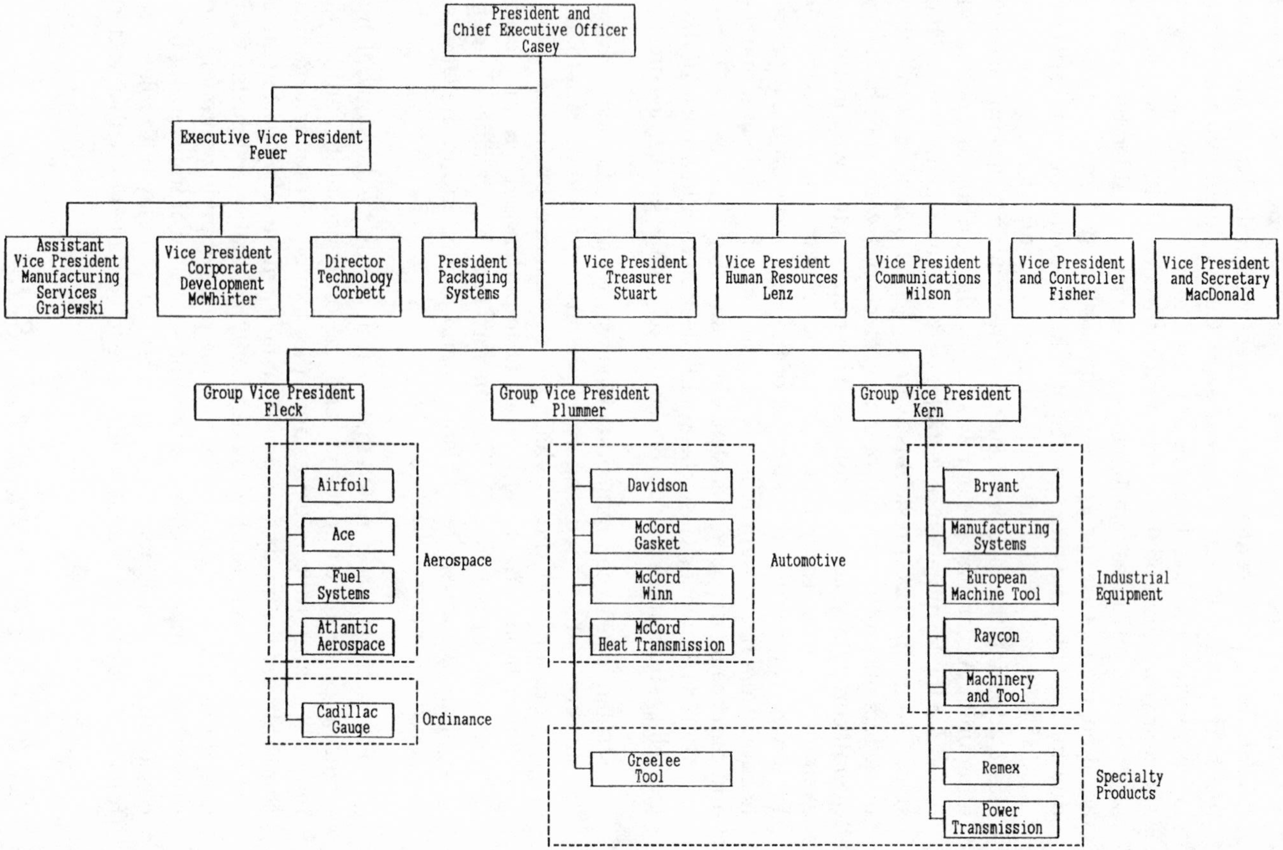

Exhibit 25.1 Ex-Cell-O Corporation (B) Organization Chart, December 1984

increase in government defense expenditures, a sharp drop in inflation, and a growing trade deficit. In the aggregate, Ex-Cell-O's sales and profits during the period through 1983 were essentially flat (see Exhibits 25.2 and 25.3). The final results for 1984 had not yet been published and were dependent in part on the outcome of the machine tool issue. It was known, however, that total sales had increased almost 20% over the previous year to $1,141 million and that operating profits, excluding the Industrial Equipment Group, were up approximately 23%.

On the other hand, the performance of individual operating groups had varied widely over this same period and not always along the lines anticipated earlier (see Exhibit 25.4). For instance, the Automotive Components Group suffered an operating loss in 1982 as the result of a steep drop in demand and a surge in the market share held by imported cars. Results gradually improved as the industry recovered in 1983. A changing attitude among the automobile manufacturers toward their suppliers also appeared to emerge at the depths of the recession. In exchange for more stable relationships, selected suppliers were required to assume greater responsibility for quality, design engineering, and, in some cases, even styling. Led by its Davidson Division, which accounted for nearly three-quarters of the group's sales, operating profits in 1984 finally surpassed the previous high recorded in 1979.

As anticipated, the Aerospace Group delivered increased sales and operating profits in most years during this period. Continued weakness in commercial markets was more than offset by strength in government procurement; by 1984 the latter accounted for approximately 55% of group revenues. Progress had been made through improved manufacturing techniques which afforded the closer tolerances and more uniform quality needed for engine fuel efficiency. Although there had been some success in broadening the customer base to other jet engine manufacturers, such as GE and Rolls Royce, the group still relied on Pratt & Whitney for about 75% of its sales. Nevertheless, the replacement market had grown to roughly 50% of sales which, it was hoped, would contribute to future stability.

Sales for the Ordnance Group increased sharply in 1981 and again in 1982. The following year, the division developed its first tracked vehicle, a lightweight high performance tank. This product was expected to result in significant sales in 1987 and beyond.

Performance for the Specialty Products Group was mixed. Greenlee Tool, the largest division, suffered through a difficult period during the 1982–83 recession when sales of construction equipment and woodworking tools were severely curtailed. Costs were cut, and new products developed, all contributing to an impressive turnaround in 1983. The second largest unit, Power Transmission, experienced similar pressures. A major program was undertaken to modernize machinery and manufacturing processes, and by 1984 positive results were becoming evident.

Exhibit 25.2
EX-CELL-O CORPORATION (B)
Financial Summary, 1978–1983

(thousands of dollars)	1983	1982	1981	1980	1979	1978[a]
Sales	$ 953,803	$ 1,027,123	$ 1,124,494	$ 1,020,677	$ 961,867	$ 729,792
Operating profit	87,006	97,804	106,797	97,646	111,341	82,515
Earnings before income taxes	87,001	85,664	102,898	88,064	100,968	75,068
Net earnings	49,815	48,202	56,411	49,992	54,212	39,412
Dividends declared	22,681	23,153	22,069	20,297	18,712	15,563
Total assets	689,627	697,633	725,039	708,926	618,845	533,643
Shareholders' equity	427,335	415,904	409,563	381,799	351,780	313,312
Net working capital	269,713	251,436	241,654	232,757	220,415	190,823
Property, plant & equip., net	175,891	179,738	189,375	181,986	173,504	164,855
Capital expenditures	29,512	29,223	41,313	38,390	41,944	28,090
Depreciation	32,222	30,744	29,395	28,552	26,979	27,082
Long-term debt	52,188	49,415	59,908	60,080	62,163	52,007
Research and development	**27,356**	**28,236**	**21,000**	**15,184**	**13,552**	**12,052**
(dollars per share)						
Net earnings[b]	$ 3.51	$ 3.25	$ 3.68	$ 3.25	$ 3.54	$ 2.71
Cash dividends declared	1.60	1.57	1.44	1.32	1.22	1.03
Shareholders' equity[c]	30.15	29.06	27.08	24.83	22.99	20.80
Common stock price-high	44 1/2	28 1/2	36 1/4	30 7/8	25 3/8	23 1/8
Common stock price - low	**24 1/2**	**18 1/4**	**21 3/8**	**17 7/8**	**16 7/8**	**14**
(percent)						
Return on sales	5.2	4.7	5.0	4.9	5.6	5.4
Dividend payout	45.5	48.0	39.1	40.6	34.5	39.5
Return on beginning equity	12.0	11.8	14.8	14.2	17.3	13.6
Debt to total capital	12.1	13.6	14.5	16.4	15.8	14.9
Effective tax rate	**42.7**	**43.7**	**45.2**	**43.2**	**46.3**	**47.5**
Average number of employees	13,100	14,100	16,300	16,800	16,900	14,300
No. shareholders, year end	13,253	13,965	14,676	15,097	15,977	16,685
Weighted ave. no. shares outstanding (000)	14,182	14,838	15,318	15,396	15,324	14,538

[a]On January 27, 1978, McCord Corporation became a wholly owned subsidiary of Ex-Cell-O.
[b]Based on weighted average number of shares outstanding during the year.
[c]Based on shares outstanding at year end.

Exhibit 25.3
EX-CELL-O CORPORATION (B)
Consolidated Balance Sheets
(thousands of dollars except per share amounts)

	November 30,	
ASSETS	1983	1982
Current Assets:		
Cash and marketable securities	$119,940	$119,442
Receivables, net	123,618	126,832
Inventories	144,569	149,121
Other current assets	54,818	51,825
Total current assets	$442,945	$447,220
Investments	26,014	29,489
Property, plant and equipment, net	175,891	179,738
Other assets	44,777	41,186
	$689,627	$697,633
LIABILITIES AND SHAREHOLDERS' EQUITY		
Current Liabilities:		
Notes payable and current portion of long-term debt	$ 6,553	$ 16,097
Accounts payable and accrued liabilities	123,872	121,388
Customer deposits	31,924	45,351
Income taxes	10,883	12,948
Total current liabilities	$173,232	$195,784
Long-term debt	52,188	49,415
Deferred items	36,872	36,530
Shareholders' Equity:		
Preferred stock, no par value:		
Authorized and unissued—5,000,000 shares	-	-
Common stock, par value $3 a share:		
Authorized—50,000,000 shares		
Issued—15,363,535 shares	46,091	46,091
Additional paid-in capital	57,648	57,343
Earnings reinvested in the business	364,237	337,103
Foreign currency translation adjustment	(12,423)	-
	$455,553	$440,537
Less cost of treasury stock—1,191,739 shares in 1983:		
1,050,876 shares in 1982	28,218	24,633
Total shareholders' equity	$427,355	$415,904
	$689,627	$697,633

Exhibit 25.4
EX-CELL-O CORPORATION (B)
Industry Segments Information

Segments:				Sales		
	1984	1983	1982	1981	1980	1979
Industrial Equipment[a]	$ 214,523	$185,047	$ 295,518	$379,861	$ 387,296	$321,798
Automotive Component	371,512	278,939	224,119	245,256	216,321	241,642
Aerospace	263,519	231,980	242,770	223,305	197,464	167,008
Ordnance	152,550	136,231	143,230	114,916	62,996	81,022
Specialty Products	138,954	121,606	121,486	161,156	156,600	150,397
Total	$1,141,058	$953,803	$1,027,123	$1,124,494	$1,020,677	$961,867

Segments:		Operating	Profit	(Loss)	Before Taxes	
	1984[b]	1983	1982	1981	1980	1979
Industrial Equipment[a]	$ (6,784)	$(10,736)	$ 26,776	$ 41,162	$ 51,243	$ 37,129
Automotive Components	27,345	14,855	(2,861)	10,593	6,051	19,940
Aerospace	51,604	44,611	42,164	22,273	19,013	21,068
Ordnance	23,208	28,081	28,229	19,674	5,182	12,546
Specialty Products	15,848	8,107	473	8,546	10,702	14,603
Total	$ 111,221	84,918	94,781	102,248	92,191	105,286
Corporate expenses	(26,054)	(22,670)	(32,129)[c]	(19,549)	(14,190)	(17,643)
Interest expense	(5,329)	(5,244)	(6,209)	(7,164)	(7,679)	(5,769)
Miscellaneous income, net	20,739	29,997	29,221	27,363	18,521	19,094
Consolidated	$ 100,577	$ 87,001	$ 85,664	$ 102,898	$ 88,843	$100,968

Segments:			Identifiable	Assets		
	1984	1983	1982	1981	1980	1979
Industrial Equipment[a]	NA	$145,535	$158,149	$ 224,016	$ 258,858	$236,168
Automotive Components	NA	137,840	129,082	131,580	127,853	133,109
Aerospace	NA	83,955	86,948	106,157	96,545	77,089
Ordnance	NA	46,062	47,059	50,596	37,404	24,012
Specialty Products	NA	63,996	60,899	70,138	90,142	94,240
Total	NA	$477,388	$482,137	$ 582,487	$ 610,802	$564,618
Corporate	NA	212,239	215,496	142,552	94,608	54,227
Consolidated[d]	NA	$689,627	$697,633	$ 725,039	$ 705,410	$618,845

Segments:			Capital	Expenditures		
	1984	1983	1982	1981	1980	1979
Industrial Equipment[a]	$ 10,700	$ 9,259	$ 9,355	$ 13,050	$ 12,526	$ 10,360
Automotive Components	17,055	8,833	8,446	8,602	10,198	11,396
Aerospace	11,194	3,479	5,744	9,133	10,497	7,694
Ordnance	4,121	3,678	1,638	4,117	1,328	734
Specialty Products	5,941	3,658	5,069	5,791	5,199	8,320
Total	$ 49,011	$ 28,907	$ 30,252	$ 40,693	$ 39,748	$ 38,504
Corporate	1,936	605	(1,029)	620	(1,358)	3,440
Consolidated	$ 50,947	$ 29,512	$ 29,223	$ 41,313	$ 38,390	$ 41,944

[a]Includes the Packaging Systems Division (Pure Pak). Sales in 1983 were approximately $46 million.
[b]1984 figures do not include charges for the restructuring operations.
[c]Includes a charge of $14.4 million to cover the cost of plant closings and consolidation of certain manufacturing facilities and a reduction in carrying value of related assets.
[d]Primarily cash and investments.

The status of the remaining Specialty Products divisions were significantly changed. The Remex Division's efforts to develop flexible computer disk drives was discontinued in 1983, and attention was focused on its mature line of paper tape equipment used to load numerical control programs into machine tools. At this point the unit's activities became closely associated with those of the Industrial Equipment Group. The Plastic Components Division was consolidated into Davidson.

Machine Tool Markets

The machine tool industry had been in turmoil since the first oil shock in 1973–1974. A sharp recession was followed by a strong recovery in the capital goods markets in 1978–1980, accompanied by a burgeoning demand for production equipment. In addition to the enormous investment programs undertaken by the automobile companies, machine tool makers benefited from the prosperity enjoyed by the aerospace, ordnance, packaging, metal fabricating, semiconductor, and energy industries. So great were the tooling needs in these areas that U.S. producers were swamped with business, causing backlogs to grow and customers to look elsewhere for suppliers. Indeed, Ex-Cell-O managers generally attributed the noticeable market share secured for the first time by Japanese and other foreign machine tool companies to the opening provided by this capacity shortfall.

Boom was followed by bust. With a few exceptions, such as defense/aerospace, the capital goods and metal working industries then entered a period of weak demand, overcapacity, and escalating foreign competition. As a result, machine tool sales in the United States fell to $1.8 billion in 1983 from a peak of $5.1 billion in 1981. Import penetration, which rose from 26.7% to 37.5% of domestic consumption in this period, further reduced the revenues of domestic suppliers (see Exhibit 25.5).

The key success factors for the leaders in the industry were their orientation to customers' needs, their ability to solve problems through the

Exhibit 25.5
EX-CELL-O CORPORATION (B)
Machine Tool Trends

	1980	1981	1982	1983	1984
The U.S. Industry					
Shipments (billions $)	4.7	5.1	3.6	1.8	2.3
EBT (% of sales)	12.9	12.2	5.0	(9.6)	NA
Employment (thousands)	99.7	98.3	78.2	62.7	64.6
Import Penetration (% of domestic consumption)	24.8	26.7	29.0	37.5	41.9

engineering of technical solutions, and their dedication to precision and quality. Historically, these had been achieved through adapting individual machines to the user's manufacturing process with an eye toward reducing throughput times and waste, and extending capabilities in terms of tolerances, materials, and shapes. In recent years, however, market requirements had been changing rapidly. Factory automation, production flexibility, in-line quality controls, and electronic instrumentation became increasingly important as U.S. manufacturers struggled to respond to offshore competition, product proliferation, and shorter life cycles.

The machine tool industry had also identified a significant new market in flexible manufacturing systems (FMS), a key component of the "factory of the future." An article that was carefully studied by Ex-Cell-O executives noted in part:

> Success in the 1970s was having the right product . . . at the right time. But in the 1980s and beyond, many observers feel that success will increasingly be derived from manufacturing . . .
>
> Flexible Manufacturing Systems (FMS) are regarded by many experts as the best way to meet the conflicting demands of low-volume but also low-cost production generated by proliferating product lines and frequent—often unpredictable—changes in the marketplace. At the same time, FMS addresses the issues of reducing manufacturing costs and improving product quality, which [have been termed] the most crucial concerns facing manufacturing managers today . . .
>
> Although a precise definition of FMS has yet to be written, the generalized FMS manufactures parts in random order, moving them between discrete machines with an automated handling system. In its simplest form, it might consist of two lathes, serviced by a single robot, all controlled by a programmable controller. In its most complex form, an FMS might include multiple CNC machining centers, special machine tools, inspection machines, and various types of automated material handling devices, all controlled by a computer . . .
>
> FMS demands absolute commitment and sustained effort by the user if the installation is to be successful. FMS also requires substantial front-end engineering and managerial resources, both from the vendor and the user. And it requires a level of cooperation and exchange of sensitive business planning information between vendor and user heretofore unheard of in typical manufacturing equipment acquisitions . . .
>
> It isn't uncommon, especially for the first-time FMS user, to spend 12 to 18 months in this planning phase. And after the final proposal is accepted, it will typically take 12 months or more to build, deliver, install, and debug the system. So the entire project

can easily take 2 1/2 years or longer, which emphasizes the importance not only of having a team, but also of having each team member be as familiar as possible with the entire project—one of them may retire, or find another position . . .

The number of FMS installed has doubled about every three years or less, but the results of a Delphi Study conducted recently by the Society of Manufacturing Engineers and the University of Michigan imply that the growth rate may increase. The study forecasts that by about 1987:

- Approximately 15% of total machine tool production will be going into flexible systems.
- Noncontact high-speed on-line inspection systems with closed-loop feedback to the machine control system will be in wide use.
- Approximately 38% of all FMS will be equipped with diagnostic sensors and associated software for implementing process alterations in real time.

And, finally, the Delphi Study suggests that by 1990, 20% of the machine tools sold will be capable of running fully unmanned systems . . .

The fact is that we are facing major changes in the ways American manufacturers have to do business. And it seems we may still lack a clear understanding of the problems and opportunities, and of the risk of not doing anything versus the risk of doing something.[2]

For most machine tool companies, FMS represented a challenge because few of them possessed all of the requisite skills and capabilities to service the emerging market. The approaches to meeting this challenge varied. For instance, Bendix (later merged into Allied Corporation) sought joint agreements with and partial ownership of other companies such as Caman, Toyota, and Yaswac to gain rapid market entry with proven technology and to minimize investment in R&D. Similarly, Cincinnati Milacron paired up with IBM to incorporate software and computer technology in its manufacturing systems. On the other hand, Cross & Trecker had, over a 10-year period, sought to integrate its machinery components with common software and a coordinated marketing effort. Mazak, a Japanese firm, had relied on state of the art systems engineering, and a comprehensive worldwide marketing effort, backed by exceptionally good service.

[2]Tom Hughes and Don Hegland, "Flexible Manufacturing—The Way to the Winner's Circle," *Production Engineering,* September 1983.

Casey indicated that the approach to the design and manufacture and the receptivity of the marketplace for production equipment in Germany and Japan differed considerably from that in the United States.

> In Japan there is no special machine tool industry per se. That's an exaggeration, of course, but machine tool technical leadership there is in the hands of the components manufacturers who develop machines to make their own products. If they are successful, then the equipment is sold on the outside. Japanese car companies, for instance, design the manufacturing process and make machine tools to operate it.
>
> In Germany, when the components manufacturers see an opportunity to upgrade their machine tools and manufacturing systems, they are eager to try it regardless of the cost. As a result of this receptivity, computers and FMS have been accepted more easily on the factory floor.

Industrial Equipment Group

The financial performance of the machine tool divisions mirrored that of the U.S. industry. After achieving record sales and earnings in 1980, the incoming order rate deteriorated rapidly, and by 1983 sales had fallen 60% and the group in total was incurring sizable losses. Although the German subsidiary remained profitable, albeit with narrower margins, the setbacks experienced by other divisions were severe, worse, it seemed, than in previous recessions.

As backlogs shrank, consideration was given to consolidating manufacturing facilities and reevaluating product lines. The intent was to hold market share in promising areas where Ex-Cell-O enjoyed a leadership position in technology and withdraw from those that offered little hope of competitive advantage. By 1982 Ex-Cell-O had shut down seven machine tool plants. If there were products manufactured in them with established market niches and favorable prospects, provisions were made to move them to other locations. The cost of these closings was reflected that year in an extraordinary charge of $14.4 million.

Among the shuttered plants was a central machine shop in Goshen, Indiana, which had been constructed in the mid-1970s to manufacture components for the Industrial Equipment divisions. The concept of a common parts unit had been neither popular nor successful. The other divisions resented being forced to buy from it. Moreover, Goshen soon became the recipient of used Ex-Cell-O machines which had been returned by customers for being unreliable and which its management was in no position to resell.

In August 1983, Ex-Cell-O acquired Raycon, a small, entrepreneurial company with a strong base in electronics and software and a highly regarded line of electronic discharge machines. It was also developing noncontact laser, fiber optic, and video gauging equipment for use in inspection and machine monitoring operations. Casey hoped that this unit would provide the group with technology and skills in areas of importance for the future, particularly in flexible manufacturing systems. On the other hand, plans for a machine tool technology center had been put on hold, in part because Otto Kern, group vice president, was skeptical about an early systems-led recovery for the industry and was reluctant to proceed with a major capital project during a period of contraction.

Production facilities and product lines following the consolidation and the addition of Raycon are described in Exhibit 25.6.

FMS Focus Session

In October 1983, Kern, Feuer, and Casey met with the machine tool division managers and members of the corporate planning staff, for three days to formulate a program for expanding Ex-Cell-O's participation in FMS. The meeting was one of four "focus sessions" held during the year to identify and develop strategies for the core businesses that Ex-Cell-O would concentrate on for future growth. The operating managers were asked to make presentations on the opportunities available to the company and the role that each division was to play in pursuing them.

Chuck Patterson, director of strategic planning, summarized some of the issues raised in a follow-up memorandum to Casey:

A. Future Trends

- Our economy is changing from a focus on consumption to a focus on productivity. This will create opportunities for companies like Ex-Cell-O—particularly our manufacturing equipment business segment.
- The nature of metal cutting is going to completely change by the end of the decade. Electronics will play a key role in machine tools of the future.
- We do not have a clearly perceived group machine tool strategy, and because we have closed down many plants over the last few years, we have a real credibility problem. Many people are saying Ex-Cell-O is going out of the machine tool business.
- Ex-Cell-O has been successful because we have provided solutions to customer problems through precision and quality and engineering innovations. This gave Ex-Cell-O, over the years, the competitive edge. However, in today's turbulent world, we find this extremely difficult to continue implementing because the customer no longer knows what his needs are.

Exhibit 25.6
EX-CELL-O CORPORATION (B)
Manufacturing Facilities
Industrial Equipment Group

Division	Manufacturing Locations	Size (sq.ft.)	Employment	Major Product Lines
Bryant	Springfield, VT	181,000	600	Precision grinding machines
Machine and Tool	Holland, MI	160,000	240	Honing machines Die casting machines Roto-Flo cold-forming machines
	Berne, IN	64,300	176	Gauging, assembly and parts handling equipment Electrical discharge machines Milling machines Lapping machines
Manufacturing Systems	Rockford, IL	468,000	490	Flexible manufacturing systems Transfer lines Planers, plotters, slotters, and shapers Computer NC machining centers
	Ontario, Canada	160,000	249	Milling machines Precision boring machines Vertical turning machines Flexible manufacturing systems Transfer lines
Raycon	Ann Arbor, MI Owosso, MI	20,000 20,000	48 38	Electrical discharge machines (EDM) Laser machining centers Noncontact laser, fiber optic and video gauging
European Machine Tool	Eislingen, Germany	240,000	800	Flexible manufacturing systems Transfer lines Roto-Flo cold-forming machines Computer NC machining centers
	Leicester, England	117,000	271	Boring machines Transfer lines Computer NC grinders

B. Flexible Manufacturing Systems

- The FMS market is an emerging growth market and will carry good profit margin potential—particularly in the electronic and software content.
- The metal cutting FMS market is here today and is being successfully pursued by our European and Manufacturing Systems Divisions.
- We need to focus on proprietary content—especially the software (electronics). Sources of good margins in the FMS business will be proprietary content, innovation, problem solving, involvement with the customer, special application niches, software and electronics, and hardware/software marriage.

The presentations also addressed both the specific opportunities for Ex-Cell-O in the FMS market, and some of the obstacles to be overcome:

Bryant Grinder was the leading U.S. producer of internal grinding machines. Although division management felt the immediate impact of FMS on Bryant's market niche was minimal, they indicated that there might be a potential in the future. The division's strengths were in its individual machines; software capability was limited.

The Machinery and Tool Division was expert in stand-alone die casting, honing, and gauging equipment. One quote had been made on a flexible die casting system in collaboration with Raycon which included robotic loading and unloading, palletizing, and inspection steps, but another supplier who had been working with the customer on process design won the order. However, the division had some electronics capability and the assembly facilities to accommodate FMS. On the other hand, it did not have a lot of experience in systems sales; generating proposals which incorporated other vendors' equipment had proven difficult.

Remex, although not officially a member of the machine tool group, was included in the meeting because its line of paper tape numerical control equipment was installed in approximately 75% of the nation's custom machine tool shops. The division was attempting to develop a system for converting machines operating with paper tape controls to computers that would permit this large installed base to be integrated into FMS. To exploit the market opportunity, Remex needed additional software talent, which it hoped to obtain through consultants, and a greater understanding of machine tools which it anticipated acquiring through joint efforts with the machine tool divisions.

Raycon had strength in electronics and some software capability which had been applied to the development of sophisticated electronic discharge machining and noncontact gauging systems. Raycon hoped to support the other divisions with new products and related software, especially in quality assurance, monitoring, and process controls, which were important elements in the design of automated production lines.

Manufacturing Systems, the largest and oldest unit in the group, produced a broad range of machine tools and transfer lines but was committed to growth through systems sales. A major undertaking, then in process, involved upgrading the various product lines to FMS capability with compatible, flexible software. A prototype advanced work center system had been built and displayed at a trade show earlier in the month and had generated considerable interest. Although dependent on outsiders for software at the time, the division planned to add its own staff and work with the other units on integrated systems for the metal removal FMS market. Mindful of the capacity shortage experienced several years earlier, the division manager had kept his sizable engineering department in place despite current losses in anticipation of the recovery that some industry analysts foresaw in the months ahead.

The European Machine Tool Division was also dedicated to the FMS concept and had been successful in obtaining one order for an automatic blade line and another for automotive parts machining and assembly totaling nearly $10 million. In fact, FMS inquiries exceeded the division's capacity to produce them in Germany, while those for conventional machines were decreasing. The division reorganized its sales organization to focus on systems rather than individual machines and increased the capability of its proposal engineers to specify them. The division's major concern was building an FMS base quickly enough to take advantage of the shakeout predicted in the European machine tool industry.

At the end of the meeting Casey addressed the issue of the corporation's commitment to the machine tool industry:

> Perhaps the clearest sign of our corporate commitment is the fact that we are tolerating, although uncomfortably, some rather significant losses in some of the divisions. If we didn't have the faith that there was going to be a real future beyond the valley we would . . . insist that we cut back and control their losses to a much greater degree. I think we would have to do that if we were just a machine tool company. Fortunately we have other segments, but I can assure you with complete conviction that we are committed to this business . . .
>
> Manufacturing equipment, more than any other single segment—although we have a lot of good things in other segments—can make Ex-Cell-O the kind of company we want to be. The fact that we don't see our ultimate goal clearly is not as important as the fact that we are moving in that direction.

Chuck Patterson listed the conclusions reached at the meeting on the steps to be taken by the Industrial Equipment Group:

a. Develop and implement a material processing FMS business plan. European Machine Tool and the Manufacturing Systems Division in the meantime will concentrate on the metal removal FMS business.

b. Transfer Raycon technology and capabilities into the other units of Ex-Cell-O.

c. Emphasize the opportunities for our more advanced product (FMS) while gradually deemphasizing traditional products.

d. We need to address the issue of software. Possibly we need our own software company.

e. In the FMS business we need to act as a group instead of as separate divisions.

More specifically, Bob Williams, corporate vice president of administration, was to chair a committee of division operating managers to formulate a program for approaching the nonmetal FMS market, e.g., the machining of plastics and composites. Casey hoped that this effort would also suggest additional avenues for cooperation among the units. In addition, plans were made for designing and installing an advanced FMS in the Power Transmission Division to improve that division's manufacturing process and to serve as a showcase installation for the Industrial Equipment Group. As these efforts proceeded, a second review meeting was anticipated, probably at the end of 1983.

Machine Tool Review—Fall 1984

The follow-up meeting was not held as anticipated. Williams died suddenly a week after the focus session, and efforts at the operating level, although continuing, did not warrant a second general review. Despite an improving economy in 1984, operating losses in the Industrial Equipment Group continued unabated at a rate of $1.0 million or more a month, and by mid-year, with the support and encouragement of his board, Casey once again began to examine its outlook.

In September, Feuer, Kern, and Dick McWhirter, vice president of corporate development, met at Casey's suggestion to evaluate the machine tool situation and in particular that of the Manufacturing Systems Division. They reasoned that to be successful in the industry a unit had to have a distinctive competence, which could be either a "central distinctive core technology" serving many markets (such as IBM) or a "central core market" served by many technologies (such as McDonnell Douglas). None of the Ex-Cell-O divisions fit the second category. On the other hand, they concluded that all facilities except those in England and Canada had, or had the potential for achieving, the former. Each division and some of the major product lines were rated as shown in Exhibit 25.7. Arrangements were set for a full review in December.

The December meeting was attended by all of the top corporate officers, the Manufacturing Systems and European Machine Tool Division

Exhibit 25.7
EX-CELL-O CORPORATION (B)
Industrial Equipment Group Expenditures

Division (Product Line)	Sales Potential (millions)[a]	Distinctive Competence (Technological)[b] Past	Future	Market Position Past	Future
Bryant	$48	+	++	Leader	Leader
Machine and Tool—Holland	30	+	+	Middle	Leader
(Roto Flo)	12	++	++	Leader	Leader
(Die Casting)	12	0	+	Middle	Leader
Manufacturing Systems (Transfer Lines) (FMS)	96	0	+	Leader Also Ran	Leader Leader(?)
Raycon	18	+	++	Leader	Leader
Machine and Tool—Berne	12	++	+	Middle	Middle
Germany	72	++	+	Leader	Leader
England	24	0	=	Also Ran	Leader
Canada	30	+	-	Middle	Leader
	354				

[a]Sales based on three good capital investment years.
[b]Best (++) Worst (=)

managers, and an outside director. At the outset, the objective for the machine tool units was reiterated: "Shift the major focus of the business from traditional machine tools to advanced computer controlled FMS cells and machining centers while maintaining a leadership position in selected segments of the traditional machine tool business."

From an analysis of market and competitive trends such an objective appeared to be sound. The biennial International Machine Tool Show in October had been decidedly more upbeat than the one in 1982; exhibitors generally reported increased interest in innovative equipment, particularly FMS. Some industry observers were forecasting that an upturn was finally about to begin. Yet the automobile companies which provided more than 75% of the Manufacturing Systems Division's revenues had been slow to release tooling orders and reluctant to work with Ex-Cell-O on process design. Among their concerns were a myriad of major technical uncertainties about automobile design that had significant implications for manufacturing. For instance, would body panels be made from coated steel or reinforced plastics? Would continuously variable transmissions, that were then under development in Europe, be introduced in the U.S.? Balanced against their fear of tooling up for an obsolete design was the desire to replace old, inefficient process equipment for cost and quality reasons.

The Manufacturing Systems Division had not made the anticipated progress in upgrading its product line to accommodate FMS or in overcoming the coordination difficulties among the machine tool divisions. It also appeared that the FMS systems being developed in the United States might not be compatible with the ones designed by the European division. In addition, Remex had not completed the technical work on its computer adaptation product. Summary financial information for the machine tool divisions is provided in Exhibit 25.8.

On the other hand, several of the divisions were projecting improved performance (Exhibit 25.8). A new assessment of capabilities relative to competitive requirements suggested numerous strengths (see Exhibit 25.9), and work seemed to be progressing satisfactorily on the FMS system for the Power Transmission Division. Questions were raised, however, about the feasibility of remaining simply as producers of individual machine tools. Stand-alone machinery, such as that manufactured by Bryant and the Machine and Tool Division, were increasingly being specified as components of larger systems. Investment would be required in electronics and software to insure that these products could be adapted to FMS in the future.

For Casey the future of the machine tool business in Ex-Cell-O had implications that extended beyond the Industrial Equipment Group:

> If Ex-Cell-O is to be a world class aerospace components parts manufacturer, we have to have in-house machine tool capability. It's been like pulling teeth to get the machine tool people to make machinery specially for our aerospace divisions. They want to develop products for the market and sell them to everyone, including our competitors.

The meeting adjourned without a final decision on a course of action. However, a number of conclusions were reached. First, a master plan had to be developed promptly that would fix the concept, structure, research requirements, and expectations for the group. Second, losses in the Manufacturing Systems Division had to be stopped. Third, the possibility of divestments and plant closings had to be acknowledged and consideration given to establishing a reserve for restructuring to be included in the 1984 financial statements. If a reserve were set up, its burden would be eased by an after-tax $17.7 million tax credit due to a change in the tax law that was to be recognized in the year-end figures.

A Visit to General Motors

Shortly after the meeting, Casey and Kern met with the top purchasing group at General Motors to propose a new procurement system for machine tools. (Casey had earlier been disturbed to learn that General Motors had

Exhibit 25.8
EX-CELL-O CORPORATION (B)
Machine Tool Division Financial Performance[a]

I. SALES	Plan 1985	1984	1983	1982	1981
Bryant Grinder	$ 53,744	$ 21,242	$ 26,344	$ 49,757	$ 49,602
Machine and Tool	53,994	50,862[b]	24,535	31,116	34,505
Manufacturing Systems					
Rockford	48,952	27,462	16,142	66,466	82,001
London	20,831	14,975	12,562	17,382	31,488
Raycon	14,760	5,174	814		
European Machine Tool					
Germany	49,818	37,620	41,236	56,183	63,830
England	5,610	12,128	11,986	20,400	19,855
Total	$247,709	$169,463	$133,619	$241,304	$281,281

II. OPERATING PROFIT	Plan 1985	1984	1983	1982	1981
Bryant Grinder	$ 4,136	$ (4,495)	$ (3,439)	$ 10,859	$ 10,312
Machine and Tool	4,392	3,232	(1,242)	3,690	8,027
Manufacturing Systems					
Rockford	(7,018)	(13,433)	(10,780)	12,178	20,309
London	(73)	(2,713)	(3,380)	(734)	3,982
Raycon	(1,136)	(3,181)	(767)		
European Machine Tool					
Germany	2,780	1,156	1,277	7,409	7,445
England	(960)	581	(492)	(1,286)	(1,242)
Total	$ 2,121	$(18,853)	$(18,823)	$ 32,116	$ 48,833

III. CAPITAL EXPENDITURES	Plan 1985	1984	1983	1982	1981
Bryant Grinder	$ 3,365	$ 641	$ 2,057	$ 1,870	$ 1,114
Machine and Tool	2,540	1,091	791	1,168	836
Manufacturing Systems					
Rockford	596	792	3,305	545	2,966
London	1,079	1,016	112	450	2,605
Raycon	1,489	781	47		
European Machine Tool					
Germany	2,570	1,421	863	2,368	2,384
England	1,262	140	476	624	2,020
Total	$ 12,901	$ 5,882	$ 8,514	$ 7,025	$ 11,925

IV: R&D EXPENSES	Plan 1985	1984	1983	1982	1981
Bryant Grinder	$ 2,060	$ 1,436	$ 1,216	$ 1,924	$ 836
Machine and Tool	1,206	1,093	896	947	444
Manufacturing Systems					
Rockford	1,020	2,368	1,289	1,676	1,532
London	180	184	214	407	168
Raycon	1,772	1,655	107		
European Machine Tool					
Germany	1,454	974	1,009	739	204
England	454	67	198	209	112
Total	$ 8,146	$ 7,777	$ 4,929	$ 5,902	$ 3,296

(continued)

Exhibit 25.8 *(continued)*

V: CASH CONTRIBUTION	Plan 1985	1984	1983	1982	1981	Net Assets 11/30/84
Bryant Grinder	$ 2,036	(9,901)	(802)	10,088	3,668	28,420
Machine and Tool	(113)	(6,617)	(2,856)	5,594	12,776	31,592
Manufacturing Systems	(19,325)	(9,286)	(7,796)	12,367	4,320	
Rockford	*	*	*	*	*	38,822
London	*	*	*	*	*	20,855
Raycon	(4,964)	(3,100)				7,963
European Machine Tool						
Germany	98	(1,565)	6,270	11,849	(11,381)	30,320
England	(2,180)	2,710	814	(4,855)	(2,022)	8,750
Total	$(24,448)	$(27,759)	$ (4,370)	$ 35,043	$ 7,361	$166,722

aFigures have been disguised.
bSales increases from 1983 to 1984 reflect sales of products transferred from discontinued operations.
*Amount included in Manufacturing Systems Division total.

bypassed the U.S. industry entirely in favor of an Italian supplier for the retooling of its Tonawanda assembly plant.) The Ex-Cell-O managers suggested a partnership relationship through which the two companies would work closely together throughout the life of a project to adapt the latest technology to the needs of the manufacturing process. The advantages of this procedure over the traditional "arms length" competitive bidding system were emphasized during the presentation (Exhibit 25.10).

Casey indicated to the General Motors executives that their encouragement would be an important element in his decision about the future of Ex-Cell-O's machine tool business. They received the proposal with interest and promised to review it over the next several months.

Alternatives

There appeared to be three general alternatives for the machine tool divisions. The first was to continue with the existing objective of exploiting specialty niches in stand-alone machines and becoming a factor in the metal removal FMS business in the 1990s. The plans submitted by the divisions forecast a return to profitability in 1985 (see Exhibit 25.8) as well as increased expenditures for capital equipment and R & D. In this case, the company might seek a pairing with another firm that could provide software and computer skills, which appeared to be deficient at Ex-Cell-O. Changes in management and organization might also be necessary.

Second, Ex-Cell-O could take action in the short term to reduce the losses but retain a position in the machine tool industry. In this case, the Manufacturing Systems Division might be eliminated and its plants either sold or closed. Casey was not confident that a buyer could be found for the

Exhibit 25.9

EX-CELL-O CORPORATION (B)

Machine Tool Structure Analysis

<u>RATE AGAINST NEEDS</u>

	Degree of Relationship to Other Units	Product Range	New Product	Culture	Market Position	Technology Position	Quality of Work Force	Adaptability	Labor Relations	Age Structure of Work Force	Facilities
Bryant	3	3	3	3	1	1	1	3	1	3	1
Europe Machine Tool Division	3	1	1	1	1	1	1	1	1	2	1
Manufacturing Systems Division	3	1	1	1	2	2	2	2	1	3	2
Machine and Tool	2	2	1	1	1	2	1	2	1	2	2
Raycon	2	1	1	1	1	1	2	1	1	1	2

1 = Excellent.
2 = Good.
3 = Fair.

Exhibit 25.10

EX-CELL-O CORPORATION (B)

Traditional Procurement System

Process	Advantages to G.M.	Disadvantages to G.M.
The process is supposed to be "Arm's Length."	Selection process is relatively simple and straightforward.	There is little sharing of machine tool technology within G.M. resulting in constant design duplication.
Very decentralized purchasing.	G.M. can buy equipment at "low cost" by comparing one supplier's proposal to another's.	The exorbitant proposal and sales costs due to supplier duplication of effort is eventually borne by G.M.
A number of suppliers receive a part print and a specified or recommended machining process from G.M.		G.M. will normally buy yesterday's technology since that is what the supplier is asked to quote on.
Suppliers commit proposal and engineering resources to prepare a firm priced proposal for equipment.		If a supplier quotes on new technologies, he often loses the order on price or bears all the financial risk if he gets it—creating a conservative business attitude which inhibits experimentation and implementation of leading edge technologies.
G.M. reviews proposals and narrows the field of selection, sometimes combining the best features from several vendors.		Supplier investments in new technology, new products, and plant and equipment is discouraged due to competitively depressed margins and an inability to maintain proprietary confidentiality.
G.M. consults with remaining suppliers to arrive at final process, price and delivery date.		Some builders get overloaded, resulting in quality and delivery problems while others have excess capacity and have to cut organizations.
G.M. lets contract.		An unstable economic climate is created which ultimately will shrink the qualified machine tool supplier base and engineering talent to the point that it will be unable to respond to the needs of G.M.
		No provision exists for G.M. and its machine tool supplier to share technology or information on long-range business plans, needs or global strategies.

(continued)

Exhibit 25.10 (continued)

Process	Advantages to G.M.	Disadvantages to G.M.
The process is a "Partnership."	The recommended system would promote G.M.'s long-range business objectives through joint advanced planning and process development activities.	Selection process becomes more complex requiring a greater degree of mutual trust between G.M. and its suppliers and changing established purchasing practices.
Some centralized control of sourcing.		
G.M. establishes a close-working relationship with selected capital equipment suppliers by evaluating them against measurable criteria:	New technical solutions can be more readily explored, evaluated, and implemented.	
– Quality – Reputation – Reliability – Commitment – Demonstrated Capability – Technical Capability – Financial Viability and Stability	A coordinated purchasing function able to balance its purchases among vendors, promoting a healthier machine tool industry able to make greater investments in R&D, product development and production facilities.	
	G.M.'s North American operations would have access to the latest technology and manufacturing systems from U.S.-based companies that can provide superior communications, project coordination, and service.	
A machine tool builder is selected early in the life of the project.	A working partner could provide unified systems by combining diverse technologies associated with information processing, materials, machining, and forming.	
A joint development effort follows, aimed at achieving the optimum process.		
The price of the equipment is negotiated on an open book basis.	Capital equipment costs would ultimately decline as the duplication waste of multiple proposal and sales costs could be greatly reduced.	

division as a business; tentative discussions with several likely prospects suggested that, if there was interest at all, Ex-Cell-O would have to guarantee a profit in the backlog and assume other onerous covenants. Bryant might be scaled back to reduce annual expenses by approximately $2.0 million, and Remex might be sold. On the other hand, the European Machine Tool Division could continue to develop and sell advanced systems and conceivably export them to the United States. The other divisions would remain, but under tight cost and investment controls. The pretax charge for discontinuing the Manufacturing Systems Division and downsizing other operations was calculated to be on the order of $37 million. There were, of course, variations on this plan. For instance, closing the Ontario facility and transferring its work to a reconfigured Rockford plant might lower the special charge by $10 million.

Third, Ex-Cell-O could divest the entire machine tool business. The financial consequences in this case would depend on the existence of buyers and the terms of sale. The book value of identifiable assets, however, was on the order of $140 million. Such a move would eliminate the risk of further losses in the short run. Moreover, it would certainly provide convincing evidence to the financial community that Ex-Cell-O should no longer be classified as a low growth machine tool company.

As Casey evaluated these alternatives, he considered the impact each would have on the company's other divisions and on its relationships with its major customers. For instance, if Ex-Cell-O were to withdraw from machine tools altogether, would that signal a reduced commitment to the automotive industry? Would the European Machine Tool Division by itself have enough muscle to be a credible factor in the U.S. market if the Manufacturing Systems Division were discontinued? Would the company be sacrificing machining and process design skills that might be needed by its growing aerospace components businesses? And would it be passing up a role in an industry poised for a dramatic recovery as the dollar weakened and U.S. manufacturers finally began to retool?

Time was now of the essence. The annual report was due to be released soon, and decisions were necessary to complete the financial statements. Other parts of the company demanded Casey's attention, and he was anxious to put a plan in place for the machine tool segment that would clarify its position for the foreseeable future.

CHAPTER 26

Medical Products Company

A T THE BEGINNING OF their three-day meeting in March 1990, Mr. Roberto Hausman, the president of the Disposable Devices Sector of the Medical Products Company (MPC), welcomed the group assembled around the conference table.

This promises to be a very productive meeting. A window of opportunity has opened up for us, and it appears that we finally have a chance to resolve, once and for all, some of the issues our European organization has been struggling with over at least the last six years. The recent acceleration in the projected growth rate for our hypodermic and diabetic products makes it possible to discuss possible changes without having to worry about consolidating plants or making substantial reductions in personnel at any plant. We now operate within an organizational structure that allows us to deal with the problem as a whole, and all the key people who will be involved in implementing the changes that may be required are in this room, participating in the design of those changes. You collectively control all the resources necessary to make it happen. Now I charge you with that responsibility.

The task force assembled to plan the reorganization of European manufacturing for hypodermic products included the president for Disposable Devices in Europe, the managers of all the European factories producing hypodermic products, and several senior managers (including those responsible for strategic planning) that coordinated European activities with those in other parts of the world. It had been preceded by a three-day meeting in Europe, attended by about 20 managers drawn from the

Professor Robert H. Hayes prepared this case as the basis for class discussion rather than to illustrate either effective or ineffective handling of an administrative situation. Certain names and numbers have been disguised.

same factories as well as a group from MPC's European headquarters, where the same issues had been discussed and alternative solutions proposed. In a larger sense, however, it had been preceded by a number of meetings and studies over the previous decade that had attempted to negotiate—without enduring success—the evolving, and often conflicting, needs and concerns of the company's European plant network.

MPC's International Organization

MPC was a major supplier of diagnostics systems and disposable medical devices to health care institutions such as hospitals, physician's offices, clinical laboratories, and pharmacies. In 1990 the combined sales of its two product sectors, Disposable and Diagnostics, were slightly over $2 billion (Exhibit 26.1 provides a summary of financial information). After a decade of rapid growth, MPC's sales outside the United States now approached 40% of the total, two-thirds of which took place in Europe.

Most of the growth in European sales had taken place since 1980, when the company had decided to become much more aggressive in expanding its presence there. At that time European operations were organized by country, with strong country managers overseeing domestic marketing and sales activities for all products. The factories producing hypodermic products (which, at that time, comprised most of the MPC products made in Europe) also reported to them. MPC's top management decided that it no longer made sense for local managers to make product marketing decisions that could have spillover effects on other countries. Also, they were concerned because different quality, cost, and delivery standards had been adopted by different plants producing the same product.

Therefore, during the early 1980s an SBU (Strategic Business Unit) structure similar to the one that previously had been established in the United States was overlaid on the existing country organization. An SBU president was created for each of MPC's key product lines and given sales and profit responsibility for all the sales and marketing organizations associated with that product line in Europe. They reported to the president of European Operations (located in Lyons, France), on the same level as the country managers. The European president, in turn, reported to MPC's president for International Operations at its U.S. headquarters. The managers of the European factories, on the other hand, now reported to the Hypodermic Products Division president in the United States.

This structure was soon found to be confusing and unwieldy, involving as it did both an existing group (country managers) having strong personalities and a new group of SBU presidents that was generally less knowledgeable about the specifics of each individual country's markets, clinical practices, and regulatory policies. Moreover, the European organization felt itself somewhat isolated from U.S. operations: it received low priority in the delivery of products from U.S. factories, and products

Exhibit 26.1 Medical Products Company
Summary of Selected Financial Data Year Ended
September 30 (thousands of dollars, except per share amounts)

	1989	1988	1987	1986
Operations				
Net sales	$1,811,456	$1,709,368	$1,462,882	$1,203,943
Gross profit margin	45.7%	46.5%	46.5%	46.1%
Operating income	225,795	239,041	200,006	146,531
Interest expense, net	34,527	27,657	54,714	15,673
Income from continuing operations before income taxes	227,786	206,252	187,999	149,308
Income tax provision	69,784	57,296	51,053	38,445[b]
Income from continuing operations	158,002	148,856	136,946	100,846
Net income	213,596[a]	161,943	148,164	121,930[b]
Earnings per share				
- Continuing operations	4.00	3.69	3.30	2.36
- Net income	5.40[a]	4.01	3.57	2.85[b]
Dividends per common share	1.00	.86	.74	.66
Average common and common equivalent shares outstanding	39,586	40,401	41,548	42,903
Financial Position				
Current assets	868,630	882,992	842,304	782,795
Current liabilities	567,761	525,771	493,016	445,419
Current ratio	1.5	1.7	1.7	1.8
Property, plant, and equipment, net	1,100,567	925,447	754,872	631,306
Total assets	2,270,130	2,067,533	1,891,478	1,690,916
Long-term debt	516,047	499,969	479,559	391,664
Shareholders' equity	1,071,497	959,803	861,284	803,925
Book value per common share	27.99	24.33	31.62	19.62
Financial Relationships				
Income from continuing operations before income taxes as a percent of sales	12.6%	12.1%	12.9%	12.4%
Return on total assets[c]	14.0	14.6	14.3[d]	14.1
Return on equity	17.0[d]	17.8	16.0[d]	16.4
Additional Data				
Depreciation and amortization	$ 121,947	$ 109,217	$ 91,911	$ 71,312
Capital expenditures	314,267	272,538	190,968	139,032
Research and development expense	97,543	93,255	82,825	68,890
Number of employees	18,800	20,600	19,900	19,300
Number of shareholders	7,134	8,451	7,872	8,175

Source: 1989 *Annual Report*
[a]Includes after-tax gain of $44,658 or $1.12 per share, on the sale of Advor subsidiary.
[b]Includes extraordinary credit from utilization of tax loss carryforwards of $10,017, or $.23 per share.
[c]Earnings before interest expense and taxes as a percent of average total assets.
[d]Excludes gains on sales of Advar and Devon in 1989 and 1987, respectively.

designed in the United States did not sufficiently reflect the standards required by individual countries.

In an attempt to smooth coordination and avoid these sorts of conflicts, around 1986 this structure was integrated with cross-functional teams created for each of the company's major product lines. Drawn from around the world, each team was asked to formulate a worldwide strategy and coordinate several of the activities for its products. The rationale behind the creation of these teams was that some decisions were properly made at a local level while others ought to be made globally, and that a rigid structure composed of members having different allegiances could not easily differentiate the two. It was felt that a team of people who worked together more informally and could develop close personal relationships with one another was better equipped to mediate such issues.

Although the team concept resolved some of the difficulties that had been experienced, the various teams ended up operating quite differently and with varying degrees of success. They also were felt to add significantly to the time each manager spent in meetings. Then, in early 1989 a whole new corporate organizational structure was created. The International Sector was eliminated and the company was organized into the current two worldwide product sectors. In addition, the responsibilities of the European President were transferred to the five European SBU presidents, each of whom reported to the president of the appropriate Product Sector. The five SBU presidents formed a European Management Committee, which became a forum for discussing and managing Europewide issues. The role of the country manager remained as before, but factory managers (who previously had reported to the U.S. product organization) now reported to the appropriate European SBU president.

Despite the many benefits of this worldwide product organization, concerns continued to be expressed (primarily by former country managers and their staffs) that MPC was no longer sufficiently responsive to local market, labor, and legal issues. Moreover, the five European division presidents sometimes found it difficult to resolve issues that had ramifications throughout Europe as a whole—for example, the restructuring of the European plant network and the development of a European central distribution and information system.

European Hypodermic Products

MPC's Disposable Devices Sector accounted for about 55% of its total sales in 1990, and was organized around five core businesses: hypodermic syringes and needles, diabetic care products, IV (intravenous) catheters, PSD (prefillable syringes), and medical gloves. It was the world leader, in terms of market share, for all these products except medical gloves.

Hypodermic products included both needles and syringes. In simple terms, a needle was formed by attaching a cannula (a thin, hollow metal tube, pointed and sharpened at one end) to a plastic device that allowed it to be attached to the barrel of a syringe. A syringe, in turn, consisted of a glass or plastic barrel into which a plunger was inserted. If the needle were not already attached to the syringe at the factory, a medical technician would attach a sterilized needle to the bottom of the barrel; then s/he would draw the appropriate amount of a prescribed drug into the barrel, insert the needle into the patient, and press on the plunger to push the drug out of the barrel into the patient. Medication could also be given through IV lines.

Thousands of different combinations of cannula, needle, and syringe were possible. The cannula, for example, could be many different thicknesses and lengths, and could be coated with different substances that made its penetration of human skin easier and less painful. The wide assortment of needle stockkeeping units (SKUs) reflected the different types of cannulae, the fact that needles could be equipped with different mechanisms for attaching them to a syringe, and they could be packaged in a variety of ways (e.g., individually, in bulk, or in packages that varied by type, language, and graphics). The cost of needles varied according to their size and configuration, but generally cost about $15 per 1000. Needles and cannulae were "truly transnational products," according to one company manager. "They are used everywhere and are easy to ship."

Similarly, syringes differed by size, by the barrel material used (glass or plastic), by whether or not they incorporated a nonremovable needle, by other design features, and by type of packaging. Insulin syringes, for example, were designed specifically for self-injection of dosages appropriate for diabetics. They were characterized by simple, low cost designs and were produced in very high volumes on dedicated lines.

The syringes required for European markets tended to have different sizes and designs than those sold in the United States, so it was difficult to supply one region from the other on short notice. Europeans, for example, generally preferred separate needles while in the United States needles were usually attached to syringes at the factory. In the United States, moreover, syringe designs that prevented the transmission of diseases by making reuse impossible and/or by protecting the health care provider from accidental needle sticks were becoming increasingly popular. Representative costs associated with transporting various types of MPC products among the different regions of the world are provided in Exhibits 26.2A and 26.2B.

Within the company, syringes were described in terms of their size, usually specified by the maximum number of thousandths of a liter—or, equivalently, cubic centimeters, (abbreviated as ml and cc) that could be contained within the barrel, and number of parts. The traditional syringe design incorporated three parts (not including the needle, if attached): a plastic injection-molded barrel, a plastic molded plunger, and a rubber gasket (called a "stopper") that was attached to the bottom of the plunger and prevented fluid from flowing back around the plunger as it was pushed through the barrel. In the 1970s a new 2-pc (two-piece) design

Exhibit 26.2A Freight Cost Per 40 Foot Container (top number in box) and 1000 5cc Syringes ("M" in bottom number represents 1000 units)

From:	United States	Europe (Belgium)	Singapore	Mexico	Brazil	North Latin America (Ecuador)	South Latin America (Chile)
				TO:			
United States	$0.00	$1,618 $ 2.02/M	$2,164 $ 2.71/M	$2,817 $3.52/M	$4,880 $ 6.10/M	$5,170 $ 6.46/M	$4,595 $ 5.74/M
Europe	$3,100 $ 2.95/M	$0.00	$1,032 $ 0.98/M	$3,000 $ 2.86/M	$5,300 $ 5.05/M	$4,800 $ 4.57/M	$5,300 $ 5.05/M
Singapore	$3,081 $ 2.93/M	$2,880 $ 2.74/M	$0.00	$5,898[a] $ 5.62/M	$7,044[a] $ 6.71/M	$7,402 $ 7.05/M	$8,252[a] $ 7.86/M
Mexico	$3,235 $ 4.04/M	$2,844 $ 3.56/M	$4,981[a] $ 6.23/M	$0.00	$8,100[a] $10.13/M	$3,500 $ 4.38/M	$7,988 $ 9.99/M
Brazil	$5,082 $ 6.35/M	$2,890 $ 3.61/M	$7,246[a] $ 9.06/M	$7,899[a] $ 9.87/M	$ 0.00	$5,890 $ 7.36/M	$2,931 $ 3.66/M
North Latin America	N/A	N/A	N/A	N/A	N/A	$ 0.00	N/A
South Latin America	N/A	N/A	N/A	N/A	N/A	N/A	N/A

[a]No direct service offered; shipped via other port. All rates based upon MPC paying freight to customer.

Exhibit 26.2B Hypodermic Products Duty Cost (% of Landed Value)

						North	**South**
		Europe				**Latin America**	**Latin America**
From:	**United States**	**(Belgium)**	**Singapore**	**Mexico**	**Brazil**	**(Ecuador)**	**(Chile)**
United States	0%	5.3%	0%	15.8%	35%	10%	15%
Europe	8.4%	0%	0%	15.8%	35%	10%	15%
Singapore	8.4%	0%	0%	15.8%	35%	10%	15%
Mexico	0%	0%	0%	0%	35%	10%	15%
Brazil	0%	0%	0%	15.8%	0%	10%	10.5%
North Latin America	N/A	N/A	N/A	N/A	N/A	0%	N/A
South Latin America	N/A	N/A	N/A	N/A	N/A	N/A	0%

TO:

Source: Company report.

became available, which incorporated the stopper into the plunger. This design was inherently cheaper to produce than the 3-pc because it eliminated both the need for the costly rubber stopper and the assembly step required to attach it to the plunger. As a result, even though the 2-pc design did not permit the same dosage precision or variety of applications that was possible with 3-pc syringes, it rapidly gained market share in certain countries (particularly Spain and Germany), and accounted for nearly all the growth in MPC's sales during the 1980s. Whereas a typical 5 cc 3-pc. syringe might cost $.05 to produce, a similarly sized 2-pc syringe would only cost about $.035. Raw materials accounted for about 40% of the total cost and factory wages for another 20%.

MPC's factories originally had been organized by process stage. At one end of the factory was the plastic molding department, where batches of barrels and plungers were produced in injection molding machines. These parts were then transported by carts to an assembly area and assembled with rubber stoppers and cannula (if necessary) into finished products. At some point during assembly, the product/company name and markings indicating the gradations in capacity were printed on the barrels. Then the assembled syringes were transported to a packaging area. Finally, the packaged products were sterilized, using either cobalt radiation or a sterilizing gas.

A sterilization facility could cost from $1.2 million (for a small gas unit that, operating around the clock, could process from 200 million to 500 million units per year, depending on their type and size) to almost $7 million for a large cobalt unit that could process from 700 million to almost 2 billion units per year. As a result, only the larger plants had their own facilities. Smaller plants either sent their output to sister plants for sterilization or used external contractors.

Over time this batch production process had evolved in two interrelated ways. First, machines were developed to perform many of the individual steps (e.g., assembly, printing, and packaging) that previously had been carried out manually. Second, the complexity and time delays that were inherent in batch production had led increasingly to the use of so-called in-line processes, where plastic molding machines were dedicated to the production of specific parts, which then were transported directly by conveyors or air chutes to an automatic assembly and marking operation, and finally on to packaging. This conversion usually occurred in a series of steps, as various stages of the process were automated and then hooked together.

There were few economies of scale possible under either approach, except through the spreading of a plant's overhead. Once an assemblage of molding, assembly/marking, and packaging equipment had been balanced to the needs of a specified output of a given set of products and was running efficiently seven days a week, the only way to increase production was to add another balanced mix of similar equipment. Capital costs varied by product, but in early 1990 it was estimated that buying new equipment to produce 200 million annual units (running 120 hours a week) of 3-pc syringes would cost about $4.5 million, while equipment for producing the same amount of 2-pc syringes would cost about $3.5 million. Of this, molding equipment accounted for about 50% of the total, while assembly/marking and packaging each accounted for about 25%.

"The key to an effective hypodermic plant," argued one manufacturing expert, "is uninterrupted, around-the-clock, in-line operation with high uptime. In particular, high, efficient utilization of molding operations, where the bulk of the plant's assets are located, is essential. We ought to achieve over 99% mold cavity utilization [the percentage of good output from a single injection molding cycle, where the mold might contain over a hundred cavities for a certain type of barrel or plunger], and preferably at least 95% equipment uptime. Currently our mold cavity utilization is running in the low 90s, and our uptime in the mid-'70s, so we have a long way to go." He also suggested that a plant whose capacity was more than 1,500 million units did not benefit from additional economies of scale.

MPC produced cannulae in only four factories, the largest being its plant in Wichita, Kansas. The cannulae used by its European plants were all imported from MPC's plants in Singapore, Brazil, and Wichita. The European plant network had gradually grown over the years into six plants, one of which specialized in glass-barreled syringes that were sent to pharmaceutical companies to be filled prior to delivery to health care providers. Because of its glass-forming capability, the products manufactured there could not be produced at the other European plants, which made only plastic syringes. Each plant specialized in certain sizes and types of products (see Exhibit 26.3A), but because they had been added to the network one by one over time, sometimes by acquisition, there was considerable overlap in the products produced. Capsule descriptions of each plant now follow, in the order they joined the network.

Ennis, Ireland (1964)

The town of Ennis is located on Ireland's west coast, 20 miles north of Shannon. The plant was established in 1964 to assemble (manually) all sizes of 3-pc hypodermic syringes and needles for the European market. Ireland was chosen as the location of the plant because of its relatively low labor costs, initial freedom from income taxes, and the fact that the spoken language was English. Initially all components were purchased, but in 1967 the plant began molding syringe barrels and plungers. In 1970 the plant was expanded and the first automatic needle assembly equipment was added. A year later the production of 3, 5, and 10 ml 3-pc syringes was transferred to its new sister plant in Limerick. In 1982 Ennis was expanded again and most of its production was converted to a semi in-line process (molding and assembly were connected, but packaging was separate).

Exhibit 26.3A Capacity, Production and Days Operating per Year by Plant (mil. units), 1989

	Ennis (240 day/year)		Limerick (240 day/year)		San Miguel (240 day/year)		Zaragoza (322 day/year)		Kraus (240 day/year)		Total	
	Capacity	Production	Capacity	Production	Capacity	Production	Capacity	Production	Capacity	Production	Capacity	Production
Needles												
Assembled	1,926	1,907					578	578			2,504	2,485
Packaged	1,391	1,370					910	910			2,301	2,280
Syringes												
3 Piece:												
1ml (not insulin)			137	86							137	86
2ml	195	188									195	188
5ml	156	124			122	122					278	246
10ml	122	73			75	75					197	148
20ml			90	58							90	58
30ml			26	11							26	11
50ml/60ml			81	58							81	58
2 Piece:												
2ml							289	252	263	203	552	455
5ml							289	274	263	223	552	497
10ml							133	120	205	155	338	275
20ml							66	66	54	26	120	92
Total	473	385	334	213	197	197	777	712	785	617	2,566	2,114
Sterilization	No		Yes		Yes		Yes		No			

Exhibit 26.3B Plant Comparisons, 1990

| | 3-Piece Syringes | | | | 2-Piece Syringes | |
	Ennis	Limerick	San Miguel	Singapore	Zaragoza	Kraus
Workforce:						
Direct	87	65	30	60	85	125
Total	123	92	55	125	140	158
Engineering capability	Weak to OK	Good	Very good	Being developed	Very good	Weak
Culture	MPC + Ireland	MPC + Ireland	Entrepreneurial + MPC	Entrepreneurial/MPC	Entrepreneurial	Entrepreneurial
Rate of improvement	Slow	Slow to good	Good	Slow start-up	Very good	Slow
Average wage and fringes (US$/hour)	$16.00	$16.00	$14.00	$6.00	$14.00	$17.00
Million syringes per direct employee/year (average)	4.4	3.3	6.5	5.0	8.4	4.9
Relative product cost normalized to low-cost plant	1.40	1.40	1.20	1.00	1.00	1.35

Limerick, Ireland (1971)

Limerick was nearby, about 10 miles east of Shannon. The plant was built in 1971 to produce 3-, 5-, and 10-ml 3-pc syringes using a batch form of automated assembly. Three years later the plant began producing 2-pc 2, 5, and 10 ml syringes as well, using a semi in-line automated process. This production of 2-pc models was discontinued shortly thereafter. In 1978 the plant was expanded and began producing 1 cc insulin syringes; these were sold by MPC's Consumer Products Division rather than by its Hypodermic Products Division, which had the responsibility for managing the plant. A major production crisis was experienced in 1980–1981, but eventually it was corrected and the plant expanded again. In 1983, the production of large 3-pc syringes was moved back to Ennis. Limerick was equipped with a sterilization facility, which served both Irish plants and was operating at about 60% of capacity in early 1990.

San Miguel, Spain (1982)

By 1980 the Spanish market for hypodermic products had grown into the fifth largest in the world. Since Spanish producers at that time were protected by high tariff barriers, in 1982 MPC established a manufacturing operation at San Miguel, about 20 miles east of Madrid. This plant was dedicated to the production of a limited range of 3-pc products, and organized for semi in-line processing right from the beginning.

During the early 1980s MPC's sales grew rapidly, and it maintained its position as the second largest hypodermic products company in Europe. Its market shares in most product categories were in the range of 12% (for 2-, 5-, and 10-ml. 3-pc syringes) to 22% for needles and large (30 and 50 ml.) 3-pc syringes. Profit margins varied by product and country, but were generally between 35% and 55%. MPC's two major competitors were Braun, a German company whose market share was from 50% to 100% higher than MPC's for most products, and Terumo, Japan's largest hypodermic manufacturer. Braun supplied all European demand from its modern, high volume, in-line factory in northeast Germany. Terumo's market share in Europe had risen rapidly—to about half MPC's share in most product categories—after building a plant near Brussels during the early 1980s. Other competitors included Sherwood (a subsidiary of American Home Products), Pharmaplast, and Fabersanitas, none of which held a market share greater than 10% in any major product category.

The 1984 Review

Despite its market success, MPC was concerned by the low profitability of its European operations and so in 1984 set up a task force to review European manufacturing. This group concluded that MPC's major problem was simply that it had too much production capacity in Europe; the average utilization of its three plants was only about 60%. Therefore, the task force recommended closing one of the three plants and consolidating production in the remaining two. There was sharp disagreement, however, as to which plant should be closed; the economics suggested that closing San Miguel would reduce costs the most, but this would also severely impair MPC's ability to compete for business in Spain.

The task force also observed that the fastest growing market in Spain was for 2-pc designs, which the San Miguel plant was not set up to produce. Even though the manufacture of 2-pc and 3-pc products might appear to be very similar on the surface, in practice the two types required very different processes and skills—as MPC had learned when it tried to introduce 2-pc products into the Limerick plant. The task force therefore suggested that the fastest way to enter the market for 2-pc products in Spain would be to acquire a factory that was already producing them.

This last recommendation turned out to be the only one that was fully implemented. All three existing plants redoubled their efforts to reduce their costs. As part of these efforts, the Irish plants redistributed products between them so that each could focus its attention on a narrower range, and the San Miguel plant integrated backward into producing its own rubber stoppers (which was subsequently discontinued).

Zaragoza, Spain (1986)

In 1986, MPC acquired the Fabersanitas plant in Zaragoza, about halfway from Madrid to Barcelona, which was producing 2-pc syringes. The plant had been built in 1979, and had operated under a management philosophy that was very different from MPC's. That was to run the plant at full capacity so as to minimize costs, and then sell the resulting output at whatever price was necessary to clear the market. The confusion that resulted from acquiring and assimilating this acquisition into MPC's European plant network took several years to resolve, but eventually the Zaragoza plant became quite efficient and profitable. It was equipped with its own sterilization facility.

Kraus, Germany (1987)

Meanwhile, before the overcapacity situation in Europe had been resolved, the fast growth of demand for 2-pc syringes in Germany and the desire to improve its ability to compete with Braun led MPC to acquire a hypodermic plant in Kraus, about 100 miles south of Hannover, in 1987. This facility, originally built by Voigtlander to produce 35mm. cameras, had been leased by Pharmaplast (another of MPC's small competitors) in the mid-1970s and converted to the production of 2-pc and 3-pc syringes.

Although MPC knew that the old three-storey plant was not ideally designed for syringe manufacturing, it didn't realize until after taking it over how cost inefficient it really was. Aside from having the highest labor rates in Europe, its process flow was poorly designed, plastic molding was being carried out in an inappropriate location, and its sterilization facility was not safe to use. Unfortunately, there was no room to expand and no other sterilization facility was available nearby. In order to make it a low-cost producer, it appeared that major changes in plant, equipment, and work organization would be required.

As a result of these two acquisitions, MPC had been able to increase dramatically its capacity for 2-pc products, as well as its ability to penetrate the German and Spanish markets, two of the largest in Europe. Its overcapacity situation—which now applied to all syringe products—and profitability problems, however, had been exacerbated. The growth of the total European market for hypodermic products had slowed from over 10% per year in the early 1980s to under 5% by 1988.

Making the company's worldwide capacity situation even worse had been the opening of its modern, high-volume factory in Singapore in 1988. This facility, which cost almost $60 million, was designed to produce over 2 billion cannulae per year, as well as over 1 billion needles and 500 million medium-sized (3, 5, and 10 ml.) 3-pc syringes using a continuous, in-line process. Sterilization was provided, under a long term contract, by a nearby plant belonging to another U.S.-based health care company. The plant enjoyed a relatively low wage rate (then averaging less than $4 an hour, including all fringes), an excellent communications and shipping infrastructure, worker training grants, and freedom from income taxes for at least 10 years.

The original purpose of the plant had been to provide a world class facility that could deliver lower cost products than any of MPC's competitors, and provide a source of supply for attacking the rapidly growing markets in Asia. After Singapore's start up, however, it was decided that entering the Japanese market would take too long and prove too expensive, so Singapore's excess capacity was available to supply other regions of the world. In early 1990 it was operating at about 60% of its design capacity.

In 1988, a new study was initiated to help decide how to deal with all these problems. It reaffirmed the tax advantages of producing in Ireland and the importance of maintaining production operations in Germany and Spain. It also concluded that production volume differences and high fixed overhead costs were the primary cause of the cost differentials among its European plants. Therefore, it proposed that all plants should be kept open but that various products be moved from one plant to another so as to achieve a better balance of capacities, and that new equipment be purchased to reduce costs and improve yields.

The cost of implementing these recommendations, which included the financial costs associated with both buying new production equipment, moving existing equipment between plants (in addition to the cost of physically moving the equipment, this included the cost of training operators in its use, the cost of the temporary additional inventory required to cover the period of reduced production, and the cost of the disruption caused at both the sending and the receiving plants), and the human costs associated with resizing plants, was estimated at between $15 and $20 million. MPC's top management was reluctant to commit to such costs given the uncertain external (market) and internal (organizational) environment of the late 1980s.

Therefore, the decision was made simply to adjust the production rates of various products to bring supply into better balance with demand and to proceed with the on-going efforts to improve the operational effectiveness of the two Irish plants. The Zaragoza plant, for example, was shut down for four weeks. Kraus's workforce was reduced slowly through attrition and by eliminating all part-time workers, and the plant moved to a four-day workweek. No other changes were proposed there, except to implement a changeover to the same 2-pc design that was then being produced at Zaragoza, until there was a clearer understanding of what was happening to the market for its products.

The Situation in Late 1989

The manufacturing situation was essentially the same in late 1989. Total European demand for both 2-pc and 3-pc designs had grown less than 10% over the previous two years, and excess industry capacity was putting increasing pressure on prices. Whereas MPC had competed primarily on the basis of the superior designs and consistent high quality of its products, price was becoming increasingly critical for most products and it appeared that it was likely to be at least equal to quality in importance in the future. The ability to introduce new products rapidly, or to adjust quickly to changes in product mix or volume levels, was regarded as much less important.

The gross margins of 2-pc products, for example, had shrunk to about 20%, and increasingly customers appeared to regard them as commodity products. Small capacity (10cc or less) syringes appeared to be following the same path. The situation for insulin syringes was less clear, as marketing personnel felt that, because of MPC's extensive consumer education program and the cost reimbursements to diabetics by European governments, the individuals who purchased such syringes were less price sensitive than the institutional purchasers of other types of syringes; gross margins for these products approached 50%. Others disagreed, however, arguing that forces similar to those that were placing increased emphasis on price in other product lines would soon affect insulin syringes as well.

MPC's major competitors were scrambling for market share, and in that volatile environment MPC found itself with excess inventories of some products and backorders of others. Its European operations were barely profitable. "How can we develop a manufacturing strategy," asked one exasperated factory manager, "when we don't even have a marketing strategy?" A comparison of the different plants along various dimensions is contained in Exhibits 26.3A and 26.3B.

Manufacturing costs at the two Irish plants were still unacceptably high and their delivered quality, although good on average, was inconsistent. "Everything seems to be going O.K. and suddenly something goes wrong," observed one U.S. manager. The combined workforce at the two plants had been cut in half since 1983 and millions of dollars had been invested in new in-line equipment, but the productivity of both plants was still lower than that of other MPC plants. It was estimated, for example, that the Wichita plant could produce the same output for $3 million less per year. This cost penalty was becoming of increasing concern because of speculation that Terumo would soon be introducing a line of 2-pc syringes and expanding its Belgian factory to include needle manufacturing. MPC's Irish operations continued to be profitable, however, largely because of the high gross margins enjoyed by insulin syringes. They were now paying income tax at the rate of 10%, far below the rates in other European countries.

One of the major causes of the Ennis plant's high costs was its complex product mix (it now manufactured 120 different items), which required a much higher proportion of time spent on changeovers, and its high labor costs. In addition, it experienced somewhat lower yields (that is, higher reject levels) than other plants. This was attributed to poor process controls, as well as poor worker attitudes and work habits, outdated equipment technology, and inadequate preventive maintenance. On the other hand, the cost of closing the Ennis plant was estimated to be in the vicinity of $10 million.

Although Limerick produced a more limited product range (16 insulin SKUs and nine 3-pc SKUs), it experienced poor molding efficiency and a high rate of line stops. Its overall utilization rate was only 70%. As a result, its manufacturing cost for insulin syringes was about 30% higher than that in the United States. Similarly, its cost of producing 3-pc syringes was estimated to be higher than Terumo's.

Kraus provided consistently good quality but still had the highest manufacturing costs in the company. More important, its cost of producing 2-pc syringes was estimated to be substantially higher than Braun's. This appeared to be due primarily to its low rate of capacity utilization, together with an inappropriate facility and old equipment. Kraus's skill levels, worker attitudes, and work ethic were good, however, as was its equipment maintenance.

There had been some support for a proposal to relocate the Kraus facility into a new, modern facility located nearby. The town indicated that it would be willing to provide the land for such a facility at a low cost (unemployment in the area was over 20%), but MPC's initial estimate of the cost of constructing a greenfield facility having roughly the same capacity as the old plant was over $20 million. This was considered to be a much too costly alternative, given the company's excess capacity in Europe and top management's increasing emphasis on improving corporate ROI. On the other hand, closing the plant would also be expensive; under German law its 160 employees would be entitled to large severance benefits (averaging over $25,000 each because of their long seniority at the plant), and an $8 million writedown in assets would be required.

The San Miguel and Zaragoza plants, on the other hand, had improved remarkably. Both were under the direction of the same manager and were characterized by excellent skill levels and work habits and well designed equipment procurement, development , and maintenance policies. San Miguel had focused its attention on a very narrow range of products (11 SKUs belonging to two product families), and produced them on four automated production lines that operated around the clock. The Zaragoza plant made a wider range of products but had become the lowest cost producer of 2-pc syringes in the world. This had been achieved through high quality and reliability, low waste, and a low frequency of line stops, while operating seven days a week at high capacity utilization. Both Spanish plants had sufficient building space to more than double their existing capacity, if necessary, and had developed the capability to design, modify, and build much of their own production equipment.

"MPC traditionally has tended to try to solve operating problems by investing money in new equipment," commented a senior manufacturing manager. "Zaragoza has demonstrated that, using existing equipment and people, you can also solve problems by investing engineering resources, by proper preventive maintenance, and by extensive operator training."

Early 1990: The Impact of a New Sales Forecast

Suddenly a burst of optimism was injected into the rather pessimistic scenario that appeared to be unfolding. The collapse of communism in Russia and Eastern Europe had opened up a huge new market for health care products (particularly in the former East Germany), and these people appeared eager to buy better designs and quality than had previously been available to them. Moreover, rising prosperity and the increasing adoption of modern medical practices in the Middle East had led to a rapid increase in the market for MPC's products there, particularly in Turkey. Whereas in 1989 MPC Europe had sold over 2.1 billion units of various syringes, in early 1990 it began to appear that it could sell over 2.5 billion units that year. About 40% of the projected increase was expected to come from the expansion of demand in Eastern Europe, primarily for 2-pc

Exhibit 26.4A   *Scenario A* Sales: Europe/M.E.A./Eastern Europe (mil. units)

	1990	1991	1992	1993	1994
Needles					
Packaged	3,249.2	3,452.9	3,609.7	3,761.9	3,923.9
Bulk	500.8	522.2	468.7	460.1	470.8
Total (assembled)	3,749.9	3,975.1	4,078.4	4,222.0	4,394.7
Syringes					
3 Piece:					
1ml	179.3	189.2	199.9	211.0	222.8
2ml/3ml	231.1	247.2	264.3	282.9	302.6
5ml	277.6	250.2	266.6	284.2	303.0
10ml	169.3	180.2	185.8	191.5	197.7
20ml	70.0	72.1	74.3	76.6	79.0
30ml	13.7	13.9	14.3	14.6	15.0
50ml/60ml	69.8	74.0	78.3	83.0	88.0
Total 3 Piece	1,010.7	1,026.8	1,083.5	1,143.8	1,208.0
2 Piece:					
2ml	636.9	683.9	726.5	761.6	799.9
5ml	571.2	615.0	649.9	683.7	716.0
10ml	258.9	274.1	289.8	303.5	317.8
20ml	92.0	95.2	98.4	101.7	107.4
Total 2 Piece	1,559.0	1,668.3	1,764.6	1,850.5	1,941.2
TOTAL SYRINGES					
(3 Piece/2 Piece)	2,569.7	2,695.1	2,848.1	2,994.3	3,149.2

syringes, while another 40% was expected to come from sales to the Middle East. Demand from Africa and the expansion of MPC's share of traditional markets accounted for the remainder.

MPC's major European competitors found themselves hampered by a lack of production capacity, while what MPC had thought to be its great manufacturing disadvantage—its considerable excess capacity—suddenly became a source of opportunity. Revised sales forecasts suggested that rather than growing at an average rate of about 5% per year, its sales might well grow at almost twice that rate over the period 1990–1995. Two possible future scenarios for demand had been developed (see Exhibits 26.4A and 26.4B). Scenario A, which was considered the more likely one, envisioned continued moderate growth in both 3-pc and 2-pc syringes. Scenario B, on the other hand, projected a faster overall growth rate together with a shift from 3-pc to 2-pc designs. The debate about what to do about MPC's manu-facturing problems in Europe abruptly shifted from which plant to close to how to increase efficiency and capacity within the existing structure. To deal with the impending capacity shortfall, plans were being drawn up to have all plants operate seven days a week (21 shifts) rather than the usual

Exhibit 26.4B *Scenario B* Sales: Europe/M.E.A./Eastern Europe (mil. units)

	1990	1991	1992	1993	1994
Needles					
Packaged	3,256.5	3,810.5	4,002.4	4,228.0	4,456.1
Bulk	500.8	950.2	1,324.7	1,742.0	1,849.0
Total (assembled)	3,757.2	4,760.6	5,327.1	5,970.0	6,305.1
Syringes					
3 Piece:					
1ml	179.3	89.5	95.6	102.1	109.1
2ml/3ml	231.1	250.4	271.1	294.0	319.1
5ml	281.8	257.4	277.6	299.6	323.4
10ml	169.3	182.5	196.7	212.3	229.2
20ml	70.0	74.3	78.5	83.2	88.4
30ml	13.7	14.3	15.2	15.8	16.7
50ml/60ml	69.8	75.3	81.3	87.7	94.6
Total 3 Piece	1,015.0	943.8	1,016.0	1,094.8	1,180.4
2 Piece:					
2ml	647.8	833.3	884.5	930.7	980.5
5ml	575.4	733.8	770.2	816.0	858.6
10ml	263.2	293.6	307.1	325.3	339.6
20ml	92.0	99.5	102.7	105.9	111.7
Total 2 Piece	1,578.5	1,960.2	2,064.5	2,177.9	2,290.4
TOTAL SYRINGES					
(3 Piece/2 Piece)	2,593.5	2,904.0	3,080.5	3,272.7	3,470.8

five (15 shifts). Because of the large number of vacation days required by law in most European countries, however, it would probably not be possible to run the plants more than about 325 days a year.

It was in this, more buoyant, environment that Mr. Hausman called for a meeting to readdress MPC's European manufacturing strategy.

CHAPTER 27

Strategic Planning— Forward in Reverse?

Are Corporate Planners Going About Things the Wrong Way 'Round?

Robert H. Hayes

With all the time and resources that American manufacturing companies spend on strategic planning, why has their competitive position been deteriorating? Certainly not because the idea of doing such planning is itself misguided. Nor because the managers involved are not up to the task. Drawing on his long experience with the nuts and bolts of operations deep inside American and foreign companies, the author proposes a different answer. Perhaps the problem lies in how managers typically approach the work of planning: first by selecting objectives or ends, then by defining the strategies or ways of accomplishing them, and lastly by developing the necessary resources or means. A hard look at what the new industrial competition requires might suggest, instead, an approach to planning based on a means-ways-ends sequence.

S INCE I BEGAN to study American industry almost 30 years ago, there has been a revolution in the science and practice of management and, especially, in the attraction of bright, professionally trained managers to the work of strategic planning. Yet as corporate staffs have flourished and as the notion of strategy has come to dominate business

Mr. Hayes is the William Barclay Harding Professor of Management of Technology at the Harvard Business School. He is the author or coauthor of three McKinsey Award-winning articles in *HBR* and, with Steven C. Wheelwright, of *Restoring Our Competitive Edge* (Wiley, 1984), which was selected by the Association of American Publishers as the best book on business, management, and economics published in 1984.

education and practice, our factories have steadily lost ground to those in other countries where strategy receives far less emphasis and the "professionalization" of management is far less advanced.

Over the years, I have prowled through hundreds of American factories and talked at length with innumerable line managers. Of late, I have been increasingly troubled by a recurring theme in the explanations they give for their companies' competitive difficulties. Again and again they argue that many of those difficulties—particularly in their manufacturing organizations—stem from their companies' strategic planning processes. Their complaint, however, is not about the *mis*functioning of strategic planning but about the harmful aspects of its *proper* functioning.

In explaining why they continue to use old, often obsolete equipment and systems in their factories, some of these managers assert that their corporate strategic plans call for major investments elsewhere: in acquisitions, new lines of business, new plants in new locations, or simply the subsidization of other parts of their organizations. Their job, they say, is to "manage for cash," not to upgrade the capabilities of their existing plants. Others complain that their companies' strategic plans force on them new products and equipment that require capabilities their organizations do not have (or, worse, no longer have). Still others report that they must assimilate acquired companies that "do not fit" or must grow faster than is prudent or even possible. With money being thrown at them faster than they can absorb it, much of it is poorly spent.

These comments do not come from ineffective managers who are looking for excuses. Nor are their companies unsophisticated in the art of strategic planning. Most of them have been at it for a long time and are widely regarded as experts. How, then, are we to make sense of the fact that, although the United States has poured more resources—both in total and on a per company basis—into strategic planning over the past 20 years than has any other country in the world, a growing number of our industries and companies today find themselves more vulnerable strategically than when they started? Not only do they fall short of goals, but they also lag behind competitors, largely of foreign origin, that place much less emphasis on strategic planning.[1]

Consider, for example, the experience of one company that, for a dozen years, emphasized the expansion of its market and the achievement of "low-cost-producer" status while allowing its R&D budget to fall to just over half its previous level (in constant dollars). The company has now

[1]A number of studies suggest there is either no relationship between planning and various measures of organizational performance or a negative one. See, for example, P. H. Grinyer and D. Norbum, "Planning for Existing Markets: Perceptions of Executives and Financial Performance," *Journal of the Royal Statistical Society (A)* 138, pt 1 (1975), p. 70; Ernest A. Kallman and H. Jack Shapiro, "The Motor Freight Industry—A Case Against Planning," *Long Range Planning*, February 1978, p. 81; Ronald J. Kudla, "The Effects of Strategic Planning on Common Stock Returns," *Academy of Management Journal*, March 1980, p. 5; Milton Leontiades and Ahmet Tezel, "Planning Perceptions and Planning Results," *Strategic Management Journal*, January–March 1980, p. 65; Leslie W. Rue and Robert M. Fulmer, "Is Long-Range Planning Profitable?" *Academy of Management Proceedings* (1973), p. 66.

come to realize that the high-volume, low-cost end of its business has moved irretrievably offshore and that its only hope for survival lies in rapid product innovation. There is, however, little innovative spark left in the organization, and neither increases in the R&D budget nor additions of new people appear to have had much impact. In desperation, the company is contemplating a merger with another company that has a better record of product innovation, but it is finding stiff resistance to its advances because of its reputation as a "researchers' graveyard."

Or consider the experience of another company that has a reputation for having modern production facilities and for being in the forefront of product technology in its fast-changing industry. As soon as it tests out the process for making a new product, management builds a new factory dedicated to that product. Unfortunately, once in place, this new facility tends to ossify because management also believes that the product life cycle in its industry is so short that continual investment in process improvement is uneconomic. As a result, the company has recently found itself losing market position to competitors that have pushed ahead in process technology. Although loath to cede business to those who came later, it has so far been unable to muster the ability (or, some say, the commitment) to keep up with its challengers' processing capabilities. Worse, management is realizing that the next generation of new products will require many of the manufacturing skills that it has neglected and its competitors have forced themselves to master.

How can these well-run companies that impose on themselves the rigorous discipline—and employ the sophisticated techniques—of modern strategic planning end up worse off than when they started? Is this a statistical accident or is there something about the process itself that is bad for corporate health? In this article, I will argue that, under certain circumstances, the methodology of formal strategic planning and, even worse, the organizational attitudes and relationships that it often cultivates can impair a company's ability to compete. Moreover, the circumstances under which this occurs is true for much of U.S. industry today.

To understand the damaging effects of that methodology, we must take a hard look at the logic that shapes it. The traditional strategic planning process rests on an "ends-ways-means" model: establish corporate objectives (ends); given those objectives, develop a strategy (ways) for attaining them; then marshal the resources (means) necessary to implement this strategy.

There are two familiar lines of argument for keeping these three elements of the planning process (ends, ways, means) in their current order. First, ends should precede ways because managers must know what their objectives are before deciding how to go about attaining them. A generation of MBA students has had pounded into their heads the story of Lewis Carroll's logician, the Cheshire Cat, in *Alice in Wonderland*. When Alice comes upon the Cat and asks, "Would you tell me, please, which way I ought to go from here?" the Cat responds, "That depends . . . on where you want to get to." Alice answers, "I really don't much care where," and the Cat tells her, "Then it doesn't matter which way you go!"

The second argument has a different basis: to maximize efficiency, the choice of strategy should precede the assembling of the resources for carrying it out. Because each strategy is likely to require a different mix of resources, developing resources before choosing one of them exposes a company to the risk that it will be short of some resources and have too much of others.

What is wrong with this model? Let me raise questions about four of its aspects: (1) the ends that companies usually select, (2) the ways they try to attain those ends, (3) the means through which they carry out those ways, and (4) the logic that strings these elements together in the ends-ways-means order.

Choosing Ends

Most companies select goals that are too short term. It is almost impossible for a company to create a truly sustainable competitive advantage—one that is highly difficult for its competitors to copy—in just five to ten years (the time frame that most companies use). Goals that can be achieved within five years are usually either too easy or based on buying and selling something. Anything that a company can buy or sell, however, is probably available for purchase or sale by its competitors as well.

A series of short-term goals also encourages episodic thinking. When attention focuses on meeting immediate objectives, organizations often find the successive hurdles they have set for themselves increasingly difficult to surmount. Finally, the accumulated weight of deferred changes and seemingly innocuous compromises becomes too great, and managers trip badly on a hurdle that seemed no higher than the rest.

In most of the companies that I have observed, the goals are not only short term but also highly quantitative, focusing on rates of growth in profitability, return on investment, and market share. Unfortunately, quantitative goals follow Gresham's Law: they tend to drive out nonquantitative goals. It is easy for an organization tied to quantitative goals to believe (or to act as if it believes) that anything that is not quantitative is not important.

In practice, the danger is that hard numbers will encourage managers to forget that different kinds of goals have different values at different levels in an organization. Goals like return on investment have great meaning and value for senior managers, who understand the need to allocate capital efficiently and who are themselves evaluated on their ability to do so. ROI has almost no meaning for production workers, however, whose only contact with investment decisions is indirect: roofs that leak, old equipment that does not hold tolerances, new equipment that creates more problems than it solves. What does have meaning for these workers is quality (getting the work done correctly), timing (meeting delivery schedules), the working environment, and the satisfaction that comes from doing a good job as part of an appreciative organization. Objectives that have little meaning for large segments of an organization cannot be shared and cannot weld it together. Nor, for that matter, can episodic goals ("last year's emphasis was on quality, but this year's emphasis is on productivity"), which succeed only in diffusing commitment.

What Makes The Grass Grow

Attempts at despotism . . . represent, as it were, the drunkenness of responsibility. It is when men . . . are overwhelmed with the difficulties and blunders of humanity, that they fall back upon a wild desire to manage everything themselves . . .

This belief, that all would go right if we could only get the strings into our own hands, is a fallacy almost without exception. . . . The sin and sorrow of despotism is not that it does not love men, but that it loves them too much and trusts them too little . . .

When a man begins to think that the grass will not grow at night unless he lies awake to watch it, he generally ends either in an asylum or on the throne of an emperor.

—From G.K. Chesterton, *Robert Browning* (1903)

Developing Ways

Short-term goals also work to back companies into a mode of thinking that is based on forecasts (What do we think is going to happen?) rather than on visions (What do we want to happen?). Unfortunately, even though the usual five- to ten-year time periods are too short to achieve truly strategic objectives, they are much too long to obtain accurate forecasts.

Consider, for example, the forecasts made more than a decade ago of a stable, slow-moving enterprise: the U.S. economy. In 1970, when a number of eminent economists tried to predict how the economy would fare during "the sizzling seventies," their consensus was that inflation would continue at about 2.5%, productivity growth would average about 3%, and real growth in GNP would approach 4.5%. Instead, inflation averaged 8%, productivity growth only 1.3%, and real GNP a bit over 3%. As a result, the average American in 1980 enjoyed an income nearly 15% less than that predicted ten years before.

In the early 1970s, many U.S. corporations based their strategies on comparable forecasts of economic growth, as well as on their own forecasts of the much less predictable behavior of particular markets and competitors. Should we be surprised that most of their forecasts were totally off the mark, as were the elaborate strategies to which they gave rise? I suspect that the surge in domestic merger and acquisition activity in the late 1970s reflected in part the growing frustration of American managers who realized they could not reach the forecast-driven goals they had set for their companies and themselves through internal activities alone.

Inevitably, quantitative goals and reliance on long-term forecasts, combined with too-short planning horizons, lead corporate strategists to spend most of their time worrying about structural, rather than behavioral, means for achieving their objectives. After all, they reason, specific, measurable results come through "hard," measurable efforts: investments in new plants and equipment, the introduction of new products, the redesign of organization charts, and so on. This leads them to neglect less easily measured factors like performance evaluation and reward systems, work-force policies, information systems, and management selection and development policies. As the recent interest in "corporate culture" suggests, however, real strategic advantage comes from changing the way a company behaves, a task far more difficult and time-consuming than simply making a few structural decisions.

Another problem with today's strategic planning processes is that they reduce a company's flexibility. Like all organizational processes, strategic planning is subject to the first law of bureaucracy: if you give a smart, ambitious person a job to do, no matter how meaningless, he or she will try to make it bigger and more important. Jack Welch learned this lesson soon after he became chairman and CEO at General Electric. According to Welch, "Once written, the strategic document can take on a life of its own, and it may not lend itself to flexibility. . . . An organization can begin to focus on form rather than substance."[2] He also described to a group of Harvard MBA students how GE's strategic plans had become less and less useful as they got bigger and bigger, as more and more hours went into preparing them, and as planners embellished them with increasingly sophisticated graphics and fancy covers.

William Bricker, chairman and CEO of Diamond Shamrock, has much the same reaction: "Why has our vision been narrowed? Why has our flexibility been constricted? To my mind there is one central reason: our strategies have become too rigid. . . . A detailed strategy [is] like a road map . . . [telling] us every turn we must take to get to our goal. . . . The entrepreneur, on the other hand, views strategic planning not as a road map but as a compass . . . and is always looking for the new road."[3] This is a provocative analogy: when you are lost on a highway, a road map is very useful; but when you are lost in a swamp whose topography is constantly chang-

[2]"Managing Change," keynote address, Dedication Convocation, Fuqua School of Business, Duke University, April 21, 1983.

[3]Entrepreneurs Needed," *Oil and Gas Digest*, November 15, 1982.

ing, a road map is of little help. A simple compass—which indicates the general direction to be taken and allows you to use your own ingenuity in overcoming various difficulties—is much more valuable.

Strategic Leaps or Small Steps?

The difficulties that highly visible U.S. industries are now experiencing surprise and puzzle many Americans. Why is the nation that put a man on the moon and invented genetic engineering unable to produce a consumer videocassette recorder (all those sold by U.S. companies are imported, even though a U.S. company produced the first commercial videotape machine 30 years ago) or even a better small car than Toyota? One possible reason, of course, is that we *can* put a man on the moon. The very skills and psychology that enable us to conceive and carry out something like the Apollo project may hamper us when we are in a competitive environment that bases success more on a series of small steps than on a few dramatic breakthroughs.

Consider the graph in Exhibit 27.1, where the horizontal axis measures the passage of time and the vertical, competitive effectiveness (lower cost, better quality, more features, faster delivery). In a free market, a company's competitive effectiveness should improve over time—that is, it will move from a position in the lower left of the graph to a position in the upper right. Now, how does a company accomplish this movement?

One approach, shown in Exhibit 27.2, is through a series of strategic leaps, a few giant upward steps at critical moments. These leaps may take a variety of forms: a product redesign, a large-scale factory modernization or expansion, a move to another location that promises great improvement in wage rates or labor relations, an acquisition of a supplier of a critical material or component, or adoption of a new manufacturing technology. Between taking these giant steps, managers seek only incidental improvements in competitiveness, as the company digests the last step and contemplates the next.

At the opposite extreme, as shown in Exhibit 27.3, a company may try to progress through a series of small steps whose cumulative impact will be just as great. Rather than rely on a series of discontinuities, such a company continuously strives to bolster its competitive position through a variety of incremental improvements.

Which approach is best? Both can get you to the same point, but each places different demands on an organization and exposes it to very different risks.

Strategic Leaps. Each step in Exhibit 27.2 is highly visible and usually requires a major expenditure of funds. Thus the timing of the change becomes important. A decline in profits, a potential acquisition, a sudden surge of orders that pushes the organization to the limit of its resources—

Exhibit 27.1   Competitive Progress

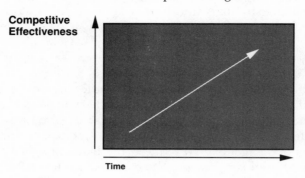

Exhibit 27.2   Progress Through Strategic Leaps

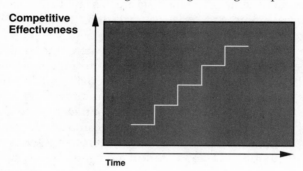

Exhibit 27.3   Progress Through Incremental Improvements

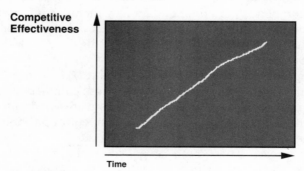

any such development can delay the project or put it on hold. Further, managers at all levels in an organization must get involved in analyzing and approving the decision to take the step. Extensive staff involvement is also essential, as is the expertise of many specialists—financial analysts, strategic planners, legal experts, scientists, outside consultants, and public relations personnel—who often have more allegiance to their own "professions" than to the company itself.

Because each step is so big and so visible, whoever proposes the change takes on an enormous risk in return for the chance to reap huge rewards. Success creates heroes; failure brings severe consequences. The people who rise to the top in such organizations usually fall into one of two camps: they are either "lucky gamblers," who were involved in two or three successful leaps, or "corporate kibitzers," who managed to avoid entanglement in any disasters.

Such companies regard the corporate staff as an elite group and treat assignments of line managers to staff positions as promotions. At lower levels in the organization, however, there is little need for outstanding, highly trained people. The task of people at these levels is simply to operate the structure that top management and its staff of experts have created. It does not seem necessary in such companies to put much time and effort into training and upgrading factory workers or managers because the next strategic leap may make their newly developed skills obsolete. Nor do personnel policies that reward employee longevity seem particularly desirable because they reduce the company's flexibility—its ability, say, to pull up stakes and move to a new location, to sell the business, or to implement a significant reduction in employment as part of an automation program.

In similar fashion, a reliance on strategic leaps makes it unnecessary for workers or lower level managers to have a detailed understanding of how their own operations affect—and are affected by—other parts of the organization. The same logic robs employee suggestion programs of their usefulness, for workers cannot possibly understand how the changes they may propose fit into the company's overall strategy, much less the leap it is contemplating next.

Small Steps. If, however, a company follows an incremental approach to improvement, few of the steps it takes are highly visible or risky. Because major capital authorization requests are seldom necessary, there is little need for much staff assistance or outside advice. Rather than put massive resources into the development of elaborate plans in the rarefied atmosphere of a remote headquarters, such a company expects the bulk of its improvements to bubble up, in an entrepreneurial fashion, from lower levels in the organization. Its corporate staff is much smaller and less powerful than that of a strategic leap organization. Its main role is to offer support services. In effect, the organization charts of these companies look more like tables than pyramids.

This incremental approach requires immense low-level expertise—not expertise *of* a low level, but expertise *at* low levels. Developing this kind of expertise takes a long time. Executives need to expend great effort on recruiting people who are both loyal and trainable, and on continuously improving their capabilities once hired—through both formal education programs and job assignments that provide a broad understanding of the company's products, processes, and competitive environment. In turn, top management needs to augment this understanding and keep it up to date by disseminating information about current financial results, market behavior, and competitors' activities.

Having made so extensive an investment in low-level expertise, a company will do its best to retain the people who have it. Long-time employees have another advantage: over time, through their multiple job assignments, they develop relationships with people in different parts of the organization. These relationships make it easier to implement the small changes that require communication and cooperation among several different groups.

Incremental projects generally require so little capital that managers can often fund them out of a plant's annual operating budget. It stands to reason that plant managers will support such efforts if they are intimately familiar with the production systems and people involved and are committed to the plant's long-term success because they expect to stay in their jobs for a long time. Such projects are also more likely to thrive if workers, plant engineers, and lower level managers participate in developing them—through suggestion programs, quality circles, and the like—and if they identify the company's long-term success with their own.

This kind of company does not believe that many of its problems can be solved by top management. The information and expertise needed for dealing with them reside lower down in the organization, and the problems themselves are continuously evolving. Therefore, top management's role is less to spot and solve problems than to create an organization that can spot and solve its own problems.

The Tortoise and the Hare

Up to this point, I have been describing, rather abstractly, two contrasting "pure" strategies. In practice, of course, few companies choose approaches so extreme; most strategies fall somewhere along the spectrum between them. U.S. companies do, however, tend to adopt approaches toward the strategic leap end; those of our two most powerful international competitors, Germany and Japan, tend to seek incremental improvements within an existing structure and technology. They are the tortoise; we are the hare.

In the fable, as we may recall with some apprehension, the tortoise won the race. Are we to share the hare's fate? To answer that question, let us examine the risks and rewards of each approach.

The central risk of following the incremental approach is that a company will be "leap-frogged" and left behind by a competitor that abandons its traditional technology, location, or corporate strategy and adopts a new and more successful one. The folklore of American business is full of such examples: the replacement of piston engines by jet engines, of vacuum tubes by transistors, of ditto machines by xerography, of New England textile companies by those that moved south. The list goes on and on.

Conversely, the central risk of following the strategic leap approach is that a breakthrough may not always be available exactly when it is needed. After seizing a major competitive advantage, a company may see its lead nibbled away by competitors that gradually adapt themselves to the new technology or strategy and then push it beyond its initial limits. This is the time to make another leap, but what if the company's technicians and strategists reach into their hats and find nothing there?

One obvious response to this predicament is to use an incremental approach, like that of the competition, until a breakthrough does become available. Doing so, however, is not easy for a company that has organized itself around the expectation of repeated breakthroughs. As I have argued, the kind of organization adept at making strategic leaps bears little resemblance to one that takes the incremental approach. Entrepreneurship from below cannot be "ordered" by managers from above—particularly when, as is usually the case, top-down, staff-dominated planning and control systems have caused most of the entrepreneurs to leave.

Unfortunately, the reverse is not true. As our Japanese and German competitors are demonstrating all too well, companies that adopt an incremental approach *can* eventually accommodate themselves to a new technology. As a rule, they are not as fast but, if given the time, they can do it. In other words, the ability to progress through incremental change does not preclude, although it may slow down, a company's ability to master discontinuous change. In fact, an organization that is used to continuous small changes and that has balanced strategic expertise at the top with operating expertise and entrepreneurship at the bottom is probably better prepared for a big leap than is an organization that has gone for several years without any change at all.

Assembling Means

The third element (after ends and ways) in the strategic planning paradigm is the selection and assembling of the resources necessary to implement the chosen strategy. Although a strategy will usually require many different types of resources, strategic planning in most corporations devotes most of its attention to just one: financial wherewithal. There are two reasons for this.

First, since managers usually state their ultimate objectives in financial terms, it is natural for them to state required resources in financial terms as well. Second, resources get used most efficiently when management provides only those that are absolutely necessary. Understandably, companies try to maintain their resources in as liquid (that is, financial) a form as possible for as long as possible, for doing so gives them maximum flexibility to convert liquid resources into the desired form at just the moment they are needed.

Such a practice works well if reasonably efficient markets exist for important assets like market position, worker or manager skills, and technological capabilities. Many companies have come to realize, however, that technology, market position, and organizational skills are not as transferable as they had expected. As a result, those that try to buy them often run into the infrastructure problems I described earlier.

Informed businesspeople, who understand well the danger of trying to place a modern steel mill in a less developed country like Bangladesh, have sometimes been willing to try to implant advanced new technologies in organizations that are unprepared to receive them. In most cases, these organizations respond by starving the new technology of understanding and resources—just as the human body tries to reject a heart transplant that is essential to its survival. No matter how brilliant its technological underpinnings, a new product will fail if the company's manufacturing organization is unable to make that product efficiently or if the company's sales force is unable to sell it effectively. Such capabilities cannot be bought from the outside. They must be grown from within, and growing them takes time.

The Logic of Ends-Ways-Means

When managers in strategic planning demand that ends should precede ways and both should precede means, they make certain assumptions about the environment and the nature of competition. First, they assume that the world of competition is predictable and that clear paths can be charted across it much like a highway system across a road map. Equally important, they assume that reasonable objectives, arrived at by thoughtful people, can be achieved through purposeful activity and that progress toward those objectives is both measurable and controllable.

The managerial logic of ends-ways-means also attributes a certain stability to the company itself. There is an expectation that the company's values and needs will not change over the planning horizon and that the objectives it sets will seem as desirable up close as they do from afar. Managers can, therefore, concern themselves with "static optimization"—that is, with making a few key decisions and then holding to them. There is a further expectation that, once these objectives and the strategies for achieving them are in place, managers can assemble the necessary resources in the required time frame and convert them into the appropriate form.

Underlying all these assumptions is the belief that responsibility for organizational success rests primarily on the shoulders of top management. This "command-and-control" mentality allocates all major decisions to top management, which imposes them on the organization and monitors them through elaborate planning, budgeting, and control systems. In many ways this logic is similar to that which underlies modern conventional warfare: generals set the strategy, provide the resources, establish the detailed plan of action, and continuously monitor the progress of engagements as they occur.

Does this logic make sense? Earlier I questioned the notion that means should follow ways on the ground that important resources—technology, skills, and effective working relationships—cannot always be purchased when needed. Now I also question whether managers should decide on ends before selecting ways.

Taken to an extreme, these questions could turn into a general attack on logic as applied to business planning. Such attacks are more and more common these days, from *In Search of Excellence*'s claim that "detached, analytical justification for all decisions . . . has arguably led us seriously astray" to the *Washington Post*'s insistence that "preoccupation with logic has helped to improve and reform the world, but it has also put professionals dangerously out of touch with the gritty everyday world." My point is not to disparage the relevance of all logic to planning but to suggest that there may be alternative logics worth exploring. One of them, in fact, is to turn the ends-ways-means paradigm on its head: means-ways-ends.

How might such a logic work? First, it suggests that a company should begin by investing in the development of its capabilities along a broad front (means). It should train workers and managers in a variety of jobs; educate them about the general competitive situation and the actions of specific competitors; teach them how to identify problems, how to develop solutions for them, and how to persuade others to follow their recommendations. It should acquire and experiment with new technologies and techniques so that workers and managers gain experience with them and come to understand their capabilities and constraints. It should focus R&D activity on fewer lines but spread it more widely throughout the organization. Managers should have cross-functional assignments so that they develop a broad understanding of the company's markets, technologies, and factories.

Second, as these capabilities develop and as technological and market opportunities appear, the company should encourage managers well down in the organization to exploit matches wherever they occur (ways). Top management's job, then, is to facilitate this kind of entrepreneurial activity, provide it with resources from other parts of the company, and, where feasible, encourage cooperative activities. In short, the logic here is, Do not develop plans and then seek capabilities; instead, build capabilities and then encourage the development of plans for exploiting them. Do not try to develop optimal strategies on the assumption of a static environment; instead, seek continuous improvement in a dynamic environment.

The guiding force throughout such disparate activities will not come from a set of directions or controls. To the contrary, it will come from a balance between integration, which arises out of a sense of organizational unity and camaraderie, an instinctive banding together in the face of common enemies, and direction, which arises out of a set of shared values rooted in a long-term vision of the kind of company that its people want it to become—in short, group cohesion and a compass. A compass, remember, is not an end; it only provides a sense of direction, a means to a variety of possible ends.

Under what circumstances might such a means-ways-ends logic be effective? When the competitive world is like a swamp that is shifting in unpredictable ways, particular objectives are likely to lose their attractiveness over time. Even so, a common vision can keep people moving ahead, moving around unforeseen obstacles and beyond immediate (largely because they are visible) objectives.

Is Guerrilla Warfare Always Better?

An organization that takes a means-ways-ends approach to strategic planning assumes everybody is responsible for its prosperity. Its success rests on its ability to exploit opportunities as they arise, on its ingenuity, on its capacity to learn, on its determination and persistence.

There is an obvious analogy here with guerrilla warfare. It would, of course, be wrong to suggest that strategic planning based on a strategic leap approach is always less effective than that based on an incremental approach. Even in guerrilla warfare, someone must decide where to fight and which goals to seek. Someone must select and train leaders and rally soldiers to the cause. On occasion, conventional pitched battles are perfectly appropriate.

Sometimes companies must change their objectives; they may decide to enter a new business or abandon an old one. These decisions seldom bubble up from the bottom. Instead, they flow down from the top. The trick, of course, to managing such discontinuities without alienating the organization or undermining its capabilities is to employ a patient, consensus-seeking decision process in which all parties have an opportunity to be heard. More important, everyone must regard a necessary leap as the exception, not the rule. Once a guerrilla army decides that the only person with any real authority is the supreme leader, its field commanders lose their credibility.

Therefore, I suspect that the Japanese and German companies that are currently studying the American approach to strategic planning do not intend to make it a way of life. They intend simply to graft it onto their existing systems so they can be better prepared for dealing with the discontinuities that sometimes confront them. What they may not appreciate is how seductive such an approach can be for top management. When the balance of power begins to shift, when the "counters" gain ascendancy over the "doers," the best doers may seek to become counters. Or they go elsewhere, where they can do it *their* way.

Further, in most mature industries, the development of markets and technology is not discontinuous but moves forward in a steady, almost predictable manner. Even in high-technology industries like semiconductors and computers, for example, progress during the past decade has taken place within technological frameworks that were essentially in place more than 15 years ago. The opportunities for dramatic breakthroughs and strategic "end runs" have diminished as sophisticated multinational companies have identified most of the untapped markets and have uncovered most of the unexploited pools of low-cost labor in the world. They are running out of islands to move to.

Seen in this light, the present struggle between U.S. companies and their foreign competitors can be likened to a battle between a bunch of hares, trained in conventional warfare and equipped with road maps, and an unknown number of tortoises, equipped with compasses and an expertise in guerrilla warfare. Unfortunately, the battle is taking place in a swamp and not on a well-defined highway system.

The logic of ends-ways-means that got the hares into this situation is unlikely to get them out. They will need to explore a new logic, possibly a reverse logic, and be willing to question the basis of formal strategic planning as it is practiced today. Perhaps they should return to the approaches they used to follow—when they spent less time developing strategies but their industrial capabilities were the envy of the world.

Backing into the Future

If, in conclusion, I may give for what they are worth the impressions of a brief visit to Washington, I believe that there is much devoted and intelligent work in progress there, and that the fittest ideas and the fittest men are tending to survive. In many parts of the world the old order has passed away. But, of all the experiments to evolve a new order, it is the experiment of young America which most attracts my own deepest sympathy. For they are occupied with the task of trying to make the economic order work tolerably well, while preserving freedom of individual initiative and liberty of thought and criticism.

The older generation of living Americans accomplished the great task of solving the technical problem of how to produce economic goods on a scale adequate to human needs. It is the task of the younger generation to bring to actual realization the potential blessings of having solved the technical side of the problem of poverty. The central control which the latter requires involves an essentially changed method and outlook. The minds and energies which have found their fulfillment in the achievements of American business are not likely to be equally well adapted to the further task. That must be, as it should be, the fulfillment of the next generation.

The new men will often appear to be at war with the ideas and convictions of their seniors. This cannot be helped. But I hope that these seniors will look as sympathetically as they can at a sincere attempt—I cannot view it otherwise—to complete, and not to destroy, what they themselves have created.

—From John Maynard Keynes, *New York Times,* June 10, 1934

Exploiting Capabilities: Strategic Hinges and Long-term Flexibility

Introduction

VIEWING THE FIRM AS a collection of operating capabilities provides us with a powerful model for how a company might take advantage of its *existing* set of abilities to create new opportunities. This is a very different view of the world than existed 10 or 20 years ago, when the primary focus was on deciding which markets or technologies a company wanted to operate in. The challenge then became one of assembling the appropriate resources needed to support that strategy. Over time, firms have recognized that a sustainable operations advantage tends to be built through a meticulous combination of structural and infrastructural elements of the firm. Unfortunately, such capabilities take time to build, so the old model of identifying an opportunity without regard to the abilities extant in the firm starts to look increasingly fragile. In addition, opportunities disappear faster than the necessary capabilities can be created.

In reality, firms use both of these mechanisms. They identify new opportunities and assemble the resources they need to implement their plans (and learn new things as a result of this), but they also take into account their existing capabilities and continuously look for opportunities to exploit them. The balance between the two approaches depends to a great extent on the characteristics of the business in which the firm operates. Volatile, unpredictable markets and technologies tend to favor exploiting existing capabilities (see Figure C.1).

An analogy we find useful here (and one that underscores the need for an appropriate balance) is that of a person's career: Few of us are doing today what we planned to be or do when we were, say, 14 years old. A career tends to evolve over time through a combination of cultivating the specific capabilities required to prepare us for what we would like to do and some analysis of what we are good at, as that becomes clear over time. We have a plan, try it out, then discover that we are better or worse at particular roles and adapt our plans to conform. In addition, opportunities arise as time goes which may not have been anticipated, and some of these

Figure C.1   The Balance between Planning and Exploiting Existing Capabilities

Capabilities/Opportunity Based More Appropriate	Planning-Based More Appropriate

$$\longleftrightarrow$$

• Turbulent Competitive Environment	• Stable Competitive Environment
• Rapid Technological Change	• Stable Technology
• Short Term Technology Cycles	• Long Term Technology Cycles
• Limited Cap-X Commitments	• Large Cap-X Reqmts.
	• Heavy Sunk Capital

Examples: Software, Electronics   *Examples: Aircraft, Petrochemicals*

will provide such a good fit with our abilities and evolving interests that it makes no sense to stick with the original plan. Taking action on this new opportunity will also help develop new abilities, which may be exploited in the future, and so on. Most people use a combination of planning and opportunism in building their career (though we suspect that post-rationalization often makes us underestimate the latter!). Either extreme has its dangers.

One can imagine people so determined to become musicians that they doggedly set about developing the necessary skills to achieve that end, regardless of the fact that they have no talent. Although one might admire their determination, they are more likely than others to remain starving artists. On the other hand, pure opportunists who use existing talents to take advantage of anything they can do in the short term pay a heavy price. First, they do not necessarily develop any new abilities. Second, their lack of consistency means that any abilities they do develop are muddled and unfocused.

This section of the course looks at companies going through processes of strategic change over time, and in particular at firms faced with the opportunity to exploit their capabilities and/or develop new ones along the way.

A Structure for Mapping Strategic Change: Strategic Hinges

When you listen to Mozart or Bach, the pleasant sound you hear is not only a result of their artistry, but also a result of certain rules of music theory. One rule goes something like this: if you switch from one key to the next, without using a good mechanism to get there, it will sound dreadful to the listener. One of the mechanisms used to avoid this is a "hinge note." This is a particular note that one chord has in common with the next, despite the fact that all of the other notes have changed. The disjunction then doesn't seem so bad. Many composers use hinge notes as a way of changing the key of their music.

Let's develop this analogy for companies. A firm may be seen as a collection of capabilities, which usually undergoes change as it moves into a new business. Some of the capabilities needed will be new, while some capabilities are common to the old and new businesses. Such common capabilities might be knowledge of a particular market, expertise in a type of manufacturing technology, an ability to set up plants in remote locations, or a particular engineering design expertise. Stealing a term from the music theorists, we call these capabilities *hinge capabilities*. Firms do not make successful transitions without a strong hinge that exists in common between the two businesses. The key to a successful transition is not only the identification of a good opportunity, but also the judicious choice of a hinge that will be used to get into the new business, and, by implication, understanding what new capabilities must be developed. An understanding of the prospective hinges allows a firm to focus its search for new opportunities in particular directions, consistent with a path over time, as we will see below.

Let us use an example from earlier in the book to illustrate the idea, along with a diagrammatic way of analyzing this situation. In "Whistler," as you may remember, management were facing something of a dilemma. They were sitting on a shrinking market, being attacked on all sides by low-cost competition exploiting the maturation of the technology in radar detectors. While Whistler had experienced a number of "golden years" when it exploited its technical engineering prowess to gain an innovative edge, the opportunities to do this in radar detectors were diminishing. Whistler needed to develop something else to do. Whistler's own description of its capabilities differed depending on whom you spoke to—as is usually the case. Some said its competence was in the automobile accessories market (a *market-based* competence), and it should therefore look to make products like portable tire pumps and gauges. Others were convinced that Whistler's abilities were in microwave technology (an *engineering-based* competence) and it should therefore consider new microwave applications such as collision-avoidance detectors for backing up trucks. Still others were convinced that Whistler was actually good at *making* tightly-packed electronic circuit boards in small lots (a *manufacturing-based* competence) and that it should therefore go into the business of assembling other small-scale electronic devices.

Each of these capabilities provided Whistler with a prospective hinge to move into a new business, but each implied different sets of new things that needed to be learned, and different paths over time. We can show this on a simple *hinge diagram,* as shown in Figure C.2.

The diagram illustrates a number of features concerning Whistler's strategic dilemma. The first is that it identifies the hinges that are implic-

Figure C.2 Hinge Map for Whistler

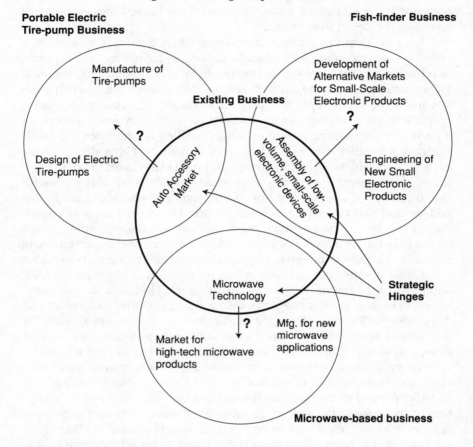

itly being used in going into each new business. When a firm is looking to move into a new arena, it is important to ask the question "What hinge are they using?"—what does the new business have in common with the old in terms of capabilities. The general rule for this is fairly obvious, but not always followed: it should be something the firm is particularly good at. A strong hinge is critical for a successful transition, as this is what provides the beachhead for advance.

Second, each of the prospective hinges and new businesses together define the new capabilities that must be developed. These are shown in the diagram outside the circle of the existing business, but in the circle for the new businesses. The question the firm must ask is—can we acquire these new capabilities well enough, and fast enough? That is, what kinds of things are we good at learning—and will our ability be sufficient to perform well in the new business?

Third, what future path does this imply for the firm? Will the new business itself define a set of competencies from which we will pick another hinge? Or will it, in future, exploit another hinge within the existing business? Firms follow both patterns in making transitions, as we see in the various cases in this section.

Fourth, the diagram shows us what sets of capabilities might have to be "let go" if the new business starts to dominate. The danger of trying to manage the larger set of capabilities is that the firm becomes unfocused. Companies often have difficulty "letting go" of the capabilities that supported past victories, and the diagram helps us see which abilities are not consistent with the new path.

Transitional Capabilities

Implicit in the above is that a good hinge should:

- Be a strong, existing capability
- Provide clear competitive advantage in the new business
- Be consistent with the general future direction that the firm plans to follow

Over time, firms develop not only "core capabilities" but also, *transitional capabilities.* There are certain kinds of transition that a firm becomes practiced in making. For example, a firm that consistently uses its manufacturing capabilities as a hinge will become practiced at learning about new markets. Firms that always use their marketing focus as a hinge will become good at developing new manufacturing and engineering capabilities. An awareness of "what we are good at learning" provides firms with a much better analysis of the prospective hinges they might use over time. As we mentioned above, firms follow a variety of strategies for developing businesses over time, as shown in Figure C.3.

The strategy they use depends not only on their ability to learn, but also on the nature of the capabilities that they can learn. John Deere, for example, would be more likely to employ strategy A—it has a strong set of capabilities in the agricultural-equipment business, and would be unlikely to hop onto a new "lily pad" that took it further away from that core. U.S. Robotic's entrepreneurial spirit might well have carried them on a path that looked like Strategy B, where each new business grows to provide hinge capabilities for subsequent businesses. In the cases that follow, we suggest you sketch out maps of the strategic capabilities and the hinges that are being used by the firms as they make their transitions. This will help identify the new things that must be learned, the consistency with previous paths, and the nature of abilities that the firms learns well. It will also provide clues about candidate transitions for the future.

Figure C.3   Example Strategies

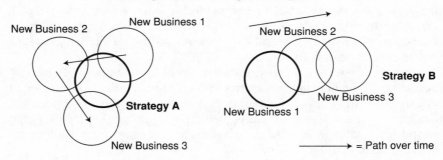

The Cases

"US Robotics (USR)." This case provides us with an excellent example of a firm facing the end of a successful run of opportunism, which must now commit to a particular strategy. The question is: what strategy? USR has been successful over the past decade by using a combination of good engineers, market knowledge, and quick-witted management to adapt to the bewilderingly volatile modem business. From manufacturer to distributor and back to manufacturer, it has had an uncanny ability to adapt quickly to new circumstances. Indeed, many in USR are quite proud that they do not have an Operations Strategy (is this true?). But perhaps the time has come for USR to commit to a particular path. As the old saying tells us: "you cannot keep all of your options open all of the time." The question for USR is what structure it should commit to. Should it build a new manufacturing operation, and develop real excellence in quality and cost? Or should it split up into single business units and grow new "little USRs," which can remain as innovative as ever through close links between R&D and manufacturing? Each path means giving up opportunities—not at all comfortable for such a "roll with the punches" company! But what kinds of opportunities does USR give up by committing to each of the proposed plans?

John Deere. This company had the inverse problem: in this case, we see a company which has had a strong focus on planning, and an historical sense of its role in the world, that is suddenly faced with an opportunity to exploit one of the capabilities it developed along the way. What might have been a straightforward decision for USR is much more difficult for John Deere, and for good reason. The new opportunity might defocus the organization and detract from what its historical strengths have been. At the same time, it may be difficult to stop the train now that it's rolling. A lot of people in the organization are anxious to sell their Manufacturing Systems capabilities outside John Deere. "Deere" gives us a chance to make a decision about such opportunism, and to see the kind of trade-offs that firms must make in developing new abilities.

Australian Paper Manufacturers (APM). This concern has traditionally been part of a packaging company. But part of being a good packaging company is making good paper and cardboard. APM found itself in a shrinking market for brown bag paper, leaving some of its capacity idle. Fortunately, there was another market (new to APM), the fine-paper market, that had been dominated by a sleepy monopolist. APM saw an opportunity and seized it. Not only did they attack the market, but they were very successful at it, using the strengths they had developed in making paper for packaging to meet the new challenges of making fine paper. Their marketing innovativeness allowed them to rethink the way that paper was sold, much to the chagrin of the incumbent. Having established a beachhead, APM must now decide how to consolidate it, and how to turn an opportunistic move into a core business.

APM provides us with one of the best examples of success through exploitation of existing capabilities. Since they were not operating in the industry they entered, the incumbent did not even consider them to be a threat. All the while, APM had been developing the capabilities needed to operate in fine paper through their packaging business, which required the ability to make first-rate paper. When the opportunity arose to exploit the capability, it not only took the incumbent by surprise, but perhaps APM as well!

"Micom Caribe." This case shows a company in the process of building capabilities ripe for exploitation. Like APM, they have been developing new capabilities as they responded to a quality crisis. But in fixing their quality problem, they have developed capabilities in excess of those needed in the existing business. The question is how to exploit those abilities. Tom Moschetti's pivotal role as plant manager underscores the fact that strategy is not just formulated by "the company" (as if there really were an all-powerful controller at the top!) but rather is the result of decisions being made throughout the organization. Moschetti must decide how best to exploit his plant's abilities while still supporting MCC's overall strategic objectives.

CHAPTER 28

U. S. Robotics Inc.

*Our manufacturing strategy? We bought most of our equipment
at 30 cents on the dollar from people who thought they had a
manufacturing strategy.*

—John McCartney, CFO

"**S**LEEP FASTER—that was our motto in the early days." Casey
Cowell, President and CEO of U.S. Robotics (USR), reminisced
about the turbulent beginnings of what had become, by 1991,
an $80 million company. USR was the second largest American manufac-
turer of modems. Over the 15 years since USR's founding, its entrepreneurial style had generated remarkable results. Despite a capricious
market and a rapidly changing technology, USR had prospered through a
chameleon-like ability to adapt to its environment. Now, with the aggressive growth target of "5 by 5" ($500 million dollars in sales by 1995),
Cowell pondered the company's future.

First, how could USR maintain its extraordinary flexibility as it grew
six-fold in size? Second, while it was clear that growth would maintain
USR's momentum, many other firms in the industry had mysteriously
failed or been acquired as they reached $150m in sales. Some were suffo-
cated in mushrooming overhead costs, while others simply became arthritic
in a tangle of bureaucracy. Still others over-committed themselves to new
manufacturing equipment, only to see their technology become outdated or
under-utilized during sales slumps. How would USR avoid such problems?
Finally, and most urgently, it was becoming clear that USR's core operations
were growing too large to remain on its single site in Skokie, Illinois. How
should USR reorganize to begin building a world-class multi-site network—
and what skills should it now concentrate on building?

Cowell was optimistic about the rapidly growing firm, but knew that the manufacturing expansion plan on his desk was a harbinger of many difficult decisions that would shape USR's operations strategy in the years to come. While it was unclear which capabilities USR should develop, with such an ambitious growth goal, sleeping faster might again be among them.

The Data Communications Industry

For a number of years, computer-based information and the ability to manage it were recognized as increasingly valuable assets to organizations. The process of collecting, analyzing and distributing information effectively had become more challenging due to the wide dispersion of organizational computer systems resulting from rapid declines in the cost and increases in the power of desktop computers. To capitalize on the full potential of distributed computing environments, users had to be able to communicate reliably and effectively at high speeds.

Data were processed by computers in digital form, and therefore needed to be modulated into analog form before being transmitted over a standard telephone network. Similarly, data had to be demodulated back into digital form for the receiving computer (hence mo-dem: modulator-demodulator). Two types of networks were used for such transmissions: dedicated leased lines and dial-up connections over the public switched telephone network. In the early 1980's, dedicated leased lines prevailed because high speed communications required the more constant, higher quality channel conditions generally available only on such lines. More recently, however, dial-up modem technology had allowed fast and effective communication over the public networks, thus increasing the cost effectiveness and accessibility of fast data transmission for companies without access to leased lines.

Since 1980, standards set by the CCITT (the international data communications standard setting body) for dial-up data transmission speeds had increased from 1200 bits per second to 14,400 bits per second. These increases reflected advances in modem performance as well as the introduction of effective network management systems. The changes had resulted in a major increase in data communications over the public switched telephone network. The sources of this growth included telecommuting professionals working from homes and decentralized offices, the increasing number of portable computer users, and the proliferation of information databases and communications services accessible via the public telephone network such as CompuServe, MCI Mail, Lexis, Nexis, and Dialog.

Enhancements in the public switched network enabled the introduction of even faster dial-up services, with speeds of 56,000 bits per second and above. It was expected that demand would increase for products delivering higher data transmission rates over analog lines. It was also expected that the availability of all-digital circuits would gradually increase. There would thus be significant opportunities in the future for companies to develop and market hybrid network management systems that could accommodate both dial-up analog and digital transmission technologies simultaneously.

The U. S. Robotics Story

USR had never made a robot—the company was named after the fictitious corporation in Isaac Asimov's "I, Robot." "It gave us a high tech image at a time when people really didn't know what 'robotics' meant," noted Cowell. USR was founded in 1976, the result of a collaboration by five recent college graduates.

> None of us were really sure what to do with our lives—I was on my way to grad school to be an academic. One of my friends convinced me that if I got my Ph.D. in Economics as I'd planned, I'd have been the only guy in the unemployment line who knew why he was there.

Cowell decided against an academic career. The partners' attributes were clear: intelligence, enthusiasm and a desire to succeed.

As luck would have it, in 1976, a Federal Communications Commission (FCC) decision allowed independent manufacturers to make devices that plugged directly into the telephone network. This created the market opportunity for all-electronic modems. Spotting this opportunity, the partners set out to manufacture one of the first all-electronic modems. After designing the device, the partners soldered capacitors, resistors, transistors and integrated circuits onto home-made printed circuit boards to make their first product, which was shipped in Spring, 1978. Cowell recalled the early days in Hyde Park in Chicago: "It was all done in a small apartment—a very small apartment!"

"None of us were engineers," noted Cowell, "we just had to figure it out by trial and error." This method of trial and, particularly, error cost the young USR dearly. USR found their costs exceeding target prices. Despite these "teething problems," as the partners viewed them, USR survived to correct itself. From then on USR adhered to an enduring standard formula: use existing microprocessor technology, cleverly put together, to produce a superior product.

As USR learned about the modem business, a new opportunity arose. In the late seventies, users usually bought premium-priced terminals from the company who supplied their computer. This prompted a clutch of independent manufacturers to produce cost-competitive terminals which users could purchase separately.

As we sold our modems, people asked us which terminal we recommended. After a while, we decided to distribute other people's terminals, as well as our own modems. This was a great opportunity. We began selling terminals for Televideo, GE, DEC, and Perkin-Elmer and a few other companies.

Distribution soon became the bulk of USR's business. It gave the young company a flow of cash which enabled it to survive and grow. More importantly, the organization learned about its market through distribution of other people's products.

When the products didn't work, the users called us directly. We learned all the reasons people had problems, what they liked and what they didn't like. We were really developing an ability to work with users and understand what they really wanted.

Changing Tack: The Move from Distribution

By 1981, 75% of the young manufacturer's sales were in distribution; only the remaining fourth was generated from manufacturing its own products. Cowell became wary of the course USR was taking:

We were getting blurred. While we were learning a lot about distribution, and making money from it, we needed to decide if this was what we wanted to be. It wasn't.

We decided that we wanted to be a designer and manufacturer of data communications products, focusing on the small-computer market. We now wanted to sell our products through the distribution companies we had just been competing with. We had to completely reposition ourselves and tell them, 'Remember us? Your worst enemy? Well, now we want to be your best friend.'

By 1983, through a growing ability to produce and market superior products, the re-focusing was a success. Another opportunity soon arose: Original Equipment Manufacturers such as Apple, Commodore and Zenith asked USR to provide modems specifically configured to their requirements. By 1984, this business made up over 50% of USR's sales. A $20 million contract with Apple Computer alone accounted for 45% of USR's sales during fiscal years 1984 and 1985.

To support its business re-positioning, USR moved its headquarters and manufacturing facilities from Chicago to a larger site in Skokie, Illinois.

Changing Tack: Hard Times

In 1985, the personal computer industry slumped. The downturn hit USR's OEM business hard, and prompted another review of USR's course:

> It wasn't only the loss of revenue that was a problem. Somehow, again, we had gotten ourselves into two businesses at once. In the OEM business, you have a few large customers and you do what they want. In brand-name sales, you create an organization good at finding where the market is headed, and develop products accordingly. That means you need a different sales expertise. Your Engineering group has to be different, and interact more with marketing, since you're trying to follow the market yourself, not follow someone else who's following the market.
>
> It's hard to run an organization that's trying to do two different things. You're more likely to succeed if you're doing a few things well rather than several things in a mediocre way. We needed to concentrate on building something we were really good at. The OEM nose-dive made the direction clear: build an organization that is truly excellent in engineering—which makes the best products on the market—and gets them there fast."

USR flexed itself and used the slump in the personal computer industry as an opportunity to refocus. Direct sales grew to 95% of revenues. USR began to build an engineering group that would prove difficult for competitors to catch—a mission which had continued into the 1990's.

Engineering Engineering

Cowell described the development of Engineering at USR:

> While we were in the distribution business, we were learning a lot about designing and building modems. In fact, it was this set of skills that won us the Apple contract. We proposed to Apple that we build their modems, which they would then re-sell under their name. We had to convince them that we were the guys for the job. We did it by building perfect prototype modems with outstanding features. Our capabilities in engineering let us pounce on this great opportunity.

While USR's Engineering group was already good, the exacting standards of the Apple project propelled it to excellence.

> We really had the best product—the only really big problem was in manufacturing: We had to ramp up from 1,000 boards a month to 22,000. We went to three shifts but we had to sub-contract out some assembly work. Still, we got the job done.

The Courier 2400 project

When the OEM market evaporated in 1985, USR set about building up its Engineering group.

> We decided to build faster modems. We set our R&D team a challenge—to produce a new Courier 2400 baud modem. They developed a great product.

USR stayed with its standard formula: Use off-the-shelf microprocessors, together with an in-house designed data-pump—the technical heart of the product. The data-pump carried out filtering, modulation and demodulation of the data stream. Because USR was one of few companies that designed its own data pump, it had a great advantage in matching and exceeding the industry standards for data-transfer rates.

> The data pump has been the real source of our competitive advantage. We have been able to stay one jump ahead of the competition with faster, more reliable modems through innovation in data pump design and standard microprocessor technology.

Getting Better at Getting Faster

Managing the Critical Path. As USR realized the increasing competitive importance of its engineering capability, it set about managing its innovative heart carefully. To meet and beat the competition, new faster, more fully-featured products needed to be introduced every 9 to 12 months. It was clear that USR needed to develop its ability to adapt to such rapidly changing markets.

To ensure that time to market was as short as possible, each development project was planned on a PERT[1] chart, and the critical path was found. Projects were color coded: when one of the eighty engineers was on the critical path for a given model, a colored plaque was placed on his or her door. Claudia Newland, an engineer on the team, commented on the importance of the plaques:

> If you need to talk to me, better make it relevant to the project I'm on! That's the message these plaques send.

Modular Design. In addition to improved project planning and resource management, the introduction of modular design techniques avoided the traditional duplication of design effort across products. Mike Levi of the Technical Support Group had carried out a study to find out what took up engineers' time:

[1]Production Evaluation and Review Technique

We looked at a whole range of factors to see if we could figure out what feature of a board design correlated most strongly with the time it took to get the design done. It turned out to be pretty simple: the number of components. New boards took 1.4 days per component across a wide range of products.

Many of the auxiliary features of modems made for the North American market, such as the modem interfaces to telephone lines, remained unchanged across designs. Other modem sub-systems, such as the data pump, distinguished one model from the next. In 1991, USR introduced a motherboard/daughterboard system in which a standard carrierboard (mother) held a specialized daughter board. "The introduction of the mother-daughter system stops our engineers from re-inventing the wheel every time a new product comes out.

The new system meant not only fewer and shorter design decisions and better thought-out designs, but also more straightforward manufacturing as USR built expertise in motherboard production.

In-House Prototyping. Prototype manufacturing used to be contracted out to local vendors. USR's R&D group found that information about problems in manufacturing was often too slow in coming back to be useful. In 1990, prototype manufacturing was brought in-house and carried out on the full-scale manufacturing lines. The benefits were immediate.

Now, manufacturing can say to us "Hey, this component is a really tight fit" or "Why can't we turn this component around?" This is the kind of thing we can fix very easily. They'll often have a list of 20–30 problems that need attention. They're the kind of things that you just let slide when the prototypes are made outside.

Levi summarized the Engineering organization which USR had built:

Speed has been the key for us. It has given us the ability to respond to the market flexibly. Because we have a fast engineering department, we can hit the window of opportunity for faster modems more quickly than anyone else. And having manufacturing under the same roof makes us even faster.

Manufacturing

There were three stages in the manufacturing process at USR. The first stage, *PCB assembly,* involved placing and soldering purchased components onto a printed circuit board. The second stage was *product test* in which the boards were checked: first, to ensure that they were electronically correct, with components in the right places and second, to ensure that the

Exhibit 28.1   Revenue History

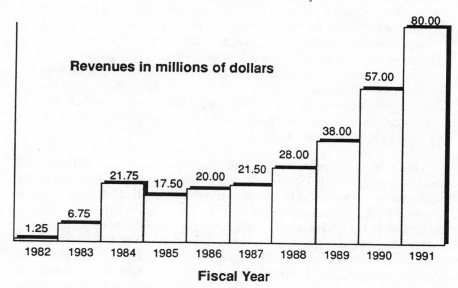

Revenues in millions of dollars

Fiscal Year	Revenue
1982	1.25
1983	6.75
1984	21.75
1985	17.50
1986	20.00
1987	21.50
1988	28.00
1989	38.00
1990	57.00
1991	80.00

boards functioned correctly. The third stage, *final assembly,* was the assembly of completed PCBs and auxiliary components into a modem enclosure.

As late as 1989, 75% of PCB assembly work was being carried out by a subcontractor in Mexico. Boards and components were shipped to Mexico, where PCB assembly was carried out and they were shipped back to Skokie for final assembly.

Exhibit 28.2   Products and Brands

Low		Functional Complexity	High
Home Office/ Small Business	Portable	Organizational Desktop	Network & Data Center
Sportster	*WorldPort*	*Courier*	*Total Control*
Individual Desktop Communications	*Laptop/Notebook Communications*	*Corporate Desktop Communications*	*Network Managment Systems*
	BLAST *Communications Software for All Market Sectors $99 to $9,995*		
$139 to $649	*$159 to $699*	*$349 to $1,295*	*$5,000 to $20,000*

We were assembling PCBs in a low labor-cost country for the obvious reason, but we started to figure out that there were some less obvious reasons for moving it back here. First, we just couldn't live with the time lag of sending the work down there and, more importantly, sending it *back* down when there were quality problems. Communication was slow and difficult. Recurring problems just took a long time to get fixed. So we did the opposite of what everyone else was doing and brought PCB assembly back to the States, though we maintained our relationship with our subcontractors for surge capacity.

By 1990, both prototype manufacturing and all high-volume PCB work was back in-house at the Skokie facility. Having all manufacturing under the same roof as design and marketing brought USR unanticipated benefits. First, product quality improved—since quality problems could be immediately tracked to their source, difficulties could be resolved immediately. Second, design-for-manufacturability issues became clearer and could be quickly sorted out with the engineers. Third, (as the plant learned about production), costs quickly became comparable to those in Mexico. Fourth, product development cycles were shortened as prototypes were made on actual production equipment.

USR made prototype production painless by linking its computer-aided design (CAD) system to the shop floor. CAD files representing prototypes were electronically routed to production equipment, where a prototype run of 15 to 50 units could be completed in about an hour.

By 1991, over 95% of USR's sales were manufactured in Skokie. Of the 110,000 square feet at Skokie, 45,000 square feet were used for manufacturing, 25,000 square feet for product development, and the remainder for all other departments. In 1991, the Skokie plant was producing 1,500 modems per day.

Process Technology

Capital investment for USR is a quarter of that of our competitors. Ongoing we expect to be able to purchase SMT lines at 50 to 60 cents on the dollar.

—Gary Boss, Vice-President of Manufacturing

PCB assembly at Skokie was carried out on two separate manufacturing lines: a fully integrated *surface mount* (SMT) line and another 2 lines which accommodated both surface mount and *through-hole* technology (see Exhibit 28.3). Through-hole was the traditional technology for PCB production. Pins from components passed through holes drilled in the board; components were then mechanically and electrically connected to the board by molten solder, which formed pools around the pins on the other side of the board and then solidified. Soldering was carried out in a wave soldering machine, where boards were passed over a miniature river of molten solder. SMT was a newer technology, in which components were affixed directly to the board with a solder paste. The pins of the components rested on small pads on the top of the printed circuit board. This assembly was then passed through a reflow oven to melt the solder paste and create a permanent electrical and mechanical contact. USR's hybrid line accommodated surface mount components by affixing them to the board with an adhesive and soldering SMT components with through-hole components in the wave solderer.

The advantage of SMT over through-hole was that much greater component density could be achieved, and hence miniaturization enhanced. The precision required for SMT necessitated automatic placement of components. However, once an SMT line was working well, it would produce fewer defects than a through-hole line of equivalent capacity. Surface mount manufacturing technology was improving all the time, and was expected to continue to produce boards of higher quality and component density.

Not all components were available in packages suitable for surface

Exhibit 28.3   Board Assembly Process at USR

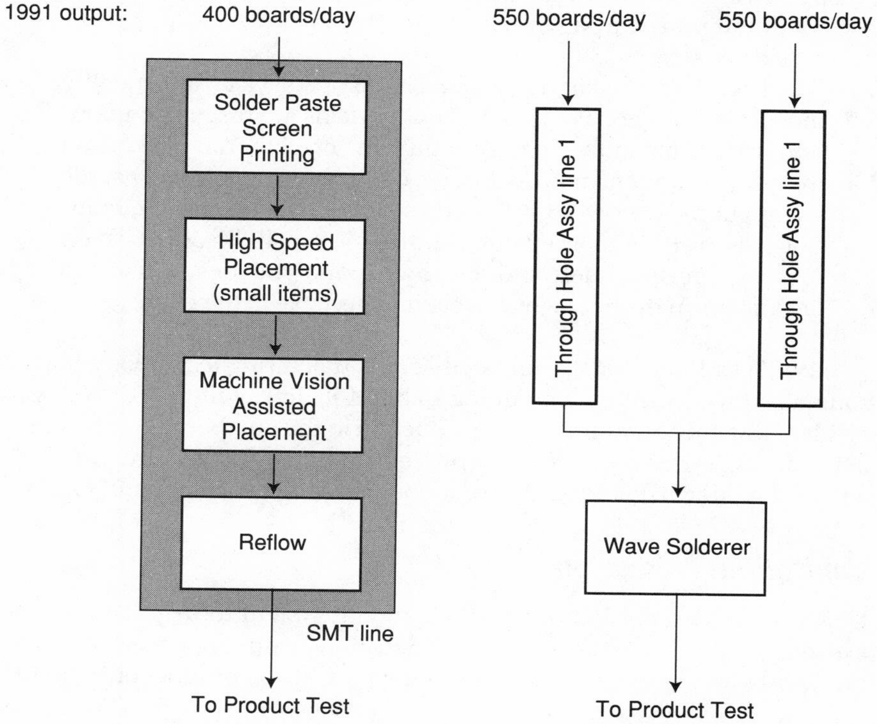

mount, however, and many were expensive in this form, so USR continued to use through-hole technology, although newer products were progressively employing more and more SMT components. The SMT line was more highly automated than the hybrid line, and was producing 400 boards/day in August, 1991. The hybrid lines produced 550 boards/day each. Most production was carried out on an extended 9-hour shift, though a second skeleton crew completed daily production and cleaned up the work area in preparation for the next day's production.

USR kept its investment in manufacturing low by buying used equipment at a discount from its network of equipment brokers. This still enabled it to stay comparatively up to date with newer and higher speed PCB assembly lines, without too much capital investment or the risk of untested technology. The existing SMT lines at USR ran at 10,000 components/hour. The latest generation of SMT lines were 50% faster, required 15% more space and cost $1.5m when bought new. Gary Boss commented on this policy:

> Of course, it would be great to buy new equipment—you get a lot of support from the manufacturer, so you can get up and running faster. We are really a generation behind on SMT. On the other hand, to buy new you often have to commit yourself 12 months in advance. If we buy used, we can stay flexible. I can usually find used equipment in a couple of months, and we can put work outside as a contingency.
>
> If we had to start focussing on first-pass yield and quality though, we might have to change. Our yields are really good now, but they are not in the "parts per million" bracket. You really need the newest equipment to do this. We can inspect out any bad boards we might make now, so we can do without these levels of quality. But it is really important for another reason: PPM defect levels mean you really understand the process, and you are less likely to get failures in the field which were undetectable in the plant.

While USR continually updated its manufacturing technology, it also sought improvement by continuing to build its links with R&D. A direct result of this collaboration was the reduction in the number of components in products despite progressive improvement in product features. In 1991, a typical modem contained 200 components—35% fewer than in 1986.

Controlling Production

USR used a Material Requirements Planning system to help it plan and execute production. Each month, production controllers met with the marketing and sales group to determine and revise production requirements for the next 6 to 8 months. At this meeting, production planners would "freeze" the build schedule for the fourth month ahead, allowing only minor changes in production quantities. The plan for two months ahead was firmly fixed, so that no changes in any product's planned production volumes were possible. Production Controllers maintained a four-week supply of finished goods inventory to satisfy any unanticipated demand.

USR's Markets

Product Line

By 1991, USR provided one of the broadest product ranges in the industry. There were four key markets in which USR participated: Home Office, Organizational/Desktop, Portable and Data-Center. Exhibit 28.2 (p. 601) shows the brands offered by USR and Exhibit 28.4 lists competitors in various segments.

Home Office. The home office/small business market contributed 15% of USR's sales. This was the high volume, low cost segment in which USR's Sportster brand had 1–2% share, with units ranging in price from $80 to $400 (see Exhibit 28.8). An example of a small business end user was Peapod Delivery Systems, an on-line service that enabled a subscriber with a personal computer and modem to order groceries from home or work. Peapod used Sportster 2400 modems to transmit data to and from its customers. Availability and cost were critical in this market.

Organizational Desktop. The organizational desktop market demanded speed and reliability, and thus quality was crucial. USR's Courier brand covered this segment (see Exhibit 28.10). Courier made up more than 50% of USR's sales and commanded a 20% share of this market, offering units priced between $250 and $1200. An example end-user was General Electric Medical Systems' Nuclear and X-Ray Divisions which used Courier V.32bis modems for remote equipment diagnostics in both their integrated nuclear imaging and X-ray systems. The Courier modem link was designed to permit offsite GE technicians supporting these systems to analyze equipment malfunctions and to determine the components necessary for repair prior to the on-site visit.

Portable Computer. The need for a product in the portable computer market had been apparent for a number of years. In 1990, USR acquired Touchbase Systems, a company specializing in the design and manufacture of modems for portable computers. WorldPort, the Touchbase brand, had a 15% segment share and quickly garnered 15% of USR's sales (see Exhibit

Exhibit 28.4   USR's Markets and Competitors

Market	Company	Sales ($m)	Growth
Personal/ Home Use	Practical Peripherals	20	18%
	US Robotics	7	
	ATI	10	
	Zoom	20	
	Taiwanese Clones (total)	20	
Organizational/ Desktop	UDS (Motorola)	120	at low end (<9600 baud) -5% at high end (> 9600 baud) 30%
	Hayes	100	
	US Robotics	56	
	Microcom	40	
	Telebit (niche player)	40	
	Multitech	40	
Portable	US Robotics	12	100%
	Megahertz	10	
	Hayes	8	
	Practical Peripherals	5	
	10-15 cloners	5	
Data Center	Opticom	20	
	UDS (Motorola)	10	
	Microcom	5	
	US Robotics	4	
Leased Line (Robotics not currently participating)	Paradyne (AT&T)	400	
	CODEX (Motorola)	350	
	General Data Com.	$200m (public)	
	Gandalf	150	
	US Robotics	0	

28.9). One end user was SYSCO, an institutional food distributor serving the hotel and restaurant industries. The use of laptop computers equipped with internal 2400 bit per second WorldPort modems enabled members of SYSCO's sales force to place orders, access current product pricing and availability, and upload information to the corporate mainframe.

Exhibit 28.5   Balance Sheets

U.S. Robotics, Inc. and Subsidiaries

CONSOLIDATED BALANCE SHEETS

	September 30,		June 30, 1991
	1989	1990	
ASSETS			
CURRENT ASSETS			
Cash and cash equivalents	$ 330,873	$ 3,080,703	$ 1,661,572
Accounts receivable, less allowance for doubtful receivables of $76,615, $291,693 and $663,748 for 1989, 1990 and 1991, respectively	4,227,888	5,455,344	8,063,942
Inventories			
Finished products	2,122,720	2,174,205	4,407,783
Work-in-process	1,115,159	1,939,039	2,293,185
Raw materials	3,185,081	2,239,264	3,535,578
	6,422,960	6,352,508	10,236,546
Deferred income taxes	403,000	452,000	764,000
Prepaid expenses	201,768	428,238	600,683
Total current assets	11,586,489	15,768,793	21,326,743
PROPERTY AND EQUIPMENT — AT COST			
Land and building	4,580,241	4,777,922	5,182,889
Computer, test and factory equipment	3,242,255	4,495,463	6,069,137
Furniture and fixtures	241,224	381,185	496,923
	8,063,720	9,654,570	11,748,949
Less accumulated depreciation and amortization	2,514,488	3,703,610	4,677,045
	5,549,232	5,950,960	7,071,904
OTHER ASSETS	147,968	2,563,139	3,184,229
	$17,283,689	$24,282,892	$31,582,876

(continued)

Exhibit 28.5 Balance Sheets *(continued)*

LIABILITIES AND STOCKHOLDERS' EQUITY

CURRENT LIABILITIES			
Note payable to bank	$ 250,000	$ —	$ —
Other notes payable	—	1,491,994	558,258
Current maturities of long-term obligations	330,249	602,297	5,163,930
Accounts payable — trade	2,278,161	2,680,618	3,888,886
Accrued liabilities	1,498,840	2,782,753	2,191,096
Income taxes payable	639,609	215,702	
Total current liabilities	4,996,859	7,773,364	11,802,170
LONG-TERM OBLIGATIONS	3,994,039	3,521,307	3,526,590
DEFERRED INCOME TAXES	74,400	79,400	109,000
COMMITMENTS AND CONTINGENCIES			
STOCKHOLDERS' EQUITY			
Preferred stock — $.01 par value; 2,000,000 shares authorized; issuable in series, none issued	—	—	—
Common stock — $.01 par value; 23,000,000 shares authorized; 8,301,114, 8,216,814 and 6,573,714 issued and outstanding in 1989, 1990 and 1991, respectively	83,011	82,168	65,737
Additional contributed capital	2,654,691	2,624,682	2,396,355
Retained earnings	5,512,099	10,170,748	13,760,955
	8,249,801	12,877,598	16,223,050
Deferred compensation under restricted stock plans	(29,695)	(13,204)	(10,640)
Foreign currency translation adjustment	(1,715)	44,427	(67,294)
Total stockholders' equity	8,218,391	12,908,821	16,145,116
	$17,263,659	$24,282,892	$31,582,876

Exhibit 28.6 Statements of Earnings

CONSOLIDATED STATEMENTS OF EARNINGS

	Year ended September 30,			Nine months ended June 30,	
	1988	1989	1990	1990 (unaudited)	1991
Net sales	$28,793,304	$37,532,758	$56,359,105	$40,460,366	$57,177,876
Cost of goods sold	17,273,114	21,901,651	28,552,486	20,761,723	26,785,193
Gross profit	11,520,190	15,631,107	27,806,619	19,698,643	30,392,683
Operating expenses					
Selling and marketing	5,151,272	6,419,964	9,715,773	6,758,259	10,252,096
General and administrative	2,408,027	2,638,929	4,881,720	3,373,574	5,779,453
Research and development	2,226,284	2,991,179	4,671,288	3,292,324	4,824,611
	9,785,583	12,050,072	19,268,781	13,424,157	20,856,160
Operating profit	1,734,607	3,581,035	8,537,838	6,274,486	9,536,523
Interest income	—	—	(84,397)	(77,199)	(171,714)
Interest expense	321,501	477,366	558,141	439,988	375,504
Other expense	3,881	98,052	240,727	177,638	310,091
Earnings before income taxes	1,409,225	3,005,617	7,823,367	5,734,059	9,022,642
Income tax expense	370,000	1,070,000	3,096,000	2,236,000	3,533,000
Net earnings	$ 1,039,225	$ 1,935,617	$ 4,727,367	$ 3,498,059	$ 5,489,642
Earnings per common share	$ 0.09	$ 0.17	$ 0.44	$ 0.33	$ 0.56
Shares used in per share calculation	11,771,369	11,119,390	10,674,671	10,682,947	9,824,737

Exhibit 28.7 Background of Officers

Casey G. Cowell	38	Chairman of the Board, President, Chief Executive Officer and Director
John McCartney	39	Executive Vice President, European Operations, Chief Financial Officer, Secretary and Director
Jonathan N. Zakin	42	Executive Vice President, Sales and Marketing and Director
Dale M. Walsh	55	Vice President, Advanced Development
Gary R. Boss	50	Vice President, Manufacturing
Robert P. Polychron	44	Vice President, Sales
Ross W. Manire	39	Vice President, Finance
Semir Sirazi	37	Vice President, Research and Development
Peter I. Mason	39	Director
James C. Tyree	33	Director
Gian Fulgoni	43	Director
Paul G. Yovovich	37	Director

Cowell, a founder of the Company, had served as Chairman of the Board, President, Chief Executive Officer and a director of the Company since 1983. Cowell also served as a director of Platinum Technology, Inc. and several private companies. Cowell also had served on the National Board of Directors of the American Electronics Association. Cowell had a B.A. from the University of Chicago.

McCartney had been a Vice President and Chief Financial Officer of the Company since 1984 and a director since 1985. He had held the positions of Executive Vice President since 1988, Executive Vice-President, European Operations since 1990 and Secretary since 1989. He was previously a Manager at Grant Thornton, a public accounting firm. McCartney had an M.B.A. from the Wharton School of the University of Pennsylvania and a B.A. from Davidson College. He was a certified public accountant.

Zakin joined the Company as Vice President, Sales in 1987. He had served as the Company's Executive Vice President, Sales and Marketing since 1989 and had been a director since 1988. Prior to joining the Company, Zakin was a Vice President and Chief Financial Officer of Winterhalter, Inc., a computer communications company. Before joining Winterhalter, Zakin was President of Cosma International, an international management consulting firm specializing in marketing computer products. Zakin received an M.B.A. from Harvard University and a B.S. from New York University.

Walsh had been a Vice President of the Company since 1983. He currently served as the Company's Vice President, Advanced Development, a position he had held since 1989. Prior to that, Walsh served as Vice President, Engineering. Before joining U.S. Robotics, Walsh was senior scientist at General Datacomm, Inc. Previously, he was manager for modem development at Paradyne. Walsh was a member and past chairman of the Electronics Industry Association committee which developed modem standards recommendations for the CCITT. Walsh held a B.S. from the University of Illinois, Urbana and a B.S.M.E. from the University of South Florida.

Boss joined the Company in 1987 as Director of Manufacturing Operations. He was appointed Vice President, Manufacturing in 1990. Previously, he was Vice President, Manufacturing, at Oak Industries, Inc.'s Oak Switch Systems Division. Boss holds a B.S E.E. from the Milwaukee School of Engineering.

Polychron joined the Company in 1987 as National Sales Director. He was appointed Vice President, Sales in 1990. Previously he was East Coast Sales Manager of Telebit Corporation. Prior to that, he held sales management positions with a number of technology companies. Polychron holds a B.S. from Hofstra University.

Data-Center. The Total Control brand was aimed at the data-center segment and comprised 15% of USR's sales. These products, which were ideal for corporate computer centers, had average selling prices between $5,000 and $15,000 (see Exhibit 28.11). Total Control had 1–2% share of the data-center segment. The data-center segment very much drove demand in the organizational desktop segment, as more corporate users were able to access their computer center directly using a Courier style modem.

Exhibit 28.8   Sportster Sales Flyer

Exhbit 28.9   WorldPort modem

Exhibit 28.10   Courier Sales Literature

BLAST data communications software provided the capability to manage a network of modems. Prices ranged from $99 to $9,995. BLAST had less than a 5% share of the software segment. An example of an end user was Exxon Corporation, where many Exxon-owned service stations used personal computers to collect retail information and monitor fuel inventory. BLAST communications software linked these retail locations to Exxon's IBM data center in Houston.

Distribution and Competition

USR's products traditionally reached end users through a two-tiered distribution channel. USR sold to distributors which in turn sold to resellers such as superstores, computer chains, franchise organizations, and value added resellers. These resellers generally sold directly to end users, including corporate and individual purchasers. USR increasingly sold directly to key corporate accounts.

In North America USR sold to approximately 30 national and regional distributors, which in turn sold to over 5,000 resellers. USR provided technical support to resellers and end users. Outside of North America USR's products were marketed, sold, and serviced by over 20 distributors. These distributors sold both to large end users and through resellers. The inter-

Exhibit 28.11   Total Control Sales Literature

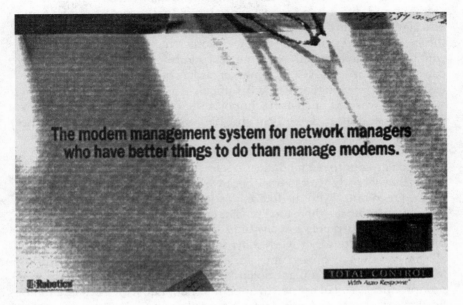

national distributors had data communication technical expertise and provided first line technical support to international customers.

The data communications industry was fiercely competitive and was characterized by rapid technological change and emerging industry standards. Many of USR's competitors had access to large financial and technological resources. Competitors included Codex and Universal Data Systems (both subsidiaries of Motorola), AT&T/Paradyne, Microcom, Telebit, Hayes Microcomputer Products and Multi-Tech Systems. As USR expanded its product offerings, it expected to begin to compete with many additional well-established companies—particularly at the more sophisticated end of its product range.

Market Trends

As USR grew, it saw its market changing in a number of ways. First, and most important, was the increase in variety of products being sold. "We can provide for customers' needs much more effectively by providing a broad range of products in each market" pointed out Jon Zakin, Executive Vice-President of Sales and Marketing. The number of active SKUs being produced had gone from 220 to 500 in 12 months and continued to increase.

Second was an increasing focus on the corporate customer. Rather than selling a small range of products to a myriad of individual users, products were increasingly sold to institutions. This made individual orders larger and more specialized. Demand had become much more "lumpy" and difficult to forecast, since individual corporate orders could be a significant portion of a particular period's demand. At the same time, the increasing specialization to the customer meant that manufacturing run lengths were small. As large, corporate customers progressively constituted more of USR's total market, orders became sporadic, and forecasting was becoming increasingly difficult.

Third was the increasing importance of international customers. International sales in 1989, 1990 and 1991 were 4%, 12% and 18% of net sales respectively. As international sales grew, engineers became aware of the change in their work patterns. Engineers had to tailor each modem for a particular country's standards. While such changes were usually not major, they were difficult to track because of their sheer number. One engineer pointed out, "With the international work, the plaque has moved on before you know it—there aren't major changes but there are a lot of them coming down the pipeline at any time. It's getting pretty difficult to schedule this in with the other work—and it's kind of difficult to keep track of all the product changes and variants." Dave Price, Manufacturing Manager at the Skokie plant noted, "Every month, we get three or four new products. A lot of the new work is international, with just slight modifications to other models—but from a control point of view, they are just as difficult as a whole new model." Zakin predicted that international sales would provide USR with 40% of its business by 1995.

The fourth trend was the increasing commoditization at the low-end of the market. In the Home Office market commoditization was such that distributors placed orders with whichever manufacturer could deliver quickest—features and price being a given. "It's tough at this end now," remarked Zakin, "products are undifferentiated and stockouts are costly."

The fifth trend (of which everyone in the organization was aware) was the relentless shortening of product life-cycles: by 1991, some products would last only six months in the market place before they were superceded.

Zakin underlined the growing need for flexibility in manufacturing:

> There are really four ways in which USR needs to be flexible. First, we need to provide a broad range of products for the marketplace. Second, we need the ability to introduce new products quickly. We are already among the best in the industry at this, but with more products coming into the range at an increasing rate, we'll have to get better still. Third, we want to be able to cover unexpected surges in demand: we're getting more and more big order opportunities which would be very lucrative if we could respond fast in manufacturing, and produce in volume quickly enough. Fourth, we need to be able to change the mix of products our system

produces—this really means being able to re-schedule quickly and effectively, and set up our manufacturing lines faster.

Growing the Market

Zakin's marketing organization was enthusiastic about "5 by 5": "It sets a high benchmark for the organization and, what's more, I think we can do it." The group had developed a clear idea of how marketing would support achieving $500 million in sales by 1995. USR would continue to expand sales in its differentiated high-end products (such as Total Control) while reducing participation in the commoditized low-end such as the Sportster range. "It's important for us to move up the food chain," commented a member of the marketing group. In addition to a shift in sales mix, USR had a number of possible opportunities to develop new markets. They included vertical applications of USR's modem technology, such as the development of point of sale terminals for retailers. The high-end leased-line segment was worth over $1 billion (see Exhibit 28.4), and USR had not yet begun to apply its talents there. New markets also included going beyond leased-lines into the private network segment such as American Airlines' SABRE reservation system.

5 by 5

5 by 5 is really a war-cry—it reflects an underlying philosophy for the company. It's very clear to us that we have to grow in order to thrive in this business. Smaller companies are too fragile—there comes a point where you cannot be a small, family concern anymore—you have to grow to be credible and strong—as well as to have some direction.

—John McCartney

All of the USR management team recognized the need to grow, and intended to make an Initial Public Offering to raise capital for the expansion. The IPO was to be made in October 1991, to raise $26 million. All were concerned, however, that so many companies in the electronics industry had found it difficult to manage growth beyond $150m in sales. "There are quite a few firms smaller than $150m, and a number of bigger players above $500m—but not very many in the middle." The reasons for the failure of other growing companies were unclear. Many businesses attracted excessive overhead as they moved from single-unit to multi-site operations. Some firms over-estimated the market for their products and invested in expensive manufacturing technology which they were later unable to utilize fully. Firms which "failed" were taken over by larger firms or were liquidated. Indeed, it was from such companies that USR was able to obtain its manufacturing technology at highly discounted prices. Cowell described one such failure:

> MicLan put in too much infrastructure. Two years ago, they were fine. A year ago they just fell away. All of their overheads ballooned—sales, marketing, manufacturing. Then their sales went flat. People were more worried about their jobs than anything else.
>
> USR is tremendously lean as far as people go, " said Jon Zakin, "we have a good understanding of what happens when you take on too many people, but we also have to be really careful about burn out. People are working very hard here and some of them are beginning to feel the strain.

Acquisitions

USR intended that one-third of the growth towards 5 by 5 would be provided by acquisitions. These acquisitions would be used to complement and accelerate its internal product development efforts as well as to provide access to new geographic markets. Since August 1989, USR had already completed and integrated three such acquisitions:

* In August 1989, USR acquired Miracom Limited, a U. K. manufacturer of low speed modem products. Miracom was acquired to provide a solid base for USR's operations in the U.K. Miracom operated a small manufacturing facility in Ipswich, U. K.
* In January 1990, Communications Research Group (CRG) of Baton Rouge, Louisiana was purchased. CRG developed and marketed communications software products marketed under the brand name BLAST; its software development expertise would provide USR with the ability to provide integration of hardware and software across a broad range of platforms.
* In May 1991, USR acquired Touchbase Systems, Inc., a leading manufacturer of modems for the portable computing market with $9.2 million in revenues in 1991. Touchbase was headquartered in Northport, New York. The WorldPort brand was recognized internationally for its pocket-size, battery powered V.32 modems—USR believed it to be the only manufacturer shipping a V.32 modem at the time. The Touchbase acquisition complemented the Miracom purchase, since it provided marketing and technical expertise in France, and so aided further expansion in Europe.

USR integrated these acquisitions by reorganizing senior and middle management, streamlining manufacturing functions and merging the marketing, distribution and product planning and development functions with those of USR. The management team at USR continued to look for new acquisitions to complement its operations.

Growing Pains

Bursting at the Seams

While continued growth and expansion of the product range were enthusiastically welcomed, manufacturing and the Skokie facility as a whole were beginning to feel the strain. It was clear to USR's tight-knit team that there was a major problem—Skokie was simply running out of room.

By August 1991, finished goods and work-in-progress had begun to seep into the corridors and production planners battled to keep it under control. The increase in product variety, the increasing speed with which products were being brought to market, the change in demand patterns and the increasing difficulty in forecasting had made the job of Production Controllers increasingly arduous. Work-in-progress levels began to rise and it was becoming difficult to schedule and plan production to satisfy the market while keeping inventory low. It was also difficult to keep track of the myriad of orders for USR's growing product range.

In addition, there was a clear need to consolidate and standardize the production of portable modems from the recently-acquired Touchbase. This production needed to be carried out with the Sportster range, to maintain consistent quality and take advantage of the commonality in the two ranges. WorldPort had to be brought in-house.

"Clearly, we need to find a solution to our space problem," commented Boss. "The great thing about USR is that we always seem to turn this kind of a problem into an opportunity—although, I must admit, we're in a tough spot."

Fortunately, there was a facility nearby which would provide 86,000 square feet of extra space (the existing facility was 110,000 square feet). The building was available for purchase. The question was—what should move out?

Breaking Up is Hard to Do

Suzanne Purdy was a recently-hired business school graduate with a keen interest in manufacturing. Purdy had spent some time in the steel industry before coming to USR as operations planner, reporting to Gary Boss. Cowell and Boss had charged her with developing a plan for USR's operations over the next four years—specifically, to make recommendations about the space problem.

"As I see it," noted Purdy, "there are three options available to us. First, we could simply move all of manufacturing into the new facility. The problem with this is that we might lose some of the advantages we've found from having R&D and manufacturing in the same place. This has been much more advantageous than everyone thought it would be and it would be hard to give it up. This is especially important to USR now—our product range is broadening fast to service the internationals, and there are more and more new designs which are being produced faster and faster.

Second, we could build a 'business unit' in the new facility—we could move Total Control and Courier products across, and provide groups of people from marketing and R&D to support that range. This would keep R&D, marketing and manufacturing together in a group for those products, while keeping Sportster & WorldPort back here. The advantage of this would be that we would maintain a team, and keep the strong day-to-day links between design, marketing and manufacturing. Unfortunately, this will break up our marketing group and engineering group—and a lot of work is carried out in common across all products. The R&D people in particular feel that they are very much part of a team of engineers and they might be reluctant to move away from their critical mass. As well as this, it is not only manufacturing capacity which we switch between products when unpredictable things happen—we can move marketing and R&D people to work on whichever project is most urgent. We would lose some of that ability if we split them up. We are also bound to have some duplication of overhead as a result of having two R&D and marketing groups.

Third, we could simply sub-contract the manufacture of all our stable, mature products—these may simply need to be made by a source better set up for volume manufacture, where we don't need quite the day-to-day interaction that we need for more volatile products. Even so, there are still some changes in these products, and we could probably manufacture them as effectively as anyone else now—if only we had the space."

Process Technology & Flexibility

Boss was philosophical about the problem, but was tackling some issues of his own.

"No matter what we do—if we continue to do all of our own manufacturing—we will have to buy more capacity and more SMT lines. The question is, is it finally time to invest in state-of-the-art manufacturing equipment and buy the stuff new? If we start moving into the high-end leased-line markets, we will be up against some real heavy-hitters—with really outstanding first-time quality. We may need the best equipment money can buy.

"At the same time, we have been successful by avoiding getting too grand about manufacturing. We've stayed flexible because we've never over-committed ourselves. We don't want egg on our faces if some of these new markets don't pan out. Maybe we'd be better off concentrating on what has always worked: second-hand equipment producing first-rate products."

Looking to the Future

Cowell commented on the challenge of growing USR's operations:

> USR has been great at taking advantage of opportunities as they arise—we can do this a lot better than other people. Even so, it seems like we get our feet on two lily pads at once! It happened when we got into distribution and it happened when we were manufacturing for the OEMs—in both cases, we lost one of the lily pads and found the right thing to focus on. Now, we want to grow, and we might need all the lily pads—but how do we manage them all?
>
> At some point, we will have to break the business up: It will just get too big to manage it as we are now, on one site. But the question is, how should we split it? Should we segment it into business units? or should we divide it up functionally? If we break up into businesses, we risk duplicating a lot of functions, and taking on a lot of the overhead that we've seen strangle other firms. As well as this, there are a lot of subtle interactions between the businesses that we can't ignore. For example, the market for Total Control is a driver for the Courier market. If we break it up into functional departments, say, by moving manufacturing out again, we might lose everything we have gained by having manufacturing on site. We've seen a lot of advantages from having everyone together—marketing, development and manufacturing—you need to lean across the table and see people. You don't see their pupils contract in a memo!
>
> Then we need to think about the longer term and the international market. Should we continue to grow manufacturing in Europe or should we keep manufacturing only in the States?"

As Purdy made her way to Cowell's office to make her recommendations, she bumped into a stack of Total Control boards waiting for rework in the corridor. "Damn!" It was going to be a long morning.

CHAPTER 29

Deere & Company (A)

The Computer-Aided Manufacturing Services Division (Abridged)

"A Window to the World"

*S*TRIDING BRISKLY ACROSS the glass-encased bridge leading to the main building of the Deere & Co. Administrative Center, Bill Rankin betrayed, in a broad smile, elation at having just received conditional approval to proceed with a plan to market some of the software and systems his division had developed over the past five years. Tom Hein and Dave Scott, managers in the Computer-Aided Manufacturing Service Division, were returning with Rankin from the meeting with some of the firm's senior executives. They had presented a business plan, developed with input from their engineers, that projected financial returns too good to be rejected. Nevertheless, their presentation had not been without some anxiety, for becoming a manufacturing systems software vendor represented a major departure from the John Deere tradition of being one of the world's foremost manufacturers of heavy duty agricultural and industrial equipment.

Rankin's presentation had stressed the potential benefits of the proposal beyond the revenues it could be expected to generate. He had argued that the venture would be "a window to the world" that, if properly exploited, would assure Deere of remaining a dominant manufacturing force internationally. Their conviction notwithstanding, Rankin and his managers were aware that final approval had been influenced as much by a prolonged depression in the firm's principal markets as by the strength of their arguments. The firm's earnings per share had fallen to a record low in the past year, and business conditions were not expected to improve in the short term.

Professor Robert Hayes prepared this abridged case as the basis for class discussion rather than to illustrate either effective or ineffective handling of an administrative situation. It is based on a case prepared by Doctoral Candidate Gordon Shirley under the supervision of Professor Ramchandran Jaikumar.

A booming farm economy had encouraged farmers to invest in massive amounts of farm equipment during the 1970s. But as federal programs changed in the 1980s, consumer preferences in farm machinery shifted away from large "fully loaded" products toward equipment that performed basic tasks more productively and cost effectively. A similar trend toward smaller, more productive equipment also was evident in the industrial equipment market in which Deere competed, and was accompanied by vigorous price competition.

After a prolonged period of striving to adjust to the deepest farm recession in decades by reducing costs in its core business, Deere began to explore some additional sources of revenue, such as new product lines and services. Of particular interest were ventures that would provide some protection against the cyclical nature of its traditional businesses. A joint venture to manufacture diesel engines with General Motors was under investigation, along with plans to make the firm an even more dominant force in the lawn care products industry. Approval of the CAM services plan was in keeping with this willingness to entertain new ideas.

Rankin was aware that a number of problems remained unresolved. The conditional nature of the approval created a need to generate early sales, which was particularly worrisome because a ban on recruiting from outside the firm would force him to draw the salesforce from the existing group of engineers, none of whom had any sales experience. This would undoubtedly put some strain on the engineering resources available to the group, and Rankin was concerned that progress on new projects might be impaired. He also had to consider how to exploit the large potential market for his organization's services so as to maximize the benefits to Deere.

The Growth of a Giant

In 1836, a young blacksmith, discouraged by the depressed business conditions in Vermont and the fires that twice had destroyed his shop, decided to seek his fortune in the West. Captivated by the beauty and fertility of the Rock River Valley, John Deere and some fellow Vermonters decided to settle in the small commune of Grand Detour, Illinois, where Deere established a new blacksmith shop. He soon learned that the plows brought west by the pioneers would not scour in the rich black soil of the prairies. Every few steps the iron moldboards, designed for sandy eastern soil, had to be scraped of the heavy soil that stuck to them. Many farmers were quitting the area in despair.

After experimenting with different shapes and materials for plow bottoms, in 1837, Deere developed the first successful self-polishing steel plow. In its first trial, the black earth fell smoothly away from the highly polished surface and curved shape of the moldboard and share. This "self-polishing plow" helped open the West to agricultural development.

As demand for his new ploughs increased, in 1847 Deere moved to Moline, Illinois, to take advantage of the transportation and water power provided by the Mississippi river. By 1850 production had reached 1,600 plows per year using special steel rolled to Deere's specifications by mills in Pittsburgh. Subsequently, Deere introduced the reaper and thresher as alternatives to more primitive harvesting methods. Over the next hundred years Deere and Company evolved into the largest producer of farm equipment in the world and a leading manufacturer of industrial equipment. In the decade of the 1970s alone, Deere's sales grew from $1.5 billion to $5.4 billion and its market share in farm equipment increased an estimated 35%. Its construction and industrial products businesses grew too, though less dramatically.

As Deere's volumes increased and new products were introduced, its factories tended to become larger and more complex. (See Exhibit 29.1.) Rankin observed:

> We're a very traditional company, and as we've grown slowly and deliberately, so also we've grown outward. With every increment of growth you don't have time to go back and erase the blackboard and redesign the facility. As product volumes change over time, and new products get introduced, things tend to get added on the periphery, resulting in a great deal of process complexity. If you take a top view of a traditional manufacturing facility, like many of ours at the time, you'll see a complex material flow with material moving from building to building without any apparent rational pattern.

When the problem became pronounced in the early 1970s, Deere initiated a major modernization and reorganization program. At its largest manufacturing facility in Waterloo, Iowa, two new plants were constructed to simplify and "focus" manufacturing operations for a line of diesel engines and tractor assembly, while at the same time freeing space for other manufacturing activities.

The Group Technology Approach

To aid in rationalizing the organization of the remainder of the factory, the Administrative Services Division proposed that "Group Technology" be utilized. This was a software-driven system for analyzing and classifying parts into groups, which facilitated the identification of parts whose function could be performed by other parts, the design of new parts that could replace several existing ones, and the creation of production processes that were customized to the needs of a part group.

Subsequently, a reorganization of machine tools in one part of the factory was undertaken using manufacturing cells as the fundamental building blocks. This involved moving away from large process-based

Exhibit 29.1 Deere's Engineering and Technology Organization Chart

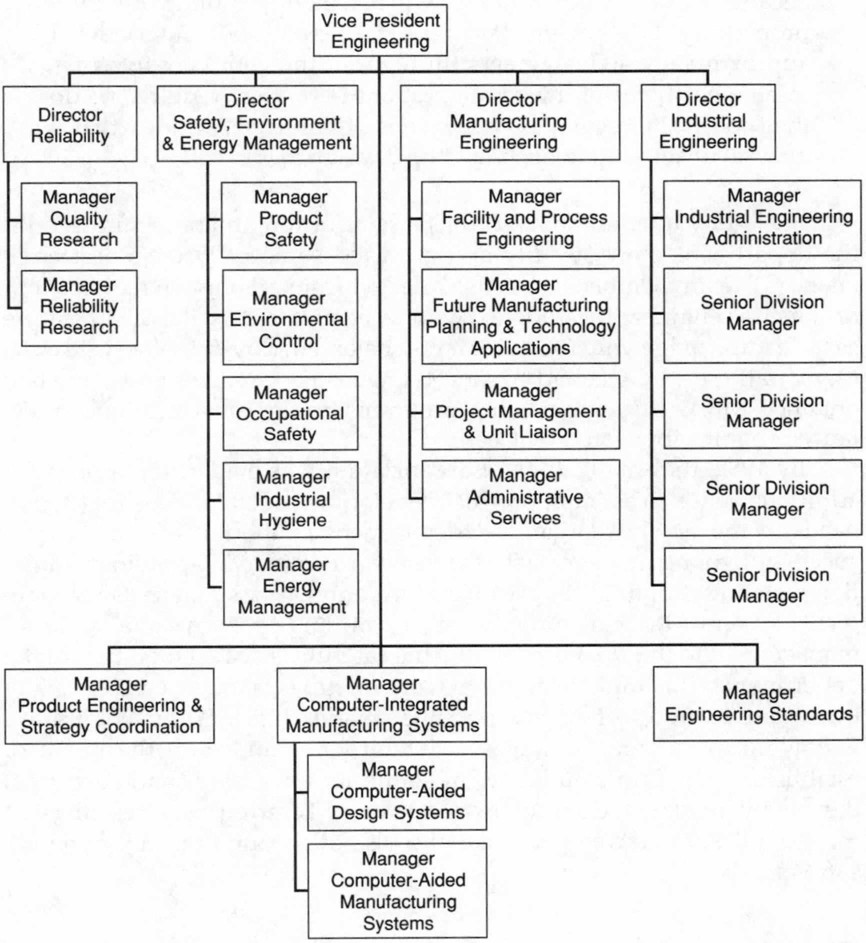

organizational units to individual operating units that were designed to transform raw stock into finished parts as efficiently as possible. To minimize cross flow, manufacturing cells were designed to incorporate all, or nearly all, of the operations in their assigned part families. Encouraged by the success of these two projects, a Group Technology System department was established to advance the technique and make it more accessible to other divisions.

Tom Hein explained the objective of the group at the time.

Group Technology was initially introduced simply because we had a reorganization problem in the plant and GT looked like the way to solve that problem. As we looked at other, related problems, however, the shortcomings of [our initial] system quickly became evident and, in 1978, we began developing our own proprietary GT system. As a starting point, we interviewed approximately 400 engineers throughout the company to determine what types of information about parts they required to do their jobs. The results of this exercise reinforced the idea that a new set of software tools had to be developed.

Fueled by internal demand for help in forming manufacturing cells, the department grew steadily and attracted some of Deere's best engineers. GT team members were also selected from among the region's top-of-the-class engineering students, who were attracted by the firm's stature as a leading edge manufacturer and major employer in the Midwest. Many of these students had advanced engineering degrees and some had obtained MBAs through evening programs, under an educational assistance program sponsored by Deere.

By 1982, the small, strained organization was evidencing a need for additional skills to assist in product development. Rankin was selected to head up the newly reorganized department in the fall of that year. A successful young manager with extensive experience in applying simulation techniques both in the Army and in John Deere's materials management system, Rankin brought an open and participative style of management to the job. He provided the carefully selected members of the department with ample freedom to work on projects they were personally interested in and, whenever possible, made decisions by committee. Following the reorganization (see Exhibit 29.2), and with the intent of establishing the firm as a leader in computer-integrated manufacturing, the newly renamed Computer-Aided Manufacturing Services division moved quickly to develop a range of tools built around the enhanced GT software.

The John Deere Group Technology System

The nature of the set of products that constituted the Deere Group Technology system was elaborated by Tom Hein, manager of software development.

The heart of our package is a classification and coding system designed to capture key geometric characteristics of a part. Working from engineering drawings at a computer terminal, part coders at any one of our factories can input data on new and revised parts through an interactive menu-driven program. The system generates a 35-digit code that acts as a reference to a part's features. In addition to creating the code, our system, unlike other commercially available GT packages, retains complete, detailed,

Exhibit 29.2 CAM Services Organization Chart

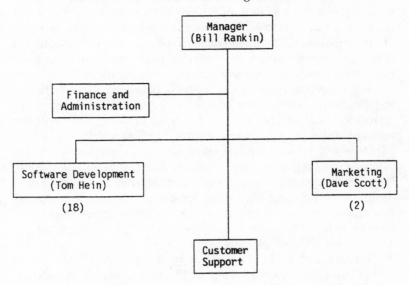

geometric data about the part that can be used routinely for selection and analysis. The system is also designed to access, from other corporate and factory data bases, additional production data, including standard costs, weights, routings, future requirements, etc. for parts.

To analyze this augmented GT data base, we have developed a variety of flexible retrieval and analysis programs that are available to all Deere engineers. The software comprises thirty major programs organized in six modules (see Exhibit 29.3) that variously provide the capability to put data into the system, modify data already in it, isolate groups of parts based on any combination of geometric features and/or production data, and perform statistical, graphical and sensitivity analyses. The system also incorporates a number of sophisticated file management routines . . . and "help" screens containing comprehensive on-line instructions and definitions.

Currently, the system is accessed daily by nearly all of Deere's factories in the United States and Europe, providing reference data for process planning, facilities and capacity planning studies, procurement of machine tools, and to control parts proliferation and assess new manufacturing technologies.

A more specific accounting of the benefits of the GT system was provided by the group's new marketing manager, Dave Scott. "The GT system," Scott said,

. . . has been the key to the firm's movement toward cellular manufacturing and the adoption of just-in-time production concepts. It
has been a major contributing factor in the increased productivity
of our engineers, allowing analyses to be performed that couldn't
even be conceived before its existence. Our tools have been cred-
ited with providing major savings to the corporation.

For example, because our code is based on manufacturing
features, such as holes, threads, splines, and slots, a designer can
go to a terminal and get a listing, in the terminology that he or she
normally thinks in, of all the parts that fit the description of a new
part that's being designed. Several things can happen when this
occurs. First, an existing part might be found that will do the job.
When this happens, besides eliminating the need to create a new
design and the associated downstream paperwork for tooling,
processing, etc., it allows us to exploit economies-of-scale by
increasing the production requirements for the existing part, or to
go to a more efficient process.

I have heard industry estimates, by the way, that the manhour
cost of launching a new part design through tooling, process engineering, and manufacturing is about $11,000. So an up-front
savings of this amount comes every time we avoid a new design.

Exhibit 29.3   The John Deere/Group Technology System
(JD/GTS) Software Package

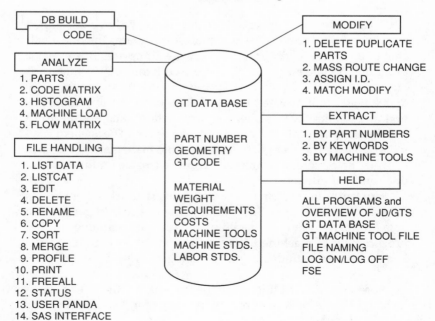

Similar, though I imagine lower, savings are realized when, by modifying an existing design to meet the new part function, we can fit the part into a family and still get the economies of scale. Eventually we might find that a part designed for a product manufactured at one plant is being made at another because it fits into an existing family at that plant.

Perhaps most importantly, though, the GT system has provided a foundation for computer-integrated manufacturing (CIM) at Deere. GT's feature-based representation of parts provides a common neutral "language" to bridge computer-aided design (CAD) and computer-aided manufacturing (CAM), a fundamental requirement for CIM. With our system, the design data base becomes the same base used for manufacturing. What this means is that eventually, instead of trying to create families of parts by design similarities, we can think in terms of families that lend themselves to similar processing.

Computer-aided Process Planning

With GT as an experience base, the group began to develop computerized process planning tools. Process planning was the link between design and manufacturing. It entailed the conversion of design data into manufacturing plans and costs; as Hein had put it, "It's where CAD meets CAM."

A process plan, the specification of the manufacturing operations to be performed in the production of a given part, was developed by a planner who used a blueprint supplied by the designer to decide how each feature should be produced, which machine to use, and what machine settings to apply. Typically in excess of 50% of a company's manufacturing engineering manpower was consumed by this task, which drove all downstream functions. It was usually based on the experience of a few critical people, and yielded inconsistent results.

The logic required to develop an "optimal" process plan was frequently quite complex. The philosophy behind the John Deere Process Planning System (JD/PPS) was to decompose the task into smaller problems, each comprising a module. Thus, a process plan for a part that required turning, milling, and drilling would be developed using three logic modules, one for each of the different tasks. This approach had a number of advantages. One was that the logic of any single module was less complex than that of the whole plan. Another was that efficiency increased when a plan's development could be distributed among several engineers. Finally, developing logic modules for generic classes of operations, and providing a flexible method of integrating the modules, made the system usable in any manufacturing environment.

Two logic modules had already been developed, one for drilling, the other for turning. Hein explained:

Let's say a process engineer wants to drill a hole in 4140 stainless steel. The hole is to be 1/2" diameter and a coolant will be used in the process. The engineer also specifies the machine on which the job is to be done. Having been provided with this information, the JD/PPS system calculates, based on stored information about the capabilities of the particular machine, the most appropriate speed and feed rates for drilling the hole in the specified material. This information allows the engineer to determine what capabilities new equipment should have, and is useful in process design.

We began with these two modules because quite a bit of research had already been done on the processes, providing us with a scientific base of knowledge. Much of production, though, is more art than science, and for these operations the JD/PPS was designed to capture rules used by an "expert." It was here that the modular decomposition feature paid the greatest dividends, since a system engineer could work on a particular process with experts, possibly drawn from different Deere facilities, to develop and maintain logic modules. In addition, the modular structure of the system allowed us to develop and add new modules for new technologies as they became available.

The problem with all of this is the magnitude of the task involved. I estimate it will take another five years before we have a system we're fully satisfied with, and this assumes we'll have the system engineers to work continuously on it. Nevertheless, we feel this is key to Deere being able to fully optimize its manufacturing operations.

Computer-Integrated Manufacturing (CIM)

Group technology and computer-aided process planning provided valuable data and tools for improving communications among the design, planning, and manufacturing functions. "The problem," Hein said,

> is that the language of CAD is geometry based. Data input by the designer is stored by the computer in the form of points and equations that allow lines, arcs, and circles to be combined and displayed to represent a finished part. Interpreting these line diagrams presents a great deal of difficulty for manufacturing, as there the language is based on manufacturable "features."

To provide a communication link between CAD and CAM, the group had begun to develop a feature-oriented part description data base that was a logical extension of the GT data base.

To help resolve its hardware interfacing problems, Deere was the first company to implement a Manufacturing Automated Protocol (MAP) local area network. Scott remarked: "When fully implemented, the MAP network will allow us to simply plug in the computers and hardware for both CAD and CAM systems and be off and running." Following the first MAP installation at the Harvester Works, Deere's CAM systems engineers undertook a number of installations in other facilities.

Flexible Manufacturing Systems (FMS)

The members of the CAM systems group were aware that many of the successes of CIM to date had been achieved by focusing on very narrow families of parts. "Flexible manufacturing systems are effective through similar focusing," Hein had said.

Deere had been one of the first users of FMS technology. Its first system was installed in the Waterloo facility in 1981, when many local firms were just learning of the existence of the technology. In addition, the firm had a number of flexible manufacturing cells in operation at other locations. Its Waterloo installation was perhaps the most publicized American system in the trade journals, and Deere was widely consulted by other firms interested in installing FMSs. As it had been involved in the development and implementation of some of these projects, the CAM systems group had significant experience with the technology.

A Typical Consulting Project

The group's reputation spread rapidly by word of mouth. As news of the results achieved in the reorganizing of the Waterloo manufacturing facility was publicized throughout the decentralized organization, requests for the group's assistance in analyzing and developing reorganization plans for other operating facilities began to come in. The case of the hydraulic cylinder cell was typical.

Hydraulic cylinders were integral components on a wide range of heavy industrial and agricultural equipment such as that manufactured by Deere. They converted fluid power into directed motion to move backhoe arms, and to lift and tilt front end loader and bulldozer blades. (See Exhibit 29.4.) Consistent with its tradition of customer service, the company retained on its active parts list almost every cylinder used in any of its products for the last 50 years.

Traditionally, hydraulic cylinders were manufactured by an unwieldy batch process carried out in a 340 thousand square foot, three-floor factory. The functionally laid out plant suffered from all the shortcomings of batch processes. Lead time for production was long, work in process inventory was enormous, and a large indirect labor pool was employed in machine set-up and teardown, material movement, tool crib attendance, inspection, and maintenance. The need for expediting remained high despite having intro-duced a sophisticated MRP program. Jobs were often very late or even lost.

Exhibit 29.4   The Hydraulic Cylinder

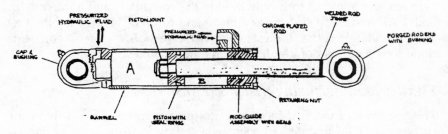

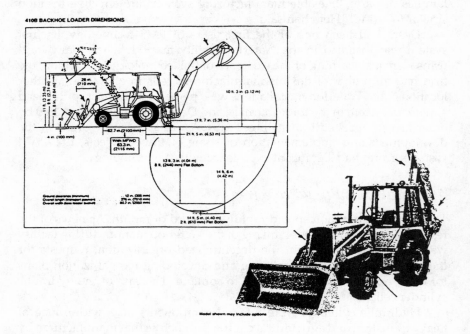

After coding all the cylinders and performing a preliminary analysis, the CAM engineers decided to develop a cell for manufacturing the heavy duty agricultural cylinders. These products constituted a significant portion of the regular production workload and shared common physical and manufacturing characteristics. A few days later, they learned that another CAM engineer was in the middle of a related project to control the proliferation of cylinders by forming design families. While the set of cylinder designs being "standardized" by the group was used primarily in medium-duty industrial equipment, there nevertheless was a considerable overlap in design specifications for the two groups of cylinders.

The industrial and agricultural products that used these cylinders were produced in geographically and organizationally separate facilities. Product designers in one division typically had been unwilling to "compromise" their designs to incorporate components designed for another, even if manufacturing efficiencies would result. This had begun to change as the firm's business environment increased pressure for improved efficiency.

Out of these efforts emerged a new cylinder class—the 120 series— which doubled as a medium duty mobile construction equipment cylinder and a heavy duty agricultural equipment cylinder. Designed for ease of manufacture, these cylinders reflected a greater awareness of the constraints and capabilities of the manufacturing system. For example, a new cylinder design could be quickly developed by selecting the appropriate component from each family, or by modifying a "standard" family design where an appropriate component did not already exist. In either case, the task would be easier than designing a product from scratch, and since all the products would conform, within limits, to a standard design, manufacturing efficiencies would also be achieved.

A manufacturing cell was then developed to produce this new family. Of the 62 machine tools that comprised the cell, 37 were existing machines that had been relocated and 25 were newly acquired. Results of the change are shown in Exhibit 29.5. The part count fell from 405 to 75, and nonstandard parts were eliminated. Manufacturing was rationalized by minimizing the number of product routings. Routing simplification is illustrated in Exhibit 29.6, which compares the barrel routings in the batch process with that in the 120 series cell. The ratio of direct to indirect workers went from 123:50 to 57:1, and all material handling, set-up, and tool changing was done by the direct work force. Two process planners scheduled work through the cell, compared to seven to schedule an equivalent workload through the batch process. Making the work force responsible for inspecting the quality of its own work eliminated the need for roving inspectors. By allowing defects to be identified immediately, this approach facilitated a just-in-time system, in which work pieces moved almost immediately to adjacent workstations.

The manufacturing cell was managed by four supervisors (two on the day shift, one on each of the other shifts), and staffed by two programmers

Exhibit 29.5 Summary Statistics for Modular Manufacturing Implementation

| | GT Cell Cost Reduction | |
	Before	After
Inventory	21 Days	10 days
Material handling	26%	14.5%
Scrap	51%	14% (last 3 months, less than 10%)
Maintenance	36%	22%
Inspection	17%	3%
Crib attendants	17.4%	0%

All costs are stated as a percent of the total direct labor charges/week incurred in the cell.

Exhibit 29.6 Example of Routing Simplification/Standardization

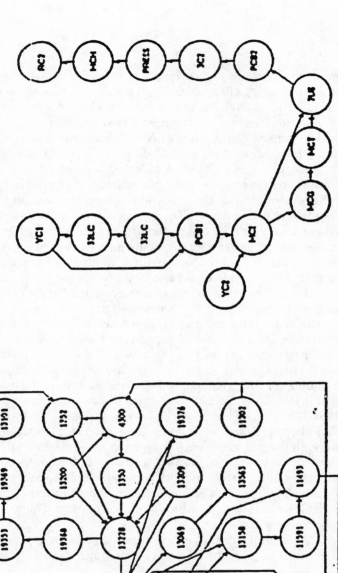

DEPARTMENT 120
BARREL ROUTING

CURRENT BARREL ROUTINGS

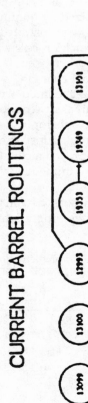

and two engineers. Engineering projects had previously been performed by engineers from a centralized pool who serviced the entire Plow and Planter facility. This limited continuity of interest in a particular project, and substantial delays between identifying needs and implementing projects were common. Under the new approach, as soon as a project was identified one of the engineers immediately became involved. Over time the two engineers developed an intimate knowledge of the system and developed close working relationships with the supervisors. By combining their more scientific perspective with the extensive process experience of the supervisors, who viewed manufacturing as essentially an art, they quickly became "experts" in the specific processes within the cell.

Based on this success, the Plow and Planter Works, in association with the Hydraulic Design division, decided to develop a second cell for manufacturing heavier duty cylinders. Only 38% of the design engineering resources and 8% of the manufacturing engineering resources consumed in the first cell's development were required to develop the second.

Exploiting the Potential

Marketing the group's services within the firm had not been a problem, given its string of successes, and now Rankin, Hein, and Scott contemplated how to exploit Deere's external market. The potential market seemed huge. All three were convinced of the value of their systems and tools and, with the revamping of the U.S. and European industrial bases in response to the competitive threat from the Far East, demand for such services could be enormous. A number of small companies had begun to offer engineering systems software for specific niche markets but, except for some quite sophisticated CAD tools, most of the software was primitive compared to Deere's. The flurry of activity in the area had also attracted a large number of independent consultants into the market.

Deere's excellent position derived from its long involvement and record of success. All Deere systems and software tools were tested internally, and customers could see them in action in Deere facilities. None of the firm's competitors was positioned to offer this kind of "live" demonstration. Consequently, Deere considered all segments of the market open to exploitation. Though estimates of market potential varied widely in the various segments, all were very high and anticipated rapid growth.

Opinions varied on the marketing issue. Scott favored pricing the integrated GT software package at the high end to reflect the inherent quality of the product, and providing training and consulting at cost. Some of the engineers, however, recommended pricing the software low enough to generate quick sales and charging substantially higher rates, commensurate with management consulting fees, for after sales service. Hein also was concerned by what he perceived to be an accelerating shift away from developing new systems toward modifying existing tools for applications outside the metal fabrication industry. He was under pressure from Scott, for example, to allocate some resources to the development of a new code structure for the GT system that would make it applicable to the electronics industry. Rankin, however, felt that marketing, at least initially, should be concentrated in the metal fabrication industry to allow engineering resources to be focused on projects directly relevant to the firm's own operation. This, he believed, would make it easier to leverage Deere's huge experience and parts base.

Earlier in the year, Brian Rugh, one of Rankin's engineers, had demonstrated some of the newer GT tools at a Deere operation in France. When Rugh keyed in from a product blueprint the dimensions of a part used by the French plant, the system generated a list of 15 parts used at the Dubuque facility that fit the criteria. Keying in another feature of the part reduced the number to three. Rugh had then called up the tools, routing, production plan, and standard hours involved in the manufacture of one of the parts and from these calculated its cost. This experience had convinced both Rugh and Rankin that the 200,000 part number data base already coded and residing in the company's computer was a potentially marketable resource that could easily be augmented with data on customer products. A number of uses could be made of this database. A client interested in analyzing cell arrangements for the production of a family of parts, for example, could use the database to extract illustrative costs and production times for a similar set of parts, thereby significantly reducing the data collection required.

About another possibility, Rankin was less sure. The depressed state of the firm's core business coupled with the success of its "reorganizing" and "refocusing" projects had left many of Deere's manufacturing facilities (including the Cylinder plant at the Plow and Planter Works) with excess capacity. With the high overheads they had to carry, some of the division managers had begun manufacturing related products for outside consumption. Rankin suspected that the knowledge of firms' needs obtained through his group's sales and consulting activities could be exploited by matching those needs with the capabilities of Deere facilities. The CAM Systems group, inasmuch as it controlled the common data base for the entire firm, might serve as a broker for this service.

However, the most important contribution his group could make, he believed, was in improving Deer's ability to keep abreast of the latest advances in production technology. New processes and techniques were appearing with greater frequency. In order to exploit them for competitive advantage it would be necessary to learn about them as soon as they appeared, and to capture this knowledge in a form that would make it more widely available within Deere. As its engineers provided consulting services to other firms, they would be able to identify new technologies and gain access to the knowledge of the experts in these new processes. Rankin wondered what long-term impact this might have on Deere.

CHAPTER 30

Micom Caribe (A)

You'll never be where you think you are if you stay where you are.
—Tom Moschetti,[1] Micom Caribe Plant Manager

"WE HAVE A QUALITY PROBLEM with the Micom Box," came the accusatory voice from corporate offices in California.
"What's the problem?" asked Tom Moschetti.
"It's a quality problem," the voice responded tautly, "you people down there just need to get it fixed!"

Though only a memory by January 1991, calls like these had so bombarded Micom Caribe (Caribe), the Puerto Rican manufacturing facility for Micom Communications Corporation (MCC), that their echoes still resounded in Moschetti's ears. Quality problems had plagued the 1987 introduction of the Micom Box, and the tantalizing ambiguity of these "quality problems" had compelled Caribe[2] to develop an entirely different manufacturing operation.

This new structure had been a great success. The latest MCC product introduction—perhaps the most important in company history—would finally give Caribe the chance to demonstrate its newfound quality and flexibility.

While the plant was consumed with the new product launch, Moschetti and the rest of the steering committee debated how Caribe should chart a strategy to build on its emerging capabilities—and at last weld manufacturing firmly into MCC's competitive strategy.

Micom Caribe

Micom Caribe, the only manufacturing facility of Micom Communications Corporation, bought components, assembled them into circuit boards, and

---

[1]Pronounced *Mosketti.*

[2]Pronounceld *Kah-ree-bay.*

Professor David Upton and Research Associate Joshua Margolis prepared this case as the basis for class discussion rather than as an illustration of either effective or ineffective handling of an administrative situation.

Exhibit 30.1 Map of Puerto Rico

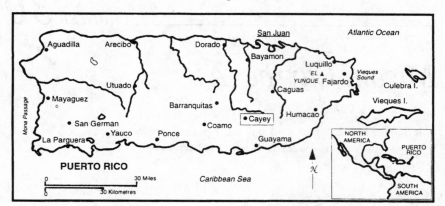

manufactured MCC products using those boards and other purchased components (power sources and outer casings, for example).

Caribe first began operating in 1981 when the plant opened fittingly in April, Puerto Rico's Month of Industry. As sales grew from $1.5 million in 1982 to $23.6 million in 1990, Caribe moved from an original space of 11,000 square feet to a 75,000 square-foot facility, both provided by Puerto Rico's Economic Development Administration. Located in the town of Cayey, 45 minutes from San Juan, the plant employed 214 people. (See Exhibit 30.1 for map of Puerto Rico.)

Micom Communications Corporation (MCC)

Although based in Simi Valley, California, Micom Communications Corporation could have come straight from the pages of a Silicon Valley success story. Founded in 1973, MCC had been a world pioneer in the data communications industry. Its products connected many different types of data and communications equipment using one "box" rather than a complex system, which reduced communications costs. This box, filled with circuit boards, took information and concentrated it so it could travel easily between pieces of equipment. The Micro800 Data Concentrator, for example, connected remote users to a host computer, creating wide-area networks (WAN); MCC's other major product, INSTANET, created local-area networks (LAN) by connecting personal computers, work stations, data terminals, and mainframe computers located within a building or campus.

MCC made its first public stock offering in 1981, the same year it moved manufacturing to Puerto Rico. In 1988 Odyssey Partners, a private investment firm, acquired the company in a leveraged buy-out (LBO). Through three sets of ownership, MCC continued to concentrate on simple, full-featured products in a market dominated by expensive, complicated equipment.

Customers and Competitors

MCC had over 400 customers. Sixty percent of sales came from independent distributors and 40% from original equipment manufacturers (OEMs) who incorporated MCC products into equipment that they assembled and sold. IBM and AT&T were MCC's two largest OEM customers, but others included Digital Equipment Corporation, Prime Computer, Sun, and Hewlett-Packard.

In August 1989 MCC shipped its 200,000th multiplexor, a total that surpassed all competitors' sales combined.[3] But constant innovation and rapid change characterized the entire computer and communications industry—and was becoming faster as time went on. Fleeting market dominance would not secure MCC's future.

Puerto Rico, MCC and Manufacturing

Since 1898, Puerto Rico had been affiliated with the United States, first as a colony and then as a free associated commonwealth. Situated in the Caribbean Sea, Puerto Rico covered 3,435 square miles,[4] roughly two-thirds the size of Connecticut. With a population of 3.3 million in 1988, Puerto Rico had a density of 951 people per square mile, compared to 70 for the United States mainland.[5]

Operation Bootstrap

When Spanish forces conquered Puerto Rico in the early 1500s, they introduced sugar cane and used African slaves and native Taino Indians to work the fields. Until the 1940s, sugar remained the island's main economic product. But in 1942 the government of Puerto Rico initiated "Operation Bootstrap," a self-help program designed to improve the standard of living by attracting industrial development to the island. By 1985 manufacturing comprised 39% of the gross domestic product, making it the single largest sector, while agriculture comprised just 2%. The administrative body known as Fomento ("development") managed the industrialization effort and included two organizations. The Economic Development Administration (EDA) promoted industrial projects, reaching out to foreign investors and coordinating all necessary activity and

[3]Richard S. Borden, "Micom Communications Corporation: Corporate Backgrounder."

[4]8,897 square kilometers.

[5]Puerto Rico's population density: 1,531 per square kilometer. U.S. population density: 111 per square kilometer.

resources. The Puerto Rico Industrial Development Company (PRIDCO) actually constructed physical facilities and offered cash incentives to participating companies. PRIDCO built 99 industrial parks, including the one in which Micom Caribe operated. PRIDCO provided inexpensive leases (as low as $0.25 per square foot in 1990) and offered cash incentives for leasehold improvements, employee training, and start up costs.[6]

Section 936

A second component of Puerto Rico's rapid development revolved around Section 936 of the U.S. Internal Revenue Code: with certain stipulations, all profits earned in Puerto Rico were not subject to federal tax. The government of Puerto Rico supplemented those tax incentives with its own exemptions from commonwealth and local taxes.[7]

Progress and Potential

From a one-crop economy at mid-century, Puerto Rico emerged to become the hub of industrial activity in the Caribbean Basin. Life expectancy in the 1940s was just 46, but by the mid-1970s it reached 72, on a par with that of the U.S. mainland. Net income per capita had grown from $121 in 1940 to $4,200 in 1985. Although that paled in comparison to the U.S. figure of $14,565, Puerto Rico's cumulative economic growth between 1985 and 1989 (16.4%) surpassed that of the United States (14.5%). Gross domestic product hit $30 billion in 1990 and gross national product reached $21 billion.[8]

Puerto Rico's economic affairs and political status were intimately connected well beyond the ramifications of special tax privileges, and Micom Caribe reflected their relationship. Just as the economy as a whole depended largely on exports to the U.S. and on tax privileges accorded by the U.S. government, individual firms recapitulated this relationship. MCC initially situated a plant on Puerto Rico as a tax haven for its most profitable products. MCC leased a plant built by PRIDCO and enjoyed

[6]Jonathan Goldman, "Puerto Rico," *Institutional Investor,* December 1990. Government Development Bank for Puerto Rico. *1990 Annual Report.* Puerto Rico Industrial Development Company, *1987 Annual Report* and *1990 Annual Report.*

[7]Jonathan Goldman, "Puerto Rico," *Institutional Investor,* December 1990.

[8]Gross domestic product (GDP) calculates the output of production attributable to all labor and property located in the commonwealth. Gross national product (GNP) calculates the output of production attributable to entities owned by citizens of the commonwealth. Because U.S. companies owned many of the businesses on Puerto Rico, GDP for Puerto Rico was higher than GNP. Earl Parker Hanson, Puerto Rico, *Encyclopedia Americana,* 1990 ed. The Economist Intelligence Unit, *Cuba, Dominican Republic, Haiti, Puerto Rico: Country Report* (London, England: Economist Intelligence Unit, 1990). No. 1 Jonathan Goldman, "Puerto Rico," *Institutional Investor,* December 1990. *Information Please Almanac, Atlas, and Yearbook* (Boston, MA: Houghton, Mifflin Company, 1991). Bureau of the Census, *Statistical Abstract of the United States, 1990* (Washington, D.C.: U.S. Department of Commerce, 1990). 110th edition. The Economist, *The World in Figures* (London, England: The Economist Publications, Ltd., 1987). Commonwealth of Puerto Rico, *Public Improvement Bonds of 1991.*

reduced leases and handsome tax exemptions. But Caribe had developed into an expert manufacturing facility, one whose products generated 95% of the parent company's revenues.

Despite all of Micom Caribe's advantages and accomplishments, like Puerto Rico itself the plant still labored under a disparity in status, only part of which could be attributed to the very real facts of economic dependency. It was a widely held view that culturally ingrained attitudes on both sides of the ocean had to be considered significant. One manager at Micom Caribe, a native of Puerto Rico and a long-time veteran of Micom Caribe, echoed the views of many at the plant:

> Most Puerto Rican plants are treated like sub-contractors of U.S. firms, and they see themselves that way. There's a mentality of colonialism. "The gringos arrived, and we must bow to them." U.S. firms are the fathers, the only people with right and reason, no one else.
>
> Micom Caribe began as a child to MCC. The message was clear from California: "We are to teach. You are to follow." We've done something different than the parent company, though. We joke that we decolonized the island.
>
> We may never be free of the U.S. belief that we have not advanced. Any little thing that happens between MCC corporate and Micom Caribe gets exaggerated. Our doubt is always there that they will not see we have made a lot of progress. Bleeding was there—their approach left wounds—so any time a problem arises, it bleeds a little.

Puerto Ricans filled over 90% of all management positions within the U.S., European, and Japanese factories on the island,[9] and all managers and directors at Micom Caribe except Moschetti were native Puerto Ricans. Nonetheless, industry as a whole in Puerto Rico, and Micom Caribe as one example, struggled with the legacy of what Puerto Rico continued to confront politically: making real the 1953 ruling by the United Nations that Puerto Rico was no longer a colony.

Manufacturing Operations

At first, MCC intended to produce only high-volume, stable products in its Caribe facility—that is, those products simple to manufacture. But like the historical evolution of Puerto Rican industry, Caribe became a highly skilled plant, gradually supplanting other MCC facilities in the United States, Mexico, and Singapore—each originally vaunted for its superior technology, worker training, and/or lower wages. Caribe proved itself

[9]Jonathan Goldman, "Puerto Rico," *Institutional Investor*, December 1990.

more effective and more profitable, before taxes, than any of the other MCC plants. MCC had initially wanted Caribe to account for no more than 30% of gross revenues, but by 1990 Caribe products generated 95% of MCC revenues. Plant Manager Tom Moschetti underscored the significance of the plant's accomplishments: "MCC is now in Puerto Rico not because of taxes but because we at Caribe are the most efficient and effective organization."

Understanding, Learning, and Quality

> We have to ensure that operators do not see themselves as victims
> of the factory.
>
> —Tom Moschetti

Accusatory phone calls and customer complaints had made the Micom Box problem the critical turning point in the plant's development. Until 1987, Micom Caribe had operated more or less as a manufacturing service to the California-based engineering and marketing groups. MCC designed the products and provided the stream of innovations which had been the traditional source of its competitive edge. Caribe's job was simply to manufacture the product—to take the specifications and to build in quantity. MCC saw manufacturing as a matter of simply keeping machines running and meeting delivery dates. There was little dialogue between design engineers and the plant.

The structure of MCC's Puerto Rican manufacturing facility had reflected the subsidiary role of manufacturing in MCC's competitive strategy. Like many similar plants in Puerto Rico, Caribe had been set up to hit budgets and deadlines by tightly controlling costs and schedules. This had been achieved through an infrastructure based on a strictly hierarchical organization and through a direct labour force trained to do only one task well. Coordination and scheduling were carried out by "pushing" work onto the floor, while quality systems relied on traditional techniques such as Acceptable Quality Levels (AQL) and inspection. Caribe was little different from hundreds of other plants in Puerto Rico: traditional, static and hierarchical—designed to provide low cost over a stable range of products. Then, in 1987, came the Micom Box.

The Micom Box

The Micom Box differed from the manufacturing Caribe had been accustomed to: it was much more exacting of the manufacturing process. In addition, the schedule for introducing the Micom Box was more aggressive than Caribe was used to—reflecting the need of MCC to serve the quickening pace of innovation in the industry. While its function was very similar to the previous generation of devices, the Micom Box was based on a novel modular electronic design, which made it easy to configure to a wide variety of applications. To distinguish the Micom Box from the products of its increasingly innovative competitors, MCC's new managers focused on its quality, touting the product as the company's best ever—as the one device that would satisfy all customer needs for connecting computer and communication equipment. MCC promoted the Micom Box as "*the* quality product."

Customers awaited the "quality" product they had heard so much about, yet what they received instead, they told sales representatives, was not quality. Complaints deluged MCC. Moschetti recalled the confusion and frustration Caribe experienced. "Customers were using the language MCC had given them. They expected quality, and they were telling the company, 'This isn't a quality product.' But that was a marketing term, not an operations term." Accusations within MCC amplified intense customer complaints as all fingers pointed to the plant. It took Caribe six months to locate the origin of the problem. "We realized then that none of us—engineering, marketing or manufacturing—knew what quality meant," recalled Moschetti.

As MCC lost market share, Caribe scrambled to fix the problem. MCC's new president and his management team knew little about manufacturing and provided no guidance. Edwin Franceschi, Caribe's director of technical services commented: "The information being provided by Marketing wasn't of any use. They didn't know how to communicate in a way that would help us pin-point the manufacturing problems. By the time we had figured out what the problem was, a new one had appeared. We just couldn't seem to get feedback fast enough, or in the right form."

The plant was running out of fingers to put in the dike. It was time for a radical change of approach. Although Moschetti had worked under six different vice presidents in six years, he realized this situation was different. "I always expected corporate to provide leadership. It's easy to do what others tell you to do. But now the people above me knew nothing about manufacturing and assumed it was just about 'running the equipment', so I had to go out and learn what we should do." Caribe could no longer survive by fighting intermittent fires without ever really tracking down their sources; it had to learn more about its own manufacturing operation and why things went awry.

Zen and the Art of Operations Strategy

From his days as a student, Moschetti had been fascinated by eastern philosophy and, in particular, by Zen Buddhism. As Caribe delved beneath the symptoms of its manufacturing ignorance, Moschetti drew on the Zen notion of Ka, acceptance of the unknown. He explained the orientation it suggested: "The relationship of the things I know is a tiny piece of the universe. The relationship of things I don't know is Ka. Knowing and respecting what you don't know is an asset."

As Caribe concentrated on improving production of the Micom Box, Moschetti also mapped out a long-term plan to change the plant's fundamental approach to manufacturing. He wanted to remove the mystery behind quality and provide people with the knowledge they would need to manufacture flawless products. He wanted employees to concentrate on how they were doing what they were doing rather than on a particular goal they were trying to achieve, and to realize that it was good to negotiate and experiment; that it was good to ask questions and not just blindly follow standard procedures; that it was even OK to fail.

Participation and democracy lay at the heart of his plans to manufacture better products. Operators had to contribute (see Exhibit 30.2). Employees had long been told, at least tacitly, that they were incapable of making decisions on their own; Moschetti even wondered whether they would have sufficient confidence in their own abilities. Managers had to accept participation and needed to share authority and responsibility. Caribe's metamorphosis would require managers to encourage non-managers to offer ideas for improvement. The people actually putting the products together knew the most about the process; they therefore were most likely to have the best ideas for improvement, reasoned Moschetti, and it was management's responsibility to elicit contributions.

Exhibit 30.2   Carmen Olmeda—An Assembly Operator

Moschetti had a strong belief in the plant, but knew he would have to take specific actions to put in place an infrastructure in which improvement could flourish and become the natural way of doing things. To set up an environment conducive to this he initially set about making changes in the following areas:

- Encouraging senior managers to concentrate on developing a manufacturing strategy
- Increasing middle management responsibility
- Providing tools for quality improvement
- Installing manufacturing cells and teams, and
- Introducing cross-training of direct labour.

Getting middle managers to take responsibility would be difficult, since they tended to rely on the directors to guide them in running the plant. The directors were equally loath to give up their perceived responsibility of managing the plant, despite the need for them to be free to concentrate on longer-term strategic issues. While a firm believer in direct, honest approaches to management, this problem forced Moschetti to resort to subterfuge.

Managing Middle Management

Efforts to expand involvement began in early 1987 with the second tier of managers: ten people who comprised the plant's operating committee and reported to the directors of each function (see Exhibit 30.3). This operating committee was set up to manage the day-to-day running of the plant. However, it soon became clear that the steering committee, composed of the functional directors, had either refused or were finding it difficult to relinquish de facto control. The plant's directors were called to a conference in New Orleans with MCC management, and Moschetti deviously asked his directors who would run the plant, since they had previously insisted that the managers were not qualified. Everyone involved knew they had only one option: leave the plant in the managers' hands. With daily telephone conversations between New Orleans and Cayey, managers proved more than capable. From then on the operating committee took control of daily operations, freeing the steering committee to chart policy and attend to the plant's strategy for the future.

By 1990 the ten members of the Operating Committee met every day from 3:30 until 5:00 to discuss issues of mutual concern—everything from unexpected surges in orders to equipment assessment. "We came with the impression," one member commented, "of 'why waste an hour and a half when we have better things to do?' But we learned that only by extending our view of what a company does could we broaden our abilities to

Exhibit 30.3   Organization Chart

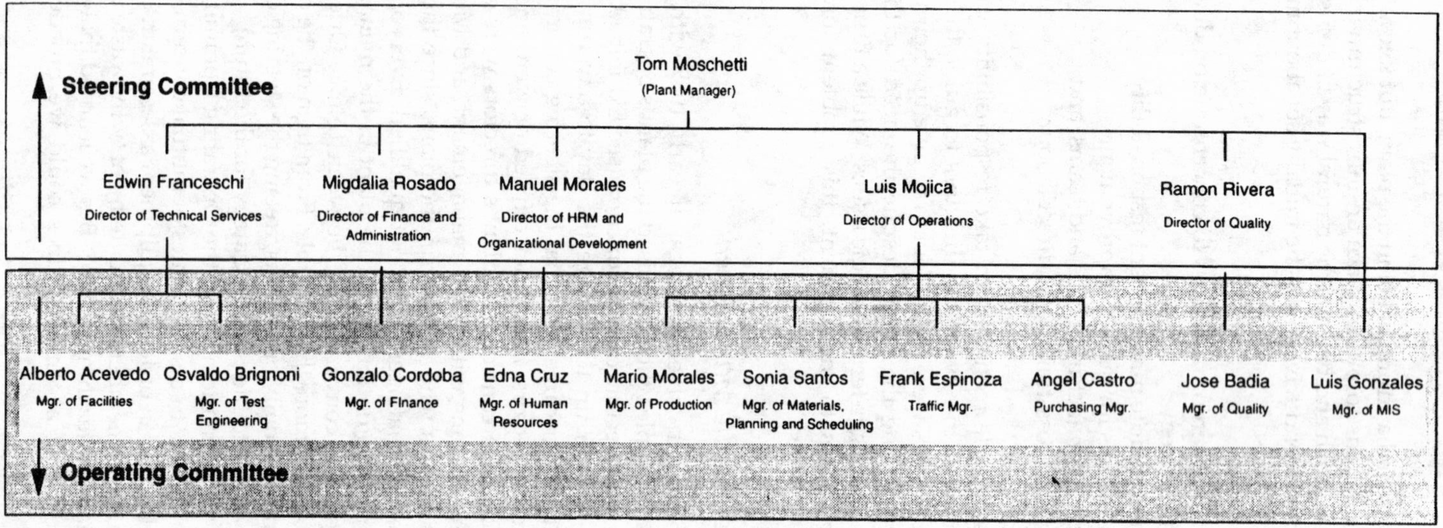

Tom Moschetti
(Plant Manager)

Steering Committee

Edwin Franceschi	Migdalia Rosado	Manuel Morales	Luis Mojica	Ramon Rivera
Director of Technical Services	Director of Finance and Administration	Director of HRM and Organizational Development	Director of Operations	Director of Quality

Operating Committee

Alberto Acevedo	Osvaldo Brignoni	Gonzalo Cordoba	Edna Cruz	Mario Morales	Sonia Santos	Frank Espinoza	Angel Castro	Jose Badia	Luis Gonzales
Mgr. of Facilities	Mgr. of Test Engineering	Mgr. of Finance	Mgr. of Human Resources	Mgr. of Production	Mgr. of Materials, Planning and Scheduling	Traffic Mgr.	Purchasing Mgr.	Mgr. of Quality	Mgr. of MIS

perform in our function." Their knowledge had broadened to such an extent—in part because committee leadership rotated—that Gonzalo Cordova, accounting manager in finance, had accepted additional responsibility as a manager of production control in the operations department.

Each manager on the operating committee had been accustomed to making decisions on his or her own, based only on his or her expertise. Although it had taken the group several years to coalesce, they did indeed feel comfortable working together to run the plant. One member commented, "Divergent views rather than convergent views bring us together." Another member put it simply, "We fight a lot." Noted one member, "It's more natural to ask your people to work in teams if you set the example. You're more familiar with the conflicts and pressures."

Tools for Quality Improvement

To weave quality into the fabric of the plant's ongoing operation, Moschetti, Manuel Morales, director of human resources, and Ramon Rivera, director of quality assurance, investigated quality programs and chose Philip Crosby's Quality Improvement Process (QIP). Although only one of many quality schemes popular among corporations, and though criticized by some, the Crosby approach appealed to Caribe because it was easy to understand, fitting, and came in the form of a product on which everyone could be trained. Crosby's system featured a gradual process for imparting sensitivity to quality, with 14 steps carefully mapped out. (See Exhibit 30.4 for Crosby's 14 steps.) Crosby stressed the importance of fundamental changes in a plant's culture, which coincided with Caribe's own intentions. Crosby's QIP aimed at involving everyone at the plant—just what Moschetti sought—but followed traditional paths of authority to get there, which conformed with Caribe's culture at the time.

Crosby preached that quality could not be described in relative terms: quality standards had to reflect market requirements; either a product conformed to those standards or it did not; either the product had quality, or it did not; products could not be said to be better or worse in quality. In Crosby's system, quality could be measured by adding up the costs of all activities that could be eliminated if products were produced without problems. By using zero defects as a principle, rather than a slogan, Crosby believed people would see the folly of tolerating a percentage of errors. Instead they would search for ways to make products correctly to begin with. Just as people do not expect doctors and nurses to drop a certain percentage of babies delivered, neither should they expect a certain percentage of products to be damaged. Companies, he argued, should find ways to make the manufacturing process work correctly.[10]

---

[10]Philip B. Crosby, *Quality Is Free: The Art of Making Quality Certain* (New York: McGraw-Hill Book Company, 1979). Philip B. Crosby, *Quality Without Tears: The Art of Hassle-Free Management* (New York: McGraw-Hill Book Company, 1984).

Exhibit 30.4   Steps of the Crosby Quality Improvement Process

1.	Management Commitment	8.	Supervisor Training
2.	Quality Improvement Team	9.	Zero Defects Day
3.	Quality Measurement	10.	Goal Setting
4.	Cost of Quality Evaluation	11.	Error Cause Removal
5.	Quality Awareness	12.	Recognition
6.	Corrective Action	13.	Quality Councils
7.	Committee on the Zero Defects Program	14.	Do It Over Again[a]

[a]Philip B. Crosby, *Quality Is Free: The Art of Making Quality Certain* (New York: McGraw Hill Book Company. 1979). Philip B. Crosby. *Quality Without Tears: The Art of Hassle-Free Management* (New York: McGraw-Hill Book Company, 1984)

Caribe followed Crosby's approach, first eliciting senior plant management's commitment to quality, then establishing an infrastructure for recognizing problems with quality, and finally imparting techniques and mechanisms for identifying and solving problems. Directors and managers formed the Quality Improvement Team (QIT), which set and managed a master plan. The QIT appointed a chairperson for each of Crosby's steps, and that person would then recruit a team to implement the step. Quality assurance engineers at the plant trained production operators in the fundamental steps and tools of collecting information about problems, using statistical process control, and taking corrective action.

For the first time in Caribe's history, directors alone were not setting policy. Even more important, the QIP embraced every layer of the organization; everyone from floor workers to Moschetti became equipped with skills and mechanisms for introducing changes. The QIP sanctioned any change, suggested by anyone, if it improved quality. Process performance measures were developed to monitor each change and provide evidence for the value of a changed process. This reinforced the importance of contributions from anyone at the plant, finally making real Moschetti's aim of worker involvement.

Manufacturing Cells

Caribe had initially configured manufacturing in a rigid line and relied on automatic conveyors to transport material from station to station. But in 1987 Caribe swapped automated sizzle for flexible cells and cross-training. The plant was re-organized into 15 cells: 2 sequential cells for sub-assembly, 12 product-oriented cells for assembly and 1 cell for special testing. Each cell had from five to eight people, who worked together as a team— rather than as peas in a pod, as they had previously. (See Exhibit 30.5 for the revised plant layout.)

For sub-assembly, workers in the insertion cell inserted components

Exhibit 30.5 Micom Caribe Plant Layout in 1990

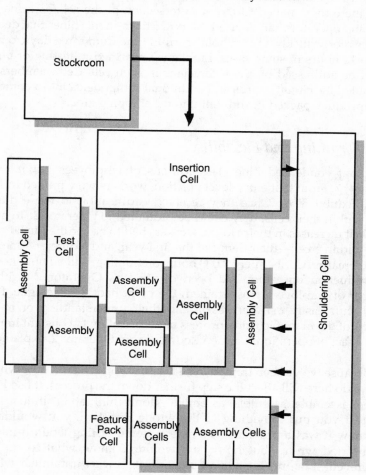

into circuit boards. Then the boards moved to the soldering cell, where they went through the wave-soldering machine.[11] Members of the soldering cell then cut the circuit boards into the different shapes needed for MCC products and prepared the boards for further assembly.

In the 12 assembly cells, completed circuit boards were made into MCC's finished products. When the boards came out of sub-assembly, they went to a U-shaped cell dedicated to one particular type of product. All other parts peculiar to the cell's products were gathered from the stockroom as needed.

---

[11]In a wave soldering machine, the circuit board traveled above a bath of molten metal about 6 inches long and 18 inches wide. A paddle pushed waves of the metal down the bath, lightly soaking the board and thereby soldering the inserted components in place.

Once in a cell, circuit boards went through an initial functional test. From there they moved to the burn-in section of the cell.[12] Caribe engineers and operators had devised their own burn-in machines that detected failures more quickly and cut total burn-in time from three days to two—and to 12 hours in some cases. Problems unearthed in testing or burn-in would be addressed by the technicians in each cell. Cell members then assembled the circuit boards and additional components into a completed MCC product, packed it, and sent it to the shipping area.

Cross-Training and Flexibility

The plant condensed nine classifications of employees down to one, Operator 1. From that entry-level position, workers were trained in 12 key skills (Exhibit 30.6). Once they received certification in those different areas within their cells, they could be promoted to Operator 2. To qualify for merit increases in their wages, workers had to be certified in 80% of all skills within a cell—their own cell the first year, and a different one every year thereafter. Caribe spent 7,000 hours on training, and all but one of the 90 production operators had been certified as Operator 2. With that number of employees cross-trained, the plant had become agile. People could shift easily between tasks, and their understanding of multiple aspects of the manufacturing process made attention to constant improvement a fact of operation. Carmen Rodríguez, an Operator 2, explained:

> Because we've been trained in all areas, we understand how what we do here will affect the step further down the process. It used to be, assemble, assemble, assemble—don't think about it, just do it. If you put something in the wrong direction, you wouldn't know it was a problem. The person doing testing would find it inserted wrong, but he or she wouldn't know what to do to prevent it happening again because testers were unfamiliar with prior processes.

Under a traditional manufacturing system, such as an assembly line, the absence of one person could disrupt the entire line. Because Caribe workers were trained in many processes, workers could easily be shifted among tasks to accommodate the most subtle of changes and thereby balance all steps of the process. Although this also made Caribe workers attractive to other firms, Caribe enjoyed a 4% turnover rate, 2% below the industry standard in Puerto Rico. By 1989, Caribe had built one of the most agile plants on the island.

---

[12]Circuit boards experienced a high rate of failure in the initial hours and days of their use. Manufacturers of any equipment involving circuit boards therefore ran their products for several days in a process known as "burn-in," which eliminated all faulty units and moved the products past the initial period of high failure.

Exhibit 30.6 Components of Operator Certification

1. Material Handling
2. Mechanical Skills
3. Document Interpretation
4. Packing Skills
5. Quality Criteria in Metal Parts
6. Soldering Skills
7. Testing and Procedure Interpretation
8. Machine Operator Skills
9. Group Concept Training and Problem Solving Skills
10. Quality Awareness
11. Self Inspection
12. Safety Awareness

Hurricane Hugo. Hurricane Hugo lashed Puerto Rico at the most inopportune time for Micom Caribe. Under new ownership, MCC was rebounding from several disappointing years. To reinforce the company's renewed vigor, management offered a gain-sharing program that depended upon meeting certain revenue and profit goals. Initial distributions were to come in October 1989. The expected bonuses had created a sense of euphoria throughout the company.

MCC was on the verge of achieving the prescribed goal, and pressure was mounting on the plant. The sales had been made, and the orders were set to hit Caribe during the final week of September. But Hurricane Hugo hit first. The factory was completely disabled. Some MCC managers in California had all along doubted that Caribe could achieve the target. "We've done our jobs," Moschetti recalled hearing, "they won't do theirs." Even those who had faith in the plant now knew the hurricane would impede its efforts.

Communication lines were all down, and a week's delay existed in relaying information. Sales orders could not reach the plant. Raw materials could not be delivered because the airport had been closed. When Caribe finally received the sales orders, the plant faced a stack of orders for the Micom Box. The cell that assembled the Micom Box simply lacked the capacity to meet the orders.

Spontaneously, operators from other cells designed a second Micom Box cell. That same afternoon, the new cell—staffed by engineers, secretaries, maintenance technicians, and manufacturing operators from other cells—began producing Micom Boxes. Caribe made its shipments, MCC achieved its targets, and everyone in the company received the promised bonus. Caribe had proven itself capable, building credibility and trust with corporate management. In addition, operators had built confidence in the system and a deeper trust began to develop between workers and managers. With the tools to improve quality and the confidence and desire to do so, quality began to spread through the plant like a flame in a tinder box. The Process Improvement Teams were the spark to the flame.

Improvement Spreads: the Process Improvement Teams

Caribe continued to move methodically through the 14 steps of Crosby's system, and in the autumn of 1989 every cell formed its own Process Improvement Team (PIT), the fundamental rubric of the quality improvement process. Cell members would meet to identify problems, discuss ways to solve them, and track their progress. Gerardo Batista, an Operator 2 certified in two different cells, described the radical change PITs and the whole quality process had made: "Before, employees couldn't have insights. They did not matter to Micom. But now I know that if my idea is good, it will be adopted." Rafael Rios, a manager for human resources, commented on the metamorphosis he had witnessed.

> People in manufacturing used to be treated like children. They were given everything in their hand, and they expected everything. Caribe used to go out of its way to be parental: 'Let me make the decision for you.' Now people are solving problems on their own.

Every cell had a simple chart printed on an 8 1/2 × 11 sheet of paper: the corrective action sheet. Cell members kept track of every problem they encountered as soon as it arose. Six columns detailed the status of each problem. The first column named the problem; the second defined the problem; the third listed the quick-fix (the temporary solution); the fourth listed the cause, once discovered; the fifth column gave the corrective action (the solution addressing the underlying cause); and the final column detailed any later follow-up (see Exhibit 30.7).

Negotiation and Experimentation

Moschetti succinctly characterized the plant's approach to quality: "While we have learned that quality for us is 'conformance to requirements,' we have also realized that the goal of quality is customer satisfaction, and the customer is the next operation." Every step in the manufacturing process was defined as a customer of prior steps and a supplier for future steps. Whoever found a problem had to take responsibility for solving it, which meant finding the source of the problem, physically getting together with the people responsible for that process, and solving the problem.

Exhibit 30.7 Corrective Action Report

CUSTOMER	SALES ORDER	PROBLEM DEFINITION	QUICK FIX	ROOT CAUSE
MST	6852	Customer received incorrect product.	Packer w/o training was replaced. Shipping audit was performed.	- Lack of awareness in some personnel. - Part numbers stocked in the same location.
BLACK BOX	65893	Customer received incomplete order.	Personal awareness.	- Shipping audit not performed in some cases. - Lack of awareness in some personnel.
BLACK BOX	65893	Customer received correct product with incorrect label.	New personnel were trained for rush periods. Shipping audit was performed.	- Not trained personnel at assembly areas in rush periods. - Inspection and sampling plans not followed by production personnel.
HEWLETT-PACKARD	58736	Customer received incorrect product.	Shipping audit was performed.	- Shipping inspection not performed in some cases.
AQUILA	67568	Customer received incomplete order.	Audit at shipping area. Physical inventory performed in the cell for this part number.	- Lack of awareness in some personnel. - Some doubts due to new product.

Prepared by Lucy Guerrero.

Whenever an operator learned of a problem, he or she had to address the problem, just as a supplier would.

Caribe employees were encouraged to look for solutions through knowledge, negotiation, and experimentation. When a quality problem arose, those affected by it in the downstream step had to be precise about their problem. Operators had to define precisely what they needed from their "supplier" and why, so their suppliers could meet those needs. Once the objectives were understood, both supplier and customer had to work together to determine together whether they had the technical knowledge necessary to reach the objective. If they lacked knowledge, they both had to experiment until they found a solution.

Negotiation and experimentation formed the plant's common language, replacing traditional talk of action items and results. "When most people face a problem, they think they know where they're going and exactly how to get there," Moschetti observed. "But we learned you cannot do that with quality—so much of the difficulty is a result of the absence of knowledge." Improving quality meant accepting that absence and working through it. If people encountered a problem with quality, they had to explore why it arose: What did they not know about "customer" needs? What requirements had to be clarified for "suppliers"? What technical knowledge did they lack that caused the problem to arise? How could they acquire that knowledge? Only by engaging these questions could they actually move to a point of knowing what they wanted to do and how to do it. People began to accept that questioning, learning and changing were a normal part of their job. As Moschetti put it, "The only way to get there is to get out of thinking you're there."

An Example of the Quality Improvement Process: The Feature Pack Cell

MCC's Feature Pack was a small rectangular device the size of a candy bar that enhanced the capabilities of MCC's multiplexors. The Feature Pack production cell looked like every other cell in the plant—except for the blue and silver Micom Caribe banner hanging overhead. The U-shaped cell area had a corrective action sheet and two flip charts (giant pads of paper on easels): one tracing the ongoing work done by the cell's PIT; the other, hanging at the cell's entrance, listing the questions the cell had for engineers—a list engineers roaming through the plant would check.

Like all other PITs in the plant, when the Feature Pack team held their first meeting, cell members listed all of the problems that prevented them from doing their jobs effectively or resulted in defective products. These were listed on a flip chart, and then each team member assigned a rating, from one to five, to each problem. The team tallied scores and ranked the 19 major problems they had identified. The team chose 12 problems to address first, from a lack of tools to inadequate visual aids—problems common to many PIT lists.

After culling these "vital few" impediments most responsible for their quality problems, the team gathered data about each impediment: how it hindered them, how it affected their work, how often it occurred. They probed for the root cause, experimented with solutions, and sought support from the plant's engineers when necessary. For example, the team worked with the manufacturing engineers to develop succinct, clear visual aids (diagrams) in colour for any of the cell members to follow when assembling the Feature Pack. When asked what people did before the visual aids had been available, the only operator formerly responsible for assembly pointed to her head and remarked, "If I wasn't here, no one could do the work." Now the five members of the cell produced 1,500 Feature Packs every month, and as the PIT leader remarked, "We all know the same essential things." Like all others in the plant, the cell used Pareto charts to determine which defects in the Feature Pack they should focus on most intently (see Exhibit 30.8). They also drew on Caribe's unique model for negotiating better quality.

Exhibit 30.8   Feature Pack Pareto Chart (December 1989–May 1990)

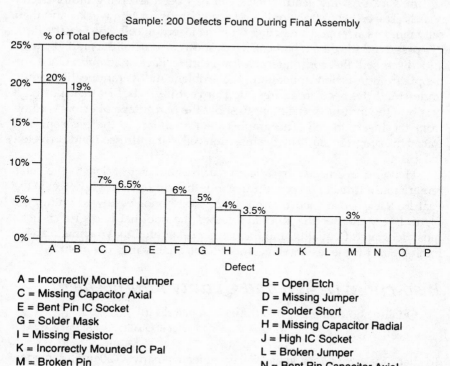

A = Incorrectly Mounted Jumper
C = Missing Capacitor Axial
E = Bent Pin IC Socket
G = Solder Mask
I = Missing Resistor
K = Incorrectly Mounted IC Pal
M = Broken Pin
O = Etch Short

B = Open Etch
D = Missing Jumper
F = Solder Short
H = Missing Capacitor Radial
J = High IC Socket
L = Broken Jumper
N = Bent Pin Capacitor Axial
P = Pin Over Etch

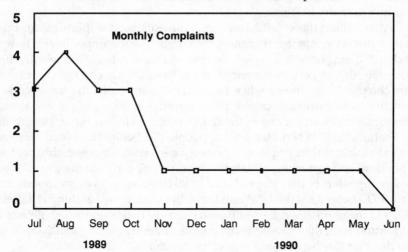

Exhibit 30.9   Feature Pack: Customer Complaints

    In May 1990 the Feature Pack cell had been receiving faulty circuit boards. The cell kept track of the rejected boards for two weeks, and then cell members arranged a meeting with the insertion cell. The Feature Pack PIT presented the data it had collected, showed some of the faulty boards, and discussed the consequences for Feature Pack assembly. Once the people from insertion understood the problem and its ramifications, they understood the need to address it. The Feature Pack PIT then posted a graph in the middle of the plant to show the percentage of errors coming from the insertion cell. The graph called attention to the problem and traced the progress made by the insertion cell as it addressed and corrected the error.

    Hanging overhead, the Micom Caribe banner testified to the cell's remarkable efforts. Eight consecutive months without a single defect in the Feature Pack had earned the cell the highest honor bestowed within the plant. Every quarter the 15 cells selected the one that had proven itself most dedicated to quality, and the banner celebrated that distinction. (See Exhibit 30.9 for the results of Feature Pack's quality improvement.)

Inspection, Design and Quality Improvement

> Quality should be like breathing. You just do it.
> —Ramon Rivera, Director of Quality Assurance

To check for errors, Caribe had once needed as many as 30 quality inspectors. By mid-1990 it had none. The number of circuit boards that required trouble-shooting dropped by 82%. The plant had cut inventory by 68%

and could respond to customer requests from 25% to 50% faster. Caribe cut throughput time from 18 days to fewer than 8. On-time delivery improved by 21%. Warranty returns dropped by 30%. (Exhibits 30.10, 30.11 and 30.12 show summary data on quality improvement.) "Most people get high on the results of our quality process," Moschetti concluded. "But even more significant, it relaxed our resistance to change."

The personal efforts behind the statistics underscored Caribe's accomplishments. Members of the soldering cell, for example, typified the plant's dedication to quality. Production operators would take boards from the wave soldering machine, and using a fixture—a frame that fastened the circuit board in place and served as something like a stencil— they would maneuver a router to create the appropriate shape. Caribe had traditionally ordered fixtures from professional manufacturers specializing in them. Each fixture cost between $400 and $600 and took a month or more to make. Not only did operators have difficulty using the professional fixtures, which never seemed perfectly tailored when they arrived, but there were never enough fixtures to match the different boards Caribe manufactured each day. Worse yet, some ordered fixtures would simply never arrive.

By the spring of 1990, just six months after workers in the soldering cell had formed their process improvement team, they had eliminated those problems. Whenever the cell needed a new fixture, one of the operators, Carlos Torres, would make a finely tailored fixture from otherwise discarded materials—scrap circuit boards and wood panels from incoming shipping crates. In about 30 minutes, Torres could produce a superior fixture, all for a cost of $2 in materials. Perhaps as important as the savings and better fit, the home-made fixtures reduced the time it took to perform the cutting task from 1 minute 58 seconds to just 48 seconds. Because he worked in the cell itself and understood the processes involved, Torres made fixtures that produced more reliable products. In addition, problems and urgent demands could be addressed immediately within the cell.

Exhibit 30.10 Manufacturing Improvements Micom Caribe, 1988–1990

Indicator	1988	1990	% Reduction
Work-In-Process Inventory	$3.97m	$1.27m	68
Total Inventory	$10.85m	$7.56	30
Scrap (Annualized)	$700k	$175k	75
Manufacturing Lead Time (Days)	18	6	66
Internal Rejections (%)	1.86%	1.1%	41
Printed Circuit Boards Requiring Trouble Shooting	1602	288	82
Warranty Returns (Units)	189	132	30

Exhibit 30.11   Quality Improvement at Micom Caribe, 1987–1990

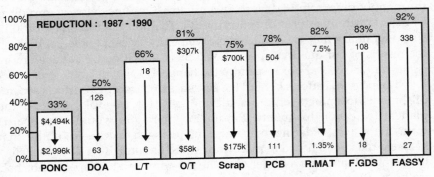

PONC =   Price of Non-Conformance (costs associated with correcting errors)
DOA=   Dead on Arrival (units that fail at customer sites within first three months)
L/T=   Lead Time, Days
O/T=   Overtime, Annualized
PCB=   Printed Circuit Boards (sub-assembly failures), units monthly
R.MAT=   Raw Material (rejection rate of materials received from suppliers)
F.GDS=   Finished Goods (shipment verified to contain exactly what customer ordered), units/monthly
F.ASSY=   Final Assembly failures, units/monthly

Design for Manufacturability. As an extension of its quality effort, Caribe established a Design For Manufacturability plan. It provided a structured way of linking the plant with corporate design teams in California. Caribe had pursued a closer relationship with California, and despite considerable skepticism from the U.S. engineers, Caribe finally convinced designers to visit the plant. As Edwin Franceschi, director of technical services, commented, "We wanted to show them that we don't have monkeys in the trees around here. We wanted to give them some idea of our new capabilities." A formal channel now existed to relate suggestions from factory workers on this team to the corporate development group. In its first nine months, the first product designed with Caribe's input recorded no failures in the field, and the streak had yet to be broken. Micom Caribe had passed down an average of 250 engineering change orders[13] per month in 1988, but by the end of 1990 that figure had dropped to just 40.

Breathing

In June 1990, Caribe detected a recurring problem in one particular circuit board. A tele-conference between engineers in California and operators and engineers at Caribe clarified the problem and the flaw was eliminated.

---

[13]An engineering change order (ECO) informed design engineers of a problem encountered in manufacturing and attributable to design of the product or process. The ECO requested a change to rectify the problem.

Exhibit 30.12 Manufacturing Quality Indicators: Non-Conformance

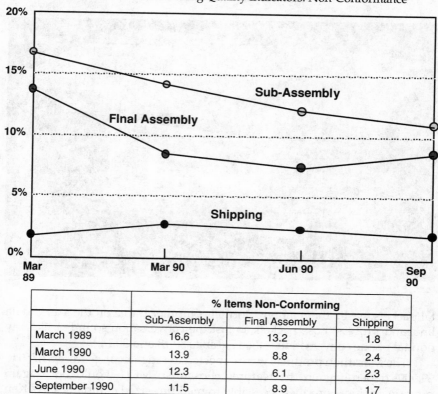

	% Items Non-Conforming		
	Sub-Assembly	Final Assembly	Shipping
March 1989	16.6	13.2	1.8
March 1990	13.9	8.8	2.4
June 1990	12.3	6.1	2.3
September 1990	11.5	8.9	1.7

Later that month, a manager from MCC's California offices called Moschetti and asked him for samples of the bad circuit boards. Moschetti went to a test engineer and asked him if he was aware of the request. The test engineer candidly responded, "We don't build bad boards. Do you want me to make some fail?" Caribe was breathing.

Marathon

In the summer of 1990, MCC again revolutionized the industry when it announced its Marathon series of data/voice network servers (DVNS). MCC would be the first company to link voice and data communication on a data line. Because voice could not tolerate transmission delays acceptable for data, voice could not be carried along with data and fax transmissions, except on special lines (called T1) too expensive for all but the largest companies. Like MCC's other products, the Marathon 5K was a box containing numerous circuit boards with communication chips. A digital signal processor lay at its core, allowing the Marathon 5K to take voice, break it into digi-

Exhibit 30.13   Marathon 5K

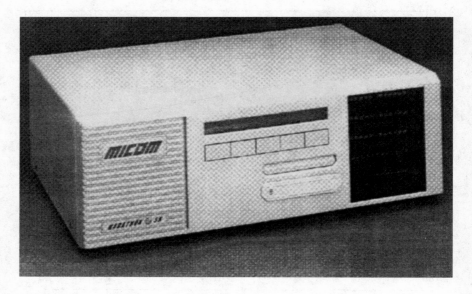

tal packets, nestle them among normal computer traffic on the leased data line, and process those packets so fast the conversation sounded like any normal phone conversation.[14] (See Exhibits 30.13 and 30.14.)

The Marathon products were expected to range in price from $2,750 to $9,900, depending on the features chosen, so MCC would once again provide a critical product accessible to medium-sized companies. As Ken Guy, vice president for corporate strategy and business development, explained, "The T1 companies are aimed at the Fortune 500. We are aimed at the Unfortunate 500,000."[15]

To make room for production of the Marathon series, Caribe needed to clear 20% of floor space. The plant's engineers usually rearranged plant layout, spending a tremendous amount of time and effort to complete work-flow and work-space analyses. Luis Mojica, director of operations, went to the PITs instead. "You have complained about your work space in the past," each cell was told, "and now you have permission to rearrange your area in a way that's best for you. But can you create a 20% savings in space?" Within five days, the PITs had created a 30% reduction in space.

Marathon provided a special opportunity for Caribe. The Marathon

[14]Micom Communications Corporation, news release: "New Product Developed to Curb Office Communications Costs," November 2, 1990. Audio Video Reporting Services, "Chip Talk," KNX Radio, December 12, 1990, Harry Newton, "Every Man's Network," *Data Communications*, supplement to November 1990, p. 4.

[15]John T. Mulqueen, "Micom Integrates Voice, Data, and Fax at Low Speeds," *DataCommunications*, November 1990.

Exhibit 30.14 Data Voice Networking

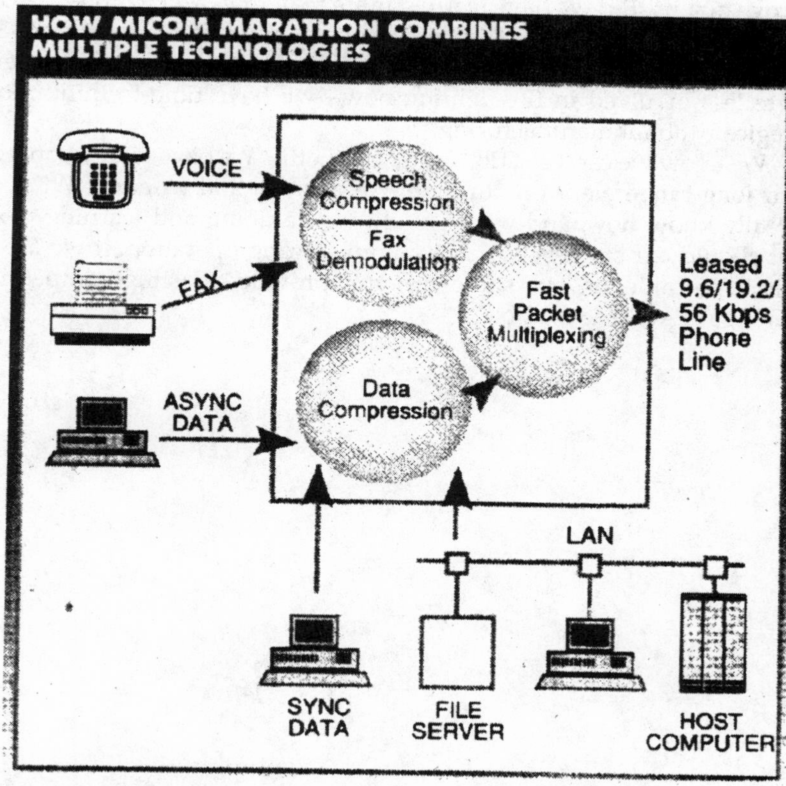

Source: Data Communications November 1990.

product development team had asked Edwin Franceschi to join them, and in addition to Franceschi's frequent visits to California, two manufacturing engineers from Caribe spent six months in Simi Valley. Even more important, Marathon promised to compensate for declining sales of other MCC products.

Charting a Course

Caribe was now a plant to be proud of. Marathon would finally provide it with an opportunity to demonstrate that its new way of running operations could provide a clear, competitive advantage to its parent: world-class quality—with enough flexibility to beat the competition to the marketplace. While the Marathon launch had the plant enthusiastically consumed—with everyone intent on showing MCC the plant's new mettle, Moschetti was more reflective:

"When we set out on this journey, we wanted to know how to improve quality. But we have learned more than that. Much more. We can now do things which we would never have thought possible before 1987. I am sure we have capabilities that none of us are aware of. As managers, we are less involved in fire-fighting now—we have time to think more strategically about manufacturing.

"We know we can't sit still," said Moschetti. "We have to develop a lot of our long-range plans on our own. We often sit and wonder: 'What do we really know now, and what should we be doing and learning next? What should *our* strategy be, as a manufacturing operation, if we are to continue to build on our successes, and provide a lasting competitive advantage to MCC as a whole? '"

CHAPTER 31

Australian Paper Manufacturers (A)

K EN MCRAE, GROUP GENERAL MANAGER for Australian Paper manufacturers (APM), smiled as he re-read the headlines one winter morning in June 1990: "Report Savages PCA" and "Kayser Mill 'the
dirtiest in the country.'" Accompanying articles in the Advocate and the
Examiner had chronicled the toxic chemical problems that confronted the
Paper Company of Australia (PCA). Although the controversy had
signalled another possible opening for McRae and APM, it seemed to raise
as many questions as it answered.

Just three years earlier, McRae had invaded PCA's market area, fine
papers. APM was equipped with the most advanced manufacturing technology in Australia and had taken a daring marketing approach. Now,
with four established fine-paper products, McRae was considering APM's
next move. Should he expand APM's uncoated, fine paper capacity? How
would he maintain APM's environmental record amid growing concerns
over toxic chemicals, forestry, and recycling?

Australian Paper Industry Prior to 1987

Before 1987, the Australian paper industry was divided neatly into three
companies.

1. Australian Newsprint Mills (ANM) supplied newsprint. News-
    print was made by a mechanical process, and because it still
    contained a large proportion of the original wood, it was termed a
    "wood-containing" paper.
2. Australian Paper Manufacturers (APM) produced paper packag-
    ing, referred to as "paperboard." Paperboard was made using a

This case was prepared by Professor David Upton and research associate Joshua Margolis as a basis for
class discussion rather than an illustration of either effective or ineffective handling of an administrative
situation. Data have been disguised.

Figure 31.A Types of Paper and Pulping Processes

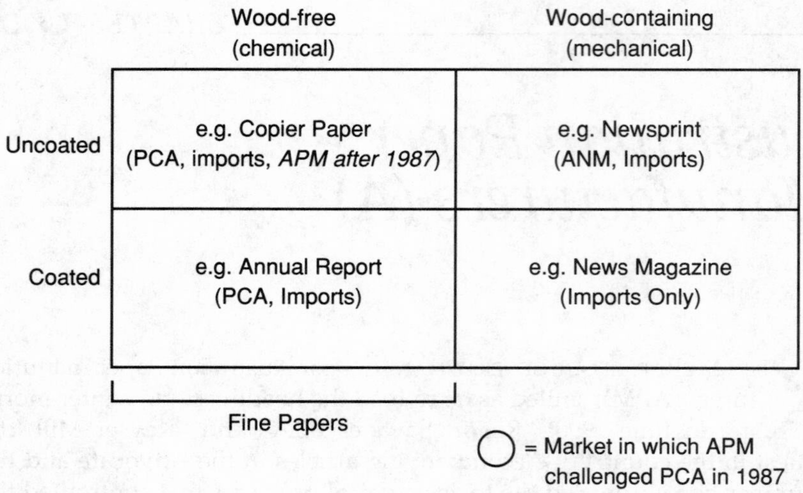

	Wood-free (chemical)	Wood-containing (mechanical)
Uncoated	e.g. Copier Paper (PCA, imports, *APM after 1987*)	e.g. Newsprint (ANM, Imports)
Coated	e.g. Annual Report (PCA, Imports)	e.g. News Magazine (Imports Only)

Fine Papers

◯ = Market in which APM challenged PCA in 1987

chemical process, which eliminated all wood but the required fibers and rendered a stronger product.

3. Paper Company of Australia (PCA) dominated fine-papers. Fine papers were also made using the chemical process. Because the chemical process eliminated all wood but the required fibers, the resulting product, when compared to newsprint, was termed "wood-free" paper. This wood-free or fine paper was used by businesses for printing and writing, and it was divided into two types: those that had a special outer coating ("coated"), such as paper for an annual report, and those without any special coating ("uncoated"), such as copier paper.

Low average tariffs allowed imports to compete with domestic supply. The three Australian companies, however, kept to their own markets, which created cordial relations among them. In total, the three companies produced 1.7 million tonnes[1] of paper and paperboard in 1986.[2]

PCA and APM

PCA and APM were subsidiaries of major Australian corporations. Maitland Industries owned PCA and termed itself a "diversified resources group."

---

[1]A metric tonne is equal to 1000 kilograms or about 1.1 U.S. tons.

[2]Food and Agriculture Organization of the United Nations, *Pulp, Paper and Paperboard Capacity Survey 1986–1991* (Rome: FAO, 1987), p. 95.

Along with paper production, Maitland Industries operated nine mines in Australia, ranging from gold and silver to copper, bismuth, and iron ore, and owned a manufacturer of industrial slurry pumps. Another Maitland subsidiary, Australian Energy Resources, was the country's largest producer of uranium and a major exporter to the United States and Europe.

PCA represented 25% of Maitland's sales (19.4% of operating profit) and dominated production of fine papers in Australia. In 1986, PCA held 75% of the 179,000 ton uncoated, fine-papers market, and recorded A$495 million in total sales (A$51 million in operating profit).[3] Sales were divided roughly 60% and 40% between uncoated and coated fine papers. Whatever PCA did not produce for the Australian market, imports gobbled up.

Amcor Limited, Australia's largest forest products and packaging company, owned APM. Amcor held extensive packaging interests throughout the world and produced metal, plastic, and paper packaging. From aluminum beverage cans and plastic jars, to fast-food containers and corrugated boxes, Amcor continued to extend its reach throughout Australasia, Europe, and North America. Amcor's total sales reached A$2.4 billion in 1986, with operating profit of A$163 million. As Amcor's paper division, APM manufactured products such as cardboard consumer packages and corrugated shipping boxes. For 1986, APM recorded sales of A$600 million and operating profit of A$75 million.[4]

To enter another area of the paper industry—uncoated fine papers— APM could draw on its strength in paperboard manufacturing. But making fine papers required careful attention to the manufacturing process and to growing concerns about the environment.

Making Paper

The first step in making paper and paperboard, after the wood was cut, involved "pulping." This process refined the wood so that only the fibers, the substance required in paper, remained. Wood consisted of approximately 50% cellulose fiber, the material used in paper, 30% lignin, a tough, resinous adhesive that gave structural support to the tree, and 20% extractable oils and carbohydrates. During pulping, the cellulose fiber was separated from the other components so it could be processed further; pulping could be done either mechanically, by grinding the wood, or chemically, by boiling the wood with chemicals. Although newsprint manufacturers relied on mechanical pulping, the grinding process broke the cellulose into shorter fibers when tearing them apart and left some lignin in the resulting pulp. This created a weaker paper that turned

---

[3]All monetary figures are in Australian dollars. Australian dollars had an approximate value of 0.8 U.S. dollars in 1989.

[4]Amcor Limited, *Annual Report 1989*, p. 36.

Figure 31.B   The Chemical Pulp Process

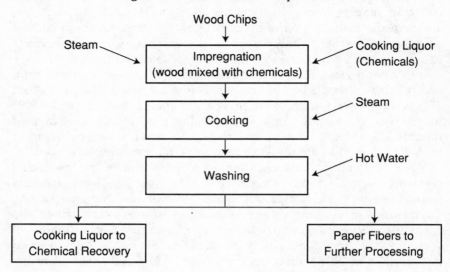

yellow more quickly. Only products with less rigid quality requirements—newspapers and telephone books, for example—used mechanical pulp.[5]

Chemical processes (shown in Figure 31.B) produced much sturdier pulp, which could be used for fine papers and packaging. Chemical reagents were added to the wood, forming soluble compounds with all of the non-cellulose materials. This left a residue of cellulose less abused and purer than mechanical pulp. Two different chemical pulping methods predominated. The soda process, used by PCA at its Kayser mill in Tasmania, added caustic soda to the wood at high temperatures. The soda was then recovered as soda ash and converted back into caustic soda using quicklime. A newer process called kraft used sodium sulfate as the cooking chemical, which yielded stronger pulp at a faster rate.[6] Unlike mechanical pulping, which used 90–95% of the wood harvested, chemical pulping used 45–50%.[7] Chemical pulp yielded 1.25 tonnes of paper per tonne of pulp because inert "fillers" were added in the process.

When transformed into fine paper—the bright white type used in business and printing—chemical pulp went through an intermediate step: bleaching (see Exhibit 31.1). Chlorine gas and chlorine dioxide were applied to the pulp, removing the remaining lignin and leaving a pure white cellulose fiber. On average, between 50 and 80 kilograms of chlorine were used

[5]*The Greenpeace Guide to Paper* (January 1990), pp. 4, 8.

[6]*The Kline Guide to the Paper Industry,* ed. Joan Huber, fourth edition (Fairfield, NJ: Charles H. Kline and Company, Inc., 1980), p. 55. "Kraft" is the German word for strong.

[7]*Greenpeace Guide to Paper,* p. 7. Skogsindustrierna [The Swedish Pulp and Paper Association], *Is Bleached Paper Dangerous?* (Aeberhard & Partners Limited, 1989), p. 20.

Exhibit 31.1   The Bleaching Process*

Bleaching of chemical pulp

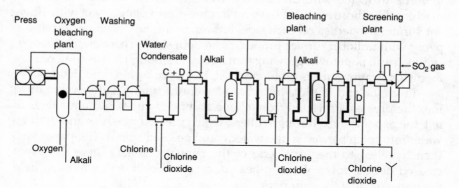

In the chemical pulp process it is impossible to remove all lignin without damaging the cellulose fibers. In the sulphate process, moreover, the pulp is coloured brown by the lignin compounds.

Paper products with very high demands on purity, brightness and permanence require 100 per cent freedom from lignin.

This is the reason why chemical pulp is bleached. The introductory bleaching is called <u>continued delignification.</u>

The example in the above diagram illustrates a bleaching plant with with six bleaching stages. The reaction time in the different stages varies from half an hour to a few hours.

1. Oxygen. Roughly half of the lignin is dissolved. If the delignification process is carried further, the fibers are weakened. The pulp is washed thoroughly.

2. Chlorine/chlorine dioxide (C + D). For environmental reasons more chlorine dioxide is charged at this stage: the chlorine dioxide is charged first, followed by the chlorine about 1 minute later to give the best effect (sequental charging). Steps 1 + 2 give the pulp some brightness.

3 + 5. The extraction stages (E) extract reaction products with alkali.

4 + 6. The chlorine dioxide stages (D) complete dissolving the lignin and in particular raise the brightness.

*Skogsindustrierna (The Swedish Pulp and Paper Association), Is Bleached Paper Dangerous? (Aeberhard & Partners Limited, 1989), p. 17. This diagram illustrates a bleaching process that includes oxygen prebleaching, also referred to as extended delignification.

to produce one tonne of bleached kraft pulp.[8] Bleached pulp allowed producers to make a strong, bright paper that did not discolor during storage or when exposed to sunlight. It thereby satisfied the needs of paper products with high demands for purity, brightness, and permanence.[9]

Once the pulp was bleached, it was processed into "stock": a suspension of fibers and additives in water. Individual fibers of pulp were suspended in water and then "beaten" and refined to produce fibers with the proper characteristics of length, flexibility, surface area, and density. Chemicals could then be added to the stock: rosin, aluminum sulphate, or synthetics to reduce absorbency for writing papers; starch to add strength; dyes for colored paper. At the end of this process, stock could be made into a sheet of paper.

To produce a finished sheet of paper, a paper machine had to remove water from the stock—between 100 and 500 tonnes of water for every tonne of pulp. Water was removed by three methods in sequence: first by gravity, second by squeezing, and finally by heating. In the "wet" end of the paper

[8]*Greenpeace Guide to Paper,* p. 13.

[9]*Is Bleached Paper Dangerous?* p. 17.

machine, the stock was deposited on a "wire"—a continuous belt of mesh material—and together with inclined blades of metal or plastic ("foils") underneath it, the wire drained the water from the stock. A single-wire machine, like those in all of PCA's mills, produced a paper sheet with different surface properties on each side. Newer, twin-wire machines produced paper with uniform surface properties on both sides. This double-sided, or symmetrical, paper was growing more popular; though it was unnecessary for all applications, users preferred its stability, uniformity, and flatness.

From the end of the wire, what was now a fragile paper web moved into the presses. Protected from above and below by continuous belts of felt, the paper moved through rollers, which pressed the sheet and drained water into catch basins (so the water could be used again). The paper web then travelled to the "dry" end of the paper machine. There the paper crossed double rows of steam-heated, cast-iron cylinders while felt held the paper against the cylinders.

In the calender section, the paper was pressed further, as a set of hardened cast-iron rollers improved the surface-finish of the paper. From there the paper was wound onto a steel spool. In the final step of making paper, broadly called "finishing," large reels of paper were rewound into smaller reels, some were made into stacks of sheets (reams), and the paper was inspected.[10]

Before most paper could be used it was often "converted" into the end product. First, the paper manufacturer applied a coating appropriate to the paper's use—a pigment for fine papers and a barrier coating for packaging materials. With packaging materials, either the primary producer, such as APM, or an independent converter would then mechanically construct the paper into products: bags, boxes, and envelopes. Fine paper, once properly coated, inspected, and packaged, was sold to merchants, who supplied end-users.[11]

In Australia, annual consumption of fine paper—paper made of bleached, chemical-processed pulp—rose to 358,000 tonnes in 1987. Uncoated fine paper, such as photocopy paper, stationery, and offset printing paper, comprised 52% of that market, while coated fine paper, the type used in an annual report, comprised the rest. From its Kayser, Bridport, and Kiama mills, PCA could supply 230,000 tonnes of fine papers per year, with the total divided 61% (140,000 tonnes) for uncoated and 39% (90,000 tonnes) for coated.

Paper and the Environment

When chemical pulp was bleached to produce wood-free paper, approximately 10% of the chlorine used combined with organic molecules from

---

[10]Note on Process Control in Pulp and Paper Making. Harvard Business School Case 687–061 (President and Fellows of Harvard College, 1987), pp. 5–10.

[11]The Kline Guide to the Paper Industry, p. 63.

Exhibit 31.2   Map of Australia

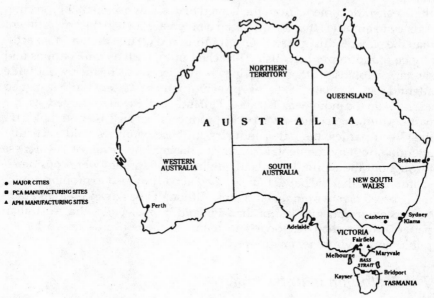

the wood, which was then discharged as effluent from the mill. Bleaching thereby produced as many as 1,000 toxic chlorine compounds called "organochlorines." Chemical pulp mills typically discharged between five and eight kilograms of these organochlorines per tonne of bleached pulp. Because the pulping process required large amounts of water to flush chemicals from the pulp, companies situated mills near rivers, lakes, and oceans; the effluent then ran directly into these bodies of water, such as Bass Strait near PCA's Kayser Mill (See Exhibit 31.2 for map of Australia).

Only 300 organochlorines had been formally identified, the most notorious of which was dioxin. Known most for its use in the Vietnam War, under the name Agent Orange, dioxin served as a defoliant to remove all ground growth. But dioxin had also been found to cause reproductive disorders in animals and to suppress their immune systems, leaving them more susceptible to infection. Fish found in waters off Sweden suffered reproductive and liver damage, skeletal abnormalities in offspring, and impaired immune systems—symptoms attributable, at least in part, to organochlorines released by the paper industry. Further, organochlorines were bioaccumulative: they remained in the bodies of organisms that ingested them, and contamination levels rose with every step of the food chain.[12]

Fears about dioxin's connection to pulp bleaching first arose in 1970 but gained renewed attention in 1987 when Greenpeace published No

[12]*Greenpeace Guide to Paper,* pp. 13–16.

Margin of Safety, a report on the United States paper industry. Greenpeace cited leaked documents from the United States' Environmental Protection Agency to argue (1) that dioxin posed a far greater risk to the environment than the paper industry had been admitting and (2) that dioxin could actually be found in products using bleached pulp, such as milk cartons and sanitary napkins.[13] Organochlorines began receiving further worldwide attention in the late 1980s as pro-environment Green parties gained strength in Scandinavia. Because Finland and Sweden served as the world's number six and seven paper producers[14] as well as strongholds for the Green parties, the paper industry in those countries paid particular attention to environmental concerns, raising the level of awareness throughout the world. In Finland, environmental issues were considered so important that the paper industry had already agreed to prohibit advertising based on environmental claims. Although less advanced in its attention to environmental issues than Finland and Sweden, the Australian paper industry had responded to many of the concerns raised by the public and environmental groups.

The Australian Industry's Efforts

Both Maitland (PCA's parent) and Amcor (APM's parent) had experience responding to environmental concerns. Maitland had instituted strict environmental procedures in connection with uranium mining: to prevent potential contamination, the company collected every drop of rainwater that fell on its mines. In the 1970s, PCA had introduced a bond writing paper from 100% recycled fibers, but it failed to gain market acceptance.[15] Amcor had responded to a series of concerns over packaging, ranging from the release of chlorofluorocarbons (CFCs) by aerosol cans to the waste created with the use of polystyrene (styrofoam). Amcor's annual report was frequently prefaced by a two-page discussion of environmental issues. In addition, Amcor held international patents for Corrishell, a paper-based alternative to polystyrene for products such as fast-food containers.[16]

Organochlorines. The Australian paper industry cited studies that recorded a dioxin level in the average daily intake of food ten times higher than in the average daily amount of paper used. APM and PCA also noted that studies had not yet provided conclusive proof linking dioxin to adverse effects upon humans. Nonetheless, both companies abided by

[13]*Greenpeace Guide to Paper*, p. 17.

[14]Behind the United States, Canada, Japan, U.S.S.R., and China, "World Pulp, Paper, and Board Industry At A Glance," *Pulp and Paper*, August 1988, pp. 54, 55.

[15]APPM, *Paper and the Environment* (September 1989), p. 41.

[16]Amcor Limited, *Annual Report 1989*, p. 12.

strict government standards, continually sampled emissions from their mills, and distributed pamphlets to inform consumers of the companies' environmental efforts. Rough estimates put APM's expenditures on environmental protection at A$60 million for the 1980s, compared to total capital expenditures of A$300 million.

Chlorine provided the only means for producing traditional white business paper, and though new technologies and process modifications promised alternatives in the future, a capital intensive industry like the pulp and paper industry would require time to implement the changes. The drastic 50% reduction of chlorine levels in Sweden, for example, took ten years to implement with the technology available at the time (1979).[17] But new intermediate measures, while not the ultimate solution environmentalists sought, could reduce the use of chlorine. Greenpeace estimated, for example, that half of all chlorine could be replaced by extending and repeating the oxygen stage of bleaching.[18] The paper produced from oxygen-bleached pulp, they asserted, could fulfill the same business requirements as chlorine-bleached paper. Environmental concerns with paper, however, extended beyond fears of dioxin to the issues of deforestation and recycling.

Deforestation. Four tonnes of wood produced one tonne of paper, and during a period of increasing anxiety over the greenhouse effect, this seemingly wanton use of forests came under increasing scrutiny.[19] The production of one tonne of paper from discarded waste paper, when compared to production from virgin wood, used half as much energy and water. It created 74% less air pollution, 35% less water pollution, and saved the 17 pulp trees which would have been used.[20]

APM and PCA recognized the growing public interest in forest preservation and tried to inform Australians of the forestry management methods the companies used. As Australia's largest private forest plantation owner,[21] APM paid particular attention to forestry management, and PCA, with large forestry operations in Tasmania, showed similar attentiveness. Less than 30% of Australia's 25.6 million hectares[22] of public native forests were managed for wood production, and only about 1% of that managed portion was harvested in any one year.[23] To ensure future

[17]Clive Capps, "Chlorine's bleaching days are numbered," *Pulp & Paper International,* April 1990, pp. 60, 61.

[18]*Greenpeace Guide to Paper,* p. 20.

[19]The greenhouse effect refers to the warming of the earth's surface as levels of certain gases, such as carbon dioxide, increase. Trees take in carbon dioxide and replace it with oxygen, thereby serving as the earth's "lungs."

[20]*Greenpeace Guide to Paper,* p. 40.

[21]*Amcor and the Environment,* p. 3.

[22]1 hectare = 2.47 acres

[23]Forest Industries of Australia, *Forest Facts: The Series—Overview,* March 1990.

supply, both companies had to commit themselves to regrowth programs: five eucalyptus trees planted for every one harvested, five pine trees for every four harvested.[24] Recent studies had even uncovered the advantages of managed forests, where young, active growth—which consumed high levels of carbon dioxide and released oxygen—replaced older trees that consumed less carbon dioxide, or even released it as they decayed.[25]

Although the paper industry nurtured its forests carefully and continued to conduct tree-breeding research, to generate stronger trees with improved yields and resistance to diseases, environmentalists worried about "monocultures," the dependence upon one variety of tree in all replanting efforts. In contrast to an array of robust varieties that could support all forms of life and resist potential disease and soil depletion, monocultures would be unable to provide the same support to the ecosystem as natural growth and could be wiped out by a single, potent disease.

Recycling. Australia recycled 30% of all recoverable paper, putting it in the same range as the United States and Finland, ahead of Canada, New Zealand, and China, and behind Sweden, Japan, and the Netherlands.[26] To recycle paper, manufacturers had to remove ink, fillers, and coating materials from the old paper. Waste paper was washed in detergent to remove the ink, and if necessary, bleached to brighten it. High quality, white recycled paper often indicated heavy use of detergents and bleaching to transform the waste back into bright paper. Between 10% and 25% of collected waste paper was lost in recycling plants, most of that fillers and coating material.[27] In addition, continued use and recycling sapped the strength of paper fibers, which could therefore be reused a maximum of five to ten times. Often, companies combined virgin and recycled pulp.

Throughout the world, most paper fashionably labelled "recycled" stretched the definition somewhat. Most recycled paper contained a limited proportion of recycled fibers, and most of those came from "preconsumer" sources. Scrap from paper mills and book-printers constituted such "pre-consumer" waste: it had never in fact gone through consumers. Environmentalists called special attention to "post-consumer" waste: paper collected from households and offices. Whereas the paper industry had always relied on pre-consumer waste as a source of pulp, it was only just beginning to harness post-consumer waste. That in turn was creating growing demand for used paper and was providing the impetus for broader recycling efforts. Although Australia used a high percentage of post-consumer waste, inefficient collection and sorting methods, together

---

[24]*Amcor and the Environment*, p. 3.

[25]*Forest Facts: #1—The Greenhouse Effect*, March 1990, APPM, *Paper and the Environment*, p. 11.

[26]*Amcor and the Environment*, p. 4, *Greenpeace Guide to Paper*, p. 41.

[27]Here coating materials refer to those added during the "converting" stage. "Coated" fine paper, such as that used in an annual report, could not be recycled at all.

with the lower pulp to paper yield, made it an expensive resource. One tonne of waste pulp cost A$760 but only yielded 0.75 tonnes of recycled paper. One tonne of bleached virgin pulp cost roughly A$1120 but yielded 1.25 tonnes of paper.

The Australian paper industry continued to address the public's concerns about environmental issues, but a basic gap separated environmental groups and the industry. Environmental groups questioned the very need for bleached, white paper. They felt that kraft pulp bleached with oxygen rather than chlorine provided an ivory color paper suitable for business uses, yet gentler on the environment. Greenpeace and other groups felt that few office papers required extreme brightness. The paper industry, they felt, created the demand for extreme brightness, and, they argued, with some marketing attention and consumer education, paper companies could provide oxygen-bleached paper, ultimately abandon chlorine bleaching, and satisfy current business requirements with ivory-colored paper. APM and PCA both cited previous attempts to introduce less chemically-treated products into Australia and their failure to receive consumer support. As one industry document promised, "To the extent that the Australian market demonstrates a preference for off-white or unbleached products, [we are] able and pleased to meet that demand."[28]

Australians remained particularly concerned about the environment. Many considered their country a pristine frontier to be left free of the tainting influence they felt industry had brought to bear upon other developed countries. While business leaders pushed for an approach which balanced economic growth and environmental protection, polls revealed that Australians favored protecting the environment at the expense of economic growth, if a choice had to be made.[29] Just over half of all Australians also reported purchasing products that did not damage the environment, with 40% of respondents saying that the products had been more expensive.[30]

APM Enters The Uncoated, Fine-papers Business

In 1984, APM completed a A$163 million modernization of its kraft pulp plant in Maryvale, Victoria. The improvement added 140,000 tonnes per year of kraft pulp capacity, bringing the Maryvale plant's total output to 350,000 tonnes per year. At the time, most of this pulp was used for packaging materials in one of APM's paper machines or sold on the pulp market. Pulp could generally be sold profitably on the world market,

---

[28]*Amcor and the Environment*, p. 6.

[29]"Economic Growth and the Environment," Business Council of Australia Environment Task Force, Melbourne, 14 June 1990. Philip McIntosh, "Most prepared to put environment ahead of growth," *Sydney Morning Herald*, 15 June 1990, p. 5.

[30]Philip McIntosh, "Most prepared to put environment ahead of growth," *Sydney Morning Herald*, 15 June 1990, p. 5.

although it could be used most beneficially in the company's own machines. APM included stringent emissions and effluent controls in its improvement program. When the Australian government issued strict effluent guidelines in 1989, the Maryvale plant already met them.[31] According to the mill manager, the pulp from Maryvale contained no detectable dioxin in parts per quadrillion (10^{15})—equivalent to the thickness of a credit card compared to the distance to the moon.

The Maryvale plant had four paper machines, and in 1986 APM turned its attention to Paper Machine 3. Originally built in 1972 to produce brown shopping bags, Machine 3 had a capacity of 31,000 tonnes per year. By the mid-1980s, though, people had stopped using these "checkout" bags (preferring plastic), and between Machines 1 and 2, the company could cover demand. This left Machine 3 ripe for transformation. APM seized the opportunity, upgraded Machine 3, and used it to take them into the heart of PCA's fine-papers market.

McRae commented:

APM was fundamentally part of a packaging company. But we were extremely good papermakers too. We had a brand-new pulp plant and there was no point hanging around getting beaten up in a shrinking market so we thought—why not use the skills we've built up making bag paper and learn how to make fine paper?

People in the plant were convinced it could be done, and that their years of experience in making bag paper could be adapted to such a closely allied process. A number of trial runs were made in order to determine the general viability of the idea. Once it was proven feasible, APM sanctioned the investment. Between May 1986 and July 1987, APM spent A$50 million to rebuild Maryvale's Machine 3, converting it from making bag paper to producing white wood-free paper.

As each addition of capital equipment took place (from new controllers to new drier drums), trial runs were made to ensure that the improvement process was on track. Stage by stage, the trials were made with the team of operators who would finally run the process full-time. The team became intimately involved with the problems of installing the new equipment, and already knew many of the new tricks of the trade when it came time to run pre-production trials. Slowly, but surely, the crew learned what to do: how to make a thin, uniform sheet without tearing the paper in the machine and how to get just the right drying rate to make a sheet without wrinkles. Each experiment was carefully recorded by the team, and even the most minor problems with the final sheet were regarded as nuggets of information to be fed back into the improvement

[31]"Maryvale mill starts new pulp line," *Pulp & Paper International*, June 1984, pp. 42–43. Australian Paper Manufacturers, *APM Papers Group*, p. 18, Amcor Limited, *Annual Report 1989*, p. 17.

process. By July 1987, they had done it. They had learned how to make fine paper better than anyone else in Australia.

The upgrading of Maryvale's Machine 3 had not simply put APM next to PCA as the second domestic supplier of uncoated fine paper.[32] It also made APM the owner of Australia's largest and most technologically advanced fine-paper machine. The 70,000 tonnes per year of Machine 3 capacity gave APM the product it needed to steal from imports—the company's primary goal in entering the fine-papers market.[33] Customers had been accustomed to buying some of their paper from PCA and some from overseas, but PCA had not kept pace with the growth in demand. Although aiming to replace imports, McRae, director of marketing for APM papers group at the time, knew his toughest job lay in establishing APM's fine papers amid a market dominated by PCA.

Ken McRae's Challenge

PCA produced three-quarters of all fine papers consumed in Australia and even controlled 80% of the copier paper market, with its Prism brand copier paper. PCA owned the country's second and third largest paper merchants, Grafton Paper and PaperSource, which reinforced the company's market share. These two merchants distributed 40% of Australia's fine paper and made competition with PCA a formidable task.

To steer APM around PCA's strengths and into the expanding fine-papers market, McRae designed an innovative marketing strategy, restructured the method of distribution, and plotted a careful ramp-up of demand for output. He outlined the essential elements of his plan—quality and service:

> Our technology gave us an edge in quality. We had the kraft pulping process in Maryvale, which gave us a stronger pulp than the soda process used by the competition. PCA still relied on old soda-process machines, which had been installed in the 1950s. Our paper machine, Maryvale 3, also gave us a better quality paper. It's the only twin-wire machine in Australia, a Voith duo-former, which takes water out of both sides, producing a paper with the same surface finish on both sides, unlike more traditional machines that remove water from the bottom side only, giving a different surface on one side of the sheet. With the pulping process and the paper machines PCA had, they just couldn't produce the quality of paper we could.
>
> We offered better service. You used to tell customers, "We are

---

[32]*Pulp & Paper International,* December 1986, p. 48, "Rebuilt PM starting up at Maryvale," *Pulp & Paper International,* July 1987, p. 17.

[33]*APM Papers Group,* pp. 18–20.

making product category X at a specific time, so get your order in." Now we say, "Tell us what you want, and we will make it." We attempted to bring the lead-time down so they could hold less stock. We also benefitted from having fewer sub-divisions of products than PCA. We began with just three basic products. Maryvale Machine 3 was designed to make changeovers with relative ease compared to older paper machines.

McRae enhanced APM's emphasis on service by replacing merchants with direct customer contact. Paper merchants served as intermediaries between the manufacturers and customers, typically taking bulk orders, placing it with a mill, and receiving the invoice. The customer paid the mill price, while the mill paid the merchant a 3–5% commission. McRae described his plan:

> We went out and asked customers, "How would you like to do business directly with us?" We decided to ignore the merchants. We offered much better response to customers. We serviced everything, had a toll-free number and a computerized order-taking system. We had a simple policy: To be a direct customer, you had to buy a minimum of 500 tonnes of a single product.
>
> Merchants responded angrily. They felt we were leaving them with scraps. We asked, "How do you add value? If you add value, how come people are only paying you the mill price?" Nonetheless, we were prepared to work with them for new markets. We did need them to help us set up the distribution network.

APM wanted to deliver 95% of all orders on time, and if delays arose, APM's goal was to warn customers 100% of the time. Toward that end, McRae reorganized APM's customer service operation. Instead of having a sales office in each of Australia's seven states, McRae situated all sales representatives and order-input clerks in the same office—the same office where production-planning people worked. APM established a nation-wide toll-free number. McRae then instituted an advanced computer-based information system, which allowed APM to enter an order, assess the volume it would absorb on the machine-cycle for that month, and offer a specific date for delivery. "The intention," McRae explained, "was to do it all live with the customer, so when the customer got off the telephone, he or she could know precisely when to expect the delivery, at least within a three-day window."

Ramp-up. In August 1987, APM inaugurated its move into the fine-papers market. McRae developed a careful plan for ramping up to full capacity on Maryvale 3. APM intended to be producing at 40,000 tonnes annual rate by

August 1988, starting with three crews working Monday through Friday and eventually moving to four and then five crews. Like all of Maryvale's other paper machines, Machine 3 would eventually operate 24 hours a day, 365 days a year.

APM began by selling PrintRight, an offset printing paper. "We felt it was the easiest product to make," McRae explained, "and one we could get into the marketplace fairly easily. We wanted to get practice making that, refine things on the machine, and then go to the sheets that required greater technical expertise." Just three months later, the company introduced its continuous forms (computer) product, DataRight, which brought total annualized output to 8,000 tonnes. McRae next introduced CopyRight, APM's copier paper, in June 1988, and sales surged to the annual equivalent of 32,000 tonnes. By August 1988, Maryvale Machine 3 was producing at a rate of 50,000 tonnes per year, and by March 1989 it had reached its capacity of 70,000 tonnes per year. (See Table 31.1.)

Markets. Beyond ramping up to desired capacity, McRae also had to encourage consumer acceptance of APM's new product. As he put it, "We had three very different audiences all being supplied off the one machine." CopyRight catered to the white-collar office worker; PrintRight served a blue-collar, predominantly male, audience; and DataRight was aimed at technically-oriented users. Customers, however, tended to stick with the brand they were using, as much out of inertia as from brand loyalty. McRae outlined his approach:

> For the offset printers, we distributed photographs on PrintRight with just a hint of color around the profile—a really difficult shot to print. We knew this would impress them, and it did indeed attract them to our product.
>
> We talked about the technical benefit of the sheet itself when we marketed DataRight. We were selling it to people who take the paper and turn it into forms.

CopyRight had to be directed at a broader audience, one that would consume close to 85,000 tonnes in 1989, but McRae's innovative approach gained APM the acceptance and name recognition it sought.

> PCA packed their copier paper in 10-ream boxes, which weighed 15 kilograms, just under the maximum of 16 kilograms allowed by the government. Although we knew it would double packaging and distribution costs, we started selling 5-ream boxes, a far more manageable weight for office workers. We also put a perforated panel into the box so people could remove the packets easily.
>
> When we launched the product, we took out full-page advertisements in the daily newspapers. We took out ads in trade maga-

Table 31.1 Uncoated Fine Papers Ramp-up (annual equivalent in tonnes)[a]

	8/87	11/87	6/88	8/88	3/89
APM Brands					
PrintRight	200	4,000	10,000	12,000	17,000
DataRight	0	4,000	15,000	24,000	28,000
CopyRight	0	0	7,000	14,000	25,000
APM Total	200	8,000	32,000	50,000	70,000
Imports Total	46,000	36,000	32,000	24,000	22,000
PCA Total	140,000	130,000	120,000	144,000	108,000
Market Total	186,000	174,000	184,000	218,000	200,000

[a]annual equivalent = the month's production x 12.

zines for the dealers. We also advertised on the radio. In areas teeming with office workers, we handed out balloons with "CopyRight" printed on them. We wanted to get this great name "CopyRight" recognized, so we could get the product moving.

APM spent over A$1 million to launch CopyRight, but McRae saw the introduction as well worth the expense.

We were experimenting with the market. We had to find out how much PCA's Prism name was really worth, and we wanted the market to perceive us through CopyRight. PrintRight and DataRight depended upon that market.

By the end of the first quarter of 1989, APM had established itself in the fine-papers market. The A$50 million investment in Machine 3 appeared to be paying off (see Table 31.1 and Exhibit 31.3).

Race to Expand

The uncoated fine-papers market was projected to grow at 6.5% annually through the 1990s, leading McRae to conclude that battle lines had only just been drawn between APM and PCA.

If either of the companies makes a significant commitment to expanding its capacity, the first step would be to put in a pulp mill of maybe 300,000 or 400,000 tonnes. That would have to be followed up very quickly with a paper machine, although capacity destined for the new machine could produce pulp for the market in the interim.

By 1995, imports will begin to grow at the expense of domes-

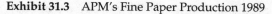

Exhibit 31.3   APM's Fine Paper Production 1989

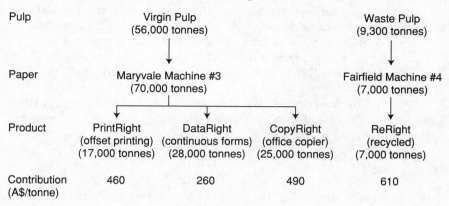

Pulp	Virgin Pulp (56,000 tonnes)			Waste Pulp (9,300 tonnes)
Paper	Maryvale Machine #3 (70,000 tonnes)			Fairfield Machine #4 (7,000 tonnes)
Product	PrintRight (offset printing) (17,000 tonnes)	DataRight (continuous forms) (28,000 tonnes)	CopyRight (office copier) (25,000 tonnes)	ReRight (recycled) (7,000 tonnes)
Contribution (A$/tonne)	460	260	490	610

tic supply, so there's room for somebody to do it. Whoever does it will have to go in with a world-scale machine—a machine capable of making 150,000 tonnes of paper per year. Otherwise you cannot get the economies of scale. But whoever does that will knock out competitors for a decade.

PCA's Bridport Proposal

As early as 1987, PCA had begun making plans for a kraft pulp mill of its own. The new mill, to be located in Bridport, Tasmania, was projected to have a total pulp capacity of 400,000 tonnes.[34] PCA had solicited foreign partners from Japan, Canada, and the United States to participate in the project, and by October 1988, joined by a Canadian company, PCA had mapped out a A$1 billion proposal. The mill, geared toward domestic supply and export to Japan, promised to be the largest single manufacturing project ever undertaken by private enterprise in the country. Australia's Prime Minister, Bob Hawke, heralded it as a venture of "major national significance."[35]

But the Bridport mill encountered unexpected public opposition. Although financial plans were completed, environmental guidelines had not been set. Environmentalists and local residents demanded stringent regulations, and the Tasmanian government responded, outlining "nonnegotiable" standards. PCA said the regulations threatened the project, and the company listed 45 objections. The two sides narrowed their differences to four points, but they remained most opposed over dioxin. One newspaper account summarized the dispute:

[34]"Bridport pulp mill plan dropped," *Pulp & Paper International*, May 1989, p. 21.

[35]Chris Sherwell, "Tasmanian pulp mill controversy sinks into confusion," *Financial Times*, 15 February 1989, p. 6.

The most problematic [difference] concerned emissions of dioxin, an organo-chlorine by-product of the plant's bleaching process. The government said there was to be no increase in the ambient level of dioxin in the marine environment. The companies said they could not guarantee this, but if there was an emission, it would be so small as to be harmless to the marine ecology.[36]

Political battles between the state and federal governments further complicated the dispute, and in April 1989, under great public pressure, the project was scrapped.[37]

ReRight

Just one month later (May 18, 1989), APM introduced its newest entry in the fine-papers market, ReRight. ReRight was Australia's first stationery paper made from 100% recycled paper—post-consumer recycled paper that was produced without chemicals and was neither de-inked nor bleached. The World Wildlife Fund endorsed ReRight, and the product generated significant interest and publicity. As McRae explained, however, ReRight represented only the most visible aspect of a deeper strategy.

> We could see environmental concerns coming more and more to the fore—the whole thing was gathering momentum. We had an infrastructure already in place because we'd been recycling paper in Australia for 60 years, and we knew how to make recycled paper on our machines. We'd just never tried to make it for office use. As we saw the public pressure mounting for more environmentally acceptable products, we picked May 1989 as about the right time to get in and launch the paper.
>
> We also knew that all the easy paper in Australia was already being collected for recycling. We were getting everything out of the supermarket. I think we had about the highest recycling rate in the world of used boxes from supermarkets. We were doing door-to-door collections around the metropolitan areas, and PCA had always bought a lot of the waste from printing plants. So most of the easy stuff was captured. Most of the paper used in offices, though, was going to landfill. So within a week of when we launched ReRight, we also started the "APM Office Paper Chase." We set up a collection structure for us to go into offices in all the

[36]Chris Sherwell, "Tasmanian pulp mill controversy sinks into confusion," *Financial Times*, 15 February 1989, p. 6.

[37]"Bridport pulp mill plan dropped," *Pulp & Paper International*, May 1989, p. 21.

major cities. We used this to say, "Look, if you want to use recycled paper, what you've got to do is give us your used paper, so we can turn it back into a sheet that you can use again."

We had thought the whole thing through and had a compelling story to tell. We were eliminating a lot of waste in society because this stuff normally went from the office straight into the landfill. We're now capturing it, bringing it back, and making paper out of it. In Australia, we've reduced waste and the cost of waste-disposal, and we're generating more paper domestically, which means Australia doesn't have to import as much as it did previously.

McRae appeared all over the media during May, and despite ReRight's higher cost, it grabbed a 3% market share (7,000 tonnes per year) of the uncoated fine papers market. To recoup its research and development expense, APM charged 20% more for ReRight than for comparable, non-recycled paper. ReRight's immediate acceptance inspired APM to introduce ReRight-Form in the spring of 1990, a recycled computer paper.

PCA's Kayser Plant

While APM expanded its recycling efforts, PCA suffered yet another blow on the environmental front. Greenpeace released a surprise report on PCA's Kayser soda pulp mill on the coast of Tasmania, declaring it the dirtiest mill of its type in Australia. Greenpeace found Kayser discharging 11.5 tonnes of organochlorines per day into the sea, at times reaching a level 80% above government standards. Greenpeace also decried the presence of chloroform, a cancer causing agent, in the effluent, and cited it as a health risk to PCA's workers. The environmental group called upon the government to monitor the mill's effluent levels more closely and demanded that the company reduce its discharge of organochlorines to a maximum of one kilogram per tonne of pulp. Greenpeace also recommended complete elimination of organochlorine discharges by 1993 and asked the government to review employees' medical records to search for abnormal incidence of cancers attributable to organochlorines, such as chloroform.[38]

Though surprised by the report, PCA managers responded virtually point by point to Greenpeace. First, they disputed the figures on effluent levels. Company data, much of it based on tests by government laboratories, revealed effluent levels below legal limits. PCA further noted that chlorine bleaching met the market demand for high quality paper and no

[38]Peter Hazelwood, "Report savages PCA" and "Greenpeace motives questioned," *Advocate*, 23 March 1990, Steven Dally, "Kayser mill 'the dirtiest in the country,'" *Examiner*, 23 March 1990, pp. 1, 2.

Exhibit 31.4   Long-Term Uncoated Fine Papers Market in Australia (000 tonnes)

Category	1986				1989				Forecast 1995
	PCA	Imports	APM	Total	PCA	Imports	APM	Total	Total
Offset Printing	50	19	0	69	20	7	17	44	44
Continuous Forms	40	15	0	55	37	7	28	72	78
Copier	44	11	0	55	51	8	25	84	150
Recycled	0	0	0	0	0	0	7	7	30
Total	134	45	0	179	108	22	77	207	302

alternative existed to produce paper of similar quality. In response to
concerns about chloroform, the company noted that it was commonly
found in chlorinated drinking water and swimming pools, and that only
extensive exposure to chloroform posed a health risk. The company
welcomed a government inquiry and cited its ongoing A$300,000 study of
the mill's environmental impact as proof of its environmental efforts.
Kayser's 50-year presence in Tasmania had created no apparent effect on
the marine environment, according to PCA, which was planning construction of a A$16 million plant to combat the rising level of suspended
solids—pieces of wood matter—in the mill's emissions.[39]

The government responded by hiring additional inspectors to monitor pollution in the Kayser region.[40] Alan Andrews, manager of the Kayser
mill, and Robert Cartmel, paper expert for Greenpeace, drew different
conclusions from the Kayser controversy. Andrews criticized Cartmel's
methods:

> Mr. Cartmel visited our research unit last year at the invitation of
> the mill and was fully briefed on the mill performance and its
> objectives.
>
> He went out of his way to create the impression he was a man
> who would give a balanced view.[41]

[39]"Greenpeace pulp claims 'impossible,'" *Advocate,* 24 March 1990, "Greenpeace motives questioned,"
Advocate, 23 March 1990.

[40]Andrew Darby, "Kayser mill worst, says Greenpeace," *Age,* 23 March 1990.

[41]"Greenpeace motives questioned," *Advocate,* 23 March 1990.

Cartmel believed he had indeed presented a balanced view and continued to condemn the Kayser plant: "It is a question of the shareholders accepting a lower profit margin in order to maintain the environment."[42]

McRae Looks Ahead

Encouraged by APM's success, Amcor had provided A$50 million to APM to consolidate the investment that had carried it into fine papers, though a pre-tax return of at least 20% per year was expected. While larger sums could always be requested, it was understood that larger sums required more attractive returns—as had been the case when APM originally entered the market by upgrading Machine 3. Further expansion into fine-papers loomed as a possibility. Copier paper alone promised 10% annual growth and recycled paper continued to grow in popularity. The uncoated fine-papers market as a whole was projected to grow at a rate of 6.5% annually through the year 2000. "Sitting on our hands is no good. If our influence in the market declines, customers will push us around."

McRae weighed his immediate options for the capital budget:

1. The capacity of Machine 3 at Maryvale could be expanded up to 100,000 tonnes. Initial estimates put the cost of increasing from the existing capacity of 70,000 tonnes at A$35 million. McRae would have to decide how he would use this extra capacity.

2. APM was producing 7,000 tonnes of recycled paper at its Fairfield plant, and increasing capacity to 15,000 tonnes would cost A$18 million.

3. In addition to APM's recycling efforts, McRae focused on ways to reduce APM's discharge of organochlorines. APM could reduce its dependence on chlorine by substituting oxygen in one of two ways:

    a. To replace chlorine through oxygen pre-bleaching, APM would have to spend A$15 million in development and implementation. Oxygen pre-bleaching[43] would reduce chlorine use by 50%. Pulp output at Maryvale would drop by 5%, from 350,000 tonnes to 332,500 tonnes, but many engineers at the plant had expressed keen interest in learning about the technology. Pulp contribution at Maryvale was A$200 per tonne of pulp.

    b. Alternatively, APM could intensify the use of oxygen during bleaching, which would reduce the level of chlorine by 15% and cost approximately A$8 million. Pulp output would be unaffected.

---

[42]"Report Savages PCA," *Advocate*, 23 March 1990.

[43]Oxygen pre-bleaching was also known as extended delignification. See Exhibit 31.1.

Exhibit 31.5 Editorial from Pulp and Paper International—June 1990

Chlorine bleaching has to go

Drastic actions are needed if mills are to become truly environmentally friendly. Renate Kroesa of Greenpeace outlined some of the changes environmentalists would like to see the industry introduce at PPI's Market Pulp conference held in Brussels in May.

ENVIRONMENTALISTS HAVE difficulty understanding why industry is resisting so much the introduction of less bleached paper goods into the market, since such a move would actually provide reductions in production costs in the form of saved energy and saved bleaching chemicals.

Bleaching to a lower level would also enable the mills to close the loop, since the elimination of all chlorine bleaching would also eliminate corrosion-causing chloride ions. Such a closed-loop system would also greatly reduce the amount of fresh water needed by the mill.

Consumers are prepared to accept less bright paper products, if given the choice and if educated accordingly. Opinion polls have shown again and again that consumers are more than prepared to shop consciously and that the onus is on industry to produce such products.

Very few paper products require high brightness, high quality printing papers being one of these. Yet, as we are able to see from the example of the West German company Hannoversche Papierfabrik, even this market can be satisfied by using chlorine-free sulfite pulp.

In fact, the Swedish Chemical Inspectorate published a study last year, which investigated different kinds of paper and whether these could be produced without the use of chlorine. This government study concluded that there was not one single paper product that could not also have been produced without chlorine.

Aside from eliminating chlorine-based bleaching, it is essential that all mills install secondary treatment facilities to degrade and detoxify the remaining effluent. It is encouraging to see that Canada is now following the lead of other countries to require secondary treatment for all mills, and not only those that are located along rivers and smaller streams. It is less encouraging to see that Sweden, which has done so much work with regard to reducing the generation of chlorinated compounds at source, is still not forcing its mills along the Baltic Sea to employ secondary treatment.

A sophisticated effluent treatment system is also of particular importance for CTMP mills, which have benefitted greatly from the growing market demand for chlorine-free pulp, but often do not employ the kind of sophisticated secondary treatment necessary to degrade the high acute toxicity of this effluent. A newly-proposed CTMP mill in Canada has promised to install the first chemical recovery for CTMP mills.

Instead of full-heartedly pursuing further development of chlorine-free bleaching technologies and the marketing of less bleached products, the industry is investing vast amounts of money in the construction of new, huge kraft mills, again designed to produce highly bleached market pulp, and again using chlorine-based bleaching technologies.

Even with technology that would guarantee AOX discharges of between 1.5 and 1.0 kg AOX/ton of pulp, the sheer size of these new mills will make them become another point source of large-scale discharges of organochlorine compounds.

At the same time, existing kraft mills use the fact that they have to install better bleaching technologies as an excuse to double the original capacity, thus offsetting any improvement with regard to the overall discharge of organochlorines.

Greenpeace views new kraft mill proposals as incompatible with the concept of sustainable development for other reasons as well. Due to their sheer size, these proposed new kraft mills will require either large scale clear-cut logging of virgin and old-growth forests or intensive tree plantations, both of which are incompatible with sustainable forest management practices. Both wipe out eco-systems to replace them with monocultures.

At the same time, our waste mountains are ever growing. Many cities have recently introduced recycling programs, or will soon do so. But the collected wastepaper is already exceeding the absorption capacity of existing recycling mills. At the same time, institutions and environmental groups cannot find sufficient supplies of office paper made of recycled fibers.

There can only be one conclusion to this, and that is to build recycling mills using clean recycling technologies, and at the same time to freeze the production capacity of virgin pulp, while converting the production process to become environmentally friendly and chlorine-free.

Exhibit 31.6   Editorial from Pulp and Paper International—May 1990

Why we must win public support

John Luke, president and chief executive officer of US pulp and paper producer Westvaco, looks at eight environmental challenges which will confront the pulp and paper industry in the future. Besides the development for cleaner processes and better forestry, he also stresses the importance of winning public support, and the need for positive action to overcome misconceptions about the industry's environmental record. This Viewpoint is based on a speech given to the American Paper Institute's Annual Paper Week, held in New York City, USA, in March.

LOOKING AHEAD, we shall work to build as progressive an environmental record in the future as we have in the past:

First, our products will be under constant and intensive scrutiny. They must not only be safe, they must be perceived as making a positive contribution to public health and the quality of life. Our product integrity must be beyond question.

Second, our forest management will also face increasing public scrutiny. Our forest practices will have to be progressively more environmentally sensitive.

Third, our industry will have to make on-going and measurable progress in reducing pollution both in the atmosphere around our mills and in receiving waters. We will also feel pressure from the public relating to the general problems of acid rain, global warming and toxic fear. Standards will be progressively complex and stringent, and the public more demanding.

Fourth, we will have to cope with new trace chemical challenges as advancing analytical technology identifies them and as they are cast in the role of undermining human health. We will face these trace chemical alarms in our products, in our effluents, in our solid waste disposal and throughout our mills.

Fifth, we will face growing emphasis on "environmental aesthetics"—the range of public nuisance factors which may not represent an actual threat to our natural environment, but which are perceived as having an impact on the quality of life.

Sixth are environmental accidents. The running aground of the oil tanker Valdez in Alaska is fresh in everyone's mind, and both the public and the media will be intolerant of future accidents.

Seventh is the growing pressure for environmental codes of conduct and responsibility. The momentum for these is increasing and each of us must decide whether to react to the calls of others or to take a lead in formulating our own codes. We have decided to take a lead at Westvaco. We have formed a new committee of our board of directors, called the Committee on the Environment. It meets each quarter, and we feel that it is a constructive response to the developing environmental climate.

Eighth, our environmental success in the future is going to depend on how ably we manage our effluents, on how effectively we earn support for our progress, and on how we work for sound environmental policy.

Looking at these eight factors, we know that we can manage our effluents, but developing broad public support is a newer dimension to the problem. It will mean taking steps with all of our constituencies— our employees, local communities, the media and our elected representatives at all levels. Our progress has to be recognized and not diminished by emotion and misrepresentation on the part of activists. The industry alone has the responsibility for providing the perspective, the facts and the balance necessary for clear thinking and clear action on the public's part.

The dimension of environmental policy is also new. It is critical that we help shape an environmental policy which is responsive to genuine risk and which protects the natural environment and human health, with sound science and regulatory reason as its foundation. This is essential to the future of our industry, and it is equally essential to the competitive position of all US industry in the world economy.

These new environmental dimensions are going to be just as important as the degree of measurable environmental progress we are able to accomplish. Our reputation will be the result of our actual environmental performance and the public's perception of that performance.

In the USA, we are complying with the most stringent environmental requirements in the world. No other country's paper industry has made the progress which we have made in environmental improvement.

But we now face an even more challenging environmental future, which will require us to be outspoken about our performance and to work with skill and determination to help the nation adopt soundly-based environmental policies. That is what it will take to stay on the environmental high ground.

Environmental groups lobbied for activated sludge-treatment plants to cleanse the effluent entirely of organochlorines. All pulp mills had to be equipped with primary treatment facilities, but the industry considered secondary treatment, such as activated sludge-treatment, unnecessary. Environmentalists estimated the cost of activated sludge-treatment to be A$25 million for APM. While they realized the industry would likely be unreceptive to such a large expense—for equipment which contributed few tangible benefits to the company—environmentalists did not consider it a quixotic request. One environmentalist typified the rising sentiment of Australians when he noted, "How can you put a dollar value on the sensible use of the environment?"

As he read accounts of the Kayser mill controversy, McRae reflected on long-term opportunities:

> If we sit still, we'll get hurt sometime before the year 2000. Whoever takes the next big step will have it made in Australia. We are looking toward putting in a paper machine of 150,000 tonnes. Whatever we don't use for uncoated papers could be our foundation for going into coated papers. We'd only have to add a coater at the end of the machine. Total investment would be A$350

Exhibit 31.7   Steps in the Pulp and Paper Chain for Fine Paper

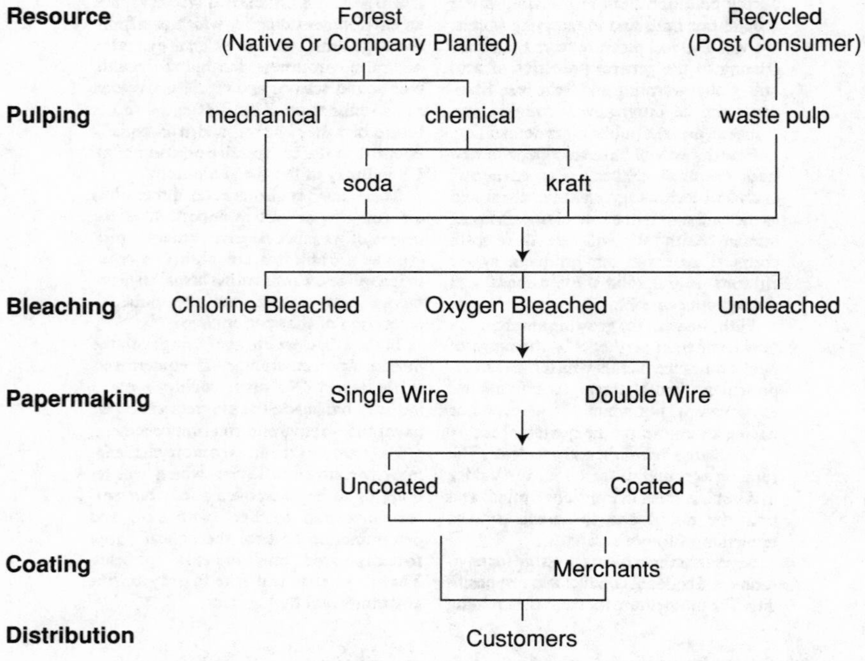

Exhibit 31.8   Precautionary Principle

The Nordic Council's Conference on Pollution of the Seas* adopted this principle as its standard for environmental protection.

> The need for an effective precautionary approach, with that important principle intended to safeguard the marine ecosystem by, among other things, eliminating and preventing pollution emissions where there is reason to believe that damage or harmful effects are likely to be caused, even where there is inadequate or inclusive scientific evidence to prove a casual link between emissions effect.

*The 1989 conference included members of parliament from Beligum, Canada, Czechoslovakia, Denmark, the Federal Republic of Germany, Finland, the German Democratic Republic, Iceland, Ireland, the Netherlands, Norway, Poland, Sweden, Switzerland, the U.S.S.R., the United Kingdom, the Faeroe Islands, and Greenland.

million, but we'd have tremendous flexibility to alternate between coated and uncoated. Of course, this would also mean a big pulp mill, but we could financially justify new pulp capacity in any case.

If PCA decides to expand, the unknown is what they would do with the capacity they've currently got. Their machines are a lot older and less efficient than ours are. Would they build two machines or will they just put in one? And will they close down all of the inefficient machines? What will their net increase be?

Some local environmentalists invoked the popular aphorism, "Think globally, act locally," to argue against any expansion of the Australian paper industry. To preserve the earth's environment, they felt, paper use worldwide had to decrease. Environmental groups throughout the world advocated a hierarchy of measures to protect the environment: reduce first, reuse second, and recycle third.

McRae put down the accounts of the Kayser affair and turned to the June issue of Pulp and Paper International (see Exhibit 31.5). Despite APM's stunning success in fine papers, McRae knew he would have to chart APM's future course very carefully.

CHAPTER 32

Beyond World Class

The New Manufacturing Strategy

Robert H. Hayes and Gary P. Pisano

URING THE 1980s, U.S. manufacturing companies rediscovered the power that comes from superior manufacturing and initiated a variety of activities to improve their competitiveness. Many announced that their "manufacturing strategy" was to become "world class"—as good, along various measures, as the best companies in their industries. In pursuing this goal, they typically adopted one or more of a growing number of improvement programs, such as TQM (Total Quality Management), JIT (Just-in-Time) production, and DFM (Design for Manufacturability), not to mention lean manufacturing, reengineering, benchmarking, and the ubiquitous team approach.

While some of these improvement efforts have been successful, the majority, according to recent surveys, have not. Even some of the Japanese companies that pioneered these approaches appear to be having second thoughts. These conflicting results have led to frustration, confusion, and a growing debate about whether the difficulties with these efforts are the result of poor management or of flaws in the programs themselves.

This debate is misdirected. The problem is not with the programs nor with the way they are implemented. The problem is that simply *improving* manufacturing—by, for example, adopting JIT, TQM, or some other three-letter acronym—is *not* a strategy for using manufacturing to achieve competitive advantage. Neither is aspiring to lean manufacturing, continuous improvement, or world-class status.

In today's turbulent competitive environment, a company more than ever needs a strategy that specifies the kind of competitive advantage that

Robert H. Hayes, the Philip Caldwell Professor of Business Administration at the Harvard Business School, specializes in manufacturing strategy and international competitiveness. This is his 16th contribution to HBR. Gary P. Pisano, associate professor at the Harvard Business School, specializes in technology and manufacturing strategy.

it is seeking in its marketplace and articulates how that advantage is to be achieved. If managers pin their competitive hopes on the implementation of a few best-practice approaches, they implicitly abandon the central concept of a strategy in favor of a generic approach to competitive success. How can a company expect to achieve any sort of competitive advantage if its only goal is to be "as good as" its toughest competitors?

We propose a new explanation for the problems that many companies have experienced with improvement programs. Our view reflects the current shift in thinking not only about manufacturing but also about the essence of competitive strategy itself. And it integrates manufacturing strategy with the notions of both core competencies and learning organizations.

The crux of the issue is that most companies focus on the *form* of their organizational assets—for example, the mechanics of JIT and TQM—rather than on their *substance*, the skills and capabilities that enable a factory to excel and make it possible for various improvement programs to achieve their desired results. The consequence of this outlook is that managers have tended to view such programs as solutions to specific problems rather than as stepping-stones *in an intended direction*.

Looking at manufacturing strategy as an intended direction has ramifications for almost every aspect of running a corporation because it implies that the key to long-term success is being able *to do certain things* better than your competitors can. Such superior organizational capabilities provide a competitive advantage that is much more sustainable than one based on something you can build or buy. You may be able to buy access to a certain technology, for example, but you cannot buy the ability to produce it efficiently, sell it effectively, or advance it over time. The road to competitive success is not paved with advanced equipment, the transfer of production to a low-wage area, or improving quality by adopting a TQM system. These are all programs that your competitors can copy relatively easily.

In a stable environment, competitive strategy is about staking out a position, and manufacturing strategy focuses on getting better at the things necessary to defend that position. In turbulent environments, however, the goal of strategy becomes *strategic flexibility*. Being world-class is not enough; a company also has to have the capability to switch gears—from, for example, rapid product development to low cost—relatively quickly and with minimal resources. The job of manufacturing is to provide that capability.

If managers consider the capabilities they want to develop or preserve, they may make very different decisions about closing a plant or exiting a business, about "make versus buy" decisions, about alliances and acquisitions, about whether to automate an operation or move it to a low-wage area, about training and management career paths. (See Box 32.1, "A New Approach to Investment.") Considering desired future capabilities can also help managers think through whether JIT or any of the other new "best practices" is the best vehicle for building the capabilities that will be central to their company's long-term success.

Box 32.1

A New Approach to Investment

Traditionally, companies have viewed investments in new facilities, technology, and R&D as the primary means to enhance their existing manufacturing capabilities. But according to the new approach to manufacturing strategy, managers should think about investments more in terms of their capacity to build new capabilities. Rarely, if ever, is a strategically worthwhile capability created through a one-shot investment. Capabilities that provide enduring sources of competitive advantage are usually built over time through a series of investments in facilities, human capital, and knowledge.

The idea of investments as crucial steps in the capability-building process conflicts with an assumption that often underlies capital-budgeting decisions: that investments can be reversed or delayed. According to traditional capital budgeting, an asset that is sold can often be bought back, and an investment can often be deferred with no penalty other than that contained in the time value of money. This may be true for certain types of assets, such as a new plant. But a company's capabilities are more than its physical assets. In fact, they are largely embodied in the collective skills and knowledge of its people and the organizational procedures that shape the way employees interact. Like muscles, capabilities embodied in human capital atrophy with disuse—and deterioration can be irreversible.

Consider a company that is contemplating closing a plant. Accounting standards require that it recognize the loss in book value resulting from that closure. But what about the loss of specialized capabilities embedded in the plant—things like skills in precision machining, a highly motivated workforce, and detailed knowledge of customer needs? If demand picks up again, the company can go out and buy a plant and equipment, but replacing the human capital that took years to build will be much more difficult.

The traditional financial models used to evaluate capital investments also ignore the fact that investments can create opportunities for learning. These opportunities are a lot like financial options: they have value, and that value increases as the future becomes more unpredictable. If a company cannot predict whether future customers will emphasize high performance or low cost, an option that would allow the company to achieve either one as the situation evolves has a very high value.

Consider a company that needs to expand capacity. One way might be to add a production line that is identical to existing lines. A second might be to invest in an R&D effort directed at improving productivity. Certainly the latter is more risky, but it also provides an opportunity to gain a deeper understanding of the production process. This new knowledge, in turn, might create opportunities for future investments, such as a new design for production equipment or the development of substitute materials. It might also open up new competitive options. Discovering a way to reduce setup times, for example, may increase capacity without additional investment. Alternatively, it could allow the company to produce smaller lot sizes without any loss in capacity. Neither of these would be options if the company expanded by adding another line just like its existing ones.

Some history is needed to help explain the forces behind this new strategic framework for manufacturing.

Until the early 1980s, most managers in the United States thought about manufacturing in terms of a paradigm whose roots went back over 100 years. The American system of manufacturing, with its emphasis on mass markets, standard designs, and high-volume production using interchangeable parts, revolutionized manufacturing in the mid-1800s. Modified and elaborated by the principles of scientific management as promulgated by Frederick Taylor and his disciples as well as by such great industrialists as Isaac Singer, Andrew Carnegie, and Henry Ford, this new paradigm helped the United States become an industrial powerhouse by the 1920s.

The following ideas were accepted as dogma: that work was most efficiently done when divided up and assigned to specialists; that managers and staff experts should do the thinking so that workers could concentrate on "doing"; that every process was characterized by a certain amount of variation, hence an irreducible rate of defects; and that communication in an organization should be tightly controlled and should proceed through a hierarchical chain of command. Manufacturing should emphasize long runs, utilize equipment designed for each process stage whose capacities are matched as closely as possible, and use inventories to buffer different stages both from each other and from the erratic behavior of suppliers and customers. Work should be organized and conducted systematically, in a logical sequence and under tight supervision.

In 1969, Wickham Skinner challenged Taylor's assertion that there was one best way to manufacture in his now-classic *HBR* article, "Manufacturing—Missing Link in Corporate Strategy" (May–June). The kernel of his argument was that: (a) companies have different strengths and weaknesses and can choose to differentiate themselves from their competitors in different ways; (b) similarly, different production systems, the composite of decisions in a number of key decision areas, have different operating characteristics; and therefore, rather than adopting an industry-standard production system, (c) the "task" for a company's manufacturing organization is to configure a production system that, through a series of interrelated and internally consistent choices, reflects the priorities and trade-offs implicit in its specific competitive situation and strategy.

Despite the emergence of a totally different world order for industrial competition, this basic framework has proven to be remarkably robust. A number of common practices used today trace their roots to it. For example, the concept of a "focused factory" follows naturally from the idea that no single organization can do all things equally well. Consider a company that markets one product line sold in a market where purchasing decisions are driven largely by price and another to people who are willing to pay a premium for high quality and customized features. Since no one plant can be expected to provide all of these characteristics equally well, the focused factory concept argues for splitting the production of the two lines into separate factories or subunits within the same plant.

Another offshoot is the idea of matching product and market evolution with manufacturing-process characteristics. The product-process life cycle suggests that as a product matures, the relative importance of competitive priorities will shift, and these shifts have important implications for manufacturing. For example, in its early stages, a product often competes on the basis of special features or innovative designs. This calls for a production process that is very flexible with respect to market shifts and design changes. Such an operation might employ highly skilled workers, general-purpose tooling, and little automation; moreover, it should be located close to R&D and, to reduce the risk of obsolescence, produce small batches. As the product matures, the market typically evolves toward a small number of high-volume products that compete with each other largely on the basis of price. To this end, factories ought to be highly automated, located in areas where labor or material costs are low, employ less skilled workers, and, in order to minimize changeover costs, schedule production around long runs.

Skinner's framework for manufacturing strategy is based on the notion of strategic fit: a company's manufacturing system should reflect its competitive position and strategy. Focus provides both a means to achieve this fit and a discipline for maintaining it in the face of a barrage of opportunities. And the product-process life cycle helps guide the adjustments in strategy and systems that will likely be required in a changing world.

It soon became clear, however, that this framework is incomplete. It does not explain, for example, why two appliance makers may adopt similar competitive strategies and choose similar production processes, but one may end up being far more successful than the other.

Japanese companies began in the late 1970s to assault world markets in a number of industries with increasing ferocity. Their secret weapon turned out to be sheer manufacturing virtuosity. Most were producing products similar to those offered by Western companies and marketing them in similar ways. What made these products attractive was not only their price but also their low incidence of defects, their reliability, and their durability.

For a while, it appeared that Japan's manufacturing superiority could be attributed to the traditional precepts of manufacturing strategy. By and large, the Japanese adopted consistent policies in their pursuit of high efficiency and quality. They also operated focused factories; in fact, their emphasis on "repetitive manufacturing," "Just-In-Time" production, and smooth work flows led them to be almost obsessive in their pursuit of long runs of standard products. And their emphasis on continuous improvement appeared, at least initially to those looking for familiar reference points, to mirror the U.S. fascination with learning curves.

But as our eyes slowly grew accustomed to the many nuances of Japanese culture and began to pick out the details of their management practices, certain paradoxes became evident. During the 1980s, a new paradigm of manufacturing that challenged both the American system of manufacturing and some of the basic tenets of manufacturing strategy began to emerge.

Are "trade-offs" really necessary? Manufacturing strategists long argued that different production systems exhibited different operating characteristics: some were good at low cost, some at high quality, and some at fast response times. In designing a production system, therefore, managers had to decide which was most important. And if there were conflicts among different objectives, they had to make tough choices based on a careful analysis of the trade-offs. But many Japanese factories practicing lean manufacturing appeared to surpass their U.S. counterparts on several dimensions: they achieved lower cost, higher quality, faster product introductions, and greater flexibility, all at the same time.

In their widely read book on the auto industry, authors Womack, Jones, and Roos (1990) describe how, in contrast to mass production, lean production

> is "lean" because it uses less of everything . . . half the human effort in the factory, half the factory space, half the investment in tools, half the engineering hours to develop a new product in half the time. Also it requires keeping far less than half the needed inventory on-site, resulting in fewer defects, and produces a greater and ever-growing variety of products.[1]

Lean manufacturing has apparently eliminated the trade-offs among productivity, investment, and variety. (See Box 32.2, "Allegheny Ludlum: Minimizing Manufacturing Trade-Offs.")

Do factories have to be focused? Although Japanese factories initially appeared to restrict product variety and encourage uninterrupted work flows, many elite Japanese companies embarked on an orgy of product proliferation in the 1980s. Sony, for example, introduced over 300 versions of its basic Walkman (disclaiming the need for market research, it simply introduced a new model and saw how it sold), and Seiko was renowned for its ability to introduce a new watch model every working day. Didn't this product proliferation refute the idea of focus? The emergence of new flexible manufacturing systems, which apparently made it possible for factories to produce a broad range of products with little loss in efficiency, also seemed to undercut the need for focused factories.

[1]Womack, Jones, and Roos (1990), p. 13.

Box 32.2

*Allegheny Ludlum: Minimizing Manufacturing Trade-Offs**

The Allegheny Ludlum Corporation is one U.S. company that has been pursuing a strategy of minimizing the trade-offs inherent in manufacturing by expanding its capabilities through a variety of tailored programs. The specialty steelmaker, which has had a consistently high return on equity in the last 13 years (a period during which many steelmakers lost money), has managed to achieve a substantial degree of flexibility (in terms of customizing individual orders) and low costs.

Allegheny's success cannot be explained by its adherence to the traditional concept of manufacturing strategy or to lean manufacturing, but by the way it has successfully integrated both. Like other companies that have embraced lean manufacturing, Allegheny emphasizes product variety, continuous efforts to reduce manufacturing costs, teamwork, and delegated decision making.

But some of Allegheny's approaches contradict conventional lean-manufacturing practices. Although the company employs the cross-functional teams favored in lean manufacturing, it maintains a primarily functional structure. And while lean manufacturing stresses "horizontal" problem solving (dealing with problems at lower levels in the organization), Allegheny's top management is very involved with all aspects of the business. Daily reports on productivity, utilization, yield, rejects, and variances flow vertically to its CEO, who uses the information to institute immediate corrective actions.

The steelmaker has made a commitment to invest in, improve, and capture (through models) its knowledge about process technology. To encourage plants to undertake technically risky experiments, the company charges their cost to a separate corporate account rather than to the plants themselves.

One such endeavor developed capabilities that enabled Allegheny to double the capacity of its melt shop without any physical expansion. This involved several projects. One focused on finding lower cost raw materials, while others concentrated on increasing batch sizes, reducing the time required between batches, and cutting the time between the completion of the melt and further processing. These projects involved experimentation on the shop floor, with the active involvement of first-line supervisors, and contributions from other departments. For example, R&D developed computer programs to increase control over the melting process. This increase in capacity gave Allegheny the option of expanding its total output of commodity steels (at a lower cost than competitors), making more customized orders, or some combination of both. When there is uncertainty about the demand for each type of product, having this option is obviously valuable.

Like companies engaged in lean manufacturing, Allegheny engages in vigorous and continuous manufacturing improvement. Unlike improvements in many of these companies, these improvements take place within a strategic framework that recognizes that the key to achieving competitive advantage is deciding which capabilities to build.

*Information for this example was obtained from the HBS case "Allegheny Ludlum Steel Corporation" (9-686-087) by Artemis March under the supervision of Professor David Garvin and the HBS case "Allegheny Ludlum: Research and Engineering Resource Allocation" (9-692-027) by Geoffrey Gill under the supervision of Professor Dorothy Leonard Barton.

Is strategic fit enough? Although the traditional manufacturing strategy framework provided a vision of the contribution that a company's manufacturing organization could make to its competitive success, it left vague certain key issues. For example, while it was clear that once a company settled on competitive strategy, it was less clear how much freedom manufacturing should have to develop competencies that went beyond the strategy's immediate requirements. And there was little discussion of the criteria that should be used to guide the selection of capabilities to be acquired.

Moreover, while many Japanese companies had built exceptional manufacturing capabilities, they did not appear to have an enduring approach to competition. Instead, the form of their attack changed, sometimes with bewildering speed, from low cost to high precision to flexibility to innovativeness. And through such changes, they were sometimes able to transform the nature of competition within an industry.

Japanese companies had apparently found an approach to manufacturing uniformly superior to the "Taylor system," which was characterized by an emphasis on speed and flexibility rather than volume and cost. According to this lean approach, people should be broadly trained rather than specialized. Staff is "overhead," and overhead is bad. Rejects are unacceptable. Communication should take place informally and horizontally among line workers rather than through prescribed hierarchical paths. Equipment should be general purpose, possibly using some form of programmable automation, and organized in cells that produce a group of similar products rather than specialized by process stage. Production throughput time is more important than labor or equipment utilization. Inventory, like rejects, is "waste." Supplier relationships should be long-term and cooperative. Activities associated with product development should be done concurrently, not sequentially, and should be carried out by cross-functional teams.

The Japanese approach has brought us full circle from the days of Frederick Taylor: speed and flexibility have replaced cost and hierarchy, but once again, we have settled on "one best way" to compete. The question, then, is what role is left for manufacturing strategy? What's the point of worrying about whether you should emphasize cost or flexibility when your competitors have adopted approaches to manufacturing that allow them to beat you on both?

In the relatively stable environment of the 1960s and early 1970s, the name of the game in strategy was to find an attractive industry position (offer the lowest cost or the highest quality) and build a competitive fortress around it. A good manufacturing strategy was one that defended a company's position through a narrowly focused set of capabilities.

When, however, the terms of competition shifted from low cost to high quality to flexibility to innovativeness, companies found that both their competitive strategy and their manufacturing strategy quickly became outdated. Centralizing production in a highly automated facility may look like a brilliant decision when customers place a premium on low price. But as the marketplace shifts and competitors adjust to provide higher quality and faster response times, while keeping their costs *reasonably* low, a centralized facility can quickly become a corporate millstone.

On the other hand, companies that choose product innovation rather than low cost as the way to compete could have the opposite problem. For example, Compaq prospered in the 1980s by being one of the fastest developers of new products in the personal computer industry. But it ran into trouble in the 1990s, when customers placed greater importance on low cost and fast response in customizing products, incrementally improving features and delivery. After great organizational turmoil, Compaq was able to realign its operations to reduce its costs and, more recently, has begun to make further changes in hopes of providing a customer responsiveness that matches rival Dell Computer's.

Unfortunately, neither the traditional approach to manufacturing strategy nor the lean-manufacturing paradigm pay much attention to bolstering an organization's strategic flexibility. In fact, both of these approaches often hinder flexibility. The early approach to manufacturing strategy led top managers to focus their companies' operations around specific competitive priorities that tended to make them vulnerable to strategic shifts. And lean manufacturing drives companies to become similar to one another.

The problem is not with lean manufacturing itself nor with any of its component practices like concurrent engineering, JIT, or TQM. The problem is the way companies apply these practices to their own problems. Companies tend to embark on such programs to correct particular weaknesses in their operations. But managers typically define their problems in terms of starting points and end points: "We need to reduce our variable cost by $1 per unit," or, "We need to reduce our defect level to 200 parts per million." And they seek solutions through the adoption of specific practices: "We're going to implement a JIT system in order to become more responsive," or, "We need a TQM program to improve our quality."

It is hard to imagine any manufacturing-improvement process progressing very far without specifying certain changes in practices and measurable goals. But thinking in terms of time periods and framing the solutions as the adoption of specific practices can lead to two types of problems. The first is equating an improvement in manufacturing capabilities with a manufacturing strategy. The second is failing to recognize that new practices build new capabilities that can form the basis of a new manufacturing strategy—*if* they are recognized and exploited.

After embarking on a major manufacturing-improvement effort, companies may find that just when they appear to have solved the problem (for example, reduced the quality gap between themselves and their competitors), they encounter new problems that require new approaches, some of which seem to contradict those just put in place. Once quality has improved, for instance, companies may find they may need to compress product-development times or reduce delivered costs.

Some would argue that such changes in priorities simply reflect the need for continuous improvement. After all, one can never expect to stop making improvements. Unfortunately for those involved—the managers, first-line supervisors, shop-floor employees—such efforts are more like continuous frustration. Despite the seemingly successful implementation of one new set of practices after another, the company always seems to be trying to catch up with its competitors.

Whistler, a U.S. consumer electronics company, faced a choice in the late 1980s when it was rapidly losing market share to Asian competitors: either improve domestic operations to achieve cost parity or move offshore, as its U.S. competitors had done. Whistler chose the former and succeeded in reducing its manufacturing costs to Asian levels over two years. Unfortunately, by the time the company achieved this, Asian competitors were taking market share by introducing a barrage of new products.

Whistler's problem was not that its improvement program was flawed or poorly implemented; it had succeeded in reducing costs dramatically. But in doing so, it had distracted management attention from new product development while Asian competitors had been able to become more innovative *and* maintain relatively low costs.

Without realizing it, Whistler's manufacturing-improvement efforts had actually resulted in a shift in its manufacturing strategy from being the first to introduce innovative products to achieving cost parity. Had the company viewed its problem in this light, it might have chosen a different path. Rather than simply trying to change its operations to become more cost competitive, but less innovative, it might have looked for ways to *change the trade-off* between cost and innovativeness.

By viewing different improvement programs as targeted solutions to specific competitive problems, managers overlook the true power of these programs: their ability to build new capabilities. Thus, a key role for a company's manufacturing strategy is to guide the selection of improvement programs.

Consider a plant that establishes the long-term goal of drastically reducing its lead times and inventories. It can proceed toward this goal in either of two directions. One might be the immediate adoption of a JIT pull system. If the plant lacks the skills that make JIT work (for example, low setup times and defect rates), this approach might be very costly. Adopting this system will, however, create strong incentives to reduce setup times and defect rates, as well as to develop other JIT-related skills and induce an ethic of continuous improvement. Over time, a true JIT system might emerge.

An alternative approach would be to begin with a manufacturing resources planning (MRP) system, a computerized production-scheduling system based on forecasts of future demand and production lead times, as well as on real-time data from the shop floor. The initial results might not be close to JIT. Lead times, in fact, might even temporarily increase, since MRP systems tend to be rather clumsy in handling schedule changes and rush orders. On the other hand, MRP exerts pressure to improve shop-floor discipline and develop better data, which facilitates better production scheduling and the transition to computer integrated manufacturing. Once MRP control has been established, the lead times in the system can be steadily whittled away until it approaches a pure JIT system.

Both approaches may eventually allow the company to respond quickly to customer demands with low inventories. However, they cultivate different capabilities over time. Adopting an MRP-type system fosters skills in using computers and managing databases, neither of which are central to a JIT approach. Pull systems, on the other hand, encourage skills in factory-floor problem solving, incremental process improvement, and fast response. Each approach, in short, leaves the organization with a different set of skills and thus a different set of strategic options in the future. A decision about which approach to pursue should not be made without considering which set of capabilities will be most valuable to the company.

Thinking about TQM, JIT, and other manufacturing-improvement programs not as *ends* in themselves, but in terms of the capabilities they both require and create drives one to think differently about solutions. Within a static framework, solutions to problems are regarded as one-shot deals. In a dynamic setting, however, solutions are viewed as part of a longer term *path* of improvement. Individual practices are adopted not just to solve an immediate problem but also to build new skills that open up new opportunities. From this perspective, manufacturing strategy is not just about aligning operations to current competitive priorities but also about selecting and creating the operating capabilities a company will need in the future. (See the Box 32.2, "Hitachi-Seiki: Building Capabilities.")

This change in perspective has tremendous implications for basic corporate decisions. Let us look at two examples.

Focused Factories

Advocates of the traditional approach to manufacturing strategy and lean manufacturing consider the idea of focus differently. The idea that factories should be focused on a narrow set of tasks or objectives continues to gain acceptance in the United States, even though it is not always clear whether a given facility should focus around products, processes, or regions. Advocates of lean manufacturing, in contrast, regard focus as an outdated concept, reflecting America's long fixation with mass production.

Despite their apparent differences, both fail to recognize that how a manufacturing system is organized affects not only its current performance but also, over time, the things it can do easily or with difficulty. Whether and how a plant should be focused depends on the capabilities it wants to build.

A plant's skills can be thought of as the set of tasks it regards as routine. Whether or not a given task is routine depends on experience and capabilities. For example, high-precision assembly may, over time, become routine for one plant but still be considered very difficult by a less experienced plant. This explains why so many poorly performing plants have been transformed by adopting the focus concept. Their poor performance reflected a lack of operating skills, and focus provided a mechanism for channeling managerial attention and resources toward mastering those skills. As an organization gains operating experience, difficult tasks become routine, and it can take on additional complexity with little performance penalty.

Vertical Integration and Sourcing

Lean manufacturing favors outsourcing and long-term relationships with suppliers. U.S. companies, on the other hand, have traditionally viewed sourcing decisions in terms of financial trade-offs and resource constraints. Again, both views downplay the dynamics of such decisions.

Consider a company that is trying to decide whether to make a component or buy it from an outside supplier. Typically, such decisions are made by analyzing the relevant production and organizational costs of the two alternatives. That kind of analysis becomes suspect, however, if one thinks not in terms of parts that get incorporated into products, but in terms of those capabilities that are closely linked and mutually reinforcing as opposed to those that can be separated. If a potential supplier possesses capabilities that are essential to a company's competitive success, the company must either work to assimilate those capabilities or develop very close, partnership-like relations with that supplier.

A decision to outsource an activity may completely alter the calculus for future decisions. Like people, organizations can forget how to do things. As skills atrophy through disuse, bringing activities back in-house at some future point becomes less feasible. So, like the decision about focused factories, outsourcing requires an evaluation of learning potential. Bringing in-house some activity with which the company has little expertise may be inefficient and less "lean" in the short term but absolutely essential over the long term because it builds critical skills that the company currently lacks.

Manufacturing strategy can no longer confine itself to guiding short-term choices between conflicting priorities like cost, quality, and flexibility. Nor can managers limit themselves to choosing which faddish improvement technique to adopt or which company to emulate. Long-term success requires that a company continually seek new ways to differentiate itself from its competitors. The companies that are able to transform their manufacturing organizations into sources of competitive advantage are those that can harness various improvement programs to the broader goal of selecting and developing unique operating capabilities. How can a company create such a strategy?

First, it must start with the idea that the primary way manufacturing adds value to an enterprise is by enabling it to do certain things better than its competitors can. Which things and how they are better will be different for individual companies, and for the same company at individual points in its evolution. Every company occasionally falls behind its competitors in some area, but for the long term, it must identify one or two areas—for instance, flexibility and innovativeness—in which it will try to be in the forefront most of the time.

Obviously, these capabilities should be ones that customers value; even better, they should be ones that are hard for competitors to duplicate. Customers may value low cost, for example, but as many consumer electronics companies learned during the 1970s and 1980s, achieving low cost by going offshore does not provide a sustainable advantage because competitors can do the same. Competitors can also license a new technology or hire those who participated in developing it. Great manufacturing strategies are built on unique skills and capabilities, not on investments in buildings, equipment, or specific individuals.

Second, a company must develop a plan for building the capabilities it wants to acquire. This is where the question of which manufacturing-improvement approaches to use and in which order comes in. A company may decide to use teams, but only after it has cultivated the capabilities that will allow teams to be effective: credibility and trust between functional groups and a cadre of effective team leaders.

Before adopting any program, managers should ask themselves, "What specific capabilities will this program create for my organization, and are these capabilities valuable in competitive terms?" Providing clear answers to such questions is usually easier if managers focus on only a few, carefully selected improvement activities. And the ones chosen will probably have to be modified to meet the company's needs. Neither capabilities nor improvement programs come in one size fits all.

In today's world, where nothing is predictable and unfamiliar competitors emerge from unexpected directions at the worst possible time, a company should think of itself as a collection of evolving capabilities, not just as a collection of products and businesses, which provide the flexibility needed to embark in new directions. Corporate strategy must provide a framework for guiding the selection, development, and exploitation of these capabilities. Since many of the capabilities with the greatest competitive value reside in a company's manufacturing organization, corporate strategy must become much more explicit about, and reliant on, manufacturing considerations than in the past.

Reference

1. Womack, James, Daniel Jones, and Daniel Roos (1990). *The Machine That Changed the World.* New York: Macmillan, p. 13.

Box 32.3 _____

*Hitachi-Seiki: Building Capabilities**

Many Japanese companies have realized that by expanding the range of their manufacturing capabilities, they increase their strategic options. Even so, few have created strategies that spell out exactly which capabilities they should develop to enhance their strategic flexibility. Hitachi-Seiki seems to be one of the exceptions. A relatively obscure manufacturer of machine tools in the 1950s, by the mid-1980s, the company had become one of the world's leading suppliers of flexible manufacturing systems, computer-controlled equipment that can perform a variable sequence of machining tasks.

As early as 1952, when the first numerically controlled machine tool was developed at MIT, Hitachi-Seiki set for itself the extremely ambitious goal of developing the capabilities required to become a leader in computerized automation. It began by embarking on basic research in automated production, some of which was done in collaboration with other Japanese manufacturers through a consortium organized by the Ministry of International Trade and Industry. After the consortium disbanded and despite the fact that the many problems with the new technology led most companies to stick with traditional manufacturing processes, Hitachi-Seiki continued to build its knowledge base.

Recognizing early on that successful automation would require the integration of mechanical design (the traditional machine tool technology) and electronics, the company began hiring electrical engineers. And in 1967, it set up a new engineering discipline, which it called "mechatronics."

The company's earliest efforts in flexible manufacturing systems failed. Its first system, developed in 1972, had only slightly better productivity than conventional machinery and was plagued by reliability and coordination problems. Yet developing that system built capabilities for future projects. For example, it brought together for the first time some of the company's top engineers from different disciplines to write software. They encountered difficulties in coordinating their efforts. But through this early experience, Hitachi-Seiki was able to cultivate engineers with broad skills and perspectives.

The company's second project incorporated some of the lessons learned from the first. While the results were slightly better, it also fell short of its goals, and its productivity was still not high enough to generate an adequate return on investment. But the company again learned critical lessons. One was that viewing flexible manufacturing as a set of purely technical prob-

(continued)

lems that could be solved with technical expertise was a mistake. Instead, the company needed to take a systems approach to development that combined manufacturing and engineering perspectives.

For its third project, Hitachi-Seiki created a development team that brought together a variety of functions, including manufacturing, machine design, software engineering, and tool design. The project leader was trained as a mechanical engineer but had experience in tool design and manufacturing.

The team had learned from the prior projects that it would be difficult to develop one system that could achieve all the desired performance targets. These included automatic tool changing, flexible fixtures that could hold materials of different sizes, and the ability to operate untended. So the team members decided to develop three systems and created separate teams to tackle each. All three systems were finished in record time and met their financial and performance targets.

The lesson of the Hitachi-Seiki story is not simply, "If at first you don't succeed, try, try again." The company had a long-term goal, but lacked the capabilities to achieve it. Early projects were vehicles for building these capabilities. With each project, the company expanded its knowledge of technical matters (i.e., computer software) and organizational issues (i.e., how to integrate disciplines to solve problems). And with each successive project, engineers who began as specialists gradually became generalists.

After developing the company's first commercially successful flexible manufacturing system, many of the project team members were transferred to the Customer Service Department, where they designed and built systems to customers' specifications. This leveraged the skills they had developed and broadened their understanding of customer needs. It also ensured that a new group of engineers would begin to learn how to develop flexible manufacturing systems.

---

*Information for this example was obtained from the HBS case "Hitachi-Seiki" (Abridged: 9-690-067) by Robert Hayes. This case appears in this volume as No. 24.

CHAPTER 33

Mechanisms for Building and Sustaining Operations Improvement

David M. Upton

*T*HE NEED TO IMPROVE the effectiveness of operations has, over time, given rise to a series of philosophies, tools and techniques. Many of these appeared, at the time, to offer "the solution" to the continuing problems of ailing manufacturing performance. The faddish nature of such panaceas as Value Engineering, Quality Circles, Flexible Manufacturing Systems, Total Quality Management and Worker Empowerment often led to wide swings in managers' perception of their value—from "good" to "bad"—in just a few years. Each new technique, however, left its mark, and found its way into the operations manager's toolbox. The steady stream and changing nature of these methods and techniques vividly illustrate the evolution of the role of operations in corporations, and provide a window of insight into the general practical problems of building new operational capabilities.

This paper describes some common approaches to improving operations at the operating unit level and sustaining that improvement. The first part of the paper looks at the recent history of operating improvement; the second section describes common starting points for building improvement. The final section examines the challenges of sustaining an improvement path, and describes three models of continuous improvement.

1. The Background of Operations Improvement Techniques

Having experimented with a number of management fads, such as collecting firms, like stocks and bonds, into diversified portfolios, many Western

The research reported in this paper was supported by the Division of Research, Harvard Business School.

managers realized that corporate success was inherently transitory if not under-pinned by sound operational abilities at the operating-unit level. Various approaches for creating such capabilities may be divided into three distinct phases or philosophies, which overlap yet dominate their times.

A. Structural Solutions to Infrastructural Problems

In the 1970s, firms frequently attacked the problem of operations performance by addressing structural aspects of their operations strategy. In particular, a firm's facilities and sourcing strategies were often adjusted, chopped or wrenchingly changed as regimes of new managers stepped in to "fix" specific operations problems. Sudden, dramatic restructurings led to organizational units being selected for survival on the basis of their cost (and occasionally quality) performance and under-performing units were closed or sold-off. Components, even whole products, were often 'outsourced' to overseas suppliers, who could produce them at lower cost and thus provide an immediate apparent saving (see Chandler Home Products (B) [5][1]).

Such methods did rid operating networks of many poorly performing units which were unlikely to get better over time. Unfortunately, many potentially healthy babies were thrown out with the bathwater. A reliance solely on structural methods for improving operating performance fails for a number of reasons, not least of which is a failure to incorporate the fact that operations management is a *dynamic* activity. Organizational units are often unable to improve or perform because of the nature of the tasks assigned to them, as well as the measures used to evaluate their performance. Units may perform poorly because they have received the runt's share of investment capital, which leads to poor performance, resulting in less investment, and so on. Second, "poorly performing" units are often required to produce a wide variety of low-volume products or services. Although unprofitable according to traditional cost-accounting methods, they are justified as providing support to the product range as a whole. Finally, the most common performance measurements often single out as stars those units who happened to perform well on dimensions such as return on assets (often a bizarre fiction negotiated through transfer prices) or cost per unit (at the whim of cost accountants' allocation of overhead). Sometimes, *utilization* measures are used—which usually penalizes units that are required to deliver a wide variety of products or services.

This sledgehammer approach to pruning assets often resulted in haphazard "gardens" of factories in which the gardener not only weeded without cultivating, but also selected plants based on how green their leaves looked. Although many networks were indeed made leaner and meaner, in others valuable technical capabilities were thrown away and

---

[1]Numbers in square brackets refer to entries in References listed at end of this article.

good managers were lost. In addition, the units that remained were forced to suffer the less visible costs due to the loss of focus that results when a servicing unit is forced to take over some of the dead unit's responsibilities. In the worst cases, little was done to help improve a unit's performance aside from the usual corporate sticks and carrots.

Michigan Manufacturing Corporation [2], for example, had for many year struggled with what to do about an old plant which performed poorly according to its traditional measures. Finally in an attempt to improve the aggregate performance of the division, it "rationalized" its plant network by closing that plant. After the fact, it became clear that this plant had been providing a wide range of important services to the network, from new product development to the manufacture of spare parts. It was taken over by the ex-employees, who reorganized the plant, eliminated some products and processes, and sold the remaining products back to Michigan Manufacturing at several times their previous transfer prices.

Such restructurings were often justified by the beneficial effect they had on the careers of those leading them. Something, after all, was being done to solve the operations "problem." It was dramatic, and that was what the times required. Unfortunately, it was not enough. Despite occasional (although unpredictable) beneficial effects, operations' performance languished as a result of such short-term vision. Something more than "restructuring" was needed in order to cultivate operations performance at the unit level.

B. Systems Solutions

In the early 1980s, technology apparently rode to the rescue on a silicon chip-studded robot. Computers and associated networking technologies had been applied for many years to process-control in commodity and chemical industries, as well as to the manufacture of a broad range of parts by Computer-Numerically Controlled (CNC) machining centers. Now systems in which computers controlled not only individual processes but also the coordination of different processes, started to look like a likely prospect for salvation. The unmanned factory—implicitly seeing people as a problem rather than a resource—became a goal in itself (see [16]).

Thousands of engineers throughout the world worked to develop (at great expense) robots able to pick individual objects from a cluttered floor, or wrote software that would supposedly slice through the complexity of managing a job-shop by controlling everything that happened within it. Yamazaki's manufacturing system for producing machine tools at one time employed more employees who worked as visitor guides than as operators [9]. Automated systems, which wrested control away from mistake-prone operators while at the same time improving productivity and quality, were touted to be the new panacea.

A flood of technological TLAs (Three Letter Acronyms) beset manufacturing managers (MRP, MRPII, FMS, CIM) each promising huge competitive leaps in performance. While it is inevitable that a focus on such computer-based schemes would detract from other concerns, the faith in the software engineers' craft was astonishing (at least in retrospect). A number of problems began to arise very quickly.

MRP (Material Requirements Planning) systems, it was said, demanded "discipline" in a plant to stop the remaining operators from running a parallel system on the back of cigarette packs when the computer running the MRP program failed to complete on time [3]. FMS was found to be flexible in that it could switch quickly among the products for which it was originally designed—yet was relatively inflexible once new products were required [13]. The very thing that made such systems flexible in the short term—their software—became an iron cage that required tremendous effort to bend to new requirements.

The revolution that pinned its hopes on computer integrated automation in the 1980s began to lose steam. While these new systems provided great advantages in tackling the informational complexities of manufacturing systems that made a broad range of products, and often improved the trade-off between cost and variety, they failed to embody some critical elements of manufacturing competitiveness.

First, many firms bought turnkey systems from software vendors, machine-tool companies and computer firms. With such systems widely available, firms lost some of their ability to differentiate themselves from their competitors. Manufacturers were reduced to being servants of their systems. Worse still, a whole range of new skills in software engineering was required—skills that many firms found difficult to acquire. They became, in essence, untrained caretakers of alien technologies.

Second, as noted above, the systems approach ignored the dynamic nature of manufacturing. In a world of capricious markets and fast-changing technology, firms found their heavy investments in CIM to be less than versatile, in the long term, despite exhibiting some degree of flexibility in the short term.

Finally, few computerized systems guided the way to further improvement. By limiting the involvement of skilled people (other than computer experts), a reliance on automation was just another instrument for gaining "control," and providing a step change in operations effectiveness. Unfortunately, the resulting systems were usually difficult to improve once in operation. In fact, the complexity and interrelated nature of the software systems that controlled their behavior discouraged attempts to make even simple improvements. A single patch could have pernicious and unexpected consequences—and patches on top of other patches could conspire to bring the whole system to a halt.

Despite these problems, computer integration has become a necessary, rather than sufficient, condition for success in many operations [10].

Long-term success, however, demands the creation of ever-more powerful systems—ones that are difficult for competitors to replicate and are steadily being improved. It involves the effective management of all the resources available to managers. At the heart of such an engine are the people in the organization, who alone have the capacity to build new abilities as time moves on. While technology may yet prove us wrong, at present, such relentless improvement is strongly reliant on the involvement of human beings and their ability to learn new tasks and develop new skills. This is why many plants that relied solely on technology and systems have foundered as market requirements evolved.

One technique from the "systems" school merits further attention, since it straddles both the systems approach and "continuous improvement" philosophies. Just-In-Time production (JIT) grew out of the Toyota Production System, which began as a system for production-control yet evolved into the foundation for a new philosophy in manufacturing. Through the approach it took—triggering the production of parts while at the same time controlling inventories—JIT spurned "central control" computing monoliths and distributed production control throughout the plant. Even more heretical, it put much of that control back in the hands of operators, who often rose to the challenge and created the constantly improving organization for which many firms had been searching.

C. Improvement by Philosophy

While many western firms tried to replicate the successes of 'JIT' approaches using Kanbans and cellular manufacturing, most were disappointed with the results. In particular, those who viewed JIT as just another "system" achieved only modest performance improvements. Something was missing, something about the way in which people viewed their work and the philosophy that encouraged them to seek out improvement had been lost. The failure of the pure systems approach hailed a new wave of improvement philosophies. *Empowerment, agility, total quality, "world-class," and reengineering* [4] each aimed to radically alter the *culture* of operations, as well as provide a different approach for building new infrastructural abilities.

At their best, these new philosophies and techniques provided structures and motivation for the improvement efforts of ailing organizations. At their worst, they became fuzzy clouds of semantic overkill—consultant-fuelled fashions against which people found it difficult to argue, yet which failed to provide a clear path and specific steps for improvement.

There is no shortage of texts that describe each of the above approaches in detail, and they have been tremendously influential and beneficial for many operations. However, in the absence of specific recommendations, they can become hollow sweet-sounding exhortations, critically reliant on particular individuals whose leadership, vision and experience blended with the chosen philosophy. This made it difficult for those who sought clear prescriptions for improvement, since it implies that the replicability of success is strongly limited (probably inevitably) by key individuals in the particular organization. Even those with the potential for leadership were often unable to help; the very best managers are often unconvincing in their rationalization of what makes them so able. Their descriptions of their approaches frequently boil down to fairly vague statements of 'philosophy' and 'belief systems' without pinning down the improvement methodology in a way that is transferrable to others.

Infrastructural improvement relies heavily on a synthesis of each of the above approaches. It is of little use to "empower" an unnecessary plant, or seek computer integration without thought to the implications this will have for future improvement opportunities for the people who work in a plant.

The most important decision for a manager embarking on any improvement path is that of selecting a *direction* for that path. As Hayes and Pisano describe [7], the danger of improvement themes like "world-class" is that they do little to ensure that the long-term direction of improvement will fit with the competitive needs of the business. Any improvement strategy should be closely tailored, in direction and nature, to the peculiarities of the individual firm's situation. The most difficult challenge is often that of building an appropriate infrastructure (systems, policies, routines and common values of understandings) rather than the installation of machines, plant and equipment. It is here that the greatest opportunity exists for continuing improvement and where the greatest number of people can be directly involved in the improvement effort and the development of new organizational capabilities.

At the foundation of such development is the individual operating unit. The plant is the primary unit from which manufacturing enterprises draw their strength. It is where most people go to work and focus their attention each day, whether the back office of a financial services company, a restaurant, or any other individual facility where people work together to produce or deliver a product or service by concerted effort.

At the lowest level, an operating unit is a *collection of inputs.* Investments of productive machinery, labor and materials combine in one place to create new value. At the next level, it may be seen as a collection of *intellectual knowledge, routines* and *systems* which are forged together more or less informally to generate and exploit competitive capabilities. At another (and inconveniently vague level for the mechanistic of mind) it is a *community* of people. It may have all manner of systems, intellectual capital, and hard capital, yet absent the sense of common purpose and community it can fail to improve and flounder against competitors. In one factory producing consumer products, productivity blossomed by 15% after being ceremoniously named for the village in which it was sited, rather than the impersonal "Canning Plant #14." Good operations managers are constantly aware of each of these levels of abstraction as they build improvement in their operations.

Even given a clear vision of how an operation might progress, the question facing most operations managers is where and how to begin their improvement. The following section describes some common embarkation points and outlines some of their advantages and particular challenges. These common improvement thrusts draw techniques from each of the historical themes described above.

2. Common Approaches to Building Improvement

The starting points described below are usually employed in combination, and in particular circumstances, one may simply be a subset of another. In general, however, an initiative is characterized primarily by one of these approaches, with others as subsidiaries. Some of these approaches are described in more detail by Hayes, Wheelwright and Clark [8].

(1) Reconfiguring the Structure of the Operations Strategy

A common "top down" approach to boosting the performance of an operation is a wholesale re-structuring of the operating strategy: through plant rationalization and construction, the installation of new technology and greenfield sites. The key challenge here is to provide a platform that will permit and encourage continued improvement once the structural change is in place. The adage often used when setting up a new structure is "Do it first, do it fast, do it right." The reasoning behind the aphorism is well-founded. It is extraordinarily difficult to build or maintain any operation in an environment of great uncertainty, particularly as far as job security is concerned. Whether one is a line-worker concerned about the continued existence of the plant, a production controller concerned about the skills

Table 33.1 Common Approaches to Building Improvement

Primary Approach	Focus
1. Reconfiguration of structure	Broad change in facilities, equipment & process technology
2. Demonstration Project	New technology of method of operation
3. Continuous Benchmarking	"Physical" performance of other operations
4. Functional Improvement	Particular function of department
5. Business Process Improvement	Selected (cross-functional) process
6. Grass-roots Improvement	Broad training and involvement of lowest levels in the operation

one might need when the "new system" comes in, or even a manager worried that the plant's role may be undermined with the outsourcing of a large proportion of its work—one common feature emerges. People will underperform (even counter-perform) until the uncertainty goes away. It is therefore critical in "step-change" improvement to either get it right in one fell swoop, or make the series of changes that are clear and credible to the organization at the outset.

The idea of making a "step-change" in performance through investment in new production technology is also not without fundamental problems, particularly in the short term. Hayes and Clark [6] discovered that many factories experience deep, long dips in performance when installing new manufacturing equipment into an existing operation. Others, however, installed similar equipment much faster and more successfully. The difference appeared to be due to careful planning, clear direction setting, and forceful leadership.

(2) Demonstration Projects

Demonstration projects provide an opportunity for a company to make a bold leap in its manufacturing or operating capabilities. Such projects focus on one part of a company's total operation, usually in a particular department or shop. In the 'island' created by the project, it will assemble the very best people, ideas and technologies to show what can be done and how the operation may be carried out in a radically different way than the operations extant in the organization.

Such projects have the advantage that they can "break free" of existing inhibitive norms in the company. They also challenge and motivate the most able people in the organization to become pioneers and free themselves of the bureaucratic bonds which may have been stifling their imagination and careers. They provide tremendous focus on individual problems, and in doing so, generate much learning which might otherwise have been diffused over time. On the other hand, the "acid test" for the success of any such project is its ability to cease to be simply a *demonstration* project and for the new approach to spread to the rest of the organization.

(3) Continuous Benchmarking Initiatives

While benchmarking is usually thought of as a diagnostic method for assessing what degree of improvement is possible, it can also provide the beginnings of an improvement method in itself.

The most valuable form of benchmarking for operations improvement is operational benchmarking, which compares one's own operations with another using physical, clearly measurable characteristics such as lead times, variable costs, yields, defects, and physical inventory levels.

Physical measures tend to be more clearly and broadly understood than financial measures, which may lose credibility because they reflect different cost structures and engender misunderstandings about how the figures are calculated and what they mean. On the basis of a benchmarking study, Daewoo Shipbuilding and Heavy Machinery [14] classed themselves as the fastest improving shipyard in the world. They ensured that all benchmarking was carried out by the people who would act on the information, so that both the right data would be collected and that every opportunity for learning from these comparisons could be exploited.

Continual benchmarking of this sort serves to constantly expose an organization to comparison with the leader in various operations practices, and illuminates the mechanisms through which it can improve its performance along measures over which it has some control. Benchmarking works well when the structure of the operations strategy and its fit with the competitive requirements are good, but the operation still lags in performance. Exposure to the performance levels that other operations have been able to achieve encourages people to seek causes (providing the basis for new learning) and allows them to assimilate entirely different ways of performing comparable tasks.

(4) Functional Improvement Initiatives

Occasionally, the shortcomings in a firm's operations performance on its principal competitive thrust lie primarily with one function. In such circumstances, it makes sense to concentrate on that area, and provide it with the help and support it needs from the rest of the organization. Improvements in a particular function can often provide an instructive example of how radical a change is possible (and hence provide motivation for other groups). Most importantly, however, they require the identification of a serious competitive issue with one particular functional group. The danger is that this group, by being "singled-out," may feel threatened and become uncertain of the role of the group as a whole. Many Information Technology groups that provide support to operations have undertaken dramatic changes in the functions they perform and the way they work with the rest of the operation. Caught up in a revolutionary change in the nature of information technology, it has made sense for many firms to focus on improving this particular function as its role becomes increasingly important to operations whether competitiveness, through building new production control architectures or electronic data interchange systems. While there are still situations in which one can say "the problem here is the bottleneck in the toolroom—fix that and everything will be fine," more likely are those which demand attention across traditional functional boundaries, viewing operation as a collection of interrelated processes provides a better focus for improvement.

(5) Business Process Improvement

There are probably an infinity of ways to slice an operation up into its constituent processes. Some processes, however, clearly dominate an operation, and these processes often provide an excellent starting point for an improvement path. One process that is key for firms compelled to provide quick response, for example, is the order-fulfillment process, which cuts across the operation from order entry in the Sales department to dispatch and delivery from Finished Goods. This is the approach which has recently been termed "reengineering."

The focus on Process Improvement rather than Functional Improvement grows from the fact the traditional departmental subdivision of operations has become an increasingly frayed approximation to the optimal. For quick response, for example, it may make much more sense to organize an operation around the process that delivers the order (through a small, mini-factory focused on a small set of jobs, from order entry to delivery) rather than glean the load-sharing advantages of a larger "manufacturing" shop which might have been appropriate for increased asset utilization but a disaster for lead times and responsiveness to customers.

(6) Bottom-up Improvement

Building improvement from the ground up is the implicit objective behind the empowerment craze of the early 1990s. Many firms have shown tremendous improvement in performance as a result of what might be termed "grass-roots" improvement efforts. People in the operation are given more autonomy to seek out opportunities, either in teams or individually, and improve the operation's effectiveness. Responsibility for improvement lies squarely with those who work on the processes. Any ground-up improvement initiative involves a political campaign of one form or another, which should (like all political campaigns) have a clear, understandable message. The strategy must address: why the change must occur; what is it that needs to be improved; how the improvement will take place; and how the change will affect each individual's job. There seems to be an almost magic component in the most successful bottom-up schemes. In many cases (see John Crane (UK) Limited [12] or Micom Caribe [15]), the impression is one of a smouldering effort bursting into flame. The conflagration of improvement then develops so much energy that it can become hard to know how to direct it! While the search for this ingredient is ongoing, a number of features of successful ground-up improvement initiatives are readily identifiable.

Choice of Direction. A clear, credible plan of campaign is critical for a consistent message to be communicated to people. Vague terms like *empowerment* and *reengineering* have little meaning to people who have to implement concrete changes. Vagueness will quickly destroy the credibility of an initiative.

The Trojan Horse. The reason that generic schemes such as TQM and Lean Production can often be good starting points for motivating a workforce to commit to improvement is that they provide structure (how) and focus (what) to an improvement path. This structure and clarity is a tremendously powerful tool for unifying a workforce. Quite often, the scheme is simply a Trojan Horse: it gets improvement rolling in the plant, which quickly triggers a range of other, more important, improvements.

Training. On the surface, training simply provides the skills that people need in order to carry out the new tasks they might be assigned (such as Statistical Process Control or Just-in-Time production). Its ancillary roles are much more important. First, it builds confidence: it is hard to try new things if you are scared of exposing your own ignorance—there is no gain worth that risk for most people. Second, it establishes credibility and a communication channel with people. Finally, it builds an esprit de corps—a sense of common purpose and experience which is critical in overcoming difficult times as the path is followed.

Structures to Stop Backsliding. At each step along the path, there must be a mechanism that removes the "old-way of doing things" as an option. If computers are involved, this can mean the removal of the manual system; If work-in-progress reduction is the objective, it might be the fact that a new layout has no *space* to put incomplete parts. In any case, where the old way remains feasible, there is the possibility of slipping back and any mechanisms that preclude this will provide both continued momentum and an increased sense of urgency.

Using the Skills of Middle Managers. It is usually rather easy to enlist the cooperation of operators in making a change because it generally reflects an attempt to improve their situation (though it may be hard to sustain that motivation). Most changes are more interesting than a humdrum job. Upper management are exposed to the competitive imperatives and so understand the necessity for change. It is in middle management that the real, unanticipated problem arises. These people are threatened with the loss of their power base, their functional position, and their base of expertise—in effect, they are disempowered by "empowerment." This is a critical issue. These managers are often important sources of knowledge in the plant, and the danger is that their skills can be lost—analogous to the way that a closed-down plant's capabilities can be lost when networks are restructured. The solutions often revolve around re-training supervisors and foremen to become trainers and provide technical support. Again, the important principle is that people should be told what will happen to them as soon as possible, before the uncertainty eats away at their commitment and they have time to commit themselves publicly to an opposing position.

Each of these considerations reinforces the general concerns of why the plant needs to improve, what and how it will improve and "what's going to happen to me." In this kind of improvement initiative an understanding of the operating unit as a community is much more valuable than a model of an economic unit or technical system.

None of the above approaches is independent. Pieces of each are used in any improvement strategy and it is in synthesis of the approaches that the real art of operations management shows itself. However, one or two of the approaches usually dominate any initiative, and a quick recognition of the improvement philosophy and development path can provide important clues about the potential problems that need to be addressed as well as the opportunities that exist to encourage continued improvement in the future.

3. Sustaining Improvement

Most improvement initiatives comprise a series of subprojects, which might be as simple as teaching operators to set up their own machines (changing the role of machine-setters to setter/operators) to the installation of new computer equipment. Each subproject is directed towards achieving the prevailing goal, for example, responsiveness, conformance quality or low-cost. The subproject manager might be an individual operator or a department manager. Periodically, at least once a year, an evaluation is made of the existing initiatives and plans are developed for new projects to be undertaken during the next period, so that the forward thrust is sustained (to build continuous improvement over time).

Even though a number of the starting points discussed above (particularly continuous benchmarking and grass-roots improvement) are associated with "continuous improvement," there are—in reality—very different models and mindsets underlying such improvement which affect both the sustainability of the initiative and its ultimate benefit. Three such models are described below. While the patterns described may not actually continue indefinitely, they represent the underlying view of how improvement takes place that is implicit in the actions of both managers and operators.

Model 1. Continuous Improvement: Exhausting the Pool of Opportunities

This improvement model is based on the assumption that the opportunities for improvement in the plant are static, and that improvement involves picking the "lowest hanging fruit" first, and then progressively moving to the more difficult projects. Selection of subprojects is thus based on how difficult those projects are expected to be to implement and how fast the payback is expected to be. Easy subprojects get done, difficult ones don't. This model is very common in plants suffering from *scheme exhaustion*. People in the plant will have lived through a series of improvement schemes (often for other performance dimensions) and the new initiative appears to be more of the same to them.

Despite being labeled "continuous improvement," both managers and employees assume that while the new initiative will show gains at first, over time the pool of easy wins will become exhausted. After a year or two, it becomes difficult to make improvement on the original dimension, so opportunities to improve on other dimensions seem much more attractive and productive. "World-class" provides an excellent reason to change tack, and launch a new improvement initiative. Unfortunately, this new initiative may not be improving the most important competitive char-

Table 33.2 Three Models of Continuous Improvement Initiatives

	Model I	Model II	Model III
Performance Improvement	Convex, decreasing gains	Linear	Accelerating
Long-term objectives	Inconsistent over time	Consistent over time	Consistent over time
Provision of new opportunities for improvement	Opportunistic	Reactive, Unplanned	Planned
Sub-project selection criteria (periodic)	Ease of implementation Speed of payback "Low-hanging fruit"	Extent to which sub-projects provide direct improvement in chosen direction	Extent to which sub-project provides direct improvement in chosen direction Extent to which the sub-project provides a platform for future gains
Approach	Get the easy things done Drain the Pool of Opportunities "It was something else last year, and it'll be something else next year."	"We must *try* harder to improve our performance on this measure. ...and keep finding (and stumbling on) new opportunities to improve the operation."	"We must sow the seeds for new improvement opportunities for the future and still improve every day..."

Figure 33.1   Continuous Improvement (I): Pool Exhaustion

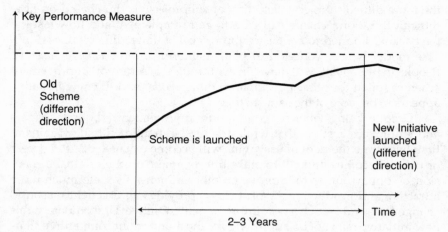

acteristic of the operation. Even so, it is in the "stalled" stages of old initiatives that new fashions—TQM, reengineering—find the most fertile ground: it feels better to see something improve (even on a less important dimension), than to watch a tired old scheme founder as improvement becomes harder and harder. Firms in these situations often do not have a clear idea of how they compete, and become easily diverted by the latest fad. They subject their plants to a series of psychologically exhausting schemes (though the new managers or consultants that bring them may see them as new and exciting).

Quality Circles, an improvement fad in the late 1970s, provides a good example of such an initiative. Many operations found the idea of cross-functional meetings to discuss how quality might be improved to be productive—at first. Over time, however, quality circles often degenerated as the easier subprojects disappeared and it became harder and harder to produce noticeable results. The dispirited team would then become aimless and the initiative would be tagged "a waste of time." The scene would thus be set for the next scheme to take hold.

2. Continuous Improvement (II): Linear, Focused Improvement

Firms with this model of improvement have a very clear, long-lasting view of how they compete, and communicate it well to people through the operation. There is a shared understanding that improvement may become more difficult as time goes on, but that at each step on the path, new opportunities will show themselves (somehow) and fuel sustained improvement. The fact that the difficulties of sustaining improvement are generally understood guards against the disenchantment that can quickly take the wind out of the sails of the initiative. A faith in "getting better

Figure 33.2   Continuous Improvement (II): Linear Improvement

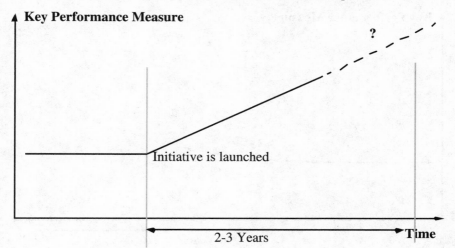

every day" and "stretch goals" keeps the improvement moving forward for as long as people are prepared to put relentless effort into overcoming increasingly difficult obstacles.

The problem with this model of improvement is that a reactive, "we'll cross that bridge when we get to it" view forces the operation to deal with a series of progressively more difficult hurdles, and little attention is paid at each stage to sowing the seeds that will provide longer-term opportunities. This kind of improvement path is often seen in new operations where the skepticism resulting from a series of schemes has not had the chance to set in.

Strong, charismatic leaders are critical for this mode of improvement, since people need to believe that there can always be a better way of doing things. Such leaders are often characterized as "obsessive" as they try to squeeze more and more blood out of the increasingly dry stone [1]. The danger comes further down the road than it does for model I. Although the organization does not immediately jump to improve on another competitive dimension when things become difficult, it ultimately has to deal with a situation which has not been planned for or dealt with proactively: what happens when it becomes exceptionally difficult to improve further in a given direction?

AT&T's Universal Card Services operation [11] provides an excellent example of such an initiative. After winning the Baldrige Award for quality in 1992, the operation found it progressively more difficult to improve. Indeed, there was evidence that many people in the organization felt at odds with the zealots leading the quality campaign on the grounds that bonuses were becoming more and more difficult to achieve as they were pushed to continue improving quality. While such perseverance and focus

Figure 33.3   Continuous Improvement (III): Accelerating Improvement

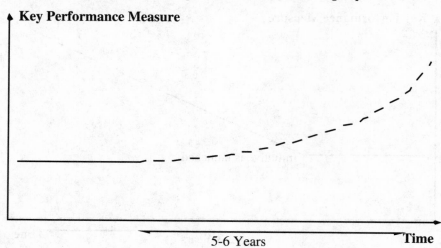

is a marked improvement over Model I, it still does not plan for the day when the opportunity well runs dry by encouraging people to lay a long-term foundation for improvement.

3. Continuous Improvement (III): Accelerating Improvement

Few firms employ this model. The key feature is that, at each period, subprojects are selected based on two factors:

- The extent to which the project delivers direct improvement along a chosen dimension
- The extent to which it generates future opportunities for improvement.

By using these selection criteria, firms ensure that improvement occurs continuously, but also proactively provide opportunities for further improvement. Teams working in this environment discuss not only the improvement plans for this year, but the improvement plans for the following years, knowing that they will have to increase the rate of improvement every year. To do this, they lay the groundwork for further improvement down the road, and may often select projects with little immediate benefit, and even projects that appear to drag the operation along an improvement path headed in the wrong direction. But this is done strategically and judiciously, in order to build capabilities, in the long term, which will provide opportunities for further improvement on the appropriate dimension. This is very different from selecting a subproject because it is an easy thing to do. The combination of progressive improvement, and the provision of launch pads to provide future opportunities is very powerful, but very difficult to do well. However, this improvement mentality can provide an explosive, exponential performance improvement. The prime difficulty is that, because of the initial effort put into building long-term improvement opportunities, results may be slow at first. In the longer term, this approach will generate rapidly improving performance.

Daewoo Shipbuilding and Heavy Machinery [14] on Okpo island in Korea used this approach explicitly when rescuing the plant from the brink of disaster in 1987, to make it one of the most productive and fastest improving shipyards in the world by 1994. While its improvement trajectory did falter here and there (see Figure 33.4), Daewoo's strict policy was that each subproject should also provide a foundation for further improve-

Figure 33.4   Daewoo Shipbuilding and Heavy Machinery: Improvement Results

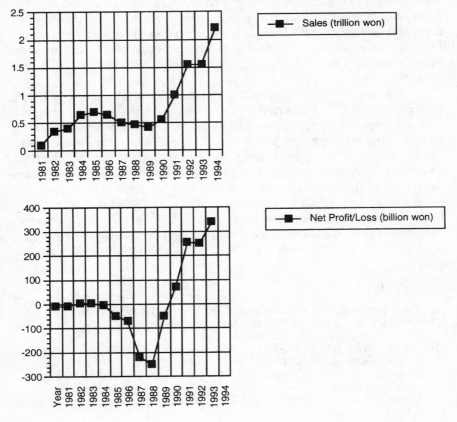

ment, and the teams responsible for the project should also be responsible for exploiting its platform benefits. An example of such a project was the improvement of welding quality in the plant. While the quality of welding was not a major problem, a progressive improvement in welding quality would allow the removal of entire assembly processes in subsequent years, thus providing a postponed, but large jump in productivity in the long term. The welding quality project went ahead on this basis. A progressive shop-floor learning project to control the way in which welding structures distorted ultimately allowed the yard to install propellers in parallel with other components, rather than after distortion had settled down, saving valuable weeks of factory time. The above models are stereotypical, and most firms will fall between the lines, using a combination of both philosophies. However, the dominant philosophy is usually easy to recognize in an operation, and provides important clues about how the improvement process may itself be improved. It is important to remember that none of the models can sustain itself indefinitely since no firm can continue to improve forever from a given structural base: there are ultimately limits to how much an operation can glean from a particular platform of technology. While the improvement process is going on, good companies are continually looking for ways to make their own technology, facilities and processes obsolete. These constantly revisited structures then provide new platforms from which to use the improvement engines that have been built.

While most managers would agree that doing something is better than doing nothing to improve performance, it is important to remember that any improvement initiative has a long-term cost, in particular on the morale of the operation and people's willingness to commit themselves to future initiatives. For this reason, it is critical that the improvement be shaped in a way that is sustainable and focused over a longer period than the tenure of the current manager. While improvement fads can provide the impetus that encourages static organizations to move, it is critically important that sufficient attention is paid to building a common understanding of how the improvement will be kept on course and sustained over time.

References

[1]   The Economist, "The Straining of Quality," January 14, 1995: 55–56.
[2]   Christensen, Clayton M. (1994). "Michigan Manufacturing Corp.: The Pontiac Plant." Harvard Business School Case 9-694-051.
[3]   Garvin, David (1988). "Digital Equipment Corporation (A): The Endpoint Model." Harvard Business School Case 9-688-059.
[4]   Hammer, Michael and James Champy (1993). Reengineering the Corporation. New York, HarperCollins.
[5]   Hayes, Robert H. (1980). "Chandler Home Products (B)." Harvard Business School Case 9-680-048.

[6] Hayes, Robert H. and Kim B. Clark (1986). *"Why Some Factories Are More Productive Than Others."* Harvard Business Review (Reprint 86508).

[7] Hayes, Robert H. and Gary P. Pisano (1994). *"Beyond World-Class: The New Manufacturing Strategy."* Harvard Business Review (Reprint 94104).

[8] Hayes, Robert H., Steven C. Wheelwright and Kim B. Clark (1988). *Dynamic Manufacturing,* Free Press.

[9] Jaikumar, Ramchandran (1986). *"Yamazaki Mazak."* Harvard Business School Case 9-686-083.

[10] Rogers, Paul, David M. Upton and David J. Williams (1992). Computer Integrated Manufacturing. *Handbook of Industrial Engineering.* New York, John Wiley and Sons: 647–671.

[11] Rosegrant, Susan (1993). *"A Measure of Delight: The Pursuit of Quality at AT&T Universal Card Services."* Harvard Business School Case 9-694-047.

[12] Upton, David M. (1991). *"John Crane (UK) Limited: The CAD-CAM Link."* Harvard Business School Case 9-691-021.

[13] Upton, David M. (1992). *"A Flexible Structure for Computer-Controlled Manufacturing Systems."* Manufacturing Review 5(1): 58–74.

[14] Upton, David M. and Bowon Kim (1994). *"Daewoo Shipbuilding and Heavy Machinery."* Harvard Business School Case 9-695-001.

[15] Upton, David M. and Joshua Margolis (1991). *"Micom Caribe (A), (B) and (C)."* Harvard Business School Cases 692–002, 692–003, 692–043.

[16] Williams, David J. (1988). *Manufacturing Systems: An Introduction to the Technologies.* New York, Halsted Press: 131–132.

INDEX